MOON

DOMINICAN REPUBLIC

LEBAWIT LILY GIRMA

Contents

the Dominican Republic

It's no surprise that the Dominican Republic now ranks as the most visited country in the Caribbean. The diamond white beaches and lavish resorts from Punta Cana to La Romana attract millions of sun worshippers every year. And while the blue waves, breezy palm trees, and sparkling sand are worth the trip, it's the rest of the country that will make you fall in love.

The capital's Colonial City is brimming with grand Spanish-style architecture, 16th-century cathedrals, and wrought-iron balconies. Outside the capital, beaches are lined with rows of *frituras* (fried food shacks) selling the day's catch, along with red onion-spiced avocados and *tostones* (crispy fried plantains). Avid surfers and divers flock to the north, while the countryside offers enriching cultural expeditions to cacao and coffee plantations. Adventure awaits in the mountainous heart of the country, where you can hike through cloud forests and horseback ride to crisp, cool waterfalls. In the southwestern corner of the island, the possibility of sheer isolation still exists among the peaks, sand dunes, and deserted beaches.

Clockwise from top left: the Colonial City; a kitesurfer in Cabarete; Calle El Conde; Charcos de los Militares; Carnaval; rolling cigars.

Regardless of where you find yourself in the DR, at the center of it all are unmistakably Dominican experiences. The constant stream of merengue and bachata in the air invites you to dance, whether in the middle of a park or at a *rancho típico* (open-air, roadside club). People gather on street corners, playing dominoes and throwing back Brugal rum or ice cold Presidente beers from the *colmado* (corner shop). You'll find constant celebration, most notably during February's countrywide carnivals, which offer a glimpse into the country's eclectic African, Taíno, and Spanish heritage. Music mixes with laughter to create the daily soundtrack, because Dominicans enjoy every day to the fullest.

The Dominican Republic oozes life. They say New York City never sleeps, but the DR never stops dancing.

Clockwise from top left: Puerto Plata; a bright countryside home; Santo Domingo; Isla Saona.

Planning Your Trip

Where to Go

Santo Domingo

Santo Domingo was the first city of the Americas, and today, it is the most dynamic, cosmopolitan city in the Caribbean. The **Cuidad Colonial,** declared an UNESCO World Heritage Site in 1990, displays Spanish colonial and gothic architecture in its sprawling plazas and bustling streetscapes. The upscale **Piantini** district in the center of the city offers modern casinos, boutique hotels, and sleek bistros and lounges. On the weekends, city dwellers flock to the nearby beaches of **Juan Dolio, Guayacanes,** and **Boca Chica.** Santo Domingo is just a two-hour drive from Punta Cana via the Coral Highway.

Punta Cana and the Southeast Coast

On the southeast and eastern coasts of the island are the DR's most visited regions: Punta Cana, Bayahibe, and La Romana. **Punta Cana** is the crown jewel of Dominican tourism, covering 30 miles of powdery soft sand with all-inclusive resorts, with a handful of independent hotels in **Bávaro. La Romana** offers luxury inland with world-class resorts and golf courses. **Bayahibe** also boasts many resorts and tourists, though its colorful village center still provides a cultural window into the DR. Many take day trips from Bayahibe to the stunning **Saona and Catalina Islands,** both of which offer beautiful beaches and great diving.

The Samaná Peninsula

Jutting out of the northeast corner of the island is the Samaná Peninsula, with uncrowded beaches flanked by cliffs and coconut plantations. This

Juan Dolio

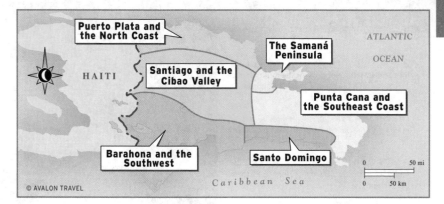

Puerto Plata and the North Coast

The Samaná Peninsula

ATLANTIC OCEAN

HAITI

Santiago and the Cibao Valley

Punta Cana and the Southeast Coast

Barahona and the Southwest

Santo Domingo

Caribbean Sea

0   50 mi

0   50 km

© AVALON TRAVEL

region is a haven for European expats and independent travelers. There are three main areas: **Samaná town,** known for its seasonal humpback whale-watching; **Las Terrenas,** a funky and cosmopolitan town; and **Las Galeras,** home to top beaches like **Playa Rincón** and **Playa Frontón.** Offshore, the towering rocks of **Los Haitises National Park** are worth a boat trip for bird-watching and Taíno history. The Carretera Samaná links the peninsula to Santo Domingo in two and a half hours, and JetBlue flies direct to Samaná's El Catey International Airport.

Puerto Plata and the North Coast

The North Coast of the Dominican Republic is the most well-rounded destination in the country. There are historical sights in **Puerto Plata city,** water sports in nearby **Cabarete** and **Sosúa,** and cultural excursions to amber mines and coffee and cacao plantations in the province's various municipalities. Puerto Plata city is also attractive for its **Playa Dorada** resorts and beaches. If you're a wildlife-lover, head west of Puerto Plata city to see manatees at the **Estero Hondo Marine Mammal Sanctuary** and mangrove swamps in **Monte Cristi.** Heading west there are even more beautiful beaches and offshore islands

Santiago and the Cibao Valley

The mountainous **Cibao Valley,** known as the breadbasket of the country, offers all kinds of adventure. There are a handful of national parks in and around **Jarabacoa**—including the tallest peak in the region, **Pico Duarte**—with freshwater rivers and lush hills for rafting and hiking. Nearby **Constanza** sits at 4,000 feet high, covered in pine forests, vegetable farms, and flower plantations. The **Valle Nuevo National Park** welcomes hikers to cooler temperatures and cabins with chimney fires. The Cibao Valley's major gateway, **Santiago,** is the DR's second largest city, a commercial hub known for its cigars and active nightlife.

Barahona and the Southwest

The least developed area of the Dominican Republic straddles the Haitian border in the southwestern corner of the country. It is also the most unique geographically, with a landscape that includes sand dunes, pebblestone beaches, and mountains in **Barahona,** to a host of lagoons, national parks, and roads lined with cactus in **Pedernales.** The country's largest protected park, **Parque Nacional Jaragua,** is home to turtle nesting beaches and flamingos at **Laguna Oviedo.** American crocodiles glide in the salty **Lago Enriquillo,** the lowest point in the Caribbean, while 30 endemic bird species roam the **Sierra de Bahoruco.** The southwest's best highlight is the remote **Bahía de las Águilas,** considered the best beach in the Dominican Republic.

If You Are...

- **A CULTURE BUFF:** Visit Puerto Plata province and stay in Tubagua; visit the mountains of Jarabacoa and Constanza; book a homestay in Barahona.

- **HONEYMOONING:** Stay in a luxury resort in Punta Cana; pick out a boutique hotel in Las Terrenas.

- **A CITY OR NIGHTLIFE LOVER:** Dance the night away in Santo Domingo, Puerto Plata, or Las Terrenas.

- **ON A BUDGET:** Visit Bayahibe and go island hopping; head to Las Galeras for beautiful beaches; stay at a beachfront cabin in Punta Rucia.

- **AN OUTDOORS LOVER:** Visit the Cibao Valley for waterfalls, river-rafting, and mountain hiking; stay in Barahona and the southwest for national parks, lagoons, and swimming holes.

Playa Blanca, Punta Cana

When to Go

The Dominican Republic is blessed with **sunny, warm weather year-round,** with average temperatures in the mid-80s. It gets extremely humid and hot in the summertime, while cooler sea breezes make mid-November through January more pleasant. The **rainy season** has become unpredictable, with more rainstorms happening now in November than in **hurricane season,** which normally peaks in September and October. In the central mountains or the Cibao Valley, days are cooler and drier, but temperatures can drop to below freezing at night in December.

High **tourist season** runs from mid-December through mid-March—expect higher rates during this time. But it's worth it if you're coming for the **humpback whale mating season** in Samaná (which ends mid-March), or for **Dominican Carnaval,** which runs every Sunday in February around the island.

During Easter holidays or **Semana Santa**—Holy Week or the week preceding Easter Sunday—hotels fill up in popular areas from Juan Dolio to La Romana and Las Terrenas (look out for beach closures due to a high level of boozing that weekend). In Santo Domingo, the Malecón is partly turned into a pedestrian zone, and becomes a beach party in the city with games and music. It's also a dangerous time to be on the road, so be wary.

The **low tourist season** (summertime) brings with it attractive airfare and slashed hotel rates, if you can bear the heat and humidity. Catch the **merengue festival** in Santo Domingo in July. November to mid-December is the best compromise between seasons, with fewer tourists, ideal weather, and good rates before the **end of year holidays**—not to mention the Dominican Republic Jazz Festival on the North Coast.

Before You Go

PASSPORTS AND TOURIST CARDS

Valid passports that won't expire for an additional six months from your travel dates are required. North American or Western European travelers do not need a visa, but you must purchase a US$10 **tourist card** online or upon arrival at the airport. These cards are valid for a 30-day period; overstays will result in paying an exit fee at the airport upon departure, calculated according to the amount of time extended (up to US$110 for four additional months). For complete visa requirements, visit www.godominican-republic.com.

VACCINATIONS

There are no required vaccinations for entry to the Dominican Republic. However, it is recommended that you always keep up to date with routine shots for measles, mumps, and rabies. For longer stays, it is recommended that you also get hepatitis A and B, tetanus-diphtheria, chicken pox, and typhoid shots.

Note that the CDC issued an alert in 2015 for pregnant women or women who plan to conceive, advising that they postpone travel to many parts of the Caribbean, including the Dominican Republic, due to the spread of the **Zika virus.**

All other travelers should practice enhanced precautions to avoid **mosquito bites.** Always be sure to use insect repellent, wear protective clothing when venturing into the outdoors, and keep mosquitoes outside.

TRANSPORTATION

Transportation options abound: there's always a bus, car, bike, or coach bus heading to your destination. The DR boasts **10 international and domestic airports** at convenient points close to beach resort towns and cities. **Taxis** are easy to spot, and airport fares are displayed as you exit. Around town or cities, they have set fares; but these become open for negotiation for longer distances, especially in low season—agree on a price before entering any taxi to avoid being overcharged.

There are numerous public transportation options. Hop in the *carritos*, or **shared public taxis,** or the *guaguas*, **shared minivan buses,** that are sometimes beat up. These modes of transportation are dirt cheap, cramming up to seven people in one sedan, or up to 30 in a minivan, and run set routes while picking up passengers anywhere along the way. *Motoconchos* or **motorbike taxis** are popular among locals, and while they are the most cost-effective and fast way to get to your destination, they are the least safe, especially for big cities or highways (with no helmets provided).

Two major coach **bus companies,** Caribe Tours and Metro Tours, offer convenient itineraries between major cities and hubs. Traveling to the smaller towns is easily done by *guagua*—a private white van business, air-conditioned, with wireless Internet on many routes. There are express *guaguas* or regular ones that stop at every passenger hollering on the roadside.

Renting a car is a definite possibility, with major brands present around the island and its airports. Driving offers more flexibility in your itinerary. But beware that accident rates are high in the DR due to speeding, drunk driving, and multiple road obstacles (cows and bikes). It is safer to invest in a local driver. Gas prices are also high.

WHAT TO PACK

Pack any prescription drugs, sunscreen, a hat, and mosquito spray. Throw in some wipes for those long road trips, for when bathroom supplies might be lacking on the way.

Bring **lightweight clothes,** as well as long-sleeve cover-ups if you plan on taking any boat and catamaran excursions or hiking. If you're heading to Jarabacoa and the beautiful mountainous

Motorbike taxis often accommodate more than one person.

central area, or even at a lodge in the hills of Puerto Plata, you'll want **warmer clothes,** as it can get chilly at night. Mountain hiking, to Pico Duarte for instance, requires proper hiking boots, while sneakers are a must for the national parks and forests you plan on exploring.

Bring **nice outfits:** at resorts, some à la carte restaurants require it, and in the cities, Dominicans dress up. Clubs can even refuse entry if you show up in shorts. Sightseeing in cities also means not dressing like you're going to the beach, especially if you plan on entering churches and cathedrals. Of course, on beaches or in beach towns, the **dress is casual,** but walking around in your bathing suit is frowned upon unless you're actually on the beach. Nudity is forbidden altogether (but often overlooked in areas like Punta Cana).

The Best of the Dominican Republic

The Dominican Republic is a huge country—the second largest in the Caribbean—and the most diverse geographically. This 10-day itinerary will give you a solid glimpse into the DR's beaches, culture, and adventure. It can also be used for a 4- or 7-day trip.

Santo Domingo: Culture and Nightlife

DAY 1

Arrive in **Santo Domingo** mid-morning and check into **El Beaterio** in the **Ciudad Colonial.** Grab an outdoor Dominican lunch on the sidewalk terrace of **Cafetería El Conde** and enjoy the views of the **Parque Colón** and the **Catedral Primada de América** while you eat. Walk lunch off by exploring the area's stunning architecture and museums on foot, or rent a bike from **Zona Bici.** Make your way down **Calle Las Damas,** visiting the **Fortaleza Ozama, Museo de las Casas Reales,** and **Alcázar de Colón,** the former palatial home of Diego Colón, son of Christopher Columbus. For dinner, indulge in the seafood tasting menu at **Pat'e Palo,** the first-ever tavern in the Americas. Afterward, walk over to **Lulú Tasting Bar** for a cocktail on a colonial terrace. If it's a Friday or Saturday, catch the free **Santo Domingo de Fiesta** folkloric dance show on the far end of **Plaza de España.** If it's a Sunday, walk over to the **San Francisco Ruins** for the city's most popular outdoor merengue, son, and salsa concert.

The Samaná Peninsula: Beaches and Seaside Landscapes

DAY 2

Rise early and walk down Santo Domingo's **Malecón,** the waterfront promenade, to the neoclassical, neighboring **Gazcue district.** Have a Dominican breakfast at **Hermanos Villar,** a

Santo Domingo's Malecón

fishing on Playa El Valle

cafeteria buffet with staples such as fried cheese and *mangú*. Ready for those sugary white beaches? Head north to the **Samaná Peninsula** by coach bus with **Caribe Tours** or by rental car (get your toll change ready). Enjoy spectacular views of coconut plantations on the 3-hour journey before arriving in **Las Galeras.** Check into **Villa Serena** and have lunch there. Walk to the main village beach and arrange for your next day boat ride to three of the area's most beautiful beaches, and then spend the afternoon at nearby **La Playita,** a less crowded stretch of white sand with shallow turquoise waters. If you'd rather have a little more adventure, spend the afternoon horseback riding along the shoreline with **Rudy's Rancho.** At sunset, walk back to the **main village beach bar** and join the locals with some rum and loud merengue or bachata music. For dinner, enjoy a casual Italian meal in the village at **Ristorante Roma.**

DAY 3

From the main beach, get whisked off to the Atlantic shores and towering cliffs of Las Galeras. You'll have an entire day swimming, sunbathing, and snorkeling at three postcard-perfect beaches: **Playa Madama, Playa Frontón,** and **Playa Rincón.** After your excursion, have dinner at a romantic cliff-top table at **El Cabito** and take in Las Galeras one last time.

DAY 4

Hop in a private taxi or catch a *guagua* (local bus) to funky **Las Terrenas.** Check into your cabin at **Casas del Mar Neptunia** and walk over to the beachfront. Stroll its length down to **Playa Las Ballenas** and have an affordable French gourmet lunch at **La Vela Blanca.** Spend an afternoon swimming and sunning on the beach. For dinner, grab a seafront table at **La Terrasse** along the lively **Pueblo de los Pescadores** restaurant row. Head over to **Replay** and dance the night away to Dominican and international tunes. Arrange for a taxi to El Catey Airport the next day, or continue on your trip.

Puerto Plata and Cabarete: Cultural Tourism and Water Sports

DAY 5

Rise at dawn and head to **Puerto Plata,** four

hours by car and five hours by public bus. Admire the rustic beauty of the North Coast as you pass multiple fishing villages. Once in Puerto Plata, grab lunch at **Café Tropical** and then continue on to **Tubagua village** by taxi or car, another 20 minutes into the countryside. Drop your bags in your cabin at **Tubagua Eco Lodge** and take in the panoramic hilltop and sea views. The lodge's local guide Juanin will take you on a three-hour hike through Tubagua village to gorgeous falls and pools at **Charcos de los Militares.** If you'd prefer to see the DR's famous amber mines or a nearby coffee plantation, you can arrange it through your host at the lodge. Return to the lodge to enjoy the sunset while soaking in the pool tub.

DAY 6

Head out early by car or taxi to explore the northwest coast, stopping first at the **Estero Hondo Marine Mammal Sanctuary.** Go on a guided hike around the reserve's mangroves and observe over a dozen manatees from a lookout tower. Continue on to nearby **Playa Ensenada,** for a Dominican lunch at one of several beachfront

food shacks. After lunch, head to adjacent **Punta Rucia Beach,** where you will find boat captains ready to take you to offshore **Cayo Arena.** The boat will take you through the mangrove channels of the **Monte Cristi National Park.** Spend the rest of the afternoon snorkeling around the gorgeous corals off this tiny cay. Head back to Puerto Plata city and check into **Boutique Hotel El Palacio.** Walk over to **Skina** for dinner. This longtime local favorite serves authentic Dominican and Latin dishes.

DAY 7

If you're up for it, catch the sunrise along Puerto Plata's **Malecón.** Grab a morning breakfast and admire the Victorian architecture at **Heladeria Mariposa,** across from **Parque Independencia.** Head to Puerto Plata airport for your flight home, or continue your trip and hop into a *carrito* (local shared taxi) heading to **Cabarete.** Check into the beachfront **Villa Taina Hotel** and grab a light sandwich at **Mojito Bar,** a short walk away. Spend the day learning how to windsurf or kitesurf at **Kite Beach.** Later, have a beachfront dinner at **La Casita de Papi**

Salto de Baiguate

Punta Rucia

Constanza's farmland

for authentic Dominican seafood; burn the calories off at the two-story **Lax Ojo dance club, Onno's Bar,** or one of the other numerous beachfront dance spots.

Jarabacoa and Constanza: Countryside Lifestyle

DAY 8

Experience the stunning mountainside of the DR in **Jarabacoa,** about a two-hour trip by car or bus. Check into **Jarabacoa Mountain Hostel** and head out for a casual Dominican lunch at **El Taíno.** From there, meet up with local guide David from **Jarabacoa Eco Adventures,** who will take you on a horseback or motorbike ride to **Salto de Baiguate** for a swim in refreshingly cool waters. In the evening, hop in a taxi for dinner at the mountaintop **Aroma de la Montaña.** Pick a candlelit table on the outdoor terrace and dine with views of the **Cordillera Central.**

DAY 9

After breakfast at the hostel, head out to neighboring **Constanza** by car or with César of Sindi-Taxi, riding through **El Tireo village** and its vast fields of vegetable crops and flower plantations. Once there, enjoy a fresh vegetable pizza and strawberry *batida* at **Antojitos de Lauren.** Drive up to **El Divino Niño Monument,** just outside of the town center, to meet the 48-feet high statue overlooking Constanza's hills. Head back to town for a local Ferringer brew at the funky **La Esquina bar,** a local favorite. If you're able to rent an all-terrain vehicle, drive to **Valle Nuevo National Park,** one of the DR's natural wonders, and hike through its pine forests with a guide from **Villa Pajón Eco-Lodge.** Head back to Jarabacoa for the night and have dinner at **Pizza and Pepperoni.**

DAY 10

Grab an early coffee and breakfast from **La Tinaja** in downtown Jarabacoa before heading back to **Santiago** for your flight home. Hop on Caribe Tours (the bus terminal is a short walk from La Tinaja) or get a private taxi ride to the airport.

PUNTA CANA AND BAYAHIBE

Playa Bávaro (page 92)
One of the most well-known beaches in the DR, Playa Bávaro hosts many resorts, but that doesn't take away from its glorious stretch. The crystal clear water is the perfect temperature for a dip.

Playa Macao (page 90)
The undeveloped Playa Macao is great for surfing or taking a stroll along the palm-studded blond sand. It also has some of the best fish shacks on the Punta Cana coastline.

Playa Juanillo (page 105)
On the southern tip of the Punta Cana coastline, the long, shiny white stretch of Playa Juanillo is dotted with towering, leaning coconut trees—a poster-worthy sight.

Isla Saona (page 132)
A quick boat ride off the coast of Bayahibe, Isla Saona's beaches are a brilliant white, dotted with tall coconut trees and facing a turquoise Caribbean Sea. The best of all is the uncrowded, beautiful Canto de la Playa at the edge of the island.

THE SAMANÁ PENINSULA

Playa Rincón (page 163)
The crown jewel of the Samaná Peninsula's beaches, Playa Rincón is a two-mile-long strip of white, soft sand and leaning coconut trees, just 10 minutes by boat from Las Galeras. Visit in the after-noon for fewer crowds.

Playa Cosón (page 172)
The most stunning beach in Las Terrenas is Playa Cosón, a long, dreamy, blond stretch, dotted with a handful of luxury boutique resorts. Locals flock to the undeveloped stretch on Sundays to swim and indulge in the best fish shacks in the region.

Playa El Valle (page 154)
Tucked north of Samaná town, Playa El Valle is an ultra-remote, undeveloped golden beach, sitting at the foot of the towering, lush hills of El Valle. It is not a swimming spot due to riptides, but it makes for a lovely walk.

THE NORTH COAST

Punta Rucia and Cayo Arena (pages 243 and 244)
Playa Punta Rucia is a jumping-off point to the off-

Playa Cosón in Las Terrenas

shore Cayo Arena, and each stuns on its own. The uncrowded Punta Rucia offers miles of unshaded white sand, which sparkles even brighter in the hot sun. The tiny Cayo Arena has beautiful turquoise waters and some of the best snorkeling in the DR.

Playa Cambiaso (page 198)
Getting to Playa Cambiaso requires a bumpy, 1.5-hour ride from Puerto Plata city, but the remoteness of this stunning stretch is what makes it unique. Locals flock here on Sundays for swimming and seafood, but on weekdays you'll have the beach to yourself—save for a couple of wild donkeys to keep you company.

Playa El Morro (page 246)
Hugged by El Morro, a towering limestone mesa, the reddish blond eponymous beach offers breath-taking scenery. Soft stones shift from one half of the beach to the other with the tide.

THE SOUTHEAST

Bahia de las Águilas (page 321)
The remotest of them all, and often said to be the most gorgeous beach in the DR, is Bahia de las Águilas, a protected, undeveloped stretch facing a stunning bay and hugged by a magnificent rocky landscape. The water is so clear that you can see your toes.

Romancing the DR

Intimate Lodgings

- **Santo Domingo:** Restored 16th-century quarters in verdant colonial courtyards await at **Hostal Nicolas de Ovando,** set on the first paved street in the Americas. **El Beaterio**'s charming convent turned guesthouse is small and peaceful, with a tranquil rooftop terrace.

- **Punta Cana: Excellence Punta Cana** offers sexy luxurious perks, like in-room spa tubs, a butler to draw your bath at turndown, and a shower with a see-through glass wall facing the bedroom.

- **Samaná Peninsula:** Lounge poolside or seaside at the charming **Villa Serena,** tucked at the edge of Las Galeras Beach. In Las Terrenas, glam it up at sumptuous **Peninsula House,** relaxing on your private sea-view veranda. Shack up in your cliff-top treehouse at **El Cabito,** taking in the views of Rincon Bay while the wind blows.

- **Puerto Plata:** At the hilltop **Tubagua Eco Lodge,** shower alfresco while staring at panoramic views of Puerto Plata or take a dip in the Jacuzzi at sunset.

- **Punta Rucia:** Enjoy a glorious sea view at **Casa Libre,** where you can take a stony path from your wooden cabin down to the beach. You likely won't find another soul there.

- **Jarabacoa and Constanza:** Stay at villa turned guesthouse **Jarabacoa Mountain Hostel** and soak in your fancy bathtub. Snuggle by the chimney fire inside your cabin at **Villa Pajón Eco-Lodge,** surrounded with pine trees and mountains inside Valle Nuevo National Park, 2,286 meters (7,500 feet) above sea level.

- **Pedernales:** Glamp in the remote southwest of the DR at **Eco Del Mar,** with bed-furnished tents set right on La Cueva Beach.

the beach at Eco del Mar in Pedernales

Many resorts offer complimentary snorkeling gear, as well as introductory PADI open water lessons. But the best underwater marinelife in the DR is often found away from resorts and in areas that aren't visited as frequently. You'll find at least two or three reputable PADI dive shops in each of these areas.

PUNTA CANA AND BAYAHIBE

Bayahibe is one of the best places in the DR for snorkeling as well as diving. The offshore, protected Saona and Catalina Islands, part of the Parque Nacional Del Este, offer colorful 40-meter (130-foot) wall dives—the Catalina Wall is especially impressive—local reefs teeming with critters, and several neat shipwrecks to explore.

- Sign up for an excursion around the islands with ScubaFun, which offers diving excursions daily, even in the slow season.

- Casa Daniel offers snorkeling excursions along the Dominicus Reef and to the Aquarium off Isla Catalina.

- Snorkel off Saona Island's stunning beaches away from crowds on a Saona Crusoe VIP day trip with Seavis Tours.

Punta Cana's best snorkeling can be found at The Aquarium, a five-minute boat ride off the Westin Puntacana Resort's beach.

- Explore with Blue Vision Adventures.

THE SAMANÁ PENINSULA

The Samaná Peninsula offers more diving than snorkeling—particularly off Las Galeras, where you will find some of the most challenging but rewarding dives around Cabo Cabrón and Cabo Samaná. The reef facing Playa Frontón, at a depth of up to 12 meters (39 feet), is made up of tall elkhorn corals and is visited by spotted eagle rays. An advanced dive teeming with coral and marinelife is Piedra Bonita, at a depth of over 30 meters (100 feet). The reef is home to turtles, Creole wrasse, jacks, and other Caribbean critters.

- Go with Las Galeras Divers, who are experts in this region.

a diving boat in Punta Cana

THE NORTH COAST

On the northwestern coast, off Punta Rucia beach is Cayo Arena, where you will experience some of the best snorkeling in the country with a vibrant reef and tropical fish.

- Hop on a boat to Cayo Arena with local captains parked on Punta Rucia or La Ensenada beaches.

- Arrange a day trip through Bávaro Runners in Puerto Plata.

An hour farther northwest, snorkelers and divers will find bliss off the coast of Monte Cristi, around the offshore islands of the Cayos Siete Hermanos.

- Sign up in advance with Soraya y Santos Tours for a snorkel tour of the islands.

- Go with Galleon Divers for advanced dives.

Candlelit Dinners

- **Santo Domingo:** Reserve a table in the lantern-lit courtyard of **La Casita de Papi,** set in a 16th-century building. For an alfresco dinner, it doesn't get more memorable than a table along **Plaza de España**'s row of outdoor restaurants at dusk, facing the beautifully lit Alcázar de Colón palace.

- **Punta Cana:** Get serenaded by a Dominican guitar duo while feasting on fresh conch or curried lobster at the candlelit, waterfront **La Yola,** while the fish swim underneath the illuminated dock.

- **La Romana:** Reserve the only table for two on the lower level of the outdoor deck at **La Casita,** away from other diners, and enjoy seafood alfresco beside moored million-dollar yachts inside the illustrious Casa de Campo Marina. Indulge in fresh homemade pasta while taking in the panoramic views of the Chavón River from the romantic outdoor terrace at **La Piazetta.**

- **Samaná Peninsula:** In Las Terrenas, it's hard to beat the beachfront setting of the restaurant row in Pueblo de los Pescadores, and **La Terrasse** is the best pick of all. Sit in a corner of the wooden deck and enjoy a French-Dominican menu under dim lanterns and cooling breezes. Over in Las Galeras, **El Cabito**'s tables perched at 14 meters (46 feet) above sea level offer a memorable sunset view of this fishing village's dramatic cliffs and the Atlantic Ocean.

- **Puerto Plata and Cabarete:** Dine by candlelight in a lush garden away from the Puerto Plata city noise at **Mares,** where renowned Dominican chef Vasquez creates exquisite local cuisine with a twist—sit poolside and sample his Brugal rum-soaked goat stew or flambé baby lobsters. Catch the sunset and the open ocean views from the dimly lit, thatched roof dining room of **La Otra Cosa,** and feast on seared tuna in a ginger and flambé rum sauce.

- **Punta Rucia:** Go to **Lino's** for a tiki torchlit dinner—barefoot if you choose—and feast on homemade Italian pizza.

- **Jarabacoa:** It doesn't get more romantic

sunset in Monte Cristi

than dining on the terrace at **Aroma de la Montaña,** perched 1,219 meters (4,000 feet) above sea level, while the night lights of all Jarabacoa flicker below.

Sexy Beaches

- **Samaná Peninsula:** The most beautiful, romantic stretches of sand are **La Playita** in Las Galeras and **Playa Las Ballenas** in Las Terrenas—a long shoreline with a lot of privacy.

- **Puerto Plata:** The bumpy ride to **Playa Cambiaso** will be worthwhile, particularly on the weekdays when your only company will be wild donkeys.

- **Río San Juan: Playa Preciosa**—adjacent to the better-known and busy Playa Grande—rewards with complete privacy and tranquility.

- **Miches:** The virgin beaches of **Miches** are far from the madding crowd of Punta Cana. Take a short drive and spend the day in bliss.

- **Punta Rucia:** Visitors primarily use **Punta Rucia** beach as a jumping-off point to Cayo Arena, but during the day it's a stunning, uncrowded white stretch with shallow turquoise waters. Sunset is not to be missed—complete with a fiery red ball.

Secluded Escapes

- **Bayahibe:** Book a **private sailing trip to Saona Island** on the gorgeous 51-foot *Dragonsmoke* through Seavis Tours.

- **Monte Cristi:** Go off the beaten track and charter a boat for an excursion to the remote **Cayos Siete Hermanos,** off the coast of Monte Cristi. Spend a blissful day of sunning and snorkeling with no one else around.

- **Constanza:** Experience the highest altitude in the Caribbean and bundle up in a cozy mountain cabin at **Villa Pajón,** tucked inside a protected national park. Spend the day hiking in pine forests and return to hot cocoa by your chimney.

Bayahibe village

Roots and Rhythms

The Dominican Republic is a cultural melting pot, where numerous aspects of daily life are a blend of European, African, and native traditions or beliefs. Dance to merengue beats, snack on a plate of plantain-based *tostones*, and venture into the markets to explore the *botánicas*, or herbal remedy shops. This is the real pulse of the Dominican Republic.

Day 1

Arrive in **Santo Domingo** on a Saturday morning and sample your first Dominican lunch *cafeteria* at **Hermanos Villar** in the charming **Gazcue district;** have a plate of rice and beans with chicken, or slices of *chicharrón* (pork) with sides of yucca. Walk to the **Ciudad Colonial** and check into the **Hotel Conde de Peñalba.** Take a sunset stroll through this historical area, down **Calle Las Damas** and to the **Fortaleza Ozama.** Walk back up Calle Las Damas and indulge in a romantic dinner at one of the bistros lining **Plaza de España—Pura Tasca** and

Pat'e Palo are delicious options—imbibing *chinola* (passion fruit) sangria. After dinner check out the free outdoor folkloric dance performance by the **Ballet Folklórico,** also at the plaza. An alternative is to reserve a table at the lively **El Conuco** for Dominican food—try the *sancocho* stew—and a live merengue dance show. You may even be pulled onto the floor.

Day 2

Enjoy a rich Dominican breakfast of *mangú,* fried eggs, fried cheese, and ham or sausage, with a cup of Café Santo Domingo on the outdoor terrace of **Cafetería El Conde.** Walk to the **Mercado Modelo,** close to Chinatown, and shop for larimar or amber jewelry or Dominican-made ceramics. Don't miss the clamor of the outdoor fruit and vegetable market, where *botánicas*, or traditional healers, have also set up shops selling mysterious potions. Have a toasted sub sandwich and a *batida,* or fruit smoothie, at **Barra Payán.** Visit nearby museums, starting with the **Museo**

Carnaval performers

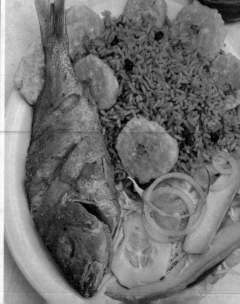

a plate of fried fish, avocado, and *tostones*

Social Impact Tourism

You'll quickly discover a diverse country that is much more than its beaches. Where to begin? Venture beyond the tourist zones and sign up for an excursion with one of the rural cooperatives that have mushroomed around the country. These inspiring entrepreneurial groups offer visitors experiences unique to their respective villages and towns—from cacao plantation visits to off-the-beaten path hikes. The income generated helps fund jobs and is reinvested into the cooperative. This evolving, exciting concept of community tourism is a win-win for travelers looking to experience the real Dominican Republic and locals working to secure a sustainable future. Find more information online at dominicantreasures.com.

PUERTO PLATA (PAGE 200)

Take a community tour through the Community Tourism Network of Puerto Plata (Red de Turismo Comunitario, tel. 809/696-6932, www.popreport.com/turisopp). They offer seven experiences unique to the province's various towns:

- Dominican baseball: Visit Bartolo Colón's home town and the stadium he built for his community.

- Cacao: Learn all about the production of organic cacao in the DR. Plant a pod, sample some chocolate, and get a chocolate mud treatment!

- Merengue: Spend the day immersed in all things merengue in a village that has produced generations of traditional merengue musicians.

- Columbus' first home: Enjoy clifftop views and tour the ruins of Christopher Columbus' home.

- Manatees: Hike two trails, paddleboard among the mangroves, visit a secluded beach, and witness dozens of manatees from a lookout tower at the Estero Hondo Marine Mammal Sanctuary.

- Amber: Tour the only place in the world where blue amber is found and where amber is actually mined.

- Coffee: Learn about the production of organic coffee in the DR from bean to cup.

JARABACOA (PAGE 276)

Stay in green lodging near the Rio Yaque del Norte at the Sonido del Yaque (Sonido del Yaque, tel. 829/727-7413, sonidodelyaque@gmail.com), run by the Club de Mujeres Nueva Esperanza, a cooperative of 30 women. They offer 10 rustic cabins tucked into the lush countryside, which are off the grid, using renewable energy and water sources. They also have a riverfront restaurant that provides organic, locally-sourced meals and they also provide local excursions.

BARAHONA PROVINCE (PAGE 311)

Arrange a homestay with local cooperative COOPDECI (Cooperativa para el Desarollo de La Ciénaga, tel. 829/560-3560, www.guanaventuras.com), based in La Ciénaga. You'll get your own room and bathroom in the house of a cooperative member, and a unique perspective on the DR.

The cooperative also manages a tour operating arm, Guanaventuras. Tours are with a licensed local guide, who can take you on a range of excursions, including snorkeling in La Ciénaga, hiking to the Cueva de la Virgen on an exclusive trail, and visiting the larimar mines.

You can learn to make artisan marmalade with the women, or grab lunch at their local restaurant, Delicias Mi Siembra.

de las Casas Reales and the Alcázar de Colón to learn about the DR's history from the colonial days, and then the Museo de la Resistencia, an excellent look at the DR's political journey post-independence. Grab an early dinner at Mesón D'Bari, serving tasty Dominican seafood and meat dishes—try the goat stew. At 7pm, head over to the San Francisco Monastery Ruins and enjoy the best outdoor live merengue and son concert with the band Grupo Bonyé. Enjoy

BAGGING A PEAK

If you're a thrill-seeker, hike to Pico Duarte, the tallest peak in the Caribbean at 10,105 feet. The excursion takes two days, beginning in Manabao just outside Jarabacoa. Local guide David Durán of Jarabacoa Eco Adventures is your best bet for a customized and affordable Pico Duarte trip. David can also take you on a climb to El Mogote—shorter yet more challenging than Pico Duarte, due to its steep and rocky terrain. You'll be rewarded with a stunning 3,815-foot summit panoramic view of Jarabacoa.

SPELUNKING

One of the most thrilling and remote caves to explore is Cueva Fun Fun inside Los Haitises National Park. Contact Rancho Capote to book a tour. The adventure begins with a horseback ride, then a hike through a wet forest, and finally a rappel down a narrow opening 28 feet below ground. You'll spot critters while hiking past Taíno petroglyphs and pictographs. There are additional caving opportunities (with freshwater lagoons) inside the Parque Nacional Del Este. The southwest is home to the least visited caves at El Pomier and Las Caritas de los Indios.

CANYONING

The North Coast is ideal for rock climbing and canyoning off waterfalls. Both Cabarete and Puerto Plata are solid bases for trips to Damajagua Falls and lesser visited falls like the Big Bastard. Visit with popular outfitter Iguana Mama.

RIVER RAFTING

Take an exhilarating rafting excursion on Jarabacoa's Río Yaque del Norte, the longest river in the DR. Contact Rancho Baiguate or Rancho Jarabacoa to book a tour.

MOUNTAIN BIKING

Hop on a mountain bike and brave the hills of the Cordillera Central. Out of Cabarete, Iguana Mama's exhilarating 31-mile "Max Endurance" takes you on an uphill, downhill, and off-road ride through Cabarete's El Choco National Park.

Jarabacoa

PARAGLIDING

Fly over Jarabacoa's mountains and verdant scenery, above waterfalls and valleys, with Flying Tony (www.flyindr.com). Tony takes you on a 25-minute drive from Jarabacoa to Paso Alto where the exciting liftoff takes place. He will also take you out to Constanza.

ZIPLINING

Ziplining above the hills of Samaná's dense El Valle forests and hills will have you screaming at the top of your lungs. Samana Zipline has the best engineered zipline in the country, which will take you 122 meters (400 feet) above El Valle over 12 lines. Flip upside down or ride together as a couple—the integrated braking system means all you have to do is focus on the panoramic views.

ATV AND QUAD RIDING

Riding at high speed down bumpy dirt roads and village tracks in an all-terrain vehicle is a fun way to get lost in nature and explore the DR countryside. In Puerto Plata, Outback Adventures offers ATV rides through the hills of Muñoz village, with visits to a local home. Samaná and Jarabacoa are also great landscapes to enjoy by ATV—rent your own from Jessie Car Rental.

some Presidente beers and twirl away on the cobblestoned streets with the locals. Night owls can keep the party going afterward at **Parada 77.**

Day 3

Rise at dawn and head north to **Puerto Plata** via Caribe Tours or Metro Tours, unless you're driving. From the city, hop in a taxi, rental car, or combine *guagua* and *motoconcho* rides to reach the hilltop **Tubagua Eco Lodge.** Drop your bags and head on a three-hour afternoon hike through the village with the lodge's local guide. You'll meet the locals, sample fruit from the trees, and trek beside river streams. Grab a cold Bohemia beer or soda at the village *colmado* along the way and continue until you reach the stunning blue sinkholes and falls of **Charcos de los Militares.** After the hike, drive 10 minutes up the **Ruta Panorámica** to the small community of **Yásica** and feast on *carne salada* at **Zero Discusión,** washed down with some Brugal rum. Or stick to the lodge for a home-cooked meal in the palapa dining room, with panoramic starlit views of Puerto Plata.

Day 4

In the morning, head out on a day trip to the small town of **Guananico** with Puerto Plata's local cooperative, **Red de Turismo Comunitario.** You'll first stop at **Hacienda Cufa** for a chocolate tour and tasting at a cacao farm. After a Dominican lunch, you'll head over to **Rincón Caliente,** where you'll experience an afternoon of merengue *típico* with renowned merengue artists, and learn about drum making, accordion playing, and dancing to merengue. Head back to **Tubagua** for the night.

Day 5

Leaving Tubagua, drive south on the winding, bumpy **Ruta Panorámica,** with glorious views of the Cordillera Septentrional mountain range, lined with small villages and colorful roadside fruit and souvenir shacks. The road leads to **Santiago,** where you should stop for lunch at **Rancho Chito,** the region's best *lechonera,* a restaurant specializing in pork roasted on a pit. The *chivo* or goat is delicious. Belly full, drive 10 minutes outside of the city to **Higüerito,** where you'll find local potters and doll makers spinning wheels. Stop for *guineos* (bananas) roadside on your way back to Santiago. At this point, head for the airport or continue your trip to **Jarabacoa** and **Constanza**—see Day 8 of the Best of Itinerary for more details.

Santo Domingo

S anto Domingo, the first city of the Americas, is the most dynamic and exhilarating city in the Caribbean. A palpable energy blankets its multifaceted neighborhoods, from the cobblestoned streets of the Ciudad Colonial to the sleek restaurants, hotel bars, and cigar lounges of the Polígono Central. No matter where you are, merengue pours out into the streets, keeping the pulse of the city.

Beyond its quaint charm lies a city with a fiercely independent spirit—thrown into relief by the statues of heroes that dot the horizon and stand for the struggle for freedom from dictatorship. The Spanish conquistadores used it as a base for conquering the Caribbean region and parts of the Americas. Santo Domingo was home to the first cathedral, the first convent for nuns, the first university, the first street in the New World, and was the first urban design template. It's a city that many fought over and occupied, including British buccaneer Sir Francis Drake, the French, and even neighboring Haiti, but it has always fought back for independence.

Today, *La Capital,* as it is affectionately called, is a bustling metropolis of 2.5 million inhabitants. It's the most cosmopolitan city in the Caribbean, with shopping malls that rival those in North America, fine dining, and more nightlife than your dancing feet could handle in one visit. Santo Domingo excels in and prides itself with promoting Dominican culture. There are festivals year-round, open museum nights, art exhibits, theatrical performances, and plenty more.

History buffs, culture lovers, shopaholics, music aficionados, and night owls—nearly every traveler will find their bliss here. Santo Domingo is a city of contrasts; it combines the past and present, the lifestyles of a seaside town and a modern metropolis, and Dominican culture with international influence.

Full of surprises: that's Santo Domingo.

PLANNING YOUR TIME

Most of the city's major sights and activities are in adjacent areas or at least a short taxi ride

---

Previous: restaurants in the Colonial City; El Malecón. **Above:** dancing at Santo Domingo de Fiesta.

Look for ★ to find recommended sights, activities, dining, and lodging.

Highlights

© AVALON TRAVEL

★ **Ciudad Colonial:** Stroll amid restored Spanish colonial buildings and bougain-villea-shaded alleys in an area that was once Christopher Columbus' stomping grounds (page 33).

★ **Parque Colón:** Surrounded by stunning architecture, centuries of Dominican history, and boutique sidewalk restaurants, the leafy Parque Colón offers a slice of Dominican life (page 33).

★ **Catedral Primada de América:** Admire the ornate interior of the first cathedral in the New World (page 35).

★ **Museo de las Casas Reales:** Journey through the Dominican Republic's history, from the arrival of Spanish colonialists to the Trujillo years, at this museum housed in a former 16th-century royal court (page 36).

★ **Alcázar de Colón:** Immerse yourself in 16th-century royal culture by touring Diego Colón's former home—the most impressive structure in the Colonial City (page 36).

★ **Parque de la Independencia/Altar de la Patria:** Pay your respects at the mauso-leum of the Dominican Republic's three independence heroes (page 40).

★ **El Malecón:** Stroll down Santo Domingo's famed Malecón, a seafront promenade home to parks, casinos, and restaurants. Buy a fresh coconut roadside and enjoy the Caribbean Sea breeze (page 42).

★ **Los Tres Ojos:** These ancient Taíno caves once used for rituals reveal a stunning ecosys-tem. Hike past giant caverns and stalagmites, marvel at the freshwater lakes, and look for turtles (page 46).

★ **Live Merengue and Son with Grupo Bonyé:** Head to the San Francisco Ruins to enjoy Grupo Bonyé's outdoor concert, held every Sunday from sunset until 10pm (page 49).

★ **Playa Boca Chica:** Relax on miles of white sand and indulge in fresh seafood at the bustling Boca Chica (page 76).

Santo Domingo

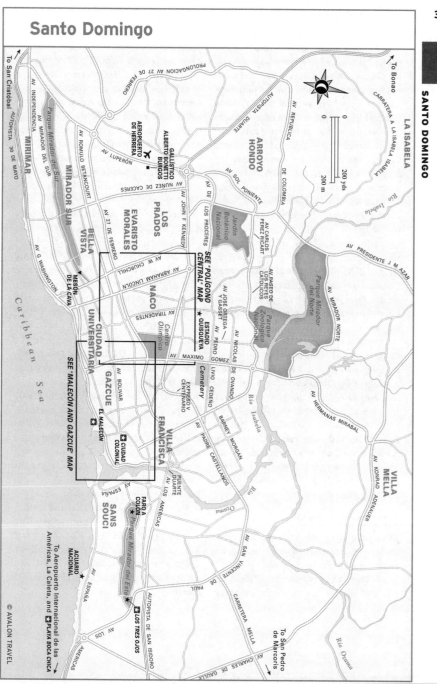

away from one another—but expect city traffic delays in the daytime.

If you have a few days or more, your best bet is to pick one of several boutique hotels in the **Ciudad Colonial** as your base and spend a morning or evening checking out the nearby **Gazcue** neighborhood and the **Polígono Central,** comprised of three upscale neighborhoods. You'll want to save a minimum of two days to fully appreciate the Cuidad Colonial and its parks, museums, plazas, and centuries-old architecture. Even if you're not much of an arts and culture buff, you should spend at least half a day in this area—after all, this is where the first city of the Americas took shape.

Finally, spend a day or two exploring nature—in the caves at the nearby **Los Tres Ojos** or at the beaches of **Boca Chica** or **Juan Dolio.** You could also opt for an excursion to a cacao farm in the lush *campo* or countryside of San Francisco de Macorís northeast of the capital.

Only have a day? Spend the morning in the Ciudad Colonial—have breakfast at a sidewalk café, then walk up and down Calle Las Damas to visit the Fortaleza Ozama, the Museo de las Casas Reales, and the Altar de la Patria. Have lunch on the Malecón, a 10-minute walk away, then head to the Museo del Hombre Dominicano in the city center and relax in the gardens of the Plaza de la Cultura. For a sunset cocktail, hit Vertygo 101 Bar in the Piantini District or head back to the Ciudad Colonial for more options.

ORIENTATION

Santo Domingo was the first planned urban space in the Americas, designed as a square, and is actually easy to navigate.

The Ozama River divides the city into east and west. West of the river are the main areas frequented by tourists: the **Ciudad Colonial,** the **Malecón,** and the **city center**—essentially the area around the major arteries of Avenidas John F. Kennedy, 27 de Febrero, Winston Churchill, and Máximo Gomez.

Arriving from Las Américas International Airport and Avenida Las Américas, whether you're heading to the Ciudad Colonial or the Malecón, you'll cross the river bridge going west along the Ozama River and down Avenida Francisco Alberto Caamaño, which heads along the Ciudad Colonial's outer edges, and turns into Avenida George Washington or the Malecón.

Heading over to the street parallel to the Malecón lands you on Avenida Independencia, where the tree-lined **Gazcue** neighborhood stretches all along the main thoroughfare as well as its side streets. It's home to several budget guesthouses, affordable local restaurants, and bustling commercial services interspersed with neighborhood corner bars. The Gazcue neighborhood is 10-minute walk to the Ciudad Colonial. Use **Independence Park** as your landmark—it faces the pedestrian street of Calle El Conde.

Avenida Winston Churchill and Avenida George Washington will connect you to the city's trendiest hubs, the three neighborhoods of Naco, Paraíso, and Piantini, making up the **Polígono Central.** Think upscale shopping malls, trendy bistros, and cigar lounges, plus movie theaters and the latest string of brand hotels with infinity pools.

Heading back east of the river and a stone's throw outside of Santo Domingo is where you'll find **Los Tres Ojos.** Continuing east leads to the city dwellers' beach escapes: **Boca Chica, Guayacanes,** and **Juan Dolio,** all a string of white sand beaches that begin just 20 minutes outside the capital.

Sights

★ CIUDAD COLONIAL

The capital's historic district—the Colonial City, formally called **Ciudad Colonial** though some locals still refer to it as "la Zona Colonial" or even just "la Zona"—stretches approximately 10 blocks, starting along the west bank of the Ozama River and spanning west up to Parque de la Independencia (Calle Palo Hincado), and bordered north and south by Avenida Mella and the Malécon (Paseo Billini). It was declared an UNESCO World Heritage Site in 1990. Sure enough, it's one heck of an architectural, historical, and visual feast to marvel at. This is the section of Santo Domingo where conquistadores like Christopher Columbus, his son Diego Colón, and first governor of the Americas Nicolas de Ovando ruled over the first city of the Americas and plotted their growing empire in the Caribbean region. So of course, it is filled with 16th-century edifices in the form of churches (including 22 chapels), palaces, and courthouses, as well as statues of key historical figures. Most of these colonial buildings have transformed into shops, museums, galleries, and boutique hotels.

Stroll along the cobblestoned **Calle El Conde**—a pedestrian haven of shops and cafés running through the heart of the area reminiscent of Barcelona's Las Ramblas. Idle away some time on a park bench alongside locals or sit at a sidewalk café with a cold Presidente and take in the seamless blend of old and new among the cathedrals and museums and wrought-iron balconies alive with flowers.

There's never a dull moment in this formerly walled, historic zone. *Guagua* or local bus conductors shout and hiss as their slim bodies hang over the edge of the vans while looking for passengers. Men slam dominoes in the shade and whisper sweet nothings as women pass by. *Motoconchos* buzz about, while merengue echoes out of restaurants and bars. *Limpiabotas*—shoeshine boys—polish away while patrons read the paper or smoke a fat cigar.

In this single area, you'll find most of what is iconic to the Dominican Republic: the interplay of life at cigar shops, sidewalk cafés, larimar and amber jewelry stores, mobile vendors selling *chicharrón* or pork rinds, Helados Bon ice cream carts, and *colmados,* the DR's iconic corner store shops that double as bars.

Note that the Calle El Conde's pedestrian buzz doesn't get going until around 10am, and if you head there early, you'll find only a couple of cafés open while all the other businesses have iron gates pulled down. Art vendors start wheeling out their wares later in the morning.

★ Parque Colón

Undoubtedly one of the best people-watching spots and most popular parks in Santo Domingo, conveniently set along the pedestrian's path on Calle El Conde, **Parque Colón** (Calle El Conde, from corner of Arzobispo Meriño) is where you'll get a glimpse of Dominicans engaging in one of their favorite pastimes: taking a break with their loved ones under the shade, while indulging in sweet treats like *palitos de coco,* listening to local musicians' ballads, and watching the world go by—from tourists to vendors and artists on easels. Sometimes you might even catch a play.. At the heart of this large square is a statue of Christopher Columbus—pointing south as he did when he first spotted the Dominican Republic from his ship—and at his feet the beautiful and valiant Taíno chief, Anacaona, who was sadly betrayed. Surrounding the park are notable buildings, including the first cathedral of the New World. Parque Colón is also where you'll find licensed tour guides—look for their khaki pants, blue shirts, and a badge hanging from their neck. Feel free to barter for a tour of the Ciudad Colonial on foot, especially if it's closer to sunset. At

Ciudad Colonial

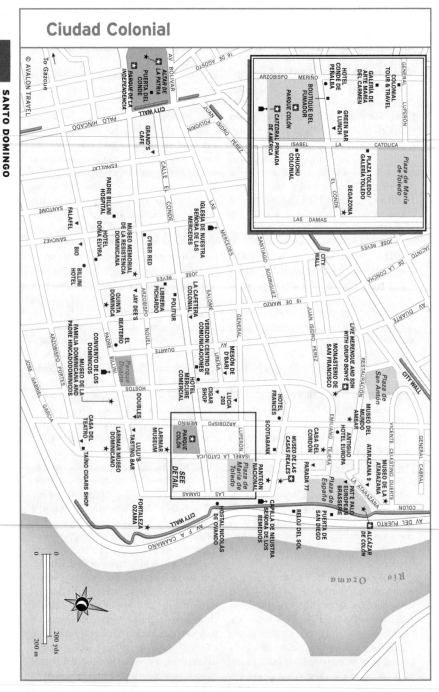

© AVALON TRAVEL

To Gazcue

0   200 yds
0   200 m

Río Ozama

night, the park is no less lively, when couples stroll after work and young Dominicans hang on corners with their beverage of choice. Whether it's just to laze away on a bench or to meet up with friends, there's no place in the city like Parque Colón.

★ Catedral Primada de América

Standing tall on the south side of Parque Colón is the first cathedral ever built in the Americas—La Basilica Catedral Santa María de la Incarnación or **Catedral Primada de América** (Calle Isabel La Católica, 9am-5pm daily, US$1.30 or 60 pesos, includes audio). It's worth shelling out the small entry fee to tour this architectural wonder, with a guide and/or with your English audio headphones. Construction launched in 1512 and was completed in 1540. The end result is one of the most ornate buildings in the Americas, showing a gothic influence and coral rock facade. It is said to have once harbored the ashes of Christopher Columbus. If you only have time for one room, look inside the sacred Chapel 12—or the chapel for prayers—and prepare to gawk at the lavish designs. As an added bonus, the sanctuary is now nicely air-conditioned.

Calle Las Damas

Known as the oldest and first paved street of the Americas, the **Calle Las Damas** or "Street of the Ladies" is where Maria de Toledo and her 39 *compañeras* would spend the evening strolling up and down from the palace. The street has kept its charm and is one of the loveliest in the Zona Colonial. You won't see frocks and wigs, but you will still pass horse-drawn carriages. On this street you will also find venerable churches, colonial buildings-turned-upscale boutique hotels, and notable sights like the Fortaleza Ozama and the Panteón Nacional. The old-world glamour remains amid the restored colonial buildings. Taking a walk down Calle Las Damas is a must.

Fortaleza Ozama

The first military fortress in the Americas and the oldest military structure, the **Fortaleza Ozama** (Calle Las Damas, 9am-5pm Tues.-Sat., 10am-3pm Sun., US$1.50) was built between 1502 and 1507 by the city's first governor, Nicolas de Ovando, to resemble a medieval castle. It has a central tower, standing tall on a bluff above the river—the Torre de Homenaje—at nearly 19 meters (61 feet). At the fort's entrance is a statue of Gonzalo

Catedral Primada de América

Fernandez de Oviedo, known for authoring "The natural and general history of the Indies"—a key document in Santo Domingo's colonial history. Climb the stairs to the top of the tower—it's more fun to use the interior spiral staircase—and take in the panoramic views of the Ozama River on one side, facing the cannons and a view of the more recent port built in 1937, and the sprawling lawns on the other. Grab a pamphlet at the entrance, if you don't need a guide—although they are usually ready and waiting for willing tourists.

Panteón Nacional

If you're a history and architectural buff, you'll immediately notice the **Panteón Nacional** (Calle Las Damas, 9am-6pm Tues.-Sun, free), an impressive, towering limestone building with a neoclassical facade. This 18th-century Jesuit church-turned-national mausoleum is said to keep the remains of over 40 famous Dominicans and national heroes who played a big part in the struggle for independence, like Gregorio Luperón. Eugenio María de Hostos, and María Trinidad Sánchez. In the doorway there will be a handsome, standing, uniformed presidential honor guard holding a Dominican flag (if you want his photo, be courteous and gesture to him if you can, they usually don't mind). Take a quick peek at the vaulted ceilings bearing a stunning mural of the Resurrection and Last Judgment by Spanish painter Rafael Pellicer. You'll also notice a giant lamp that was donated by former Spanish head of state Francisco Franco. Shorts and sleeveless tops are not always allowed, so dress appropriately.

★ Museo de las Casas Reales (Museum of Royal Houses)

Once the Royal Court and first courthouse of the Americas, dating back to the 16th century, as well as the governors' office, the **Museo de las Casas Reales** (Calle Las Damas, tel. 809/682-4202, 9am-5pm daily, US$2.20 or 100 pesos, includes English audio) covers the colonial history of the DR, from the arrival of Columbus' three ships in 1492—replicas of

La Pinta, La Niña, and *La Santa María* are on display—to the mapping of the first cities founded by Columbus and the brutal days of slavery. On the second floor, the reception hall of the governors or Gran Salón del Trono y Recepciones is a breathtaking display of opulence. Portraits of Spanish kings covering the walls look out onto mahogany floors, sparkling chandeliers, and windows opening onto the Ozama River. Directly across, the Salón de Armas houses armaments of various periods, including from Trujillo himself. Like most restored museums in the Ciudad Colonial, you'll find various open courtyards, ideal for taking a breather.

★ Alcázar de Colón

One of the most visited sights in Santo Domingo and the most impressive structures in the Ciudad Colonial is the **Alcázar de Colón** (Calle La Atarazana, Plaza de España, tel. 809/682-4750, 9am-5pm Tues.-Sun., US$2.25), the former and restored palatial home of Columbus's son Diego Colón and his wife María de Toledo, niece of King Ferdinand of Spain. The building of the palace—a soft coral limestone structure—began in 1510, a year after Colón became governor and viceroy of the colony. Columbus himself died before getting a chance to see his son's home, which held lavish events for the Spanish aristocracy, including the likes of Cortes, Balboa, and Ponce de León. The palace was ransacked around 1915 by Sir Francis Drake and immaculately restored in 1952. The rooms display artifacts and period furniture, as well as paintings and musical instruments. You can tour María de Toledo's bedroom, as well as Diego Colón's—with rare items like an elephant skin covered trunk imported from North Africa in the 17th century. Don't miss the reception hall. A spiral staircase leads to a wide veranda with a lovely view of the Ozama River and the highway buzz of the modern city below. Buy entry tickets in the white building across from the museum, and avoid Tuesday and Saturday if you dislike big crowds.

Plaza de España

At the end of Calle Las Damas and starting immediately after the Museo de las Casas Reales, **Plaza de España** (Calle La Atarazana) faces the majestic riverfront Alcázar de Colón museum and former palace and captures the old romance and the modern allure of Santo Domingo in a wide-open, unshaded square that is indeed reminiscent of Spain. Pedestrians stroll the plaza while diners relax at one of a half dozen trendy, upscale restaurants and cafés in restored warehouse buildings lining the square. Plaza de España is favored for live performances and holiday events, including a twice weekly free folkloric dance show on Friday and Saturday evenings. It is particularly delightful to walk the space after sundown, when the gas lanterns glow over couples or dog lovers take a promenade. The sidewalk terraces fill with diners enjoying their meals al fresco with a stunning view of the illuminated palace across the way. At the center of the plaza is the obligatory statue: this time, a large bronze portrait of Nicolas de Ovando, the city's first governor, known as the founder of the new Santo Domingo, but also the man said to have been behind the extermination of the Taíno. It's incredible to think that just a few hundred years ago, Europe's most famous conquistadores occupied this same space and walked the same ground.

Monasterio de San Francisco

The impressive ruins of **Monasterio de San Francisco** (Calle Hostos, Calle Duarte, and Calle Restauración) tower above several blocks of the Ciudad Colonial. Walk straight up Calle Hostos, up the hill past the Calle El Conde intersection, and you'll end up there. Built in the 16th century, the first monastery of the New World was home to the first order of Franciscans to move to the Dominican Republic. Over the years, it suffered fire—at the hands of Sir Francis Drake when he took Santo Domingo—as well as several devastating earthquakes in 1673 and 1751. It was then used as a mental asylum from 1881 through 1930—the chains used on inmates can still be seen scattered inside the site. Today, the ruins serve as a dramatic backdrop and stage for outdoor concerts every Sunday evening as well as performances and even weddings.

Parque Duarte

A nicely shaded square, tucked a couple of blocks away from the central hustle and bustle of Calle El Conde, **Parque Duarte** (Calle Padre Bellini, corner of Av. Duarte) is

The Alcázar de Colón is lit at night.

Touring the Ciudad Colonial

There are numerous ways to explore the museums, churches, and cobblestoned streets of Santo Domingo's Ciudad Colonial. You can pick one of these alternatives, or combine them if you have time to spare and depending on your level of comfort. It's easy to explore on your own, but if you prefer having company, there are guided options as well. The beauty of the area may have you returning more than once.

- **Take a self-guided walk:** It's perfectly safe to explore the details of La Zona at your own pace. You'll get plenty of information on the various museums via the English audio headsets included in your entrance fee. The easiest path is to begin at **Calle El Conde,** across Independence Park, and walk all the way down the pedestrian street to admire the shops, sidewalk art, cafés, and restored colonial homes, until you reach **Parque Colón.** From there, you can head into the cathedral facing the park before continuing on down Calle El Conde onto **Calle Las Damas,** where more iconic sights await—including Fortaleza Ozama, the Panteón Nacional, and the Museo de las Casas Reales. After visiting the latter, walk to the edge of Calle Las Damas and you'll stumble onto the grand **Plaza de España.** Wander over to the Alcázar de Colón Museum office for tickets, before entering the actual palace museum. Take a break and enjoy cocktails and bites on the terrace at one of the outdoor restaurants on Plaza de España. It's easy to explore the entire area on foot. Don't miss seeing the area at night—it's truly romantic. Note that you should stay away from the seedier outlying parts and stick to the center of the Colonial City and its main sights, day or night.

- **Hire a private tour guide:** If you're a history buff, a writer, or someone with an insatiable thirst for an in-depth knowledge of places beyond the usual basic tourist information, contact the passionate local historian **Miguel Roman** (tel. 809/299-4906, miguelfroman@gmail.com, US$20/hour), a former college professor in the United States turned freelance guide, for a private walking tour. Otherwise, you can head to Parque Colón and find a guide by looking for blue shirts and khaki pants. These folks are licensed by the tourism board and will usually spot you before you spot them. Pick one that speaks your language well and bargain for your walking tour. Prices start at US$10 and may rise, depending on your haggling skills and the guide. Guides are enthusiastic about their city and full of valuable information you might not glean from an audio recording. You might need to tell them to slow down if they speak too fast, but they also don't mind stopping for your dozens of photos. If you can, tour closer to sunset—the golden

a low-key favorite among the area's older residents during the day, and by night, a popular hangout with occasional drumming. It was once DR founding father Juan Pablo Duarte's "headquarters," where he would meet with fellow independence heroes Mella and Sánchez. The park faces spectacular colonial buildings like the first convent of the Dominican Order in the Americas, built in 1510, and the first university. At the center of the park is a statue of Duarte.

There's more buzz after sunset and later in the week, when groups of friends of all ages gather around drinks they bring from the *colmado* across the park. It's also a popular pre-party rendezvous spot for gay Dominicans,

especially on the weekends. Stick around at night instead of going to the disco and you might make some friends or end up dancing to impromptu drumming from a group of Rastafarians. It is a space that welcomes all to come to take in the beauty of the surrounding Ciudad Colonial. You'll find local guides here as well during the day, but if you're not interested, a simple no thanks will suffice.

Convento de los Dominicos

Set in a stunning brick and white colonial building on Parque Duarte is the church of the **Convento de los Dominicos** (Calle Padre Billini, corner of Avenida Duarte, tel. 809/683-1817, 8:30am-noon, 3pm-pm Mon.-Sat., light shining on the colonial buildings makes the area even more beautiful and the heat more bearable. A reliable local guide I've used and who is often onsite is **Socrates Valenzuela** (tel. 829/393-9629 or 809/407-8570)—you can ask around the park for him.

- **"Trikke" your way through history:** Sign up for a three-wheeled electric scooter tour of the area—day or night—one of the new fun ways to explore Santo Domingo. **Trikke Colonial** (Calle Padre Billini 54, tel. 809/221-8097, www.trikke.do, 9am-10pm Mon.-Sat., 9am-8pm Sun., US$35-45) has one-hour or 90-minute tours that come with headgear, a guide, audio, and water. Solo travelers can also show up at any time of day and get a one-on-one tour. Young and dynamic bilingual guides will lead you to the Zona's main sights—including the cathedral, Calle El Conde, Plaza de España—occasionally stopping to take in some history and snap some photos. Soak up plenty of cultural tidbits along the way. I was nervous hopping on a motorized scooter and navigating the busy streets, but you get to warm up and practice for about 10 minutes before taking off. You'll be relieved to know that cars are more inclined to slow down for Trikke riders than for pedestrians!

- **Hop on the train:** The **Chu Chu Colonial** (Calle El Conde 60, corner of Isabela La Católica, across Parque Colón, tel. 809/686-2303, www.chuchucolonial.com, 9am-5pm daily, US$12) is a train-like wagon that may look a little touristy, but it's a fun way (for children in particular) to imagine the lives of Spanish conquistadores as you glide past ancient buildings to the sound of hooves on cobblestone. You'll be placed in sections according to language preference for the audio recording. If you're not up for walking in the sun or have kids and prefer a quick 45-minute historical tour in English that you can retrace on foot another day, then this is a nice option to get the lay of the land, if a tad pricey by local standards. Tours run throughout the day, every hour on the hour.

- **Cruise on a bicycle:** Rent a beautiful turquoise beach cruiser bicycle from **Zona Bici** (Calle Salomé Ureña, corner of Reyes, tel. 809/979-1260, 9am-1pm, 3pm-7pm daily, US$6.60/ hour per bike, includes helmet and water bottle), the latest ecofriendly way to get around in this historical neighborhood. It's conveniently located in the heart of the Zona, so you can zip through the small alleys and hidden corners at your own pace, with or without a guide. They also have a tricycle for those who might be a tad nervous, and 2- to 4-year-old baby seats if you need them. Bike locks are included, as well as a basket for any items you might be carrying.

US$3.40). The Dominican friars arrived in Santo Domingo in 1510, and established the oldest Catholic church as well as the first university in the Americas—one of its wings remains open, but the rest of the university was relocated. The friars were the greatest advocates for the Taíno, who were suffering at the hands of the Spaniards. One of the most outspoken was Friar Anto Montesino, whose gigantic statue you can see at the start of the Malecón. Inside, the church is a testament to Roman and Gothic architecture, with a vaulted ceiling, mahogany altar, and statue of Santo Domingo de Guzmán, the founder of the Dominican order. There are five chapels, and masses are held every morning and Sunday evenings.

Quinta Dominica

You might miss this spot unless you walk slow and observe. The **Quinta Dominica** (Calle Padre Billini No. 202, tel. 809/687-5944, http://quintadominica.com, 9:30am-6pm Mon.-Sat., free) just steps across from Parque Duarte is a delightful one-floor 16th-century former home turned gallery with rotating art such as portraits of various Spanish and British royalty, including one of Columbus himself. There are no English audio guides or labels, but the visual display is sufficient to appreciate. Most beautiful of all, however, is the open courtyard and its lush gardens at the back of the property. Grab a bench and take a respite in nature—right in the city, yet away from everything and everyone.

Museo del Mundo Ambar

Museo del Mundo Ambar (Calle Arzobizpo Meriño 452, tel. 809/682-3309, www.amberworldmuseum.com, US$1.10) is worth the stop if you have time to spare. This lovely 17th-century colonial building turned private museum houses a jewelry store and souvenir shop on the ground floor, and up a flight of stairs is the museum. Inaugurated in 1996 by Jorge Caridad, who worked with amber from age 12, this comprehensive display of stones of various sizes from various countries is well displayed with bilingual captions and includes details on the formation of amber. Look for the Dominican Hall corner for a display dedicated to Dominican amber and its history.

★ Parque de la Independencia/ Altar de la Patria

At the start of Calle El Conde, the **Parque de la Independencia** (Calle El Conde and Calle Palo Hincado, 8:30am-6pm) faces the busiest transportation hub and avenue in the city. *Motoconchos, guaguas,* and cars are almost incessantly zipping by at this intersection between old and new, past a park commemorating the Dominican Republic's struggle for independence. At the park's entrance, also facing Calle El Conde, you'll notice a stunning arched entrance known as the **Puerta del Conde.** It indicates the start of the Ciudad Colonial and is one of the most symbolic locations in the country's long history to freedom. It is here that Count of Peñalba defended against an invading British force in 1655. It is also here that in February 1844, independence fighters executed a coup against occupying Haiti and liberated the country to form an independent Dominican Republic. The first Dominican flag was raised on top of Puerta del Conde.

Inside the gated park, up a series of steps on the west end, you'll find the impressive **Altar de la Patria,** a white marble mausoleum. In the mausoleum, there are large statues of the country's Founding Fathers, each of which is holding their respective remains: Juan Pablo Duarte, Matías Ramón Mella, and Francisco del Rosario Sánchez. On Independence Day, the president stops here to lay a wreath on the tomb of the Founding Fathers. Interestingly, Independence Park is considered the "kilometer zero" marker, or the geographical point

Parque de la Independencia

Santa Bárbara's Murals

one of Santa Bárbara's murals

On the northern edge of the Zona Colonial and directly facing the port behind ancient walls and cannons is the once forgotten and neglected neighborhood of Santa Bárbara. Home to the Santa Bárbara Church, where the DR's Father of Independence Juan Pablo Duarte was baptized, and the Santa Bárbara Fort, which helped protect the city, it became known later as *el eslabón perdido*, or the missing link.

In April 2015, the area's visibly run-down walls benefitted from a weeklong community revival art project, sponsored in part by the Ministry of Culture, called "Hoy Santa Bárbara." Artists from the DR and the Latin Caribbean—including Esteban del Valle, Vero Rivera, Dominican Natalie Ramirez, and Bik Ismo—set up shop in the streets and painted vibrant murals, most of them representative of Dominican culture.

Thanks to the colorful murals, which increasingly bring local photographers for creative shoots, the area has seen a rapid transformation. Walk all the way past the Alcázar de Colón, take the stairs down to street level and keep straight without exiting the Colonial City. Within a block and a half, on your left hand side you'll begin to spot Santa Bárbara's new colorful walls. The murals can be found across a few side streets, so feel free to stroll around to view all of them—the locals are now used to tourists wandering up this way for photo ops.

from which all distances on roads and highways are measured.

MALECÓN AND GAZCUE
Palacio Nacional

The **Palacio Nacional** (Av. Dr. Delgado)—often a quick roadside stop included in city tours—is a regal building in Gazcue that stretches across an entire block. Inaugurated in 1947, the palace was built of roseate marble extracted from the Samaná Peninsula and designed in a neoclassical style by Italian architect Guido D'Alessandro. The building is now used as the offices of the Executive Branch of the Dominican Republic. An outside view and photo is likely all you'll get, I'm afraid, as tours are not allowed.

Museo Memorial de La Resistencia Dominicana

If you're a political buff or want to understand the key moments in history that impacted Dominicans during the brutal Trujillo regime and after it, visit the **Museo Memorial de la**

Resistencia Dominicana (Calle Arzobispo Nouel 210, tel. 809/688-4440, 9:30am-6pm Tues.-Sun., US$3.30 or RD$150, with audio). The most striking exhibit features a wall of heroes who fought against Trujillo and perished, and the gruesome history of the dictator's regime, including the Haitian genocide of 1937 and the murder of the Mirabal sisters in 1960.

★ El Malecón

An iconic landmark of Santo Domingo is the city's seafront Avenida George Washington, known as **El Malecón.** Facing the Caribbean Sea and dotted with large hotels, casinos, seafront restaurants, and movie theaters, this is where locals escape the heat of urban life and catch some fun when they can. It's also where you'll see them getting some exercise or dancing by the sea after sundown. The Malecón is one of the features that contributed to Santo Domingo being declared the 2010 Culture Capital of the Americas. It's come a long way, and while there's still visible pollution along the promenade and in the sea—you'll see plastic bottles, Styrofoam lunch boxes and other waste scattered in certain areas—it has seen some major improvement and remains a lovely place to walk and catch the breeze. Coconut vendors set up here, and there are parks and entertainment for families—notably, Plaza Juan Barón and Playa Güibia. It's a safe area during the day, but don't wear jewelry or carry valuables; thieves have been known to jump curbs to grab unsuspecting tourists' cameras. The liveliest, and perhaps safest, stretch of the Malecón is near the Hilton Hotel, at Güibia Beach, with a playground for kids, workout machines for adults, and live Zumba classes, not to mention a stretch of beach good enough to sink your toes in. But remember: don't bathe in these parts as the waters are polluted and the currents strong.

Plaza Juan Barón and the Obelisk

Facing the Caribbean Sea and renovated in 2009 as part of a large-scale effort to revitalize the Malecón, **Plaza Juan Barón** (Av. George Washington, Malecón, 4pm-midnight Sun.-Thurs., 4pm-2am Fri.-Sat.) is an outdoor recreational area for all, and particularly ideal for families. The kids can enjoy pizza and hot dogs, ride mechanical horses, zip around go-kart racing, biking and more. There are also various food stands. The cliff-top location is a dream for those seeking a break from the city madness. Events and karaoke nights are frequent, and there's an onsite bar where you

Santo Domingo's Malecón

Malecón and Gazcue

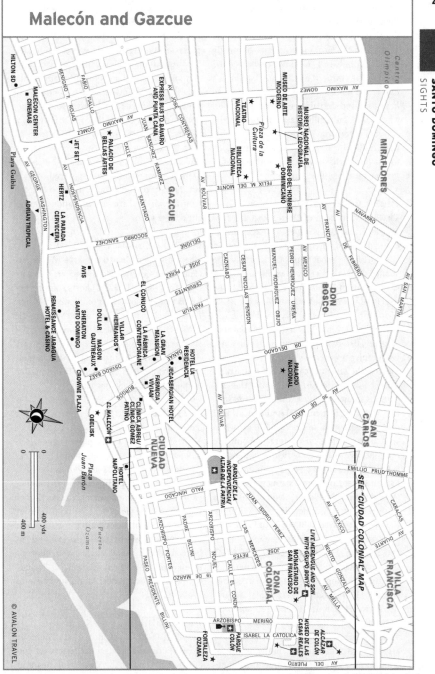

HILTON SD •

MALECON CENTER
■ CINEMAS

Playa Gúibia

ADRIAN TROPICAL

AV. GEORGE WASHINGTON

Centro Olímpico

MIRAFLORES

BENIGNO F. ROJAS

FABIO FIALLO

AV. JOSE CONTRERAS

EXPRESS BUS TO BAVARO
AND PUNTA CANA

JUAN SANCHEZ RAMIREZ

CALLE

AV. MAXIMO GOMEZ

MUSEO DE ARTE
MODERNO ★

MUSEO NACIONAL DE
HISTORIA Y GEOGRAFIA ★

AV. MAXIMO GOMEZ

TEATRO
NACIONAL ★

Plaza de la
Cultura

MUSEO DEL HOMBRE
DOMINICANO ★

BIBLIOTECA
NACIONAL ★

★ JET SET

★ PALACIO DE
BELLAS ARTES

GAZCUE

AV. INDEPENDENCIA

HERTZ ▲

LA PARADA
CERVECERA ▼

SANTIAGO

SOCORRO SANCHEZ

FELIX M. DEL MONTE

AV. BOLIVAR

AV. FRANCIA

NAVARRO

AV. 27 DE FEBRERO

AVIS ■

JOSE J. PEREZ

CERVANTES

PASTEUR

DELIGNE

EL CONUCO ■

CAONABO

CESAR NICOLAS PENSON

MANUEL RODRIGUEZ OBJIO

PEDRO HENRIQUEZ UREÑA

AV. MEXICO

DON
BOSCO

AV. SAN MARTIN

RENAISSANCE JARAGUA
HOTEL & CASINO ●

SHERATON
SANTO DOMINGO ■

DOLLAR ■

MASON
GAUTREAUX ▼

OSVALDO BAEZ

VILLAR
HERMANOS ▼

LA FABRICA
CONTEMPORANE ▼

LA GRAN
MANSION ▼

DANAE

BURGOS

HOTEL LA
RESIDENCIA ●

FARMACIA
VIVIAN ■

DR. DELGADO

PALACIO
NACIONAL ★

▼JECASERGIAN HOTEL

CROWNE PLAZA ●

OBELISK ■

EL MALECON ■
CLINICA ABREU/
CLINICA GOMEZ ✚
CLINICA GOMEZ/
PATINO

CIUDAD
NUEVA

AV. 30 DE MAYO

AV. BOLIVAR

SAN
CARLOS

HOTEL
NAPOLITANO ●

Plaza
Juan Barón

Puerto
Ozama

PALO HINCADO

✚

PARQUE DE LA
INDEPENDENCIA/
ALTAR DE LA PATRIA ★

JUAN ISIDRO PEREZ

ARZOBISPO NOUEL

ARZOBISPO PORTES

ARZOBISPO MERIÑO

PADRE BILLINI

PASEO PRESIDENTE BILLINI

19 DE MARZO

LAS MERCEDES

CALLE EL CONDE

NOUEL

REYES

JOSE
REYES

EMILLIO PRUD'THOMME

SEE "CIUDAD COLONIAL" MAP

AV. MEXICO

BENITO GONZALES

LIVE MERENGUE AND SON
WITH GRUPO BONYE ●

MONASTARIO DE
SAN FRANCISCO ✚

ZONA
COLONIAL

MUSEO DE LAS
CASAS REALES ✚

ALCAZAR
DE COLON ✚

ISABEL LA CATOLICA

PARQUE
COLON ✚

FORTALEZA
OZAMA ★

AV. DEL PUERTO

CARACAS

AV. DUARTE

AV. MELLA

VILLA
FRANCISCA

0   0

400 yds
400 m

© AVALON TRAVEL

can sit and drink the night away. Across the Plaza is the iconic 40-meter-tall (130-foot) **Obelisk** of Santo Domingo—known locally as *Obelisco Macho* or male obelisk—originally built by Trujillo in 1935 when he renamed the capital after himself as Ciudad Trujillo. It's one of the few dictator-built monuments to have survived destruction after his murder. The current mural illustrations represent the Mirabal sisters who spoke out loudly against the Trujillo dictatorship and were murdered for it. The obelisk serves as a reminder of *la lucha*—the struggle for freedom.

Plaza de la Cultura

This treasure trove of Dominican art, history, and museums is centered on a gated, verdant courtyard where all that is Dominican is showcased. What you'll find in this one space, officially known as **Plaza de la Cultura Juan Pablo Duarte,** is the Museo del Hombre Dominicano, the Museo de Arte Moderno, the Teatro Nacional Eduardo Brito, the National Library, the Museum of Natural History, the Museum of History and Geography, a cinema showing Dominican movies, the cinema's café, and a restaurant. I like to call it the Smithsonian of the DR. With its sprawling lawns, fountains, and statues, it is a perfect cultural and educational oasis. Expect it to be busy on Friday, when students from the various area schools are brought here on a weekly field trip. Plaza de la Cultura also hosts a popular annual Book Fair in the spring. There's a metro stop and station within the Plaza called the Casandra Damirón stop, convenient if you want to try the first metro system in the Caribbean.

MUSEO DEL HOMBRE DOMINICANO

If you only have time for one modern museum in Santo Domingo, make it the **Museo del Hombre Dominicano** (Plaza de la Cultura, Av. Pedro Henríquez Ureña, tel. 809/687-3622, 10am-5pm Tues.-Sun., US$2.30 or 100 pesos). Three floors of this spacious building are filled with information on the origins of Dominicans, from the first Taíno inhabitants to present-day DR through a detailed showcase of history, culture, and religion. The first two floors house Taíno pieces and rituals displays—including body decor, ceramics, and artwork. All the labels are in Spanish, but you can follow along thanks to an English audio recording device included in your entry fee. If time is short, head straight to the fourth floor and spend most of your time in the Ethnology Room covering the history of the DR from its so-called discovery by the Spanish to modern-day Dominican life. The Carnival displays alone are worthwhile, with hundreds of colorful masks covering the walls and costumes from the various carnival celebrations around the country.

MUSEO DE ARTE MODERNO

The four-story **Museo de Arte Moderno** (Plaza de la Cultura, tel. 809/685-2154, 10am-5pm Tues.-Sun., US$2.30) hosts rotating exhibits from various parts of the world. When I visited, I stumbled on an exhibition on Ethiopia in the basement. The most impressive permanent displays are of Dominican art dating from 1844 all the way to the present. There's no coffee shop here, so bring a water bottle with you if you need it.

Museo Bellapart

The private **Museo Bellapart** (Av. J. F. Kennedy corner of Dr. Lembert Peguero, tel. 809/541-7721, ext. 296, 9am-6pm Mon.-Fri., 9am-noon Sat., free) is housed on the fifth floor of a Honda building and hosts rotating exhibits as well as a permanent collection of more than 2,000 pieces of Dominican art from paintings to sculptures dating from the 19th century all the way to 1980s. It's a great way to learn about the various stages in the country's history and about its renowned artists, including Jaime Colson, Yoryi Morel, and Celeste Woss y Gil.

Playa Güibia

Playa Güibia is a seaside park and outdoor gym where you can feel the breeze as you enjoy the views of the Caribbean Sea and mingle with locals. The park livens up in the evening after sunset, particularly on the weekends, and turns into a giant entertainment center on public holidays, with street closures.

AROUND SANTO DOMINGO
Faro a Colón (Columbus Lighthouse)

This stand-alone, 204-meter-tall (670-foot) memorial building is an oddity in a desolate neighborhood and commemorates the life of Christopher Columbus. It was inaugurated on the 500th anniversary of his arrival to the Dominican Republic. Guards stand outside the cross-shaped **Faro a Colón** (Av. España, tel. 809/591-1492, US$2.25). It is said to house Columbus' remains, although Spain and Cuba have previously disputed that fact. Another controversial aspect of this gigantic building is its lighting mechanism, which is said to project a cross straight up into the sky that can be seen as far away as Puerto Rico. Turning it on causes a complete black out in Santo Domingo, though, so it's never lit. The most interesting part of this sight are the various chambers displaying—ironically—indigenous artifacts and history from each country in Latin America and the Caribbean. The surrounding neighborhood isn't one to wander around in at any time of day. The Faro a Colón is a bizarre sight at best, and not worth a special trip. But if you are going, a taxi ride from the Ciudad Colonial would cost around US$5; you can negotiate to have your taxi wait for you.

Jardín Botánico Nacional

The largest botanical garden in the Caribbean and the fourth biggest in the world, the **Jardín Botánico Nacional** (Av. República de Argentina, esq. Av. Los Próceres, tel. 809/385-2611, www.jbn.gob.do, 9am-6pm daily, trolley departs every 30 min., US$5) is a lush 640-acre expanse of native trees, flowers, and plants from around the island. There are over 5,000 flower trees, including 360 species of orchids and over 100 species of palm trees. Founded in 1976, the full name of the garden is the Dr. Rafael Ma. Moscoso National Botanical Garden, named after the first Dominican botanist who documented and catalogued all the DR's flora in 1943. You may also see the national bird, the *cigua palmera*—or palmchat bird—nesting atop a royal palm. Entry tickets include a guided tour of the museum—worthwhile to get a quick introduction to varied topography of

Los Tres Ojos

the DR's six regions—and a 30-minute open trolley ride (with a guide on loudspeaker, whose English you might not always get) that will take you through the gardens' various sections. The Japanese garden is not to be missed—the trolley stops here and you get to walk around long enough for photo ops. From there, you can hop off anywhere you like to continue wandering on your own. There's a free guided birding hike every Sunday—meet at the main entrance at 7am.

★ Los Tres Ojos

A trip to **Los Tres Ojos** (Parque Mirador del Este, 8am-5pm daily, US$2.30) is one of the most popular tours closest to Santo Domingo and actually one of the most worthwhile.

Prepare to gasp as you step onto a narrow staircase that leads you all the way down into a series of three limestone caves once used by the Taíno for sacred ceremonies. Hike around giant grottoes filled with stalactites and stalagmites and dotted with three phosphorescent blue freshwater lakes (hence the name, The Three Eyes). Look closely in these waters and you'll spot turtles; they swim closer to the edge if you're lucky.

You can hop onto a hand-cranked wooden barge for US$0.50 to reach a fourth, separate cave with the most beautiful emerald lake. There's a local who stays in the cave every day who will dive into one of the lakes if you tip him. It's a gorgeous spot for photos and a lovely nature break from the city.

Entertainment and Events

Dominicans from around the island will tell you: they love Santo Domingo at night. Whether it's the live music, the trendy clubs, or sidewalk bistros facing lantern lit, cobblestoned plazas—there's something magical and energizing about this city after dusk. Blame it on the romantic ballads and catchy beats of the country's national music ringing all over its neighborhoods. Each day of the week in La Capital brings another "place to be," so keep an eye out for the latest, including happy hour specials, by consulting www.quehacerhoy.com.do.

NIGHTLIFE
Bars and Clubs

Get started by hitting up a *colmado* for some cold Presidente beers, music, and local vibes—there are some fantastic no-name ones in the Ciudad Colonial, particularly on Calle Pale Hincado, at the corner of Arzobispo Portes. Then go for a happy hour al fresco in the Ciudad Colonial or at a fancy hotel bar on the Malecón or in the Piantini District. And *then* go dancing.

In the Ciudad Colonial, you'll find a whole row of bars on Calle Hostos, which intersects with Calle El Conde, and some fancy spots a block north of the Parque Colón. For a night of seeing and being seen, dress casual chic and head to **Lulú Tasting Bar** (Calle Arzobispo Meriño 151, corner of Padre Billini, www.lulu.do, 6pm-3am daily), one of the trendiest lounge-like places to hang out after work hours or on weekends with a gorgeous outdoor terrace and an equally attractive interior of tables and dim lit bars filled with top liquors. The bartenders are friendly and the food here is good. For live merengue music with bites, there's the brand-new **Jalao** (Calle El Conde 103, tel. 809/689-9509, www.jalao.do, no cover), conveniently located across Parque Colón, opened by the owners of Lulu's and Pat'e Palo. Dress appropriately for this one if you go in the evening.

For more of a chill-out bar party vibe, the popular chain **Onno's** (Ciudad Colonial, Calle Hostos 57, corner of Calle El Conde, tel. 809/689-1183, www.onnosbar.com/zonacolonial, 9pm-3am, drinks US$4-10) never disappoints and attracts more foreigners.

Barhopping Circuit

Lulú Tasting Bar

Santo Domingo is has the best nightlife in the DR. Start off in the Colonial City, where the happy hour buzz gets going at sunset—have a beer at a local *colmado* to warm up, and then go for some sangria at Tasca, overlooking the lit Alcázar de Colón. Afterwards, head over to Lulú Tasting Bar where the young and fabulous mingle over tapas and wine or a number of premium cocktails on an outdoor colonial terrace. From there, walk over to Doubles, a popular bar that fills up early.

Take it up a notch with a taxi ride to the Malecón and park yourself at Parada Cerveza, for some Brugal rum or Bohemia over loud merengue and the sea breeze blowing from across the avenue. Feel like a fancier vibe? Continue on with a taxi hop to the open-air Vertygo 101 Lounge & Bar, at JW Marriott, with panoramic views over the city center.

When you're ready and warmed up for more music with your drinks, grab another taxi and head to the first drive-through bar in the Dominican Republic at El Trompo (Av. Tiradentes, Ensanche Naco, tel. 809/878-5827), with happy hour from 6pm-10pm. You could also end your night back in the Ciudad Colonial, where patrons are packed on small dance floors under dim lights while the salsa, son, and merengue echo out onto the cobblestoned streets, starting with Onno's. Then stumble down to Bio—just a couple of steps over—to dance some more. If you're able to leave the exhilarating mood there, walk over to Parada 77 for even more dancing, some of which spills onto the sidewalk, or grab a taxi to La Cacibajagua—a hip and funky lounge set in a colonial building, with a DJ spinning old-school R&B to world beats.

The volume and the mood rise as the clock strikes twelve, like at most watering holes in the area.

La Cacibajagua (Calle Mercedes #319, corner of Sánchez, tel. 809/333-9060, Tue.-Sun., 10pm-2am) is another solid bet for a laid back and funky atmosphere, with DJs spinning rock, old school, and alternative music in a dim lit, cozy colonial building that spreads out into a courtyard. Expect a diverse,

eclectic, 30-something crowd, and occasional live music.

You won't see a sign outside, but El Sartén (Calle Hostos 153, tel. 809-686-9621, 10pm-2am, no cover) is a local dance spot and bar for the older crowd, playing Latin beats in a small space that gets crowded late at night. Most head here after Onno's, just a couple of doors down. If you're up for dancing in a crowded and more hip space, the small disco Bio Bar (across Falafel Restaurant, Calle Sanchez 125, tel. 829/766-8122, 11pm-3am, no cover) works for after midnight stops. The DJ spins a variety of international dance tunes while the light and smoke effects are full on. Head to the second floor and dance freely wherever you're standing.

Parada 77 (Calle Isabela La Católica 255, one street before Plaza de España, tel. 809/221-7880, 7pm-1am Mon.-Thurs. and Sun., 7pm-3am Sat., no cover) is the preferred, casual hot spot in the Ciudad Colonial, with a twenty to thirty-something crowd dancing the night away to merengue, bachata, and salsa on a dimly lit open floor inside a colonial building. There's a doorway to a back courtyard, as well, where you'll find more couples twirling under the stars on a second floor. If you're solo, don't be afraid to ask a guy or gal to dance! Many also like to take a breather outside on the sidewalk with their drinks. This is a popular stop on Sundays after the outdoor Bonyé concert at the nearby San Francisco Ruins. Look out for any weekday live bands on the social media site.

Club Murcielago (formerly Guacara Taína, Av. Mirador del Sur 655, tel.809/533-1051, 9pm-2am Tues.-Sun., www.guacara-taina.net, US$7) was popular in its heyday, but is now more of a tourist club, where newcomers experience the thrill of dancing inside a cavernous chamber underneath the Parque Mirador del Sur. Music ranges from merengue to contemporary genres like rap.

Jet Set (Av. Independencia 2253, tel. 809/535-4145, 9pm-3am daily, US$7) is the one nightclub that remains while others come and go like the wind—it's been around at least 40 years. Skyline views of the city add to excellent live merengue and salsa bands during the week, including a popular live bachata night on Mondays that's not to be missed.

Speaking of a jet-set crowd, mix and mingle with Dominican professionals and business travelers at the gorgeous **Vertygo 101** (JW Marriott, Av. Winston Churchill 93, Piantini District, tel. 809/807-1717, drinks US$6-20). Bring your bathing suit if you dare, for a dip in the transparent infinity pool while you sip on cocktails and nibble from the tasty bar bite menu. And don't forget to stand on the glass floor terrace, where you can stare at your toes 101 feet above Avenida Winston Churchill.

East of the Ozama River, across the bridge and off the beaten path from the tourist-trail of the Malecón is another favorite among young Dominicans, **Euphoria** (Calle Venezuela #15, across from Burger King, euphoritard@hotmail.com), on a street famous for its string of clubs and bars, most of which are ultra-local and play Dominican beats. Just say "La Venezuela" to a taxi driver and he'll know where to go. Leave the valuables at home and go with a local if you can.

If you're a salsa fan, the place to be is **Discoteca El Águila** (Av. San Vincente de Paul 20, tel. 829/578-3434, infoaguilard@gmail.com, 9pm-4am Wed., 9pm-3am Fri.-Sat., 3pm-1am Sun., no cover), where you'll see some of the country's best *salseros*.

Live Music

One of Santo Domingo's best features is its affinity for live music; it's a big part of the capital's culture. A number of restaurants and lounges across the city offer regular performances. Quite a few take place in the Ciudad Colonial, usually in some spectacularly romantic outdoor courtyard. From merengue to salsa and son, city dwellers love any excuse to enjoy dancing to bands all week long.

Owned by the same folks as Mesón D'Bari, **Lucía 203** (Calle Hostos 203, tel. 809/689-5546, 10pm-1am Thurs., no cover) is a must for dancing, if you're lucky to be in the capital on a Thursday. It's the most popular live music spot and evening in the Zona and for good reason—a fantastic band performs son, as well as merengue, inside a beautiful colonial building, with seating centered around an open Spanish courtyard. The dancing usually kicks off around 11pm on a small but packed floor with a nice crowd of all ages. Reserved seating is available, but you'll find plenty of space if you arrive early. Drinks and food are available all night, while you twirl the night away with friends or with others you meet there.

Earlier on Thursdays is the weekly **Live Jazz in the Colonial City** (Calle El Conde, 6pm, no cover), with various talents performing Afro-Caribbean rhythms, from rumba to son and samba, on the Escalinatas del Conde, or the stairs at the very end of Calle El Conde, just past the intersection with Calle Las Damas. You'll often find a young international crowd gathered here, from neighboring hostels and local meetups.

Las Terrazas at Mesón de la Cava (Av. Mirador Sur 1, tel. 809/533-2818, www.elmesondelacava.com, 8:30pm-midnight, no cover) hosts local band Sonbossarengue, Tuesday through Friday, outdoors on its breathtaking, mood-lit garden dining terrace. Expect to eventually rise from your seat and burn off your meal with some hard-to-resist Latin beats.

Along the Malecón, on the poolside restaurant terrace of the **Hotel Napolitano** (Av. George Washington 51, tel. 809/687-1131, reservas@napolitano.do, Thurs.-Sat. 8:30pm-midnight, no cover) is a live merengue band that attracts plenty of locals on the weekends. It's hard to beat dancing al fresco with the Caribbean Sea breeze blowing away.

Located inside a lively casino, **Merengue Bar** (Gran Casino Jaragua, Av. George Washington 367, tel. 809/221-1435, no cover) serves up plenty of cocktails and meal specials all week, but it also offers a live merengue band and ample dance floor every single evening starting at 9pm. The floor gets pretty packed with locals, pre- or post-gambling.

★ LIVE MERENGUE AND SON WITH GRUPO BONYÉ

Bars and dance clubs there are aplenty in the Ciudad Colonial, but you won't find a more lively and exhilarating ambience than the weekly outdoor Sunday night concert and bash with popular local band **Grupo Bonyé** (Calle Hostos, 5:30pm-10pm Sun., free) performing against the backdrop of the sprawling Ruins of San Francisco. For four hours, city dwellers from all corners to gather at this historic spot to dance from sundown to evening to merengue, son, and salsa. This brilliant cultural event is sponsored by the Ministry of Tourism and attracts everyone out of their respective neighborhoods across the city: tourists, locals, expats, rich and poor, young and old. It's a safe environment to party in—just mind your purses and pockets. Ladies, you might be asked

Grupo Bonyé at the San Francisco Ruins

to dance, and it's perfectly fine to accept or decline. Plastic tables and chairs are laid out across the plaza starting around 5pm—come early if you want to save space for your group. The dance floor gets filled with avid dancers almost as soon as the band hits their instruments, and the neon stage lighting glowing on the ruins, under starry skies, gives the place an atmosphere unlike any other. There are food vendors onsite, and drinks flow from Presidente booths, as well as small local bars set directly across from the event—order your jumbo Presidente bottle from the **Riconcito de Don Guillermo** for quicker service. This is one event you do not want to miss.

Gay and Lesbian

There's a solid gay and lesbian community in the city, as in any major metropolitan hub. While clubs and bars come and go, there are a couple of favorite gathering spots.

Parque Duarte (Ciudad Colonial, Calle Duarte and Calle Billini) is one of the popular meeting points and pre-party hangouts for young and old gay Dominicans, particularly on weekends. One long-standing bar is **Esedeku** (Calle Las Mercedes 341, a block north of Calle El Conde, tel. 809/763-8292, esedekubar@gmail.com, 9pm-1am Wed.-Sun., 3am close on Fri.-Sat.), named after the Spanish pronunciation of SDQ, Santo Domingo's acronym. It calls itself "more than a bar" and a meeting place. You'll find a young and lively, up-market crowd, often residents, mingling indoors and on a rooftop lounge. Be sure to dress appropriately—no tees and sneakers—as with other nightlife venues in the city. The Sunday karaoke nights are popular as well.

Click Bar (Calle Vincente Duarte, close to Plaza de España, tel. 829/449-5154, 9pm-3am Thurs.-Sun., no cover) is primarily for lesbians, but anyone is also welcome to come and mingle in this trendy club setting. Occasional male and female strip shows and drink specials are offered.

For a night of loud clubbing with a young crowd, head to **Fogoo Discotec** (Calle Arzobispo Nouel 307, 10pm-4am Thurs.-Sun., US$3 cover on Fri.-Sat.), always busy with plenty of sidewalk hustle and bustle, and special events or theme nights posted on social media channels. Adjacent is **G Lounge** (Calle Arzobispo Nouel 305, tel. 829/550-5565, 10pm-3am Thurs.-Sun., no charge), attracting crowds with fun drag shows and male strippers in barely-there thongs. Police have been known to shut the place down for noise.

For more on the gay and lesbian scene in Santo Domingo, check www.monaga.net.

THEATER

The **Teatro Nacional Eduardo Brito** (Av. Máximo Gómez 35, tel. 809/687-3191, www.teatro.com.do) hosts plays and musical performances year-round at the country's most prestigious facility. The stunning building is within the Plaza de la Cultura complex, with three air-conditioned halls—the largest seats 1,800 people—and excellent acoustics. Check the website for scheduled plays. There's a metro stop right by the theater, if you're feeling adventurous.

On any given day of the week, there are multiple events at the active **Casa de Teatro** (Calle Arzobispo Meriño 110, tel. 809/689-3430) in the Ciudad Colonial. It's one of the most active artistic centers in the city, founded in 1974. You'll find art and photo exhibits, movie nights, plays, and a café hosting live music most nights. The calendar is updated often, so stay tuned to social media sites.

Other smaller and reputable theaters in the city offer plays every month, including **Teatro Las Máscaras** (Calle Arzobispo Portes 56, next to Plaza de la Cultura, US$10) holding just 50 seats, and **Teatro Guloya** (Calle Arzobispo Portes 205, between Hostos and 19 de Marzo, tel. 809/685-4856, teatroguloya@yahoo.com), with plays for children and adults.

For the latest plays, check the frequently updated online schedule on http://teatro.com.do.

CINEMAS

The **Palacio del Cine** (http://palaciodelcine. com.do) chain is your best bet—these theaters are exactly like the ones you find in the United States, with ultra-comfortable seats, air-conditioned rooms, your usual popcorn and soda stops—except they also sell beer. The latest movies are on display and show in English, with Spanish subtitles. One of my favorite locations has seven showings inside the **Ágora Mall** (Av. John F. Kennedy, corner of Abraham Lincoln, tel. 809/732-0800, US$5.50, US$7 for 3D). Other solid picks are the **Blue Mall's Palacio del Cine** (Av. Winston Churchill, corner Gustavo M. Ricart, tel. 809/955-3086, US$5.50-10)—where there's a separate VIP section, and the first IMAX theatre in the country at **Caribbean Cinemas** on the second floor of **Galería 360** (Av. John F. Kennedy, tel. 809/567-0162, www. caribbeancinemas.com.do, US$5-7) or at the **Acropolis Center** (Av. Winston Churchill, tel. 809/955-1010, US$3-5).

A block away from the Fortaleza Ozama, tucked inside a restored colonial building, the **Colonial Gate 4D Cinema** (Calle Isabel la Católica and Padre Billini, tel. 809/565-0746, info@thecolonialgate.com, 9am-5pm daily, every 15 min., US$8) jolts you back to 1586 when Sir Francis Drake invaded the walled city of Santo Domingo. This is probably the most exhilarating five minutes I've experienced in a movie theater, from sudden seat movements to water mists in the air as pirate ships roam the seas by the Dominican Republic. The movie is available in both English and Spanish. There's a lovely outdoor courtyard you can enjoy after the movie, as well as a photography display of various regions of the Dominican Republic.

CASINOS

The 24-hour **Gran Casino Jaragua** (Av. George Washington 367, www.casinojaragua. com, tel. 809/230-5383) facing the Malecón is one of the best and liveliest casinos in Santo Domingo. It's beside the Renaissance Jaragua. Here, anytime any day of the week, you'll find plenty of Dominicans trying their luck at slot machines as well as blackjack tables, roulette, and a closed-off VIP room. The atmosphere is laid-back, and the nicely air-conditioned space and free drinks while you gamble are delightful after a hot walk under the sun. On the weekends, twirl to a live Dominican band at the onsite Merengue Bar, from 9pm.

The smaller **Crowne Plaza's Casino** (Av. George Washington 218, U.S. tel. 877/859-5095 or 809/221-0000, 24 hours) is another option, located across the Malecón, and with slot machines, roulette, blackjack, and poker tables. A tad livelier is the casino at the **Napolitano Hotel** (Av. George Washington 51, tel. 809/687-1131, www.napolitano.com. do).

FESTIVALS AND EVENTS

Santo Domingo de Fiesta

Sponsored by the Tourism Ministry, **Santo Domingo de Fiesta** (Plaza de España, no phone, 9pm-midnight Fri.-Sat., free) is an incredibly entertaining two-hour folkloric dance show covering the history, geography, and cultural heritage of the DR—from indigenous to African and Spanish—through music and dance. This free show is held twice a week under the starry skies on the far edge of Plaza de España. The vibrant performances are ones you won't forget anytime soon—grab a seat and indulge in this visual feast. If you stay till the end, you'll see the night end with the audience—including you—pulled onto the floor for merengue with the professional dancers, until everyone goes home close to midnight. This is a real treat for those interested in the music, history, and diversity of the DR.

Carnival and Independence Day

The Dominican Republic's biggest, most significant and festive celebrations take place during the month of February, with **Carnival parades** every Sunday until the first weekend of March, and Independence Day Parades celebrated on February 27. This makes for one long week (and actually, even a month) of parties and shenanigans. In Santo Domingo, the main Carnival revelry takes place along the Malecón, part of which is closed off for the festivities on Sunday afternoons. Show up around 4:30pm and watch from the block along the Hilton Hotel or Güibia Park.

On **Independence Day,** head to the Puerta del Conde around 1:30pm to catch a glimpse of the president and the pomp and circumstance while he passes to pay tribute to the Founding Fathers. Otherwise, the best Independence Day event to catch is at 4pm along the Malecón: an impressive, colorful military parade begins at the Obelisco Macho and stretches all the way down the waterfront avenue. It lasts until 7pm. Expect surprises—including ships offshore blasting canons and fighter jets and helicopters overhead—while the parade goes on. It's a great time to catch the energy of this city, with tons of folks spread out along the Malecón, and plenty of vendors and local scenes. You can bring your cameras and smartphones but keep an eye on your surroundings.

Semana Santa

The festivities of **Semana Santa** or Holy Week roll out every year, starting with a street procession on Palm Sunday through the Gazcue and Ciudad Colonial neighborhoods. Good Friday has the most impressive procession of all, starting at dusk at Iglesia de las Mercedes, running through the streets of the Colonial City, and ending back at the cathedral across Parque Colón for the 8pm official mass and concert. The concert is one of the most popular events of the week; get there early if you want seats. Easter Week is otherwise quiet within Santo Domingo, as most Dominicans head to the *campo* or countryside and to nearby area beaches with family. You'll find many of them at Boca Chica to Juan Dolio. There will also be plenty of action and company at Playa Güibia, where the streets are closed and the seafront venue transforms into a giant outdoor pool and amusement park for the enjoyment of local families who can't afford or weren't able to travel.

Merengue Festival

Held in late July, Santo Domingo's **Merengue Festival** is a celebration of Caribbean rhythms, from the country's bachata and merengue sounds to salsa, reggae, and reggaeton. Major Dominican artists, as well as visiting ones, perform on a massive

Semana Santa processions

stage at Plaza Juan Barón over a weekend—usually Friday and Saturday—along the Malecón. But festival-related events and mini concerts can start as much as a week or two earlier, with food vendors selling Dominican fare, artisan booths, and plenty of rum to keep the merengue fever going. Book your rooms early as this is one popular event.

Festival Presidente

If you want to see just how much the Dominicans love their Latin music, you'll have to attend **Festival Presidente,** a three-day concert and festival held every other year in October at the gigantic Felix Sánchez Olympic Stadium. You'll gasp at the sight of over 50,000 dancing fans, clapping and screaming to lyrics as major Dominican artists perform, as well as visiting international stars like Maná and Bruno Mars. It's a jolly fun time—complete with the most amazing fireworks mid-concert, water jets splashing the standing audience in front of the stage, and green Presidente balloons to wave around with the rest of the crowd. You'll see people dancing in the aisles or from their seats, and pizza vendors will pass by with slices and drinks for sale if you'd prefer not to leave your seat to go to the downstairs food court area. Buy tickets in advance, bring small change, and don't carry anything of value—cameras are not allowed at all within the venue and security checks are strict, so stick to your smartphone.

Colonial Fest

The celebration of all things Ciudad Colonial takes place over three days in late November at **Colonial Fest,** with concerts and ballet dancing performances by the cathedral, artisan products, food specials, and even historical reenactments in period costumes. There are also culinary lessons at various locations within the neighborhood. Every day of the fest, the night ends with a free outdoor concert on Plaza de España. The events begin at 10am and go on until midnight, and sometimes 1am.

Noche Larga de los Museos

If you're lucky, you'll be in town when the **Noche Larga de los Museos** hits the Ciudad Colonial. During the long night at the museums held one day in each season—spring (March), summer (June), fall (September), and winter (December), the Colonial City's major museums open their doors to the public until midnight, free of charge. Additional events are also in place at each venue to celebrate. It's a lively time to be out and about on foot.

Shopping

Shopping in Santo Domingo is plentiful, and it's the main hub for most expats who otherwise live in other parts of the country. You'll find discount fashion shops and lots of shoe shopping all along Calle El Conde, in the Ciudad Colonial. Arts and crafts, as well as souvenir and jewelry shops, are also well represented all over this area. For American and foreign chains like Forever 21 and Zara, go to the U.S.-style malls listed below in the Piantini downtown district.

ARTS AND CRAFTS

Galería de Arte Maria del Carmen (Arzobispo Meriño 207, Ciudad Colonial, tel. 809/682-7609, artemariadelcarmen.com.do, marthopm@hotmail.com, 8am-8pm daily) is a charming 30-year-old gallery, hosted in a restored colonial home, carrying original and certified works of art from Dominican artists such as Luis Oviedo and Miguel Gomez, as well as Cuban and Haitian works from Bernard Sejourne. The paintings come in all sizes and are each breathtaking, from abstract to vibrant portraits. You could easily miss this gem of a gallery as it's up a side street from Parque Colón and has no sign on the outside. Ask lovely host Nuri Jacob to show you her own paintings—they've been exhibited at the city's top museums, including Museo del Hombre Dominicano. Shipment is available by FedEx.

On a parallel street tucked away in the corner of Plaza Maria de Toledo is **Galería Toledo** (formerly Bettye's Galería, Calle Isabel la Católica 163, tel. 809/688-7649, www.galeriatoledo.com) selling both Dominican and Haitian art, including pieces by Luis Oviedo. The store also carries souvenir trinkets, handmade purses, and jewelry.

Tucked away from the pedestrian throngs of the Ciudad Colonial, yet a block away from the action, **Galería Bolos** (Calle Isabel La Católica 15, tel. 809/686-5073, 9am-8pm daily, http://galeriabolos.blogspot.com) is a fantastic place to get a unique, handmade piece of Dominican or Haitian art, sculpture, and crafts made across the country. From recycled wood mirrors to paintings depicting Dominican scenes prepare to spend quite a bit of time in this colonial building. They also have carnival devil figurines made of papier-mâché and handmade purses. Bring your wallet.

La Placita Mercadito Colonial (Calle Isabel La Católica 151, Ciudad Colonial, tel. 809/686-2406, carmellymorel@gmail.com, 9am-10pm) is a large, lively souvenir store where you're sure to find a classic DR gift for every member of your family from Dominican rum to mamajuana (you can sample them), T-shirts to cups, larimar jewelry to art. Walking through the store alone is sheer fun. It stretches far enough that it takes at least five minutes to get to the back, where you'll end up on a different street.

Galería de Arte Nader (22 Rafael Augusto Sánchez, tel. 809/544-0878, 9am-7pm Mon.-Fri., 10am-1pm Sat.) showcases work by Dominican artists.

BOOKS AND MUSIC

The megastore **La Sirena** (Av. Mella 258, tel. 809/221-3232, 8am-8pm Mon.-Sat., 8:30am-3pm Sun. and holidays, www.tiendalasirena.com) has a book aisle in most of its locations. Offerings consist of a mix of Dominican history and education books, as well as international authors and children's tales.

In the heart of the city, **Librería Cuesta** (Av. 27 de Febrero, corner of Av. Abraham

Ágora Mall

Lincoln, tel. 809/473-4020, 9am-9pm Mon.-Sat., 10am-7pm Sun., www.cuestalibros.com) is the best bookstore chain in the capital, with a two-level Barnes & Noble type of design, complete with a café and an audiovisual music listening room.

The annual **International Book Fair** (Feria Internacional del Libro, ferilibro@gmail.com) hosts all the bookstores gathered in one place at Plaza de la Cultura, during this weeklong festival of all things literary, music and theater. See the website to find out when the fair will take place.

CLOTHING AND ACCESSORIES

You'll find all of your favorite U.S. stores—including Forever 21, Zara, Mango, Nine West—at the popular **Ágora Mall** (Av. Abraham Lincoln, tel. 809/363-2323, www.agora.com.do, 8am-9pm daily) offering the best range of affordable apparel and shoes. Another option is **Galería 360** (Av. John F. Kennedy, tel. 829/995-7360, www.galeria360.com.do, 10am-9pm Mon.-Sat. and 11am-8pm Sun.). For higher-end designer labels, head to the posh **Blue Mall** (Av. Winston Churchill, corner of Calle Gustavo Mejía Ricart, tel. 809/955-3000,

www.bluemall.com.do, 10am-9pm Mon.-Sat., 11am-8pm Sun.).

Pick up summer dresses and accessories with a Caribbean flair designed by Dominican designer Jenny Polanco at **JP Project Ciudad Colonial** (tel. 809/221-3796, call for hours, www.jennypolanco.com.do) a boutique tucked a block away from Calle Las Damas. There are also locations throughout the island.

MARKETS

Spare at least thirty minutes for a colorful, lively Dominican experience shopping at the **Mercado Modelo** (Av. Mella, Mon.-Sat. 9am-6pm, noon close on Sun.), originally built in 1942 by Rafael Trujillo as one of Santo Domingo's first tourist venues. On the northern edge of the Ciudad Colonial, you'll go up a flight of yellow-painted stairs and end up in an old covered market building filled with souvenir stalls selling all things Dominican—from larimar jewelry to wood carvings and carnival masks, including some Haitian art. Be sure to bargain hard, and prepare for various vendors to call out "mi amor" and insist on you viewing their wares. Politely decline if you're not interested. Note that the prices here are some of the best you'll find after you

fruits at the Mercado Modelo

bargain, and you would be supporting the locals. Head to the back of the market for the food section—from fish to fruits and obscure "cure-alls" or love potions—and watch Dominicans doing their own haggling, amid banter and passing traffic. The neighborhood isn't so safe at night, so stick to daytime hours. It's an easy walk back to the Ciudad Colonial from here, if you continue up a couple of blocks from the market's front entrance and turn right on Calle Duarte.

La Sirena (Av. Mella 258, tel. 809/221-3232, 8am-8pm Mon.-Sat., 8:30am-3pm Sun. and holidays, www.tiendalasirena.com) is the DR's version of K-Mart—you can find absolutely anything here, from a fully stocked supermarket to apparel, electronics, and household items. There are at least a dozen locations throughout Santo Domingo, but my favorite is the large one across from the Blue Mall, complete with a food court.

CIGARS

You can watch a *tabaquero* roll cigars by hand in the Dominican style at **La Leyenda del Cigarro** (Calle El Conde 161, corner of Calle Hostos, across from Mercure Hotel, tel. 809/682-9932, www.laleyendadelcigarro.com, 9am-9pm daily). Sample a variety, and sit and enjoy your cigar purchase with wine or rum at the back tables or out on the sidewalk. Brands unique to the store are El Secreto Cubano. There are artisanal cigars you can buy as singles, if you prefer not to purchase a whole box. Hats and larimar jewelry are also for sale.

CHOCOLATE AND SWEETS

The **ChocoMuseo** (Calle Arzobispo Meriño 254, corner of El Conde, tel. 809/221-8222, www.chocomuseo.com, 10am-7pm Mon.-Sun.) is a great place to get a quick, free taste of Dominican cacao—one of the country's four largest exports. It's not a museum by any stretch of the imagination. Instead it's a store where you can get some background on organic cacao farms in the country and sample some organic chocolate made right here in the DR. Chocolate bars and other treats are on sale.

La Casa de los Dulces (Calle Emiliano Tejera and Arz. Meriño, tel. 809/685-0785, 9am-5pm Mon.-Sat.) displays over 20 different types of Dominican desserts and sweet-tooth snacks on its shelves, just like a supermarket. Choose from dried fruits to blocks of *dulce de leche* and mini coconut cakes. Get a cultural lesson while you indulge. You can also shop for reasonably priced souvenirs.

Sports and Recreation

BASEBALL

Passions run deep for baseball in the Dominican Republic, and this fervor for the sport goes back to the late 19th century. Some attribute this to the U.S. occupation of the DR in 1916, but it's more likely that it came earlier from Cuban immigrants who fled their country in the late 1890s. Either way baseball is a sport that Dominicans took to and integrated into their culture over 100 years ago. Dictator Rafael Trujillo had a solid hand in modernizing and solidifying the game, building the first major stadium in the capital, which he called Estadio Trujillo (later renamed Estadio Quisqueya). The major leap and source of pride for the DR came in 1956 when Ozzie Virgil joined the New York Giants as an infielder, becoming the first Dominican to play in Major League Baseball. Since then, the DR has contributed more players to the major leagues than any other country, or even combined Latin American countries.

From rich to poor, cities to countryside, baseball unites all Dominicans in conversation or in person at a game. In the cities and towns, the green patches where young adults train are a guaranteed sight. Beyond the fun of the sport itself, baseball also represents hope for economic salvation from a life of poverty—for the player, his family and community—and a dream of becoming famous. It certainly was a dream come true for players like Sammy Sosa, Bartolo Colón, and Pedro Martinez, to name a few.

Six teams from around the DR make up the Liga de Béisbol Profesional de la Republica Dominicana, the country's professional league, and compete each season. They are the Águilas Cibaeñas (Santiago/Estadio Cibao), Gigantes del Cibao (San Francisco de Macorís/Estadio Tetelo Vargas), Estrellas Orientales (San Pedro de Macorís/Estadio Julian Javier), Toros del Este (La Romana), Leones del Escogido and Tigres del Licey (both Santo Domingo/Estadio Quisqueya). Ask a local about favorite teams and it's a sure conversation starter. The winner of the season's games goes on to play in the Caribbean Series.

The baseball season in the Dominican Republic runs from the end of November through the end of March, so if you're visiting during these months, you should absolutely catch a game with Licey or Escogido at **Estadio Quisqueya** (Av. Tiradentes, tel. 809/540-5772, www.estadioquisqueya.com. do, 5pm Sun. or 8pm Tues.-Sat. except Thurs., US$5-20). Purchase your tickets ahead of time, though you can also snag them at the door as the games begin. A baseball game in the DR, particularly in Santo Domingo, is livelier than any in the United States—with a marching band in the stands, fans waving flags while swigging beers, mascots and cheerleaders shaking their behinds on the field, and vendors roaming the aisles with pizza slices. Going to a baseball game is a quintessential Dominican experience.

GOLFING

One of the closest and best picks for golfing is one hour east of Santo Domingo, in the beach resort town of Juan Dolio. **Guavaberry Golf and Country Club** (Nueva Autovía del Este Juan Dolio, tel. 829/547-0000 or 809/333-4653, www.guavaberrygolf.com.do, US$95/18 holes) is a championship course designed by the legendary Gary Player. It borders a nature reserve and is famous for one signature holes played over a 15-foot waterfall. Onsite are a clubhouse with pool, private beach club, restaurant, and bar. Golfers often purchase package stays with the nearby Coral Costa Caribe Resort.

Estadio Quisqueya

DIVING

One of the most popular dives is a mere 12 miles from Santo Domingo's shores at **Parque Nacional Submarino La Caleta** (Autopista Las Américas Km. 25, tel. 829/278-4874, info@reefcheckdr.org). It's considered one of the best dive spots in the country. It's also a popular spot for beginner PADI lessons with a depth of just up to 20 feet and a protected bay. The chief attraction here is a 1984 shipwreck, the *Hickory,* as well as several underwater Taíno sculptures.

You'll find the closest independent dive shops in **Boca Chica**—and the more economical way to explore this shipwreck. Call ahead to check on scheduled dives with **Tropical Sea Divers** (Beachfront, Calle Duarte 35, tel. 829/697-9522, www.tropicalseadivers.com, 8am-5pm daily, 2-tank dive US$64 or US$150/5-dive package, plus applicable transport), because the weather determines whether or not they head out to La Caleta. If they are, hop on an early *guagua* from Parque Enriquillo and reach Boca Chica in time for the boat.

COCKFIGHTING

Everyone tells you that baseball is the primary sport in the Dominican Republic. But lo and behold, there's another activity just as iconic: cockfighting. It remains fairly hush-hush, and those who participate are usually countryside folk who seem to just know where and when to go. If it's not your cup of tea, it's easy to ignore. Otherwise, there are cockfighting rings *(club gallistico)* in nearly every major city and village—but some of the most authentic in decor are in Santo Domingo. Those who are interested shouldn't miss the 42-year-old **Coliseo Gallístico de Santo Domingo Alberto Bonetti Burgos** (Av. Luperón, tel. 809/563-1503, www.gallerosoy.com); the season calendar is online, with sessions running from October through August. Another place to experience local ambience—sans sign or name, as is often the case—is just a couple of steps **adjacent to the National Zoo** (Av. Paseo de los Reyes Católicos, from 2pm Sat.-Sun., between US$4.50-11). It's in a semi-dodgy area so bring your driver. There's no charge to stand by the gate and quickly take a peek inside.

THE CACAO TRAIL

A two-hour drive north of the city, **El Sendero del Cacao** (tel. 809/547-2166, www.cacaotour.com, year-round, from US$89) takes Santo Domingo visitors out of

cacao pods at El Sendero del Cacao

the city hustle and bustle and into the great Dominican *campo*—one that is lush with cacao trees in the northwestern province of San Francisco de Macorís. Hacienda La Esmeralda Garcia Jimenez, one of the oldest family-owned cacao farms in the country, is a 100-acre plantations—with 2,400 acres on yet another piece of land. It runs a chocolate factory onsite where it harvests, processes, and exports 80 percent of its product overseas to Europe, mostly France. A guide will walk you through the actual plantation, where you'll learn about cacao pods and trees, how it's harvested "family style" in the DR, and the three challenges facing the crop on the island. You'll get to walk through the ancient Maya way of making chocolate—pounding the mortar and pestle to crush the beans—and the fermentation process, before ending up in the factory where modern chocolate bars are made. The obligatory gift shop is where you can purchase these rarely sold organic chocolate bars. If you visit on a Friday, you might run into school groups, but it makes for a livelier visit. It's a trip that will give you a solid glimpse into the fertile and lush Dominican countryside and one of its four most important crops.

HIKING

Head just one hour southwest of Santo Domingo to **Dunas de las Calderas national park,** better known as **Las Dunas de Baní** for a unique landscape not found elsewhere in the Caribbean. Hike sand dunes as if you're in the desert and take in the splendid surrounding Caribbean sea views. It's an easy day trip, whether in your rental car or by public transportation. The buses to the town of Baní leave from Parque Enriquillo, and also pass along the Malecón for pickups anywhere you flag them down. Once in Baní, switch to a *guagua* to Las Calderas (the driver will know where to drop you off).

Food

CIUDAD COLONIAL
Cafés

Noah D'Bari (Calle El Conde 155, tel. 809/688-5712, 8am-9pm daily, US$0.90-2) is conveniently located a stone's throw from Parque Colón. It's perfect for a quick, affordable coffee, sandwich, and pastries—including chicken or beef empanadas—before hitting the alleys of the Ciudad Colonial.

La Cafetera Colonial (Calle El Conde, 7am-5pm daily, from US$2), affectionately called "La Cafetera," is your historic Dominican diner. Founded in the 1930s, it was once a favorite gathering place for the country's artists, politicians, and writers. It remains a staple of the area, no matter how many trendy sidewalk digs show up. You'll find the cheapest and tastiest coffee and greasy breakfast here, from Dominican fried cheese to simple eggs on toast. Sit at the counter if you can bear the hard stools and don't mind the not-so-chatty servers, or grab a table at the back for more privacy. It's perfect if you're short on time. Right outside is the pedestrian buzz of Calle El Conde.

Café La Marielle (Calle El Conde, 9am-6pm daily, US$2-10) is an ideal pit stop with affordable gourmet snacks from European-style square pizza slices to French pastries, baguette sandwiches, coffee, and fresh-squeezed juices. The open-air, cozy seating area allows some people watching without being obvious, unless you prefer to sit outdoors at one of the sidewalk tables.

Grand's Cafetería & Bar (Calle El Conde 516, tel. 809/685-5577, 24-hour daily, US$2-15) is a lively, affordably priced café at the very start of Calle El Conde across the hub of Avenida Independencia. Meals are served inside or al fresco along its sidewalk tables if you want more action. You can also join the locals sitting at the counter with the day's newspaper

El Plato Dominicano

A blend of Taíno, European, African, and even Middle Eastern influences, Dominican food isn't complicated—it's hearty comfort food, made from fresh homegrown ingredients. Much of it is fried, stewed, and served with plenty of meats (pork and goat are favorites) and starches to fill your belly up fast (like cassava bread and *batatas*, or potatoes). A great online resource on all things Dominican food is www.dominicancooking.com. Here are a few basics to get your exploration started:

- *Desayuno criollo/Dominicano:* The typical Dominican breakfast consists of fried eggs, fried salami slices, fried cheese (*queso frito*), and a couple of *mangú* mounds, topped with sautéed red onions. *Mangú* is mashed plantains, seasoned with salt, lemon, and butter. Some throw in avocado slices. You'll find these rich breakfasts sold roadside and at restaurants.

- *La Bandera Dominicana:* "The Dominican Flag" is the national dish. It's a plate of rice and beans served with meat stew (often beef or chicken). It usually comes with a side salad, like *ensalada rusa,* a creamy potato salad with eggs, peas, and carrots. It's sold cheaply at around US$3.27 and easy to find anywhere in the DR. *Note:* You can also ask for *concón*—the slightly burned, scraped crispy bottom coat of the rice in the pan.

- *Chicharrón:* These are bits of pork fat and rinds, deep-fried to perfection. You'll find street vendors pushing their *chicharrón*-topped carts or carrying them on a platter on their heads. Only the strong of stomach should try these.

- *Sancocho:* This hearty soup is the holy grail of Dominican cuisine. Often served at holidays, celebrations, and family gatherings, it's a thick concoction combining multiple ingredients seasoned and cooked in one pot: chicken, pork, potatoes, green plantain, yucca, yam, onions, and green peppers. The bowl of *sancocho* is topped with an avocado slice and a spoonful of white rice. This dish is a good cure for hangovers.

- *Pica pollo:* Deep-fried chicken with a thick, crispy skin is a popular street food, and one of the cheapest meals you'll find in the DR.

- *Locrio de pollo:* The Dominican equivalent of paella—seasoned rice mixed with chicken.

- *Quipes:* The Middle Eastern migration to the south of the island in the 19th century brought the Lebanese kibbeh—a delicious croquette snack, crispy on the outside and mushy meat fillings on the inside. These snacks are found roadside and at restaurants.

- *Pasteles en hoja:* Frequently served at Christmastime are *pasteles en hoja*—"Dominican tamales" made with plantain dough, filled with meat, and wrapped in a plantain leaf.

to read and a delicious, cheap cup of coffee while the merengue beats on. Just like the menu, this place is a slice of Dominican life.

Not up for crowds? **Córner Cafe** (Paseo Colonial, behind Calle Padre Billini, tel. 809/338-4040, US$0.50-4) is a darling new spot tucked in one of the prettiest and quietest alleys in the Ciudad Colonial, directly behind the Billini Hotel's courtyard. There are two sidewalk tables shaded by pink bougainvillea, as well as indoor seating. Snacks range from mini almond croissants to pies, quiche slices, freshly baked bread, and, of course, gourmet coffee, tea, and wine. The breakfast combos and prices are super-reasonable.

Dominican

Popular with locals and tourists, **Cafetería El Conde** (Calle El Conde 111, tel. 809/688-7121, www.condepenalba.com, 24-hour daily, US$3-15), at the foot of Hotel Conde de Peñalba, has the best-looking outdoor terrace and buzz in the Zona. Its umbrella-shaded tables sit smack by the Parque Colón

A common Dominican breakfast consists of fried cheese, fried salami, eggs, and a pile of *mangú*, or mashed plantains.

- *Tostones:* Served as a side, these are plantains that are mashed, fried, and refried to make them crispy.

- *Aguacate:* Avocados are wonderfully abundant and large in the DR, making them a common side dish on menus. You'll also spot the avocado vendor on the street, selling freshly sliced portions to munch on along your route.

- *Mofongo:* Plantains mashed with garlic—the mixture can be combined with meat or shrimp (*camarofongo*).

- *Batida:* Dominicans have a sweet tooth; they love *batidas,* or fruit smoothies with a splash of condensed milk. A popular kind is the *morir soñando*—"dying while dreaming"—an orange juice smoothie with a splash of condensed milk.

- *Dulce de coco:* Crunchy bits of coconut, a popular dessert snack.

- *Palitos de coco:* Coconut balls with a caramelized outer shell.

- *Habichuelas con dulce:* Sweet creamed beans, served during Easter.

with its constant foot traffic, musical events, and nonstop action. It's a great place to grab a Dominican meal and a beer and admire the colonial buildings surrounding the square. The affordable menu specializes in local fare, but also offers burgers and sandwiches. The Dominican breakfast here is excellent.

Directly across the popular Parque Colón, the outdoor, casual **Green Bar & Lunch** (Calle El Conde, 101 Plaza Colón, tel. 809/221-9677, greenbarlunch@gmail.com, 7am-midnight daily, US$5-7) can be described with the "three B's" as is said in the DR: *bueno, bonito, barato* (tasty, pretty, and cheap). Grab a sidewalk table on the lively cobblestoned street and pick from an affordable menu of Dominican and sandwich and burger options. Don't forget to ask about the *plato del día* or Dominican dish of the day. Throw back a Presidente and do some people watching in the colonial zone. The vibe here is laidback, upbeat, and local. If you're out touring the museums and want a quick option, this would be it.

Offering European-style tapas with a Dominican touch, newcomer **Mercado Colón** (Calle Arzobispo Nouel 105, tel. 809/685-1103, www.mercadocolonge.com, 12pm-1am Mon.-Sat., closed Sun., US$2-8) is an indoor market and restaurant that has converted itself in the hottest place to eat in the Ciudad Colonial. Set in a restored colonial building with original tiles, part coral stone walls, and Dominican decor, the tavern-like wood interior is split into six stands including a Dominican dessert stop and three air-conditioned bar and seating areas (including a wine bar and imported beer stand). Hugging the outdoor patio—with seven to eight wooden tables under a covered, leafy terrace—are three windows where you can place your order for the tapas menu of your choice from hot to cold bites. To die for are the *montaditos* or units of three tapas topped on house-baked bread—like The Dominican, combining osso buco, avocado, and fried plantains. There is also a wood-fired pizza station for personal-size pizzas. The later it gets in the day—particularly after 9pm Friday through Sunday—the more well-heeled city dwellers flock here to spend time "sharing good food without leaving the wallet hanging," as its co-owner described it.

★ **Mesón D'Bari** (Calle Hostos 302, Ciudad Colonial, US$15-30), once featured on the Travel Channel, serves tasty Dominican dishes. Try the stewed goat in a *criollo* sauce, or one of the many seafood options. Set in a colonial home for over 30 years, the bar is popular with locals, but this restaurant is where you'd go for a special night out surrounded with art, dim lighting, and live merengue music on weekends. It's just a block away from Calle El Conde, yet tucked away from the crowds and the street noise.

For seafood lovers, the arrival of **La Casita de Papi** (Calle Hostos 356, corner of Calle Mercedes, tel. 809/221-0079, 7pm-midnight daily, US$11-13), which earned its fame in Cabarete, is great news. The restaurant, set in a romantic colonial building that formerly housed La Taverna Vasca restaurant, serves up Dominican seafood dishes that rival its original location, as well as steaks and pastas. Grab a table in the dim leafy courtyard and order the signature *langostina* or *camarones a la Papi.*

Made famous thanks to an episode of Anthony Bourdain's *No Reservations,* the original **Barra Payán** (30 de Marzo 140, tel. 809/689-6654, 24-hour daily, US$3) is an open Dominican diner dating back to the 1960s, complete with red stools and a silver-lined counter. It serves toasted baguette sandwiches stuffed with a choice of fillings, from chicken and cheese to ham, pork, salami, and burgers. Wash it down with fruit juice squeezed on the spot—shaken with ice or with condensed milk Dominican-style. Or do like other locals and pull into the parking lot while a server rushes to your car window to take your order. It's perfect for those late-night snacks that soak up the alcohol after a night of dancing.

Newcomer **Jalao** (Calle El Conde 103, tel. 809/689-9509, www.jalao.do, noon-1am, Tues.-Sun., US$5-12), run by the same owners as popular Lulu's and Pat'e Palo, has an ideal location directly across from Parque Colón, where the old Hard Rock Cafe was located, and promises a menu and ambience that is *100 D'aquí*—100 percent from here. While the decor is Dominican and the service friendly, the huge two-story restaurant feels impersonal and more like a tourist trap than an authentic local hangout. Still, some dishes are worth the try, including the yucca croquettes stuffed with cheddar, and the Jalao Burger topped with a slice of fried plantain. A loud live band entertains on weekend nights.

International

The pizza is tasty and comes in generous portions at the sidewalk restaurant and bar at **Segazona** (Calle El Conde 54, tel. 809/685-4461, 9am-1am Mon.-Thurs., later close Fri.-Sat., US$3-15), stretching along the last and most romantic block of Calle El Conde beneath trees and flowered balconies. It's a great place to throw back a Presidente or a mojito, grab a bite, and watch the crowds that pass on their way to Calle Las Damas. There is indoor seating, if you prefer, with only glimpses of the sidewalk.

If you're in a rush, you won't be disappointed with the local chain **Pizzarelli** (Calle El Conde, across from Parque Colón, tel. 809/544-1111, www.pizzarelli.com.do, 11am-11pm Mon.-Thurs., later close Fri.-Sat., US$3-10), offering other Italian staples from pastas to calzones, even though the pizzas are your best bet. They have various locations throughout the city, including a Malecón outpost a stone's throw from the row of hotels. Or you could order for delivery.

You haven't been to Santo Domingo until you've indulged in a night of dining al fresco on the romantic terraces facing Plaza de España. Pick ★ **Pat'e Palo European Brasserie** (Atarazana 25, tel. 809/687-8089, www.patepalo.com, noon-midnight daily, US$10-30), popular with well-heeled Dominicans and serving tapas-size dishes as well as entrées like seafood pastas and steaks. Service can be hit-or-miss, but the view of the Alcázar de Colón at night makes that less noticeable. After all, this is possibly the first tavern in the Americas.

Pura Tasca's (Calle Emiliano Tejera 51, tel. 809/333-8494, US$2.50-20) corner outdoor terrace facing Plaza de España and adjacent to a row of trendy restaurants is where you'll find city dwellers indulging in the two for one sangria specials at happy hour every Tuesday, as well as just over US$2 per tapas plate. Note: The sangria special sometimes carries over to every day of the week. The restaurant offers a full menu as well, and it's quite tasty. Just remember when your bill comes that you're paying for the premium location and view.

If you want to wine and dine fabulously in a lounge atmosphere, try **Lulú Tasting Bar** (Calle Arzobispo Meriño 151, corner of Padre Billini, tel. 809/687-8360, www.lulu.do, 6pm-3am daily, US$10). There is an eclectic gourmet tapas menu, from escargot to octopus carpaccio and stuffed jalapeños, along with top-shelf liquor and fantastic cocktails. The outdoor, leafy terrace surrounded with colonial buildings is certainly the major draw,

but the atmosphere is no less cozy inside with the friendly bartenders and light Latin music.

Sitting on a quiet corner, **Falafel** (Ciudad Colonial, Calle Sánchez, corner of Padre Billini, tel. 809/688-9714, falafelzonacolonial@gmail.com, 4:30pm-midnight daily, US$5-8) has one of the most drop-dead beautiful and romantic open-air dining rooms in the area: multilevel platforms hold tables that center around a lantern-lit Spanish courtyard decorated with plants, paintings, and masks. The falafel sandwich is good—portions are small but filling. Other Lebanese specials include shawarma, flatbreads, hummus and meat platters. Sit on the top level for the views, and don't forget to look up at least once to marvel at the starry skies while you dine amid colonial ruins.

Vegan and Vegetarian

A welcome addition to the Ciudad Colonial is the five-table, Rastafarian-owned **Kalenda** (19 de Marzo, corner of Arzobispo Portes, tel. 809/688-7975, kalendasd@gmail.com, 8:30am-9pm Mon. and Wed.-Fri, 9am-4pm Sun., US$5-7), good for the vegetarian, vegan, and gluten-free crowd—as well as anyone in search of a healthy meal. Everything is made fresh daily on the spot by owner-chef Mikael. A set daily menu is posted on a board outdoors, and comes at US$6.50 a plate with rice, sides, and a soup entrée. Expect to feast on flavorful, beautifully presented meals from falafel balls, spring rolls, sushi, and corn cakes in eggplant sauce with world music for ambience. Menu options also include steamed or sautéed vegetables, tortillas, soups, and pastas. Portions are generous. Ask about their guava sorbet.

MALECÓN AND GAZCUE
Cafés
Benefruta (Av. Doctor Delgado and corner of Calle Santiago, Gazcue, tel. 809/338-0907, benefruta@hotmail.com, 7am-11pm daily, US$1-5) calls itself a "fruit market cafeteria" and indeed, it's a colorful place where you can pick your fresh fruits from a vibrant sidewalk

window, or go inside the diner-like setup and order a range of freshly squeezed juices—natural or sweetened—smoothies and *batidas* along with affordable sandwiches and other healthy granola snacks.

Villar Hermanos (Av. Independencia 312, Gazcue, tel. 809/682-1433, 7am-11pm daily, from US$3) is a great spot for a quick morning coffee and a fresh-made pastry, whether to eat there or to go. You could also sample a Dominican breakfast, with *mangú*, eggs, and all sorts of fried sausage, buffet or à la carte.

Dominican

★ **La Fábrica Contemporánea** (Calle Danae 4, near corner of Av. Independencia, tel. 809/328-9929, lafabricacontemporanea@gmail.com, 12pm-4:30pm and 6pm-11pm Mon.-Sat., closed Sun., US$2-8US$2-8) is a small and funky local restaurant run by Ana de León and Angela Tavárez, two young Dominican artists. It's tucked on a side street you might otherwise not notice. This gem of a place serves succulent Dominican and Latin dishes—fajitas, burritos, *mofongo*—and daily *bandera dominicana* lunch plates at just US$3. Vegetarian options are also plenty—such as roasted eggplant and salads. Nights are for a la carte and live music. Don't miss sampling

the "house tea" or *te de la casa*, with or without rum. While you wait for your made-to-order meal, admire the creative bohemian space filled with recycled and repurposed furniture like barrels painted and turned into cushioned seats. Taíno masks and other art adorn the outdoor patio. If you're up for it and can sing a tune, show up at dinnertime and grab the open mic.

Adrian Tropical (Malecón/Av. George Washington, tel. 809/221-1764, 7am-2am daily, US$2.50-20) has a stunning backdrop, with a dining terrace perched on cliffs above the Caribbean along the city's famed Malecón. Grab one of the outdoor tables and order a *mofongo* specialty—the *camarofongo* is good—or from a range of pastas, sandwiches, seafood dishes, and burgers. There is interior seating if you must, but that wouldn't make sense unless it's busy (or at the second location in the city center and not on the water). Service can be slow and erratic, but it's a nice spot for a romantic lunch or dinner, with a slightly trendy vibe.

A street behind the Crowne Plaza and thus ideal if you are staying on the Malecón, ★ **Villar Hermanos** (Av. Independencia 312, Gazcue, tel. 809/682-1433, 7am-11pm daily, from US$3) is a typical Dominican

Adrian Tropical

cafetería—with food displayed buffet style—but also an à la carte casual restaurant, with a dessert section and bakery in the back. It's incredibly affordable; takeaway lunch items are charged by weight or by the lunch box if you pick the day's special (you choose three items). Come early and don't be afraid to ask the servers about the menu items.

You'll have a blast at ★ **El Conuco** (Calle Casimiro de Moya 152, Gazcue, tel. 809/686-0129, www.elconuco.com.do, 7am-midnight daily, US$5-20). This restaurant tucked in a residential neighborhood is all things Dominican, from its decor—red and blue flag colors, hymns and sayings painted on walls, an outdoor *fogón* or fire hearth—to its dishes and warm service. Dominican specialties are listed on the bilingual menu, and the cocktails are divine. Some call this place touristy, but it's a great spot to get immersed in Dominican culture within your first week of arrival. A lively merengue dance show takes place starting around 9pm, with diners often pulled onto the dance floor by the attractive waitstaff. Reservations aren't required, but it might be safest to do so. The owners of El Conuco opened a similar restaurant called **Buche' Perico** in March 2016 in the Ciudad Colonial on Calle El Conde at the corner of Calle Las Damas.

Have you ever dined in a cave? You'll long remember your experience at Santo Domingo's iconic ★ **Mesón de la Cava** (Av. Mirador Sur 1, tel. 501/533-2818, www.elmesondelacava.com, noon-midnight Sun.-Fri., noon-2am Sat., US$15-25), from a tasty menu to the stunningly romantic limestone interior. A spiral staircase leads you underground from the entrance, where tables await under stalactites. The menu offers Dominican specials—try a fish fillet in a coconut Creole sauce—as well as contemporary seafood, pasta, and steak options. A wide selection of wines and champagne are available. When making reservations, which are required, be sure to specify the restaurant, and on your next visit try

the adjacent outdoor La Terraza, with live music and set in a beautifully lit garden.

POLÍGONO CENTRAL

The center of Santo Domingo is exploding with upscale gourmet restaurants, bistros, and cafés—and there seems to be a new hottest place to be every month. These are the best picks that have stuck around and are sure not to disappoint.

Cafés

Grab a pricey but fun brunch or breakfast at the popular, Euro-chic **Julieta Brasserie** (Av. Gustavo M. Ricart 124, corner of Manuel J. Troncoso, tel. 809/475-1007, 8am-11pm Mon.-Fri., 8am-mindnight Sat.-Sun., US$5.50-10). Expect omelets, waffles, pancakes, smoothies, Dominican-style *mangú* with fried cheese, and a myriad of other morning treats. Sit in an air-conditioned room or outdoors, although the traffic and noise can be a bit much on the weekdays. There's live music occasionally, and it gets crowded so arrive as early as possible.

Dominican

★ **Buen Provecho** (Av. Gustavo Mejia Ricart 59, tel. 809/562-4848, 7am-4pm Mon.-Sun., US$3-15) is my favorite Dominican restaurant in the city. It's set in a simple yet cozy and unpretentious dining room. There's also a shaded outdoor patio shielded from street noise with a wall of potted flowers. The tasty and authentic Dominican fare at an affordable price in an otherwise pricey and trendy area is quite the find. It's hard to say which meals are better: the Dominican breakfast (there are international breakfast options too) or the colorful lunch buffet of all things rice, *mangú*, chicken stews, and other local specialties. Don't be afraid to ask the waiters for a menu translation on any items; they're very friendly.

International

★ **Mitre Restaurant & Wine Bar** (Abraham Lincoln 1001, corner of Gustavo Mejia Ricart, tel. 809/472-1787, www.mitre.com.do, noon-1am daily, US$10-30) is a place

Polígono Central

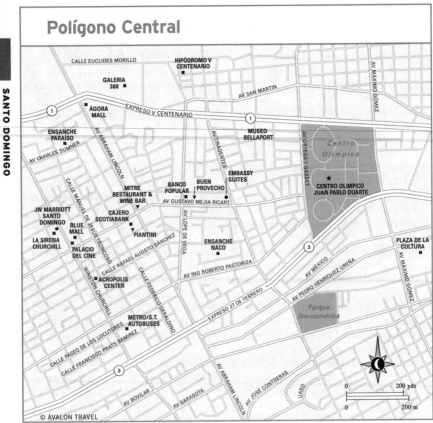

CALLE EUCLIDES MORILLO
HIPÓDROMO V CENTENARIO
GALERIA 360
AV SAN MARTIN
AV MÁXIMO GÓMEZ
ÁGORA MALL
EXPRESO V CENTENARIO
1
1
ENSANCHE PARAÍSO
MUSEO BELLAPORT
AV ORTEGA Y GASSET
Centro Olímpico
AV CHARLES SUMNER
AV ABRAHAM LINCOLN
AV TIRADENTES
EMBASSY SUITES
CENTRO OLÍMPICO JUAN PABLO DUARTE
MITRE RESTAURANT & WINE BAR
BANCO POPULAR
BUEN PROVECHO
AV GUSTAVO MEJIA RICART
CALLE MANUEL DE JESÚS TRONCOSO
CAJERO SCOTIABANK
CALLE RAFAEL AUGSTO SÁNCHEZ
AV LOPE DE VEGA
JW MARRIOTT SANTO DOMINGO
BLUE MALL
PIANTINI
ENSANCHE NACO
3
PLAZA DE LA CULTURA
AV MÉXICO
AV MÁXIMO GÓMEZ
LA SIRENA CHURCHILL
PALACIO DEL CINE
AV ING ROBERTO PASTORIZA
WINSTON CHURCHILL
ACROPOLIS CENTER
CALLE FEDERICO GERALDINO
AV PEDRO HENRIQUEZ UREÑA
EXPRESO 27 DE FEBRERO
Parque Iberoamérica
METRO/S.T. AUTOBUSES
CALLE PASEO DE LOS LOCUTORES
CALLE FRANCISCO PRATS RAMIREZ
3
AV BOLIVAR
AV SARASOTA
AV ABRAHAM LINCOLN
AV JOSÉ CONTRERAS
UASD
0   200 yds
0   200 m
© AVALON TRAVEL

to dress up and mingle among the jet set of the city or celebrate a special occasion. Nibble on foie gras before indulging in a choice of pastas, risotto, steaks, and seafood.

Inside the luxurious JW Marriott, **Winston Grill & Patio** (Av. Winston Churchill 91, tel. 809/807-1717, US$10-21) serves international and Dominican fusion plates made while you watch the chefs at work in the open, live kitchen. The shrimp risotto and filet mignon *a la parilla* are delicious. Sip it down with wine or champagne, available by the glass under the light pouring in from the floor-to-ceiling glass wall. Head out to the infinity-pool adorned terrace post meal and take in the city views.

Grilled fish and meat lovers will also enjoy **Victoria by Porter House** (Av. Gustavo M. Ricart, tel. 809/542-6000, www.victoria.do, noon-midnight daily, 2am close on weekends, US$6-25). The burgers and dry-aged rib eye are sure bets. There are also pasta and salad options, as well as a children's menu.

Vegan and Vegetarian

Thanks to the active Taiwanese community in the DR, there are a few solid choices in the city for those of you who are gluten-free, vegan, and vegetarian eaters.

Jardín Jazmin (Av Núñez de Cáceres corner of Luis F. Thomen, tel. 809/732-0701, noon-10:30pm Tues.-Sun., US$2-5) is a popular Taiwanese-owned vegan restaurant. The large menu includes everything from veggie dumplings to fried tofu. They serve excellent fruit smoothies, fresh juices (pineapple/papaya mix is heavenly), and bubble milk tea.

Restaurante Bambú by Meli (Av. Rómulo Bentancourt 2064, tel. 809/482-0049, 5pm-10pm Tues.-Fri., noon-10pm Sat.-Sun., US$1.50-5) is a favorite as far as vegan eats go—so good even meat lovers won't notice. Set in what looks like someone's backyard garden with mismatched wooden tables, stools, and chairs, this off-the-beaten-track verdant spot attracts the healthy, trendy food lovers of the city. Treats here are a healthy variation on Latin eats. Think *quipes* filled with plantain and cheese, vegetable empanadas with soy, or burritos stuffed with soy meat and beans. The Vietnamese rolls are huge and delicious. Order a variety of these bites and share, tapas style.

Accommodations

CIUDAD COLONIAL

Staying in the Ciudad Colonial is a sure bet if this is your first time in Santo Domingo. It's a short walk to the Malecón and Gazcue—or just about $3.30 for a one-way taxi—and there's something to be said for being a stone's throw from the pedestrian Calle El Conde with its all-around Dominican buzz.

Under US$50

Island Life Backpackers' Hostel (Ciudad Colonial, Isabel La Católica 356, tel. 809/333-9374, www.islandlifebackpackershostel.com, US$15-45) is a short walk to Plaza de España and the heart of the area. A bar and lounge welcomes you as you enter, leading to a spacious Spanish courtyard with yet another bar. Stairs head to the rooms, ranging from dorms to private. The bunk beds have thick mattresses, and all three sets of dorms share a living room and bathrooms. Travelers' favorite sayings are scattered about on the walls wherever you turn, including in the bathrooms, making you feel right at home.

US$50-100

Hotel Conde de Peñalba (Calle El Conde 111, tel. 809/688-7121, www.condedepenalba. com, US$54-89, includes breakfast) was my first hotel in Santo Domingo and a perfect pick for a solo traveler and first-timer in La Capital. It's ideally located across from Parque Colón. You'll immediately notice its popular outdoor dining terrace, sharing a sidewalk with the park's passersby. Upstairs, the hotel's old, even if slightly worn, colonial charm is undeniable, with its winding staircase, period art, and wooden floors. The single rooms are small, but ideal for solo travelers spending little time in their rooms. Remember to climb the stairs all the way to the rooftop for a panoramic view of the park.

The delightful ★ **El Beaterio** (Calle Duarte 8, tel. 809/687-8657, www.elbeaterio. fr, US$75-100, breakfast included) is a 16th-century former home turned into a cozy guesthouse you will have a hard time leaving. Situated across from quiet Parque Duarte, the value is excellent. Immaculate rooms are centered on an open courtyard and ooze of romance with elegant yet simple bedding, air-conditioning, and decent-sized baths. Pick the more spacious upstairs suites, and head to the rooftop terrace for a drink and a view. The friendly Haitian staff here is a highlight.

Set in the heart of the Colonial City, **Boutique Hotel Palacio** (Calle Duarte 106, tel. 809/682-4730, www.hotel-palacio. com, US$72-111) is delightfully decorated, with rooms and suites in simple whites and dark wood colors, with air-conditioning, patio views, queen- or king-size beds, wireless Internet, and phones. The highlights are the Spanish courtyard relaxation area and the rooftop swimming pool area. Free coffee and parking are additional perks. Walk in after 7pm for a one-night stay and you'll get a discounted rate of US$65.

A bargain, if other rooms are booked in this rate category, is the **Mercure Hotel** (pronounced *Mercury* in Spanish, Calle Hostos, tel. 809/688-5500, www.mercure.com, from US$55) in the heart of Calle El Conde. It is convenient to sidewalk cafés and museums. Air-conditioned rooms are worn but clean, and the onsite restaurant—with a sidewalk café of its own opening on Calle El Conde—is a decent pick on this drag. The hotel does seem to attract more single male travelers.

US$100 and Up

The award-winning ★ **Hostal Nicolas de Ovando** (Calle Las Damas, tel. 809/685-9955, www.accorhotels.com, US$165) raises the bar in the Ciudad Colonial. It's evident from the moment you step inside the famed former governor's home turned luxury hotel. Located on the oldest street in the Americas, the hotel consists of three villas, the first of which was built in 1502. The main entrance leads to the first courtyard, where the **Cibao Bar,** lounge, and swimming pool attract the majority of the clientele. Scattered through this maze of mansions are several gardens and courtyards, ideal for strolls. The dim, colonial hallways leading to rooms with arched doorways that ooze history, even if their interiors are more modern. There are a handful of presidential suites—two-story plush lofts with king-size beds and private balconies, where Brangelina stayed overnight, as well as other dignitaries like UN Secretary Ban Ki Moon. Onsite is a French restaurant, **La Residence,** open to the public, and art exhibits are often hosted throughout the year.

Billini Hotel (Calle Padre Billini 256-258, tel. 809/338-4040, www.billinihotel.com, US$170-190) is the newest renovation and addition in the handful of luxurious escapes in the Ciudad Colonial. A 17th-century colonial home that was once used for several purposes from guesthouse for clergy to schools, it's now your ultra-sleek, white and red posh and avant-garde hotel, complete with a rooftop pool and bar, onsite restaurant, and staff in red and black uniforms. The rooms are equally bright and modern, outfitted with all the electronic bells and whistles, including private patios although the view isn't as spectacular. Perks include 24-hour room service, free airport transfers, Bang Olufsen speakers, and L'Occitane bath products, if that's your beat.

The adults-only **Casa Sánchez** (Calle Sanchez 260, www.casasanchezhotel.com, US$90-130, includes breakfast) luxury boutique hotel has high-ceiling standard rooms and self-catering suites. Pick a poolside Colonial Room, with air-conditioning, wireless Internet, flat-screen TV, power showers, and gorgeous original tiles. The show stealer is the hotel's swimming pool set in a Spanish courtyard with powerful water jets. The multicolor pool lights are gorgeous at night. On the rooftop is a garden for more relaxation.

MALECÓN AND GAZCUE

The Malecón has a row of high-rise brand-name hotels and casinos, which attract business travelers, while Gazcue offers extremely affordable guesthouses out of the public eye. Gazcue is generally safe to walk around, but be more cautious on the Malecón, where there are occasional peddlers, and don't display any valuables. Both areas are about a 15-minute stroll away from the Ciudad Colonial west of Independence Park.

Under US$50

Almost straddling the Malecón, up a side street behind the Crowne Plaza, is the all-white, charming colonial ★ **Maison Gautreaux** (Calle Felix Mariano Lluberes, tel. 809/412-7838, www.maisongautreaux.net, US$45, breakfast included)—an amazing deal for being just a block up from the main seafront avenue lined with pricier brand hotels and within walking distance to the Ciudad Colonial. Rooms are well appointed, with air-conditioning, wireless Internet, and cable TV. They also have an onsite restaurant and rooftop Jacuzzi.

La Gran Mansión (Calle Danae 26, tel. 809/682-2033, johanny_v@hotmail.com,

US$31) is a gated white residence turned guesthouse, with all ground-level, clean, and spacious rooms. Bedding is basic, but you have all you need for a roof over your head and a warm shower in an equally wide bathroom. There is Internet access and cable TV, and a small outdoor terrace.

On the next block over, **Hotel La Residence** (Calle Danae 62, tel. 809/412-7298, willianaresidencia@yahoo.com, US$25) welcomes you with a large outdoor, covered patio where you'll find guests and locals relaxing with a newspaper. Rooms and bathrooms are visibly older, but the basics are there—including air-conditioning, wireless Internet, and small bathrooms with hot and cold water.

A much better value and the best deal in Gazcue is across the street at the hard-to-pronounce ★ **Jecasergian Hotel** (Calle Danae 31, between Av. Independencia and Calle Santiago, tel. 809/338-9144, jecasergian@gmail.com, US$25) with 13 modern rooms that include air-conditioning, wireless Internet, cable TV, double beds and a decent-size bathroom. You won't find this gem online, so call ahead to reserve or walk in if there are no big events in town. A stone's throw away are a handful of restaurants, including supermarkets, roadside fruit vendors, major hotel restaurants a block or two away, and it's a 15-minute walk to the Ciudad Colonial.

US$50-100

Hotel Napolitano (Av. George Washington 51, tel. 809/687-1131, www.napolitano.com. do, US$95-155) is an old-school Dominican favorite, but don't get the wrong idea—there's not much that's old school about its grounds. Its popularity is mostly due to its breezy, spacious seafront, poolside terrace—**La Terraza,** where a restaurant hosts live Dominican bands on the weekends for some dining and dancing al fresco and serves up a mix of Dominican dishes, seafood, pasta, steaks, and desserts. The atmosphere is laid-back, the staff friendly, and it's a great place to spend the day. Nonguests can purchase a day pass for US$20, which includes a meal

with dessert, a drink, and pool and gym use. The seafront rooms are a good bang for your buck. Amenities include an onsite casino and a nightclub that goes until 6am. To top it off, you're a 10-minute walk from the Ciudad Colonial.

If you're looking for a low-key but modern, solid value hotel on the Malecón within easy walk of the Ciudad Colonial and Gazcue's local restaurants, the **Crowne Plaza** (Av. George Washington 218, tel. 809/221-0000, www.crowneplaza.com, US$129-198) doesn't disappoint. The staff is the highlight here, aside from the well-appointed oceanview rooms—with air-conditioning, TV, wireless Internet, full shower tub, minibars, and stereos. There are adjoining connections for families if needed. There's an onsite restaurant with a full breakfast spread (mimosas included) and a rooftop swimming pool and lounge. To splurge, ask about the executive club and presidential suites.

US$100 and Up

The Renaissance Jaragua Hotel & Casino (Av. George Washington 367, tel. 809/221-2222, www.marriott.com/sdqgw, from US$119), the most popular and iconic hotel on the Malecón open since 1942, underwent a US$40 million, yearlong renovation in 2014 and has reopened with 300 newly furnished rooms and junior and presidential suites. Stay in the tower section if you can, the extra splurge (about US$30 a night) is worth it. On the grounds are a renovated, spacious pool and bar-restaurant area with sea views, a fully equipped fitness center, and three restaurants, along with an often-busy casino with live music at the Merengue Bar.

Hilton Santo Domingo (Av. George Washington 500, tel. 809/685-0000, www. hiltonsantodomingo.com, US$159-219) is a solid pick for a modern, safe, and convenient location on Santo Domingo's waterfront. Located directly across from the sea, all rooms get a sea view. But the most glorious "corner rooms"—ask for 1713 or 1715—offer a panoramic ceiling-to-floor window view of the

Caribbean outside, including from the bathroom, as well as a glorious view of the coconut-tree lined avenue. The onsite, pricey **Sol y Sombra** restaurant, open to all, has stunning seafront views for a lunch or dinner rendezvous. Amenities also include a swimming pool and bar—with water views from the seventh floor—and a 24-hour gym.

The redesigned, modern open lobby and lounge seating at the **Sheraton Santo Domingo** (Av. George Washington 365, 809/221-6666, US$120-800) are an initial draw. The hotel location is excellent, on the main drag of Santo Domingo yet walking distance to the Ciudad Colonial and Gazcue. And the rooms have all the comfort and amenities of the Sheraton brand. Food is average here at best, but the staff and the pool terrace with a view of the Malecón might just make up for it. Note some rooms are currently undergoing renovations.

POLÍGONO CENTRAL
US$150 and Up

Inside the fancy Blue Mall and accurately boasting "unpretentious luxury," the 150-room ★ **JW Marriott Santo Domingo** (Av. Winston Churchill 93, Piantini District, tel. 809/807-1717, US$299)—the first in the

Caribbean region—is a great deal for your fancy buck and is the most beautifully detailed, luxurious property downtown. It's hard to say what's more impressive here—the vertical gardens and marble wall entrances, the standard rooms with an open bathroom design and mirrors with in-built plasma TV, or the onsite **Vertygo 101 Lounge & Bar,** set on an outdoor terrace 101 feet above Avenida Winston Churchill. The bar has an infinity pool with impressive city views, and is an après-work hangout of trendy Dominicans. Don't miss the **Winston Grill & Patio Restaurant,** where a Mexican Peruvian chef and his open, live kitchen delights palates with dishes such as oriental duck tacos and shrimp risotto. The hotel is connected to the Blue Mall via three entrances, at least one of which is a private escalator, giving guests access to a multitude of shopping and entertainment options, including a full movie theater.

One of the newest kids on the luxury business hotel block of modern Santo Domingo opened in 2014. **Embassy Suites by Hilton** (Av. Tiradentes 32, Silver Sun Building, tel. 809/685-0001, www.santodomingo.embassysuites.com, US$159-200, includes breakfast) is housed within the tallest commercial building in the capital, along the

the JW Marriott Santo Domingo

popular Avenida Mejia Ricart, next to several trendy lounges, cigar bars, and restaurants. Sumptuous touches include marble floors, high ceilings, shining corridors and funky ceiling lightbulbs. The all-suites hotel attracts a business clientele—there are conference rooms, a bar, and restaurant onsite—and has a somewhat austere feel. Suites are spacious and furnished in brown and cream colors. Views are of unfinished high-rises across the way. The highlight, aside from location, is perhaps the fancy infinity pool on the seventh floor, with skyline views of downtown Santo Domingo.

Information and Services

TOURISM

Colonial Tour & Travel (Arzobispo Meriño 209, a few steps from Parque Colón, tel. 809/688-5285, www.colonialtours.com.do, 9am-5pm Mon.-Fri.) is a popular travel and tour agency. It offers various full-day excursions from Santo Domingo to interesting sights including Isla Saona, 27 Charcos de Damajagua, and inland cultural tours. The website is pretty advanced, and you can book tours online. Keep an eye on their Facebook page for the latest options and departures.

Blue Travel Partner Services (tel. 809/200-1778, www.bluetps.com, 24-hour call center) is a destination management company offering numerous services from airport transfers to organized sightseeing tours around the Dominican Republic. Offices are located islandwide. They are reliable, friendly, and always on time.

Grab a map of the city at the **GoDominicanRepublic Tourism Booth** (Calle Las Damas, corner of Calle El Conde), which includes the downtown area by zones, and the colonial section. Feel free to ask for any other booklets and pamphlets of other regions of the DR you might be visiting. They have a *Guía Turística* magazine that is bilingual and also quite useful.

TravelNet (Calle Rafael A. Sánchez 102, tel. 809/534-7440, www.travelnetdr.com, 8:30am-5:30pm Mon.-Fri., 8:30am-12:30pm Sat.) is a travel agency specializing in hotel packages with excursions, flights, car rentals, and cruises to other destinations—including exclusive offers on Royal Caribbean.

MONEY

For your banking and ATM needs, go to **Banco Popular** (corner of Calle El Conde and Calle Duarte, tel. 809/544-8917) or **Scotiabank** (Calle Isabel La Católica, across from Hotel Frances). In Gazcue, try the inside ATM at the **Crowne Plaza** (Av. George Washington 218, tel. 809/221-0000). There's also an excellent 24-hour pharmacy close to the Zona, **Farmacia Carol** (Av. Independencia 57, tel. 809/685-8165, www.farmaciacarol.com), and an Orange desk inside if you need to purchase a SIM card (just remember to bring your passport ID).

GROCERIES

A new branch of **Supermercado Nacional** (Calle Duarte 106, corner of Calle El Conde, tel. 809/221-2224, 8am-9pm daily) is an excellent addition to the area—offering a full supermarket within the popular Ciudad Colonial area, stocked with full groceries, toiletry needs, wines, liquor, and a deli counter. For an even larger supermarket, if you need it, there is **La Sirena** (Av. Mella 258, tel. 809/221-3232, 8am-8pm Mon.-Sat., 8:30am-3pm Sun. and holidays, www.tiendalasirena.com)—though it is in a dodgier neighborhood. There are also smaller stores up and down Calle El Conde, including pharmacies, fashion stores, Internet cafés, and pretty much anything a traveler might need.

Safety in the City

Every Dominican you run into in the city will warn you: be careful, Santo Domingo isn't safe. Yes, there is petty theft and some distracted tourists have been known to get their cameras snatched out of their hands at sights like the seafront Malecón. But as in any big city you might visit and wander around, common sense rules. Don't flash valuables. Don't walk late at night. Taxis run 24 hours and appear within minutes of a call. This city isn't any more dangerous than Chicago or Washington DC, as long as you stick to well frequented zones—including the Ciudad Colonial, Gazcue, and the Malecón. Downtown Santo Domingo is fine by day, and fine by night as long as you have a ride. If you're headed east of the Ozama River, *always* catch a taxi and arrange for a return pickup.

For the woman traveler: if you're going to walk around, prepare to be catcalled and propositioned for marriage every 5-10 minutes and at every corner block where men might be gathered outside. This is a frequent occurrence in Santo Domingo. If it's just a Buen Día greeting, then responding while continuing on your way is fine. Otherwise, your best bet is not to respond and to continue without stopping. Street talk is annoying, but in the Dominican Republic it's mostly harmless. Of course, always be sure to practice good safety habits; don't walk alone after dark or in isolated areas, and don't display valuables (including smartphones) if possible.

Transportation

GETTING THERE
Air
Aeropuerto Internacional de Las Américas (tel. 809/947-2225, www.aerodom.com) is the main entry point into Santo Domingo, located east of the city. The drive from the airport into the metropolitan area is actually quite pleasant with views of the Caribbean Sea. Major carriers to Santo Domingo include American Airlines (tel. 809/542-5151), Delta (tel. 809/955-1500), US Airways (tel. 809/622-1015), Jet Blue (tel. 809/200-9898), Spirit (tel. 809/549-2046), Air France (tel. 809/686-8432), Lufthansa (tel. 809/689-9625), and Iberia (tel. 809/508-0288).

It's important to note that after you land at las Américas, and before you get in line at immigration, you must first purchase a Tourist Card for US$10, unless you've already purchased one online. You can get one from one of the automated ticket booths if you have the exact change, or from a representative at a counter—look for the sign and desk just before you enter the queue for immigration. If you miss this, you'll be sent back to get one and lose your place in the often-long immigration line.

Ferry
There is a ferry service from Santo Domingo to San Juan or Mayaguez, Puerto Rico, and round-trip via **America Cruise Ferries** (Puerto Don Diego, tel. 809/688-4400, www. acferries.com, US$190 adults, US$174 children). It's a 12-hour journey, departing from the port in Santo Domingo across the Fortaleza Ozama.

Bus
Metro Tours (Av. Winston Churchill, tel. 809/227-0101, http://metroserviciosturisticos. com) and **Caribe Tours** (Av. 27 de Febrero, corner of Leopoldo Navarro, tel. 809/221-4422, www.caribetours.com.do) service long distances between Santo Domingo and other parts of the country. Metro Tours will take you north to Puerto Plata, with stops in Santiago and Sosúa (bring a sweater for the full air-conditioning blast), while Caribe Tours makes runs from the city to Puerto

Plata, Samaná, and Barahona, among other destinations.

Expreso Bávaro (Calle Juan Sánchez Ramirez 31, tel. 809/682-9670 in city, tel. 809-552-1678 in Bávaro, www.expresobavaro.com, 6:30am-4pm daily, approx. US$9 one-way) takes you to the Punta Cana region, more precisely to Bávaro area hotels, north of Punta Cana airport. The trip takes just 2.5 hours along a new highway, with three departures in the morning and three in the afternoon.

You'll find numerous other express *guaguas* running frequently throughout the day that head to nearby cities such as La Romana. Head to Parque Enriquillo for more information or hop on one, but keep valuables out of plain sight.

Car

Car rentals are easily found at the airport, as well as in the city. You'll find major brands such as **Avis** (airport tel. 809/549-0468; Av. George Washington 517, tel. 809/535-7191), **Hertz** (airport tel. 809/549-0454; Jose Maria Heredia 1, tel. 809/221-5333), **Dollar** (airport tel. 809/221-7368), and **Budget** (airport tel. 809/549-0351).

GETTING AROUND
Car

Unless you have nerves of steel and more than a decade of experience driving in the Caribbean—and even then—I highly recommend hopping in a taxi over driving your own car in Santo Domingo. Unlike the outskirts where highways rule and everything is well indicated, the city is a maze of mad drivers each trying to outrun the other and occasionally burning through red lights at massive intersections at night. It's nerve-wracking enough being a passenger, much less getting behind the wheel. The capital is well served with three major thoroughfares—Avenida George Washington, Avenida 27 de Febrero, and Avenida John F. Kennedy—but it can be very confusing if you're new to the city. Leave the in-city maneuvering to Dominicans. If you're heading to Boca Chica, Juan Dolio,

and nearby La Romana, however, you will be better off getting your own car as taxis are expensive for long journeys, and the highways are well marked and smooth.

Taxi

The airport ride from Las Américas to your hotel in the Ciudad Colonial or on the Malecón will cost approximately US$25-30, depending on your haggling skills, although these fares are usually standard *from* the airport to the city, and more flexible when you head back. When you get out of baggage claim with your stash, walk confidently straight toward the exit and do not go with anyone who randomly solicits you as you're walking. Once you are close to the exit doors, you'll see an official taxi booth with dispatchers ready to direct you to the right cab according to your destination. Inquire about the fare before you get in and before they grab your bags. Insist if you don't get an immediate answer, so there's no confusion at the end of your ride.

Aside from the pricey airport taxi fare for a half-hour ride, the rest is good news: taxis are incredibly cheap when exploring within Santo Domingo. There are several car companies that are on call and available 24 hours, which is handy in a spot with plenty of nightlife. The most popular of these companies, recommended the most by locals, is **Apolo Taxi** (tel. 809/537-0000, www.apolotaxi.com, 24 hours, from US$3-5). When you call, be sure to get a price quote for your destination and they will also give you the car number, color, and arrival time (they speak fast—if you need help, ask a local). Be ready before you call, as they usually have drivers within every zone of the city. There are no meters, so the price is set according to neighborhoods (usually about US$3 or 150 pesos from the Ciudad Colonial to Gazcue or US$4 from the Ciudad Colonial to downtown Santo Domingo, which is incredibly cheap). Prices do go slightly up at night, as expected. There may be times when you have to call twice and the cab is a no-show, but for the most part, they are on point and know all the shortcuts to get you to your destination safely. If you don't speak Spanish, hand the phone over to a local or ask your hotel to call the taxi company. Don't grab one parked right outside the Ciudad Colonial hotels or the Malecón hotels—they charge almost triple the price.

Uber has recently arrived in Santo Domingo—but be aware that the individual drivers who show up might not know the city or your destination well, and you'll end up spending more getting lost around the city. At the time of publication, drivers were on strike due to newly reduced fares.

Guagua (Local Bus)

The most economical way to get around, safer than the motorbike taxis, is the minivan buses. They are often white, beat-up Toyotas with a conductor who hauls people onto the van and hollers for the destination as the driver speeds along avenues. If you're claustrophobic, you'll likely have a panic attack at the amount of people who are crammed inside the *guagua*, at times sitting on complete strangers' laps. But the merengue beats on above the interior chatter, and the van always gets you to your destination. While *guaguas* can be safe on longer distances—to say, Boca Chica and nearby beaches—the local, city *guaguas* are rougher and I don't recommend them for novice travelers. But if you're traveling light and looking for a cultural experience, by all means, be my guest. And save some money while you're at it.

Motoconcho (Motorbike Taxi)

They are all over the Dominican Republic: *motoconchos,* or motorbike taxis. They'll take you at similar taxi distances or shorter for chump change. They usually park on street corners and will holler at pedestrians within their view (much like the *guagua* conductors and shared taxi drivers). They don't provide helmets, however, and they also cram several passengers onto one bike—some of whom may have big bags or other items to carry— be aware of the risks you are taking. I don't recommend them in Santo Domingo's insane traffic and aggressive driving shenanigans. Shelling out five bucks for a cab is worth it.

Metro

Clean and sleek, Santo Domingo's **metro** (www.metrosantodomingo.com, 6am-10:30pm daily, US$1.30 for a rechargeable metro card, US$0.90 round-trip)—the only one in the Caribbean—opened in 2008 under President Leonel Fernandez and an initial outlay of US$700 million to the dismay of many at first. It now consists of two lines, with more on the way. Before you get excited: it doesn't yet connect all of the areas that are relevant to tourists, but it has been useful to daily workers commuting from the suburbs to the city center. It's still a fun way to experience this large city and get a sense of just how much more modern it is than its Caribbean counterparts. The first line consists of 16 stations, named after historical Dominican figures, and begins at Centro de Los Heroes, passes through downtown, and ends in Villa Mella, with an exit along the way at the National Theater and Plaza de la Cultura. The second line has 14 stops. Rides cost 20 pesos one-way (approximately US$0.50), and no food or drinks are allowed.

East of Santo Domingo

BOCA CHICA

Twenty-five minutes' drive from Santo Domingo—and less than 10 miles from the international airport—is a beautiful white sand, swimmable Caribbean beach, and the average city dweller's number one escape: Boca Chica. Once a free-spirited fishing village, tourism has long spiked in Boca Chica. Dotting the near two-mile-long stretch are al fresco cafés, thatched-roof restaurants, *frituras* or fried fish shacks, dive shops, and midsize resorts, with plenty of music echoing along the way. Dominican families, lovers, friends, teenagers, and toddlers: everyone loves a day's escape to Boca Chica from neighboring Santo Domingo.

Boca Chica gets a bad rep for its high prostitution levels, but it's only bad at night. Everyone just keeps about their business and plenty of families frequent Boca Chica. If you're a Caucasian male, you'll be approached more often by the working ladies, but you are free to say no and keep your eyes on your pockets and belongings. If anything, Boca Chica's beach is clean, well maintained, and safe for kids. The town has become a lot more tourist-oriented over the years.

It is safe to walk around the main drag and the beach during the day, as well as the main drag of Calle Duarte at night. Just remain vigilant and bring few valuables to the beach. At night, the beat moves over to Calle Duarte and a handful of outdoor bars and clubs. A portion of the main drag is blocked off every night after sundown, and tables are placed in the middle of the street for those who want to dine amid all the night action.

Weekdays are ideal if you seek a less crowded scene, while Sunday is the liveliest, most exhilarating day to experience Boca Chica in all its Dominican glory.

Orientation

Arriving from the main highway, the Autopista de las Américas, you'll turn right at the traffic light onto Avenida Caracoles, which curves right and turns into Calle Duarte after you take another right. This is the main drag where you'll find most of the restaurants, shops, bars, pizzerias, *colmados,* local *pica pollo* restaurants, a Central Park—across from Banco Popular—and small hotels. Take any side street on foot from Duarte, and end up at the beach. Along Avenida San Rafael, parallel to Duarte, are a few more local sidewalk cafés and the north side of the park, where buses run all day long, as well as guesthouses nearby.

Knowing where to relax on the beach and where to mingle won't take long to figure out. On the far eastern end is a quiet pocket by the casual seafront terrace at The Boat House Restaurant, where you can sit and watch paddleboarders and boats pass in the distance. Going west, past the restaurant and Tropical Sea Drivers, is a lively, local stretch of beach restaurants—serving everything from pizza to fresh fish—and eventually you'll hit the Don Juan Beach Resort, which sits at about the halfway point.

Across the resort is a tranquil dockside restaurant and lounge, as well as a stone pier where kids gather to jump into the water. Past this area farther west, a wide-open expanse of beach is a refreshing break from the crowded restaurants. This is where the Sporting Club crowd relaxes with lunch and private beach chairs. Beyond them, the local decibel goes up, and soon at the very western edge of the beach, you'll find yourself amid larger crowds of Dominicans. They gather around a table and under the shade playing dominoes, while others are closer to the beach with their coolers, Tupperware, and boom boxes sharing lounge chairs. Vendors make their way through the beachgoers, offering everything from massages to plates of food and beer from the nearby row of *frituras.*

East of Santo Domingo

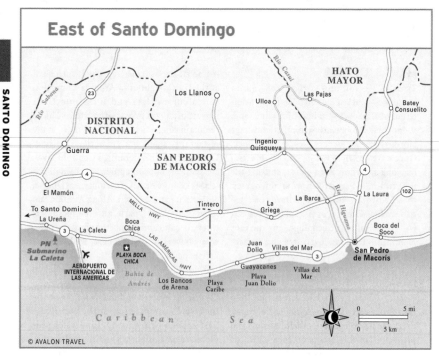

© AVALON TRAVEL

Back on the far eastern end of Boca Chica, past the beach, is the glamorous side: three overwater dock restaurants—Neptuno is the best pick—where well-heeled Dominicans come to spend their Saturday or Sunday afternoons away from the public beach to indulge in gourmet meals, pricey cocktails, soaking in Jacuzzi tubs, and swim right off the dock.

★ Playa Boca Chica

Part of the reason **Playa Boca Chica** is so popular, aside from its powder-soft sand, is that it faces a coral reef in Caucedo Bay that catches the waves and thereby creates a natural lagoon safe for all to enjoy. The water is still a glorious island turquoise hue and shallow. It's under one meter (four feet) deep, so you can wade out from the beach over to La Matica, a mangrove and bird cay across the way.

The daily scenes on Boca Chica beach are authentically Caribbean and Dominican. The merengue and bachata music waft on the sea breeze. There is a constant stream of activity as locals play dominoes in the shade, frolic with their infants in the water, play beach football and volleyball, and throw back their mixed Brugal cocktails while standing in the sea together at sunset. Vendors hawk pretty much everything from sunglass racks to floaties, candy, ice cream, coconut, fruits, massages. Still others are in the water, selling banana boat rides. It's one of the best people-watching beaches in the DR.

Lounge chairs and umbrellas are available for rent at various points along the beach—they average between RD$250-300 for two, all day (US$5.50-6.50). Your beach chair vendor also functions as a *camarero* or beach waiter, ready to bring anything you need—from food to drinks—for an extra fee. A simple *no gracias* will keep most vendors at bay. You might also encounter the occasional child begging. They can be persistent and follow you around. Decide in advance whether to give or not because you will be setting a pattern.

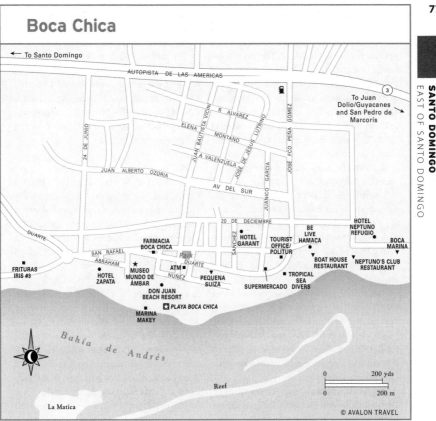

Boca Chica

← To Santo Domingo

AUTOPISTA DE LAS AMERICAS

To Juan
Dolio/Guyacanes
and San Pedro de
Marcoris →

R ALVAREZ
ELENA
MONTANO
JUAN BAUTISTA VICINI
A VALENZUELA
JOSE DE JESUS LUTRIMO
JUANICO GARCIA
JOSE FCO PEÑA GOMEZ
24 DE JUNIO
JUAN ALBERTO OZORIA
AV DEL SUR
20 DE DICIEMBRE
SANCHEZ

DUARTE
SAN RAFAEL
ABRAHAM
FRITURAS
IRIS #3
HOTEL
ZAPATA
FARMACIA
BOCA CHICA
Park
DUARTE
MUSEO
MUNDO DE
ÁMBAR
ATM
NUÑEZ
PEQUENA
SUIZA
DON JUAN
BEACH RESORT
★ PLAYA BOCA CHICA
MARINA
MAKEY

HOTEL
GARANT
TOURIST
OFFICE/
POLITUR
BE
LIVE
HAMACA
SUPERMERCADO
TROPICAL
SEA
DIVERS
BOAT HOUSE
RESTAURANT
HOTEL
NEPTUNO
REFUGIO
NEPTUNO'S CLUB
RESTAURANT
BOCA
MARINA

Bahía de Andrés

Reef

La Matica

0   200 yds
0   200 m

© AVALON TRAVEL

Sights

Museo Mundo de Ámbar (across from Don Juan Beach Resort Reception, Calle Juan Bautista Vicini, corner of 20 de Diciembre, tel. 809/523-5668, www.amberworldmuseum.com, 9am-5pm Mon.-Sat., free) steps from the beach is just about the only traditional sight you'll find. It's worth a stop if you haven't yet learned about the DR's semiprecious stones. The small room is split into a museum and a jewelry store. Prices for the gems are higher than you'll find in Santo Domingo, but if you're pressed for time, this is a decent option.

Sports and Recreation

Although it's as easy as parking yourself on the beach to feel entertained by the crowds and the people watching, there's also plenty to do for those who love to be active on the water. And the good news is, most tour operators and dive shops in Boca Chica are bilingual, even trilingual thanks to a solid North American and European expat community.

Boca Chica's calm waters, as well as its closeness to a reef, make it an ideal place to get into water sports. There are over 20 local dive spots less than 10 minutes away from shore, just outside the reef to start. Check in with Swiss-owned **Tropical Sea Divers** (Beachfront, Calle Duarte 35, tel. 829/697-9522, www.tropicalseadivers.com, 8am-5pm daily, 2-tank dive US$64 or US$150/5-dive package, plus applicable transport). They have three PADI-licensed dive instructors and are the most highly recommended dive shop in

Boca Chica as well as the most organized I've seen. This small operation offers excursions for beginners to the coral gardens nearby and options for the experienced, including two-tank dives at **Catalina Island** (US$68/tour plus $64 for the dives), shipwreck exploration at Parque Nacional Submarino La Caleta, and cave diving at La Cueva Taína. You can also rent snorkel gear (US$10/day), digital cameras (US$10), or aqua scooters and explore on your own, but be sure not to venture beyond the reef. Onsite facilities include showers, bathrooms, and a coffee and tea station.

Caribbean Divers (Calle Duarte 44, tel. 809/854-3483, www.caribbeandivers. de, markushaemmerle2@yahoo.de, US$88/2 dives, US$20 snorkel) offer diving and snorkeling trips to sites just beyond the reef. Keep in mind that they often have walk-in seasonal specials.

You'll find plenty of other casual water sports like banana boat rides, water bikes, and paddleboarding from vendors along the beach. Head over to **Flyboard Dominicana** (at Boca Marina, tel. 809/649-8511, cell tel. 829/861-2636, noon-6pm Sat.-Sun.) for some jet boarding adventures.

Anglers can book fishing charters through **Don Juan Beach Resort** (Calle Abraham Nunez 4, tel. 809/687-9157, www.donjuan-beachresort.com). Trips depart from **Marina Makey** across from the resort.

For day of golf, you're in luck: only a 15-minute drive away is one of the country's top golf courses at **Guavaberry Country Club** (Nueva Autovía del Este Juan Dolio, tel. 829/547-0000 or 809/333-4653, www.guava-berrygolf.com.do, US$95/18 holes) in the beach town of Juan Dolio.

Food

The handful of restaurants and cafés in Boca Chica, whether facing the beach or on Calle Duarte, offer seafood, shellfish, and plenty of Italian food. You'll find numerous casual dining options on the beach—feel free to experiment—but these few selections will set you on the right path.

Start with an authentic Boca Chica whole fish meal at the row of **Frituras by Cafetería Perla Marina** (Calle Duarte, intersection of Av. 24 de Junio and Av. San Rafael, 12pm-4pm daily, US$3) on the western end of the beach—not to be mistaken with some of the other fried foods shacks you'll spot around Boca Chica. Along this long row, where each shack is numbered at the top, find **Fritura Iris #3** (tel. 829/636-4843, US$3)—Iris (whose full

Playa Boca Chica

name is Juliana Olivero Mercedes) is at the beginning of the strip and makes the tastiest, best seasoned steamed or fried whole fish—pick from dorado, snapper, and other catches of the day. A plate comes with sides of *tostones* and avocado. Grab a table behind her shack at Perla Marina, and order your beers there while watching scene unfold around you.

The Boat House (Calle Duarte 34, next to Tropical Sea Divers, tel. 809/523-6986, www.tbhbar.webs.com, lawrencederijk@gmail.com, 8am-11pm daily, US$3-15) is ideal for a morning coffee and breakfast with glorious sea views—or any meal for that matter, and anytime you want to escape the crowds. Although directly on the beach, it's tucked in a corner away from the noise of the main strip and a favorite among U.S. expats and locals. Meal prices are reasonable, and choices include Dominican specials as well as tasty pizza. Look out for the daily lunch offer at just US$3.50. There's a giant screen that comes on in the evening for the sports fanatics, but it isn't disruptive to those who aren't. Portions are generous, and the atmosphere is laid-back. Friday evenings are the liveliest here, when happy hour specials and free *bocas*—mini plates of the chef's choosing, like pasta carbonara—kick in at 6pm and attract a loyal crowd of local characters as well as residents from nearby Juan Dolio.

Makey Bar & Grill (across from Don Juan Beach Resort, Marina Makey, tel. 809/687-9157, 10am-9pm daily, US$5-25) is set over the water on a dock and marina a stone's throw from the beach. It's a tad pricier than the beach restaurants, but you're paying for those gorgeous views. Besides, the food is worth it from the chicken croquettes to the seafood paella. The breeze and jazzy music lull you into that relaxed Dominican pace.

Pequeña Suiza (Calle Duarte, tel. 809/523-4619, pequenasuiza@bocachicaplaya.com, 9am-10pm daily, US$5-20) offers a delightful respite from the sun for lunch or a romantic dinner setting with tables in a leafy, romantic courtyard (there's even mosquito repellent provided on the tables). There's an air-conditioned dining room as well, if you prefer. But the best thing about this place is the Italian menu of delicious pastas and fish and the staff. There's an outdoor breakfast counter for some morning action, and tables set directly on the street when the strip closes to traffic after dark.

Get your beach glam on and spend the day on the overwater deck of **Neptuno's Club Restaurant** (Calle Duarte 12, tel.

whole fried fish from one of Boca Chica's *frituras*

809/523-4703, 11am-midnight, US$10-20) on the eastern tip of Boca Chica. One of three upscale waterfront restaurants on this end, it doubles as beach club where you'll find all an all-white decor with curtains, plush seafront couches and beds, sunning platforms, Jacuzzi tubs smack in the middle of the restaurant where you can get served your cocktails. There are even steps directly beside your dining table for a dip in the Caribbean sea pre- or post-meal. All these bells and whistles come at a hefty menu price, of course. The food is decent—including lobster linguini and lasagna—though not quite as impressive to your taste buds as a casual meal from the local fry fish shack.

Accommodations

Just a couple of blocks from the beach, **Hotel Garant & Suites** (Calle Sánchez 9, tel. 809/523-5544, www.hotelgarant.com, US$57-77) is a no-frills, safe place to stay in a convenient location. The basic amenities include a spacious room with satellite TV, refrigerator, air-conditioning, hot water, and wireless Internet. The "luxury rooms" aren't lavish; they just have access to a shared veranda and a view of the small swimming pool below. There's an outdoor patio facing the street for morning coffee and breakfast, if you so choose. A street up from the hotel is Calle Duarte and its central park, bank, and convenience stores.

The 224-room **Don Juan Beach Resort** (Calle Abraham Nunez 4, tel. 809/687-9157, www.donjuanbeachresort.com, US$150) is right at the heart of the beach strip and offers an all-inclusive escape in the middle of the local action. The rooms are basic—request one with a beachfront balcony—and the buildings are old, but the location is ideal. Particularly if you'd rather not eat out every day, this could be an option. There are specials year-round, so be sure to ask if you are walking in without reservations.

Information and Services

There's a Banco Popular branch and ATM across from Central Park, and you'll find all you need—from groceries to a pharmacy and phone stores—along Calle Duarte, the main street in Boca Chica, one block from the beach.

Getting Around

Getting around Boca Chica's main drag and the beach is a breeze: use your feet, as the locals do. It's generally safe at reasonable hours. Don't walk alone late at night. *Motoconchos* or motorbike taxis are another mode of transportation, though I don't recommend these particularly on the highway. You'll see them parked by the Central Park or along various street corners off Calle Duarte.

JUAN DOLIO AND GUAYACANES

Approximately 40 minutes from Santo Domingo and a mere 15 minutes from Boca Chica is the small and quiet resort town of Juan Dolio, favored by the wealthier Dominicans of Santo Domingo. The chief attraction here is a six-mile-long stretch of powdery, thick white sand, dotted with just a handful of restaurants, beach bars, condominiums, and resorts. In recent years, Juan Dolio suffered a major decline in tourism, with major resorts shutting doors, including the Barceló. But in 2015, Juan Dolio began reviving, with the opening of a new Hodelpa boutique resort, and more new properties on the way.

The area remains safe and the beach is as pretty as ever. Santo Domingo residents with a bit more buck flock here on the weekends or on a free weekday. The president keeps a vacation house along the stretch just beside the Coral Costa Caribe Resort. In March 2015, Juan Dolio became the home to Pinewood Studios' largest underwater film studio in the Caribbean and Latin America, and with that comes the hope that this beachside community will soon see a tourism boom.

The resort side of Juan Dolio runs all along Calle Principal. The western side, facing the more public beach areas, is known as **Old**

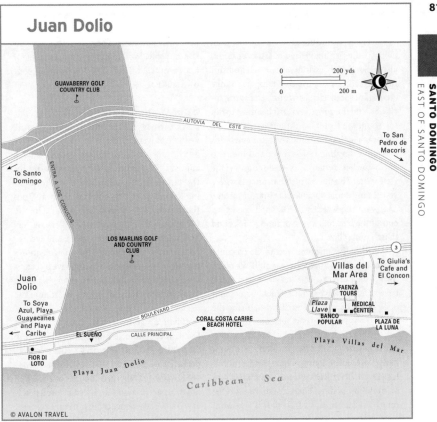

Juan Dolio

Juan Dolio and home to some of the longer-lasting small hotels and resorts. On the eastern end of the drag is **Juan Dolio Nuevo,** starting with the Banco Popular branch and a string of mini shopping plazas, with supermarkets, hair salons, and more of the higher-end restaurants and condominiums along Calle Principal. The beach on this end—also referred to as Villa Real—is also cleaner than the main public stretch (you won't see piles of trash tossed at the back of the beach). You can access it even if you're not staying at the resorts here—all beaches in the DR are public. There's a passage right beside Club Hemmingway. Be on alert when swimming here: stay close to shore, as there are strong currents.

It's easy to get up and down Juan Dolio's main beach. You'll find entry points—and two separate parking lots—on Calle Principal running parallel to the main highway. The more "public" side of the beach is dotted with chairs and umbrellas for rent as well as a handful of restaurants. Walking west, the stretch becomes more deserted for a good while—facing gated apartment buildings or abandoned hotels—before you reach the Coral Costa Caribe Resort. Continuing on farther takes you all the way to Club Hemmingway. Don't walk it alone.

You'll find everything you need on the main drag of Calle Principal, which is easy to get around. Walking is an option but it does get superhot. Using a bicycle—ask your host—or taking a *motoconcho* ride is recommended to get to Juan Dolio Nuevo.

Barely a 10-minute ride west from Juan Dolio is the fishing village of **Guayacanes,** also blessed with a white sand beach and sufficient facilities for the day-tripper: lounge chairs and umbrellas, *frituras,* changing facilities, and the gorgeous Caribbean sea to dip in. You'll see fishers and their canoes along the beach, going back and forth for catch. It's a low-key daytime-only escape and home to one of the best restaurants in the country: the Deli Swiss. The main beach entrance is where you'll find most locals relaxing on lounge chairs on the weekends. On the far eastern end of the beach is a row of food shacks and thatch umbrellas.

Another five minutes west of Guayacanes before reaching Boca Chica, you'll see signs for **Playa Caribe**—this beach faces a small cove offering waves that attract surfers and boogie boarders on the weekends. During the week, it's as tranquil as it gets, and the scene is breathtaking. Yuri and Rai are the attendants here (cell tel. 829/926-9891, 7am-6pm daily), providing lounge chairs and umbrellas (US$6.70 or RD$300 for two chairs and an umbrella all day). There are surfboards for rent (US$2.25/hour or RD$100) if you want to give the waves a twirl. Yuri can give you a lesson if you ask. He doesn't charge, but tip him what you wish. There's a restaurant on-site, but call ahead to make arrangements for a plate of fried fish (US$6.70), or bring your own snacks.

Sports and Recreation

Los Delfines Water and Entertainment Park (Autovía del Este, Km. 15, tel. 829/520-8481, www.losdelfinespark.com, US$19 adults, US$16 children 4-12 years) is fun for the family and worthwhile if you're looking to keep your kids entertained away from the beach. The largest water park in the Caribbean, it counts up to 17 roller-coaster-like water slides, a children's pool, and average restaurants good enough for an afternoon's trip. Bring your own towels, and save by catching a *guagua* or public bus from the highway. They will stop for you directly in front of the park.

If you're a golfer, you've come to the right town. Juan Dolio is home to the stunning **Guavaberry Golf Country Club** (Autovia del Este Km. 55, tel. 829/547-0000 or 809/333-4653, www.guavaberrygolf.com.do, US$95/18 holes), a par-72 course designed by the legendary Gary Player bordering a nature reserve.

the beach at Guayacanes

Surfers flock to Playa Caribe.

The entire course blends seamlessly with its surroundings—one of the course's signature holes is played over a 15-foot waterfall and indigenous coral rock formations.

Inquire about hopping on dive trips with **Juan Dolio Divers** (Calle Principal, U.S. tel. 888/774-0040 or 809/526-1948, www.juandoliodiversrd.com, US$40/dive or US$16/snorkel equipment) at Coral Costa Caribe Resort. There are over 20 sites to explore up and down the Juan Dolio coast less than a 10-minute boat ride away.

Independent operator **Faenza Tours** (Calle Principal, Villas del Mar area, tel. 809/526-1713 or cell tel. 829/292-5000, faenzarentacar@yahoo.com) offers reasonably priced excursions from Juan Dolio, including ATV tours to San Pedro de Macorís (US$50, 2 persons min.) and Isla Saona (US$60).

Entertainment and Events

There is very little entertainment in Juan Dolio. It's not a party town like Boca Chica. The chief activity after dark is to barhop.

Among the watering holes, **Bar Cacique** (Beachfront, Calle Principal, 12pm-12am daily) is good for a cold beer or local mixed drinks with a view. The bar attracts a usual cast of characters, with plenty of local women and older expat men. Other popular haunts include **Paladart** (Carretera Nueva, tel. 809/526-1855, 11:30am-12am Tues.-Sun., closed Mon.), an Argentinean tapas bar on the roadside.

You can have drinks while trying your luck at the small **Dreams Casino** (Coral Costa Caribe Resort, tel. 809/526-3318, 7pm-midnight); ask about their free shuttle service.

Food

You can get a cheap buffet lunch of rice and beans with stew at **La Differencia Pica Pollo** (Calle Principal, across from Bar Cacique, US$2.25). They also have fresh-squeezed juices daily.

Giulia's Cafe and Sports Bar (Plaza Hispaniola, Calle Principal, tel. 809/526-1492, 7am-5pm Thurs.-Tues., US$6-12) is a convivial place to grab a traditional Dominican breakfast, as well as omelettes and pancakes. Lunchtime offer burgers, sandwiches, pasta, and steak. It's located on the street side, but the atmosphere makes up for the lack of a sea view. You can watch sports, get on free wireless Internet, and when you're ready for the beach, cross the street and walk south for a couple of minutes.

A longtimer in the area, **El Mesón** (Across from Club Hemmingway, Calle Principal, tel. 809/526-2666, 11am-11pm daily, US$8-15) offers Spanish specialties, including paellas and imported sausages.

The Italian bistro ★ **El Sueño** (Calle Principal, across from beach parking entrance, tel. 809/526-3903, noon-11pm daily, US$5-15) serves up delicious wood oven-fired pizza. You can see yours being made right in the main dining room. The service is prompt and pleasant, and the location directly across the entrance to Juan Dolio's miles of white sand can't be beat.

It is my hope that **Soya Azul** (Calle

Principal, going west from Fior di Loto, tel. 809/526-2101, 11am-6pm daily, occasional evenings, US$6-15) will be around for a long time to come. This Asian restaurant sits on a gorgeous, calm portion of Juan Dolio Beach facing beautifully tranquil waters ideal for a swim. The food is a wonderful change from local fare, and ranges from spicy Thai fried rice to spicy tuna rolls, ceviche, and conch with Thai curry.

Chef Walker Kleinert's ★ **Deli Swiss** (Guayacanes Beach, Calle Central 338, tel. 809/526-1226, 11am-9pm Wed.-Sun., US$10-20) is without doubt one of the best gourmet restaurants in the Dominican Republic. Set on an idyllic terrace facing a quiet corner of Guayacanes beach where the only sound is waves gently crashing below, specials include duck and chicken pâté, crab quiche, clam chowder, and delicious homemade breads, among other options. The restaurant is renowned for its wine cellar, a selection that has earned it eight consecutive excellence awards from *Wine Spectator* magazine. After your meal, relax on one of the lounge chairs, take a dip, and walk the beach. This is one blissful and romantic place to spend the day.

Accommodations

By the time you leave ★ **Fior di Loto** (entrance to Juan Dolio, first turnoff after the Shell gas station, Calle Principal 517, tel. 809/526-1146, www.fiordilotohotels.com, US$15-40), you will have gained a friend in the lovely Mara Sandri, owner and longtime expat from Italy. Her budget hotel, decorated in all things India in honor of the nonprofit school for girls that she single-handedly launched in Pushkar, shines with its stunning murals, paintings, colorful daybeds in the reception area, and plenty of Indian and astrological motifs. Rooms range from a shared dorm to double beds and apartments. There's a gorgeous gymnasium on the top floor where Mara teaches yoga three times a week for free (4:30pm-6:30pm Mon.-Wed.). Basic breakfast and coffee are available for a small fee, as well as sodas and beer. Mara

is a wealth of DR knowledge and her all-Dominican staff is equally charming. It's a great place for independent solo or couple travelers and attracts guests of all ages, as well as plenty of Europeans and Peace Corps volunteers. There's a 24-hour front desk for added security.

Coral Costa Caribe Resort (Calle Principal, tel. 888/774-0040, US$80) is an average all-inclusive at best, although it faces a clean and swimmable part of Juan Dolio's beach. There are a couple of swimming pools, three restaurants—Mexican, Italian, and Dominican—and an onsite dive shop. Kayaking and snorkeling gear are provided. The nightclub **Boom** occasionally opens to the public on the weekends for a cover charge. Across the street from the resort, you'll find tennis courts and a casino. If you are looking for an affordable weekend resort escape close to Santo Domingo, this would be a decent pick.

Emotions Beach Resort (U.S. tel. 800/801-1971, www.hodelpa.com, US$134-186), a Hodelpa property, is a welcome new addition to Juan Dolio Beach and a sign that the area might rebound. This already popular boutique hotel is set in the heart of Juan Dolio's main white sand stretch, as well as roadside, and has intimate and immaculate grounds with sleek superior or deluxe rooms and suites. There are three swimming pools with in-water loungers and five restaurants, including options for Dominican fusion, seafood, Italian, and organic for the health-conscious. There's also a spa onsite, bicycles, tennis courts, and a billiards room. For a notch up, get an Essential Club beachfront room with an exclusive beach and pool space and other perks thrown in like a free tour to Santo Domingo's Ciudad Colonial.

Information and Services

There aren't a ton of services in this area, but you'll find the basics. There's an ATM at the **Banco Popular** branch (Calle Principal), halfway between the old and new Juan Dolio, as well as a couple of supermarkets and plazas along the way. Right in Old Juan Dolio is the sparsely stocked Naito supermarket. Farther down the main drag in Juan Dolio Nuevo is **Plaza Llave** for Internet access, beauty salon services, and a supermarket.

For car rentals, head to **Faenza Tours** (Calle Principal, Villas del Mar area, tel. 809/526-1713 or cell tel. 829/292-5000, faenzarentacar@yahoo.com, US$49/day, discounts for longer-term). They also rent scooters (US$25/day or US$100/week).

Getting There

If you're driving from Santo Domingo, take Avenida George Washington going toward the bridge and port, leading outside the city. Go right along Avenida España, where you'll begin to enjoy gorgeous views along sea. Take the exit for Boca Chica and keep straight. You'll hit tolls (30 pesos or US$.065 per car), and past that will be Boca Chica signs. You'll see *colmados,* shops and casual restaurants on both sides of highway, until you reach the light at Avenida Caracoles where you'll turn right towards Calle Duarte and the beach.

To catch a *guagua* to Boca Chica, head to Parque Enriquillo in the Chinatown neighborhood, within walking distance from the Ciudad Colonial if you don't have heavy bags. You'll see them parked all around on the street parallel to Calle Duarte. Ask anyone where to catch the Boca Chica buses heading east, as it can be confusing to find them. If you'd prefer a private ride to Boca Chica, call **Apolo Taxi** (tel. 809/537-0000).

To catch a *guagua* heading back to Santo Domingo (RD$70, every 15 minutes from 6am to 11pm), head to the north side of Parque Central, along Avenida San Rafael. Some of them are marked express and only require

one terminal switch. You'll see these minivans stop and the conductor coming out.

Heading back to the city or to Boca Chica from Juan Dolio, you can hail a *guagua* along the highway, going west. If you're headed to the airport, let the conductor know to drop you close to it. You'll have to walk the remainder of the way to the terminal, or catch a *motoconcho* down.

Getting Around

The heart of Boca Chica consists of the main strip running all along the beach and the main road Avenida/Calle Duarte, where all the hotels, restaurants, and activities are strung from west to east. You won't need more than your feet to get around.

There are taxis or motorbike taxis available if you plan to go out at night from one end to another; they are usually parked at the main entrance to Boca Chica. You can also find private taxis at the intersection of Avenida San Rafael and Avenida Caracoles, or even parked outside your hotel. Alternatively, call the **Sindicato Transporte Turístico de Boca Chica** (SITRATUBOCHZA, tel. 809/523-5313) or one of its licensed drivers, **Miguel Rijo** (cell tel. 829/701-6616). Fares include Aeropuerto Internacional Las Américas (US$25), Santo Domingo (US$40), and Juan Dolio (US$30).

If you want to continue on your adventures from Boca Chica going east, wait for the *guaguas* at the intersection of the highway and Avenida Caracoles. They go to Juan Dolio (RD$30, 20 minutes), San Pedro de Macorís (RD$60, one hour), La Romana (RD$140, one hour), and Higüey (RD$250, two hours). *Guaguas* pass from dawn until about 6pm. There aren't any at night.

Punta Cana and the Southeast Coast

Diamond white beaches, infinite blue skies, and a slew of five-star all-inclusive resorts draw millions to postcard-perfect Punta Cana. This area is largely responsible for making the DR the crown of Caribbean tourism destinations.

There are actually two distinct areas to "Punta Cana": Bávaro, north of the Punta Cana Airport, and Punta Cana proper, south of the airport. Either way, as locals and residents will tell you any chance they get, "this isn't the Dominican Republic, it's *Punta Cana.*" The area's relatively high prices and exclusive resorts echo this. For those who want to venture outside and look past the Punta Cana resorts, there are small, local beach enclaves in Bávaro, such as Los Corales and Cortecito, which welcome the independent explorer.

The area jutting south of Punta Cana is more typically Dominican. The seaside fishing villages of Boca de Yuma and Bayahibe are a stone's throw from the Parque Nacional del Este and offer easy access to hiking, birding, diving, snorkeling, and cave exploration for Taíno pictographs. Hit the links at the renowned Teeth of the Dog at Casa de Campo, shop for Dominican art in La Romana, catch a baseball game, or dine at the riverfront Altos de Chavón. And Bayahibe's most special attractions are the offshore, protected Saona and Catalina Islands, which offer unbelievably beautiful beaches and incredible snorkeling opportunities.

PLANNING YOUR TIME

It's obvious that most who head to Punta Cana and La Romana do it for one reason: the beaches. Sure enough, there are more white sand stretches and corresponding beachfront resorts here than in any other portion of the country. It's tempting to kick back and relax with all the pampering you could imagine just a couple of steps away from your lounge chair.

Still, save a half day at least to wander up and down Bávaro's Los Corales and Cortecito beaches, both in the day and night, for a glimpse of the remaining local vibe in this touristed part of the DR, as well as much better dining options and some dancing

---

Previous: cave at eastern entrance of Parque Nacional del Este; Playa Juanillo. **Above:** a boat off of Saona Island.

Look for ★ to find recommended sights, activities, dining, and lodging.

Highlights

★ **Playa Macao:** A popular spot for surfers, development-free Macao is one of the most beautiful beaches in the DR (page 90).

★ **Playa Bávaro:** The famous Playa Bávaro hosts many resorts, but that doesn't take away from its glorious stretch—ideal for laying in the sun or swimming in crystal clear, temperate waters (page 92).

★ **Indigenous Eyes Ecological Reserve:** Hike through subtropical forest on this private reserve, once home to the indigenous Taíno people, to reach twelve freshwater lagoons (page 104).

★ **Playa Juanillo:** With its iridescent white sand and luminous blue ocean, this uncrowded beach makes for a perfect photo op (page 105).

★ **Altos de Chavón:** Marvel at the architectural wonders of this Mediterranean village replica, perched 91 meters (300 feet) above the majestic Río Chavón (page 116).

★ **La Punta de Bayahibe:** Sample life in an authentic Dominican fishing village—stroll down alleys lined with colorful wooden homes, fish with locals, and watch the sun go down over the bay with a cocktail in hand (page 128).

★ **Sendero del Padre Nuestro:** Explore the beautiful forests and freshwater Taíno caves of the Parque Nacional del Este on this hiking trail (page 131).

★ **Isla Saona:** You'll find it difficult to put down your camera as you journey from one diamond white sand beach to another on the largest offshore island of the DR (page 132).

Punta Cana and the Southeast Coast

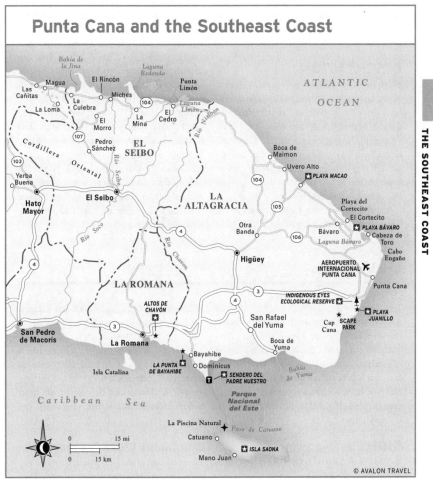

Dominican-style. While in Punta Cana, also make time for a countryside excursion to visit Higüey's basilica, its roadside butcher shops in La Otra Banda, and its cacao and sugarcane plantations. Plenty of safari tours are around, and most offer a solid glimpse of *campo* life in the DR. If you can spare another day, or a few hours on the way to Bayahibe, stop in the fishing village of Boca de Yuma and explore this untouristed part of the south. Birders, nature lovers, and pirate enthusiasts will enjoy their time here; you can also sample the freshest fish there is and visit

one of the largest caves within the Parque Nacional del Este.

For those who crave nice beaches but love culture, adventure, and water sports even more, make time for at least a one- or two-night stay in Bayahibe. You'll get a good feel for a small but bustling Dominican fishing village, while also having easier (and more affordable) access to prime snorkeling and dive sites and the offshore islands of Saona and Catalina. These islands are an incredibly long day trip from Punta Cana—something that tour operators in Bávaro don't always make clear. The bonus is enjoying some of the prettiest sunsets on this side of the Dominican Republic.

ORIENTATION

The Punta Cana Airport is your point of reference when deciding where to stay or how far to head along the long Punta Cana/Bávaro main drag. Whether you decide to set yourself up on the southern tip of the area in Cap Cana or north in Üvero Alto will make an impact on your stay in terms of what activities will be closest to you or how often you'll dip into your wallet for gasoline refills.

North of the Punta Cana Airport is the Bávaro area, with most of the all-inclusive resorts as well as a couple of hideaways for independent travelers. A portion of Bávaro is home to small beach communities like Cortecito and Los Corales where you can come and go from your hotel as you please. *Guaguas* running along the main drag in Bávaro are another advantage for staying in this area, as well as local restaurants and beachfronts that are easily accessed at various intervals. North of Bávaro is Üvero Alto.

South of the Punta Cana Airport is the area labeled Punta Cana proper, and south of that, Cap Cana. These two exclusive regions don't have any public transportation running along the main road and are more isolated than Bávaro.

Bávaro

The neighborhood north of Punta Cana Airport is called Bávaro, after its biggest beach stretch of Playa Bávaro. Here you'll find a concentration of resorts, small hotels, a multitude of local and international restaurants, the pedestrian beach village towns of Los Corales and Cortecito, and a local atmosphere in an area that is sufficiently connected by public transportation.

SIGHTS

Bávaro Adventure Park

Bávaro Adventure Park (Entrada Boulevard Turístico km 8.5, tel. 809/933-3040, www.bavaroadventurepark.com, 8am-6pm daily, US$99 for package of three activities) offers a host of activities in one gated park. Fly over the landscape up high on a zipline or skim it on a mountain bike or Segway. You can even try "zorbing" (rolling downhill inside a giant ball). It's not so much a trip into nature as it is an outing for those seeking an adrenaline rush close to the hotel.

ChocoMuseo

Located inside the Mundo Auténtico tourism complex and housing Dominican coffee and the renowned Don Lucas Cigar Factory, the ChocoMuseo chain (Downtown Punta Cana, tel. 809/480-9708, www.chocomuseo. com, 9am-7pm daily) is more a store than a museum, but you can get a free 10-minute introduction and walk through on the making of organic Dominican chocolate from bean to bar, followed by tastings. Don't miss the mamajuana and chocolate-blended drinks.

Don Lucas Cigar Factory

The president of the Dominican Republic has been spotted smoking the handmade Don Lucas cigar brands, among one of the oldest and most respected cigar brands in the country. There's only one place where a Don Lucas cigar is rolled and sold, and this Don Lucas Cigar Factory location (Av. Barceló, tel. 809/200-0129, www.donlucascigars.com. do, 9am-6pm daily, free resort pickups and tour) is it. Watch the men methodically creating each cigar before heading on to the shop to buy your own, if you so choose.

BEACHES

★ Playa Macao

Playa Macao is one of the most beautiful

Bávaro

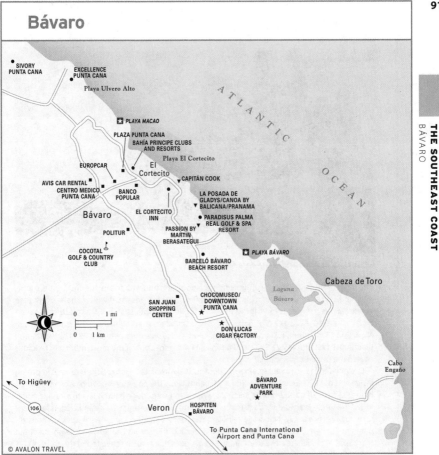

ATLANTIC OCEAN

SIVORY PUNTA CANA

EXCELLENCE PUNTA CANA

Playa Ulvero Alto

PLAYA MACAO

PLAZA PUNTA CANA

BAHÍA PRINCIPE CLUBS AND RESORTS

Playa El Cortecito

EUROPCAR

El Cortecito

AVIS CAR RENTAL

CAPITÁN COOK

CENTRO MEDICO PUNTA CANA

BANCO POPULAR

LA POSADA DE GLADYS/CANOA BY BALICANA/PRANAMA

Bávaro

EL CORTECITO INN

PARADISUS PALMA REAL GOLF & SPA RESORT

POLITUR

PASSION BY MARTIN BERASATEGUI

COCOTAL GOLF & COUNTRY CLUB

PLAYA BÁVARO

BARCELÓ BÁVARO BEACH RESORT

Laguna Bávaro

Cabeza de Toro

0   1 mi

0   1 km

SAN JUAN SHOPPING CENTER

CHOCOMUSEO/ DOWNTOWN PUNTA CANA

DON LUCAS CIGAR FACTORY

Cabo Engaño

To Higüey

BÁVARO ADVENTURE PARK

106

Veron

HOSPITEN BÁVARO

To Punta Cana International Airport and Punta Cana

© AVALON TRAVEL

beaches in the Dominican Republic. Even UNESCO agrees this spot is a jewel—they declared it one of the best beaches in the Caribbean. Prepare to gasp as you approach the top of the hill and get an initial glimpse of the deep blue ocean, golden sands, and coconut trees ahead. There are no hotels or buildings here or anywhere near the beach, and that's what makes it special. There have unfortunately been rumors that a US$35 million investment purchase has been made and a resort might be in the works soon. Beach vendors, local businesses, and concerned citizens have been holding strikes and protests, but the results are yet to be seen.

Macao is also a popular surf spot. You'll get to see some serious wave action here. You can rent equipment and get lessons onsite with **Macao Surf Camp** (Üvero Alto, beachfront, tel. 809/430-9017 or 829/556-0406, www.macaosurfcamp.com, 8am-4pm daily, US$115 two-hour class, US$300 three-day course). Beware of rip currents while in the water, however. Drownings have occurred when people have gone too far out from shore, so if you decide to take a dip, stick close to the shore but don't venture out alone or at off-hours.

If you want to avoid the bulk of the crowd, head to the beach in the morning and stay for lunch. One of the highlights at Macao

Higüey

Basílica Catedral Nuestra Señora de la Altagracia

The town of Higüey is an agricultural and transportation hub with the hustle and bustle, traffic, and modern conveniences of a big city. One of the only reasons you'd venture here, other than making a bus transfer, is to visit the basilica of Higüey, or the **Basílica Catedral Nuestra Señora de la Altagracia** (8am-6pm Mon.-Sat., 8am-8pm Sun., mass 6:30am, 8am, 6pm Mon.-Fri.; 10am, noon, 5:30pm weekends). The basilica was built between 1954 and 1971 and inaugurated on January 21, 1971, by Pope John Paul, and is one of the most important religious sites in the Dominican Republic.

Designed by French architects Pierre Dupré and Dovnoyer de Segonzac, the basilica is imposing inside and out. The exterior, including royal palms along the entrance, encompasses a 69-meter-high (225-foot) arch and a bronze and 24 karat gold entrance. Inside is an altar with a framed painting of the Virgin Mary dating back to the 16th century. Believers get in line and wait as long as it takes for a chance to say their prayers and requests before her. There are several stories of how this painting got here. The most commonly told is that a sick child was healed after seeing the Virgin Mary appear at this site close to an orange tree. Under that tree, the child found the painting.

Within the compound the **Altagracia Museum** (US$10) is well worth a stop for some religious history of the DR, as well as an outdoor candle lighting prayer area.

Every **January 21,** Dominicans and Catholics from around the world descend on the basilica to pay their respects. The day turns into a party in the streets, with the usual music, food—with plenty of oranges—and drinks.

Many tours from Punta Cana include a brief stop and tour of the basilica. If you're not appropriately dressed and showing skin above the knees, you will be handed a long skirt cover-up at the entrance to the church.

is the fresh seafood restaurants on the beach, where you can indulge in fried fish, Dominican-style.

★ Playa Bávaro

One of the most well-known beaches in the Dominican Republic is **Playa Bávaro.** Playa Bávaro's stunning long miles of white sands are the most developed in this area, dotted with all-inclusive hotels, but that doesn't take away from its glorious stretch. You'd have to stay here to truly enjoy this beach, sought after for its reef-protected calm and temperate turquoise waters. You wouldn't be alone, unless you head to the beach early in the morning or stay on at lunchtime while everyone crowds the restaurants.

Other Beaches

Also in the Bávaro area, a stone's throw north of Playa Bávaro, are two public stretches offering a more cultural beat than all the others: Playa Los Corales and Playa El Cortecito. Both of these beaches and their small communities are ideal for independent travelers who want space to throw their towel, with or without a rented chair if they choose, and enjoy some people watching, local restaurants, and an ultra-local vibe. **Playa Los Corales** is dotted with small restaurants and resorts. You may spot tourists parasailing above boating activity. The stretch is home to a small number of trendy beachfront lounges and cafés, but it still has a less overwhelming big-conclave feel than farther south on the Punta Cana trail.

You'll know you've reached the end of Los Corales and entered the Blue Flag Certified **Playa del Cortecito**—one of my favorites—when you spot more foot traffic and more mobile vendors holler out their offerings without being overbearing. This area has a bustling Dominican vibe. It is one of the only two truly public beach communities left on this eastern coast. Playa del Cortecito is home to some favorite local and expat haunts both by day and night, including Capitán Cook and Onno's. There are souvenir shacks, small hotels, and dive and glass-bottom boats waiting to scoop you up. But the atmosphere is authentic, the beach wider and clean with impossibly tall coconut trees, and water that makes it all postcard-worthy. Don't miss posing by the "I heart RD" sign at the first souvenir shack on the beach.

SPORTS AND RECREATION
Diving and Snorkeling

There are three main PADI dive shops in the Bávaro area, and they offer similar dive excursions: local, in the Atlantic, or in the Caribbean Sea with an excursion all the way south. Options south include diving off Calatina Island (US$209 all-inclusive, 9am-5:30pm) or local dives off the fishing village of Bayahibe, as well as cave diving in the Parque Nacional del Este (for those certified for cave diving). Call by 4pm the day before to see what's available and to reserve a space. One place to try is **Global Divers** (Barceló Dominican Beach Resort, tel. 809/618-9092, www.globaldiverspuntacana.

Playa Macao

com, US$135 3-dive package, Discover Scuba US$225 2-tank dive). **VIP Divers** (Cortecito Beach, Hotel Vista Sol, tel. 809/763-0752, vipdivers@gmail.com, US$60/dive, US$200 Catalina 2-tank dive) are popular for certification classes, and **SeaPro Divers** (Los Corales, next to Barceló Dominican, tel. 809/223-5696, www.seaprodivers.com, US$100 2-tank dive) gets rave reviews for both its diving and snorkeling excursions to Saona and Catalina Islands, with two-tank dives every morning.

You can hop on glass-bottom boat snorkeling trips with **Global Divers** (US$45 pp) right off the coast, followed by a natural pool on the tip of Playa Bávaro. The excursion lasts just a couple of hours.

Parasailing

Happiness is floating 46 meters (150 feet) above the Coconut Coast with **Global Divers** (Barceló Dominican Beach Resort, tel. 809/618-9092, www.globaldiverspuntacana.com, 8am-4pm, US$45 pp or $85 for two). You'll be airborne for about 10 minutes. It's quite memorable to see all those miles of pearl white sand beaches from above. Another option is the independent **SeaPro Divers** (Los Corales, next to Barceló Dominican, tel. 809/223-5696, www.seaprodivers.com, 9am-5pm Mon.-Sat., US$100 for two).

Sailing

Sailing with **Ocean Adventures** (next to Huracán Cafe, Corales Beach in Bávaro, tel. 809/390-7418, www.oapc.com.do, US$90) takes you aboard a FreeStyle III catamaran to explore the popular (and often crowded) "natural pool"—a sandbank on shallow waters—off the beach of Bávaro. For a party boat, look up **SeaPro Divers** (sailing locations at Now Larimar and Occidental Grand resorts, tel. 809/223-5696, www.seaprodivers.com, US$55), which has an all-inclusive run with a stop at the natural pool for more merriment.

Surfing and Kitesurfing

Run by surf enthusiasts and pioneers of the sport in the DR, the **Macao Surf Camp**
(Üvero Alto, beachfront, tel. 809/430-9017 or 829/556-0406,www.macaosurfcamp.com, 8am-4pm daily, US$115 two-hour class, US$300 three-day course) offers surfing classes for all levels off the beautiful, public Playa Macao. They take everyone from beginning to competition and nearly all ages (4 to 76). Lessons can last a couple of hours or nearly an entire week. You can rent boards (US$10/hour or $25/day) and surf solo if you already know what you're doing.

North of Bávaro, check out **KBS Kite Boarding School** (Zoetry Agua Punta Cana, tel. 829/672-6133 or 829/854-6548, www.kbspuntacana.com, 8am-6pm daily, US$250 three-hour beginner, pickup available). Those who are IKO certified can rent equipment or hop on a six-night, seven-day kite cruise down to Catalina and Saona Islands (US$1,899 for four persons).

Golfing

The combination of golf and beaches with the courses facing the sea is part of this area's claim to tourist fame. There are several excellent options for some early tee times. Within Bávaro, you'll find the popular **Cocotal Golf & Country Club** (Bávaro area, tel. 809/687-4653, www.cocotalgolf.com, US$119/18 holes, golf lesson US$86, shuttle service), conveniently close to the major resorts and offering 27 holes set around lakes and coconut trees, inside a residential community.

4x4 Safaris

Colonial Tours' Super Truck Safari (tel. 809/688-5285, www.colonialtours.com.do, US$95) has knowledgeable local guides who will give you as much insight into local life as possible as you ride through the streets and down dirt roads from La Otra Banda to Higüey and into farms and sugarcane plantations. The day ends as it should on the gorgeous beach of Macao, where you'll have time to swim at your leisure and bask in the glorious Dominican sun. Pickups are available from resorts on the Bávaro or Punta Cana coastline. **Bávaro Runners** (tel.

809/833-0260, www.bavarorunners.com, US$55-135) is also popular for its safaris, albeit they are a tad more crowded because of this. Whether from Bávaro or Punta Cana, you'll head to well-known sights—including the Higüey Basilica and cacao and coffee farms.

Horseback Riding

Gallop on a virgin beach up in Üvero Alto with **Rancho Caribeño** (tel. 809/724-7564, http://xn--ranchocaribeo-tkb.com, US$65 adult, US$45 children). Beginners are welcome. The three-hour ride takes you through forested trails onto undeveloped portions of Üvero Alto Beach. To ride in a natural theme park through forest and past Taíno caves, sign up for a couple of hours with **Scape Park** (Cap Cana, tel. 809/469-7484, www.scapepark.com, US$69 adults, US$41 children, pickup included). They offer a full equestrian center with an introduction to horseback riding before you head out for two hours into its forests and shaded trails.

ENTERTAINMENT AND EVENTS
Bars and Nightclubs

For a small and laid-back beachfront bar vibe, head to **Whala!Bávaro Beach Bar** (Los Corales, tel. 809/688-1612, www.whalabavaro. com, 9pm-1am daily) where a DJ spins the best in Latin music every evening during the high season. Locals and tourists mingle here, dancing merengue in flip-flops and throwing their cares to the breeze.

The open-air **Onno's** (Playa del Cortecito, tel. 809/552-0376, www.onnosbar.com, 11am-5am daily, US$5-15) is a well-known chain in the DR, consistent in providing good food (especially pizza), DJS from 10pm, and merriment directly on the beach until the wee hours of the morning.

Soles Chill Out Bar (Playa Los Corales, tel. 809/910-4371, solesbar@gmail.com, 10am-2am daily, US$5-20) is a trendy beachfront hangout for the young, the mature, and the fabulous, with lounge beds and tables directly on the beach. A live DJ spins electronic lounge music all day and in the evening if you like that sort of beat. Just a five-minute walk over on the wide beach is **Huracán Cafe** (Playa Los Corales, tel. 809/552-1046, www.huracancafe.com, 9am-11pm daily, US$5-20) with a similar setup, but a somewhat less pretentious vibe and tasty meals to boot.

The Pearl Beach Club (Cabeza de Toro, next to Catalonia Bávaro Beach Resort, tel.

Soles Chill Out Bar

809/933-3171, www.pearlbeachclub.com, 9am-12am Sun.-Thurs., 9am-1am Fri.-Sat., no cover except for events) is the latest Miami-trendy beachfront bar addition to Punta Cana, with poolside live music or DJ themed parties (the foam type), and is also an all day and evening hangout on plush sofas. There's a Caribbean-themed restaurant on site, a sushi bar, and of course, fancy cocktails.

One of the most unique nights out in Punta Cana can be had at **Coco Bongo Show & Disco** (Downtown Punta Cana, Av. Barceló, tel. 809/466-1111, www.cocobongo.com.do, 9pm-4am Thurs.-Sun., from US$75, drinks included), the part nightclub and part Vegas-style show with performances that begin close to midnight and run until early morning. Prepare to be stunned by nonstop entertainment once you enter this small but impressive club, from the exhilarating lights, smoke, and visual effects of the nightclub during intermission to dancers and acrobats flying across the room as well as on a giant stage. Performances include tributes to Michael Jackson, Madonna, and the Moulin Rouge. There are fun moments throughout, including "kiss cams" putting patrons on the spot for a public smooch shown on two screens. Local drinks are all-inclusive, and there are tables available at an extra cost if you don't want to stand all night long. There's also an outside bar as you arrive, if you want to have a couple of drinks alfresco pre-show.

Past a glamorous fountain pool entrance, bats welcome you to **Imagine Club** (Cruce Carretera Coco Loco, no phone, www.imaginepuntacana.com, 11pm-4am Tues.-Sun., US$10 regular, US$21 all-inclusive local drinks). Dancing inside an ancient limestone cave is indeed what makes Imagine Disco a must-see-at-least-once. There are two separate cavernous chambers where DJs spin a variety of music under disco lights—from techno to merengue to R&B—as well as random dancers performing various stunts. If you're in the mood to let loose and party all night, while occasionally getting bumped by a 20-something spring break-type of crowd, that's what you

will get. At the very least, it makes for great photos.

Drink Point (Av. España, corner of Av. Francia, tel. 809/552-0920, 9pm-3am Thurs.-Sun., no cover) across from the Texaco station, is an open-air bar and nightclub that had a nice crowd when it started out. It is now a hit-or-miss dance spot with the occasional less than stellar in its audience. Still, it's good for a quick beer and casual merengue or *bachata* dancing during the week (avoid Sunday). A couple of blocks north is a better option at **El Kan Drinks House** (Carretera Bavaro Veron, tel. 809/762-1200, 6pm-4am daily, no cover), with a similar lounge and club setup but a better DJ, nicer crowd, and plenty of seating space. That includes outdoor tables on the sidewalk. Keep in mind that clubs come and go like the wind, so when in doubt, ask a local about the latest place to dance.

Looking for a more laid-back spot for cheap drinks and music? The outdoor terrace of **Batú Music & Sports Bar** (Av. Alemania, Plaza El Dorado 110, tel. 829/573-0456, 11am-2am daily, US$5-15) is popular with DJs at night, sports on a muted flat-screen, as well as delicious two-for-one pizza. Happy hour is a daily affair 6pm-11pm with the cheapest drinks in town, and Thursdays are karaoke nights.

The first-ever gay club in the Punta Cana region opened its doors in late 2015 at **Mares** (Cortecito, Av. Alemania, no phone, www.marespuntacana.com, 10:30pm-4am Wed.-Sun., no cover). It welcomes all visitors, but the crowd is mostly made up of men mingling at the bar or on the outdoor rooftop terrace, a stone's throw from the beach.

SHOPPING

The **Palma Real Shopping Village** (Av. Alemania 57, tel. 809/552-8725, www.palmarealshopping.com, 10am-10pm daily) is on the main drag running along Bávaro, just past the Cocotal Golf & Country Club, and offers a range of American and international brand stores, centered on a romantic Spanish courtyard, complete with fountains. You'll find apparel, perfume, and cigar shops. There are also banks with ATM services, a movie theater (Palacio del Cine, shows begin 4pm-10pm), and an open-air food court nicely aired with powerful fans, with a Hard Rock Cafe and Burrito Taquito. You can easily get here by *guagua* from you resort if you're within the Bávaro area. Just step outside onto the main avenue and hail the bus, usually a white minivan.

Also on the main drag and in the Los Corales area of Bávaro, **Plaza Turquesa** is a newer strip mall with a few welcome conveniences. Check out two fashion stores with cute bikinis at **Fashion by Cusie** (tel. 809/455-7346, www.cusieboutique.com, 9am-9pm daily), also selling reasonably priced contemporary shoes and beachwear accessories.

You'll find the biggest mall at **San Juan Shopping Center** (Carretera Barceló Km. 9, tel. 809/466-6000, 9am-9pm daily). Several of the big hotels offer free scheduled pickup and drop-offs. If you're driving, you can get your parking ticket validated. Here you'll find the **Super Pola Supermarket** stocked with everything from groceries to a deli counter, and wine and liquor sections. Boutiques include amber jewelry stores, cigar shops, and plenty of American designer apparel boutiques on

the second floor. Caribbean Cinemas and arts and crafts stores are also onsite. At the far western end of the strip, you'll find Noah Restaurant and ATMs.

There are plenty of local souvenirs and Dominican cigars in the beachfront local vendor-filled shopping alley at **El Galeón del Pirata** (Los Corales, Bávaro, next to Solas Cafe).

FOOD
Cafés

If you're looking for that cup of java first thing in the morning, head to the beachfront, casual **Canoa by Balicana** (beachfront, next to Barceló Dominican, tel. 809/455-7432, 8am-4pm daily, US$2-5) to enjoy it with a view. Inside Plaza Turquesa, **Dalia's Cafe** (Plaza Turquesa, Los Corales, tel. 809/466-1009, reposteriadalias@gmail.com, 7am-10pm daily, US$1.50-5) won't disappoint with its outdoor patio (though streetside) or cool interior with fresh-baked pastries, omelettes, and quiche options, in addition to gourmet coffee. **BAM Market** (Buenos, Aires Market, Plaza Turquesa, Los Corales, tel. 809/455-7344, bammarket@hotmail.com, 8am-10pm daily, US$1-4) is the pick for coffee and fresh-baked Argentinean-style empanadas stuffed

Palma Real Shopping Village has an open-air food court.

with ham and cheese or other combinations. Head to the deli counter at the back of this gourmet grocery store. If you're just in search of a cheap dollar coffee and affordable local breakfast, try **Fast Chef** (Av. Alemania, Los Corales, tel. 809/455-6635, 8am-midnight daily, US$1.50-2).

Dominican

★ **La Posada de Gladys** (Av. Alemania, Los Corales, no phone, 8am-10pm daily, US$3-10) is a charming local spot amid fancier restaurants and attracts locals every day. Just steps from the Barceló Dominican on the main drag affordable Dominican specials are served under a thatched open-air palapa hugged by a leafy wall of tall bamboo and decorated with wicker chairs and plastic over leopard print cloth-covered tables. It's worth coming here for a delicious dinner of *pescado criollo* or whole fish steamed and topped with a light tomato sauce to the sounds of *bachata* and merengue echoing in the background. You could also try the *plato del día* or the Dominican rice, beans, and stew combo.

Across the street is **Fast Chef** (Av. Alemania, Los Corales, tel. 809/455-6635, 8am-midnight daily, US$1.50-5), where budget travelers converge outdoors on the casual restaurant's shared outdoor picnic tables to enjoy orders of *mofongo* (a Dominican mashed plantain specialty), fried chicken, burgers, nachos, or the local rice and beans menu of the day, among other picks.

Downtown at the crossroads between Bávaro and Punta Cana, **El Pollo Boracho** (across from Sunix gas station, Cruce Blvd. Aeropuerto, tel. 809/754-4401, 11am-11pm Mon.-Sat.) is easily the cheapest meal in this area of resorts. And it happens to be authentic Dominican food, served cafeteria-style. Ask for the *plato del día*—usually priced at RD$150 or US$3.35—consisting of rice and beans with a choice of chicken or beef.

Caribbean and International

★ **Canoa by Balicana** (beachfront, next to Barceló Dominican, tel. 809/455-7432, 8am-4pm daily, US$3-10) is a new, funky beachfront restaurant that sits on a beautiful stretch in Los Corales and offers the perfect beach club vibe with good food, great drinks, and music. The fresh juice and coconut side bar displays a cocktail of the day, but don't miss sampling their Coco Loco, served in a coconut and the best I've had anywhere. For lunch, the shrimp coconut curry is to die for, as are the burgers, chicken fingers, and pretty much any thing you pick on this fun tropical menu. Service can be a tad forgetful and checks can have errors (check them), but the staff is always friendly. Take advantage of the beach loungers and hammocks while you wait or post meal. The restaurant is only open in the daytime.

Walk one block west and you'll find the Plaza Turquesa strip, also in the Los Corales section of Bávaro, lined with trendy but laid-back cafés and restaurants attracting the locals and expats. It's particularly lively at night, when folks come out to dine with live music or grab drinks on sidewalk terraces. Try **Cafe Dalia's** (Av. Alemania, tel. 809/466-1009, reposteriadalias@gmail.com, 7am-10pm daily, US$3-10), a European bistro with gourmet sandwiches, quiche slices, and wine that you can enjoy on the terrace or in an air-conditioned interior. There's a flat-screen TV in the all-white interior for those who prefer air-conditioning, a couch, and some football.

Next door, **Restaurante Cubano** (Plaza Turquesa, Los Corales, tel. 809/455-7373, www.donpiord.com, noon-midnight daily, US$5-12) is always lively with salsa and dishes out a menu filled with meat options, including authentic versions of *ropa vieja* and Cubano sandwiches. The roast chicken is pretty tasty as well. **BAM Market** (Plaza Turquesa, Los Corales, tel. 809/455-7344, 8am-10pm daily) is a solid bet for takeout deli sandwiches or fresh-baked empanadas and juices at the back counter.

Citrus (Plaza Turquesa, Los Corales, tel. 809/455-2026, 12pm-11pm Mon.-Sat., closed Sun., US$5-12) serves excellent bacon cheeseburgers, among other seafood options, and fills up quickly in the evening; get there around 6pm to avoid a long wait.

The beachfront lounge **Huracán Cafe** (Playa Los Corales, tel. 809/552-1046, giacomo.zatti@yahoo.it, 10am-11pm daily, US$5-15) is popular with the young and trendy, from residents to visitors. A DJ spins live on the beach while you lie back on an all-white daybed or sofa and sip on cocktails. The restaurant serves a basic menu of pastas and salads.

A two-minute walk away and tucked down a quiet alley from the noisy restaurant row, ★ **Pranama** (Plaza El Dorado, Los Corales, behind Cicolello Supermarket, tel. 809/552-6767, pranamapc@hotmail.com, 5am-11pm Mon.-Sat., US$5-10) is a wonderful addition to Bávaro's incredibly diverse cuisine scene, with authentic homemade Indian meals courtesy of chef Krishna Duddukuri, who hails from South India and moved to the DR after training in Geneva. The coconut rice is to die for, blended with shaved coconut bits and peppers. Soak it in the ghost vindaloo—a spicy, tender goat stew with potatoes, or the tikka masala, among other tempting options. Wash your meal down with a *lassi*—mango, rose, or passion fruit flavored—and plot your return.

Chez Mon Ami (Av. Alemania, Cortecito, tel. 829/741-2300, chezmonamidr@gmail.com, 11am-3pm and 5pm-2am Mon.-Fri., 6pm-3am Sat., US$5-15) surprises with its solid French gastronomy in the middle of a restaurant strip in Cortecito. Try the beef bourguignon, mussels, or salty crepes. Wine is plentiful as well, as are imported beers.

To take it up a notch for a special occasion, dress up and splurge on a dinner at ★ **Passion by Martin Berasategui** (Paradisus Palma Real, tel. 809/688-5000, US$65pp tasting menu), the AAA 4-Diamond restaurant ranking among the best in the Caribbean. The award-winning, 7-Michelin star chef's creative menu will surprise, from monkfish to perfectly seared steaks and herb-crusted tuna. Go for the seven-course tasting menu for a fun food lover's experience.

Pizza

The best thin-crust, wood-fired oven pizza you'll have is at ★ **Venezia** (Av. Alemania, Plaza Costa Bávaro, tel. 829/912-6969, 7am-midnight daily, US$5-10), a small, Italian-owned spot reached by car on a road with otherwise no other surrounding attractions. Still, it's a worthwhile and only a short motorbike ride from your Bávaro digs. There are 36 pizza combinations, baked fresh while you wait, as well as pasta, risotto, and seafood dishes. The small, leafy outdoor terrace fills up quicker than the inside air-conditioned space.

Smack in Los Corales, **Batú Music & Sports Bar** (Av. Alemania, Plaza El Dorado 110, tel. 829/573-0456, 11am-2am daily, US$5-15) also serves tasty pizzas. It has an unbeatable two for one offer on the pizza of the day Tuesday to Sunday noon-2pm. Delivery is available.

Seafood

Capitán Cook (tel. 809/552-0645, Cortecito Beach, capitancook@live.com, noon-11pm daily, US$3-15) is well-known for freshly caught fish to table meals and attracts plenty of well-to-do Dominicans. Pick your table alfresco, followed by a short walk to a giant wooden trunk filled with ice and the latest catch of the day. Your choice will be weighed to determine price—pick a size you can afford—then you sit back and relax at your table with views of Cortecito Beach and watch the world go by. You'll spot the entrance from the beach thanks to a fishnet hanging over the gate. You can also access it from the main road in Cortecito.

Noah Restaurant (San Juan Shopping Center, Av. Barceló, tel. 809/455-1060, www.noahrestaurant.com, noon-midnight daily, US$10-25) is popular for its sushi, pizza, and Sicilian pasta, among other options. The food is decent, though not outstanding, and there's both indoor and outdoor seating. Across from the restaurant, **Quicksilver Surf and Crepes** (tel. 809/466-1726, 9am-11pm daily, US$3-10) doubles as a surf apparel store and a crêperie/café. It's convenient if you're hanging out at the mall.

Vegan and Vegetarian

Vegans will find unique offerings at **AmaLuna Food Vibration** (Los Corales, tel. 809/552-0664, www.amalunarestaurant. com, 7:30pm-10:30pm Mon., Wed.-Sun., US$12-28) set inside a delightful garden turned restaurant. Five-course organic tasting menus (US$28 pp) are offered with a choice of Japanese, Indian, Italian, and Spanish cuisine options. There are also more affordable single-plate pasta dishes. The presentation is delightful though the flavors might be lacking for the non-vegan. Note that boxing up food is not favored; only order what you can finish. **Balicana Asian Restaurant** (Los Corales, tel. 809/455-7432, www.balicana.com, 10am-4pm Mon.-Sat., US$5-20) offers a taste of Thailand in a Caribbean, and the setting is delightfully romantic at night, with tables around the pool at Los Corales Apartments. Try the spicy green seafood curry or the ginger teriyaki fish.

You'll find excellent vegetarian options at **Pranama** (Plaza El Dorado, Los Corales, behind Cicolello Supermarket, tel. 809/552-6767, pranamapc@hotmail.com, 5am-11pm Mon.-Sat., US$5-10), including chickpeas curry, spinach curry, and lentils, along with coconut, mango or lemon rice, salads, and potato sides.

ACCOMMODATIONS

Note that all prices listed are for double occupancy during high season. Rates can drop dramatically during low season months, and hotels regularly list their specials online. Bávaro hosts more affordable resorts closer to the small beach towns of Cortecito and Los Corales, while Üvero Alto, the remoter area north of Bávaro, is home to a handful of luxury resorts catering mostly to couples.

Under US$50

Bávaro Hostel (behind Plaza Turquesa, Los Corales, tel. 809/552-0986, www.bavarohostel. com, US$12-35) is a welcome option in an area overrun with expensive resorts. Tucked on a side street a short walk from the beach, the entrance is gated and might seem like more of an apartment, but buzz #4A and climb the steps all the way to the fourth floor reception area. Aside from dorm rooms (US$12, includes wireless Internet, linens and towels, lockers), there are private rooms available (US$25-35) with private baths. It's a place to crash for those independent souls looking to explore on foot, as it's a five-minute walk to Los Corales Beach and to the area's multitude of restaurants.

US$50-150

One of the few affordable and small hotels in Bávaro, ★ **El Cortecito Inn** (Calle Pedro Mir 1, tel. 809/552-0639, US$50, includes breakfast) is a decent spot to lay your head while staying a stone's throw away from Cortecito Beach. It sits on the main active drag of this small beach community, steps from popular restaurants and bars like Onno's and Capitán Cook. The hotel's courtyard features a pool surrounded by tall coconut trees. Rooms are clean and basic but offer air-conditioning, as well as pool-facing balconies if you choose.

The beachfront **Los Corales Villas & Apartments** (Calle Marcio Veloz Maggiolo, tel. 809/891-5915, from US$110) are off the main drag yet still close the beach and offer a range of studios and apartments for those who wish to enjoy self-catered, spacious accommodations where you can come and go as you please. Restaurants and entertainment are nearby. There's a lovely pool onsite, and amenities include free wireless Internet and 24-hour security. The only nuisance is the additional daily US$7 electricity fee.

Barceló Dominican Beach Resort (Av. Alemania, U.S. tel. 800/227-2356 or 809/221-0714, www.barcelo.com, dominicanbeach@ barcelo.com, from US$150) is probably the most affordable of the lot for all-inclusive resorts and out of all the Barceló hotels for couples and families. It's also superconvenient, which is its greatest strength. It sits smack in the heart of Los Corales, facing its beautiful beach, and therefore within easy on-foot access to local restaurants, nightlife, shopping, and water sports. Over 700 rooms attract a young international crowd, and the resort offers seven à la carte restaurants, three buffets, and three pools. Rooms are all-white, clean, and basic and have terraces, mini fridges, and coffeemakers. You can easily hop on the local *guagua* and cheaply go up and down the Bávaro drag to San Juan Shopping Center. That also means there's plenty of noise and little privacy.

A good value for families or traveling friends, **Whala!Bávaro** (Los Corales, tel. 809/688-1612, www.whalabavaro.com, US$130-172) is a small classic beachfront all-inclusive with a lively vibe. It offers 150 double or superior rooms and suites, three bars (closing by midnight), three pools, and two restaurants. Superior rooms have balconies, and suites give the added Jacuzzi touch. All amenities are included—full bath, satellite TV, air-conditioning, and mini fridge. But wireless Internet and the safe are at an additional cost. The daily buffet restaurant provides tasty Caribbean dishes. A second, à la carte restaurant rotating Mediterranean and Dominican food is at your expense (though, as you are close to a handful of excellent local restaurants around the hotel, you should skip it).

Over US$150

With 272 rooms facing a glorious stretch of Playa Bávaro, adults-only **Iberostar Grand Bávaro** (U.S. tel. 888/774-0040, www.iberostargrandbavaro.com, from US$250-330 pp) stays true to the brand's luxurious offering. Enjoy butler service, upscale furnishings and linens, and marble baths. The oceanfront luxury suites are worth the splurge—they come with reserved poolside cabanas. Equally tempting are the pool suites with walkout access from your terrace for a private dip at all hours. The resort provides free wireless Internet for guests—a rare perk among all-inclusives—and there's an 18-hole golf course onsite. There isn't much of a party scene, but you'll want to ask about the Ship Bar.

The popular **Barceló Bávaro Beach Resort** (Bávaro Beach, U.S. tel. 800/227-2356, www.barcelobavarobeachresort.com/en, US$500-700) is actually a massive compound with five separate resorts: for couples only, for families, and for those seeking a premium club stay. Amenities include a myriad of restaurants and pools, a tennis court and spa, among other options. Golf carts shuttle guests to and from the various parts of this enormous property. For quieter, exclusive quarters, splurge in a suite over at the adults-only Barceló Bávaro Palace Deluxe, where you'll barely notice other guests and where the rooms are beautifully appointed—think open marble bathrooms and fully stocked bars.

Ideally located adjacent to the Palma Real Shopping Village and across from the Cocotal Golf & Country Club (unlimited free greens included), the luxurious ★ **Paradisus Palma Real Golf & Spa Resort** (Bávaro Beach, tel. 809/687-9923, www.paradisus.com, paradisus.punta.cana@melia.com, from US$600) oozes romance with its central courtyard opening onto the pool, sea, and towering coconut trees. Restaurants are a highlight here, notably the AAA 4-Diamond restaurant Passion by Martin Berasategui, a seven-time Michelin-starred chef. For ultra-luxurious pampering, ask about "the Royal Service experience."

Sited north of Bávaro, the luxury boutique all-inclusive **Zoetry Agua** (Üvero Alto, U.S. tel. 888/496-3879, www.zoetryresorts.com/agua, US$235-715) has a beautiful stretch of beach and is popular with couples looking to pamper themselves and decompress away from it all with the help of an assigned butler. The grounds are immaculate and include 96 thatch luxury suites with wooden floors, soaking tubs, and all the bells and whistles. Think 24-hour in-suite dining, two infinity pools, four restaurants, three bars with top-shelf liquor, and an onsite spa. The "endless privileges" perks are free wireless Internet, 20-minute massages, and a 45-minute horseback ride.

Another great pick for a honeymoon escape

is ★ **Excellence Punta Cana** (Playa Üvero Alto, U.S. tel. 866/540-2585, www.excellenceresorts.com, US$280-570). The five-star, adults-only resort on the northern tip of the whole Punta Cana area, sits along 30 miles of golden beach and is ideal if all you want to do is eat, drink, bask in the sun, and indulge in some of the most beautiful resort suites you'll experience. Think in-room jet tubs and marble bathrooms, see-through glass rain showers and a fully stocked bar. The pool snakes around the resort and is a primary attraction—floaties provided. The restaurants are decent for an all-inclusive, including the Grill and the Market. Whatever you do, don't miss experiencing the two-floor luxury spa, especially the hydrotherapy circuit. For an extra fee, Excellence Club members get the extra perks: a private butler, access to a private beach section with drink service, and a lounge with hot foods and top-shelf liquor. Wireless access is free for all throughout the property.

CHIC Punta Cana by Royalton (Playa Üvero Alto, U.S. tel. 800/558-7414, www.chic-puntacanahotel.com, US$420-900) is one of the newest adults-only boutique resorts in the ever-growing Üvero Alto area north of Punta Cana and offers 323 luxury suites all facing the Atlantic Ocean. It truly delivers on its promise of an all-exclusive experience from neon purple-lit rooms to rain showers, reservation-free fine dining—including a unique Moroccan restaurant—and free international calls home. The ultimate in exclusivity is the CHIC Mansion: a 1,068-square-meter (11,500-square-foot) villa with six luxurious rooms and seven baths, a breathtaking pool and bar area, a wine cellar. and a lounge with fully stocked premium liquor.

INFORMATION AND SERVICES
Money
You'll find ATM machines in Bávaro, in the Cortecito and Corales areas, as well as in Friusa town. Your best bet is to use the ATMs inside **Palma Real Shopping Village.** There's also one inside Super Lama supermarket on the edge of the shopping complex. Another good location is at **San Juan Shopping Center,** inside the supermarket as well as on the edge of the mall next to Noah Restaurant. You'll find a **Scotiabank** branch in Plaza Brisas, in Bávaro.

Groceries
BAM Market (Plaza Turquesa, Los Corales, tel. 809/455-7344, bammarket@hotmail.com, 8am-10pm daily) sells groceries and is also ideal for those who love deli cuts, salads to go, and a wide variety of wines, as well as over 50 imported beers. They even deliver. A few steps over on the adjacent block is **Plaza El Dorado** where you'll find **Supermercado Cicollela** (tel. 809/552-0143, 9am-10pm daily) with a small selection of groceries and drinks.

Laundry
Next to Plaza El Dorado, the **Punta Cana Laundromat** (Plaza Arenal Caribe, tel. 809/552-9970, 7am-8pm daily, US$2.23/load, US$4.50 to dry, additional US$2.23 for drop-off) can meet your needs for clean apparel. Call ahead before heading over because the owner tends to close on a whim when he needs to run an errand or have breakfast. There's open wireless access for customers if you want to wash and surf.

Health and Emergencies
For serious concerns aside from the quick clinic visits—usually available onsite at resorts—head to **Hospiten Bávaro** (Carretera Higüey-Punta Cana, tel. 809/686-1414, bavaro@hospiten.com), about 15-minute drive north from Punta Cana Airport, with a 24-hour emergency room, multilingual medical staff in various departments ranging from pediatrics to cardiology, and high-end medical equipment, including an ICU and X-ray machines. Another solid option is **Centro Médico Punta Cana** (Av. España 1, Los Corales, tel. 809/552-1506, or for emergencies tel. 809/473-7283, www.centromedicopuntacana.com) with 24-hour emergency care. There are **pharmacies** in both Los

Corales—at Plaza El Dorado—and in small Cortecito. Resorts also carry first aid kits and often have supplies of painkiller medicine and aspirin; or you can buy one from the supermarket or local stores.

A branch of the tourist police, **CESTUR** (Av. Estados Unidos, Esq. Friusa, tel. 809/688-8727) is open 24 hours next to the Bávaro Express bus terminal. There is another near the airport at Puntacana Village.

GETTING THERE
Air

The private **Punta Cana International Airport** (PUJ) serves most passengers who are flying into the southeast region. It recently expanded with a second terminal, the second largest in the Caribbean, receiving over two million passengers a year on direct flights from at least 96 cities. Check with your hotel on whether they offer a free shuttle transfer. Otherwise contact **Dominican Plus** (tel. 809/481-0707, www.dominicanplus.com) for reasonably priced transfers door-to-door nonstop for US$32 one-way to Bávaro area hotels. You can also book online.

Bus

Fly into Santo Domingo and you can hop on an express bus called **Expreso Bávaro** (Calle Juan Sánchez Ramírez, corner of Av. Máximo Gómez, Gazcue, tel. 809/682-9670, www.expresobavaro.com, departures every two hours 7am-4pm, US$8; in Bávaro, Cruce de Friusa. tel. 809/552-1678). Buses are the large coach type and nicely air-conditioned, with wireless Internet and the occasional raunchy movie showing during the three- to four-hour journey. When loading luggage, let the driver know where you're headed (hotel name or area such as Los Corales or Cortecito) as the bus makes multiple spots to accommodate travelers.

The hard-core backpackers might want to skip the fancy coach and hop on a series of *guaguas* from the capital; you'd have to switch again in Higüey, the major hub in these parts, for a second bus to the Bávaro area. It's cheaper (about US$5 to Higüey, US$2 second leg) and you'll get a full cultural experience, but if you have a lot of luggage and/or don't speak Spanish, I don't recommend it.

Car

Inaugurated in 2012, the smooth **Coral Highway** linking Santo Domingo to the Punta Cana area has cut a four-hour journey down to just 2.75 hours. The road bypasses Higüey, which helps. There are three toll roads along the way, at RD$100 each. The drive is easy and pleasant, past sugarcane fields, grazing cows, and open landscapes. This same highway will take you to La Romana in just 45 minutes.

GETTING AROUND
Taxis

Taxis are a lot more expensive in Punta Cana. You'll notice when you start paying US$10 each way within Bávaro no matter how close the ride is. Most resorts post prices to sample destinations; consult the list and agree on a fee before entering a taxi. Alternatively, befriend a local driver and negotiate a price for taking you around during your stay. Try the friendly and responsible **Juan** from **Lillian Tours and Transfers** (tel. 829/265-4621 or 829/570-4810); tell him Lily the travel journalist sent you.

Another way to save yourself a lot of money: hop on a *guagua* or local bus. It travels up and down the main drag in Bávaro to any shopping center, resort, or restaurant you want to reach in Cortecito or Los Corales. You just need the occasional dose of patience because you never know if you'll wait five minutes or 30 on the side of the road, but the low fare of RD$30 (under a dollar) will remind you of that. There are numerous tour operator minivans passing along the main road too, so don't get confused. The *guagua* will have a sign that reads "Traumabapu," on the front of the bus, as well as "Transport Higüey-Bávaro-Punta Cana" on the side. Just hail it from anywhere along the main road going in the direction you're headed. They pass every 15-20 minutes. Note that they don't travel south of the airport to Punta Cana hotels. That's considered a private access road and used only by licensed tour and taxi drivers.

Car

Most visitors choose to stick to their resorts and hop on tours to explore the vicinity, but you can get a better feel for the country by getting your own vehicle and roaming around the countryside. Rates are usually better when booked online—they start around US$35— than once you are in Punta Cana. You must be over 25 and have a valid driver's license. Try **Budget Rental Car** (PUJ airport, tel. 809/480-8153, www.budget.com.do, 7am-9pm daily), **Avis** (Av. Barceló Km 6.5, tel. 809/688-1354, 8am-5pm daily, or at PUJ airport, tel. 809/959-0534, www.avis.com.do, 8am-9pm daily), **Europcar** (Carretera Friusa-Melia, tel. 809/686-2861, www.europcar.com.do, 8am-6pm, or at PUJ airport 8am-10pm), or the local **Melo Rent Car** (Los Corales, tel. 829/669-2723, rentcarmelo@gmail.com).

Air

Charter flights are now more popular for getting from Bávaro to other remote parts of the island such as Samaná and Puerto Plata. Contact **Dominican Plus** (tel. 809/481-0707, www.dominicanplus.com, from US$539 one-way for 1-3 to Samaná, or US$879 to Puerto Plata). Another option is **Dominican Shuttles** (tel. 809/931-4073, www.dominicanshuttles.com, from US$660 to Samaná).

Punta Cana

South of the Punta Cana Airport is the area labeled Punta Cana proper, and south of that, Cap Cana. This area is known for its beaches and exclusive resorts. But Punta Cana also offers plenty of outdoor activities, including hiking in natural parks, dipping in sinkholes, and golfing.

SIGHTS
★ Indigenous Eyes Ecological Reserve

On private property owned by the PUNTACANA Ecological Foundation, the **Indigenous Eyes Ecological Reserve** (tel. 809/959-2262, www.puntacana.org/reserve, 8am-5pm daily, US$25, free for Puntacana Resort & Club guests) is a protected 1,500-acre lowland subtropical forest with a verdant, shaded trail leading to 12 freshwater lagoons. The most stunning of those lagoons is **Ojos Indígenas**—or Indigenous Eyes, as the Taíno called these pools for their oval shape—open to the public for a delightful swim in turquoise and emerald freshwater. The 20-minute hike to reach the lagoon is easy, but requires closed-toe shoes to avoid stubbed toes on stones and other protruding bits of wood. The scenery is spectacular. Expect to stop several times for photos and to gawk at the various lagoons on your path, the flora surrounding the narrow trail. There are maps indicating your whereabouts as you progress on your hike.

Once you reach the main deck over the lagoon and are ready to swim, walk a few steps farther up the trail where a jumping platform awaits. Leap just a few feet into the tempting, crispy cool waters. There's a resident duck here, so don't be surprised when it joins you around the lagoon.

Scape Park

Nearly one million square meters large, **Scape Park** (Cap Cana, tel. 809/469-7484, www.scapepark.com, 8am-6pm daily, US$149 full day includes meals, US$59 Hoyo Azul, transport included) is a green escape ideal for a half day out of your gated Punta Cana hotel and into the great outdoors. This natural theme park—at least a 40-minute ride from Bávaro and 20 minutes from downtown Punta Cana—is set up and landscaped beautifully. Marked trails and gardens lead to various activities. The cenotes are one of the highlights here. The most visited is the **Hoyo Azul** sinkhole, 14 meters (45 feet) deep and sitting below a 75-meter-high (246-foot) limestone cliff. Locals discovered it only recently. The hike to the mineral waters of Hoyo Azul is a mere 15 minutes from the park entrance, taking you past medicinal plants, endemic species and orchids, and an impressive suspension bridge. It can get a tad crowded when tour groups arrive in the morning and afternoon, so visit here either very early or at lunchtime.

The second sinkhole on a shorter hike is a stunner: **Cenote Indígena Las Ondas** is a crispy cool pool buried deep in an ancient Taíno cave and with only a sliver of sunlight reaching it. Hence blue bulbs give it an eerier feel. The trail to this sinkhole is bordered by informative boards on Taíno history and culture, complete with mystical sounds (courtesy of hidden speakers), and an impressive winding wooden staircase leads you down to the water. So beautiful is the scenery that it beats any upscale spa you've ever visited. Look out for Taíno pictograms on rocks, possibly the face of a Taíno god.

The park also offers the longest **zipline course** in Punta Cana, with platforms atop cliffs. The **equestrian center** is home to 30 horses and probably the most professional setup I've seen with a training ring, video tutorials, and trails taking you through the forest's winding paths. **Buggies, mountain bikes,** and **caving** are available as well. Meals are included with a combo of two excursions, and shuttles are provided to all the major hotels up and down the coast. To add some sea to your inland excursions, ask about Scape Park's Juanillo VIP catamaran cruise, taking you along the glitzy Cap Cana coast and marina for a cool US$200.

BEACHES
★ Playa Juanillo

Playa Juanillo is absolutely breathtaking. Perhaps its allure is that it isn't overdeveloped and only supports a couple of restaurants. Or maybe it's that the sun shines particularly bright in this area, causing the sand to literally sparkle and the sea to turn a phosphorescent blue. With incredibly tall coconut trees, it's one of the most memorable beaches. It's

Indigenous Eyes Ecological Reserve

Punta Cana

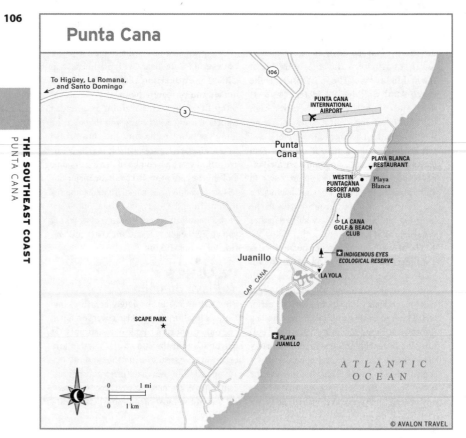

worth coming here if only for a cocktail or a fresh coconut and the view.

Other Beaches

Note that in the last year or so, the sargassum issue has spread to the Punta Cana coastline, so don't be surprised to see this particular seaweed floating in the water or piled along the shores despite daily efforts to clean up. It doesn't change the beauty of the place, but is a slight nuisance. In addition to your resort's beachfront, you'll find two additional stretches, where you can escape for more food options and more brilliant white sand in your toes.

Punta Cana Beach, in the area south of the Punta Cana Airport known as "Punta Cana proper", is actually not as impressive or

long as you'd expect, but it still offers white sand and pretty Caribbean views facing the private Westin Puntacana. Next door next to the Westin is **Playa Blanca,** a more charming and small white sand stretch delighting a blend of locals and visitors thanks to the on-site kitesurfing and paddleboarding shop, a dive center, and the excellent open-air **Playa Blanca Restaurant.** Sundays and long weekends find this beach particularly busy with Dominicans visiting from other parts of the coast and La Romana. Expect to see the young and fabulous socializing here.

SPORTS AND RECREATION
Diving and Snorkeling

On Playa Blanca in Punta Cana south of

The PUNTACANA Ecological Foundation

Launched in 1994 by Grupo PUNTACANA and located on its grounds, the PUNTACANA Ecological Foundation (tel. 809/959-9221, www.puntacana.org, fepc@puntacana.com) is a nonprofit that has been a pioneer in sustainable tourism and development on the Punta Cana coast. It has received numerous grants and awards, including the Adrian Award in 2013, as a Leader in Sustainable Tourism. Aside from an organic garden, from which the Puntacana Resort hotels procure some of their produce, the foundation runs established and pilot programs in a constant effort to conserve and mitigate the effects of tourism on the land and sea of Punta Cana. Among the most important of these is the goal to increase the population of rhinoceros iguanas, a prehistoric species once found throughout the Dominican Republic. In 2002, the foundation reintroduced the species into the area. You can visit their walled home on the grounds of the foundation, and marvel at these large creatures as they roam around in near-natural living conditions that allow them to reproduce, before later being released into the natural environment. Other projects run by the foundation, open to tours, include coral gardens and rehabilitation off Playa Blanca, worm composting and beekeeping. The last has earned them first place more than once in the DR's annual National Honey Competition. Be sure to ask about their latest lionfish women's handicraft project.

the airport, PADI dive shop **Blue Vision Adventures** (Playa Blanca, tel. 809/455-0833, www.blueadventures.net, US$80/dive, US$60 snorkeling, Discover Scuba US$220 2-tank dive) offers excellent dive and snorkeling excursions right off the reef facing the beach, just a five-minute boat ride up. **The Aquarium** is one of the most popular dive and snorkel sites, where you'll spot plenty of marinelife from rays partially covered in the sandy floor to four-eyed butterfly fish, angelfish, and snapper. There's a resident barracuda, and if you're lucky, he'll come out to show off. There's a fairly strong J-shaped current around the Aquarium, so you'll need a life jacket and solid fins to help with your swim. Adjacent to the Aquarium, the **Museum** is an underwater display of Taíno god sculptures, dropped into the sea as some sort of tribute to the first rulers of the island. It makes for fun photos. Dive excursions with Blue Vision include 18-meter (60-foot) or deeper shipwrecks all close to shore. You can also book banana boat rides, fishing trips, and wakeboarding here.

Fishing

Blue Vision Adventures (Playa Blanca, tel. 809/455-0833, www.blueadventures.net,

US$850 half-day up to 6 people) has deep-sea fishing excursions. Catch-and-release with the longtime running **Mike's Marina Fishing Charters** (tel. 809/729-5164 or 829/649-6408, www.mikesmarina.info, from US$650 4 hours for 4 people, includes private hotel transfers), and head out to Cabeza de Toro, an area popular for sportfishing.

Surfing and Kitesurfing

Kite Club Punta Cana (Beachfront Playa Blanca, next to Club Med, 829/576-6399, www.kiteclubpuntacana.com, 9am-6pm daily, US$270 three-hour lesson, US$570 two-day private lessons) offers kitesurfing classes with IKO instructors right off Playa Blanca south of Punta Cana Airport.

Parasailing

Lift up 46 meters (150 feet) above the stunning Punta Cana coastline for 10 minutes—it will seem like longer—with **SeaPro Water Sports** (www.seaprodivers.com, US$60pp or US$100 double). Transportation is provided to select hotels in the area; check listings ahead of time.

Sailing

Explore the beautiful southern tip of the coast

Boca de Yuma and the Ponce de León Museum

A 45-minute drive south from Punta Cana, the fishing village of **Boca de Yuma** is a picturesque escape for the day, far from the madding tourist crowd. This place is an Italian expat favorite; you'll find Italian seafront restaurants perched atop cliffs, with a view reminiscent of an Italian seaside town. Home to approximately 3,000 people, Boca de Yuma is more steeped in history than you might think on first glance. Where the Yuma River meets the sea, you'll see locals sit on towering rocks for a cool breeze, fishers linger along riverbanks, and undeveloped white sand beaches undeveloped where pelicans fly about. But it's also where pirates and conquistadores once roamed and launched adventures. There isn't a whole lot happening in this once- favorite Dominican weekend getaway, but it makes for an educational and relaxing day away from your resort, while offering a glimpse of local fishing life—some of the best fishing is right here—and the DR's past. Head to the river close to sunset and hire a fisherman to take you on a small motorized boat ride up and down the water (approximately US$20). Pirate Cofresí, one of the longest lasting pirates who was caught and later executed by the Americans in 1825, often navigated along the Yuma River. You'll see his impressive original ship on display on a dry dock as you cruise along the Yuma River, placed there in honor of the pirate after locals discovered it in the water in the late 1990s. Crossing to the other side of the river lands you on a small, deserted white sand beach.

For more inland adventure, drive to the entrance of the Parque Nacional del Este—right in Boca de Yuma—and hike the dry and impressive **Cueva de Berna** (US$2.30 entry fee or RD$100) where you'll see the greatest number of Taíno pictograms, particularly of Taíno faces, as you spelunk higher on the left-hand side after entering the cave. This makes it one of the most significant caves on the eastern coast, recently studied by the University of Indiana.

If you'd rather opt to explore Boca de Yuma with a tour guide, look up **Mike's Punta Cana Tours** (tel. 829/981-7989, www.puntacanamike.com, US$120). The trip begins in Punta Cana and after a couple of hours at a local school and shopping for cigars and chocolate in town, you head to Boca de Yuma for a cliff-side Italian meal, a hike through Berna Cave, and a boat ride down the Yuma River.

Those driving or catching the *guagua*—you'll have to transfer in Higüey—can head over to the town of San Rafael de Yuma and visit the former home of Spanish explorer Juan Ponce de León, turned into the **Museo Casa Ponce de León** (7am-5pm daily, US$1.50). The conquistador arrived on the island in 1493 and fought the Taíno who lived inside the Parque Nacional del Este before heading out from Boca de Yuma—then known as the Port of Higüey—in 1508 to conquer Puerto Rico and discover Florida. In the museum you can view 16th-century furniture, utensils, and other artifacts that he used.

at Cap Cana on the **Juanillo VIP** luxury catamaran trip (tel. 809/469-7231, www.scapepark.com, Mon.-Fri., US$169, includes pickup). Spend all day on the blue seas, stopping for swims and a lobster lunch as well as cocktails on the diamond stretch of Playa Juanillo. The day ends at Scape Park with a dip in the Hoyo Azul sinkhole.

Golf

In the Punta Cana proper, **La Cana Golf & Beach Club** (Puntacana Resort & Club, tel. 809/959-2222, www.puntacana.com/la-cana-golf-club.html, US$180, par 72, 27 holes) designed by the celebrated Pete Dye offers signature Caribbean Sea views—14 holes face the water—along with one of the most sustainable greens in the area. The hybrid grass can be irrigated with salt water. There's a clubhouse onsite, and nearby are beaches and excellent restaurants that are part of the resort.

Horseback Riding

Scape Park (Cap Cana, tel. 809/469-7484, www.scapepark.com, US$149 full day includes

A Day in Miches

For a full day's beach escape close to Punta Cana away from the crowds with undeveloped areas, head to the beautiful coastal town of Miches—just a 1.5-hour drive north of the Üvero Alto area of Punta Cana on a newly finished highway. Settled in the late 19th century as a fishing and agricultural community, Miches offers stunning scenery of white sand stretches along with the rolling mountains of the Cordillera Central and lagoons teeming with mangroves and wildlife. Most Punta Cana visitors don't head north to this piece of paradise now on the radar of developers, and that's why you should see it if you're able.

Contact **Rancho La Cueva** (tel. 809/519-5271, www.rancholacueva.com) to schedule your day trip. You can rent a car to reach the ranch or arrange for them to pick you up. Once there, you will hop into an all-terrain vehicle with your guide to visit a local farm or *conuco* where they plant their fruits and vegetables. You'll learn about Dominican produce and the way of life in the countryside, as well as the history of the area. After snacking on fruits and coconut, you'll hop back into the ATV and head to Montana Redonda at 305 meters (1,000 feet) for panoramic sea views that include the Samaná Peninsula. There are hammocks and a swing at this scenic stop. Pose for a few pictures, then take in the stunning expanses at your leisure.

You'll enjoy a lunch back at La Cueva, before you hop on a horse to make your way down to Playa Limon, a postcard-perfect stretch with nothing but white sand and blue waters. If you're up for it, you can continue the day by hopping on a motorboat from the beach down to the freshwater Laguna Limon amid mangroves and birds. Back on shore, you'll ride your horse back to Rancho La Cueva, for your return to Punta Cana. You'll make it in time for dinner at your resort.

Tours are limited to Monday and Friday (US$40 pp, includes lunch), but you can call ahead to negotiate other arrangements.

For more information and photos on Miches' sights, visit the local tourist board's website at www.exploramichesrd.com

meals, US$59 Hoyo Azul, transport included) offers a full equestrian center, complete with introductions to and training in horseback riding, and a stable full of gorgeous horses. If you're not up for an all-day "safari" out of town, this is the perfect choice. The dry forests and shaded paths make for an ideal place to take an hour-long ride in the bush past ancient Taíno caves. Pickups from all the major Punta Cana resorts are included.

The **Puntacana Resort & Club's El Rancho** (www.puntacana.com/horseback-riding) provides both adult-riding classes for guests and beach horseback rides.

Caving

This region was once the center of the Taíno civilization. Going north or south, this eastern area of the Dominican Republic is blessed with a handful of ancient Taíno caves previously used for ceremonies and rituals. Spelunkers will find their bliss at the **Parque Nacional del Este** (southeast entrance off dirt road after Carretera 4, 8am-5pm daily, US$2.20), at least a 1.25-hour drive south of the Punta Cana region. There, at the eastern entrance of the park in the fishing village of Boca de Yuma sits the cavernous and dry **Cueva de Berna,** one of the most important caves in the area due to its great number of petroglyphs. Along with hundreds of bats and small birds, you'll see Taíno *caritas* (little faces) carved on the walls and rocks—climb with care—on the right-hand side of the entrance. You don't need a guide to accompany you, but if you're solo, it's always best to have company.

Scape Park (Cap Cana, tel. 809/469-7484, www.scapepark.com, 9am-4pm, US$59) offers a two-hour dry cave expedition on their grounds, reached after a hike through dry forest and along an informative plant trail. The cave is equipped with a wooden staircase to lead you down into its chambers and tunnels filled with stalagmites, stalactites and resident bats.

Take it up a notch with a full-day trip north to **Cueva Fun Fun** (pronounced "foon-foon," in Spanish), located in the lush and hilly province of Hato Mayor, at the mouth of **Los Haitises National Park** (tel. 829-909-6027, www.ambiente.gob.do/ambienterd/eco-parque/parque-nacional-los-haitises, 8am-5pm daily, US$2.20). Excursions to the cave are only out of Punta Cana; book your trip with **Rancho Capote** (Calle Duarte 12, 809/553-2656, info@cuevafunfun.net, cuevafunfun.net). The cave is approximately a three-hour drive from Punta Cana, but the journey is well worth the experience of exploring the largest cave in the Dominican Republic and the longest in the Caribbean region. Fun Fun—previously known as the Devil's Cave, but renamed to describe the sound bats made flying around together—is filled with exhilarating moments not for the faint of heart nor the unfit.

The adventure begins with a 20-minute horseback ride across the private Rancho Capote's wide forestland, past fruit trees, to the beginning of the hike. You also have the option to hike this portion. From there, it's two miles uphill on foot to the southeastern entrance of Los Haitises National Park, and another 45 minutes to the mouth of the cave, walking through the park's wet forest. You'll abseil your way into a narrow cave opening 9 meters (28 feet) down in one of the most heart-pumping moments of the trip. From there, spelunking for the mile-long journey is fairly moderate and will include wading through the parts submerged by the Almirante River. Along the way you'll spot various fauna, including crabs, insects, bats, and perhaps even a stranded grass snake, as well as view pre-Columbian rock art from petroglyphs to pictographs. Bring a waterproof camera.

4x4 Safaris

Your best bet among the multitude of safaris being sold left and right in Punta Cana and Bávaro is to go through **Colonial Tours' Super Truck Safari** (tel. 809/688-5285, www.colonialtours.com.do, US$95), with local guides who will give you as much insight into local life as possible as you ride through the streets and dirt roads, from La Otra Banda to Higüey and into farms and sugarcane plantations. The day ends as it should: on the gorgeous beach of Macao, where you'll have time to swim at your leisure and bask in the glorious Dominican sun.

La Cana Golf & Beach Club

Tour Operators in Punta Cana and Bávaro

If you're staying in Bávaro or Punta Cana, you'll notice that every other white van or safari truck running down the main road is a tour company hauling its next bunch of tourists to a number of popular and often crowded excursions. Here are some tour options that stand out from the crowd:

- **Colonial Tours** (tel. 809/688-5285, www.colonialtours.com.do, US$95) offers a packed Super Truck Safari tour that offers good bang for your buck as far as organized tours are concerned. You'll ride in military-style off-road trucks blasting merengue out into the countryside of the Altagracia province. In just about 30 minutes outside of Punta Cana, you'll find yourself plunged into the real Dominican *campo* after first driving through the bustling iconic town of La Otra Banda, where the meat shops hang flesh outside, and Higüey, home to the most important shrine and basilica in the DR. Past these urban hubs, the day involves bumpy roads, pastureland with grazing cows and horses, a herd of bulls holding up traffic, coffee and cacao farms in El Bonao for tastings in a Dominican yard, sugarcane fields and horseback riding at Rancho Valencia, among other exhilarating activities and sights on this full-day trip. The day ends with a stop at the breathtaking Macao Beach, where you'll have enough time to swim and watch the surfers and boogie boarders trying their luck.

- **Ocean Adventures** (next to Huracán Cafe, Corales Beach in Bávaro, tel. 809/390-7418, www. oapc.com.do, US$90) is perhaps the busiest and most tourist-heavy operator in town. A better activity than their gimmicky pirate ship is the Bávaro Splash, where you get to maneuver your own two-seater speedboat, snorkel, and snuba all in a three-hour excursion. Don't expect to see a ton of fish since snorkeling off Bávaro's beaches isn't the best.

- **Bávaro Runners** (tel. 809/833-0260, www.bavarorunners.com, US$55-135) offer ziplining trips as well as the regular countryside safari tours. Group numbers are larger, and you will be taken to well-known sights like most other safari tour operators—including the Higüey Basilica and cacao and coffee farms—with shopping opportunities, of course. They also offer expensive trips that head all the way northeast to the Samaná Peninsula (US$285).

- **Mike's Punta Cana Tours** (tel. 809/981-7989, www.puntacanamike.com, US$89-120), albeit pricey like most tours out of Punta Cana, encourages immersion and getting out of the all-inclusive gates to understand the "real DR." Run by a Canadian expat with experience in the Punta Cana hotel industry, the tours include a similar two-part intro followed by a main destination. Whether you're ultimately headed to Boca de Yuma or out for a day at Playa Macao, it all begins in a lower-income neighborhood in Friusa, just a 10-minute drive outside of the all-inclusive enclave of Punta Cana. Here, you get an inside glimpse of the Haitian immigrant life as well as background on the Dominican Republic's geography and educational system before touring the school. Students receive donations from tourists thanks to Mike—some with suitcases filled with pencils and books. After a good hour here, the second part involves a lengthy stop at El Mundo Auténtico, which is informative but could be done solo. The value here is the main destination of the day, particularly the scenic riverside town of Boca de Yuma, for those who don't feel like driving or wandering about on their own.

Bávaro Runners (tel. 809/833-0260, www. bavarorunners.com, US$55-135) is popular for its safaris as well, although they are a tad more crowded because of this. You'll head to well-known sights—including the Higüey Basilica and cacao and coffee farms.

Spa

Almost every all-inclusive resort offers onsite spa services. But if you can spare the time, make the drive to Punta Cana proper and the Six Senses Spa (Puntacana Resort & Club, tel. 809/959-7772, www.sixsenses.com/spas/punta-cana, 9am-8pm daily, US$110), the only option in the Americas for proper pampering with an authentic Thai massage, centering your body using the Tibetan method. From the treatment rooms to the staff, this is no ordinary spa.

ENTERTAINMENT AND EVENTS

Bars and Nightclubs

Oro Nightclub (Hard Rock Hotel, Blvd. Turístico del Este Km 28, Macao, tel. 809/687-0000, www.oronightclub.com/site, US$70 with unlimited drinks from a set list) offers Vegas-style nightlife—complete with exorbitant prices for entry or for private tables. But then again, this isn't the place for those who want to feel like they are in the Dominican Republic.

A much better option is **Mangú** (Hotel Occidental Flamenco, tel. 809/221-8787, www.mangudiscobar.com, 11pm-4am Tues.-Sat.), a nightclub with a mix of Dominican music as well as international, and a down-to-earth, good-looking crowd. At least 10 notches up in posh factor is **Dux Cap Cana** (tel. 829/426-8100, reservations tel. 829/741-3044, 6pm-midnight Wed.-Sat., 3pm-midnight Sun.)—a "Chivas Club" and disco, lounge and terrace all in one, set outdoors with DJs and all-white couches surrounding a pool. Sundays are popular, starting at 3pm with an open bar for just $20.

Casinos

The majority, if not all, of the all-inclusive resorts in this area have an onsite casino, usually located beside the nightclub. There are two popular options for those who want to try their luck outside their own resort. At 4,181 square meters (45,000 square feet), the **Hard Rock Casino** (Boulevard Turístico del Este Km. 28 No.74, Macao, tel. 809/687-0000, www.hardrockhotelpuntacana.com) is the largest gaming facility in the Dominican Republic and has won best of Caribbean awards. You'll find 40 unique gaming tables as well as over 400 slots here, and when you're done, you can head over to the onsite Oro Nightclub. Another popular choice is the spotless **Princess Tower Casino** (Bávaro Princess Hotel, tel. 809/552-1111, http://towercasinos.com), offering Texas hold'em poker, blackjack, and roulette. The atmosphere is lively with music and there's a free shuttle to and from the casino.

Festivals and Cultural Events

The **Punta Cana Kite Fest** (January) is popular and gathers locals from around the country who flock to Playa Blanca to watch kiteboarders compete and show off their best stunts. The event is free and open to the public.

Carnaval Punta Cana (www.puntaca.

spicy goat stew with coconut rice at Playa Blanca Restaurant

com/punta-cana-carnival.html, second Sunday March, dates vary, free entry in general area or VIP seated area at US$40 pp) is organized by the Puntacana Group and is set up in Puntacana Village. Around 15 carnival troupes attend from around the country, including neighboring islands such as Aruba, Haiti, and St. Martin at times. It's not the same as the authentic in-the-street carnival parades in other parts of the Dominican Republic like Santiago or La Vega, but if you're in the Punta Cana area for a while and have cash to spare, it could be worth it. The event includes post-carnival concerts with merengue, *bachata,* and reggaeton artists.

SHOPPING

Aside from shopping options in town or in Bávaro, within the Punta Cana enclave is **Puntacana Village** (www.puntacanavillage.com), your one-stop shopping center with the **Galerias Puntacana** mall for souvenir shops, and onsite supermarket.

FOOD

Although not as diverse as the independent restaurant options in Bávaro—which you can still go to, with your own car or a pricey taxi— the resort areas of Punta Cana and Cap Cana hold a few of the best upscale restaurants in the area, if not the country. They may require digging a little deeper into pockets than you are used to in the DR.

The casual chic ★ **Playa Blanca Restaurant** (beachfront, tel. 809/959-2714, ext. 2234, noon-2pm and 7pm-10:30pm daily, US$6-40) is one of my favorites. This beachfront restaurant has a lovely open view of the beach and sea, and its menu offers both Dominican and beachside foods with a twist. Opt for a bowl of shrimp ceviche, yucca empanadas, or a plate of spicy goat stew with coconut rice, all washed down with the best margarita in town. The mango mojito is also to die for.

Playa Juanillo is home to a couple of spendy beachfront restaurants that double as beach clubs—with lounge chairs for a post-meal nap and beach day. The more popular one is **Juanillo Beach, Food and Drinks** (Cap Cana, tel. 809/469-7727, www.juanillo.com. do, 9am-6pm Mon.-Sun., US$6.50-21) with a real beach bar feel, decent burgers, wraps, pizza, and seafood. The "beeritas" are refreshing and huge.

Designed by Oscar de la Renta, the romantic open-air setting of AAA Three Diamond Award ★ **La Yola** (tel. 809/959-8229, www. puntacana.com/restaurants, noon-3pm 7pm-10:30pm daily, US$10-30) on a white-draped bamboo deck perched over Punta Cana Marina is only surpassed by Chef Luis' Mediterranean menu with a Dominican twist. Try the sautéed shrimp in a coconut sauce with *moro de guandules* or pigeon peas rice or the baked eggplant layered with sweet plantain and mozzarella cheese. Pick a table beside the glass floor panels and look down into the turquoise sea while a trio of Dominican musicians serenades you.

Inside **Puntacana Village** (www.puntacanavillage.com) are small, reasonably priced restaurants. **Carbon** (tel. 809/959-0018, noon-10pm daily, US$7-10), offers a Caribbean fusion menu with Dominican, Jamaican, and Cuban dishes. Try the jerk chicken, the spicy goat, or the plantains topped with beef and mozzarella. For tapas and sangria, **El Tablao** (tel. 809/959-3008, noon-10pm daily, US$7-12) doesn't disappoint—stick to the octopus, paella, or steak options. Save space for *churros* with hot chocolate for dessert.

ACCOMMODATIONS
Over US$150

In Punta Cana proper, 10 minutes' ride south from the Punta Cana Airport, the **Westin Puntacana Resort & Club** (beachfront, tel. 809/959-2262, www.westinpuntacana. com, US$275-640), part of the eponymous Puntacana Resort & Club community where the likes of Julio Iglesias and Oscar de la Renta have homes, is just three years old and its 200 rooms have ocean views facing Punta Cana Beach. The open lobby entrance will draw your attention to the view of an infinity pool in the near distance. Rooms are all-white, comfortable, and feature all the modern bells and whistles, but do retain a hotel feel.

Adjacent to the resort is the small but gorgeous **Playa Blanca,** popular for its excellent onsite restaurant with Dominican fare, water sports shops with nearby snorkeling, and a relaxed beach club vibe that welcomes outside guests. There's a fee for wireless Internet at the hotel, as with most resorts, unless you're a Starwood Preferred Guest. The convenience of amenities included is what brings families and groups here—including a nearby equestrian center, a P. B. Dye-designed La Cana Golf Course, onsite Ecological Reserve with lagoons for a cold swim, the Puntacana Village shopping and restaurant area, and some of the best fine dining à la carte restaurants in the area, for guests only, such as **Anani** and **The Grill.** The hotel offers shuttles to these various locations. Note that there isn't any nightlife at the resort, save for a cigar lounge, and you will be quite a distance from the Bávaro area and north of the airport with no public buses passing through. Prepare to stick to your immediate surroundings unless you don't mind splurging on local taxis.

INFORMATION AND SERVICES

Each resort will offer its own services, including shopping strips—but be aware that prices are superinflated. Make your dollars count and shop responsibly with local vendors whenever you are able. Most local services and shops are located in the Bávaro area, in Cortecito and Los Corales. If you're staying in the Punta Cana area south of the airport, it will cost more to get up there so throw that in your decision making when picking a hotel.

Money

For ATMs, head to the **Puntacana Village** complex (www.puntacanavillage.com). Check with your hotel if they provide complimentary rides to this shopping center.

Health and Emergencies

For serious concerns aside from the quick clinic visits—usually offered onsite at resorts—head to **Hospiten Bávaro** (Carretera Higüey-Punta Cana, tel. 809/686-1414, bavaro@hospiten.com), about 15 minutes' drive north from Punta Cana Airport, with a 24-hour emergency room, multilingual medical staff in various departments ranging from pediatrics to cardiology, and high-end

the beach at the Westin Puntacana Resort & Club

medical equipment including an ICU and X-ray machines. Another solid option is **Centro Médico Punta Cana** (Av. España 1, Los Corales, tel. 809/552-1506 or for emergencies tel. 809/473-7283, www.centromedicopuntacana.com) with 24-hour emergency care. There's a pharmacy inside **Puntacana Village** (www.puntacanavillage.com). Resorts also carry first aid kits and often have supplies of painkillers and aspirin.

A branch of the tourist police, **CESTUR** (Av. Estados Unidos, Esq. Friusa, tel. 809/688-8727) is open 24 hours next to the Bávaro Express bus terminal. There is another near the airport at Puntacana Village.

GETTING THERE
Air

The private **Punta Cana International Airport** (PUJ) serves most passengers who are flying into the southeast region. It recently expanded with a second terminal, the second largest in the Caribbean, receiving over two million passengers a year on direct flights from at least 96 cities. Check with your hotel on whether they offer a free shuttle transfer. Otherwise, taxi costs vary according to the area of Punta Cana you're headed to, with Üvero Alto north of Bávaro being the farthest out at around a 45-minute drive. You can also contact **Dominican Plus** (tel. 809/481-0707, www.dominicanplus.com), which offers reasonably priced nonstop transfers door-to-door for US$32 one-way to Bávaro area hotels. You can book online.

Bus

The **Expreso Bávaro** (Calle Juan Sánchez Ramírez, corner of Av. Máximo Gómez, Gazcue, tel. 809/682-9670, www.expresobavaro.com, departures every two hours from 7am, last bus at 4pm, US$9; in Bávaro, Cruce de Friusa. tel. 809/552-1678) takes you from Santo Domingo to the major resorts in Bávaro. From there, you'd have to take another private taxi to your Punta Cana resort. This option would be for those who started their journey elsewhere on the island—such as the capital city—but then it might make more sense to hire a driver from Santo Domingo and split the fee with your traveling group.

Car

Inaugurated in 2012, the relatively new, smooth **Coral Highway** linking Santo Domingo to Punta Cana has cut a four-hour journey to just under three hours by private car. The road bypasses Higüey, which helps. There are three toll roads along the way, at RD$100 (US$2.20) each. The drive is easy and pleasant, past sugarcane fields, open fields, and grazing cows. This same highway will take you to La Romana in just 45 minutes.

GETTING AROUND
Taxis

Taxis are a lot more expensive in Punta Cana. You'll notice when you start paying US$10 each way no matter how close the ride is. Most resorts post prices to sample destinations; consult the list and agree before getting into a taxi. Alternatively, befriend a local driver and negotiate a price for taking you around during your stay. Try the friendly and responsible **Juan** from **Lillian Tours and Transfers** (tel. 829/265-4621 or 829/570-4810); tell him Lily the travel journalist sent you.

Car Rental

Car rental rates are better when booked online (starting around US$35) than at the Punta Cana Airport. You must be over 25 and have a valid driver's license. Try **Budget Rental Car** (PUJ airport, tel. 809/480-8153, www.budget.com.do, 7am-9pm daily), **Avis** (PUJ airport, tel. 809/959-0534, www.avis.com.do, 8am-9pm daily), or **Europcar** (PUJ Airport, tel. 809/686-2861, www.europcar.com.do, 8am-10pm).

Bus

Note that there is no public transportation traveling up and down the Punta Cana resort area—the section south of the Punta Cana Airport. Public *guaguas* (small minivans shared with other passengers) only travel up and down the main road in the Bávaro area.

Air

Charter flights can take you from Punta Cana to other remote parts of the island such as Samaná and Puerto Plata. It makes sense when you are traveling in a group. Contact **Dominican Plus** (tel. 809/481-0707, www. dominicanplus.com, from US$539 one-way for 1-3 to Samaná, or US$879 to Puerto Plata). Another option is **Dominican Shuttles** (tel. 809/931-4073, www.dominicanshuttles.com, from US$660 to Samaná).

La Romana

An entirely separate destination from Punta Cana, and yet barely a 1.25-hour ride south of the *costa del coco*, La Romana province is home to some of the most well-known luxury escapes and grand sights in the Dominican Republic and in the Caribbean. Casa de Campo Resort opened in 1973 and kicked off golf tourism in the DR, and the architectural wonder of Altos de Chavón provides a completely unique experience.

The eponymous city, the third largest in the country, is a bustling commercial center offering a taste of Dominican life away from the tourism hubs. The Parque Central's baseball statues tower over coconut vendors and gritty pastel-colored buildings. *Motoconchos* and *guaguas* buzz past shops with grilled windows, lottery shacks, and fabric stores. Quieter streets harbor Dominican art galleries and boutiques. Along the edges of the city are La Romana's small marina as well as the glamorous Casa de Campo and Altos de Chavón.

If anything, the La Romana region is the laid-back and more independent sister to Punta Cana, with fewer beaches but a slew of other natural adventures on the Parque Nacional del Este trails and offshore islands teeming with mangroves and marinelife.

SIGHTS
El Obelisco

El Obelisco (Av. Libertad) is one of the first sights you'll spot as you arrive into La Romana, standing tall in the middle of a shaded and sadly abandoned-looking small park and square away from the main traffic noise of Parque Central. A few seniors hang out here on the benches. The handpainted structure is a smaller replica of the U.S. Washington Monument and depicts images of historical and modern-day Dominican life.

Parque Central

A quick walk through La Romana's **Parque Central** (Calle Duarte) is worthwhile just to see the gorgeous steel baseball statues, symbolizing the importance of the game in the DR but especially in this town. La Romana is home to local team Los Toros del Este. Indeed, it has produced numerous U.S. Major League baseball greats, such as Fernando Abad (Houston Astros), Edwin Encarnación (Toronto Blue Jays), Antonio Alfonseca (Philadelphia Phillies), and Samuel Deduno (Houston Astros). There might be a couple of undesirable characters hanging out in the park, as in any city, but this is a place frequented by all and by no means unsafe. Keep valuables to a minimum and make sure you get shots of those impressive statues.

★ Altos de Chavón

Perched on cliffs 91 meters (300 feet) above the majestic Río Chavón and bordering the east side of the prestigious Casa de Campo Resort and its Dye Fore golf course, **Altos de Chavón** (tel. 809/523-2045, www.casadecampo.com.do/altos-de-chavon, open daily) is a model 16th-century European Mediterranean village unlike anything you'll find in the Caribbean. Designed by

and Design, which hosts frequent cultural and art events and has an exchange program with New York's Parson School of Design; the **Art Gallery,** which features Dominican artists; and the breathtaking 5,000-seat Grecian-style outdoor **Altos de Chavón Amphitheatre,** which hosts big name artists year-round. The amphitheater and the entire village were inaugurated with a concert by Frank Sinatra.

Behind the church is the stunning **Museo Arqueológico Regional** (tel. 809/523-8554, www.altosdechavon.museum, 9am-8:30pm daily, US$4.50 or free for Casa de Campo guests), displaying the most comprehensive pre-Columbian and Taíno collection in the country. Exhibits at the archaeology museum date from 4000 BC to 1492 with over 3,000 pieces and the best labeling I've come across, in both English and Spanish. Dominican archaeologist Don Samuel Pion assembled them all over the course of 40 years of research in the DR. There are also displays covering the history of the DR and of Altos de Chavón. Expect to spend a good 30-45 minutes here; the room on the history and culture of the Taíno is especially captivating.

You'll also find high-end specialty boutiques selling premium cigars, designer apparel from Dominican designer Jenny Polanco, amber jewelry, and organic chocolate. For drinks, the open-air **Dye Fore Bar** has fantastic river views you can enjoy with a cocktail even if you're not a golfer. Dinner is excellent at the Italian **La Piazetta;** the antipasti spread alone is worth it, as is the outdoor dining terrace overlooking the river.

If you're staying at the Casa de Campo Resort, then you'll have easy, free access to Altos de Chavón. Otherwise, area tour operators usually offer daytime excursions to Altos de Chavón. **Colonial Tours** (tel. 809/688-5285, www.colonialtours.com.do, US$35) has a half-day tour, which is just enough time to take it all in.

Estadio Francisco A. Micheli

Inaugurated in 1979 and renovated in 2013,

Dominican architect Jose Antonio Caro and created by Italian designer Roberto Coppa, the village was completed in 1982 after six years of construction. No details were spared, from handcrafted stone paths to ironwork, custom doorframes, and period furniture. The place oozes the feel of a medieval town, with its cobblestoned streets and narrow, leafy alleys.

Aside from being an architectural wonder, the compound is home to museums, shops, and restaurants. Central features not to miss include the **St. Stanislaus Church,** built in 1979; the **Altos de Chavón School of Art**

Estadio Francisco A. Micheli (Av. Padre Abreu, tel. 809/556-6188, http://lostoros-deleste.com/estadio-francisco-micheli) is home to La Romana's baseball team Los Toros del Este (or The Bulls of the East) and has an audience capacity of 10,000. The gorgeous renovated facilities are comparable to Major League stadiums in the United States. The impeccable new field makes it one of the country's best venues. Practice begins in October for the November season. You can show up to take a sneak peak while you are in town. Sign your name on the entrance wall, beside the hundreds of other fan signatures and purchase some paraphernalia while you're at it in the on-site boutique.

BEACHES

As an inland city, La Romana doesn't have any natural beaches but there are stretches nearby. Inside Casa de Campo is the artificial Las Minitas Beach (tel. 809/523-2161, www.casadecampo.com.do/beaches). You can purchase a day pass (US$25 pp, or US$75 with a meal at Beach Club by Le Cirque, a drink, and free entry to Altos de Chavón) to indulge in a dip with the rich and fabulous, as well as an excellent lunch onsite.

SPORTS AND RECREATION

Aside from snorkeling and diving excursions that head to Bayahibe and its offshore islands, most of the inland activities and sports are found at Casa de Campo (tel. 809/523-3333 or a.concierge@ccampo.com.do for inquiries). It has the largest sports-oriented complex in the Caribbean. While not all the activities are open to nonguests, you'll find enough that are.

Golfing

One of the chief reasons visitors come to La Romana is to play the world-renowned Teeth of the Dog course (Diente de Perro in Spanish, Casa de Campo, tel. 809/523-3333 http://casadecampo.com.do/golf, 7:30am-6pm Mon.-Sun., US$255 for nonguests), ranked among the top 50 courses worldwide and first in Latin America. It is one of three Pete Dye courses at Casa de Campo. Built in 1971, this par-71 championship course stretches 6,721 meters (7,350 yards) and faces the Caribbean Sea on seven holes. It's on the bucket list of any avid golfer in the Caribbean, but even if you don't golf, take a tour of the course and you'll see what all the fuss is about—the views are unparalleled. Request your tee times well in advance.

the riverfront view from Altos de Chavón

A Land of Sugarcane

a sugarcane field in La Romana

If there were no sugarcane industry, there might not have been a Casa de Campo, an airport, or a modern seaport here. And tourism—particularly cruise tourism—wouldn't be synonymous with La Romana. The two primary industries or this province are historically linked. It all began in 1911, when La Romana started booming after the establishment of the largest sugar mill in the country. It became a primary driver of the area's economy as sugarcane prices rose steadily over the years.

In the late 1960s, Alvaro Carta, who had fled Communist Cuba to live in Miami, headed to the Dominican Republic to help run the financially troubled South Puerto Rico Sugar Company in La Romana. Later, with the financial backing of Gulf & Western, he formed a new division known as Gulf & Western Americas. The sugar mill became the single largest producing mill in the world. Carta then used the millions in revenue flowing from the operation to invest in a new industry in La Romana that would improve the town and the condition of its people: tourism. This eventually led to the six-star Casa de Campo complex and its world-renowned golf courses.

Despite the obvious bitterness that comes with the history of abuse of the Taíno, the African slave trade, and the harsh treatment of Haitian workers on sugarcane plantations in the Dominican southeast, the industry helped the town thrive and survive. Today, the sugar-producing Central Romana Corporation employs about 25,000 people, and aside from cruise tourism, sugarcane is La Romana's most important source of income.

Recently renovated in 2014, **Dye Fore** (Casa de Campo, tel. 809/523-3333, fax. 809/523-8800, http://casadecampo.com.do/golf, t.times@ccampo.com.do, US$255/18 holes for nonguests) hugs Altos de Chavón and has dramatic views of the river below, the village, and the Caribbean Sea. There are seven cliff-side holes. It's a challenging course; relax afterward at the riverfront Dye Fore Bar. **The Links** (tel. 809/523-3333, fax. 809/523-8800, http://casadecampo.com.do/golf, t.times@ccampo.com.do, US$180 for nonguests) was built five years after Teeth of the Dog, and Dye originally called it "La Barranca" or the little hill. At 6,309 meters (6,900 yards), it's an inland course featuring undulating hills and lagoons. Grass roughs and sand traps add to the challenges of this 18-hole, par 72.

Snorkeling and Diving

If you're into snorkeling or any type of

Best Golf Courses in the DR

There is little doubt that the Dominican Republic ranks among one of the top golf destinations in the Caribbean. It's also number 15 worldwide, according to the Ministry of Tourism and the Association of Golf Tour Operators. A combination of constant warm weather and varied landscapes with the Caribbean Sea make it hard to beat. The country counts 27 courses and 300 holes—52 of which front the Caribbean Sea. The majority are located on the east coast thanks to its spectacular scenery. They center around Santo Domingo's beachside escapes as well as the vacation haven of Punta Cana.

Golf tourism is big business, drawing in US$200 million in revenue a year. Resorts support courses designed by the likes of Pete Dye, Gary Player, Nick Faldo, and Jack Nicklaus and attract many a luxury traveler. Hot spots include Tortuga Bay, Eden Roc at Cap Cana, and Casa de Campo. Below is a summary of five of the best courses around the country outside of Santo Domingo. Note that rates listed are for winter season and only include greens fees.

- The world-renowned course **Teeth of the Dog** (Diente de Perro in Spanish, Casa de Campo, tel. 809-523-3333, 7:30am-6pm Mon.-Sun., htp://casadecampo.com.do, US$190) is ranked among the top 50 worldwide and one of three Pete Dye courses at the exclusive Casa de Campo. Built in 1971, this par-71 championship course stretching 6,721 meters (7,350 yards) is on the bucket list of any avid golfer in the Caribbean. Seven holes face the Caribbean Sea.

- The **Cocotal Golf & Country Club** (Bávaro, tel. 809/687-4653, www.cocotalgolf.com, US$119/18 holes, golf lesson US$86) is conveniently close to the major Punta Cana resorts and offers 27 holes set around lakes and coconut trees inside a residential community. It has a clubhouse and cafeteria. Opened in February 2000, the course was designed by six-time Spanish champion **Jose Pepe Gancedo.** Ask about shuttle services.

- The seafront **La Cana Golf Course** (Puntacana Resort & Club, US$180, par 72, 27 holes) is a beauty with panoramic views and 14 holes around the Caribbean Sea. There's a clubhouse onsite, and nearby are restaurants that are part of the Puntacana Resort & Club.

- The 18-hole, par-72 **Playa Grande Golf Course** (Río San Juan, tel. 809/582-0860, golf@playagrande.com), part of the Playa Dorada 14-resort complex, was designed by the celebrated Robert Trent Jones Sr. It has 10 holes facing the Atlantic Ocean and offers amazing vistas over its over 6,400-meter (7,000-yard) course. It was renovated under the direction of Rees Jones, the son of Robert Trent Jones Sr., in 2015.

- Another Trent Jones Sr. design, **Playa Dorada Golf Course** (Playa Dorada Resort Complex, tel. 809/320-4262, www.playadorada.com, US$75/18 holes) is an 18-hole, par 72 on the northern Puerto Plata Atlantic coast. It's surrounded by 19 restaurants as well as casinos and beaches. The complex is just a 20-minute ride from the Puerto Plata airport.

diving from wall to cave diving, you're in luck. There are more dive sites than you might have time for in this area. The various dive shops in nearby Bayahibe offer snorkeling trips to offshore islands Saona, Catalina, and Catalinita. If you are based in a La Romana hotel, **Catalina Island** is closest and might be the best option when time is limited. But none of the other sights are too far out, though they might require a full-day excursion. The closest dive shop is also one of the most attentive: **UWESCUBA** (Paseo de Mar 8, tel. 809/804-9445, www.uwescuba.com, US$110/2-tank dive) based at Casa de Campo's Marina. Award-winning instructor Uwe Rath and his staff offer all the PADI courses you might need, including cave diving and wreck diving courses. Dives will take you to nearby Bayahibe's waters and caverns.

In Bayahibe, just a 15-minute ride south of La Romana, **ScubaFun** (Calle Principal 28, Bayahibe, tel. 809/833-0003, www.scubafun.info, 2-tank dive US$80/half-day) is your best bet, with a fun diving crew who will take you on dive or snorkeling excursions to Catalina or Saona, a shipwreck exploration, and cave diving for the advanced.

Kayaking and River Boating

Those staying at Casa de Campo will benefit from the single or double kayaks provided to explore the Caribbean off the shores of Minitas Beach. Or better yet, paddle over to the stunning Chavón River—featured in major movies like *Apocalypse Now*—and get a different view of the medieval village from the water. For a speedboat ride down the river, including a tour of Casa de Campo's Marina, contact **ProExcursions Bayahibe** (tel. 829/659-4688, www.proexcursionsbayahibe.com, US$55 pp), based in the nearby beach village, for a 2.5-hour Rio de Chavón Speedboat Journey.

Sailing

Have you always wanted to charter your own boat and live it up? Casa de Campo's office at the **Casa de Campo Marina** (tel. 809/523-8646, www.marinacasadecampo.com.do, US$600-3,555 for 51 ft./15 people) has a wide selection for your dream excursion out at sea from speedboats to luxury yachts. They can find a match for all budgets and groups.

Fishing

Deep-sea and freshwater river fishing trips are available through **Casa de Campo** (tel. 809/523-3333, www.casadecampo.do, from US$700 half-day), departing from the marina. The fishing season goes from February through May, with peak months being March, April, and May. The main fish hooked include wahoo, kingfish, sailfish, marlin, and barracuda, or snooker in the river. It's a great day out for those who fish and their families.

Baseball

There's baseball everywhere in the DR. during the season is from mid-October through January. If you're visiting during baseball season (mid-October-January), you'll be able to catch a game right here in La Romana; you may even catch the ball fever that hits residents when it comes to their home team, Los Toros del Este. **Estadio Francisco A. Micheli** (Av. Padre Abreu, tel. 809/556-6188, http://lostorosdeleste.com/estadio-francisco-micheli, US$1.11-7.80), close to the center of town, is the only privately owned and funded baseball stadium. Practice sessions run in October, and regular play starts in November.

About a 45-minute drive west, the **Estadio Tetelo Vargas** (Av. Circunvalación, tel.

Estadio Francisco A. Micheli, home to Los Toros del Este

809/529-3618, www.estrellasorientales.com. do) in the industrial town of San Pedro de Macorís is home to the Estrellas Orientales and one of the major hubs for baseball in the Dominican Republic, even though it is also the smallest facility with a capacity for only 8,000. Inaugurated in 1959 in the days of Trujillo, the stadium is named after Dominican baseball great Juan Esteban Vargas, nicknamed Tetelo. He was known for his speed and strong throwing arm, which earned him the title *El Gamo Dominicano* (The Dominican Deer). His successful career took him overseas to Puerto Rico, Venezuela, Cuba, Canada, and the U.S. Negro Leagues. In 1953 at age 47, he was the league-batting champ with a .353 mark. The team won the Dominican League championship in 1954. The stadium is dubbed as the home of the Dominican Big Leaguers, because the province is the birthplace of some of the most famous Big League players out of the DR. If you're lucky to catch a game here, you will have experienced a big piece of Dominican history and culture.

Tennis

Dubbed the "Wimbledon of the Caribbean," Casa de Campo's tennis center at **La Terrazza** (tel. 809/523-3333, 7am-9pm, US$31/hour daytime, US$39 after 6pm) boasts a glorious Caribbean Sea view and features 13 fast-dry Har-Tru clay courts supported by a staff of more than 70. You can play during the day or at night, as you choose. This is a full-service luxury tennis center: there are ball boys, a spectator deck, and an onsite pro shop. Sign up for lessons if you're a newbie (US$61-76/hour); racquets are also available for rent (US$10/hour). After a game, relax with a drink or take a dip in the pool. Every year on the Thursday before Labor Day weekend, the center hosts the international Casa de Campo Cup, attracting over 200 players from 14 countries.

Tours

Runners Adventures (tel. 809/833-0260, www.runnersadventures.com/tours/ bayahibe-runners, US$85) offers a Bayahibe Runners excursion that takes you on a horseback safari into the La Romana countryside, touring a sugarcane plantation and learning about the rum-making process. Next you'll be on to coffee and cacao farms, before ending with a visit to Higüey's Basilica La Altagracia. Runners also offers a Hispaniola Explorer VIP excursion, which includes a city tour of La Romana with a stop at the Micheli Baseball Stadium and a trip to Altos de Chavón, where you'll also get to cruise down the river. It's not so much a shopping trip as it is an opportunity to see beyond the resort for those short on time.

CIGAR FACTORIES

If you're into cigars or even just curious about this prime Dominican export, visit a cigar factory and witness the rolling process firsthand. In the Punta Cana and Bávaro area, head to **Don Lucas Cigar Factory** (tel. 809/200-0129, www.donlucascigars.com.do, free tour and pickup), said to be among current DR president Danilo Medina's favorites. Remember to wear appropriate clothing when visiting factories: closed toe shoes and no bathing suits. In the La Romana area, you should tour **La Flor Dominicana** (La Estancia, Autopista del Coral, tel. 809/550-3000, www.laflordominicana.co, 8am-7pm daily) or **Tabacalera de García** (Industrial Free Zone, tel. 809/556-2127, http://tours.tabacalera-de-garcia.com, http://cigarcountrytours.com, free factory tours Tues. and Thurs., reservations required).

ENTERTAINMENT AND EVENTS
Bars and Clubs

If you find yourself in the city for a night for whatever reason, you can grab drinks and get a taste of the nightlife at the trendy **Bar Marinelli and Lounge** (Av. Santa Rosa, tel. 809/556-1891, consorciomarinelly9@gmail.com). They pour premium liquor and entice with the sounds of merengue, *bachata*, and other genres. Ask locals for the latest city dance spot, as these fluctuate as often as the

San Pedro de Macorís and the Cocolo Festival

Under an hour west of La Romana in the baseball-famous town of San Pedro de Macorís, an annual festival celebrates the unique Afro-Caribbean Cocolo culture of the Dominican Republic. The Cocolos are the descendants of enslaved Africans who emigrated to the DR in the late 19th century from the all over the British Caribbean—including Anguilla, Barbados, St. Kitts, Nevis, Tortola, Turks and Caicos, and St. Croix, among others—to work in the sugar industry. It is estimated that about 6,000 total initially immigrated to the DR.

Dominicans first gave them the name Tortolo—assumed to have derived from Tortola in the BVI—which later evolved into Cocolos, initially used in a derogatory manner. But these workers were valued for their technical know-how, and were hired as experienced drivers, chemists, and machinists. Cocolo is now a reclaimed term used with pride in this community.

The Cocolo presence resulted in a unique cultural evolution in this corner of the DR, and every year, the Cocolos' descendants celebrate their Afro-Caribbean heritage through dance troops and plays between December 25 and the first week of January, and again on June 29 to coincide with the feast of San Pedro as the town's patron saint. The performances include African-inspired folkloric dances and characters, mixed with plots and legends from medieval British literature and the Bible. The *Guloyas*, or dancers, wear vibrant costumes and feathery hats. The musical support beat various types of drums as they all celebrate and twirl through the streets. It's well worth venturing to San Pedro to witness this unique expression of Caribbean heritage. In 2005 UNESCO classified it as a masterpiece of the Oral and Intangible Heritage of Humanity.

wind, but be careful roaming around at night unless you are with a local. Over at Altos de Chavón, **Onno's** (tel. 809/523-2868, www.onnosbar.com/altos-de-chavon, noon-2am daily) is a good bet for happy hour drinks and late-night dancing, with river views and breezes.

Festivals and Cultural Events

The **ProCigar Festival** (third week of February, tel. 809/580-4754, www.procigar.org, US$895 for full program) celebrates the premium tobacco grown in the Dominican Republic, also known as Cigar Country. The ProCigar association, formed in 1992, includes the country's top cigar manufacturers such as La Flor Dominicana, Tabacalera de García, and Tabacalera Fuente, among others. The festival has been held in several areas at once, including in La Romana, Santiago, and Puerto Plata (the 2016 edition will begin in Punta Cana). Over 400 people visit from around the world and indulge in dinners, excursions, local cuisine, and nightlife, along with, of course, cigars. Events also include

cigar factory tours, and a charity auction is usually part of the event, with all proceeds donated to a nonprofit organization assisting children and the elderly. Check the website for each year's schedule of activities, full program, and cost.

Keep your eyes and ears open for the annual **Carnaval de La Romana** (every Sunday in February)—ask for location and times as these may vary, but the parades usually kick off around 4:30pm. It's a good time to see the diversity in the region, with plenty of elaborate Taíno chief costumes.

SHOPPING

You'll have access to a variety of stores in La Romana city, from high-end designer boutiques to side-of-the-road pottery and crafts stands. But the most authentic finds are the art by local creators from paintings to vibrant handmade items.

El Artístico (Km 3 1/2 Carretera La Romana, elartisticord@gmail.com, tel. 809/349-7198, 10am-6pm Mon.-Sat.) is a name everyone knows in these parts and across the DR: it's the nickname of Dominican artist Jose Ignacio Morales Reyes. Born in La Romana, the artist began playing with metal cans of tomato paste when he was a kid, and would transform them into decorative pieces he would eventually sell. Today, his lamps can be found even in the U.S. White House, among other prestigious world venues. At his headquarters a shopping arcade is filled with El Artístico handmade items: lamps, furniture, steel structures, and metal sculptures. The metals he uses the most are iron, aluminum, bronze, and copper. But a more fascinating and worthwhile sight is his actual workshop across the street, where the creations take shape. You can go inside and watch employees at work (be sure not to show up at lunchtime between noon and 1pm when it will be deserted), as well as admire some of his original works. One standout is a tree-shaped stand of the molded hands of visiting celebrity artists. El Artístico himself may be there, unless he is busy in meetings with his latest clients, which have included the president of the Dominican Republic who commission exclusive pieces to be displayed in the DR and overseas.

Another established Dominican artist, who has been in the industry for over 20 years and recently in the limelight when Casa de Campo hosted his gallery opening, Fernando Tamburini has opened his new **Arte por Tamburini** (Calle Altagracia 6, tel. 809/609-1932, www.fernandotamburini.blogspot.com, fernandotamburini@hotmail.com, 9am-9pm daily) private gallery in downtown La Romana. It is in the front section of his home; in fact, his sign is hard to spot from the road so look for a white house with a colorful artistic sign. His vibrant paintings and handmade sculpture are as delightful as Tamburini's bubbly personality. Each represents an aspect of the slow-paced, simple Caribbean life. Originally from Barahona, he graduated from the Altos de Chavón School of Art and Design after taking part in the exchange with Parson's in New York. He returned to teach art at the school and later served as director of the Altos de Chavón Art Gallery before opening up his own. Ask to see his striking handmade sculpture representing plight of Haitian *bateyes* in the Dominican Republic.

Home decorators, fashionistas, and shopaholics beware: you might not be able to leave here without taking something home: **Bibi León** (Calle Restauración 2, tel. 809/550-8393, www.bibileon.com, 9am-6pm Mon.-Fri., 9am-4pm Sat., from US$30 bracelets, US$350-600 clutches) creations are impossibly gorgeous. Set up inside a home, the entire shop is a visual feast of handpainted and handcrafted items made of caoba wood. Think unique clutches that are fit to be featured in *Vogue* and home decor pieces ranging from champagne buckets to platters and place mats, all of which bear exuberant images of nature. At the back of the boutique is the workshop area; ask to see how they paint each piece by hand with extreme precision. You can also find an outlet at Casa de Campo's Marina, in a space shared with clothing designer Jenny Polanski.

Tina Bambu's Mercado Artesanal (Calle Prof Juan Bosch, tel. 809/550-8322, 9am-6pm daily) is a popular pit stop for tourists, offering souvenirs as well as handmade pottery at a reasonable price.

If you're looking to purchase coffee or rum at the local price, the area's largest supermarket is **Jumbo** (Av. Libertad, corner of Doctor Gonzalvo, tel. 809/813-5032 or 809/333-2111, www.jumbo.com.do, 8am-10pm Mon.-Sat., 9am-8pm Sun. and holidays). Look for the big red letters you can't miss when passing through the heart of town. Locals drive from as far as Punta Cana to shop here for better prices. Much like in the La Sirena chain, you'll find everything under the sun here, from groceries to banks, a food court, an electronics store, and lockers.

Altos de Chavón (tel. 809/523-2045, www.casadecampo.com.do/altos-de-chavon, open daily) offers a handful of high-end shopping opportunities, from cigars to jewelry and designer clothing.

FOOD
Dominican

A cheap meal can be had at the Dominican-owned **Pica Pollo Rodríguez** (Calle Duarte, tel. 809/813-3493, 11am-9pm daily, US$3-5) with its signature fried chicken and fries. The meal is quite tasty and not super greasy. There's a convivial outdoor veranda if you have time to sit and eat.

International

In the city, **Shish Kebab** (Calle Castillo Marquez No. 32, tel. 809/556-2737, jgiha@hotmail.com, 10am-11pm Tues.-Sun., US$7-17) is such an iconic restaurant in these parts that Dominicans from as far as Santo Domingo will tell you that it's a sin to pass through La Romana without eating here. And they do have a point. The meat here is succulent—order ahead if you don't want a 45-minute wait for your kebabs—and you'll find all the Middle Eastern specialties, from tabbouleh to baklava desserts. The menu also includes steaks, salads, and seafood. Try one of their fresh fruit juices or Dominican *batidas* with your meal. Seating is indoors in an air-conditioned room with white tablecloths and a more formal setting or outdoors on a shaded veranda facing the street. There is open wireless Internet, and the service is friendly.

Casa de Campo's presence near the city means a host of excellent meal options, for which it's worth dipping into your pockets. For fine dining, indulge in a magical evening at **La Casita** (U.S. tel. 855/877-3643, www.casadecampo.com.do/restaurants/la-casita, 6pm-11pm daily, dress casual elegant, US$10-39)at the Casa de Campo Marina with waterfront dock seating beside pricey yachts. The menu is popular primarily for its seafood, including the paella among other fish specialties. There are also steaks, salads, and chicken entrées. Service and atmosphere are excellent, as is the light jazz that flows gently past the billowing white drapes. There's a special, more private table for two below the main platform edging the water.

Treat yourself to lunch by the beach at the ★ **Beach Club by Le Cirque** (Casa de Campo, U.S. tel. 855/877-3643, www.casadecampo.com.do/restaurants, noon-4pm and 7pm-11pm daily, US$10-60). Try the brick oven pizzas or the grilled sautéed shrimp in a white wine sauce.

Inside Altos de Chavón, ★ **La Piazetta** (tel. 809/523-3165, 6pm-11pm Fri.-Mon., US$10-26) is a cut above the rest. The charming dimly lit indoor wooden tables and stone floor win you over immediately, or choose its outdoor terrace facing the river and the evening breeze. But the authentic, homemade Italian dishes are what truly delight. The antipasti buffet is to die for with imported cheeses and cuts, while entrées range from chicken and beef fondues with mustard and blue cheese to a succulent and classic lasagna Bolognese. You'll have trouble finishing because of the huge portions. Service is excellent, and there's often a nice trio of musicians to serenade you with Latin ballads while you wait on your meal.

A couple of cobblestone paths away, the chain **Onno's** (tel. 809/523-2868, www.onnosbar.com/altos-de-chavon, noon-10pm daily) doesn't disappoint with its usual hip and lively atmosphere and a casual broad menu of burgers, pizzas, and seafood. The bar, which offers hundreds of cocktails, gets rowdier by the hour and turns into a dance spot after dinner hours (10pm-3am Fri.-Sat.). Wednesdays are ladies night. Happy hours are 6pm-8pm daily.

ACCOMMODATIONS

In truth, there's very little reason to overnight in La Romana, unless you are headed to the Casa de Campo Resort, which is at the entrance of La Romana rather than in the city center, or somehow in transit during a long-term stay.

Under US$50

The three-story **Hotel River View** (Calle Restauración 17, tel. 809/556-1181, hotelriverview@gmail.com, US$44, includes daily breakfast and dinner) is basic and dated. Expect to get tiled floors, thin bedding, and a shower and worn tubs. But it's clean if you must spend a night in La Romana town. There are more spacious rooms for the same price, if you're lucky enough to get one.

A notch better, **Hotel Olimpo** (Av. Padre Abreu, corner of Pedro Lluberes, tel. 809/550-7646, www.olimpohotel.com, US$36-43) looks impressive from the exterior, and the interior is acceptable for the price. A cool air-conditioned lobby and wrought-iron staircase lead to basic and clean rooms with double beds, peach walls, and mini fridges. There are lounge areas and inviting hallways.

US$50-100

On the western side of the Río Chavón and formerly a sugarcane plantations' surveillance post, **Hotel Vecchia Caserma** (Km. 12 Carretera La Romana-Bayahibe, tel. 809/556-6072, www.hotelvecchiacaserma.com, US$89-125, includes breakfast and wireless Internet) offers 14 rooms, as well as four triples, with air-conditioning and satellite TV. There's a small pool and an Italian restaurant onsite. The hotel is isolated so you'd need a car to get around, but it's a decent pick for a night or two.

US$100 and Up

Jet-set favorite and Leading Hotel of the World ★ **Casa de Campo** (5.5. miles from La Romana Airport, Carretera La Romana, U.S. tel. 855/877-3643 or 809/523-8698, www.casadecampo.com.do, from US$200, or US$624 all-inclusive) is one of the most prestigious properties in the Caribbean, let alone the Dominican Republic. This is where you're likely to spot celebrities from athletes to musicians and heads of state relaxing on a championship golf course or sipping cocktails at La Caña Restaurant's outdoor lounge—a Le Cirque collaboration—with views of a sprawling cascade pool. The immense 28-square-kilometer (7,000-acre) immaculately landscaped compound is an escape from everything mundane.

There are 173 rooms and 12 suites within the hotel itself. Each comes with a four-seater golf cart for exploration and face gardens or golf driving ranges. Private villas are also available for rent. The hotel offers six of its own excellent restaurants over the range of its grounds. There is also a spa, three Pete Dye-designed golf courses, including **Teeth of the Dog,** an equestrian center, three polo fields, a sailing school, movie theaters, and 13 Har-Tru tennis courts. Don't miss riding a golf cart through Teeth of the Dog for its breathtaking sea views, dining at **La Piazetta** or at **La Casita,** and getting a full, free entry and tour of **Altos de Chavón.**

Casa de Campo Marina (tel. 809/523-8646, www.marinacasadecampo.com.do) within the Casa de Campo grounds has a capacity for 350 yachts, in addition to being home to a handful of waterfront restaurants and shops. It has its own yachting club, sailing school, shopping mall, and movie theater. There are several pathways through plazas ideal for an evening or daytime stroll.

GETTING THERE

If you're driving up to La Romana from Santo Domingo, you'll hop on Highway 3 from and take it all the way. Highway 3 will turn into Avenida Padre Abreu once you enter the city limits. Turn right onto Santa Rosa Street, which will lead you to the Parque Central close to restaurants, banks, and services. If you need to continue on to Bayahibe, once you arrive into La Romana follow the signs for Casa de Campo, which will take you onto Avenida Libertad. This turns into Carretera La Romana-Higüey, and from there follow along the signs to Bayahibe just 15 minutes away.

Aeropuerto La Romana (tel. 809/813-9000, www.romanaairport.com) is just under a 20-minute drive from the center of La Romana's city, as well as Casa de Campo or Bayahibe and Dominicus resorts. Flights come in daily on carriers such as American Airlines, American Eagle, JetBlue, or Air

Canada. A host of charter flights arrive from Europe. Taxi rates from the airport to area resorts including Casa de Campo begin at US$35, and of course depend on your final destination. Prices are set and will be posted once you get past customs; double-check the rate with the driver before you depart.

From Santo Domingo, you can catch a local *guagua* (about US$5) headed to Higüey from Parque Enriquillo. Ask around to make sure you hop on the right one that makes a stop in La Romana. There's also an express to La Romana, if you're lucky enough to get to it. It leaves every half hour until 5pm. You will likely get dropped off at the Parque Central, where you can catch a taxi or a bike taxi. If you're with a group, it may be better value to pay a taxi to drive you to La Romana; rates are usually around US$135 for up to four passengers—contact Apolo Taxi (tel. 809/537-0000, www.apolotaxi.com) and get an instant quote and ride.

If you're coming south from the Punta Cana Airport or area, note that there aren't any direct public buses and you'll have to take a taxi. Contact IBK Servicios (tel. 829/926-0707, http://ibkservicios.com, US$105 one-way, 1-4 pp) for a private transfer.

GETTING AROUND

Exploring downtown La Romana is easily done on foot, but in-city taxis are also affordable. Call Santa Rosa Taxi (tel. 809/556-5313). If you choose to rent a car from La Romana, the airport has a branch of Budget (tel. 809/813-9111, 9am-5pm daily, from US$45), and there is an Avis (Francisco Castillo Marquez 35, tel. 809/550-0600, 8am-11pm daily) in town.

To go from La Romana to Bayahibe by public transportation, find the central bus gathering spot on Avenida Libertad across from the public jail. And if you're heading to Santo Domingo, there's a SICHOEM bus terminal (US$3.40 express or RD$150)—you can also ask for *la salida de La Romana*—on Avenida Abreu, which leads into Autopista del Este, next to Shell gas station. You catch an air-conditioned bus to the capital and reach it in 1.5 hours. You can also just head to the Parque Central and catch a free bus ride in front of the church to the SICHOEM terminal.

Bayahibe

One of the last Taíno strongholds in the country, Bayahibe was founded as a fishing village in 1874, when Juan Brito and his family arrived from Puerto Rico. Fishing and the traditional wooden sailboat building were primary trades. The tiny *pueblo* has since transformed into a tourist destination as more resorts realized the beauty of Bayahíbe and all of its valuable assets. The crystal clear, calm waters of its Caribbean coastline make it perfect for water sports and beachcombing. The protected national park nearby offers hiking and freshwater-filled caverns with some of the best cave diving in the Caribbean. And then there are always stunning offshore islands for day trips to paradise.

Despite the crowds of tourists and buses shuffling in and out daily to Bayahibe for day trips from neighboring Punta Cana, Dominican village life still rules. Alarm clocks are 4am roosters, followed by birds and music. The streets are dotted with colorful, traditional wooden homes and eateries. The bay, filled with boats and facing small white sand beaches, is clean and postcard-worthy. The sunsets here are some of the most spectacular in the country.

Bayahibe is *tranquilo*, as most European and Haitian expats will tell you when explaining why they made their home here decades ago. The community way of life means that this is a very hospitable and welcoming

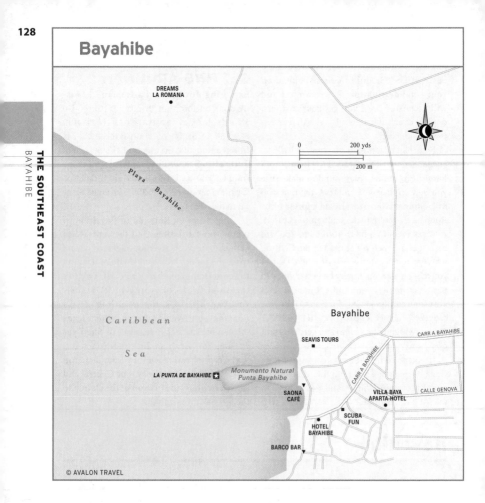

Bayahibe

DREAMS
LA ROMANA

0 ____ 200 yds
0 ____ 200 m

Playa Bayahibe

Caribbean

Sea

Bayahibe

SEAVIS TOURS

CARR A BAYAHIBE

CARR A BAYAHIBE

CALLE GENOVA

LA PUNTA DE BAYAHIBE

Monumento Natural
Punta Bayahibe

SAONA
CAFÉ

VILLA BAYA
APARTA-HOTEL

SCUBA
FUN

HOTEL
BAYAHIBE

BARCO BAR

© AVALON TRAVEL

place to stay. There's little crime here, and it is considered to be one of the safest parts of the country. Even late at night, walking is the norm (though I always advise not to do so or to carry valuables).

The main road into the village ends at a giant parking lot where tourist buses park for the day while their customers hop on boats from Bayahibe to the nearby islands. Fishing still holds key place in the village's identity, even if it isn't the primary income earner. If you're lucky, you'll arrive during Memorial Weekend in May when the fishing tournament is on.

DOWNTOWN
Casas Típicas
Stroll around the village to enjoy the visual feast of vibrant, pastel-colored **Casas Típicas** or traditional wooden homes of Bayahibe. You'll find them along the main street walking up and down in either direction. You'll also spot them on side streets off the main drag. Prepare to snap lots of pictures of these photogenic structures.

★ La Punta de Bayahibe
La Punta de Bayahibe or **La Ensenada**, is a rugged peninsula jutting out into the sea

Best Tours in Bayahibe

TOURING SAONA ISLAND

With a focus on ecofriendly tours, the multilingual-staffed Seavis Tours (beachfront, between Dreams Resort Bayahibe and town, Calle Eladia 4, tel. 829/714-4947, www.seavisbayahibe.com, US$95) offers the "Saona Crusoe VIP"—an excellent insider's take on Saona Island. They are conscious of the fact that you'd rather not be crowded in with other speedboats and tourists and find ways to avoid them. Plenty of information is provided along the way, making the trip both cultural and educational—particularly at Mano Juan, the only inhabited portion of Saona, where Seavis subsidizes a turtle nesting center. The stop at the *piscina natural* will be uncrowded because the boat heads to an area of the natural pool that is a bit more removed from everyone else. The last stop is Canto de la Playa, which is completely deserted by 3pm. It's a great time with lively guides, plenty of drinks, and a fun and mature crowd. Snorkeling gear is provided, as are drinks, snacks, and lunch.

To sail in style to Saona Island on your own charter, contact Dragonsmoke Sailing Charters (Casa de Campo Marina, tel. 829/272-9069, www.dragonsmokesailing.com, US$250 pp, four people minimum) for a blissful day drifting across the Caribbean. You can fish, snorkel, and sun yourself on a 16-meter (51-foot) yacht with fully furnished cabins and private bathrooms. The trip includes lunch, snorkeling gear, and stops at Catuano Beach and the natural pool on Saona Island.

HIKING THE JUNGLE AT SENDERO DEL PADRE NUESTRO

Another unique excursion in the Bayahibe region is to explore the former Taíno grounds and caves at the protected Padre Nuestro Trail within the Parque Nacional del Este. The only tour operator specializing in an extensive guided hiking trip—aside from the Spanish-speaking local guides by the park entrance—is Seavis Tours (beachfront, between Dreams Resort Bayahibe and town, Calle Eladia 4, tel. 829/714-4947, www.seavisbayahibe.com, US$95). Learn about the flora and fauna of the park and its prior inhabitants before being declared a protected area. Then explore stunning Taíno freshwater caves. What makes this tour even more special is that it's designed to help the local community as well. You'll visit the settlement of Benerito, just outside Bayahibe, where the locals who once lived in the park relocated and the women are now running an arts and crafts cooperative financed by USAID. The trip ends with a river excursion down the Chavón. It's a great day of local history and culture with outdoor adventure. Call ahead to check on the current status of the trail and to find out available tour dates with an English-speaking guide.

DIVING AT CATALINA ISLAND

The popular PADI five-star dive center ScubaFun (Calle Principal 28, Bayahibe, tel. 809/833-0003, www.scubafun.info) is your best bet for exploring the reefs and critters off the Bayahibe coast and some of the best diving in the DR. The two-tank dive off Catalina (US$80 2-tank dive/half-day Catalina plus US$55 excursion) includes a 40-meter (130-foot) wall dive, which you can cruise between 9 and 12 meters (30-60 feet) to see the best portions. The lunch isn't stellar but the surroundings make up for it, along with plenty of time to relax on the white sand shores and snap photos. There are also shipwreck dive excursions to the Coco Wreck and St. George Wreck. Also up to 130 feet, it's for advanced divers.

FISHING IN BAYAHIBE

Fishing is still a primary activity in this village, so much so that there's even an annual fishing tournament in the summer. Bayahibe Fishing Centre (Bayahibe Beach 2, tel. 809/833-0009 or 829/914-4162, www.bayahibefishingcentre.com, US$175 half day or US$260 full day, four people min.) and one of the best fishermen in this area in Captain Pepe take you deep-sea fishing to catch marlin, mahimahi, barracuda, and more. All fishing gear, bait, and guides are included, as well as drinks and snacks.

from the western edge of the village just after the main dock area. This area is the most historical part of the village. A pleasant trail, La Ruta La Punta Bayahibe, leads you to three of its significant points: a church, archaeological ruins, and a botanical trail. The short hike eventually leads to a glorious deck overlooking the sea and the bay ahead.

Walk up the front street, continue past the big central parking lot (behind Café Saona) and continue on that road until you reach a gate. It will be open, even if it doesn't seem so at first. As you get past it, you'll see the beautiful **Parroquia Divina Pastora** (tel. 809/833-0654, ptmariadenazaret@hotmail.com) with its entrance directly facing the sea. It was built from wood brought over from Florida and without any architectural or engineering assistance. It was the first religious institution in the area, and the oldest building in the village, and was consecrated on March 25, 1925, by Archbishop Monseñor Nouel. In 2015, the church celebrated its 90th anniversary. The most venerated item inside the church is a framed painting of the Divina Pastora or the Virgin Mary, dating from 1954. It was a gift from a Brazilian Franciscan monk who was visiting the village and moved by its *fiestas patronales*. The

church has received prominent visitors over the years, including former president of the DR Monsignor Adolfo Alejandro Nouel y Bobadilla.

After touring the church, ask to see resident Padre Antonio Villavicencio's garden at the back of the church, where he has created **La Ruta de Las Virgines:** a garden where he has planted a trail of all the matron saint figurines he has received from guests from around a dozen countries, including Portugal, Spain, Cuba, Italy, Chile, Costa Rica, Brazil, Mexico, France, and Puerto Rico. There is also one from Higüey. Each one of the figurines is labeled.

Beside the church entrance is a **Bayahibe Rose Garden.** The cactus trees carrying this national flower *(Pereskia quisqueyana)* are found only in this fishing village of the DR. Past the church, look closely and you will spot archaeological ruins left behind from the first inhabitants of the village and dating back to 2000 BC buried under overgrown shrubs. The area awaits better upkeep. Continue walking down and you'll run into a bigger garden of Bayahibe Roses. The pathway eventually leads to a covered lookout cabana and deck with breathtaking 180-degree views of Bayahibe's waters and coastline. You can walk past the

a view of the bay from La Punta de Bayahibe

lookout point along the water and circle back to the church without retracing your steps.

PARQUE NACIONAL DEL ESTE

At the southeastern tip of the country and accessible on foot from Bayahibe or via a short drive from La Romana town, the magnificent **Parque Nacional del Este** (9am-5pm daily, entry fee US$2.20) has been a protected nature reserve since 1975 and is the crown jewel of the southeastern coast. Approximately 790 square kilometers (305 square miles) of reserve encompass both land and sea. On land there is a subtropical rainforest and a dry forest that can be explored via a 2-kilometer (1.24-mile) trail known as the **Sendero del Padre Nuestro.** It will take you to Taíno caves with pictographs and the springs around which they once lived. The sea portion of the park includes the popular offshore islands of **Saona, Catalina,** and **Catalinita,** as well as the natural pool area of **La Palmilla.** There are over 400 caves within the park. The most well-known is **Cueva del Puente,** easily hiked on foot.

The park is home to at least 539 species of flowers. It also makes a great birding excursion. It is home to 144 types of birds, including unique ones such as the brown pelican, the red-footed boobie, the barn owl, and the Hispaniolan parrot. A large frigate bird colony convenes at Bahia de las Calderas, a bay on the southern coast of the park. You can also expect to see sea turtles on Saona Island. This is the most important nesting site in the country, and nesting season lasts from March through November and attracts hawksbill, green, and leatherback species. Spotted and bottlenose dolphins roam the seas surrounding the islands, as well as the rare humpback whale and manatees. On dry land, the endangered rhinoceros iguana range up to 1 meter (4.5 feet) in length and as heavy as 9 kilograms (20 pounds).

To tour the various areas of the park, whether the trail or the islands, you must be accompanied by a licensed guide. The park's own guides are available at both park entrances (from either the Boca de Yuma side or from Bayahibe). Note that camping is not permitted. The best way to tour the sea portion of the park is to hop on a boat excursion with one of the tour companies in Bayahibe. If you have time, or you're a cave diver, throw in the Padre Nuestro Trail.

If you're arriving by car, you'll use the western entrance to the park, in Bayahibe. You can reach the entrance by taxi or on foot from downtown Bayahibe also. If you're coming from the east (Punta Cana), the entrance is at Boca de Yuma, and will need to be reached by car.

Caving

There are over 400 caves within the park. The most well-known is **Cueva del Puente,** easily hiked on foot. The underground wet **Cueva de Chicho** is filled with a crystal clear *manantial* or freshwater spring, around which you can spot over 20 original Taíno petroglyphs. Open Water and Advanced Divers can indulge in 9-meter (30-foot) to over 30-meter (100-foot) waters filled with the larger Caribbean critters, along with stalactite and stalagmite formations. Contact **Scubafun** (Calle Principal 28, Bayahibe, tel. 809/833-0003, www.scubafun.info, single-tank dive, US$84pp.) for more information; they specialize in cave diving in this area.

★ Sendero del Padre Nuestro

While the islands get the most tourist attention, the **Sendero del Padre Nuestro,** also known as **Ruta Ecológica y Arqueológica de Padre Nuestro** (Carretera a Bayahibe, tel. 829/521-3398, senderopadrenuestro@explorelaromana.com, 9am-4:30pm Mon.-Sun., US$4.45 or RD$200), is also an integral and informative part of the Parque Nacional del Este. The trailhead is on the main road leading to Bayahibe and Dominicus, right after you pass Dreams La Romana on the corner of Avenida Wayne Fuller. It's easily accessible on foot from Bayahibe and Dominicus, so

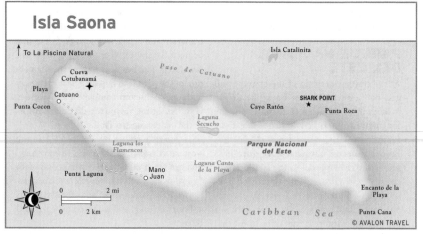

Isla Saona

To La Piscina Natural

Isla Catalinita

Paso de Catuano

Cueva
Cotubanamá

Playa
Catuano

Punta Cocon

Laguna
Secucho

Cayo Ratón

SHARK POINT

Punta Roca

Laguna los
Flamencos

**Parque Nacional
del Este**

Punta Laguna

Mano
Juan

Laguna Canto
de la Playa

0   2 mi

0   2 km

Caribbean   Sea

Encanto de la
Playa

Punta Cana

© AVALON TRAVEL

visitors can walk up to its entrance or grab a short taxi ride.

The trail is a 2-kilometer (1.24-mile), easy-to-moderate hike that takes two hours. You are required to be accompanied by one of the accredited park rangers (if you speak a little Spanish you will get the most out of the informative tour). You can also tour the park by horse with one of the rangers. **Seavis Tours** (beachfront Bayahibe, between Dreams Resort Bayahibe and town, 4 Calle Eladia, tel. 829/714-4947, www.seavisbayahibe.com/National_Park_e.htm, US$95) also offers a hiking excursion down the Padre Nuestro Trail in English.

After arriving at the Parque Nacional del Este reception area, you'll first spot several boards explaining the park's history, flora, and fauna, as well as Taíno past. The history behind the trail itself is equally interesting and plays a role in what the park has to offer today. This area was originally called Padre Nuestro, formerly a village of up to 180 families attracted by the freshwater springs—the park has an abundant underground lake and spring system—and the weather. They subsisted in the indigenous forest through hunting, beekeeping, and burning wood for coal production. Eventually, pollution from waste, deforestation, and hunting led to serious environmental impacts, not to mention

water contamination as the aquifer supplies most of the eastern portion of the DR. This was compounded by damage caused by Hurricane George. As a result, the majority of individuals were moved to modern housing about eight miles away in the village of Benerito, and in 2002, eight square kilometers of the land were legally transferred within the national park's boundaries. The trail was developed starting in 2007 with the help of USAID and inaugurated in early 2008. A new tour guide association provides jobs to displaced families, who also maintain the trail, as a means of sustainable development.

Today, a hike through Padre Nuestro takes you through areas supporting some of the DR's native plants. The guayiga plant is a root vegetable used by the Taíno to make bread. Some of the Rose of Bayahibe cacti—the national flower, endemic to this region—are over 6 meters (20 feet) tall. Charcoal sites provide a replica of what villagers once used to produce coal.

★ Isla Saona

Simply put, **Isla Saona** is a sight for sore eyes. The island sits approximately 12 miles south from the shores of Bayahibe within the Parque Nacional del Este. Its numerous beaches, turquoise waters, glorious starfish-filled sandbanks, and towering coconut trees bring approximately 3,000 visitors to the island daily via speedboat or catamaran. It's an excursion you might be tempted to repeat. Once there, visitors can snorkel, swim, and beach-hop Saona's gorgeous shores until about 4pm. Besides being the largest offshore island of the DR at 24 kilometers long (15 miles) and 5 kilometers wide (3.3 miles), it's also the most important sea turtle nesting site in the country.

A tour of the island includes stops at the **Caves of Penon, La Piscina Natural, Mano Juan Village,** and if you're lucky, **Canto de la Playa** on the southeastern tip of the island.

THE CAVES OF PEÑON

Excursions often stop along the western coastline of the Parque Nacional del Este, where you'll cruise along a series of dramatic cliffs and water-filled caves, the **Caves of Peñon.** Certified divers can explore underwater and discover an incredible amount of marinelife, including spotted eagle rays, sharks, and vibrant corals. Contact **Scubafun** (Calle Principal 28, Bayahibe, tel. 809/833-0003, www.scubafun.info, single-tank dive, US$84pp.) if you're interested in exploring these caves underwater.

LA PISCINA NATURAL

Said to be the longest or largest sandbank in the world, **La Piscina Natural,** also referred to as **La Palmilla,** offers brilliantly turquoise warm and shallow waters lined for miles with coconut trees, mangroves and underwater sea grass patches where starfish laze away at your feet. The view of this coastline is simply breathtaking and make it a sheer paradisiacal stop worth the entire trip alone. There will be other boats along the sandbank, but it's also long enough that yours could get away from the crowd and find its own pool area. Brown pelicans fly over this idyllic spot, and you can see, in the distance, the first beach on Saona a 5- to 10-minute ride away.

Past the natural pool as you travel along the Catuano Channel separating the main island and Saona, you'll notice bird nests in mangroves. The Catuano Channel is teeming with numerous species of algae, coral sponges, fish—over 100 types—including turtles manatees and dolphins. Keep your eyes peeled.

MANO JUAN

The most culturally interesting stop in Parque Nacional del Este is **Mano Juan**—another 10-minute boat ride from Catuano Beach on the south end of the island. This

Isla Saona

is Saona's sole settlement. The first inhabitants came to Mano Juan during World War II, when dictator Rafael Trujillo sent them to guard the island. Today, approximately 300 people live in pastel-colored traditional wooden houses dotting sandy streets facing the beach. It is a typically Dominican fishing village. Tourism and fishing are the main occupations here, though it's mostly vendors hawking their wares or foods to visitors. Children go to school for about four hours a day because there aren't enough teachers. The village finally got electricity in 2014, thanks to solar panels. There's still no plumbing inside the homes, and they pump well water instead.

On the very back end of Mano Juan Island, past an open field, is a turtle sanctuary. This project was established seven years ago with the help of a local fisherman and funded by Seavis Tours (so of course, they always make a stop here). Be sure to check with your chosen tour operator to make sure you get to visit the sanctuary if you're interested in conservation. About 120 to 150 eggs are laid on the beaches of Saona during turtle nesting season. Eggs were under threat due to locals eating or selling them—the belief is that this works like a drink of mamajuana—but thanks to

the center, preservation has improved and beaches are monitored regularly to protect the nests.

You can now have a Robinson Crusoe experience on this dreamy slice of Saona Island by staying overnight in the protected area. **Casa Rural El Paraíso de Saona** (contact Bayahibe Fishing Centre, tel. 809/833-0009 or 829/914-4162, bayahibefishingcentre@yahoo. com, US$60 with breakfast and dinner) offers 10 rooms in a colorful simple single-story wooden house on the beach a stone's throw from the sea. Rooms 1 and 2 have shutters with direct a sea view. Private bathrooms, linens, fans, and mosquito nets are provided (bring repellent and long sleeves for the evenings). You'll get to enjoy Saona Island before and after all the tourists have come and gone—and that's pretty special. Meals are provided at half or full board, with full board costing extra, and served on the beach. There are usually fish, chicken, and lobster options. The local *colmado* also sells affordable meals. Just don't expect to be connected to the Internet or to have cell phones coverage (though you might get a signal by the police station). Reserve ahead and arrange for pickup from Bayahibe village; you could also combine your ride with a tour of Saona Island.

Mano Juan

CANTO DE LA PLAYA

One of the beaches on the far southeastern tip of Saona, often deserted, is an absolute stunner: **Canto de la Playa** (the song of the beach). If you were ever to take sexy photos of yourself anywhere, this would be the beach to do it on. It's lined with taller, thin coconut trees than the other beaches at Saona and they continue along the shoreline as far as the eye can possibly see. The diamond white sand is near perfection, as are the calm blue waters. If you're lucky, your tour will stop here for a swim. There's only one structure on the island: the summer home of Dr. Francisco Antonio Gonzalvo, which former President Joaquín Balaguer gifted to him for curing him of a serious illness. The house sees visitors only at Easter, when the physician's daughter descends on it with her friends.

Isla Catalina

Directly off the shore at La Romana, **Isla Catalina** is part of the Parque Nacional del Este and closer to La Romana than Bayahibe—although both are possible starting points. The island is a stunner lined with thin, soft white sands and has a more rustic, undeveloped feel than Saona. On day trips you'll get to lunch and swim here at your leisure. There are some sketchy bathroom facilities. Portions of the beach are also used for cruise ship excursions during the winter season, and by resorts such as Casa de Campo, which often dock along a more "cleaned up" section of the beach. The highlight of Catalina, aside from its pristine sands, is the diving and snorkeling off its shores. Two of the prettiest dives are at the over 30-meter (100-foot) **Catalina Wall,** with hard and soft corals and colorful Caribbean fish species. On the other side of the island is the gorgeous **Aquarium,** a 9- to 12-meter (30- to 40-foot) dive where you'll spot sea horses, black urchins, and more Caribbean critters in deep blue waters.

Isla Catalinita

The smallest of the islands, **Isla Catalinita** is popular for snorkeling and diving. Visibility is excellent year-round, and you'll spot big Caribbean critters here including eagle rays, sharks, and sea turtles. The coral reefs are equally impressive. Check with **ScubaFun** (Calle Principal 28, Bayahibe, tel. 809/833-0003, www.scubafun.info) about an all-day snorkeling and diving trip out to Catalinita combined with Saona. You'll dive at Shark Point, snorkel off Catalinita, and continue on for lunch on Saona, before returning to the Piscina Natural and a last dive at the Caves of Penon on Saona (US$79/excursion).

BEACHES

There are essentially two separate beaches in Bayahibe: **Playa Bayahibe,** beginning at Dreams La Romana as you enter the Bayahibe village area and continuing into the village; and **Playa Dominicus,** occupied in large part by all-inclusive hotels (also called the "hotel zone") just south of Bayahibe. Portions of both—just 62 miles from Punta Cana Airport—have earned a European Blue Flag certification. Dominicus was the first to do so in the Caribbean region, a prestigious accolade for keeping up cleanliness and environmental standards. You'll see their certified parts designated as "Playa La Laguna."

Playa Bayahibe and Playa Dominicus are public, like all beaches in the Dominican Republic, meaning that the first 60 meters (197 feet) of shoreline are accessible and you can easily stroll past seaside hotels or even swim in the water fronting the resorts as long as you're not using their lounge chairs or going inside.

Bordering the Parque Nacional del Este on one end and the Viva Wyndham on the other, the nearly mile-long **Playa Dominicus** is easily the most stunning and longer beach of the two. The most beautiful part isn't the one facing the hotels actually, but rather the fully open, unbuilt section just past the Be Live resort. It's accessible from two parking lots: one just past the Catalonia Dominicus and the other beside the Anani Beach Restaurant. Walking the entire Playa Dominicus isn't easy in the hot sun; the beach is heavily sloped in some places and the sand is thick and coarse. Prepare for a workout, and wear plenty of sunscreen and a hat. You'll find a vendor souvenir shacks along the start of the resort-free stretch, but after that are quiet parts where you can stroll to your heart's content and swim with less company. The water at Dominicus is blissful. There are gentle rolling waves that make you feel like you are on a floatie, and the turquoise is perfectly iridescent. Alongside some of the resorts, as well as a small portion of the public area, you'll find some rocks upon entry, but they are easily avoided. You can lay your towel and relax like a Dominican or opt for a lounge chair at Anani while enjoying an Italian lunch. The far eastern end of the beach leads to an entrance into the Parque Nacional del Este, but I don't recommend wandering there on your own without a guide .

Playa Bayahibe is smaller, yet no less picture-perfect with its gorgeous bay, even if it isn't as continuous a stretch as Dominicus. Parts of the beachfront are occupied by numerous excursion boats, and in the distance, fancier catamarans. Still, there are portions where you can lay your towel and marvel at this fishing village's postcard-worthy scenery on the stretch past Dreams La Romana and

before reaching town. Want a quieter, more exclusive section where you could easily be alone on a weekday? Walk all the way west of the main street, past Mare Nostrum, and once you reach Barco Bar, make a right. You'll find idyllic white sands as well as an adjacent cove-shaped stretch.

Both Dominicus and Bayahibe beaches get rowdier on "Dominican Sundays," when locals flock from neighboring La Romana, as well as Santo Domingo, to bathe and relax.

SPORTS AND RECREATION
Diving and Snorkeling

Whether you're a beginner or looking for a fun time under the waters of Bayahibe, the American-owned **ScubaFun** (Calle Principal 28, Bayahibe, tel. 809/833-0003, www.scuba-fun.info, 2-tank dive US$80/half-day) is your best bet, with excellent staff from the desk to the dive masters. Dives head to all the offshore islands with a range of wall dives, and there are the popular Bayahibe shipwrecks *Coco* and *St. George* and the caves of Padre Nuestro to explore. An excursion fee will be tacked onto the tank-dive cost when you head to the islands, so be sure to inquire what it is and allocate funds for it.

There are local vendors on the public end of Playa Dominicus.

Diving for Treasures

Off the coast of Bayahibe, divers not only get to explore the colorful reef, walls, and fascinating caves of the Parque Nacional del Este, but also historic shipwrecks turned underwater archaeological and marine museums. These living museums play an important role in the preservation of history as well as supporting biodiversity. Whichever wreck you end up exploring, remember to always take care not to touch or remove anything. These are fragile ecosystems; a reef environment is very easily affected by the presence of humans.

A half-mile off the coast of Dominicus Beach, the *St. George* **Shipwreck** is the most popular dive and certainly one of the most colorful. Built in 1962 in Scotland to transport wheat and barley between Norway and the Americas, the 73-meter-long (240-foot) cargo ship—originally known as *M. V. Norbrae*—was later abandoned in Santo Domingo after 20 years of service. After it was destroyed by Hurricane George, which hit the DR in 1998, the ship was renamed after that disaster and eventually moved and purposely sunk off Dominicus' shores on June 12, 1999. It is now an artificial reef with sponges, corals, and attracting all sorts of Caribbean critters, particularly large barracudas. Experienced divers can literally go in and out the ship during their dive.

Opened in July 2002, the 1724 Guadalupe Underwater Archeological Preserve is directly across from the Viva Dominicus Beach Resort. The 1,000-ton, 74-gun Spanish galleon *Nuestra Señora de Guadalupe* originally set sail in 1724 from Spain to Mexico, carrying mercury used in Spain's gold and silver mines and passengers. A hurricane caused her to get stuck near Samaná Bay and sink off a reef along the coast of the DR. The majority of the passengers survived, while the mercury remained stuck in the hold. In 1976, the Dominican government hired a salvaging firm to recover any artifacts and prevent looting. They pulled up cannons, crystals, and religious objects. In 2002, Indiana University suggested that the artifacts be put back underwater as an exhibit for divers and snorkelers. They developed the preserve in about 8 meters (26 feet) of water just 0.4 kilometers (0.3 miles) off Dominicus. Today you'll spot several cannons, an anchor, cannon balls, and a deadeye from the shipwreck. These substrates attract all of the coral and marinelife you see.

Off the shores of Catalina Island is the **Captain Kidd Shipwreck: Living Museum of the Sea**, opened in 2011. The wreck lies under 3 meters (10 feet) of water and wasn't discovered for almost three centuries. A snorkeler spotted the cannons in 2007. The pirate captured this ship in 1698 in the Indian Ocean and later abandoned off the southwest of the DR. With the help of Charlie Beeker, director of Indiana University's Office of Underwater Science in Bloomington, and his Indiana University colleagues, the wreck was confirmed as Captain Kidd's. It held guns and anchors. Today, it helps the underwater sealife thrive, particularly coral.

At 13 meters (41 feet) deep, the *Atlantic Princess* is an easy wreck to navigate and swim through, therefore a good choice for Open Water divers. The former tourist boat from Bayahibe is home to numerous species of sponges, corals, and fish, schools of sergeant majors, trumpetfish, and the invasive lionfish.

In addition to making trips to the offshore islands, **Casa Daniel** (Calle Principal, bayfront, tel. 809/833-0050, www.casa-daniel.com/bayahibe, US$156-162/two-tank dives to Catalina or Saona) goes on local dive trips to coral-rich areas in the national park and along Dominicus Reef, a five-minute boat ride from Bayahibe's shores. Shipwrecks such as the *Atlantic Princess* and *St. George* are also options, as well as cave diving. You can do a combined diving and snorkeling trip (US$48-54) if you only have one diver in your group and others want to explore on the surface before getting to the islands to relax together.

Sailing

You'll be spoiled with options when it comes to sailing along Bayahibe's bay and on to its nearby dreamy islands. Nearly all of the tour operators in town will be seeking you out to sign up. Thousands descend on the village every day from nearby Punta Cana to sail these dreamy Caribbean waters.

Among your best options is **ProExcursions Bayahibe** (tel. 829/659-4688, www.proexcursionsbayahibe.com, US$195, includes all gear, meal and drinks) and their Saona Prestige trip. You'll sail to Saona Island on a 23-meter (75-foot) luxury catamaran. A notch up, and the way to explore the Caribbean Sea the way it was meant to be, is to contact **Seavis Tours** (beachfront, between Dreams Resort Bayahibe and town, Calle Eladia 4, tel. 829/714-4947, www.seavisbayahibe.com, US$1,200/day charter, includes lunch). Their private 16-meter (51-foot) Dragonsmoke sailboat accommodates up to 10 people and will head to multiple islands, if you wish, and stay as long as you like.

Paddleboarding
Bayahibe SUP (Bayahibe Beach, tel. 809/609-4045, www.bayahibesup.com, 9am-5pm Tues.-Sun., US$50 two hours with instruction or just US$20/hour) operates out of a simple shack and will take you on SUP excursions. They have everything from a "Surfari" two-hour trip along the coastline (US$50) to a paddle and snorkeling combo (US$40).

Fishing
Bayahibe Fishing Centre (tel. 809/833-0009, www.bayahibefishingcentre.com, US$175/half day pp, 4 people minimum) goes out on affordable half-day morning deep-sea fishing trips with popular Captain Pepe. You'll catch sailfish, marlin, king mackerel, mahimahi, and other big fish trolling 2-10 miles offshore. You can share the boat or charter it, with a minimum of 4 and maximum of 8 people per boat. Fishing trips can also be combined with excursions to Saona and Catalina. **ProExcursions Bayahibe** (tel. 829/659-4688, www.proexcursionsbayahibe.com, US$195, includes all gear, meal and drinks) offers a leisurely sailing, deep-sea fishing and snorkeling trip aboard a 12-meter (38-foot) catamaran that takes you from the village shores all the way to Saona Island.

ENTERTAINMENT AND EVENTS
Bayahibe is a tiny village. The little nightlife there centers around a couple of bars. The ones that aren't frequented by too many working ladies are listed here.

Bars and Nightclubs
Bayahibe's **Super Colmado** gets going every day around 5pm when employees of hotels hang here after work. They are joined by guides, fishers, and as the night goes on, the ladies of the evening. You'll get a feel of an authentic, small-town Dominican *colmado* here. Couples will dance both inside the bar/store and outside on the sidewalk as the music blasts and the beer flows incessantly all night, including spillover across the street. It's the liveliest local spot in the village, where all the usual suspects can be seen daily.

Tucked away at the western end of the main road, and yet a minute's walk from the center of the village, **Barco Bar's** (Calle La Bahia, tel. 849/875-5081, info@barco-bar.com, 8:30am-12:30am daily, US$3-15) ambience and views are hard to match. The open-air casual bar and restaurant is not much more than wooden tables and chairs but offers the best cocktails at sunset watching as well as a beach stretch right in the *pueblo*. Sit on the wooden swings if your bottom fits and take in the breeze and the bay. The food is decent, ranging from pasta to fish dishes. Free *bocas* are often served at happy hour. Wednesdays are poplar for karaoke, and Sundays and weekends are particularly busy as Dominican families come in from nearby La Romana to relax.

Café Saona (Calle Principal, bayfront, tel. 809/833-0541, www.saonacafe.com, 10am-11:45pm Tues,-Sun., 10am-2am Fri.-Sat.) is a good spot to mingle. It serves up cheap but potent cocktails to the latest tunes from happy hour on.

The Pit Stop (Carretera Bayahibe-Dominicus, tel. 809/833-0649, thepitstopbayahibe@hotmail.com, 10pm-4am Thurs.-Sun.) is where everyone ends up late at night, after

Participating anglers display their catch in the Bayahibe Torneo de Pesca.

well as chicken. A DJ blasts merengue, *bachata,* and reggaeton all day long throughout the tournament.

FOOD
Dominican

★ **El Rincón Criollo** (off main street, Calle Los Manantiales, across from Supermercado La Defensa, noon-9pm daily, US$3-5) is a must for authentic, homemade Dominican food and experiencing a local *comedor* with all of its special characters. Try *la bandera dominicana*, a plate of rice and beans with a meat stew, always on offer at lunchtime or a bowl of *sancocho,* a traditional meat and vegetable soup. There's a cheerfully painted green and pink outdoor terrace if you want to mingle and enjoy your meal with views of colorful Bayahibe.

Saona Café (Calle Principal, bayfront, tel. 809/833-0541, www.saonacafe.com, 10am-11:45pm Tues.-Sun., 2am close Fri.-Sat.,US$3.90-14.40) bills itself as a "Quebecois roots" bistro and was my favorite stop after a long day out exploring the village or the Caribbean waters. The food is cheap and tasty, and the service is friendly. There are all the usual choices from sandwiches to seafood. Be sure to ask about the lionfish, their specialty. The wide selection of mojitos don't disappoint; happy hours here are lively. It also has the best views for people watching across the bay.

International

If you're up for a good steak dinner, **Perlita Morena** (off the main street, tel. 809/833-0721, 11am-3pm and 6pm-11pm Tues.-Sun., US$10-20) serves up tasty imported Texan beef, grilled to your liking. **Mamma Mia** (next to Perlita Morena, off the main street, tel. 829/664-1694, noon-9pm Tues.-Sun., US$3-5) is probably the best deal in town for cheap but tasty Italian, served out of a small corner you might otherwise miss, one street behind the bay. Homemade dishes come out of a tiny kitchen, but portions are generous and flavorful.

a few drinks at the Super Colmado. The vibe and the music are Dominican, and the dancing goes on late. Note that Fridays get wild with a bar top strip show of near naked men and women doing all sorts of nasty acrobatics.

Festivals

The **Bayahibe Torneo de Pesca** is in its 10th year, and is a great time to visit this annual fishing tournament. Running Thursday to Sunday during the third week of May, up to 30 teams—mostly from Bayahibe, but a handful from Boca de Yuma, Saona Island, and La Romana—head out to sea to come back with the biggest and heaviest catch of the day by 5pm. I've seen catches weighing up to 14 kilograms (30 pounds), including mahimahi. The catch is weighed right in town at the entrance of the bay where the boats come in, in full view of the cafés and a highly excited local crowd of families and children. There are picnic tables set up above the bay in the grassy area, where folks go to buy a plate of freshly caught fish from the tournament, as

Mare Nostrum (Calle Principal, tel. 809/833-0055, www.marenuestro.com, noon-10:30pm Tues.-Sun., US$10-30) used to be a great spot for fine dining and the only upscale option. It still has the best view in town from an open terrace perched above the Bayahibe waters. The service leaves a little to be desired, but the ultra-long menu offers a wide choice of salads and especially seafood. Try the seafood carpaccio or lobster ravioli. There are endless pasta options, including risotto, as well as meat-free dishes.

Facing an idyllic portion of Dominicus Beach east of the all-inclusive resorts, **Anani Beach Restaurant** (beachfront, Av. Laguna, tel. 849/655-1608, 8am-midnight Fri.-Wed., US$5-10) serves up more Italian favorites, including fresh seafood. Meals and service are decent, but the location and privacy alone are worth the price of a meal on a stunning stretch. Funky yet soothing Latin beats accompany your meal, while the constant roll and crash of iridescent turquoise waves carries on a few steps away from your table. Swimming here is simply heavenly; take a dip pre- or post-meal. The restaurant also allows use of its beach chairs and showers for around US$3.

ACCOMMODATIONS

Bayahibe is pretty much divided into two zones so you'll have two choices of where to stay: at a hotel in the *pueblo* itself or at one the all-inclusive resorts lining Playa Dominicus, ranging from Iberostar to the Catalonia. Keep in mind that getting from one side of Bayahibe to the other will require a bus or an overpriced taxi. Those who stay in an all-inclusive might end up having to stick to their area or only come out once to visit the village. They also have the advantage, however, of being on the longest and prettiest beach stretch in Bayahibe. The exception among the all-inclusive resorts is Dreams La Romana, which is just a two-minute walk down the beach to the village. When you stay at Dreams or in the village proper, you'll have easy access to all the excellent local restaurants and nightlife.

Under US$50

Hotel Bayahibe (tel. 809/833-0159, www.hotelbayahibe.net/home.html, US$37) is your classic beachside hotel, but with a gorgeous art-decorated lobby and hallways cheerfully painted in tropical island colors. Rooms are equally spotless and bright, and have tiled floors and double beds, air-conditioning, mini fridges, TV. and phone. There are appealing

El Rincón Criollo

open-air balcony lounge areas on every floor. It's a good deal for the money.

The Italian-Dominican family-owned **Villa Baya Aparta-Hotel** (Calle Tamariando 1, U.S. tel. 888/790-5264 or tel. 809/833-0048, www.villabayahotel.com, US$40-50) offers a range of six well-appointed rooms, three suites with kitchen, and eight apartments inside a residential compound that is just two minutes' off the main drag and another two to the beach. The rooms are split across three-story peach buildings named after the islands off the coast of Bayahibe. There's a budget room for the solo traveler, but note that it's tiny, removed from the wireless Internet signal, and can get hot with just a fan. There's a central courtyard with a seating area, and continental breakfast and coffee are served daily with fresh fruits. Amenities include free wireless Internet and ample parking space. They can also help arrange excursions. It can get very noisy in the neighborhood, but that's what happens when you stay smack in the village.

US$100 and Up

The laid-back yet upscale ★ **Dreams La Romana** (Bayahibe Beach, tel. 809/221-8880, www.dreamsresorts.com, US$101-266) is located in Bayahibe, not in La Romana as its name suggests. The most recent, glorious addition includes an Adults Only Preferred Club section, worthwhile for those who want the perks of an all-inclusive and then some with private access to a stunning pool area, club lounge, two restaurants, a private beach section, and wireless Internet (otherwise not included). The resort is immaculately clean, spacious, and pleasant to the eye. Rooms are cozy, with comfortable beds, strong air-conditioning, flat-screen TVs, glass showers and soaking tubs, and a stocked mini fridge. The portion of Playa Bayahibe facing the resort is small but charming, although it can get crowded with lounge chairs. The farther right toward the dock you go, the quieter it is. Alternatively, you can walk a bit past the resort beach going toward the village and lay your towel there. The resort's several restaurants are quite good for an all-inclusive, and you don't need reservations for any of them. The best are Portofino and Olio. Other amenities include nightly entertainment with live music, a disco, and merengue dance classes on the beach during the day. If you're going to stay at an all-inclusive in Bayahibe or in La Romana province, this would be your best pick for a relaxing, pampered stay, only a stone's throw from the fishing village of

Dreams La Romana sits on a beautiful section of Bayahibe's beach.

Bayahibe with its own excellent local restaurants, shops, and bars.

Sandwiched among a row of beachfront resorts, **Iberostar Hacienda Dominicus** (Playa Dominicus, tel. 809/688-3600, www.iberostar.com, from US$169) is on the Dominicus side of Bayahibe, about 5 kilometers (3 miles) south of the village. It has a popular black-and-white painted lighthouse bar right on the beach that you can spot from miles away. The five-star resort is spotless and offers impressive comforts, à la Iberostar: fountains amid manicured grounds, three pools, seven restaurants, a fitness room, and nightly entertainment.

GETTING THERE AND AROUND

Getting to Bayahibe from La Romana is a mere 15-minute ride. If you're coming from La Romana Airport, expect to pay around US$30 for a taxi ride for up to five people. It's a lot cheaper to reach Bayahibe from downtown La Romana, where you can hop in a *guagua* from the Parque Central for about 60 pesos (US$1.33). If you'd rather invest in a taxi ride, contact **Gil Castillo** (tel. 809/420-0708), a taxi driver based in La Romana city, and try to negotiate; he can also shuttle you to Casa de Campo if you decide to visit Altos de Chavón or one of the restaurants (US$26 one way, 1-4 people).

If you're up for a day of sightseeing in La Romana city, find the local bus station in Bayahibe village: an orange-painted open garage labeled "ASODEMIROBAM Parada Bayahibe-Romana" located across from the giant parking lot where tourist buses park (ask anyone if you don't spot it). This will get you to La Romana for just 60 pesos (US$1.60) one way.

Getting around the village of Bayahibe itself is supereasy: just walk. No cars needed. It's a small place and you'll want to slowly wander its colorful streets and alleys and take photos of its traditional wooden homes. If you're interested in getting around by scooter or rental car, try **Dominican Emotion** (tel. 809/897-9270 or 809/452-5698, US$13/day for scooter, US$33/day sedan).

Information and Services

You'll find the answer to all of your needs right in Bayahibe village. If you're on the Dominicus side, there are plenty of small markets and services—just a tad pricier perhaps, because of the location.

In the village, there's an **Internet center** (25 pesos or US$.50/30 min., 8am-9pm Mon.-Sat.) with four or five desktop computers in a blue building on the main drag across from **CESTUR** (tel. 809/200-3500).

Supermercado La Defensa (Calle Juan Brito, tel. 809/833-0504, 7:30am-9pm daily), the local supermarket, is a few steps up from ScubaFun, next to the town's Super Colmado bar/corner store.

You'll find a **BanReservas ATM** beside Hotel Bayahibe—keep your wits about you anytime you are withdrawing money on the street.

The Samaná Peninsula

Look for ★ to find recommended sights, activities, dining, and lodging.

Highlights

★ **Cayo Levantado:** Three miles off the shores of Samaná, this dazzling island was once the site of a major Bacardi commercial—giving it the nickname "Bacardi Island" (page 151).

★ **Parque Nacional Los Haitises:** Take a boat tour to see giant mangroves and towering bluffs, teeming with birdlife and insights into the Taíno past (page 152).

★ **Playa El Valle:** The bumpy journey to this spectacular beach will reward with cliff views and authentic fishing scenes (page 154).

★ **Whale-Watching in Samaná:** Hop on a whale-watching vessel and witness the 40-ton humpbacks during their mating season from mid-January through March (page 155).

★ **Beach Hopping in Las Galeras:** Take a boat tour to three of the most beautiful beaches

in the DR: **Playa Rincón, Playa Frontón,** and **Playa Madama.** You'll spend an entire day swimming, sunbathing, and snorkeling (page 164).

★ **Pueblo de los Pescadores:** This charming beachfront row of restaurants, bars, and cafés in Las Terrenas will give you a taste of Europe in the DR (page 170).

★ **El Salto de Limón:** Horseback ride through lush forests to reach the peninsula's most spectacular waterfall, over 27 meters (90 feet) high (page 170).

★ **Playa Cosón:** Bury your toes in spongy sands and take a dip in warm waters at the most stunning beach in Las Terrenas. When you get hungry, indulge in some of the best fresh fish in the region (page 172).

Sticking out of the northeastern coast like an outstretched arm, the Samaná Peninsula is one big showcase of tropical splendor. Towering bluffs and lush green hills stand in contrast to the deep blue Atlantic. Rustic and uncrowded beaches stretch out against the horizon. Waterfalls cascade and coconut trees sway.

This coast is home to some of the country's top-rated beaches, including Playa Rincón and Playa Frontón in Las Galeras, and Playa Cosón in Las Terrenas. The rugged landscape of the peninsula, particularly in Los Haitises and El Valle, offers a lot of recreation options for those who like the outdoors. There are hard-to-reach corners, mysterious caves, glistening rivers, and far-flung beaches like Playa Morón and Playa El Valle.

The peninsula was an isolated escape before the opening of El Catey International Airport in 2006, followed by the installment of a scenic highway linking the peninsula to Santo Domingo in 2011. But Samaná's charm holds fast despite the growth. The vibe on the peninsula remains laid back. The melting pot of history, food, and cultures attracts independent and international visitors. Las Terrenas, a funky beach haven with a lively European beat, is particularly international, with boutique hotels, trendy cafés, and French bakeries. Opportunities to immerse yourself and mingle with locals abound with the peninsula's Afro-Euro Caribbean beat.

PLANNING YOUR TIME

There are three main areas you'll want to consider when planning a trip to Samaná Peninsula: the town of Santa Barbara de Samaná, Las Galeras, and Las Terrenas. The peninsula as a whole remains quite a distance from the rest of the island, but getting there has been made easier by an international airport at El Catey and a highway linking the peninsula and Santo Domingo in just 2.5 hours.

Las Galeras and Las Terrenas are your best bet for overnight stays. Samaná town doesn't have much happening unless it's humpback whale season. Passing through this scenic town to enjoy the gorgeous bay views and the

---

Previous: Playa Las Terrenas; Playa El Valle. **Above:** Playa Cosón.

The Samaná Peninsula

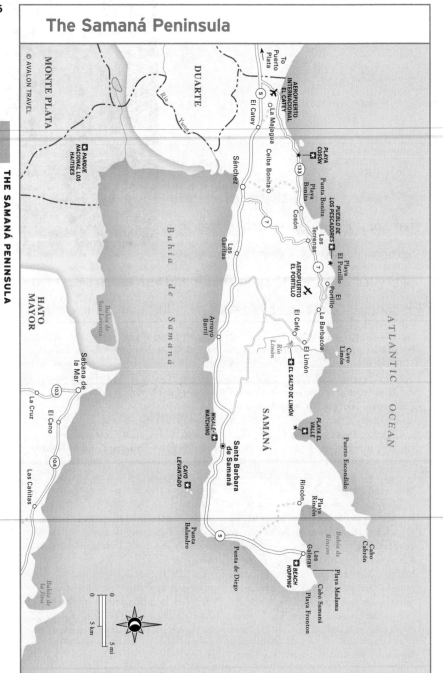

nearby El Valle region is worth it, however, even for just a day. Explore the town on foot to visit La Churcha, the Malecón, and its peculiar Bridges to Nowhere. Or head directly north to El Valle, where you can take in some of the most splendid scenery in the country at Playa El Valle.

From there, continue northeast until you reach the end of the road—literally—and you'll hit Las Galeras, a rustic and quiet fishing village blessed with amazing beaches, tucked between the Atlantic and a cliff-hugging coastline. Spend at least two days here to hike, dive, beach hop by boat, and indulge in the freshest seafood.

Head east for two more days to the more developed and trendy Las Terrenas, with its own funky, international beach vibe, where you can indulge in French cuisine, breathtaking beaches, and plenty of nightlife.

Santa Bárbara de Samaná

The Samaná Peninsula's capital, Santa Bárbara de Samaná—called Samaná for short—is a small scenic bayfront town of 15,000 inhabitants and a quiet hub where tourism, construction, and fishing are the main industries. Samaná's big moment comes once a year—from January through March—when the humpback whales make their entrance into the bay and stay there to mate and calve.

Much of the day-to-day activity in town centers along the Malecón, offering scenic strolls with views of bluffs and sea. Everyday life is simple yet authentic, with fishing and sailing boats floating in the bay, children playing soccer and baseball nearby in the center of town, and others resting up in the shade, by the water. At night, the Malecón echoes with merengue, and locals congregate by the sea for a twirl and a cold beer, particularly on the weekends. Past the small-town atmosphere, Samaná has made efforts to keep with the times, with modern European-style outdoor cafés and fine dining options lining the main drag. Freshly painted murals have given older haunts a face-lift.

It's true that not much goes on in this town when the whales aren't passing through and attracting thousands of cruise ship visitors

Samaná's bay

Santa Bárbara de Samaná

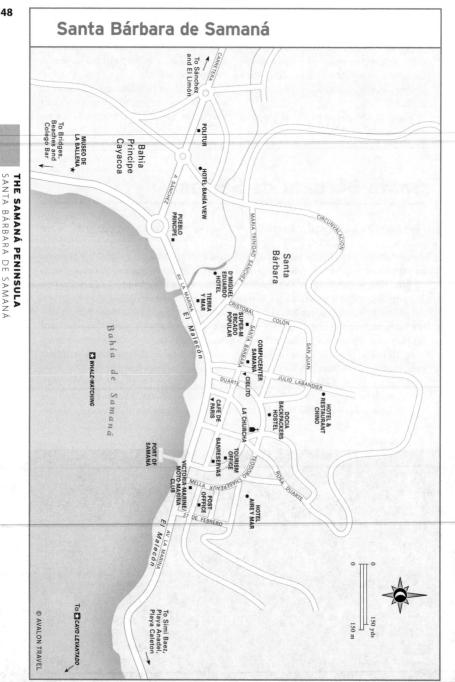

CARRETERA

To Sánchez
and El Limón

To Bridges,
Beaches and
Colego Bar

■ POLITUR

● HOTEL BAHIA VIEW

MUSEO DE
LA BALLENA

Bahía
Principe
Cayacoa

A. SÁNCHEZ

■ PUEBLO
PRÍNCIPE

CIRCUNVALACIÓN

Santa
Bárbara

MARIA TRINIDAD SÁNCHEZ

● HOTEL
EDUARDO
D'MIGUEL

▼ TIERRA
Y MAR

AV. LA MARINA   El Malecón

CRISTOBAL

COLÓN

SAN JUAN

● SUPER-M
ERCADO
POPULAR

SANTA BÁRBARA

COMPUCENTER
SAMANÁ

JULIO LABANDIER

● HOTEL &
RESTAURANT
CHINO

DUARTE

● CIELITO

B a h í a   d e   S a m a n á

✚ WHALE-WATCHING

▼ CAFE DE
PARIS

LA CHURCHA

● DOCIA
BACKPACKERS
HOSTEL

TEODORO CHASEREAUX

ROSA DUARTE

PORT OF
SAMANÁ

■ BANRESERVAS

TOURISM
OFFICE

■ VICTORIA MARINE/
MOTO MARINA
CLUB

MELLA

■ POST
OFFICE

27 DE FEBRERO

● HOTEL
AIREY MAR

AV. LA MARINA   El Malecón

To ✚ CAYO LEVANTADO

To Simi Baez,
Playa Anadel,
Playa Caleton

0   150 yds
0   150 m

© AVALON TRAVEL

and other nature lovers in the first quarter of the year. But Samaná offers easy access to Los Haitises National Park, and if you're passing through in the summer, you'll get to enjoy the unique harvest festivals celebrated by Samaná's African American descendants—complete with ginger beer, johnnycakes, and coconut treats.

Up in the hills, more guesthouses are tucked away in the neighborhood of Samaná Heights. Drive just a bit farther— past blankets of coconut trees and a string of uncrowded local beaches—and enjoy towering views over the Bahia de Samaná.

SIGHTS
El Malecón

Samaná's waterfront faces one of the most beautiful bays you'll see in the DR. Decorated with sailboats and in the distance, mangrove cays are connected by the town's famous Bridges to Nowhere. Like most *malecón* areas across the DR, it's quiet during the day as most folks relax on grassy areas under the trees away from the harsh sun yet close to the sea breeze, while the kids are jumping off the dock into the water. El Malecón comes to life at sunset with various kiosk bars and plenty of outdoor merriment along the water as well as the avenue across it. **La Ballena Blanca** is a bar on the bay open most of the day and night, with tables literally steps from the water below, under a tree. Across the street are more bars streetside, like **Tronco Móvil,** where locals play dominoes, throw back beers, and twirl to music late into the night.

Los Puentes (The Bridges to Nowhere)

Looking out from the waterfront avenue, you'll immediately notice a long bridge—in actuality, a series of two bridges, linking two small offshore cays that look like deserted mangrove isles. Soon you'll wonder just where exactly the bridges lead, because they seem to just stop at one point in the middle of the water. The answer is, nowhere! Samaná's iconic, dated bridges are a sight in and of

themselves. They do lead from town—there is public access to the stairwell to begin hiking the bridges adjacent to the Cayacoa resort—to two small cays. The first stretch alone is 200 meters (655 feet) long and takes you to the first and most frequented plot on Cayo Linares with a small beach where locals hang out and swim.

These bridges were a project of former DR president Joaquín Balaguer, who was inspired by and misread an architectural plan once put together by Napoleon. He saw Samaná's bay and surrounding hills as an ideal base for his own conquering ambitions and ordered the construction in the 1970s. Balaguer's grandiose plan included turning Samaná into a resort town, despite the difficulty of access at the time, and adding a restaurant on the first cay. Unfortunately, nothing but its shell remains (be careful climbing up those steps to the top of the first cay).

The dilapidated condition of the bridges and steps are evident as you make your way across them, and you might also wonder how they've lasted this long. But they remain sturdy and safe for now to cross and hike for stunning views of the bay. The sunrise from here is well worth it.

The Market

Samaná's small but lively, covered market reveals the abundance of the area's fresh produce, as well as its primary cultivation: the coconut. You'll find everything you need here, from local fruits and vegetables—including yams, plantains, green bananas, sweet potatoes, glandules—to fish and a butcher's shop where the meat hangs in plain view. Locals are friendly here and don't mind photos—just ask first.

Museo de la Ballena (Whale Museum & Observatory)

A bit hidden from plain view, the town's **Museo de la Ballena** (tel. 809/538-2042, www.samana.org.do, 8:30am-3pm Mon.-Fri., weekends by appointment only, US$2.20 or RD$100) is dedicated to the visiting mammals that bring in tourists three months out of the year. It's a small space, exhibiting a handful of informative billboards and photos about the history of Samaná and on the humpback whale species. It also showcases the full skeleton of Nima, found dead in February 1993 amid rocks off the coast of the peninsula between Samaná town and Las Galeras.

La Churcha

The oldest and most significant structure in Samaná is the 18th-century **La Churcha**—a Dominican play on the English word *church*—officially the Iglesia Metodista de San Pedro. It's a beautiful gothic structure brought over from England in 1901 with red corrugated iron roofing standing out against a sea of modern buildings. The story behind this place of worship, still very much used today, goes back to its founding in 1824 by freed African Americans who moved here from Philadelphia and New York at the invitation of Haiti, then-ruler of the entire island of Hispaniola. The new residents came here with their spiritual leader, Reverend Isaac Miller—his tomb remains onsite, with his wife's.

From the beginning, the denomination was the African Methodist Episcopal Church Metodista Episcopal Africana. Its historic importance led La Churcha to be declared a *patrimonio cultural* or part of the DR's cultural heritage. If you get the chance, meet the current pastor Albert Moses James Cuello, who comes from Barahona, south of the DR and is a descendant of the *cocolos,* yet another group of African descendants who came from various parts of the English-speaking Caribbean to work on the sugarcane fields of the south. The mass at La Churcha—called *culto*—is held in Spanish, with some English hymns and chants.

Inside you'll find parts from the original structure, as well as refurbished and replaced pieces. The altar is an original, as are the side pews and the two stained-glass windows. At the back of the church you will find a photo of the first structure erected before the current one was brought over from England. There are schedules posted on a notice board, as well as events. This is also where you'll find information on the harvest festivals held from June through October on the church grounds celebrating all things agriculture—as their ancestors did—with African-influenced foods including *pan inglés,* coconut dishes, and ginger beer. The church maintains additional chapels in different parts of the Samaná Peninsula in Limón and Las Galeras.

La Churcha

Samaná's African American Heritage

Between 1824 and 1825, around 200 families came from the East Coast of the United States—specifically from Philadelphia and New York—at the invitation of then-president Jean-Pierre Boyer of Haiti. At this time Haiti had control over the entire island of Hispaniola including the DR. As one of the first leaders of Haiti after the Haitian Revolution of the 19th century, the president established a pro-African immigration policy with the aim of welcoming those of who had been stripped from their native lands and sold into slavery, offering them a form of repatriation to a better place as Africa was considered too far and expensive to achieve, as well as dangerous healthwise. These families reached Samaná by boat, bringing along their traditions as well as their AME religion. Once here, they were given land.

Although the Samaná population includes many nationalities from various parts of the world, these *Americanos de Samaná*, as locals call them, had more influence on Santa Barbara de Samaná's culture than any of the others. They inspired a cuisine with typical African foods, including *pan ingles*, coconut-based meals, and ginger beer. They established their own church—La Churcha as it's famously known, now a *patrimonio cultural*—and still hold African Methodist masses. Various pastors came to serve there from Jamaica to Puerto Rico; those who spoke Spanish brought their Latin influence along.

Today, descendants of those African Americans speak Spanish and have adopted Dominican culture, but many still celebrate their own tradition of the harvest festivals, a religious celebration in which farmers give thanks to God for water, land, and agriculture, and bring fruits and produce to the church. There's plenty of outdoor cooking, and ginger beer and coconut fish are popular. The festivals take place every Sunday from July to October. A calendar is published and posted inside La Churcha for those interested in attending. The last Sunday of October is the biggest celebration of all the harvest festivals and recognized as an official holiday by the Samaná City Hall.

★ Cayo Levantado ("Bacardi Island")

This large cay off the coast of Samaná, about 10 minutes' or 6 kilometers (3.7 miles) away by boat, has one of the most stunning white sand beaches on the peninsula. Known as "Bacardi Island" because it was the site of a popular Bacardi commercial in the 1970s, it's an idyllic spot to spend a day. The island is part private—the all-inclusive Grand Bahia Principe Levantado occupies two-thirds of the island—and part public. The beach is spacious, and the turquoise waters are shallow at first, if rocky in parts. The views of the bluffs and the bay in the distance are stunning.

Walk to the back of the beach and you'll find a sort of "beach food court" where all the various fish shacks and local restaurants tempt customers with fried catch from snapper to lobster, along with all the typical Dominican sides and fresh piña coladas (US$5). There is one local restaurant that's closer to the beach than the others and comes highly recommended: **La Ballena Blanca.**

To get to Cayo Levantado, you can opt for an organized tour—most operators include a stop here along with a boat excursion to Los Haitises National Park or whale-watching in season. If you'd rather just head here solo, you can catch a boat from the Samaná Port (the main dock on the waterfront)—for about US$33 round-trip or RD$1,500 for up to three people; the larger the group, the more room you have to bargain. You'll find additional boat captains outside of Samaná town—on the road to Las Galeras, on Playa Carenero, in the village of the same name—they offer rides to the cay at a reasonable price. You can bring your own snacks, and they do sell ice on the island. Guests of the Grand Bahia Principe Levantado get a free boat ride from the resort's private marina just outside of town.

Tour excursions flock to this island, and during the high season it can be crowded with the addition of cruise ship visitors. Avoid weekends or visit in the slow season to really enjoy this gorgeous stretch.

★ Parque Nacional Los Haitises

A protected area since 1974, **Parque Nacional Los Haitises** is undoubtedly one of the most unique parks and landscapes you'll see in the Caribbean. Just 15 kilometers (9.32 miles) out from Samaná Port, there are a series of towering rock mounds—heights ranging between 40 and 335 meters (130 and 1,100 feet)—blanketed in vegetation and stretching over an area of 1,598 square kilometers (617 square miles). Birds flock overhead as fishers navigate the surfaces to and from the beaches where they camp out. Farther on, mangrove tunnels hiding ancient Taíno caves waiting to be explored.

From a Taíno word meaning highland or land of mountains, Los Haitises covers 3,217 square kilometers (1,242 square miles) and hill elevations of up to 40 meters (130 feet), and can only be reached by boat. The ecosystem of the park ranges from rainforest to coastal wetlands, and there's approximately 2,000 mm (79 inches) of rainfall every year. Mangroves cover an area of about 38 square miles (98 square kilometers); this is one of the only spots in the country to have all four species of mangrove: red, black, white, and button. The diverse environment allows for a great deal of flora and fauna within the park, spanning over 700 species of plants and 230 species of birds, including Ridgeway's hawk and the magnificent frigatebird. Underwater are coral reefs supporting fish, crustaceans, and mollusks, not to mention marine mammals such as dolphins and manatees.

The most common way to tour Los Haitises from Samaná town is to sign up for a boat excursion. If you're visiting in the off-season, you can sail to the park, and from there, hop into kayaks to get closer into the mangrove channels. There's also an entrance to Los Haitises National Park by Bayaguana on the road from Santo Domingo to Samaná, and through private property in Hato Mayor if you sign up for the Cueva Fun Fun horseback riding and spelunking excursion.

Boat tours from Samaná take you along the park's various points of interests and past the area's spectacular scenery, from the various cays with bird colonies to beaches that lead to cave access. Among the more distinctive cays are the **Boca del Infierno** and the **Isla de las Aves** or **Cayo de Pájaros**—the birds' isle—where brown boobies, pelicans, and

Cayo Levantado

Best Tours on the Samaná Peninsula

A handful of tour operators across the Samaná Peninsula offer similar excursions at competitive rates. Below are a handful of the best trips and companies. Note that if you're here in high season (winter), you might be sharing the sights with cruise ship visitors. Most operators run hotel guest excursions on different days, but check to make sure you're not booking on one of these days.

WHALE-WATCHING IN SAMANÁ BAY

Kim Beddall is your best bet for whale-watching tours, through her operation **Whale Samana** (Av. La Marina, tel. 809/538-2494, www.whalesamana.com, US$62pp, includes Marine Mammal Sanctuary fee). The marine mammal specialist hails from Canada and has observed and studied Samaná's humpback whales since 1983, as they faithfully return to give birth in Samaná's waters every year from mid-January through late March. Observe the humpbacks with Kim and her crew from a two-deck, spacious 17-meter (55-foot) boat with 360-degree views. Excursions leave at 9am or 10am, but from February through mid-March there are also 1:30pm outings.

ECOTOURS ON THE PENINSULA

Flora Tours (Calle Duarte, tel. 809/240-5482, www.flora-tours.net, US$55 pp half-day) offers nature-focused excursions. The highlight is a half-day kayak excursion down the mangrove channels of the Cosón River, just off the coast of Las Terrenas. The kayaking, good for all levels, ends at Playa Cosón. The full-day boat trip to Los Haitises National Park is also comprehensive, taking you through the unique ecosystem to get close view of birds and mangroves and making multiple stops at the various Taíno caves tucked inside this natural wonder.

BOAT TOUR OF LAS GALERAS' BEACHES

Exploring Las Galeras' top four white sand beaches, reached most easily by boat, is a bona fide adventure. Sign up with **Tour Samana with Terry** (tel. 809/538-3179, www.toursamanawith-terry.com) to brave the turquoise Atlantic with a local captain. You'll hop into a 24-foot panga-style boat and pass by gargantuan cliffs and impressive waves. The first stop is at Playa Frontón; try not to gasp as the boat turns the corner and the beach appears, with its coral-filled turquoise waters. A beach stop with snorkeling—you must pack fins to avoid stepping on sea urchins—and coconut water is in order. Next you'll head back out to Playa Madama, another small, white sand stunner. Following that is the renowned Playa Rincón, where you'll have a lobster lunch, and plenty of time to swim, snorkel, or sun yourself on a paradisiacal, two-mile white sand stretch.

HORSEBACK RIDING IN LAS GALERAS

Go deep into the rustic countryside of Las Galeras with Rudy from **Rudy's Rancho** (La Caleta, tel. 829/305-3368, rudysrancho@yahoo.com, www.rudysrancho.com, from US$20-50). Born and raised in this corner of the DR, Rudy has known the area inside out since he was a kid and has been horseback riding just as long. Now in charge of his family's horse farm, Rudy offers rides through the countryside of Las Galeras to reach its best beaches, including Playa Madama, Playa Rincón, and the less crowded La Playita. Beginners and advanced riders are welcomed.

frigates circle continuously overhead. The various caves are often visited on foot; all are easy to hike, with handrails and interiors that are well lit. The **Cueva del Ferrocarril** or **Cueva de la Línea** is considered the most significant due to having the highest number of petroglyphs and rock art. The name of the cave, which translates into "railway cave," refers to the previous existence of a railway line that ran through this area, used to carry the area's rice harvests to the dock. There's a giant opening in the ceiling of the cave 600 meters (1,969 feet) up, letting light into the chambers. Many of the drawings represent animals, especially birds, and deity masks, though many remain skeptical as to the authenticity of the drawings and what really is of Taíno origin.

BEACHES
★ Playa El Valle

Playa El Valle, 30 minutes north of Samaná town, is a sight for sore eyes. As its name suggests, this 2-kilometer (1.2-mile) stretch of golden beauty sits at the foot of a lush valley, flanked on all sides by towering cliffs. The beach is development-free and uncrowded, and the water is a turquoise green. Rocks separate the two sides of the beach, but there are openings easily crossed on foot. Playa El Valle is as rustic as Samaná itself and reflects the peninsula's true natural splendor.

The road to get here is bumpy along the second half, and it's quite a trek, which is why the beach is so uncrowded with tourists. Swimming here is dangerous during the winter season. Stick close to shore—there have been drownings in recent years—and do not go out alone. Onsite are a few local seafood restaurants—seek out the one on the far edge, **Clarissa's** (tel. 809/667-0213), a cozy palapa facing the most gorgeous part of the beach. Call her the morning before your visit to arrange food.

To get to this beach by car, head toward Dominican Tree House Village, then continue around the resort down a dirt road, crossing a dry riverbed along the way, and eventually you'll end up at the stretch. On the far western edge of the beach—cars can drive down this dirt path—you'll spot the mouth of the river El Valle.

Other Beaches

Playa Los Cayos is a lovely golden stretch facing part of the Grand Bahia Principe Cayacoa with warm waters and gorgeous views of the bridges, Samaná Bay, and Cayo Levantado in the distance. The public entrance is from town, by the bridges. Driving past the main entrance to the Grand Bahia Principe Cayacoa, you'll end up going downhill to **Playa Escondida**—also facing the hotel, from the lower level. There, you can lay your towel in the sand on the far right of the beach, on the other side of the hotel lounge chairs, and do as locals for a dip in the sea.

In town and facing part of the bay before you reach the bridges is a public stretch that is barely worth mentioning; it's visibly neglected and there's litter scattered about the shores; it's primarily to enjoy the views of boats in the bay and grab a drink at the onsite Colego Bar.

The Bridges to Nowhere lead to two small

Parque Nacional Los Haitises is a birding hotspot.

cays—**Cayo Linares and Cayo Vigia**—the first has a small strip of beach, accessed by a flight of stairs after walking the bridge. The scenery is as rustic as the bridges themselves, but the water is good to swim in. This is where Samaná's locals hang out and cool off on Sunday and public holidays. The unofficial name of this beach, according to those who grew up here, is *playa de los cueros,* or lovers' beach—couples come to this out-of-the-way spot for some memorable romantic activities.

Just five minutes outside Samaná on the road to Las Galeras is **Playa Anadel,** popular with locals. It's not the prettiest, save for the palm trees that provide some shade, but there are a couple of local restaurants and you can swim off the dark sands. Five minutes farther east, driving in the direction the Simi Baez Marina, immediately past its entrance, you'll find the slightly hidden **Playa Caletón** populated with dozens of tall coconut trees. Just drive right onto the beach and park anywhere (except under a coconut-bearing tree). It's a dark golden stretch where a few locals and fishers come to relax. An equally pretty and rustic beach is **Playa Los Grayumos,** accessible through the marina or by making a right turn before you reach the marina entrance.

SPORTS AND RECREATION
★ Whale-Watching

The number one reason to stay in the town of Santa Barbara de Samaná, and what brings thousands of tourists here every year from mid-January through end of March, is the humpback whales that make their way to Samaná's Bay to mate. There are several operators in town offering a whale-watching tour, but there's little argument about the best one to be on. You'll learn the most from marine mammal specialist Kim Beddall, owner of **Whale Samana** (Av. La Marina, tel. 809/538-2494, www.whalesamana.com, US$62, includes sanctuary fee). From aboard the *Pura Mia,* a 17-meter (55-foot) whale-watching vessel, you'll see these spectacular creatures flipper and tail lob, among other surprising moves. There's enough space on the boat that you'll move around comfortably, and the wealth of information is shared in several languages when needed. If you get seasick, take some pills; if you're not sure, there will be bags available on board.

Another popular tour operator is longtime running **Moto Marina** (Av. La Marina 3, tel. 809/538-2302, www.motomarinatours-excursionsamana.com, from $90 pp), which offers

Playa El Valle

Samaná's Humpback Whales

For three months from January through March, Samaná Bay on the extreme northeast of the DR is graced with humpback whales, or *ballenas jorbadas*. The humpback whales *(Megaptera novaeangliae)*—called this because of the way they hunch their back when diving—begin their journey months earlier, migrating from the North Atlantic to the Caribbean to mate and calve in the warm and protected shallow waters off Samaná.

Centuries ago, as early as the 17th century to be exact, whales were commercially hunted for their oil and for making flexible materials. Their numbers dropped dramatically by the 1930s, until the International Whaling Commission imposed a moratorium in 1966. More threats to these mammals include human activity like marine pollution, entanglement in fishing gear, and boat activity. In 1996, the Bay of Samaná was declared part of the 1,180-square-meter (12,700-square-foot) Marine Mammal Sanctuary of the Dominican Republic and whale-watching regulations were imposed. The Marine Mammal Sanctuary itself, comprising Banco de la Plata, Banco de la Navidad, and Bahía de Samaná surrounding Samaná, was established in 1986, prohibiting any kind of harassment of marine mammals. These regulations limit the number of vessels allowed in the bay, and there are specific guidelines on surface whale-watching and direction and speed of approach.

Every year, the whales return like clockwork, as do over 35,000 tourists who come to see them. It's a show you cannot afford to miss if passing through the area at this time. Adult humpbacks can reach up to 12 to 15 meters (39 to 49 feet) in length and weigh up to 40 tons. They feed on fish, crustaceans when they are in the North Atlantic, and can consume up to a ton in just a day. Once they reach Samaná's waters, they no longer need to feed and focus only on mating and growing their calves—the warm water helps the calves to grow fast while they feed on mother's milk—yes, they produce a thick, rich in fat milk—and gain weight and prepare for their migration back to the North Atlantic.

Their return to the bay is so regular that some have been named—including Salt, who has been visiting since 1976, and has birthed 12 calves over the last 35 years. Remember that whether or not you see the creatures making amazing dives or moves will depend on how lucky you are, but spotting their presence in the waters is guaranteed.

To learn more about these creatures, you can visit the whale museum in town, **Museo de la Ballena** (tel. 809/538-2042, www.samana.org.do, 8:30am-3pm Mon.-Fri., weekends by appointment only, US$2.20 or RD$100), a small space with informative text displays about the mammals; or better yet, sign up for a whale excursion with expert Kim Beddall and **Whale Samana** (Av. La Marina, tel. 809/538-2494, www.whalesamana.com, US$62, includes sanctuary fee). There's also an annual **Festival de las Ballenas Jorbadas** in mid-January, which officially launches humpback whale-watching season.

a combo trip to the nearby island of Cayo Levantado after the whale-watching, where you'll have plenty of swim and beach time. Trips depart at 9am.

Kayaking

Those staying at the Grand Bahia Principe Cayacoa will have access to complimentary kayaks from the water sports shack. Just hop in and explore the bay. Around the Bridges to Nowhere, stop for a break on the beaches and a swim. In the off-season, **Whale Samana** (Av. La Marina, tel. 809/538-2494, www. whalesamana.com) offers kayaking trips to

Los Haitises National Park. You'll sail over first and then explore the park's stunning mangroves up close.

If you're fortunate enough to stay at **Paraíso Caño Hondo** (tel. 829/259-8743, www.paraisocanohondo.com), within the Haitises National Park boundaries, you can hop on their kayak tour along the Cano Hondo River and the bay of San Lorenzo within the park. The trip departs at 3pm and lasts a couple of hours.

Ziplining

Just outside of town, 30 minutes up a long

Samaná's Traditional Dances

Santa Barbara de Samaná's African-influenced culture is evident during the *fiestas patronales* or town patron saint festival in the first week December, when the African drums come out. The beats and chants echo through the small town's narrow streets and seafront avenue while couples perform traditional African-influenced dances. There's the *bambula* (known as *la bambula de Samaná*), danced by both men and women. They hold hands while shaking their hips from side to side and dancing in circles as the drummers chant. The women wear long traditional dresses. You can also see this dance being performed at the church harvest festivals. Another dance, considered erotic (and obscene by some) for its suggestive movement, is the *chivo florete* or the *chivo de Samaná* (goat dance), in which the man is standing behind the woman and they both jump forward together... simulating the sexual act performed by goats.

and occasionally bumpy road, Dominican Tree House Village offers the popular **Samana Zipline** (tel. 809/542-3005, www.samanazipline.com, 8am-3pm daily, US$60 pp, US$45 under 12)—probably the best engineered zipline in the country—that sends you towering over a waterfall and 122 meters (400 feet) above the verdant hills of El Valle. Getting to the starting point of the zipline itself is a challenge on a steep 20-minute hike, but you'll soon forget that when you're soaring above the mountains. There are 12 lines and 13 stations, the longest line reaching 366 meters (1,200 feet), for a total of 2,256 meters (7,400 feet) of zipline. Lines have an integrated brake system. If you're an adrenaline junkie, this one is for you! If you sign up with **Tour Samana with Terry** (tel. 809/538-3179, www.toursamanawithterry.com, from US$100 pp), after the two-hour experience you'll stop at El Valle beach and/or swim in a waterfall, among other options.

To get to the Samana Zipline on your own, follow Route 5 through town until you come to the turn off on the left to El Valle (there's a big sign and you can't miss it). Then follow the road all the way north. It turns into a bumpy dirt road, and soon you'll see the entrance to the zipline, which is well indicated. You can also take a motorbike taxi (about US$5) or a taxi (US$20 up to 3 persons) to get there.

ENTERTAINMENT AND EVENTS
Bars and Nightclubs
The little nightlife there is in Samaná is enough to bring the town alive. You'll find most of it along the bars on the waterfront avenue, both directly facing the sea and across the main road. They are your typical Dominican-style, open-air spaces where you can get your drinks and dance to merengue, bachata, and other Latin tunes on a small floor all night. One of the most popular ones is **El Tronco Móvil** (across Malecón, tel. 809/232-0000, from 10pm, Thurs.-Sun.). Follow the sound; you won't miss the action.

Cielito Disco (Calle Rosa Duarte 2, tel. 809/849-3024, free for ladies, 9pm-4am Tues. and Fri.-Sun., US$1.10 men) is where the hardcore partygoers continue after midnight. There's almost always a time to party. Tuesday means drink specials, while Friday is ladies' night, with three free drinks 9pm-11pm.

Festivals and Events
Besides Samaná's main yearly event of the visiting humpback whales, there are a couple of cultural celebrations worth noting. In June, an annual **Marisco Ripao Festival** takes place over in the neighboring town of Sanchez, celebrating all things seafood, along with music, of course.

The African American descendants of Samaná celebrate an annual **Harvest Festival**—*fiestas a la cosecha*—every Friday starting in July through October, held outdoors in the yard of the historic La Churcha in town. The last Sunday of October—an official holiday in Samaná—is the biggest harvest festival celebration of all. Expect plenty of outdoor cooking, coconut seafood, and ginger beer.

Casinos

The casino at **Grand Bahia Principe Cayacoa** (Puerto Escondido, U.S. tel. 866/282-2442 or tel. 809/538-3131, 8pm-midnight daily) is tiny, but it's the only one in town. It is a viable option if you're really desperate to gamble the night away. The views from the hotel entrance are an added bonus.

SHOPPING

The shopping isn't mind-blowing in Samaná town. The **Plaza Pueblo Principe** (Av. La Marina, 9am-9pm Mon.-Sat.) in a row of colorful Caribbean-style shacks across the Malecón is home to a couple of souvenir stores with your usual trinkets and beach accessories. You'll also find a pharmacy here. For souvenirs, you're better off continuing up the same road for more local souvenir stores and more choices.

FOOD

On the way to Samaná from Santo Domingo, off the Autopista del Nordeste and past the first toll—you'll spot ★ **Gran Parador Bellamar** (next to Petronas gas station, Carretera Samana Km. 1, tel. 809/741-6069, 6am-11pm daily, US$6.50). Affordable, clean, and friendly, this outdoor grill and restaurant cooks a variety of meats. Patrons pull over to fill their stomach before continuing their journey. Pick among their baby back ribs, sausage, pork, or goat, with tasty sides such as mashed cassava and plantain. Wash it down with a cold Presidente.

In Samaná town, grab a cup of coffee and a croissant at **La Espiga** (Av. La Marina 3, tel. 809/538-2742, US$1.50-4), a cute, small shaded café with four tables on an outdoor terrace along the seafront boulevard. It's a good spot to start the day with wireless Internet. They have an excellent continental breakfast deal for coffee, juice, a French pastry for just US$2.65.

★ **D'Milagro Sazón** (Av. Maria Trinidad Sanchez, next to Tierra y Mar, no phone, 11am-8pm daily) is popular for affordable and tasty local fare, including the Samaná specialty *pescado al coco* (coconut whole fish). A daily dish of rice, beans, and chicken is just US$3.30 (RD$150). There's an open-air shaded seating area, and takeout is possible.

Steps from the Malecón, under a giant and spacious palapa with ceiling fans, old dining room chairs and tables on a stone covered floor, the local **Tierra y Mar** restaurant (Av. Maria Trinidad Sanchez, tel. 809/538-2436, 9am-10pm daily, US$2.25-14) offers, as its name suggests, surf and turf options. Also on the menu are pastas, local salads, soups, and a daily *bandera dominicana* lunch special—the typical plate of meat, rice, and beans (US$3.30). Service is slow but friendly; if no one comes to your table, don't hesitate to call out loud to the server as locals do.

For pizza and other basic fare, you could go to **Café de Paris** (Av. La Marina 6, tel. 809/359-9763, 8:30am-11:30pm daily, later close weekends, US$4-10), also decent for afternoon cocktails and people watching in the shade.

Tucked up in the hills, a short and steep walk from town, **Restaurante Chino** (Calle San Juan 1, tel. 809/538-2215, restaurant_chino@hotmail.com, 11am-11pm daily, US$3-20) is a longtime favorite, thanks to its spacious outdoor terrace with bay views. Service can be slow, but the excellent and reasonably priced menu ranges from Chinese options—from fried rice to lo mein dishes—to Dominican favorites like *chicharrón de pollo* or fried chicken. Portions are large.

Taberna Mediterranea (Av. La Marina, tel. 829/994-3634, 10am-11pm Tues.-Sun., US$5-20) has a rustic, Spanish tavern feel with its outdoor terrace across from the Malecón. Expect tasty seafood dishes, including paella, tapas, steaks, and pizza. The wine selection is ample, and the sea breeze and view complete the experience.

A surprisingly sophisticated dining experience in Samaná, and a favorite among well-heeled Dominicans, is ★ **La Mata Rosada**

(Av. La Marina, tel. 809/538-2388, 11am-3pm and 7pm-11pm Thurs.-Tues., US$5-15). A romantic all-white and bamboo interior draws you in immediately with its open shutters, flowing drapes, mood lighting, and a breeze that sweeps in from the sea on the other side of the street—with the occasional outside clamor. The menu, specializing in seafood, is a filled with tantalizing dishes, starting with the fish and mango tartare in vanilla oil. Ask for the *pescado al coco*, not on the menu but served if you ask; it is to die for. Pastas and turf options are also available.

ACCOMMODATIONS
Under US$50

Across from La Churcha, **Docia Backpackers Samaná** (Calle Theodore Chasereaux, tel. 809/538-2497, US$22) is the best newcomer to the area, a spot for those seeking a basic, clean place to stay. The two-year-old Dominican American-owned hostel offers four-people dorms (US$10) as well as 12 private rooms with fan (US$22), air-conditioning (US$31), and hot water. Rooms on the top floor have air-conditioning and a veranda to themselves. If you walk in, you're likely to get a lower rate. A communal kitchen and an outdoor veranda are the hostel perks you get to enjoy. There's wireless Internet in the reception area.

A better option is ★ **Samana Island Hostel** (Calle San Juan 8, corner of San Juan & Duarte, www.tropicalislandbb.com, US$20-24 pp), offering basic rooms with bunk beds accommodating up to four people, or lovely fully furnished one-bedroom studio apartments (US$40) with kitchenette, just a couple of blocks from the Malecón. Amenities for all include wireless Internet, Netflix, fridge, microwave, and coffeemaker. The owner's daughter also runs a lovely hostel (that looks more like an upscale B&B) in Jarabacoa.

Run by the jovial Spanish-speaking owner Muñeca, **Hotel D'Miguel Eduardo Hotel** (Calle Maria Trinidad Sanchez 5, tel. 809/538-2195, dmigueleduardohotel@outlook.es, from US$17) is the best deal in town for the location—just one street up from the waterfront. Bright orange and lime walls on the second floor of the building hug 13 rooms with private bath. Rooms are pricier with air-conditioning (US$28.79); some have double beds.

One block farther up is the 16-room **Hotel Samana Spring** (Calle San Cristobal 94, tel. 809/538-2946 or 829/763-2048, US$35). Rooms are basic but clean, with strong air-conditioning, hot water, cable TV, free coffee, and wireless Internet. A stone's throw from restaurants and Samaná's waterfront, with friendly staff, it's a solid pick for those on a budget.

A series of steep, narrow steps that aren't for the faint of heart lead up to the small, bright yellow **Hotel Aire y Mar** (Calle 27 de Febrero 4, tel. 809/820-7200, US$30) perched in the Samaná Hills neighborhood, set a five-minute walk from the Malecón. The location is decent and the views gorgeous, if you can deal with the stairs. There are dogs on property, but they remain inside. The better rooms have terrace views. The cheaper rooms at the back with little natural light and consist of a fan, bed, and small private bathroom. There's a shared kitchen and veranda and wireless Internet. The place is spotless and run by a nice, English-speaking Dominican couple.

US$50 and Up

Hotel Chino (Calle San Juan 1, tel. 809/538-2215, hotelchino.samana@hotmail.com, US$85-103) is a 15-minute walk uphill away from the waterfront, but its panoramic terrace views of the bay and town, tastefully decorated rooms, and onsite restaurant perhaps might justify the high price for this area. The spacious rooms offer air-conditioning, king or double beds, wireless Internet, and breakfast.

The Grand Bahia Principe Cayacoa Hotel (tel. 855/350-5535, www.bahia-principe.com, from US$95-145) has the best views of the bay and town, without a doubt. The 295-room all-inclusive hugs the Bay of Samaná and faces the town's two beautiful beaches. Any direction you look from its entrance, rooms, as well as its various terraces, offers great scenery. The elevator bridge to the beach might be slow and annoying to some, but it's a stunning view of the Atlantic Ocean as the glass panoramic elevator carries you down. If you can, stay in the oceanfront suites with a private balcony and 180-degree views over the beach and Cayo Levantado beyond, with the boats moored in Samaná Bay on the left. Rooms are cozy, ranging from standard to junior suites, with minibar, air-conditioning, cable TV, and spacious baths. Three pools allow for less crowded areas, and a second beach below the main hotel building is less crowded and quieter. Restaurants are decent for an all-inclusive—the à la carte seafood restaurant is especially good—and service is friendly. Every hour, a shuttle takes guests back and forth from the Pueblo Principe shopping plaza in town.

Dominican Tree House Village (El Valle, tel. 829/542-3005 or U.S. tel. 800/820-1357, www.dominicantreehousevillage.com, US$245) is adjacent to the most exciting zipline in the country, but it also holds its own with its dramatic jungle treehouse setting just a 30-minute drive outside of town. The lodge is a green escape from Samaná's beaches tucked inside a rainforest backdrop. Coffee and lime trees lead to a swimming pool, and suspension bridges take you to open-air tiki huts suspended in the forest, where your bedroom awaits. The cabin you pick—all 20 of which have wood floors, flowing curtains, fans, mosquito nets, and mini hammock chairs—will depend on your comfort with heights, because it is not for the faint of heart. Electricity is available all night. Breakfast and dinner are included, shared in the communal dining space. A 10-minute ride away is the stunning Playa El Valle, where you can enjoy a local seafood lunch.

Occupying two-thirds of Cayo Levantado is the 268-room **Bahia Principe Cayo Levantado** (www.bahia-principe.com, U.S. tel. 855/350-5535, from US$240), a five-star all-inclusive resort that's a favorite among honeymooners for its seclusion from the mainland and white sand beaches. To be honest, it isn't as uncrowded or idyllic as it might seem to be on a private portion of an island; the hotel is often booked solid, and the beach stretch isn't large enough to be isolated. Well-appointed rooms are divided into "villages" of deluxe suites with garden or sea views, and each gets a butler. An additional 69 new standard rooms were being built as of October 2015. There are two large pool areas, one of which is the quiet corner. The Orquidea buffet has decent options,

Hotel Aire y Mar has glorious views over the bay.

and four additional restaurants offer Italian, Mediterranean, and à la carte options. Guests are transferred to the island from the resort's private Simi Baez Marina, a short distance outside Samaná town.

INFORMATION AND SERVICES

A branch of **Farmacia Carol** (Av. El Malecón, tel. 809/538-2543, 9am-11pm daily) is located within the Pueblo Principe shopping row on the main drag.

Supermercado Mimasa (Av. Francisco del Rosario Sanchez 26, tel. 809/538-2217, or 809/538-2448 for delivery, 8am-10 pm daily) has the essentials to stock up on groceries or bathroom toiletries, and includes a bakery.

Centro de Especialidades Médicas (Calle Coronel Andrés Díaz No. 06, tel. 809/538-3999 or 809/539-3888, www.cmes. com.do) is a respected medical facility with Cuban doctors on hand and 24-hour emergency service. There's also a branch in Las Galeras.

GETTING THERE AND AROUND

Fly into Samaná's **El Catey International Airport**—also called Aeropuerto Internacional Presidente Juan Bosch—with service from various airlines including JetBlue, WestJet, and Air Canada. The airport is approximately 40 minutes' drive to Samaná town. You can hop in a taxi outside the airport or you can schedule your pickup online through **Tour Samana with Terry** (www.toursamanawithterry.com, US$85 one-way/1-4 people).

Caribe Tours (Av. El Malecón 5, Samaná, tel. 809/538-2229, US$7.80 or DP350) offers daily service between Samaná and Santo Domingo, a direct route via the new highway, with various departures. The trip is just 2.5 hours long, part of it along winding roads offering spectacularly verdant scenery.

Aside from the *boletería* or ticket booths, inside the Caribe Tours Samaná terminal is a bank teller and *cambio* for currency exchanges. The bus terminal is also just a two-minute ride away from the Grand Bahia Principe Cayacoa. Taxi drivers and bike taxis will be approaching you from the moment you begin to step off the bus.

Taxis can be costly, as is the case across the DR, and prices are set by the Samaná taxi cooperative: US$40 Simi Baez Marina round-trip, US$40 Las Galeras one-way, US$120 Playa Rincón, US$80 El Limón round-trip, US$120 Las Terrenas round-trip. One friendly and professional licensed taxi driver is **Miguel Angel Samboy** (tel. 809/827-5470)—you can set up your own custom day trip with him if you wish.

Motoconcho taxis (or *conchos* as locals like to say) are popular in these parts, because of their affordability and the small size of these fishing villages. Also the intense afternoon heat makes them somewhat more bearable to hop on than in big cities. If you want to catch one, call **Isael Jasmin** (known as "Augustin," tel. 829/228-5389, from US$1.25), a staple near the beach. He'll take you for a quick ride around the *pueblo* for around US$5, depending on your negotiation skills, and will even ride as slow as you wish if you're as afraid of motorbikes as I am.

Moto-carritos or *motoconchos de carreta* are another typical option in Samaná—motorbike drawn carriages. You can easily spot them parked along the Malecón, especially by the main dock, waiting for passersby. They cost approximately US$5 for a ride and a quick tour around town—a cheaper alternative than taxis, but not as cheap as the *motoconchos*.

Las Galeras

If there's any place that deserves to be called a "sleepy fishing village," it's Las Galeras. Located 30 minutes outside of Samaná town, at the end of the road running northeast, it's as remote as it gets on the peninsula. This rustic corner of the DR has a breathtaking Atlantic coastline and a daily *pueblo* life where all there is to do is play dominoes under the shade and throw back beers with friends after hours. Fruit and veggie shacks sit on the road next to horses and donkeys munching on grass. Taking delight in the nature that surrounds could mean hiking in the village, horseback riding through the *campo*, going fishing, or hopping on a boat ride to the area's spectacular Atlantic-facing beaches.

Las Galeras is known for being home to some of the most beautiful beaches in DR—including Playa Rincón, a popular excursion offered from all points on the peninsula. Despite the hordes of tourists who descend on it for a day's beach escape, it's still less frequented than neighboring, trendy Las Terrenas. There's just one main drag in town, dotted with most of the guesthouses, restaurants, and cafés. Spend a couple of hours in the heart of the village and the sense of community is evident—everyone knows each other by name, and you'll see the same people out and about regularly.

BEACHES

For a small village, Las Galeras is blessed with stretches that will have you gasping. There are numerous ways to get to them—consider hiking, horseback riding, or the most popular of all, boat excursion.

Please remember that when visiting any of these beaches or sights in Las Galeras, you should not go alone or at deserted times—opt for a *motoconcho* ride or sign up for a group excursion to avoid isolation and possibly robbery, which has happened in the past (the downside of beautifully isolated locations). Also, ask the locals about the weather and current conditions before you jump in—better safe than sorry.

Playa Las Galeras

The plainest of the beaches is the one right

Playa Las Galeras

Las Galeras

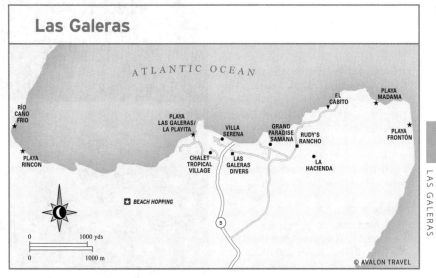

ATLANTIC OCEAN

RÍO CAÑO FRIO

PLAYA LAS GALERAS/ LA PLAYITA

VILLA SERENA

GRAND PARADISE SAMANÁ

RUDY'S RANCHO

EL CABITO

PLAYA MADAMA

PLAYA FRONTÓN

PLAYA RINCON

CHALET TROPICAL VILLAGE

LAS GALERAS DIVERS

LA HACIENDA

BEACH HOPPING

0   1000 yds
0   1000 m

© AVALON TRAVEL

in the village where the excursion boats and fishers park themselves, but even **Playa Las Galeras** holds its own. There's sea grass in parts, but the water is delightful for a swim—walk the beach all the way east to the Grand Paradise Samaná resort, where you can swim even if you can't lounge on their chairs. Sunsets are lovely here, and the village's main bar echoes that give the stretch a fun vibe.

La Playita

A favorite of mine, the perfectly white **La Playita** is 10 times more beautiful than the main beach of Las Galeras, and it's just a 10-minute walk from there. Look for the roadside sign for La Playita just off the end of the main road before you reach Las Galeras beach. Walk down the path until you hit an iron gate. Ignore the "private" sign and push open the gate, then take the first right and walk all along the pathway past some private vacation homes, down until you see a beach up ahead, past a wooded section. This pathway from town can seem a bit isolated and eerie, but it's generally safe—just don't wander here at night and use common sense. There are a couple of good restaurants on La Playita beach as well as chairs and kayaks (US$11/two

hours) for rent. Palm trees line the shore, and there are lovely views of Rincon's bay in the distance, shade under almond trees, and water in varying hues of blue. Entry is shallow and easy—follow the path that is free of sea grass. In the evening, large frogs come out to play on the beach path. To drive to the beach, take the turn off the main road that says toward Chalet Tropical and keep straight until you hit the end and the beach parking lot.

Playa Rincón

The famous **Playa Rincón,** consistently ranked as one of the DR's best beaches, is a brilliantly white, soft sandy strip located just 10 minutes by boat from Las Galeras village. Flanked by Cabo Samaná and Cabo Cabrón, you can walk the length of the beach, from the frequented side (with calmer waters and local restaurants) to a deserted stretch (don't walk it alone), before arriving at the end favored by locals, where the river meets the sea. At this end there is more wave action and bordering cliffs. There are kayaks for rent (US$20/hour) on the restaurant side—ask for Federico if you don't see anyone by the kayaks.

Most arrive at Playa Rincón from Las Galeras' beach by boat—approximately US$77 for up to five persons (contact local boat captain and well-known reliable guide **Carlos** (tel. 829/694-0254) or ask for him at the beach if you can't call). Those with sturdy cars can arrive on the other end—look for the turnoff on the road south to Samaná. If you're not one for crowds—it can feel touristy in high season—take a boat ride here around 3pm on a weekday after most of the tourist groups have left. Walk with your guide (not alone) to the far eastern end of the beach, where you can dip in Caño Frío River and perhaps even sample local food cooked over an open fire.

Playa Madama

Playa Madama is an approximately 15-minute boat ride on choppy Atlantic waters from Las Galeras' beach. It's an isolated and small crescent-shaped stretch, hiding a cave and sitting at the foot of a dense forest that some hike to reach here (do not attempt this alone due to robbery risk). The sand is pristine, the location romantic for two. But look out for the white urchins on the beach. Some hike here from La Hacienda or get here on horseback. The cliff-top views of the beach and scenery below are more breathtaking that way if you have the time.

Playa Frontón

Formerly the site of *Survivor* episodes, **Playa Frontón** rivals the beauty of Playa Rincón. If you ask me, it has a greater wow factor, hugged along its coastline by gigantic cliffs made out of *roca de mármol*—metamorphic rock with marble characteristics. The sight of this easternmost beach as your boat turns the curve on approach is breathtaking. Locals consider Playa Frontón the jewel in Las Galeras' crown. Its not being readily accessible means it has maintained its beauty. Picture the color contrast of iridescent emerald waters reflecting the corals below, against a white sand layer ahead and beyond it, near ebony rocks. You'll want to jump right in from the boat—but beware: there are small and large black sea urchins and corals teeming below, which also make it one of the best sights for snorkeling.

Playa Frontón

Wear fins if you're swimming anywhere beyond the immediate shoreline.

Behind the reef, humpback whales can be spotted from shore as they make their way to the Samaná Bay during the mating season from mid-January to mid-March. Walk on the far east of the beach, hiking through a wooded path, and you'll come across a small cave—where the *Survivor* series also filmed—and another stretch and cove where it's a lot easier to swim away from the corals.

Playa del Amor

If you ever get there, you'll likely be the only one at **Playa del Amor**—a beach only reachable by boat. As romantic as its name suggests, it's a teeny yet delightfully deserted golden stretch with white shells scattered about on the beach and sea floor. Bring your picnic cooler to spend the day. There's a lot of wave action so stick close to shore.

★ Beach-Hopping

The best way to experience Las Galeras'

beaches is by taking a boat tour to three of the most beautiful in the DR: **Playa Rincón, Playa Madama,** and **Playa Frontón.**

The most affordable option is to contact the local **Asociación de Lancheros de Las Galeras** (Playa Las Galeras, tel. 809/916-7591, US$75 for up to 4-5 persons), headquartered on the beach and offering set rates for boat tours. You can also just walk up to Las Galeras beach in the village and negotiate your boat ride with one of the captains. They don't speak a lot of English, but if you name the beaches you want to see, they'll understand. There's always one or more of them in the early morning, when tours depart, and at the end of the day between 3:30pm and 4:30pm.

For an organized all-day tour of the three beaches, with lunch and snacks included, contact **Tour Samana with Terry** (tel. 809/538-3179, www.toursamanawithterry.com, US$100 pp); owned by longtime expat and Samaná resident Terry.

RÍO CAÑO FRIO

On far end of Playa Rincón you'll find **Río Caño Frío**—this river feeding into the Atlantic dotted with mangroves and a local favorite on weekends for families seeking a cool swim in hot weather. The farther back you walk away from the beach, the more breathtaking the river water as it turns bright turquoise, and you find yourself swimming while surrounded by denser woods and mangroves. On this beach end of the river are a row of open-air shacks where Dominican women fry up fresh fish and plantains (US$9 for a plate, or US$15 for lobster; ask for **Adelsia's** stand) on open wood fire. Meals are served on shaded picnic tables, and the mood is jovial and ultra-Dominican, a far cry from the western end where your typical tourist beach chairs await.

BOCA DEL DIABLO

The Mouth of the Devil or **Boca del Diablo** is a well-known simple natural attraction: a blowhole, which on a windy, clear day, sees the sea shoot its waves straight up into it, splattering loudly above the rocks at almost 10 meters (33 feet) high. It almost sounds like a devil's roar. The surrounding wild tropical and cliff scenery is no less breathtaking as the water. Catch a *motoconcho* if you can, and leave valuables behind. The road leading up to Boca del Diablo is well past the sign for Playa Rincón in an isolated area.

Río Caño Frio

SPORTS AND RECREATION
Snorkeling and Diving

Las Galeras Divers (Main Street, Plaza Lusitania, tel. 809/538-0220 or cell tel. 809/715-4111, www.las-galeras-divers.com, from US$85/two-tank dive) sits along the main road steps from the beach, offering excursions to several of the peninsula's dive spots, including Piedra Bonita and Puerto Malo, off Cabo Cabrón, or off Playa Frontón. Two-tank dives are offered every morning in high season; stop in or call a day prior to see what's available. The shop also offers PADI certification and cave diving excursions north to Lake Dudú in Cabrera for the experienced.

ScubaLibre (Grand Paradise Samaná, tel. 809/958-9119, www.divingscubalibre.com/lasgaleras, US$70/two-tank dive) takes you snorkeling right off Las Galeras beach or diving off Cabo Cabrón and Cabo Frontón. Free pickups for off-resort guests. You can also snorkel at the **Kaio Natural Aquarium** (on Grand Paradise Samaná beach, tel. 809/883-6118, US$15)—an artificial reef created to protect marinelife, where you can observe Caribbean critters right off the beach facing Grand Paradise Samaná resort.

Windsurfing and Kayaking

You'll find a windsurfing shack on the beach at **Grand Paradise Samaná** (Playa Las Galeras, U.S. tel. 888/774-0040 or tel. 809/538-0020, $30/one-hour class); kayaks are also available for rent for nonguests ($10/hour).

Fishing

Casa Dorado (Casa Dorado B&B, Calle Playa Colorada, tel. 829/933-8678, casadorado@gmail.com, from US$280/half-day) offers some of the best deep-sea fishing in the DR. Year-round excursions take you to catch your own mahimahi, red snapper, grouper, or yellowfin tuna in 7- to 9-meter (22- to 28-foot) panga or sportfishing boats.

Horseback Riding

You'll have a better day and stay, and even gain a friend, just from meeting Rudy from **Rudy's Rancho** (La Caleta, tel. 829/305-3368, rudysrancho@yahoo.com, www.rudysrancho.com, from US$20-50), a mile from the village or a 10-minute walk up from the end of the Grand Paradise Samaná's beach. The dynamic young Dominican quit his resort job of four years to realize his dream since being a teenager: turning his family's farm—his grandparents were one of the first to move to the DR and

Horseback riding is a great way to explore Las Galeras' landscape.

Las Galeras 60 years ago—into a 10,000 square meters (2.5 acres) horse ranch and escape for those who not only love to ride but also want to experience a taste of Dominican *campo* life. It's the only Dominican-owned horse farm in Las Galeras, all the more reason to support this wonderful man's efforts. Rudy guides as well as takes you on horseback rides through the gorgeous countryside to experience a taste of Dominican life. The ranch has now been operating for five years, and Rudy's 15 horses with names like Medialuna and Chuco (warrior) aren't too huge. Onsite, the farm is set up like a typical Dominican countryside home, with an outdoor chicken coop, goats roaming, and an outdoor wood fire kitchen.

Also a little over a mile from the village, past Grand Paradise Samaná resort, **La Hacienda Hostel** (Camino al Faro, tel. 829/939-8285, www.lahaciendahostel.com, US$75 full day) is at the entrance of hiking as well as horseback riding trails into Cabo Samaná National Park. Owner Karin is a horse lover and can pick the right mounts and trail for your group, as well as take you on some of the most unique countryside back roads to the area's beaches. You can take a motorbike taxi to get here if you don't want to walk in the sun. It's a great spot for young, independent, and active travelers.

ATV Riding

You can bump and ride your way through the countryside onto Playa Rincón in your own ATV with **Tauro Tours** (tel. 849/658-8997, http://taurotours-excursionsamana.com, US$86/four hours).

FOOD

Boulangerie La Marseillaise (Main Rd., no phone, 8am-8pm daily, US$1-11) has your French croissants, baguettes, and espressos; that's when you're not tempted to stay for lunch or dinner to sample their seafood dishes. It's ideally close to a number of guesthouses and walking distance from the main beach. Farther up the drag is **Comedor Rossy** (Main Rd., tel. 809/477-0168,

11am-8pm daily) serving local fare, especially seafood, at good prices under a giant palapa. The specialty there is *camarones al ajillo* or *a la criolla*—shrimp in a garlic or tomato based sauce (US$11). They also have your usual rice and beans with stew chicken options.

Ristorante Roma (Hotel Plaza Luisitania, tel. 809/538-0178, contatti@plazalusitania. com, US$5-11) is a hop and a skip from the main village beach, and the Italian menu is surprisingly solid—particularly their thin crust pizzas, which are generous in size. Sit on the outdoor terrace and enjoy the breeze blowing in slowly from the nearby ocean.

The beachfront **La Playita Restaurant** (La Playita, tel. 849/627-2514, 9am-8pm daily, US$3-15) is a safe bet for a day on the stretch with a menu ranging from local rice and beans dishes to sandwiches and burgers.

★ **El Cabito** (tel. 809/697-9506, www.el-cabito.net, 11am-9pm Tues.-Sun., US$5-15, cash only) is one of Las Galeras' gems, and where you'd go to treat yourself to a spectacular sunset dinner with equally satisfying view of the Atlantic Ocean from your cliff-top table. The restaurant specializes in seafood—if you can, opt for the paella. A motorbike ride here shouldn't cost more than 100 pesos (US$2.20) one-way, or 500 pesos (US$11) round-trip for two in a taxi. It's a popular spot so reserve ahead.

Another idyllic restaurant with stunning panoramic views and a lounge feel perched high above the ocean is **El Monte Azul** (La Gazuma, tel. 849/249-3640, 10am-9pm daily, US$7-15, reservations recommended), run by a French and Laotian couple. It is an adventure from the moment you begin to make your way here, particularly the last stretch getting to the top of the mountain—catch a *motoconcho* or a taxi with all terrain wheels. The food is no less disappointing—once you get over the view (you might not), order the tenderloin steak, the lionfish, or a pad thai.

Treat yourself to lunch at **Villa Serena** (Playa Las Galeras, www.villaserena.com, 9am-2pm daily, US$5-15)—the salads in particular are delicious.

ACCOMMODATIONS

A stone's throw from the main village beach, ★ **El Pequeño Refugio** (Main Rd., tel. 849/267-5848, www.elpequenorefugiodesamana@gmail.com, US$35) is ideal for solo travelers on a budget. The small, partly thatch funky hotel offers artsy rooms with all you need—mosquito-netted double beds, wireless Internet, and tasteful art. There's outdoor courtyard seating in a shaded garden for a peaceful respite from the sun. Ask to stay in the loft for more space and ambience. On the ground level is a bar and lounge, where the owner serves up breakfast—from crepes to omelettes—while the bamboo walls are covered in "El Arte de Ivan" abstract creations. An outdoor shower on the ground floor is for those who can't wait to get a cocktail after a day's excursion. There are even more incredible deals on the rooms in the slow summer season.

A block away, inset off the main road, **La Isleta** (Main Rd., tel. 829/887-5058, www.laisletasamana.com, from US$82) has seven self-catering units set inside a gated residence. The overpriced, slightly dated lofts have a full kitchen, but the layout isn't as comfortable as you'd expect with a steep staircase to the bedroom and fans only (no A/C). The location is the best asset—just a two-minute walk across the hotel to reach the Las Galeras public beach.

Chalet Tropical Village (Calle Chalet Tropical, tel. 809/901-0738, www.chalet-tropical.com, US$75-155) is off the main drag and down a side road that's far enough that you'd need a bike—but the hotel's set up is unique. You'll find three *chalets* or individual thatch-roofed huts that fit up to five people—with a single bathroom, except for Chalet 3 which has two—as well as two chalet guesthouses where rooms share the villa's amenities, ideal for solo travelers. Everything is made of local wood and bamboo, while the verdant yard separating each cabana is dotted with hammocks and flowers. The hotel can arrange for whale-watching tours to Samaná in season, and it's a short distance to La Playita or Las Galeras beach.

Grand Paradise Samaná (Playa Las Galeras, U.S. tel. 888/774-0040 or tel. 809/538-0020. www.grandparadisesamana.com, US$104-192) is the only all-inclusive traditional resort in Las Galeras. Tucked on one end of Las Galeras beach, rooms range from superior to deluxe, but your best bet will be the bungalows which have a loft design for a second bedroom, a full kitchen, and a spacious outdoor terrace. Room perks include minibar, air-conditioning, satellite TV, safety deposit boxes, and hair dryers. The food across the various restaurants is average, at best, but the bartenders make stiff drinks and there are two pools available, with one tucked away from the crowds. The highlight here is undoubtedly the beach—the best stretch of Las Galeras Beach—peppered with ultra-tall coconut trees and facing calm turquoise waters. There's a sandy path that takes you directly from the beach onto the more public side of Las Galeras Beach. Note that on the eastern end of the beach, you'll find several locals renting horses, as well as a snorkel shack for trips to the Aquarium, just a mile offshore. Rudy's Rancho is also a 10-minute walk east of Grand Paradise Samaná.

The all-white, green-roofed ★ **Villa Serena** (beachfront Las Galeras, tel. 809/538-0000, www.villaserena.com, US$110-120) feels more like a friend's dreamy Victorian beachfront home than a hotel. It's also as serene as its names suggests, facing a quiet stretch of Las Galeras Beach, yet just a three-minute walk down to the village or to La Playita in the other direction. The boutique hotel has a sophisticated, old-school feel with grand staircases, wicker furniture, and four-poster beds in 21 rooms facing the sea and pool, which you can enjoy from a terrace. There's an excellent, small restaurant onsite, which although pricey, serves some of the best food I've had in Las Galeras. Rooms include air-conditioning, wireless Internet, phone, and a separate, spacious bathroom. Bikes are complimentary. It's a great spot for a couple's weekend romance getaway or for families seeking a restful escape after excursions.

INFORMATION AND SERVICES

You can find a tourist police presence on Las Galeras beach and near Grand Paradise Samaná resort. **Banco de Reservas** has a 24-hour ATM on the main drag. There's also an ATM at Grand Paradise Samaná resort.

The **pharmacy** (Main Rd., 9am-8pm Mon.-Sat., no working phone) is next to Las Galeras Divers. For medical services, contact **Centro Médico Las Galeras** (Main St., tel. 809/538-0134, lasgaleras@cmes.com.do).

GETTING THERE AND AROUND

The closest airport to Las Galeras is the **Samaná International Airport El Catey** (also known as Aeropuerto Internacional Presidente Juan Bosch, AZS, tel. 809/338-5888), about 45 miles west from Las Galeras. You'll have to find your way to Santa Barbara de Samaná town first if you're taking public transportation—from there a local minivan bus runs east to Las Galeras (US$2.20 or RD$100). Alternatively, an airport taxi ride

costs approximately US$100 one-way for up to five passengers.

There's a reason Las Galeras remains the authentic fishing village it is, and not as crowded as Las Terrenas: there are no direct coach or bus service to Las Galeras from Santo Domingo or even from Las Terrenas. You'll have to transfer through Samaná town first. **Caribe Tours** (Av. 27 de Febrero, tel. 809/576-0790, www.caribetours.com.do, RD$270 (US$5.88) one way) offers departures from Santo Domingo—and then from Samaná town you'll catch a local **bus** leaving from the market in town (as you enter the market compound, turn left and look for parked minivans). You can also hire a **taxi** driver if you prefer (US$60 round-trip to Samaná town); it's a 30-minute drive from Samaná town to Las Galeras. Call **Argenis Perez** (tel. 809/509-0187).

If you choose to rent a car and drive from Santo Domingo, the smooth **Samaná Highway** (also called DR 7 Autopista del Nordeste) takes you on a two-hour leisurely drive to Las Galeras—the route begins with Autopista de Las Americas or Highway 3 (about 18.6 miles east of Santo Domingo)—via tolls (have change ready of about five 100 pesos bills) and via Samaná town. If you're

All of Villa Serena's suites have seafront views.

coming from Puerto Plata, drive along the coastal Highway 5 all the way to Samaná (be wary of turning off into Santo Domingo when reaching Nagua). Getting around Las Galeras is easy: it's so small and everything is centered in one area. Walking is your best bet if you're just in the village. You can also use a bicycle from your hotel—it's fairly safe since there's only so much traffic down the main road or the side country roads. Motorbike taxis and taxis are also plentiful. The taxi drivers are parked by the beach entrance, at the end of the main drag in town. Prices are set to destinations, but in the low summer season you might have more room to bargain. *Motoconchos* are easy to spot, just a block before you reach the end of the main road to the beach, waiting in the shade.

Las Terrenas

With one foot in the Caribbean and the other in Europe, Las Terrenas—or *La Terrena* as Dominicans like to pronounce it—is one of those multicultural beach towns you could picture yourself spending your winters in. This town is a 24/7 flip-flop kind of place, yet trendy and cutting edge in its cuisine and nightlife. There's something to be said for its scenery—the main road hugs the coastline and white sand beaches all the way through town, stretching from Playa El Portillo to Playa Bonita, and the palm-studded Playa Cosón. After sunset, it's time to wine, dine, and eventually dance the night away on the Pueblo de los Pescadores row of beachfront bars.

The village prides itself in being multicultural and multigenerational. Expats will tell you that this is some sort of magical place outside of social norms, where age and class don't matter. What's for sure is that each year Las Terrenas attracts more and more beach-seeking tourists, trendy jet-setters from Santo Domingo, and backpackers in search of a lesser touristy and more affordable corner of the DR. Various languages can be heard while wandering around the village. There's a large French enclave in particular, as evidenced by the number of French restaurants and cafés around town, as well as the French *tabac* (tobacco shop) and newsstands inside the main shopping center, Plaza El Paseo. The transportation is as diverse as the residents; motorbikes, cars, and ATVs all fill up the streets.

★ PUEBLO DE LOS PESCADORES

You might forget you're in the Caribbean when you're hanging out at **Pueblo de los Pescadores,** the main drag of Las Terrenas. This area used to be a fisherman's village, as the name suggests, and now houses lively sea- and beachfront bars and restaurants. These places light up at night, attracting residents and visitors alike—in particular the international crowd. The range of cuisine represents the diverse nationalities of the town's residents. Here you can have a gourmet meal blending European, American, and Dominican specialties, while enjoying the sound of waves rushing to shore.

A fire destroyed the heart of the Pueblo de los Pescadores in May 2012, and its rebuilt version is less rustic and more modern—but while development continues to add shiny buildings, the laid back attitude of Las Terrenas remains.

★ EL SALTO DE LIMÓN (EL LIMÓN WATERFALL)

One of the crown jewels of Samaná, if not the entire DR, is the near 30-meter-tall (100-foot) **El Limón Waterfall.** Recognized as a natural monument in 1996, it is tucked inside a humid subtropical forest, with a cascade that gushes down moss-covered rocks into a stunning emerald-turquoise pool. The water is cold and refreshing, but not unbearable.

Las Terrenas

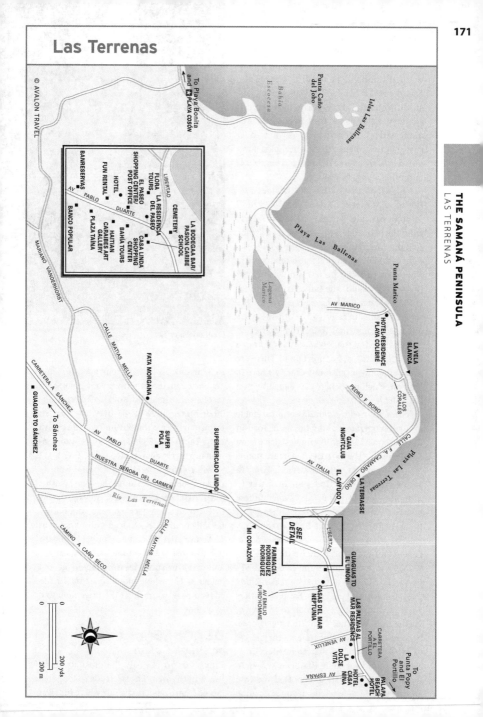

© AVALON TRAVEL

To Playa Bonita and Playa Cosón

Punta Caño del Jobo

Bahía Escocesa

Islas Las Ballenas

Playa Las Ballenas

Punta Marico

Inset detail:

LIBERTAD

CEMETERY

PASIÓN CARIBE SCHOOL

LA BODEGAA BAR/

LA RESIDENCIA DEL PASEO

FLORA

EL PASEO SHOPPING CENTER POST OFFICE

SHOPPING CENTER TOURS

HOTEL

FUN RENTAL

BANRESERVAS

BANCO POPULAR

PLAZA TAINA

HAITIAN CARAIBES ART GALLERY

BAHIA TOURS

CASA LINDA SHOPPING CENTER

AV PABLO DUARTE

AV MARICO

HOTEL-RESIDENCE PLAYA COLUBRE

LA VELA BLANCA

AV LOS CORALES

PEDRO F BONO

CALLE F.A. CAAMAÑO DEÑO

GAIA NIGHTCLUB

AV ITALIA

EL CAYUCO

LA TERRASSE

Playa Las Terrenas

CALLE MATIAS MELLA

FATA MORGANA

MARIANO VANDERHORST

CARRETERA A SÁNCHEZ

To Sánchez

GUAGUAS TO SÁNCHEZ

AV PABLO DUARTE

SUPER POLA

NUESTRA SEÑORA DEL CARMEN

Río Las Terrenas

SUPERMERCADO LINDO

CAMINO A CAÑO SECO

CALLE MATIAS MELLA

MI CORAZÓN

SEE DETAIL

FARMACIA RODRIGUEZ RODRIGUEZ

AV EMILIO PURO/HOMME

CASAS DEL MAR NEPTUNIA

LIBERTAD

GUAGUAS TO EL LIMÓN

LAS PALMAS AL MAR RESIDENCE

AV VENELUX

LA DOLCE VITA

AV ESPAÑA

HOTEL CASA NINA

PALAPA BEACH HOTEL

CARRETERA A EL PORTILLO

To Punta Popy and El Portillo

0   200 yds
0   200 m

Most excursions offer horseback riding all the way to the start of the steps leading down to the falls—a 45-minute journey on a pathway that's mostly stone and dirt—but you also have the option to hike. The walk is of moderate difficulty and allows you to fully appreciate the various plants, fruit trees, and fauna of the park at your own pace, as you wander past guava and mango trees, pineapples, hummingbirds, with more streams and honeybees humming along the way.

The last portion of the hike includes a series of steps that easily lead you down to El Limón's cascade. There, you can carefully enter the pool and swim—if you are a strong swimmer, head to the back of the pool to the right of the falls and you'll find a small cavern, where you can sit for a few minutes behind the nearby rush of the falls. As of summer 2015, the water levels have been low due the serious decline in rains (while others say it's due to environmental abuse from extraction from riverbeds). You might see a local or two jump from the top, but don't do it! There are rocks and only locals know exactly where to land on which particular day, depending on the water levels.

There are various *paradas* or local horse excursion operators along the main road in the town of El Limón, 30 minutes' drive from Las Terrenas. They are the departure points for the excursion to the waterfall. You can save a chunk if you find your own way to El Limón town by bus or car to one of these *paradas*. Among the most recommended of these are **Rancho Parada La Manzana** (tel. 829/931-6964 or 809/916-0892, alcalanuez@gmail.com) and **Santi Rancho** (tel. 829/342-9976, www.cascadalimonsamana.com, US$15 pp to hike, US$20 horseback); fees include guides, lunch, and park fees. Santi also offers a unique canyoning excursion to El Limón, via the river. Whichever outfitter you choose, be sure to call ahead of time so they know to expect you, and so that no hustlers deviate you from your route (it's been known to happen when tourists are spotted walking around in El Limón; tell them you're heading

El Limón Waterfall

to Samaná). To go with tour operators and get picked up directly from your hotel, contact locally owned **Violeta Fun Tours** (Calle 30 de Marzo, tel. 829/705-0119, www.violettafuntours.com, US$55) or **Tour Samana with Terry** (tel. 809/538-3179, www.toursamanawithterry.com, US$65 pp on Tues.).

After your waterfall tour, if you want to cool off some more, stop at the local favorite, **Manantial de Limón**—a freshwater spring by the road where locals love to cool off, especially on the weekends. It's also known as El Arroyo after the name of the bar beside the pool. Across the street are livelier *colmados* and drinking spots, blasting merengue and bachata. The whole block turns into a fun spot to park yourself in the afternoon and weekends.

BEACHES
★ Playa Cosón

Playa Cosón is easily the most stunning beach in the area. The stretch is so long that it goes from a wild, rustic side where the river runs in the background to a perfectly golden shore. Sundays are a lively time for seafood shacks—Luis' is the best—and families enjoying *la playa* Dominican-style. There's a kite-surfing shack onsite, as well as plenty of lunch tables and lounge chairs for spending the day. A 10-minute ride up the road from Playa Cosón and a half mile along is the Boulevard Turístico del Atlántico is **Mirador Cosón,** a scenic stop offering panoramic views of the coconut tree-filled hills and Cosón beach below. It's probably one of the best photo ops in Las Terrenas.

Other Beaches

Las Terrenas' beaches begin at **Playa El Portillo,** where the Grand Bahia Principe El Portillo sits, and continue along the main road and through various parts of town all the way up to Playa Bonita, which then links to Playa Cosón. As if on purpose, the beaches go from the less attractive to the most stunning. **Playa Punta Popy** is peppered with palm trees and social activity. Multiple lively open bars and restaurants line the area, and in the distance kitesurfers and paddleboarders pass on another on the open water. The sunsets here are gorgeous—ideal for watching from the Mojito Bar, mojito in hand, or from Playa Caribe Bar.

Playa Las Terrenas, in the heart of town, is decent enough, but certainly not the best for swimming or sunning all day given the choices you have. It faces the noisy village and plenty of passersby on the roadside. Continue a tad west and you'll hit **Playa Las Ballenas,** beginning beyond the Pueblo de los Pescadores and across from Hotel Alisei, stretching along that strip's vacation villas and other small hotels. The name comes from a set of three rocks jutting out of the water a few miles out from shore—they resemble the humpback whales that visit the peninsula every year. It's ideal for a swim, for a nice long beach walk or jog, and picnicking all day. It's shallow enough upon entry, which makes it good for families, and there isn't much wave action. The sunsets here are lovely, particularly across from Hotel Playa Colibri. Locals say Playa Las Ballenas is the best one in town, and I have to agree. There are no constant pestering vendors, either—save for the occasional men on bikes yelling out for fried fish or drinks, and a mobile masseuse. You'll find a handful of excellent and small beachfront restaurants scattered along the way, as well as a sailing club renting kayaks and hobies. At the edge of Las Ballenas is the stream that feeds into the ocean, a local favorite for cooling off

Playa Cosón

as if in a swimming pool and hanging out with drinks, food, and music.

A 10-minute scooter ride out of the center of town takes you to Playa Bonita—a nice long golden stretch that is less crowded during the week and attracts those who want to spend the day away from the village on a beautiful golden-white strip lined with boutique hotels, villas, and a couple of excellent restaurants. The sand has receded in parts, but it's still a gorgeous beach, with leaning coconut trees and a few almond trees providing shade for your towel. Continue walking to the far western end of the beach and you'll find the Hotel Atlantis and its famous French restaurant, and beyond that, when you reach a sandbank-like corner, Punta Bonita—which marks the point where it joins the stunning Playa Cosón.

Playa Morón is quite the trek approximately 40 minutes out of Las Terrenas by motorbike, but it's a nice ride into the countryside. The bumpy gravel roads passes farmlands and kids collecting mangoes from the trees. Once there, you'll appreciate the golden beach with its turquoise waters and tall palm trees, and the complete seclusion. Locals with horses for rent might harass you a bit to go on a ride, but just refuse politely if you're not interested. Stay close to shore as the waves can get strong here.

SPORTS AND RECREATION

Snorkeling and Diving

Snorkel or dive with Samaná Diving (front of Puerto Plaza, Caamaño Deño, tel. 809/786-1043, www.samanadiving.com, US$90/2-tank dive, US$399 Open Water Certification, US$40 snorkel). Dives take you to various shipwrecks, like the *Portillo,* as well as cave diving at Dudú in Cabrera. Be sure to book on their site to get an online discount. You can also rent snorkel masks and fins (US$15, with US$30 deposit). Over at Profundo Blue (next to Hotel Playa Caribe, Calle 27 de Febrero, cell tel. 829/349-1913, www.profundoblue, US$400/Open Water), a longtime

PADI center, you can get certified at all levels; local dives take you right off the beaches of Las Terrenas (2000 pesos (US$44)/one-tank dive).

Snorkel, beachcomb, stuff yourself with barbecue—it's a formula that Cap Caraïbes (Playa Las Ballenas, tel. 829/960-9722, www.capcaraibes-catamaran.com, US$100 pp) has perfected on their full-day catamaran excursion, which takes you to several uncrowded beaches and a natural sandbank at Puerto Escondido.

Sailing

On the end of Playa Las Ballenas, you'll find the Las Terrenas Sailing Club (next to Sol y Mar Restaurant, tel. 829/580-3065, www.lasterrenassailing.com, US$13/hour double kayak or SUP) where you can rent kayaks, hobie cats, or get a sailing lesson. Just look for the equipment parked on the beach, near the stream. Catamaran sailing trips to area beaches are offered through Cap Caraïbes (Playa Las Ballenas, tel. 829/960-9722, www.capcaraibes-catamaran.com, US$100 pp), with plenty of food, drinks, and snorkeling equipment.

Kitesurfing and Surfing

Carolina Surf School (Playa Bonita at Hotel Acaya, tel. 809/882-5467, carolinasurfschool@gmail.com, 9am-5:30pm Tues.-Sun., US$50/two-hour lesson), owned by a Dominican pro kitesurfer turned entrepreneur, offers surfing lessons for adults and kids, as well as surfboard rentals (US$13/hour), paddleboard rentals (US$25/hour). Mornings are a good time for SUP lessons, when the waters are calmer. Ask about the surf trips to the north coast, to Nagua and Río San Juan.

To see kitesurfers, head to Playa Punta Popy or Portillo Beach where you'll spot them enjoying the sweeping winds that grace this area from December through September. For lessons, there's LT'Kitesurf (Calle 27 de Febrero, tel. 809/801-5671, www.lasterrenas-kitesurf.com, US$300/six hours); you can also rent equipment if you're certified (US$70/day).

Horseback Riding

The French and Swiss duo running **Rancho Playa** (tel. 829/868-5233, ranchoplaya.lt@gmail.com, 10am-6pm daily, US$35/hour) offer beach and forest rides to of-the-beaten-track spots at an affordable price. **Flora Tours** (Calle Duarte, tel. 809/240-5482, www.flora-tours.net) offers beach horseback rides along Playa Cosón.

Whale-Watching

You can hop on a whale-watching tour with the one and only Kim Beddall of **Whale Samana** (Av. La Marina, tel. 809/538-2494, www.whalesamana.com, US$62, includes sanctuary fee), which now offers pickups in Las Terrenas. You can also travel with **Violeta Fun Tours** (Calle 30 de Marzo, tel. 829/705-0119, www.violettafuntours.com, US$90) who will also pick up from Las Terrenas.

Kayaking

Flora Tours (Calle Duarte, tel. 809/240-5482, www.flora-tours.net, US$55 pp half-day) takes you on a unique kayaking excursion down a mangrove ecosystem and river just 15 minutes from Las Terrenas. You'll spend at least 1.5 hours kayaking down the river and eventually arrive at the gorgeous Playa Cosón.

Fishing

For a fun day out sportfishing, call **CoCokite Fishing** (Calle Duarte, tel. 809/869-8031, www.cocokite-fishing.com). **Cap Caraïbes** (tel. 829/960-9722, www.capcaraibes-catama-ran.com/fishing, US$800/half day with max of five) is another top-notch operation, taking you to Puerto Escondido and other spots where you can bag your own wahoo, tuna, and other critters. Trips depart at 7:30am and return at 1:30pm.

Dancing

Las Terrenas is home to a couple of popular dance and entertainment groups, as well as dance studios. This town is for those who love to shake it. You'll get a great workout and make friends at the same time. Learn how to merengue, salsa, son, cha-cha, or bachata and partake in the village's active nightlife Wednesday through Sunday. Ask about the *noches de animación* or nights when dance groups head to a particular bar or restaurant and "host" the night by entertaining guests with their dance routines, as well as inviting them to the floor and showing them a few steps. There's usually a small cover (less than US$5). If you'd rather have formal lessons first, you have several options.

Kayaking is a great way to explore Las Terrenas' shores.

Pasion Caribe Dance School (Plaza Casa Linda, above Bodega Bar, tel. 829/548-8881 or 829/921-9984, junioraquino@pasioncaribedanceschool.com, 8am-9pm Mon.-Fri., 9am-6pm Sat.-Sun.) welcomes beginners or more advanced students with classes in salsa, bachata, merengue, cha-cha, afro palo, and *dembow*.

By Bolivar Escuela de Baile (Calle Duarte 250, tel. 809/977-9938, bybolivar@gmail.com) hosts a free "social dance" at the studio every Monday from 9:30pm, or at the Bodega Bar on Wednesday. Private classes are available all week long. You can pick up the latest schedule and flyers right outside the school.

Cockfighting

You don't hear anyone talking about it, but look closely and in every town in the Dominican Republic, you'll spot a *club gallístico*—an enclosed ring where, away from plain view, men gather and bet on cockfights. It's even more of a culturally entrenched sport than baseball. If you happen to be here on a Sunday, particularly in the mid-morning hours, head out on the road to Playa Cosón from Las Terrenas town, and you'll see hundreds of bikes parked in the area of La Ceiba, outside an enclosed ring where cockfighting takes place. If you're comfortable with the content, it's quite a cultural experience. Tickets start at RD$200 (US$4.40) depending on your chosen seat.

Spa

Janyra (tel. 809/426-4901, RD$1,200 (US$26.20)/hour or RD$600 (US$13.10)/half hour), the beach masseuse, will bring her table to your favorite corner of Playa Las Ballenas, across from the row of hotels and villas. Call ahead to set up a meeting spot; she also can often be found in the morning at the restaurant across from Hotel Playa Colibri. Soak in a Turkish bath or hammam at **Alisei Spa** (tel. 809/240-5555, www.aliseihotelspa.com, from US$65) or opt from a range of massages, Vichy showers, and other full spa services.

ENTERTAINMENT AND EVENTS

Nightlife

La Bodega Bar (Calle 27 de Febrero, corner of Calle Duarte, 9pm-2am Wed.-Sun., no cover) has the best setting in town for a club—a grand open dance floor, plenty of seating, a large bar. But it's also a regular hangout and meet-up point for prostitutes and their customers. Still, it's a good place to watch professional bachata and merengue dancers take over the floor—they host various nights here—and try a few steps while you're at it. The best nights are Thursday through Saturday. Start here before heading to the next dance spot like Son Latino or Replay.

The international crowd of Las Terrenas hangs out mostly in Pueblo de los Pescadores—a row of lively sea and beachfront bars and restaurants, ranging from French to American, that light up at night with outdoor decks. Sandwiched amid this row is **Replay** (tel. 829/717-1293, 9pm-3am Thurs.-Sun., no cover), your classic beach town dance club, with a DJ spinning everything from thumping house music to the latest R&B and some local tunes. The inside floor gets jammed after midnight, and the crowd spills over into the outdoor seafront deck.

Gaia Nightclub (Pueblo de los Pescadores, tel. 809/914-1023, www.gaialasterrenas.com, cover US$7-10) is across the street. This fancy three-level nightclub is impressive for a small place like Las Terrenas. It costs more to party here, so you won't see it as crowded on weekdays, except perhaps on Saturday when the well-heeled come here to feel exclusive.

El Son Latino (behind gas station, Calle Carmen, tel. 809/879-2135, 9pm-2am Thurs., US$2.30) has the best Dominican party vibe in Las Terrenas by far, with a mixed crowd of locals and a few expats who love to dance on the spacious, second-level floor. Thursday is the night to go—it used to be mostly karaoke but has since turned into a DJ spinning various tunes from Latin to rap. Portraits of famous Dominican artists grace the walls above the few tables reserved for bottle service.

When the night here ends at 2am, the crowd moves over to the adjacent bar and club or spills out around the gas station.

El Patio Tropical de Juampi (Calle Duarte, no phone, 6pm-midnight Thurs.-Sun., no cover) is ultra-local, with its Dominican carwash feel—a spacious thatch-roofed open-air bar, dance floor, and pool tables. Just another couple of blocks up is the similar **El Almendro Car Wash** (Calle Duarte, tel. 809/240-5478, 6pm-midnight, Thurs.-Sun., no cover) where you can enjoy a live merengue band on Sunday. The floor here is smaller and somewhat slippery, but the atmosphere is just as great, if not better because the crowd is a bit more mature.

SHOPPING

On the main street of Calle Duarte, you'll find a string of small plazas with souvenir shops, starting with Plaza Taína, as well as art and artisan boutiques with carefully selected items from both the DR and Haiti. Note that most stores close their doors at lunchtime for a good two hours, European style.

Nativ'Arte (Calle Duarte 270, tel. 829/262-3406, perla90@gmail.com,, 9am-7pm Mon.-Sat., 1pm-close Sun.) carries artisan works from various parts of DR. You'll find unique items like candles in coconut shells, and Taíno ceramic deity figures.

Haitian Caraibes Art Gallery (Calle Duarte 159, tel. 809/240-6250, 9am-7pm Mon.-Sat. except noon-3pm; noon-close Sun.) is owned by a French journalist who resides in Haiti and shuffles back and forth across the island. Collections showcase Haitian paintings, as well as Dominican items like cigars and a series of sarongs.

Inside the brightly colored Plaza Casa Linda try **Côté Soleil** (cell tel. 809/869-0160, 10am-4pm Mon.-Sat., hours vary) for some funky summer clothes including silk tunics, linen dresses, and accessories. Owner and longtime resident Chantal hails from St. Tropez and her French fashion flair is all over this boutique. She designs the clothes herself and has them manufactured in Italy. Ask her about her favorite places in Las Terrenas and you'll be hanging out here for a little while.

Puerto Plaza (Francisco Alberto Caamaño Deño, tel. 809/240-5544, www.puertoplazalasterrenas.com, 8am-6pm daily, lunchtime close until 3pm) is the gargantuan, new boat-shaped shopping mall in town (word is, a second boat is being built right behind the first). Locals call it Los Barcos, and you'll find

the boat-shaped Puerto Plaza shopping mall

a few upscale fashion stores with beachwear, as well as a 24-hour Farmacia Carol.

FOOD

You might forget you're in the Caribbean when you're out for food in Las Terrenas. There might be as many dining spots are there are nationalities; and you'll almost always enjoy it all to the sound of waves rushing to shore. **Pueblo de los Pescadores** is where you'll find a string of restaurants offering prime beachfront seats and gourmet meals blending European, American, and Dominican specialties. In Las Ballenas there are casual beachfront bistros, while Punta Popy has its own trendy restaurant row facing the sea at the entrance of town. This list below is by no means comprehensive.

For morning coffee and a pastry, head to **La Boulangerie Française** (Calle Duarte, Plaza Taína, tel. 809/876-4709, 7am-7pm Mon.-Sat., from US$2), a popular Parisian-style bakery that wins rave reviews. The java is good, but the croissants are average. Baguette sandwiches are also available among other sweet treats. The outdoor terrace has wicker chairs reminiscent of a Paris sidewalk café and faces the main drag's continuous traffic and pedestrians. Note that there's no wireless Internet here.

Sandwiched amid the Pueblo de los Pescadores, longtime favorite ★ **La Terrasse** (on Pueblo de los Pescadores, 809/240-6730, 11:30am-2:30pm and 6:30pm-11pm daily, US$20-40) has a beach chic atmosphere, with its beige and white colors, swaying lanterns and wooden deck steps from the sand. The menu offers fish, meats, and pastas, with a blend of French and Caribbean specialties. The *salade niçoise* is excellent, as is the *dorado al coco* (coconut stewed fish, a specialty in these parts). It's a lovely spot for a romantic, relaxing meal on a hot afternoon.

You can pick up a pizza any day from **Pizzeria El Pescador** (Francisco Caamaño Deñó St., tel. 809/240-6202).

Le Tre Caravelle (Punta Popy, Av. 27 de Febrero, tel. 809/917-6639, simone.mura@yahoo.it, US$5-20) serves seafood in all its forms—try the risotto. The outdoor terrace has a view of the sea and beach across the road, but there's also interior dining if you tire of the mosquitoes at sunset. It's a nice spot for a fancy dinner.

★ **La Vela Blanca** (tel. 829/633-2004, lavelablancalt@gmail.com, US$5-15) is actually a French restaurant, which locals call

La Vela Blanca offers the best beachfront lunch deal.

Lis because there's a ball court in front of it where expats gather to play in the late afternoons. Located on a quiet stretch of Las Ballenas beach, steps from Hotel Alisei, this darling small casual venue is a friendly place where food is not only finger-licking good, but plentiful and affordable. For just 300 pesos (US$6.50), a daily set two-course lunch menu, scribbled on a board, offers a choice of appetizer and an entrée, prepared by a French chef. Local tunes play while you enjoy a glass of wine or mojito with your meal and enjoy the sea breeze, toes buried in sand if you choose. It's hard to beat that. Ask about their house shot—a blend of mango, vanilla, and rum.

If you want to hear English, more of a rarity than French in Las Terrenas, head to **The Lazy Dog Beach Bar & Grill** chain (Pueblo de los Pescadores, tel. 829/877-4865, www.lazydogconcepts.net, noon-midnight Wed.-Mon., US$4-12), known for its burgers and sandwiches, though they are average, and their light rock or reggae, giving the place a classic North American diner atmosphere. The twice daily happy hour attracts expats as well as tourists.

Facing the long pedestrian boardwalk on Las Terrenas Beach, **El Cayuco** (Pueblo de los Pescadores, tel. 809/240-6885, noon-midnight daily, US$4-15) is a great spot for breakfast or for dinner when you feel like snacking from their tapas menu along with a glass of sangria. They also offer entrées that are reasonably priced.

Paco Cabana's (Calle Libertad 1, tel. 809/240-5301, pacocabana@hotmail.com, US$12-20) small thatch-roof palapa, white tablecloths, and chandelier atmosphere are enough to draw you in. But the equally small menu is decent, offering a range of seafood, pasta, and meats.

Also on the beachside of Las Terrenas, right in town, you'll find a row of shacks facing fishing canoes where locals cool off and sell fresh catch meals every day. For fresh fruits, smoothies, and veggies, find **Johnlee** (Caamaño Deño Francisco St., tel. 809/876-2751, 9am-4pm daily), a thatched open-air

market displaying its colorful produce along the entrance.

Up for some fresh fried fish on the beach, Dominican-style? The best in the area is the open-air ★ **Restaurant Luis** (no phone, 11am-6pm daily) on gorgeous Playa Cosón, where you can watch them cook outdoors on open wood fires. Pick your fresh catch and size (about US$8/pound of red snapper) and order it grilled, steamed, or fried. Head for a swim until the food is brought to your table; expect heaping sides of rice and beans, *tostones*, and avocado.

L'Atlantis Restaurant (tel. 809/240-6111, www.atlantis-hotel.com.do, noon-9pm Wed.-Mon., US$11-30) is a treat, and not to be missed when you spend the day on Playa Bonita. Sit at one of a handful of tables set in a palapa facing the sea or on a covered outdoor terrace by candlelight. The restaurant—helmed by Chef Gerard, former private chef to ex-president Francois Mitterrand—dishes out fresh seafood picked by Girard himself, French specialties, and delights like fish ceviche in a coconut sauce or grilled lobster in a butter sauce. Pastas and steaks are on offer as well. With the backdrop of the artsy hotel itself, the atmosphere is sophisticated yet intimate and casual.

Take it up a notch at the all-white **The Beach** (Playa Cosón, tel. 809/962-7447, US$10-25) for a decadent meal, whether as a long lunch or dinner. On the small terrace of this seafront restaurant with an old-world charm, house specialties include shrimp with passion fruit sauce or crab cakes with mango chutney. Sample the coconut shavings while you wait on your meal.

★ **Restaurante Mi Corazón** (Calle Duarte 7, tel. 809/240-5329, www.micorazon.com, 7pm-11pm Tues.-Sun., US$11-65) is on the far edge of the main Duarte drag and away from the beach, but the trek to this Swiss-owned, German chef-run fine dining spot is completely worth it. It is consistently ranked among the best fine dining experiences in Las Terrenas even though it might not look like much from the outside. You'll enjoy fresh-made meals inside a dimly lantern-lit, romantic Spanish courtyard. Splurge on the chef's daily Mi Corazon Tasting Menu (US$62), with almost six different dishes, including entrées like tortelloni stuffed with spiny lobster, and rib-eye steak with a spicy apple and cinnamon chutney.

ACCOMMODATIONS

Just like restaurants, rooms abound in Las Terrenas, ranging from budget accommodations to hotels offering self-catering apartments and exclusive villas. Prices have gone up in recent years, and while it's not as cheap as staying in Las Galeras, it's cheaper than staying in Punta Cana.

Under US$50

Fata Morgana (tel. 809/836-5541, www.fatamorganalasterrenas.com, US$25) is about a 7-minute walk from Playa Bonita, and you'll need a ride to get to Las Terrenas if you want more restaurant options than those at Bonita and some nightlife. But if you're just seeking a basic and spacious spot to stay, it doesn't get cheaper in this area. There are six rooms, each with its own little porch and hammock. You also get to enjoy a shared kitchen, with a barbecue and outdoor space.

★ **Casas del Mar Neptunia** (Calle Emilio Prud'Homme 1, tel. 809/240-6884, www.casasdelmarneptunia.com, US$46, includes breakfast) is a hidden gem in Las Terrenas. The 10 rooms in colorfully painted Dominican-style cottages are set in a tropical garden. Rooms have outdoor porches, king-size beds, a refrigerator, safe box, fans, hot water, and backup power supply. One of them has a kitchen option for an additional fee, if you're interested. It's ideal for solo travelers, and a short walk from the main drag in town.

US$50-100

La Residencia del Paseo (Calle Juan Pablo Duarte 272, tel. 809/240-6778, www.residenciadelpaseo.com, US$72-90) sits smack in the middle of the action on the main street in town, surrounded by hotels, shopping, restaurants, and some nightlife. For those who just want to be a hop and a skip away on foot, this could be a good choice for the price. It's two minutes' walk to the closest beach, but there are better alternatives if you can splurge for a few more dollars a day. The resort has a pool, wireless Internet, cable TV, and the self-catering apartments—kitchens and baths are dated—have balconies, fan if you pick a studio, or air-conditioning for duplexes. It's safe and a good spot if you're just passing through for a night or two. There's access from the back of the hotel to the Paseo Plaza, as well as the Pueblo de los Pescadores restaurants.

US$100-150

If you're looking for a quiet getaway for two, lazing on the beach, the whimsical yet classy white **Hotel Atlantis** (Playa Bonita, tel. 809/240-6111, http://hotel-atlantis-lasterrenas.com, US$ 135-185) is hard to miss as you walk along Playa Bonita's shore. Flanked with palm trees, 18 artsy and cozy sea-facing rooms are tucked in buildings that look straight out of a fairy tale with their funky architectural shapes. Stay in Jamaica, Quito, or Malaga, among other picks—each room offers its own decor. Onsite is the famous French restaurant run by the former chef to former French president Mitterrand. The hotel is tucked away from the main beachgoers at Playa Bonita, and at least 10 minutes' ride from town.

★ **Hotel Residence Playa Colibri** (Calle Francisco Camaaño Deño, tel. 809/240-6434, www.hotelplayacolibri.com, US$99-119) is a solid pick for families with little ones, and I love the beach vacation hotel feel it has. It is barely 10 steps across the street from a lovely stretch of Playa Ballenas. The staff is friendly, and the self-catering apartments have a full kitchen, cable TV, air-conditioning, wireless Internet, a separate living room, and en suite baths. Some are a bit dated, but the place is spotless. There's a pool at the center of this small collection of privately owned units, and the reception desk is staffed 24 hours, with security. The small restaurant shack on the beach serves up breakfast and lunch, and the sandwiches are decent. It's just a 15-minute walk from the hotel to the village, yet away from the city noise.

★ **Hotel Alisei** (Playa Las Ballenas, tel. 809/240-5555, www.aliseihotelspa.com, from US$130, includes breakfast) has a location that's hard to beat, steps from town, and within seconds of the beach. It's a clean and beautifully laid out property, with a similar setup of 54 self-catering apartments, but also onsite are a full-service spa, a restaurant, a swim-up bar, pool, and gym. Rooms are tastefully decorated and have terraces, satellite TV, air-conditioning and fans, phone, and wireless Internet. A solid pick for families.

At the smaller **Villa Eva Luna** (Playa Las Ballenas, tel. 809/978-5611, http://villa-eval-una.com, US$130, includes breakfast), you'll find five artsy, Mexican-style, one- and two-bedroom villas offering hotel services for a max of just 16 guests. Comforts include private terraces, where breakfasts are served daily, and a shaded onsite pool, although the beach is just a few steps away. It's a good pick for an entire family or a group of friends.

Hugged all around by a forest of coconut trees, the boutique **Casa Cosón** (www.ca-sacoson.com, US$140-220) appeals to honeymooners or couples seeking a dreamy escape in Las Terrenas. Facing the gorgeous Playa Cosón, the gated villa-looking hotel has an immaculate yard where you can relax on loungers with a good book, or wander to the beach. It would be easy to not leave; the meals onsite are equally enticing. Rooms all include air-conditioning and a mini fridge, while others also have oceanview terraces. If you're up for a lazy stay, this is yet another excellent choice.

US$200 and up

★ **Peninsula House** (Calle Cosón, tel. 809/962-7447, www.thepeninsulahouse.com, from US$550, breakfast included) is straight out of a movie—there's no sign from the main road leading you up a hill. This dream vacation mansion/colonial palace is as opulent as it gets, if only because of its antique and art-filled rooms—each item would tell a story if it could. The open Spanish courtyard as you enter the house is as charming as the staircase leading up to the six junior suites with private terraces that reveal spectacular garden and sea views above Playa Cosón. The family-run property is for those who seek complete exclusivity—whether for a weekend of romance or for a special family celebration. Opened in 2007, no details are spared in providing five-star (or is it six) personalized palatial service, whether it's the 19th-century ivory closets, the china service used for meals, or the turndown while you're downstairs enjoying dinner al fresco. You could easily spend hours inside exploring the various trinkets and decorative furniture pieces—I even stumbled on a wooden Ethiopian cross—accompanied by jazzy old-school music.

There's a pool onsite, with views of the ocean, and a darling beach house where you can relax, read a book, grab towels, or marvel at the African-themed decor complete with masks. Breakfast and dinner are offered, while lunch can be enjoyed at The Beach, the property's excellent restaurant directly on Playa Cosón (you'd need a car to get there or hitch a ride). Before you leave, ask to see the view of the Cosón Bay from the helipad.

The sleek **Sublime Samaná** (tel. 809/240-5050, www.sublimesamana.com, US$200-350) has for its centerpiece a series of narrow pools with sun beds facing each private villa or suite and leading from the entrance of the hotel all the way to the beach. Set on one end of Playa Cosón, the all-white resort has a posh Miami atmosphere. Meals at the onsite beach restaurant are surprisingly good, albeit pricey. There's also a small spa. Note that you'd want to have a car if you stay here, as taxi rides are to Las Terrenas town start to add up, unless you're set on unwinding in Cosón your entire stay.

INFORMATION AND SERVICES

If you're stocking up your villa for the week, head to **Super Pola** (Calle Duarte, tel.

809/472-4444, 8am-10pm Mon.-Sat., 9am-8pm Sun.). **Supermercado Lindo** (tel. 809/240-6003, Calle Juan Pablo Duarte, 8:30am-8pm Mon.-Sat., 9am-1pm Sun.) carries imported French and Spanish goods, including wines, champagne, and deli meats. They also offer free delivery.

Banco Popular has a branch and ATMs on the main Avenida Duarte; you'll find BanReservas across from it, while **Progreso Bank** has an ATM inside the El Paseo shopping plaza.

You can reach the **police** at tel. 809/240-6022. The specialized tourism police **CESTUR** (Liberty Street, tel. 809/754-3017) share headquarters with the police and have a visible presence throughout Las Terrenas. Look out for these uniformed men and feel free to ask them for directions or even to escort you at night if you need.

For medical care, there's **Centro Galeno Integral Las Terrenas** (Calle Duarte No.242, next to Banco Leon, tel. 809/240-6817, www.clinicalasterrenas.com) and the public **Hospital Las Terrenas** (Calle Mella Ramon, tel. 809/240-6474). There's a 24-hour **Farmacia Carol** right in town, inside the giant boat-shaped **Puerto Plaza** (Pueblo de los Pescadores, tel. 809/240-6688 or 809/240-5000, www.farmaciacarol.com).

GETTING THERE AND AROUND

Various airlines fly directly from North America into Samaná's **El Catey International Airport**, including JetBlue, WestJet, and Air Canada. From the airport, the Boulevard Turístico del Atlántico takes you directly to Las Terrenas (you can stop in Cosón for the scenic viewpoint).

Caribe Tours (Av. 27 de Febrero, tel. 809/576-0790, www.caribetours.com.do, RD$270 (US$5.88)/one way) has daily departures from Santo Domingo to Samaná town in big coach buses. You can then hop in a local bus or take a taxi to Las Terrenas. **Transporte Las Terrenas** (tel. 809/687-1470 in Santo Domingo, or 809/240-5302 in Las Terrenas) is a regular private minibus service with various departures from Santo Domingo (5am, 7am, 9am, 2pm, 3:30pm), as well as from Puerto Plata (6:30am). Call to check the latest pick up times and locations.

If you're driving from Santo Domingo directly to Las Terrenas, there are two options: taking the **Boulevard Turístico del Atlántico** (Route 133; bring toll money, about RD$400 or US$8.70) which connects to **Autopista del Nordeste** (Route 7) from the Santo Domingo Airport. You can also drive along the scenic, winding Sanchez-Las Terrenas road, with breathtaking twists and views of the Cordillera Samaná below. Drive slow, and take your time going around bends. The road will eventually turn into Las Terrenas' main drag of Duarte, which hugs the coastline and beaches.

Getting around on foot is easy and safe in this beach town in daylight and evening hours (just don't walk around past midnight if you have a distance to go). Still, you can rent a scooter from **Ovidio** (Av. Duarte 38, tel. 809/883-3355, ovidiorentamotors@gmail.com, about US$25/day), or cars and ATVs/quads (US$50/day) from **Indianapolis** (Hotel Los Pinos, Punta Popy, Av. 27 de Febrero, tel. 809/539-5401, indianapolisrentacar@hotmail.com) or from **Jessie Car Rental** (Pueblo de los Pescadores, tel. 809/240-6415, www.jessiecar.com). **Motorbike taxis** are also plentiful all over Las Terrenas and convenient for cheap ways to reach Playa Bonita or Playa Cosón.

As in most parts of the DR, there's a **tourist taxi association** with expensive set prices. In Las Terrenas, **ASOCHOTRATUTENA** (tel. 809/240-6391 or 809/240-6339) takes you to various popular destinations including El Portillo (US$10), Punta Bonita (US$15), Playa Cosón (US$25), Playa Morón (US$30), Samaná (US$70) and Las Galeras (US$100). Try calling **Argenis Perez** (tel. 809/509-0187) and bargain; he can take you from Las Terrenas to Las Galeras for about US$65 one-way for up to five persons.

Puerto Plata and the North Coast

Look for ★ to find recommended sights, activities, dining, and lodging.

Highlights

★ **Pico Isabel de Torres:** Ride a cable car 793 meters (2,600 feet) above the Atlantic to get a closer look at Puerto Plata's symbolic landmark: a replica of the giant Christ the Redeemer statue in Rio de Janeiro (page 188).

★ **El Malecón de Puerto Plata:** Strolling down the city's waterfront boulevard at sunset is as Puerto Plateño as it gets (page 194).

★ **27 Charcos de Damajagua:** These 27 waterfalls are the number one attraction in the DR—worth every slip, slide, jump, and spelunk (page 195).

★ **Charcos de Los Militares:** In Tubagua, hike past village scenery to reach a series of three stunning waterfalls—there won't be any tourist crowds in sight (page 196).

★ **Playa Cambiaso:** Brave the bumpy journey to this stunning beach and you'll be rewarded with seclusion—save for a few wild donkeys (page 198).

★ **Social Impact Tourism in Puerto Plata:** The Community Tourism Network offers seven unique tours in Puerto Plata, each of which has a positive social impact on local communities (page 200).

★ **Water Sports in Cabarete:** Appreciate the North Coast's sought-after winds and waves by signing up for a surfing class on world-famous Encuentro Beach, a windsurfing class on Cabarete Beach, or a kitesurfing class on Kite Beach (page 224).

★ **Estero Hondo Marine Mammal Sanctuary:** Explore this breathtaking lagoon by paddleboard or kayak and discover manatees, mangroves, and over 30 species of bird and fish (page 241).

★ **Cayo Arena:** It doesn't get more idyllic than spending a day on this small, circular plot of white sand in the middle of the ocean (page 244).

★ **Playa El Morro:** The dramatic limestone cliff of El Morro hugs this red-gold beach, making it one of the most stunning and unusual landscapes in the DR (page 246).

Puerto Plata is lovingly called *la novia del Atlántico*, or the Atlantic's darling, for its sea-hugged landscape. It's a stretch of nearly 80 kilometers (50 miles) of pristine beaches east to west along the Atlantic begs for a stopover.

Inland, verdant fields and mountains beckon with waterfalls, manatee lakes, and mangrove swamps tucked away in national parks.

This province was the birthplace of tourism in the DR, before its sunshine was eclipsed by the rapid rise and mega development of all-inclusive beach haven Punta Cana in the southeast. In 2015, Puerto Plata and its eponymous province began experiencing a revival, thanks in part to community-driven sustainable tourism initiatives, the renovation of the city's historic center and parks, and the opening of the new Amber Cove cruise port. But in truth, the North Coast, home to Christopher Columbus' second settlement in the Americas, has always packed in a lot to see and do along its breezy Atlantic shoreline.

Puerto Plata stands out for offering a window into the authentic DR, whether it's Puerto Plata city's stunning Malecón and incessant buzz of *motoconchos,* the laid-back and revived beach community life in Costambar, the multicultural restaurants of Sosúa, the wind sports hub of Cabarete, the cacao farming in Guananico, or just the merengue ringing out of bars and carwashes. At the heart of it all are the North Coast's residents, who are some of the most hospitable and charitable people you'll find in the DR.

PLANNING YOUR TIME

The North Coast is an explorer's dream and a vacationer's dilemma in terms of determining how to fit in all the fun. If you love road trips, there's no more diverse and all-encompassing spot in the Dominican Republic. In one drive, you'll experience everything from beaches to lagoons, mangrove swamps to offshore islands, water sports to hiking mountains and parks, plush resorts to jungle lodges. You won't be able to do it all, but if you plan your time right, you'll get a solid glimpse of the region and its offerings.

Determine your preferred activities and

Previous: view of the Puerto Plata countryside from Tubagua Plantation Eco Lodge; Punta Rucia beach.
Above: a sunset on the North Coast.

Puerto Plata and the North Coast

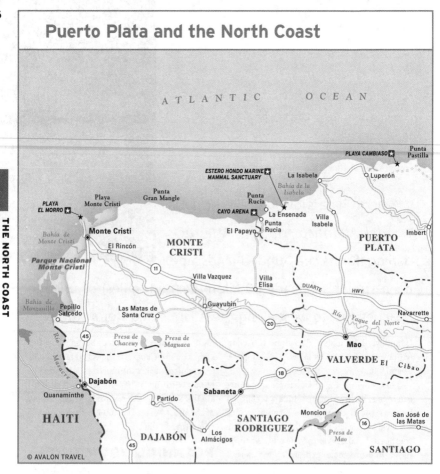

then pick a base. If you want a taste of it all, begin in the historic city of Puerto Plata. Save a couple of days to enjoy the city's museums, architecture, the beaches at Playa Dorada, and the water sports at Playa Chaparral. From there, you can head to the hills of Tubagua to hole up at Tubagua Plantation Eco Lodge, where you'll experience authentic Dominican *campo* culture and explore surrounding scenic villages. A day trip will take you to the amber mines in La Cumbre or to Guananico to make coffee or to learn how to dance merengue.

You'll want to save a couple of days to travel northwest—to the paradisiacal Estero Hondo lagoon and the beaches in Punta Rucia and offshore Cayo Arena, before ending up in wild and mountainous Monte Cristi, home to gloriously uncrowded beaches.

Still have time? A jaunt to Cabarete is worth it to see this lively water sports haven of a beach village, where kites fill the sky and surfers tumble by day and by night beachfront barhopping and dancing are the norm. If you'd rather get away from it all, head northwest to Río San Juan or Cabrera, where you'll be thrown back into the old days of a Dominican fishing village.

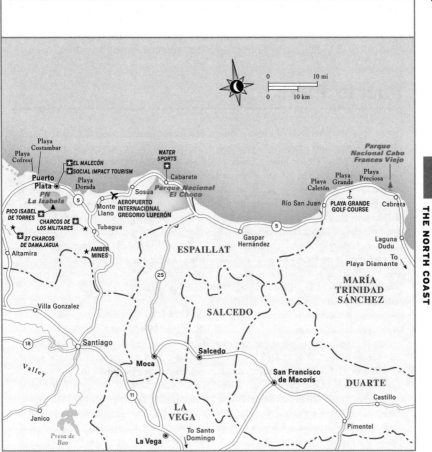

ORIENTATION

Arriving in Puerto Plata means landing at Aeropuerto Internacional Gregorio Luperón. The airport is closest to Puerto Plata town, followed by Sosúa, 20 minutes away, and Cabarete is about 40 minutes' drive, depending on traffic. It's quite easy to get up and down the North Coast wherever you choose to base yourself. If your hotel is at Playa Dorada, you'll want to account for extra fees in getting taxis to and from the touristy complex to other destinations, even to the city (you can avoid those by walking up to the highway for public transportation).

Outside of those resorts, small guesthouses abound in Puerto Plata city, as well as plenty of public transportation options, including rental cars if you'd rather day trip independently. Up in the hills above the city, you'll find Tubagua—a lovely community, home to the Tubagua Plantation Eco Lodge—and the Ruta Panorámica drive linking Puerto Plata and Santiago, offering a window into the countryside lifestyle of most Dominicans.

East of Puerto Plata, the tourist zones of Sosúa and Cabarete have the most crowds. Continue farther and you'll find yourself in more fishing villages with glorious landscapes or natural attractions, like Río San Juan and Cabrera. The same can be said heading far west of the city, onto Punta Rucia and Monte Cristi. All in all, you'll never be far from any conveniences and facilities—but you can choose just how much you'd like to lose yourself in either the countryside or the city. And that is the greatest perk of the North Coast.

Puerto Plata

Founded in 1502, the city of Puerto Plata, which bears the same name as the province, was named when Christopher Columbus looked out onto the sunny Atlantic shores and noticed the water shimmering as if it were silver. If you head just outside of town to the hills of Tubagua and look out onto the coastline, you'll see the sea does indeed resemble a silver blanket under the hot sun. Others say the silver illusion came from the sight of clouds hanging above Mount Isabel. Puerto Plata has earned numerous nicknames, including "the amber coast," for the area's richness in the precious stone. Residents affectionately call it *la tacita de plata,* or "a silver cup."

Puerto Plata was the first major tourism destination in the DR in 1974. The region thrived up until the 1990s, with tourism income surpassing that of sugar, tobacco, and cattle industries. Sadly, the decline of Puerto Plata tourism began with the development of the Punta Cana coast, as well as the drop in quality resort offerings on the North Coast.

However, there's a buzz in the air today as you travel through Puerto Plata's renovated downtown, as well as its surrounding provinces. The city is looking better than ever with repaved streets and renovated Victorian buildings in its scenic town square—there are over 100 altogether, the largest number in the Caribbean—as well as new hotels and international restaurants popping up. Off-the-beaten-track cultural activities are more within reach than ever before thanks to sustainable tourism initiatives, making this destination even more attractive for independent travelers.

The most well known area of Puerto Plata city remains the gated, all-inclusive resort and beach complexes of Costa Dorada and Playa Dorada. But there's plenty to see and do apart from them: visiting the main historical sights and museums (including a significant fortress), strolling down the stunning seafront Malecón, hiking the summit Mount Isabel, or enjoying its panoramic views by cable car, and beach hopping from nearby Costambar to Cofresí and Maimón. If you're an explorer, you're in for a treat. The adventure in and around Puerto Plata only ends when you realize you've run out of time.

SIGHTS

★ Pico Isabel de Torres

If ever there was an activity you shouldn't leave the city without experiencing, it would be a visit to **Pico Isabel de Torres** on Mount Isabel via a cable car on the **Teleférico** (Av. Manolo Tavárez Justo, Las Flores, tel. 809/970-0501, www.telefericopuertoplata. com, 8:30am-5pm daily, last ride 15 min. prior to close, US$7.80 pp or RD$350).

Drive to the entrance of Teleférico solo or get there by taxi—you don't need an organized, pricey city tour. It's a breathtaking, leisurely 10-minute ride from ground level up into the skies of Puerto Plata, at over 793 meters (2,600 feet) of altitude. The iconic panoramic view over the verdant plains of this province contrasting against the distant blue, shiny Atlantic—including a baseball field below—is one you'll long remember. Once you are at the top of Mount Isabel—one of four protected scientific reserves in the DR—a giant Christ the Redeemer statue, a replica of the one in Rio de Janeiro, welcomes you to the grounds. Walk to the top for the inevitable photo op beside the statue,

Puerto Plata

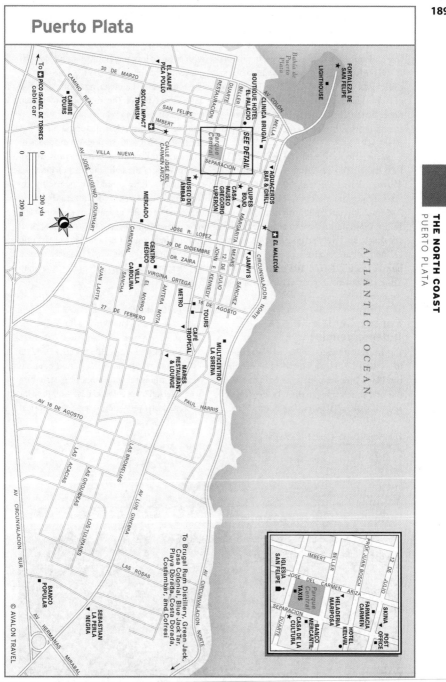

To PICO ISABEL DE TORRES
cable car

Bahía de
Puerto
Plata

30 DE MARZO

CAMINO REAL

DUARTE

BELLER

AV COLÓN

MELLA

LIGHTHOUSE

FORTALEZA DE
SAN FELIPE

EL ANAFE
PICA POLLO

CARIBE
TOURS

SOCIAL IMPACT
TOURISM

SAN FELIPE

IMBERT

BOUTIQUE HOTEL
EL PALACIO

CLINICA BRUGAL

RESTAURACIÓN

SEE DETAIL

Parque
Central

AV JOSÉ EUGENIO KOUNHART

VILLA NUEVA

CALLE JOSÉ DEL CARMEN ARIZA

SEPARACIÓN

AQUACEROS
BAR & GRILL

QUIPES

BOJO

MUSEO DE
ÁMBAR

CASA
MUSEO
GREGORIO
LUPERÓN

MARGARITA

MEARS

MERCADO

CARDENAL

JOSÉ R. LOPEZ

EL MALECÓN

20 DE DICIEMBRE

JOHN F. KENNEDY

JAMVIS

AV CIRCUNVALACIÓN NORTE

CENTRO
MEDICO

VILLA
CAROLINA

EL MORRO

SANCHA

DR. ZAIRA

VIRGINA ORTEGA

ANTERA MOTA

12 DE JULIO

SANCHEZ

MISTOR

JUAN LAFITE

27 DE FEBRERO

METRO

16 DE
AGOSTO

TOURS

CAFÉ
TROPICAL

MULTICENTRO
LA SIRENA

MARES
RESTAURANT
& LOUNGE

PAUL HARRIS

AV 16 DE AGOSTO

LAS ACACIAS

LAS BROMELIAS

LOS TULIPANES

LAS ORQUIDEAS

AV LUIS GINEBRA

ATLANTIC

OCEAN

AV CIRCUNVALACIÓN SUR

LAS ROSAS

BANCO
POPULAR

SEBASTIAN
LA PERLA
NEGRA

AV HERMANAS MIRABAL

AV CIRCUNVALACIÓN NORTE

To Brugal Rum Distillery, Green Jack,
Casa Colonial, Blue Jack Tar,
Playa Dorada, Costa Dorada,
Costambar, and Cofresi

© AVALON TRAVEL

0
0

200 yds
200 m

Detail:

IGLESIA
SAN FELIPE

IMBERT

BELLER

PROF. JUAN BOSCH

12 DE JULIO

JOSE DEL CARMEN ARIZA

TAXIS

Parque
Central

SEPARACIÓN

DUARTE

CASA DE LA
CULTURA

BANCO
MERCANTIL

HOTEL
KELVIN

HELADERIA
MARIPOSA

FARMACIA
CARMEN

SKINA

POST
OFFICE

and then continue on to the back for a hike around the botanical gardens that are part of the national park designation. You'll spot five endemic bird species—including the national bird of the DR, the *cigua palmera*, hummingbirds, and doves—and over 500 species of flora. There are souvenir shops inside the dome by the Christ the Redeemer statue—go in and browse, but be warned of the slightly pushy vendors.

Want another perspective in reaching Pico Isabel? Top adventure outfitter **Iguana Mama** (Calle Principal, tel. 809/654-2325, www.iguanamama.com, Mon. and Fri., 7:45am-3:30pm, US$80) offers a hike to the summit for intermediate to advanced hikers, starting at sea level and ending at 823 meters (2,700 feet) above after crossing through a humid tropical forest. You'll get to ride the cable car down on your return. Not a bad compromise!

Parque Central (Plaza Independencia)

The heart of downtown Puerto Plata, known to locals as **Parque Central** but officially the Plaza Independencia, is a must-see for the first-time visitor to the city, not least because it's the social hub where Puerto Plateños gather under the little shade they can find in the daytime and idle on benches after the harsh sun has gone well into the night. Lined with royal palms and flanked on all sides by gorgeous, pastel-colored Victorian-era architecture and the towering white Catedral San Felipe Apóstol, the area has grown even more beautiful every year with continuous revitalization efforts. Key historical buildings are well labeled, with impressive outdoor QR codes and information plaques providing a brief history of the sight and its interior. Take your time walking around the square, and do step inside the Casa de la Cultura, formerly the "Club Fe en El Porvenir," one of the oldest structures to remain standing and an art and cultural hub. You'll find a mobile tourist info cart in front of the church, if you need to pick up flyers on area attractions or a general map of Puerto Plata.

Fortaleza de San Felipe

Located in an area known as La Puntilla at the western edge of the Malecón, the **Fortaleza de San Felipe** (9am-4:30pm daily, US$2.25 or RD$100) was built over a period of about 16 years, and is the *only* remaining structure from Puerto Plata's colonial days—all the others were destroyed—now open as a historical

Visit Pico Isabel de Torres by cable car.

A Walking Tour of Downtown Puerto Plata

Santo Domingo has its Colonial Zone, and Puerto Plata has its Victorian architecture-filled city center. History surrounds this urban hub and spreads from the Plaza Independencia down into the characterful side streets and alleys. A handful of the 19th-century buildings have been renovated and are open for visitors, like the museums and the Casa de la Cultura, while others bear for sale signs or are slightly decayed. Either way, they add a unique charm to the city, not to mention making great photo ops for architectural buffs. Meandering your way around the city on foot for even a half day is worthwhile, and will give you the true pulse of Puerto Plata and the pride of its citizens in its ancient history of conquistadores, pirates, and freedom fighters.

On an early morning, head out to the **Plaza Independencia,** also known to locals as Parque Central, and start the day with a cup of Dominican coffee and breakfast at **Heladería Mariposa,** a great example of renovated Victorian building, directly across the street. Afterward, cross over to the park, sit on a bench, and take in the buildings hugging the square and the passing morning traffic buzz, before you start exploring the various museums. Start with the **Casa de la Cultura,** which may have an ongoing exhibit. Even if it doesn't, feel free to walk all of its levels and admire the exhibit rooms and their architectural details. Many sights have informative plaques posted outside, so you can get some insight before your self-guided tour.

When you're done, head back out and make a left on the corner onto **Calle Duarte,** where a couple of blocks down, you can visit the **Amber Museum,** one of the most well-known in the country for having collaborated with Stephen Spielberg's *Jurassic Park* in providing stones. Read about the history of the museum and get a guided tour along with the modest entrance fee.

Head back toward the square and visit the cathedral, before making your way down two blocks for a visit of the beautiful **Museo Gregorio Luperón**—one of the most stunning renovated Victorian buildings in town (in fact, the former home of Luperón's daughter, where the hero spent his last days). Enjoy the courtyard before you leave, then head one block over to **Skina** for the local rice n' beans favorite. From there, walk off lunch on the Malecón—just a five-minute walk toward the sea—with a glorious breeze sweeping in from across the boulevard. Stroll down the drag and mingle with the residents who are often found relaxing here, whether they be fishers, guides, or retired expats.

Take a seat at **La Carihuela** for *una fría*—a cold Presidente—before taking a dip at the beach. Still have energy? Walk west along the Malecón for cocktails at **Big Lee's** or head east for more beers at **Tropical Bar.**

museum for all to enjoy towering over the Atlantic Ocean.

King Philip II of Spain—after whom the fortress was named—commissioned the building in 1541 as a primary military defense structure against attackers coming in from the ocean, particularly the pirates who preyed on Puerto Plata because of all of the gold and silver mined in the area at the time. Construction of the fortress lasted 13 years, ending in 1577. Over time, the purpose of the fortress changed: In the 19th century, Dominican Republic founding father Juan Pablo Duarte was imprisoned here by General Pedro Santana, and he was one of many to suffer that fate, all the way through the Trujillo

years. In 1965, the fortress was turned into a museum. It appears small, but head inside and find several informative displays from 19th-century weapons to low ceiling chambers and an impressive panoramic view beside the original canons of the Atlantic and the surrounding areas. It's a key piece of Puerto Plata's history.

Parque de La Puntilla

Adjacent to the fortress, hugging the same Atlantic ocean views is **Parque de La Puntilla,** which was under renovation for several years and is finally nearing completion, with a brand new open air amphitheatre for outdoor concerts (similar to the one

A Dominican Hero: General Gregorio Luperón

A national hero of the Dominican Republic and son of Puerto Plata, General Gregorio Luperón (1839-1897) is loved and respected as the country's greatest leader and key player in the restoration of the DR after its annexation to Spain in 1861. He is also admired for his incredible story of rising out of humble background to the rank of general and later provisional president of the DR for 11 months from 1879 to 1880.

His foray into politics began when he was 18, when he was named assistant commander. And he was just 22 when Spain once again took over control of the territory on March 18, 1861. The annexation was at the request of General Pedro Santana in fear of another attack from Haiti. Luperón joined in rebelling against the Spanish and was eventually arrested. He escaped into exile to Haiti, Mexico, Jamaica, and New York. He returned to the Dominican Republic to continue the fight, and led the famous El Grito de Capotillo rebellion on August 16, 1863, after which he rose to the rank of general.

Forever a symbol of perseverance, patriotism, and national fervor, Luperón succumbed to cancer in his beloved Puerto Plata city at just 58 years of age. He is buried at the National Pantheon in Santo Domingo's Colonial Zone. His life and achievements, as well as relics from his home and his family, are beautifully displayed at the Casa Museo Luperón in Puerto Plata city, a restored Victorian building well worth a stop for more on this important Dominican figure. A small village outside the city is named after the hero, as is Puerto Plata's international airport.

in Altos de Chavón), paved bike trails, landscaped lawns and plenty of bench seating. It's a favorite place for local families and lovers to stroll or bike around at sunset. While some bemoan the old rustic park, the new and modern one is a welcome addition to a city where there's little urban recreation.

Casa de la Cultura

Housed in the only three-story Victorian-style wood building in downtown Puerto Plata, **Casa de la Cultura** (in front of Parque Independencia, Calle Separación, 809-261—2731, 9am-noon, 3pm-5pm daily, free), formerly called Club Fe en el Porvenir (you'll see that label outside), hosts art exhibits and musical events year-round on its three floors. The building itself is worth a look while you're meandering in the downtown area. It was originally built in 1908 as a recreational and cultural center and is one of four original buildings facing the park at the start of the 20th century. Always a center of culture, it served as a gathering place of the intellectuals who fought against the dictatorship of Ulises Heureaux, who fell from power in 1889. On

the second floor is a veranda overlooking the park and square, and on the third you'll find a library of Spanish literature. You are welcome to have a seat and consult their collection.

Museo de Ámbar

Museo de Ámbar (Calle Duarte 61, tel. 809/586-2848, www.ambermuseum.com, 9am-6pm daily, includes guided tour, US$1.10 or RD$50), housed in a gorgeous restored Victorian building, opened its doors in 1982 thanks to the Costa family, and is a small yet informative museum on the history of the Dominican stone. The fun parts include the second-floor gallery, with displays set in a cave to mimic an amber mine setting and fossilized amber pieces containing prehistoric insects, one of which was used in Stephen Spielberg's *Jurassic Park*. The movie was filmed in part in the Dominican Republic, and the museum played an important role in providing amber. The stones displayed here come from the Septentrional Mountain Range in the central highlands of the North Coast. There's a jewelry store as you exit with some unique pieces.

The **Galería de Ámbar** (Calle 12 de Julio,

Dominican Amber

In 1492, when Columbus first landed at La Isabela, he was gifted with a piece of Dominican amber, but the conquistador didn't think much of it and preferred to pursue the hunt for gold deposits. It wasn't until the mid-1900s, that interest grew in the rich amber deposits of the DR. Today, one of the most unique and popular gifts brought home from the Dominican Republic—alongside cigars, cacao, and coffee—is amber jewelry.

American entomologist George Poinar Jr. was one of the first scientists to discover the value of the Dominican stone, because of the insects and plants that were found trapped within the gems. In 1993, the scientist extracted DNA strands from a prehistoric insect found in an amber stone, making it possible to study DNA dating back to the early dinosaur period. The movie *Jurassic Park* was in fact based on that school of thought that dinosaurs could be recreated from extraction of dinosaur DNA found in amber. Dominican amber was thus made famous in Hollywood.

There are four types of amber found in the DR: yellow, red, green and blue. The most unique of them all, found nowhere else in the world, is blue amber. Blue amber isn't always blue to the sight after it's been polished; it appears as yellow under natural light yet blue under ultraviolet. It is a gorgeous stone, even worth buying unpolished—and unpolished it is a deep royal hue.

Until recently, you could only visit one of several amber museums, and their adjacent amber jewelry stores, found in every major destination of the country, from Santo Domingo to La Romana, Punta Cana and all the way up north in Puerto Plata, where the stone originates. And while that's always informative, the better alternative, now offered right here in Puerto Plata province, is to **tour the actual amber mines** of the community of La Cumbre (contact UMPC, tel. 809/696-6932, www.popreport.com/turisopp, 9am-5pm Mon.-Fri.)—that is, hike the private land on which the mines are located, including peeking inside a previously mined hole or two that aren't too deep for the average person, where you will be shown how the presence of amber is spotted as the rocks are scraped—usually a vertical line, revealing veins of black shale.

La Cumbre is known as the birthplace of Dominican blue amber, and where the best-quality stones are mined. The tour is part of a community tourism project described in this chapter, and benefits the community visited. It's a gorgeous, green drive up the Ruta Panorámica to reach La Cumbre, passing through villages while taking in views of the Cordillera Septentrional, stopping at local fruit shops if you like, and colorful roadside shacks. The road gets quite bumpy and rundown at one point, but the sights and a slow pace will distract easily from the discomfort. The area visited includes peeking down into the active 61-meter-deep (200-foot) mines where workers continue to dig daily with high hopes of unearthing brilliant stones. It's much more exciting than a museum visit, if you ask me. Miners dig without a set wage, but the stones found are worth all the hard work as the income is divided between the miners and the private landowner.

Don't forget to buy blue amber once you get up to the onsite workshop—whether it's a polished bracelet or in rock form at just US$5/gram (price varies according to the density of the amber). It's one of the most unique souvenirs you can purchase that is authentically Dominican, right from the source, and found nowhere else in the world.

tel. 809/261-2000, www.ambercollection.itgo. com, 8:30am-5pm Mon.-Fri., 2pm close Sat., from US$10) sells more larimar and amber jewelry and has one of the largest selections in town outside of the Amber Museum.

Casa Museo General Gregorio Luperón

Easily the prettiest museum in town, and a short walk from the Parque Independencia,

Casa Museo General Gregorio Luperón (Calle 12 de Julio 54, corner of Padre Castellanos, tel. 809/261-8661, museogregorioluperon@claro.net.do, 8:30am-6:30pm Tues.-Sun., US$2.25 or RD$100) is a grand tribute to the beloved Dominican military and national hero's life and times, set in yet another Victorian home restored in 2012 for up to US$2 million. The museum is actually his daughter's abode, which he gave her when she married and where he eventually died, across the street from his own home. It is said that Luperón used to love looking out onto Mount Isabel through the second-story windows. The turquoise and white museum building has perfectly polished wood floors, and displays period items. Some are original, including swords, trunks, costumes, and a model 19th-century kitchen. Luperón's life and history are on display in Spanish, but a guide is on hand to tour with you and explain it all in English for up to a full half hour if you so choose. Highlights include an outdoor courtyard facing a colorful mural depicting the life of Luperón, an upstairs photo gallery with images of Puerto Plata centuries ago—such as the Central Park area and the House of Culture—and period costumes.

★ El Malecón de Puerto Plata

Puerto Plateños will quickly tell you how much prettier their **Malecón** is compared to Santo Domingo's. One thing is for sure—the beaches are cleaner, the traffic less daunting, and yes, the sea is a prettier, striking baby blue, not to mention swimmable—making the long stretch a lovely walk in the constant fresh breeze. You can grab some fresh catch at a fraction of a restaurant's price, right by Las Yolas fishermen coop—the boats usually start rolling in around noon. Or you can stroll down the various beaches, including **Playa Cosita Rica** and **Long Beach,** and grab a cocktail and a meal at a number of bars or *casitas* dotting the Malecón. La Carihuela and Big Lee's Beach Bar are good options. Puerto Plata's Malecón certainly has a livelier and laid-back feel—though residents say it's less active than it used to be—and it's safe to cross the main avenue. In the morning and at sunset, the health-conscious jog or bike up and down the pedestrian lanes. This main drag is also where major events take place, including the Merengue Festival.

Brugal Rum Distillery

The **Brugal Rum Distillery** (Carretera Playa Dorada, no phone, www.brugal.com.do, 9am-noon and 2pm-5pm for tours) is the largest producer of rum in the DR. You can hop on one of several daily tours offered to observe the manufacturing process—the rum is aged in American white oak barrels right in Puerto Plata. It's just about 20 minutes to tour and not as fun as ending up in the adjacent store where tastings take place and you can purchase reasonably priced bottles.

Puerto Plata's Malecón

La Ruta Panorámica

Up for a scenic drive and cultural excursion you'll long remember? Rent a car, grab a guide for the Ruta Panorámica (tel. 809/696-6932, www.rutapanoramica.com), and travel up the Santiago-Puerto Plata Panoramic Route (also known as the Carretera Turística Gregorio Luperón)—an 18.6-mile drive uphill along a winding road that will take you past local villages and scenes of Dominican rural life. There are stunning views of the Cordillera Septentrional mountain range. The route begins about 7.4 miles east of Puerto Plata, going up from the Gran Parada Junction. From Gran Parada all the way to La Cumbre, the highway rises to 671 meters (2,200 feet) above sea level and connects the North Coast with the verdant Cibao Valley. You can tour a cacao farm or amber mines on the way, or just stop for local fruits, cheese, souvenirs, or drinks at a shack. Part of the road has deteriorated and is bumpy, but it also means it's less traveled as a result and therefore you can take your time. Roll down the windows, take in the fresh air and views, and immerse yourself in a true slice of Dominican countryside. You can download a map of La Ruta Panorámica directly from the website or drop by Tubagua Plantation Eco Lodge on your way up the highway and pick up a local guide there. Call ahead to schedule.

Monument to the Mirabal Sisters

This symbolic sight was inaugurated in 2008 and is worth a pit stop while you're in the area of the Ruta Panorámica linking Puerto Plata and Santiago. Located in the community of La Cumbre, the guarded Monument to the Mirabal Sisters pays tribute to the three heroines—Maria Argentina Minerva, Patria Mercedes, and Antonia Maria Teresa Mirabal—in the location above the hills where their bodies were found dumped in a wrecked car, along with their driver's, on November 26, 1960, during the Trujillo dictatorship. The sisters were known for their efforts to overthrow Trujillo, creating a resistance movement against his regime. Their murder caused indignation and ignited efforts to put an end to Trujillo's tyranny, leading to his assassination six months later in 1961. The Mirabal sisters symbolize the struggle for freedom for all Dominicans. Look closely at nearby homes in the area and you'll notice the symbol of three butterflies painted or pinned beside doorways—the sisters' code name in the secret movement was Las Mariposas or The Butterflies.

★ 27 Charcos de Damajagua

The number one sight in the Dominican Republic with over 60,000 annual visitors—it's no surprise, you won't find anything like it in the Caribbean—the Charcos de Damajagua (www.27charcos.com, 8am-3pm daily, US$6.25-10, includes gear and guide) offers a series of 27 waterfalls cascading down boulders and emptying into gorgeous pools ranging from emerald to blue hues. The adventure begins with a moderately steep hike of about 40 minutes, after which you should prepare to get wet: swimming, spelunking, jumping from up to 6 meters (20 feet) down into the water (optional) and sliding your way to and from the falls, with a guide of course. The average two-hour excursion is filled with surprises and a lot of fun, giggles, and screams. Declared a Natural Monument and therefore a protected area, since 2007 a percentage of all entrance fees (a dollar per fee; the fee varies according to how many waterfalls you climb) to the park goes directly into the community fund and helps support the surrounding villages.

As the tour begins, you'll be fitted with a life jacket and a helmet for safety, and a mandatory guide will accompany you. If you don't have water shoes, they can be rented onsite for under a dollar (bring small change). Wear your swimsuit, and if you get easily cold, put on clothes you don't mind getting wet while swimming. There are bathrooms, albeit in not always clean condition.

You'll find options to either leap off the waterfall, at your on risk, or slide down the rocks on natural slides. If you don't feel like doing either, there are staircases to bypass and continue on your merry way (some will call it "the chicken route"—peer pressure is a pest). The tours usually only take you up to the seventh fall—but if you're moderately fit, that is plenty, trust me. To venture beyond the seventh, arrange for a group of at least five to do the 4- to 5-hour adventure, or sign up with **Iguana Mama** (www.iguanamama.com, Tues. and Sat., US$89 plus tax, 10% online discount), the only outfitter authorized to go up to the 27th fall.

The throngs of visitors who descend on this North Coast gem come on safari excursions, usually in the mornings through lunchtime. But the site is easily accessed solo by public *guagua* (bus) or by taxi—they will drop you at the main highway entrance, and from there it's a short walk down a driveway to the main ticket office and the attraction. A local, trained guide will be assigned to you once you pay your ticket. Come either as the doors open or after lunch to avoid the crowds, and most definitely avoid the weekends. If you choose to visit with a tour operator, look up their various offerings and decide which works best for you.

★ Charcos de Los Militares

In the community of Tubagua is a series of three small waterfalls and glorious freshwater pools, ranging from jade to pure turquoise—Charcos de Los Militares. This area is known only to the village's residents and to guests of Tubagua Plantation Eco Lodge, who can sign up for a hike here with their local guide. The starting point for this hike is at the lodge. You can opt for either a 1.5-hour or 2.5-hour route one-way across the *campo,* past gorgeous pastureland, once-upon-a-time sugarcane fields, traditional 1970s pastel-colored Dominican wooden homes with zinc roofs, grazing cows and horses, numerous fruit trees, the village corner store, and women cooking outdoors in wood-fired ovens.

The longer route is easily one of the most unique and memorable hikes you'll ever experience here on the North Coast, and even in the Dominican Republic, in its authenticity and in the opportunity it gives to expose you to a Dominican village and its inhabitants. Once you reach the falls and pools—the last thirty minutes are the most intense of the relatively flat hike, including climbing up on rocks while holding on to a cable—you'll instantly know it was worth the effort. The first

Charcos de Los Militares

pool looks like a cenote, at about 10 feet of depth. Hiking farther up will take you to a cooler, shallower emerald pool, and falls. You can stay as long as you like and the lodge's certified guide, Tubagua-native Juanin Valbuena, is one of the best you'll find.

BEACHES
Playa Dorada

Playa Dorada is indeed a beauty. The blond sand, crystal clear water, and views of Mount Isabel make this beach a worthwhile place to visit. Playa Dorada is Puerto Plata's renowned, gated complex just a five minutes' drive from the city center. You'll find a handful of resorts ranging from all-inclusive to boutique luxury, such as five-star Casa Colonial, facing the golden Playa Dorada shoreline. Also within the compound are excellent restaurants, all open to the public—Green Jack Tar, La Tarappa, and Lucia—as well as a small shopping mall, a nightclub, a movie theater, and the Robert Trent Jones-designed Playa Dorada Golf Club. Catamaran trips also depart from these shores, and water sports are available including kitesurfing and banana boat tubing. Parking is free for patrons at the mall, and the beach is accessible to the public.

Playa Costambar

A mere 10-minute drive west of Puerto Plata town or an easy motorbike ride away, the beach community of **Costambar** (emphasis is on the second syllable) is its own getaway—with villas, shops, and casual restaurants surrounding one of the most beautiful beaches in the area. If you ask me, the white sand Playa Costambar is even prettier than Playa Dorada. The Costambar area was once hugely popular in the mid- to late 1990s, until the arrival of the Smith Enron power plant built directly behind the then Bayside Hill Hotel. Besides being a serious eyesore for guests and beach dwellers, the plant brought about significant pollution from fumes and caused respiratory problems for residents. Throw in intermittent electricity in Costambar, and villa owners slowly began to desert the area. As a result, Costambar had an abandoned feel for a long while.

In 2012, the plant finally shut down. Community residents are advocating for its complete removal, but in the meantime, Costambar not only has 24-hour power, but this beach escape is on the rise again, with new expat residents moving into renovated or new villas and businesses sprucing up their wares. CESTUR (the tourism police) has a new

Playa Costambar

outpost here, inaugurated in July 2015, and Los Mangos' nine-hole course and full wellness and spa center are bringing more traffic to the beach. The beach is as pretty as ever, and it's a great spot to spend the day, whether solo or with the family. You can reach Playa Costambar by public transportation (the shared taxi passes down Gregorio de Lora Avenue, US$0.55) or by taxi (US$6.50 one way).

★ Playa Cambiaso

Not up for crowds? You'll find your bliss at Playa Cambiaso, a well-kept secret among locals and long time residents. This absolute white sand stunner of a stretch is tricky to reach—you'll need an off road vehicle and a local driver (contact Antonio, tel. 809/252-3508). An hour's drive will lead you to a long, romantic beach, where you can swim (remain close to shore and beware of the waves), relax, and not be bothered by anyone but donkeys. There are a handful of seafood restaurants and bars onsite, and it gets livelier on Sundays. Don't forget your camera and try not to tell all your friends.

Other Beaches

The North Coast of the Dominican Republic, both west and east of Puerto Plata and along the Malecón, is blessed with a string of beaches, each with its own character and beat. From surfing havens to frenzied party stretches and deserted white sands, it's easy to get in the car or local guagua or taxi and head out to spend your days exploring these glorious playas.

Beginning with the Malecón, there are several stretches worth a swim. Playa Camacho, a short walk east of La Sirena, is popular with the locals for its wide space, white sands, and fun waves. You'll spot locals of all ages, lovers and families, picnicking and bathing close to sunset or napping under the tree shades. There are chairs for rent, but you can just lay your towel and keep it simple. Another favorite, smack in the middle of the Malecón, is Playa Cosita Rica, one of best for swimming, with fine sands, slightly calmer waters, a couple of decent restaurants and a view facing the Neptune Rock out at sea, past which kitesurfers zoom from neighboring Kite Beach. There's a volleyball net and families flock here in late afternoons. Long Beach is at the very eastern end of the Malecón and the most popular stretch with local crowds.

Sandwiched between Playa Dorada and the Iberostar Costa Dorada and lined with multicolored umbrella beach chairs along its shores, Playa Chaparral—better known to locals and taxis as El Pueblito—is a wide white sand stretch facing the local Orange Market with a series of vendors' souvenir and beach accessories shacks and a kitesurfing school. You'll also find a local bar and restaurant onsite, and the fancier Le Petit François, good for romantic dining in the evening. If you continue past the restaurant—which you should for the scenery—you'll spot apartments, more shops, and eventually the river running into the sea from below the punto verde del pueblito or a rusty but scenic green bridge. Playa Chaparral gets lively here on Sundays when locals and tourists mingle. Note that there's also a roadside public entrance for Playa Chaparral off the highway, just before you reach the Playa Dorada entrance gates.

Next up is the small Playa Cofresí within the Cofresí compound by the Lifestyle Resort and Ocean World. Named after pirate Robert Cofresí, it isn't the most attractive stretch on the North Coast—the sand is a dark bond color. But the public, resort-free side is nice for a quieter swim and sits across the seafront Los Charros Mexican restaurant, alone worth a hop to this area. The nearby Ocean World Terrace is also decent for drinks or the occasional live Dominican concert.

SPORTS AND RECREATION
Diving and Snorkeling

SeaPro Divers (tel. 809/586-1239, http://caribbeanoceanadventures.com/diving.htm, dive.pro@codetel.net.do, US$90 two-tank dive) out of Sosúa is popular with beginner divers. They will take you out into the shallow Sosúa Bay and along relatively shallow wall dives such as The Point, at 12 meters (40 feet). Puerto Plata and its neighboring areas aren't exactly the best spot in the Caribbean for diving or snorkeling, so keep your expectations in check. Sadly, much of the reef you'll see at **The Point** is brown, having died due to the sheer volume of tourists trampling on live coral. Still, you'll spot colorful Caribbean critters—including yellowtail snapper, trumpetfish, blue-striped grunts, four-eyed butterfly fish, spotted drums, and the invasive lionfish, against a beautiful, deep blue ocean.

Snorkeling stops are right off Sosúa's beaches—including in front of the new Gansevoort Playa Imbert—but you'll see a few fish, less than if you were to dive. However, the water is spectacular for swimming and incredibly clean and turquoise color that brings everyone to the Caribbean. Head out on a beautiful 16.5-meter (54-foot) catamaran with **Freestyle Catamaran Sailing Tours** (tel. 809/586-1239, http://caribbeanocean-adventures.com/catamaran.htm, US$79)—part-owned by a longtime Puerto Plateño who first came here to surf decades ago and made the DR his home. The boat leaves out of Playa Dorada and heads toward Sosúa for a two-snorkel day trip from 8:30am to 2:30pm.

Catamaran Sailing

The two popular choices for sailing down the Puerto Plata and Sosúa coasts are **Freestyle Catamaran Sailing Tours** (tel. 809/586-1239, http://caribbeanoceanadventures.com/catamaran.htm, US$79), taking you to Sosúa on a 54-ft cat, with a couple of swim and snorkel stops, or **Tip Top Catamaran Tours** (tel. 809/710-0503, www.catamarandomrep.com, US$79), offering a regular sailing trip or a VIP option complete with masseuse on board. Both make similar snorkel stops, and whichever you choose, you'll likely cross paths along the way.

Kiteboarding and Kitesurfing

Adjacent to Playa Dorada's beachfront offerings—technically sandwiched between Playa Dorada and Costa Dorada—is **Kite Legend School** (Playa Chaparral, Orange Market, a few steps before Blue Jack Tar, tel. 809/603-5860, www.kitelegendschool.com, 10am-6pm daily, US$60/hour), where IKO instructor Bibby Burgos teaches beginners out of his small kitesurfing school. His instruction ranges from learning how to hold and control a kite from the ground on the beach to becoming certified. Two assistants and four freelance instructors are on standby when the shop gets busy. Before launching his own school in 2014, Burgos taught around the DR's various kitesurfing and dive destinations, including Cabarete, Punta Cana, and Las Terrenas. You can also rent or purchase quality gear here if you're already a pro.

Golfing

Designed by Robert Trent Jones Sr., the **Playa Dorada Golf Club** (tel. 809/320-4262, www.playadoradagolf.com, US$190 3 rounds, US$60/hr lesson) opened in 1976 within the Playa Dorada complex, a stone's throw from the beach, restaurants, and hotels. The course is fairly flat, and some holes are near the ocean for pleasant views. It makes for a good morning or afternoon break for golfers.

Los Mangos Golf & Country Club (Playa Costambar, Calle Kennedy 2, tel. 809/970-3110, ext. 104, or 829/679-3184, US$25 green fee) is a nine-hole course set within the Los Mangos residential complex, and in the Playa Costambar beach community. Redesigned by Pete Dye in 2010, it's a stone's throw from the glorious white sands of Costambar and all of its beachside community conveniences. A renovated clubhouse with a restaurant, a pool with glorious views of the distant mountains of Puerto Plata, a gym, and a full service salon and spa are all onsite. You can spend the day golfing, beachcombing, and relaxing.

Horseback Riding

One of the longest-running safari tour companies, **Mega Trucks** (Plaza Turisol, tel. 809/586-3611, www.topaciotours.com,

★ Social Impact Tourism in Puerto Plata

The **Community Tourism Network of Puerto Plata** (Red de Turismo Comunitario de Puerto Plata, tel. 809/696-6932, www.popreport.com/turisopp) was born in 2009 with the aim of creating jobs and opportunities for the surrounding rural communities of Puerto Plata, all the while redefining the region's tourism offerings.

Today, the Community Tourism Network has not only built an exciting new tourism model combining sustainability and community involvement, but has also identified experiences for travelers that aren't offered anywhere else, through their **Social Impact Tours.** All of the proceeds from the tours and crafts are reinvested directly into communities to continue their growth and development.

At this time, only groups of 10 are easily accommodated, at a cost of about US$7-8 per person. Contact **Tim Hall** (tel. 809/696-6932), who spearheaded the project and will help make arrangements and/or connect you with like-minded travelers looking to participate. Some of the tours can be combined when in the same or neighboring area. Social Impact Tours also welcomes those who are interested in volunteering in these communities during their stay.

- **Baseball at Bartolo Colón's Stadium in Altamira** (9am-5pm daily): Visit the birthplace of baseball great Bartolo Colón, who originally played for the Cleveland Indians in 1997 and is now with the Mets, and tour the gorgeous stadium he built for the children in his community. There's an onsite gallery that has information about the cultural importance of baseball in the DR, and you can even see some of Colon's first uniforms and a handful of his luxury cars. Try your hand with the community boys training in the hopes of becoming the next Bartolo. And if you're lucky, the baseball great will be visiting, as he does in the off-season.

- **The Cacao Trail in Guananico** (9am-3pm Wed.-Sun.): The drive to reach Hacienda Cufa chocolate plantation is itself worth the hour and a half journey. There, you'll learn all about the production of organic cacao, its importance in the DR's economy, and you'll even get to plant your own pod, all before moving on to the fun part: sampling! Run by generations of the Mercado family, the trip includes a Dominican lunch, and if there's time, ask for a chocolate mud treatment in the outdoor jungle spa.

- **Merengue Workshop in Guananico** (10am-4pm Tues., Thurs., Sat.): Spend a day immersed in all things merengue in the village known as the *Rincón Caliente* or the "hot corner"— the birthplace of generations of traditional merengue (*merengue típico*) musicians from the award-winning Peña family. It's a super fun, high-energy day where you'll not only learn about the three instruments that make up the genre, but you'll also get to give them a try (musician Facundo Peña will show you how to play the accordion). You'll tour the workshop room where drums are made and fixed by renowed drummer Isabel Trejo Peña, who crafts instruments on demand for musicians around the country. Finally, you'll take to the dance floor across the street for lessons. The half day experience takes place in a couple of the families' homes, which were transformed just for this experience.

- **History in Luperón** (8am-4pm Mon.-Sun.): Christopher Columbus built his very first home in La Isabela in 1493, and you can tour the house's ruins at this national park, along with the ruins of the first church and replicas of his men's homes. There's a museum onsite, and you'll hike to the nearby rebuilt church or Templo de las Américas. The cliff-top views in this seafront community are stunning.

US$89) offers half a day of horseback riding on its ranch a five-minute ride away from the Damajagua Falls. The ride takes you across the property's acres of forest, past river and jungle for about 40 minutes. If you're lucky, you'll get to cool off in the river at the end. Ask about their secret little oasis where you can sip on coconuts and bathe in a freshwater pool.

Rancho Lorilar (tel. 809/320-0498 or cell tel. 809/885-9642, lorilar@gmail.com, 9am-4pm Mon.-Sat.) gets rave reviews for its beginner to advanced horseback riding options, as

Tour the DR and make a difference at the same time!

- **The Manatee Trail in Villa Isabela** (9am-5pm daily): This nature excursion will show you just how diverse the DR's landscape, flora, and fauna can be. The Estero Hondo Reserve is a sanctuary for manatees and offers breathtaking scenery from deserted white sand beaches to the coastal lagoons. You'll hike two trails at the sanctuary, accompanied by a guide, but the highlight is getting on a paddleboard and gliding across the vast, tranquil waters as you explore four species of mangroves and many different species of birds—including the Hispaniolan woodpecker, green herons, cattle egrets, and the *cigua palmera*. You'll even swim in a "natural pool" beside the mangroves while taking a break from paddling. At the end of the tour, there's a lookout tower, from which you can watch the manatees rising to the surface. If time permits, ask to squeeze in a lunch stop at nearby Playa La Ensenada.

- **The Amber Route in Yásica Arriba** (8am-5pm Mon.-Sun.): Forget the museums—you can now head to the only place in the world where amber is actually mined, in La Cumbre, and the only place where blue amber is found. You'll hike the family-owned land where the mines are located, set against the backdrop of the Cordillera Septentrional. You'll meet workers who are in the midst of mining, and they might even show you the stones they've discovered that day. You will also enter previously mined terrain and learn how amber deposits are spotted. Lastly, you'll get the unique opportunity to buy the gems onsite, polished or raw by weight, at a fraction of the price you'd find in stores. Near the mines is the Monument to the Mirabal Sisters, also worth a stop if possible.

- **The Coffee Trail in Pedro Garcia** (8am-5pm daily): Learn about reforestation and the harvesting of organic coffee in Pedro Garcia. You'll even get to make your own—from the bean to the cup.

well as its beautiful location near Maimón. It is under an hour's ride from downtown Puerto Plata.

Ziplining

Mega Trucks (Plaza Turisol 60, tel. 809/586-3611, www.topaciotours.com, US$89) has an incredible nearly two-mile-long course on its private ranch near the Damajagua Falls and the small town of Imbert. It takes you across parts of its hundreds of acres of verdant hills and forests, even above a river, on a double cabled zipline. Besides the course, there's a 27-horse stable onsite, a garden trail with Dominican fruit trees and plants, and an open-air restaurant area with stunning mountain views. Most zipline adventures are packaged into the Zip n' Ride half-day excursion combining horseback riding for beginners or pros. Before you leave the ranch, ask for a dip at the "secret garden," where you'll find a gorgeous turquoise-colored natural pool.

Up in Yásica, about 30 minutes outside of Puerto Plata along the scenic Ruta Panorámica, **Yásica Adventures** (Carretera Turística Gregorio Luperón, tel. 809/320-0000, www.yasicaadventures.com, 9am-4pm Mon.-Sat., US$84, discounts online) offers a zipline that takes you across 10 platforms, at a height ranging from 100 and 300 meters (328-984 feet) and speeds of up to 48 kph (30 mph). Speeding across this stunningly verdant, hilly part of the North Coast is a memory you'll hold long after you leave. Safety is taken seriously, and there are practice runs before you take off.

ATV Terra Cross

The hottest new way to get deeper into the countryside of the northern province is by riding your own ATV on a fun, half-day Terra Cross excursion with **Outback Adventures** (Plaza Turisol, tel. 809/320-2525, www.outbackadventuresdr.com, US$89). You'll get to ride a four-wheel ATV buggy from Puerto Plata—the headquarters are close to Playa Dorada—into the nearby village of Muñoz, dominating all sorts of terrain, from rocky paths to dusty roads, past horses, cows, pastureland, and spectacular countryside scenery. Stops are made at a traditional Dominican home, where you'll refresh with coconuts, and the Muñoz River for a swim. If you're lucky, you'll end up coming here on a Sunday to witness an authentic Dominican Sunday funday at the river, with plenty of frolicking and swimming, and outdoor cooking in big pots. Prepare your camera for the view of Puerto Plata's gorgeous coastline from the hills of Muñoz.

Ocean World Park

It's hard to miss the gigantic sign off the highway, but **Ocean World** (809/291-1000, 9am-6pm daily, admission US$69 adults, US$54 children 4-12) is your average water park where dolphins and sea lions are on display for the entertainment of families and their kids. I don't recommend such attractions where animals are sequestered—but kids

Explore the hills of Muñoz in an ATV with Outback Adventures.

generally enjoy the park. Stick to the artificial reef pool where the kids can snorkel amid colorful fish or come after lunch to swim in the pool. A better time is spent on the Ocean World Terrace restaurant and bar. Enjoy the weekly Bravissimo dance show or occasional live merengue or bachata concert.

Birding

Birders will find their bliss heading out of Puerto Plata and venturing either west or far east of the North Coast. The most beautiful birding areas include the **Estero Hondo Marine Mammal Sanctuary** (tel. 829/492-3362, 9am-5pm daily, US$5.55 or RD$250), where you can paddleboard or kayak on the lagoon and explore the birdlife amid the mangroves. You'll find up to 20 species, including the *cigua palmera,* Caspian tern, cattle egret, green heron, white ibis, red-tailed hawk, brown pelican, and Hispaniolan woodpecker. You can also hike the reserve via a couple of trails for more sightings, while you take in the manatees as well.

Río San Juan is a veritable bird sanctuary. The small fishing village is surrounded with bird sightings, but you can find them in highest concentration while cruising down the **Laguna Gri Gri**—the highlight in Río San Juan—where cattle egrets and vultures fill the mangroves and trees surrounding the lagoon. There's also a **bird sanctuary** on the other side of the Gri Gri Lagoon, heading east of Hotel Bahia Blanca and facing Playa de los Guardias. You can see plenty of egrets, including babies barely walking, as well as vultures roaming. This is the part of the lagoon that you miss when doing a boat tour; it's even better observed on foot. The collective sound of the birds echoing through the sanctuary, even as you walk past, is incredible. They tend to come out of the mangroves and trees a bit more in the early mornings or at sunset.

Cacao Tour

Chocal (Chocolate de la Cuenca de Altamira, tel. 829/308-5852, chocolatedealtamira@hotmail.com) is a small chocolate factory owned and operated by a women's cooperative, in the town of Altamira. You can arrange for a half-day visit, where you'll hike the plantation and join the women in making chocolate from bean to bar (go home with yours, or shop onsite).

Spa

The luxurious, over 929-square-meter (10,000-square-foot) space at **Baguá Spa** (Casa Colonial, Playa Dorada, tel. 809/320-3232, www.casacolonialhotel.com/spa, from US$65) is your best bet for an all-around pampering experience. There are 10 treatment rooms indoors with ocean views, including couples rooms. Outdoor massage gazebos overlook the sea and beach, surrounded by ponds and soothing fountains. Ask about the indigenous spa therapies, amber gems, honey and ocean water.

Los Mangos Golf & Country Club (Costambar, Calle Kennedy 2, tel. 809/970-3110 or 829/679-5049, US$35 60-min. massage) has a relatively new Wellness and Health Center—complete with a full-service salon and spa services. Options cover hyperbaric oxygen therapy, steam and sauna rooms, a gym, and free use of the swimming pool. The manicure, pedicure, and cleansing facial I had were excellent, as was the hair salon experience.

ENTERTAINMENT AND EVENTS
Nightlife

In Puerto Plata as in much of the DR, nightlife kicks off in full steam starting on Thursday, from local bars to dance clubs and *rancho típicos* along the highway, where merengue blasts all night long. The most popular spot in town for late-night hangouts for the young (or old) and restless is the Malecón, lined with various local or expat bars or *casetas* (they also serve bar foods). The younger and older generations often park their cars or their chairs on the far eastern end by Long Beach and blast out music from their mega speakers while the crowd relaxes seaside or dances on the boulevard.

Facing the Malecón, **Big Lee's Beach Bar** (tel. 829/868-0017, www.bigleesbeachbar.com, 9am-midnight daily) is popular among expats and tourists for its weekly karaoke Thursday and live music on Friday. A short walk over is **Tropical Bar,** where you can sit back and relax while chugging beers from all over the world. If you're up for a local beat, head to **La Casona.** These are good spots to try before you move on to more serious jamming. Also on the Malecón is **La Carihuela** with a lovely beachfront terrace where a DJ occasionally spins at night, and the crowd is eclectic. The drinks here are stiff! A few steps away on the boulevard, streetside is **Zona Acapella Club,** an open-air Dominican joint blasting out salsa and merengue—it's especially crowded on Sunday nights when there is a live merengue band. Farther up west on the Malecón, you'll find a yellow open-air terrace on the corner of Calle Separación, at **Chicharrón Light** (next to D'Angel Restaurant). It's popular, and a live *merengue típico* band turns the place out on Sunday nights.

Over in town, the young and trendy place to be is **Lust AfterWork** (Av. Manolo Tavarez Justo 104, tel. 809/261-8078, lustafterwork@gmail.com, 6pm-2am Wed.-Sun.), an outdoor lounge bar hosting live musicians and DJ dance nights on the weekends.

You can't come to Puerto Plata or the DR and not experience a true *colmado* or local bar/store–even if they are a bit quieter here than Santo Domingo's. Time seems to have stood still at the oldest one in the city: **Cafetería El Paguito** (Calle Eugenio Deschamps, no phone, noon-midnight daily) a short walk up from the waterfront. Up the steps and past the front counter, you'll find a handful of plastic tables and chairs where locals are enjoying drinks and music. Order your poison and grab a seat—a bottle of Brugal Añejo and a mixer, or some beers, the local Tigre red wine. The music echoes but it isn't superloud as folks here actually like to converse. Another option, with a dominoes table and plenty of vibes, is **Colmado Nena** (Calle Emilio Prud'Homme, esq. Sánchez, no phone, noon-midnight daily), a block south from the Malecón, facing the fire station.

At **La Casona** (Calle 27 de Febrero, corner of 12 de Julio, 8pm-midnight Thurs.-Sun.), a small bar and club space, there are enough glass walls, neon lights, and seating areas to make it seem a notch trendier. Merengue, salsa, reggaeton, and bachata dominate here. Couples love to twirl away in the tight space. Because of its early close, most head over to the next club at midnight.

Once the local bars and gas station shut down at midnight, the crowd shifts to nearby **La Esquina de Chalo** (Calle 16 de Agosto, corner of Calle Sanchez, tel. 809/586-1414, 10pm-3am Thurs.-Sun.) in an area known for its bars and not-so-shiny street scene. But the fancy club is as popular as ever and gets supercrowded on the weekends, including Sunday nights. There's no dance floor per se, but rather small tables where most sit and sway or get up and dance against passing crowds. It's not the most comfortable setup, but it's a good place to party if you're in the mood. Ladies, beware—there's a meat market vibe here.

A better pick and less pretentious, always-packed spot is the recently renovated **El Furgón** (Av. Luis Ginebra, no phone, Thur.–Sun., 10pm-2am, no cover), a cozy, single floor nightclub with spinning disco lights and a DJ playing merengue, salsa, bachata tunes all night while patrons are gathered around bottle filled tables or on the small, square dance floor. If you want to see a typical Dominican club, this is a good bet.

Ocean World Terrace (Ocean World, Cofresí, 8am-midnight daily, later close Fri.-Sat.) facing the sea is a favorite of locals, who gather here after work during the week for drinks, karaoke, and dancing. Saturdays are for the Bravíssimo Show, a Vegas-type full on-costumed dance extravaganza with all-inclusive drinks. An all-night party follows. They also host live Dominican concerts; check the online schedule for the latest.

Clubber's (Playa Dorada Plaza, Thurs.-Sat. 10pm-4am) attractive interior and solid

At the *Bomba* or the Carwash

In any city or town you end up in, it doesn't get more local in the Dominican Republic than starting the night out by heading to the *bomba* or gas station for drinks and music. There's an unusual culture of throwing back beers and rum and sometimes even being served like at a drive-through while fueling up or just parked at the gas station. In Puerto Plata, the place to begin a night of weekend partying is **La Isla Gas Station** (Av. Luis Ginebra, a street off La Sirena). You'll find the plastic chair seating and tables on ground level—directly across the pumps—or upstairs in the new, open-air lounge space where you can comfortably order your bottles and mixers and sit back and watch music videos playing (loudly, of course) on a big screen above the station. The entire area surrounding the gas station is abuzz with motorbikes, partygoers, and all-around merriment. If you're in a town and you're not sure where the party is, start with the central gas station. Another popular hangout is at the **carwash.** You'll often see them as a thatch-roofed building with an attached giant parking lot. The place goes from carwash and bar—drink while you wait!—to a full-on open-air dance spot at night, often with live merengue and bachata bands on the weekends. In Puerto Plata, **Automatic Carwash** (Av. Manolo Tavares Justo Km. 1, tel. 809/261-0152, 6pm-midnight Thurs.-Sun.) is a good example.

air-conditioning will keep you twirling away to merengue, bachata, *dembow,* hip-hop, and other genres. The nightclub attracts a nice Dominican crowd of various ages. Order your bottle and mixer, as in most clubs in the DR, grab a table, and dance till the wee hours of the morning.

Festivals and Cultural Events

Puerto Plata puts on its own **Carnival** (http://www.discoverpuertoplata.com/es/que-hacer) in February—the parades and fanfare take place every Sunday afternoon of the month along the Malecón and Parque Independencia. It's a colorful time to be in the city and a great way to experience the importance of carnival culture in the DR. Costumes are vibrant and showcase African and native Taíno influences. Various characters are represented like the Diablo Cojuelo or the limping devil, inherited from Spanish culture. Each carnival year, a new King Momo is crowned, symbolizing the person who has helped preserve tradition, along with a carnival queen. A final grand parade takes place on the fourth and last Sunday of the month, or it could end up falling during the first week of March.

The **Annual Cultural Festival** takes place the third week of June and celebrates both Dominican and Puerto Plateño culture with traditional folk music, merengue, African dances, and of course, plenty of local arts and crafts, food, and all-around merriment.

Playa Dorada's **Caribbean Cigar Night** (www.cigarnightpop.com, US$100 pp) is in March with all the major tobacco-producing brands in attendance. The evening is for wining, dancing, and dining at one of the resorts. It's a night to dress up and rub elbows with Puerto Plata's elite while celebrating all things cigar.

Held the third week of October, the annual **Merengue and Caribbean Rhythms Festival** brings all of Puerto Plata down to the Malecón for four days of merengue dancing to various live bands.

SHOPPING

Playa Dorada Plaza (Av. Manolo Tavarez Justo, tel. 809/320-6645, www.playadorada.com.do, 8am-10pm daily) has a variety of stores and kiosks spread across two levels, although only about two or three are worth a visit. But if you're pressed for time and don't have other options, you'll find all the Dominican souvenirs you're looking for, including cigars, rum, coffee, and cacao, as well as your usual beach apparel. There's a BanReservas ATM onsite. Haitian art and random clothing stores are on the second floor.

La Canoa (Calle Beller 18, tel. 809/586-3604, 9am-6pm Mon.-Sat., 9am-1pm Sun.) is a jewelry store with more larimar and amber on sale. Prices are on par with other boutiques in town. For beachside souvenir shopping, look no further than the local vendor shacks of **Orange Market** in El Pueblito-Playa Chaparral area, immediately adjacent to Playa Dorada. They sell sarongs, totes, and all the usual Dominican items, ranging from rum to cigars. Your purchases will go a lot further for the local families running their own businesses.

Get fresh fruits and vegetables from this fertile region at the lively **Mercado Viejo** (Calle Ureña and Separación, 8am-6pm), which spills out onto the streets and is a real cultural experience. Over at the adjacent concrete and less appealing **Mercado Nuevo** are souvenirs and handmade crafts.

For the food or wine items you can't find at the local **Supermercado Jose Luis** (Av. Manolo Tavarez Justo 20, tel. 809/586-3347, 8am-9pm Mon.-Sat., 8am-1pm Sun.) grocery store, there's a branch of **Multicentro La Sirena** (Av. del Malecón, tel. 809/586-6066, 8am-10pm Mon.-Sat., 8am-8pm Sun.) in town, the equivalent of a Walmart, offering full supermarket options, as well as beauty products, electronics, discount apparel, and any other items you might have forgotten along your travels. There are also other mini outlets onsite, including dry cleaning and laundry, artisan ice cream, Dominoes pizza, a food court with upstairs seating, and outdoor Banco Popular and Progreso ATMs.

The fishing cooperative **Las Yolas** (Malecón, across from Tam Tam Cafe, US$1.25-4.45) sells fresh fish daily—get there starting around lunchtime and throughout the afternoon to see what comes in. Prices are listed right by the beachfront fish cleaning station. A fun option is also to go eat at one of the famous fish shacks in Maimón, serving up fresh catch roadside. Among them **Parada Jhoan** (tel. 809/399-7141) is an excellent pick.

Get a unique Puerto Plata experience with an hour at **La Pulga** (across from the market, 8am-7pm Tues. and Thurs.), the biggest flea market in the city and what looks like the entire Caribbean! Endless rows of both new and used clothing, shoes, fashion jewelry, and house items are busy with locals of all walks of life searching for that great bargain.

FOOD
Cafés

Start your day with the sunrise, ocean views, and a hearty breakfast on the beach at **Margo's Beach Bar** (Malecón Caseta 9, margotdr@yahoo.de, 8am-10pm daily, US$3-5). Service is friendly and portions generous. It's as great a spot for families as for couples.

Facing the Parque Independencia, you can't miss the jolly pastel yellow exterior and orange furnishings at **Heladería Mariposa** (Calle Beller 38, tel. 809/970-1785, www.heladosmariposa.com, 8am-10pm. Mon.-Fri., 8am-11pm Sat.-Sun., US$3-10), a solid option for a quick cup of java any time of day or a breakfast sandwich. It's also popular for its homemade ice cream in various local fruit flavors, pastries, cakes, and brownies. You'll want to linger at the nice location across the Victorian square—which makes up for the service being slow.

One street away, **Kaffe** (Calle Profesor Juan Bosch 42, tel. 809/261-3440, comunicaciones@kaffeweb.com, 8:30am-11pm Tues.-Sun.) is a fancier spot to have coffee and desserts in town. It's set in a beautifully renovated Victorian building with funky decor all over the former mansion. The back veranda is the highlight, along with the breezy garden terrace it faces, shaded by mango trees. Colorful tables, mosaic floors, hanging potted plants, and plenty of interesting art pieces keep your attention when it's not drifting away with the soothing sounds of Latin ballads. The coffee is either Lavazza gourmet Italian or regular Nescafe. You'd come here for the setting more than anything else.

Run by a friendly Dominican couple, also within blocks from the central square is the more reasonably priced, cozy four-stool **Rinkón Cafe** (Calle José del Carmen Ariza, esq. 12 de Julio, tel. 809/320-0234, 8am-8pm daily). They offer mouth watering cakes, from chocolate to cheesecakes, homemade Dominican rice pudding, and cheap breakfast combos with Dominican pastries and gourmet coffee or tea (US$1.30-1.75). They've started offering healthy wraps for lunch.

A bit off the beaten tourist track yet nearby and worth finding for avid coffee or dessert lovers is cozy **Café Atlántico** (Av. Luis Ginebra 56, tel. 809/320-8629, info@cafedelatlantico.com, 9am-9pm daily, US$3-6), serving delicious combinations of tall iced or hot java or chocolate drinks, complete with whipped cream. The drink creations are pure works of art, and the churros are to die for. They occasionally host DJs and live music.

Dominican

A good lunch or dinner pick near the Parque Independencia is long-standing favorite ★ **Skina** (Calle Separación, corner of 12 de Julio, tel. 809/979-1950, charodeventura@gmail.com, US$3-10), set outdoors on a beautiful terrace with a leafy garden and shaded with trees. Latin sounds fill the air with videos displayed on a giant screen—the owner himself is a musician—but at soft volume. Specialties are Dominican and Latin. The *mofongo* and fajitas are excellent. And there are options such as burgers and grilled chicken sandwiches. Portions are generous and the staff friendly. It's a romantic, casual spot tucked away from foot traffic yet smack in the city center, popular with Puerto Plata's professionals. They occasionally have live music.

La Leña (across from Scotiabank, Calle 27 de Febrero 12, tel. 809/970-1013, 8:30am-11pm daily, US$2-4) is a Dominican cafeteria offering a buffet or boxed lunch to go, but there's also plenty of open-air seating for those who have time to chow down on a burger, chicken sandwich, pizza, pastas, and more. There's wireless Internet on the premises, and the coffee is decent.

A much better bet is ★ **Café Tropical** (next to Supermercado Jose Luis, Calle 27 de Febrero, corner of Beller, tel. 809/586-6667, cafetropical@claro.com.do, 8am-9pm Mon.-Sat., 8am-3pm Sun., US$5-6). The setting and Dominican lunch buffet here are attractive, and there are other buffet picks like lasagna or fried chicken. The à la carte menu is no less appetizing, with delicious sandwiches and desserts. It's conveniently close to the Metro Tours bus headquarters.

The picaderas or Dominican snacks were so good and cheap at **Amparo Delicatessen** (Calle Antera Mota 15, esq. José del Carmen Ariza, tel. 809/660-3085, from US$1.10) that the small window shack used to get jammed with waiting customers late into the night. The spot recently expanded into a lovely outdoor terrace with seating and indoor counter space, in a restored Victorian building, ideally just one street behind Puerto Plata's central square. Locals flock here for empanadas, quipes, and other starchy treats, which they enjoy on the terrace or to go. They also have batidas and sodas to wash it all down. It's a classic Dominican joint, and the service is pleasant.

Fast, cheap and tasty is also the **Pizzata food truck** (Malecón roadside, tel. 809/586-7272, US$1-2.45) dishing out empanadas and quipes (they also deliver). This roadside stop—with plastic chairs and table seating—is ideal for filling beach-hungry bellies showing up here barefoot or on scooters from across the Malecón. If you're close to the waterfront and want a satisfying, fried snack to go at über-cheap prices, this is it.

Just a couple of blocks from the Malecón, up a side street, the small **Coma en Familia** (Calle Dr. Zafra, no phone, noon-9pm daily, US$3.50) offers the cheapest Dominican-style cafeteria meals in the city. Expect to see various types of rice, stews, fried chicken, avocado, fried cheese, and even Dominican desserts. The food is oversalted here, beware. There are just five tables, and people share them all the time. If you're watching your pennies, this is a good pick.

Continue the cultural experience with a stop at ★ **El Anafe Pica Pollo** (Calle Paul

Harris, noon-11pm daily, US$1.50-3)—a true Dominican-style fried chicken joint. The succulent pieces—pick a breast or legs—are spiced, fried, and chopped fresh while you wait, and topped with sides of yucca, sliced avocado, and a red onion sauce. Take it home or sit on the roadside and dip in with your fingers. This is the tastiest fried chicken I've had in the DR, hands down, and always good before or after a night of partying. Prepare for a wait if you show up on the weekends or late in the evening.

Snack on some delicious, melt-in-your-mouth Dominican *quipes*—a twist on the Lebanese kibbeh—sold out of a family home at ★ **Quipes Bojo** (Calle Margarita Mears, 4pm-7pm Mon.-Sat., US$0.66-0.78 each). You'll see the sign as you arrive—just walk in and order the amount you'd like and meat stuffed or chicken stuffed. Take your snacks to the Malecón or the fort as the sun goes down. This place is an institution in Puerto Plata.

International

Find wrap sandwiches, panini, salads, and fruit or veggie smoothies at health-conscious **The Green Spot** (Calle Beller 52, tel. 809/261-9784, 8am-9:30pm daily, US$2.50-5). They also serve breakfast with coffee and chocolate options. Their air-conditioned space is a wonderful respite from the heat when you're out visiting museums and attractions near Parque Independencia.

Tam Tam Café's (Av. Gregorio Luperón 4, tel. 809/970-0903, tamtamcafé2012@gmail.com, 8am-1pm daily, US$4-15) sidewalk terrace, across the Malecón's glorious breeze, is a good place to take a breather, with average meals ranging from salads and steaks to seafood and pasta. Service is friendly and there might be a few vendors passing by, but the vibe is good. There's indoor seating if you prefer. A stone's throw away is the open-air **Aguaceros Bar & Grill** (Malecón, tel. 809/586-2796, US$6-11) a longtime landmark on Puerto Plata's Malecón, serving up affordable, convenient options for the starved like burritos, nachos, and fajitas.

A popular casual spot is the Mexican and Dominican fusion **Tostacos** (Calle Presidente Vásquez 3, tel. 809/261-3330, 4pm-11pm Tues.-Sun., US$5-10), popular for tacos, burgers, mofongo, and margaritas. Or relax on the open-air terrace at the casual **Kilómetro Zero** (Av. Luis Ginebra 6, tel. 809/244-4346, 10am-12am daily, except Wed., US$5-15), with any dish from its delicious menu, ranging from steaks and ribs to pastas to sandwiches.

Las Palmas (Av. Luis Ginebra 47, tel. 809/586-7065, noon-11pm daily, US$8-25) has a delightful setting for a nice dinner out or special occasion. Set in a residential home turned restaurant, the seating is indoors as well as on a veranda that continues on all the way to the back of the property to a second outdoor terrace. The pizzas are baked in a wood-fired oven, and are delicious, as are the pastas—with pick your pasta and sauce options—and seafood plates. Make reservations on weekends, as it is fills up quickly.

Il Giardino's (Av. 27 de Febrero 55, tel. 809/320-7469, 11am-10pm daily, US$4-30) small open-air terrace is framed by plants and enough foliage to distract from the fact that you're steps away from the constant traffic of the main road. Dishes here are also good: Italian staples like lasagna to tasty wood-fired oven pizza. If you're staying at nearby Villa Carolina, it's a worthwhile hop, and they also deliver. Ask about the list of daily lunch specials, running from 11:30pm to 3pm, for just US$4.45 with sides. A bit more on the romantic side yet equally welcoming, ★ **Sebastian La Perla Negra** (Av. Luis Ginebra #62, tel. 809/320-8818, 4pm-10pm daily except Tue.) serves all your pasta and pizza favorites. Here you'll find more residents than tourists; the owner himself will be on the floor working. The place has a trendy, dimlit vibe and drinks and desserts are excellent.

Italian favorite **La Tarappa** (Calle Privada 2, corner of Av. Hermanas Mirabal, tel. 809/261-2423, www.latarappa.com, 9am-11:30pm Tues.-Sun., US$3-15) serves wood-fired oven pizza, pastas, salads, steaks, calzones, and giant sandwiches, in all-around convivial, open dining room atmosphere. There's a second location inside the Playa Dorada shopping mall.

Inside the Playa Dorada resort area, ★ **Green Jack** (Playa Dorada, www.bluejacktar.com, noon-11pm daily, later close on Fri.-Sat., US$7-20) has one of the most creative menus in Puerto Plata and is reasonably priced. Whether you pick the beef carpaccio, the plantain and bacon-stuffed burger, or the Creole seafood, it's all finger-licking good.

Just before you reach the Playa Dorada you'll hit the Playa Chaparral (known locally as El Pueblito) complex, where longtimer **Le Petit François** (tel. 809/320-9612, noon-midnight Wed.-Sun., US$16-45) serves seafood specialties and a variety of French entrées on a romantic second-floor dining terrace, al fresco facing the beach or indoors. The lobster thermidor is a highlight, as are the cordon bleu and fondue options. Service is solid, and the dimly lit atmosphere, away from the tourist crowds, makes it a decent pick for a quiet evening.

You'll have the best Mexican food you've ever tasted in the DR at ★ **Los Charros y Los Pinches Chaparros** (Cofresi Beach 5, close to Ocean World, tel. 809/970-3332, eat@charros.co, noon-10pm daily, closed Mon. during low season, US$5-18). Originally from Acapulco, Mexico, Juanita uses her mother and her grandmother's recipes to fill her menu with tempting choices. Don't miss the Taquisa Los Charros, a "culinary trip through Mexico" with a plate that includes a choice of tostada, flauta, taco de cochinita pibil, and taco los charros. Wash it all down with a margarita—there are premium tequilas to pick from, of course. As for the meaning of the fun alliteration in the restaurant's name, you'll have to ask Juanita.

If you're going all out for an occasion, **Lucia** (Casa Colonial, Playa Dorada, tel. 809/320-3232, www.casacolonialhotel.com, US$10-30) is the place to do it. The all-white setting—in a dimly lit dining room with cozy booth corners and stand-alone tables—complements the outstanding Mediterranean, Dominican fusion menu. You don't want to miss trying Los Dos Chivos—with lamb simmered in an organic cacao and red wine sauce on one side of the plate and in a creole sauce on the other. There are also vegetarian options and an extensive wine list.

For a romantic night, reserve a poolside table at ★ **Mares Restaurant & Lounge** (Calle 6 Francisco Peynado, tel. 809/261-3330, www.maresrestaurant.com, 12pm-3pm and 7pm-11pm Tues.-Sun., US$10-25), set in a delightful garden. Chef Rafael Vasquez Heinsein serves a creative menu he whips up from his kitchen, which he describes as Dominican but global. Dishes include T-bone steak to lobster tail and Dominican goat with Brugal rum. It's a culinary treat and a gem in Puerto Plata.

ACCOMMODATIONS
Under $25

A reasonable budget option in town and popular with locals, ★ **Hotel Kevin** (Calle Juan Bosch 46, tel. 809/244-4159, www.hotelpuertoplatakevin.com, US$25-30) sits smack in the city center along a quiet residential street, a block from the central square and a couple more toward the seafront Malecón and its myriad cafés and restaurants. Rooms are basic, but come with air-conditioning and wireless Internet. If a roof over your head is all you're after, this is a good choice. Another solid pick for location, cleanliness, and price is **Hotel Victoriano** (Calle San Felipe 33, corner of Calle Restauracion, tel. 809/586-9752, US$13-16), a three-story hotel with 25 rooms, with or without air-conditioning, and free wireless Internet.

In a residential area about 15 minutes' walk from the central park of Puerto Plata, the family-owned **Villa Carolina** (Calle Virginia Elena Ortega 9, tel. 829/908-2200, www.villacarolina.hostel.com, US$20-30) is a solid base for solo and independent travelers on a budget. Tucked at the back of a lush yard (bring mosquito spray), past the owner's home, the dated white colonial building offers nine simple but immaculately clean rooms with queen-size beds, wood closets, and spacious bathrooms. The furniture is basic, but the low rates include a daily continental breakfast in the main living room, daily maid service, and wireless Internet (albeit spotty). Francia is a warm Dominican host who delights in helping her guests select excursions and ensuring they get around safely. The guesthouse is conveniently located just a couple of blocks away from the Metro Tours bus terminal, the local fruit and vegetables market, and a handful of local restaurants.

US$25-50

Along the seaside boulevard, **Aparta-Hotel Lomar** (Av. Malecón 8, tel. 809/320-8555, from US$30) offers both short- and long-term stays in one of its double rooms or studio apartments. It's a safe place to reside with 24-hour security. Rooms come with wireless Internet, TV, and optional air-conditioning.

Sunshine Hotel (Av. Manolo Tavarez Justo No. 78, tel. 809/586-1771, hotel.sunshine@outlook.com, US$31) is a decent budget spot for those who have transportation and don't mind being a little away from the city center, yet just a 10-minute drive out. White tiled rooms are spacious and clean, and come with a small balcony, air-conditioning, and wireless Internet, while suites have

a kitchenette. There's a popular local restaurant on the ground floor, offering an à la carte menu or an affordable daily local lunch.

US$50-100

A place like ★ **Tubagua Plantation Eco Lodge** (tel. 809/696-6932, www.tubagua.com, US$25-60) comes around once in a blue moon. Just a 30-minute ride out of the city center, the lodge is perched at the top of a hill at the heart of the Tubagua community in the central highlands of Puerto Plata. The open-air main dining room has a show-stopping panoramic view of Pico Isabel, Playa Dorada, and the Atlantic Ocean—even as far as Sosúa.

While the panoramic views steal the show, the cabins and surrounding natural environment are what make this a laid-back escape. There's a private cottage, two palapa cabins, and a long house, all on multiple levels like a traditional Dominican *campo* yard. There aren't real locks or windows, but rather drapes and funky shutters that open onto the verdant landscape. The main dining room is under a thatch-roofed wooden structure where flavorful communal meals are shared in a convivial space. A small soaking pool facing the hills is there for a cool dip or to relax beside on a lounge chair with a good book. The breeze

The panoramic views of Puerto Plata from the Tubagua Plantation Eco Lodge are unparalleled.

is frequent and the temperature refreshing, even during the hot summer months. The lodge blends in seamlessly with its environment, and your daily companions will range from roosters waking you early for the glorious sunrise views to resident dogs Mariposa and Tonta. The outdoor bathroom, shared between two cabanas, is where you'll shower atop the hills every day and marvel at the best scenery you've ever had from a toilet.

Local community tours offered to guests are among the best in the area, created by lodge owner and 30-year resident Tim Hall to help travelers immerse themselves in local culture. Don't miss the hike to Charcos de los Militares waterfalls with guide Juanin Balbuena, who will take you through the Tubagua community or on a drive down the Ruta Panorámica on visits to amber mines or a coffee plantation.

A gem in downtown Puerto Plata, worth the slight splurge from budget and a short walk from both the Central Park and the Malecón, the relatively new ★ **Boutique Hotel El Palacio** (Calle Prof. Juan Bosch 14, tel. 809/261-0942, www.hotelelpalacio.com, US$60) sets the bar high for guesthouses in the area. Six spacious rooms and a suite are set on the second floor of a gorgeous 1920s colonial building, with original floors from the turn of the 20th century. The hotel is delightfully decorated in antique furniture and trinkets—the owner's antiques store is next door—set against modern details like sliding door showers and air-conditioning. The Dutch owners have left no details spared including an outdoors terrace with a movie screen and a pool to cool off from the hot Puerto Plata sun. Breakfasts and other meals can be included upon request.

Hotel KMA (Calle #2 Urb. Reyes Caminero, tel. 809/244-4237, www.kmahotel.com, US$60) is popular for long-termers, but families or groups might appreciate its humongous apartments—1-3 bedrooms—with full kitchens and appliances, air-conditioning, and basic furniture. There's a small pool by the entrance and parking lot and laundry facilities, but that's about all for amenities. You'll need a car to stay here, or prepare to taxi to the city for dinner and entertainment.

Over US$100

Those looking to stay on the beach, with a touch of luxury, won't go wrong at one of Playa Dorada's resorts inside the gated complex, facing the golden beach, yet a stone's throw from town. But the real star here, an exclusive five-star boutique property and my own favorite, is ★ **Casa Colonial** (Playa Dorada, tel. 809/320-3232, www.casacolonialhotel.com, US$195-235), worth every penny you shell out. The stunning grounds include a lush garden hugging a mangrove lagoon, a quiet golden stretch of sand where you're free to have breakfast or lunch daily, and a third-floor infinity pool with four Jacuzzi tubs directly facing the sea ahead—the highlight for sure. The rooms come with seafront balconies and all the lavish treats expected, including daily turndown service with a dessert or snack. Last but not least, the onsite **Lucia Restaurant** is a delight in both its Zen ambience and its Mediterranean Caribbean fusion menu of dishes made from organic, homegrown ingredients as well as unique takes on Dominican specialties.

Gran Ventana VH (U.S. tel. 866/376-7831, www.granventanahotel.com, US$138) is a classic family all-inclusive choice inside Playa Dorada. If you have small kids, this is a reasonably sized resort where the main pool is the highlight, along with a nice beachfront. The rooms are in pastel beach colors and have comfortable beds, air-conditioning, and cable TV. Note that it gets really loud at the main resort, with music and entertainment during the day and nightly outdoor shows that are a stone's throw from the rooms. If you're a couple, you might prefer to stay in the separate hotel wing, across the parking lot, with a "quiet" pool and bar.

For an intimate, medium sized resort set on the gorgeous Playa Dorada, with a great onsite à la carte restaurant, stay at ★ **Blue Jack Tar** (Playa Dorada, tel. 809/320-3800, from US$154). The standard, ground floor guest rooms have a tropical feel with baby blue colors, and have all the amenities you need, including air-conditioning, TV, minibar and full bath. There's a pool onsite, a few steps away from the ocean where beds and loungers await.

Set inside the small Cofresí compound, **Lifestyle Holidays Vacation Resort** (Cofresí Beach 1, tel. 809/970-7777, www.lhvcresorts.com, US$100-400) attracts plenty of tourists for its yearlong all-inclusive deals, but probably more for its party vibe. The resort is average—the beach is one of the least attractive on the North Coast—and includes eight separate sections, such as Cofresi Palm, The Tropical, Crown Suites, Villas, and Presidential Suites. It's not close to the city. You'll need transportation to venture anywhere outside of the compound, but plenty of tours are offered. There are a couple of restaurants within the Cofresi area, and within walking distance—like the authentic Mexican restaurant Los Charros. Most travelers who are members rave about the lifestyle, while those visiting on a discount coupon often leave disenchanted. If you're going to opt for an all-inclusive or boutique resort, go for one at Playa Dorada.

INFORMATION AND SERVICES

You'll find plenty of supermarkets in Puerto Plata town. Try the locally owned **Supermercado Jose Luis** (Av. Manolo Tavares Justo 20, corner of Calle Beller, tel. 809/586-3347, 8am-9pm Mon.-Sat., 8am-1pm Sun.) with decent groceries, fruit stock, and onsite ATMs. **Casa Nelson** (across Parque Independencia, Calle Separación, 8am-8pm Mon.-Sat.) is a Puerto Plata institution. The locals' favorite discount department store, this is where you'll find everything from beauty products to school supplies, men and women's apparel, and a shoe department popular for its low prices.

For anything else you can't find, head to **Multicentro La Sirena** (Av. del Malecón,

tel. 809/586-6066, 8am-10pm Mon.-Sat., 8am-8pm Sun.), where there are additional ATMs, as well as a myriad of onsite services, including phone companies, a pharmacy, dry cleaning, and a cafeteria.

If you're staying in Playa Dorada, you'll find basic needs and shopping at **Playa Dorada Plaza** (Av. Manolo Tavarez Justo, tel. 809/320-6645, www.playadorada.com.do, 8am-10pm daily), located a short drive past the main entrance. Expect prices to be a tad higher than in the city.

Health and Emergencies

Puerto Plata has plenty of health care services. For clinic care, go to **Clínica Brugal** (Jose del Carmen Ariza 15, tel. 809/586-2519), with 24-hour emergency service, or **Centro Médico Dr. Bournigal** (Calle Antera Mota, tel. 809/586-2342), which also has a pharmacy onsite. The public hospital is **Hospital Dr. Ricardo Limardo** (tel. 809/586-2210). Inside the Playa Dorada complex, you'll find the **Urgent Care Clinic** (tel. 809/320-2222).

The tourism police, **CESTUR** (Hermanas Mirabal, tel. 809/320-4603 or tel. 809/320-0365) has a solid presence in Puerto Plata by Long Beach and is open 24 hours. You'll find plenty of CESTUR officers patrolling in downtown areas frequented by tourists like Independence Park and the Malecón.

Money

Banco Popular (across from the Central Park, Calle José del Carmen Ariza, corner of Duarte, tel. 809/586-2121) has a 24-hour ATM booth, and you'll find more ATMs available outside La Sirena supermarket. **Scotiabank** (across from La Leña, Calle 27 de Febrero, tel. 809/200-7268) is smack in town with outdoor ATMs, and Banco Progreso outlets can be found outside the supermarket Jose Luis, across the street from Scotiabank.

Tourist Information

The **Oficina de Turismo** (Calle José del Carmen Ariza 45, close to Banco Popular, tel. 809/586-3676, 9am-3pm daily) has

Public Transportation in Puerto Plata

Puerto Plata city and its surroundings are well connected by public transportation, and that's good news if you're traveling on a budget or would rather not drive. Like most parts of the DR, traveling by private taxi will cost you significantly more than braving a ride on a *motoconcho* or in a *carrito (carro)*. Both of these modes of transportation dominate on this side of the island. Whatever method you choose, **look for licensed modes of transport.**

Motoconchos (sometimes abbreviated to *conchos*), or **motorbike taxis,** can take you to places like Costambar (RD$80 or US$1.75) or Cofresí, which aren't too far out from the city. *Carritos* go as far as Sosúa (RD$50 or US$1.10) and you switch there to continue on to Cabarete. Locals often prefer to catch a ride from this motorbike taxi, despite them being more dangerous, to avoid being squashed inside a sedan with complete strangers. Motorbike taxis—they wear **neon traffic vests**—are parked on street corners around the city's main avenues. You'll also find them outside most major supermarkets, including La Sirena's parking lot. Current fares are usually displayed on a board beside their stop. They also zoom along most main streets and will likely spot you before you spot them and whistle or call out—their job is to find pedestrians. A simple "no gracias" will suffice if you're not interested.

Carritos, or **shared taxis,** pass along Calle Separación beside the Parque Central and go down Beller Road on their way to Sosúa. Ask at your hotel for the closest spot is to wave one down. When you hop into the shared taxi, pay the driver at the beginning, or at least a good while before getting off, so he's aware of where exactly to drop you along the way. The *carritos* are relatively safe modes of transport if the driver doesn't have a lead foot. Expect to get squished at times with four to five people in the backseat and up to three in the front. The discomfort never lasts long because passengers often have a different stop—and unlike the *guagua,* the car isn't likely to stop every two minutes.

Guaguas, or **public white buses** (often minivans), also go to Sosúa and Cabarete—with stops at Gran Parada, where you can catch a motorbike taxi to Tubagua—and they continue past Cabarete as far as Río San Juan and Cabrera.

Private taxis within the city of Puerto Plata itself are affordable, just like in Santo Domingo. Rates are usually around RD$150 or US$3.27 between two points of reasonable distance. Always double-check the price before you take off.

multilingual staff ready to assist you across from Independence Park. They have plenty of area brochures and maps to help with your trip. Note that as of publication time, the office has plans to relocate, so be sure to check ahead before going there.

Communications

There's a **post office** (Calle 12 de Julio, tel. 809/586-4545, 7am-5pm Mon.-Fri., 8am-noon Sat.) in town, if you care to send only postcards and nothing of value—but don't fully rely on it getting to your addressee.

GETTING THERE
Air

If you're staying on the North Coast, in Puerto Plata, Playa Dorada, Sosúa, Cabarete, or Río San Juan, you should fly into **Aeropuerto Internacional Gregorio Luperón** (tel. 809/291-0000, ext. 221, or 809/586-0175, www.aerodom.com), sandwiched between Puerto Plata town and Sosúa, and just 11 miles east or 15 minutes from Puerto Plata town and Playa Dorada. Taxi fares to and from the airport are usually posted on a board as you exit customs; as of publication time they are US$30 to Puerto Plata or US$35 to Playa Dorada. Airlines that fly here include American Airlines, Delta, United, Air Canada, Spirit, JetBlue Airways, and Copa.

Car

Coming up north from the south, take Autopista Duarte toward Santiago, then take the exit for Puerto Plata. If you're coming from Samaná, take the scenic Highway 5, all the way toward Sanchez, then Nagua, and on to the north.

Bus or *Guagua*

Getting to Puerto Plata from Santo Domingo or Santiago is easy with the in-town branch of **Metro Tours** (Calle Beller, esq. 16 de Agosto, tel. 809/586-6063, http://metroserviciosturisticos.com). There are fairly punctual departures throughout the day—starting at 6:30am. Check the website for the latest scheduled departures. You'll travel in a large air-conditioned coach bus and reach the capital in about four hours, passing through Santiago. It can be freezing cold on board, so bring a jacket and thank me later for that tip. **Caribe Tours** (Calle Camino Real, tel. 809/586-4544) also offers daily bus service to Santo Domingo—they have more frequent stops during the journey—departing every hour on the hour 6am to 7pm. Both bus companies promise wireless Internet on board, but it's hit-or-miss.

If you're coming from the Samaná Peninsula, there's a small *guagua* that runs from Las Terrenas to Puerto Plata called **Transporte Las Terrenas** (tel. 809/240-5302, or RD$300 or US$6.55 pp) departing at 6:30am (though it has been known to show up at 6am so get there early to be safe) on the main road across from Plaza Taína and Plaza del Paseo. It's a straight shot for the most part, with one break in Nagua for coffee and food, then the occasional passenger drop-off along the way. You'll reach Puerto Plata between 11:30am and noon. I've done this route myself and while it wasn't always comfortable, it was safe and just fine looking out the window at the lovely fishing villages as we made our way up. The reverse route is also possible, from Puerto Plata to Las Terrenas. A bus departs daily across from the hospital around 1:30pm, passing through Sosúa. Always inquire a day or two ahead of time, in case schedules and departure locations have changed.

If you're heading to Puerto Plata from Río San Juan or Cabrera, the smaller local *guaguas* are the only option—unless you've rented a car or a taxi, both of which are pricey. The *guaguas* take you north passing through Sosúa, Cabarete. They'll pick up and drop-off anywhere along the routes, and they are an economical way of getting around. Do be aware they are also often involved in accidents due to speeding, but for the most part it's like anywhere in the world when it comes to public or private transportation—there are no guarantees.

GETTING AROUND
Car Rentals

The big rental car companies are here, including **Avis** (tel. 809/586-4436), **Budget** (tel. 809/320-4888), and **National/Alamo** (tel. 809/586-1366). You can find them at the Puerto Plata international airport and book ahead of your vacation. For a local rental shop in the city with a good, affordable selection of SUVs, contact **Pionia Rent Car** (Av. Malecón, a block from La Sirena, tel. 809/586-3809, pioniarentcar@gmail.com, 8am-6pm Mon.-Sat., from US$35/day).

Taxis

If there are any tourist service providers in the DR that you should be wary of in terms of pricing, it's the taxis. Unfortunately, their rates are overinflated to begin with, and if they sense a DR newbie—especially if you don't speak Spanish—they pump them up even more. Always negotiate the rate *before* you get in the car, even if they insist or don't respond to your inquiry, because these taxis aren't metered. You don't want to find yourself at your destination and cornered into paying an exorbitant price. A good rule of thumb is to remember that in-town destinations are usually no more than US$3.50 (or RD$150), while rides to Playa Dorada, Costambar, and Cofresí range around US$7-10. In Puerto Plata, contact the **taxi central dispatch** (tel. 809/320-7621); they will give you the time estimate and you can ask for the rate. Always carry small change, as drivers will rarely have it.

Carros Públicos (Shared Taxis)

The originating and final destinations of the *carro público*, or shared taxi, are usually indicated at the top of the car, often a Toyota-style sedan. Most go back and forth between Puerto Plata and Sosúa (RD$50 or US$1.10)—where you can then switch to Cabarete—and stop anywhere you need along the main highway, including Playa Dorada (RD$30 or US$0.66). The main *carrito* hub to head to Sosúa is on the street corner adjacent to the Ricardo Limardo Hospital. Ask anyone for "*la parada de carros de Sosúa*." They also pass through town, however, so ask where the closest street is where you can hail one down. A good guess is Independence Park.

If you have luggage or going a distance to Cabarete, it's a better bet to go to the main exit hub by the hospital to load your suitcase and get a better seat. In general, the *carro público* is a safer alternative to *guagua* minivan buses, which can get even more crammed.

Sosúa

Sosúa's history is undoubtedly one of the most unique in the Dominican Republic and the Caribbean. The town was first settled by Jewish refugees offered a place here to escape Nazi persecution during World War II. The Dominican Republic was the only country in the world to offer to take up to 100,000 Jews as refugees in what is known as the Luperón Agreement. Between 1940 and 1945, five thousand visas were issued for displaced Jewish refugees, but only six hundred came. Most were single men from Austria and Germany, but some traveled from China and the Caribbean as well. They became Dominican citizens immediately and used this freedom to raise families and start a community in Sosúa. As Sosúa resident and descendant Joe Benjamin states, "The Luperón Agreement shows that even in those days, the DR was a country that accepted diversity and compassion." The Jewish Museum in town commemorates the settlers, who founded the meat and dairy industries of Sosúa before tourism came along, and those who left their mark here. Today about four of the original families remain, while most others have left for North America.

Today, this beachside community is a multicultural spot where expats from around the world have made their home and opened businesses. The variety of cuisine alone is testament to this. Unfortunately the town has a bad rep for heavy prostitution, but it's still a decent spot to visit in the daytime for some history and snorkeling.

ORIENTATION

Sosúa is very small; you'll be able to get around on foot with no trouble at all between the two main beaches. The main drag of Pedro Clisante is where most of the restaurants and bars are located, aside from the ones lining Playa Sosúa and facing Playa Alicia. The main street turns pedestrian as the sun goes down and the nightlife ramps up. Note that the scene might not be your cup of tea, as prostitution is obvious here.

You'll find most of the hotels and guesthouses around the streets of Pedro Clisante, Dr. Alejo Martinez, and Dr. Rosen, and there are a couple of entrances from the highway into Playa Sosúa as you approach from Puerto Plata or Cabarete or across from Supermercado Playero. You can find your way on foot between Playa Sosúa and Playa Alicia by taking the staircase up or down across from the artist alley and navigating Sosúa's small side streets.

SIGHTS
Museo de la Comunidad Judía

A great place to learn the history of the town of Sosúa and its unique cultural legacy is the Jewish Museum or **Museo de la Comunidad**

Sosúa

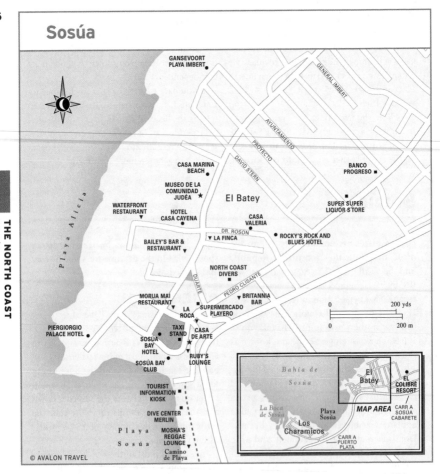

Judía (Calle Dr. Alejo Martinez, next to Casa Marina Hotel, tel. 809/571-1386, call to arrange visit, US$4), created to commemorate the Jews who were welcomed by the Dominican Republic and settled in Sosúa in the 1940s. The single-floor gallery displays the entire history of not just the families who made their home here—including names and photographs—but also of the town of Sosúa from then until the present day. The museum is under renovation until 2016, so call ahead to ensure it is open.

Casa de Arte

Inaugurated in 2013, **La Casa de Arte de** **Sosúa** (Pedro Clisante, across from Parque Las Flores, tel. 809/571-2442, 9am-noon, 1pm-6pm Mon.-Fri., 8:30am-noon Sat., free) is an exciting cultural addition to Sosúa and the brainchild of the town's mayor, Ilana Neumann, a descendant of Sosúa's Jewish settlers and herself an artist. Every month on the first floor, the cultural house hosts a rotating exhibit of Dominican artists from all around the country, including sculptors. One of the best things about this institution is its second-floor art school, where up to 200 underprivileged community kids between 8-18 years of age—those who perform best in school—get instruction with a range of free classes, from painting to ballet, jewelry making to choir singing. It's an incredible resource for the community and a shining light on Sosúa's future generations.

BEACHES

There are two beaches in Sosúa—Playa Sosúa and Playa Alicia. It's an easy, 20-minute walk from one to the other if you know the shortcuts. There's a staircase you can take across the artist alley by Playa Sosúa, which goes to the hotel side, with a 10-minute walk to Playa Alicia. The two beaches couldn't be more different from each other. **Playa Sosúa** is a beautiful golden stretch protected by a reef, making it ideal for swimming with kids and nearby snorkeling. But the beach is also more crowded and filled with vendors, cafés, bars, casual restaurants, and all-around social activity and music. Come here early in the morning if you want a quiet swim before the rush begins or stay on and join into the upbeat beach vibe.

Flanked by towering cliffs and away from the mayhem of the main drag, **Playa Alicia** is wide open—it formed over the last decade when the sea receded—and offers glorious, unobstructed views of the water. It's vendor- and hassle-free for the most part, although there are a couple of surrounding restaurants, including The Waterfront beside the Parque Mirador, built in honor of the Jewish colony who settled here in 1941. There's a staircase leading down to the beach, but the panoramic views from the top of the staircase and the park are outstanding. It's a lovely spot to take a dip or watch the sun set over beach.

SPORTS AND RECREATION
Diving and Snorkeling

Sosúa is touted as one of the best dive and snorkeling areas off the North Coast, but that praise is relative to diving and snorkeling experience elsewhere in the DR. The reef here isn't in the best of conditions, but there are still plenty of Caribbean critters to be seen and appreciated within a relatively short distance from shore. Note that all of the dive and snorkel offerings out of Puerto Plata are all available from Sosúa.

SeaPro Divers (tel. 809/586-1239, http://caribbeanoceanadventures.com/diving.htm, dive.pro@codetel.net.do, US$90 two-tank dive) is the main outfitter in the area and runs diving and snorkeling right offshore. It's popular with beginners. Dives include **The Point,**

Playa Alicia

at 12 meters (40 feet), just a few miles from the bay. Snorkeling stops abound along the coastline—the water is stunning to explore, but don't expect a multitude of fish.

You could haggle for a **glass bottom boat ride** from the beach, usually around US$20 per person. They take you to some of the popular snorkel spots, albeit in wooden boats that are less spacious. Look for the captains along Sosúa Beach.

ENTERTAINMENT AND EVENTS

There aren't major annual events in Sosúa—save for the small multicultural festival that takes place in August, celebrating art, music, and the town's international food scene. For a drink and some dancing, you'll find most of the bars and clubs along the main Pedro Clisante Street, which closes off to traffic after dusk. The scene isn't likely one you'd want to linger around too long, but there are a couple of places you can have a drink in peace and enjoy the evening if you'd rather not head to other nearby towns like Cabarete or Puerto Plata. One is **Rocky's Rock & Blues Bar** (Calle Dr. Rosen 24, tel. 809/571-2951, www.rockysbar.com, 9am-11pm daily), an expat favorite and a nice spot to mingle and have a few cocktails or beers. The other is **The Finish Line** (Ayuntamiento 5, half a block off Pedro Clisante, tel. 829/678-2975, sosua.finish.line@gmail.com, 9am-12am daily) also a North American haunt with a live rock band on Saturday afternoons from 4pm-7pm.

SHOPPING

Located down an alley now known as the artist street of Sosúa, make sure you stop at **571 Art Gallery by Leo Diaz** (tel. 809/712-3632, www.leodiazart.com, 10am-9pm daily, hours vary), where the talented self-taught Dominican sells paintings, sculptures, and other unique souvenirs bearing his art. Ask him about the story behind his "Las señoritas de Sosúa" collection of paintings, inspired by the personal stories of Sosúa's ladies of the night. Leo also teaches a painting class to community kids every week at the Casa de Arte de Sosúa.

For premium cigars, head to **Café Cubano** (Calle Pedro Clisante 27, tel. 809/571-3493 or 829/921-1763, http://sosuacigars.com, 8am-11pm Mon.-Sat.). If you're looking for sarongs, beachwear, and DR-printed totes, you'll find plenty of souvenir shops along Pedro Clisante as well as around Playa Sosúa, filled with mobile vendors and trinkets.

FOOD
Dominican

A good pick among the hundreds of casual, average food shacks dotting Playa Sosúa is **The Mofongo King** (Playa Sosúa, 9am-9pm daily, US$3-10), serving its namesake dish in a variety of ways including with chicken and pork. It's a casual spot that's just as great for a cup of coffee and some people watching. There are also beach chairs across from the café when you're ready to pass out after all that mashed plantain.

Grab some Dominican and Mexican fare on the main drag at **Bistro Típico Alberto** (Calle Pedro Clisante 12, tel. 809/571-4975, 8am-1am daily, US$3-6). Enjoy lunch or post-party grub on this sidewalk terrace.

International

Jolly Roger Bar & Grill (Calle Pedro Clisante 11, tel. 829/299-0753, www.jollyrogersosua.com, US$3-7) is popular with Canadian expats mostly thanks to its lively bar with sports screening, weekly events (including bingo), and cold beers, but it also serves decent sandwiches—try the bacon chicken burger. It's a short walk from the beach and a good setting for all, including families with kids.

Another great chill out spot on the beach, with tasty Jamaican fare from jerk to curried goat, is ★ **Mosha's Reggae Lounge** (#85 Playa Sosúa, 12pm-9pm daily, no phone); the food is cooked fresh, so relax on the beach while your meal is prepared.

The extensive, consistently good menu and service at **Scandinavian Beach Bar** (Playa

Sosúa, 9am-11pm daily, US$3-15) make it a standout on the beach. The ribs in particular win rave reviews. The spot is ideal under the shade, with free wireless Internet and a convivial atmosphere backed with music.

Captain Bailey's (Calle Alejo Martinez, 8am-midnight daily, US$5-20, cash only) has a thatch roof and sits a few steps from Banco Popular along the sidewalk. This casual open-air spot is decent if you're tired of walking in the heat and want a quick sandwich meal or coffee near your hotel. The food is average, with options ranging from burgers to Dominican specials and seafood. Note that it can get quite smoky here, and mostly foreign men congregate at the bar.

Casa Valeria (Calle Dr. Rosen 28, tel. 809/571-3565, hotelcasavaleria@gmail.com, 8am-11pm Thurs.-Tues., 8am-1pm Wed., US$5-15) is set in the leafy, cozy courtyard of its hotel. The menu offers decent priced entrées, including excellent steaks, burgers, and pastas. You can "bring you own wine"—there's no corkage fee—and if it's your birthday, the discount is your actual age—pick the better deal among the two!

Enjoy top-notch cigars and gourmet coffee at **Café Cubano** (Calle Pedro Clisante 27, tel. 809/571-3493 or 829/921-1763, http://sosuacigars.com, 8am-11pm Mon.-Sat., US$2-20)—a popular hangout of residents and visitors alike. The menu also offers plenty of sandwiches—from breakfast croissants to burgers and Cubanos—as well as desserts and cocktails. If you're a cigar aficionado, it's a good spot to learn about the various Dominican brands and find your favorite or a gift to take home.

On The Waterfront (Calle Sin Salida, tel. 809/571-3024, www.waterfrontrestaurantdr. com, noon-midnight daily) has a glorious open-air dining terrace facing Playa Alicia and the Atlantic at the end of a road on a cul-de-sac. The menu, albeit pricey, offers a wide range of entrées, but excels in grilled meats and seafood. Caesar salads are made fresh tableside. Happy hours kick in 5pm-7pm, and there are steps leading down to the beach,

making it an ideal spot to catch sunset with a drink.

Baia Lounge (Gansevoort Playa Imbert, tel. 849/816-2436, 12pm-10pm daily, US$10-30) faces the private beach and the infinity pool at this new luxury resort in Sosúa and offers a decent, varied menu ranging from Italian to Asian fusion. There's a separate sushi menu, and the wine list is extensive—ask to see the cellar on the lower level where you can dine in groups and enjoy cigars for special occasions.

Another fine dining option is at the trendy, all-white **Infiniti Blu Restaurant** (Calle Alejo Martinez/Helipuerto Sosúa, tel. 809/571-2033, 7:30am-11pm daily), serving Mediterranean, Italian, and Middle Eastern specialties, as well as breakfast treats and lunch bites from pizza to sandwiches. There's live music every Friday evening.

Tucked in a quiet corner away from the hustle of Pedro Clisante, the family-friendly, long-standing ★ **Morua Mai Restaurant** (Calle Pedro Clisante 5, across from Casa de Arte, tel. 809/571-3682, moruamai@gmail. com, US$10-25) is a solid choice for a nice meal out with fajitas, burgers, ribs, pizzas, and pastas. It's clean, service is excellent, and it's ideal if you have small kids.

ACCOMMODATIONS

The all-white **Casa Veintiuno 21** (Calle Piano 1, tel. 829/341-8551, www.casaveintiuno.com, US$119-152) is an elegant, small B&B—with just three rooms, of which two are suites—ideal for those seeking luxury away from the Sosúa strips but close enough to walk to the beach and get to the noise. Suites offer plenty of pampering, from the Egyptian cotton linens to espresso machines, plush robes, and all the electronics you need—but if you pick the 21 package, you can also get your clothes packed and unpacked for you, among other perks. There's an onsite restaurant open five days a week, as well as a lovely courtyard with a pool and plenty of loungers. The only company you'll find are the owners' two dogs.

Hotel Casa Cayena (Calle Dr. Rosen 25,

El Batey, tel. 809/571-2429, www.casacayenahotel.com, US$91-101, cash discount) is a bit dated with its peach walls, but it's a long-timer, located just a block from Playa Alicia. There's a restaurant onsite facing the hotel pool. Rooms worth booking offer king beds, mini fridges, and pool-facing balconies.

New Garden Hotel (Calle Dr. Rosen 32, El Batey, tel. 809/571-1557, www.hotelnewgarden.com, US$60-84, includes breakfast) looks like your average Floridian hotel, with rows of rooms facing a pool and an open outdoor terrace. You'll notice more single men staying here (you can guess why). Rooms have flatscreen TV, mini fridge, balcony, air-conditioning, and wireless Internet.

A few steps away, ★ **Casa Valeria** (Calle Dr. Rosen 28, tel. 809/571-3565, www.hotelcasavaleria.com, US$55-80, breakfast included) is a delightful small hotel, from the moment you reach the entrance courtyard to being in the tastefully decorated rooms—red and white hues dominate—facing the swimming pool, with air-conditioning, TV, wireless Internet, and kitchenette options. There's a good restaurant onsite as well. It's a good pick for solo travelers as well as couples who want to be away from the prostitute-and-client scene of Sosúa.

The Piergiorgio Palace Hotel (El Batey 1, tel. 809/571-2626, www.piergiorgiopalace.com, US$95-115) is a staple in Sosúa and might resemble a faded palace, but its wide, cliff-top seafront terrace still has the most breathtaking view over the Sosúa bay and beach. That alone makes it worth staying here if you're just passing through for the night, as well as the waterfront restaurant and the rooms in La Puntilla, facing the same direction and causing you to fall asleep to the hush of the ocean.

The blue and white towers at the classy ★ **Gansevoort Playa Imbert** (www.gansevoorthotelgroup.com/hotels/gansevoort-dominican-republic, US$3,000-6,000) opened in December 2014 and brought a whole new level of luxury in Sosúa with its 24 plush suites—there are 24 more to come by the end of 2016—with one and two-bedroom lofts, three-bedroom apartments with private plunge pools, and a four-bedroom penthouse with private elevator, a rooftop Jacuzzi terrace, and floor-to-ceiling windows. The resort overlooks a stunning private beach stretch while the infinity pool is the centerpiece, framed by daybeds and curtains flowing in the sea breeze. All the bells and whistles include a fifth floor gym with view of the Atlantic, butler service, daybeds and hot tubs on sea-facing terraces, rain showers, automatic blinds, state-of-the art kitchen facilities, and free wireless Internet throughout the property.

INFORMATION AND SERVICES

You'll find most services on the main streets of Calle Pedro Clisante and Calle Duarte. This is the main intersection in the tourist part of Sosúa, an area known as "El Batey." For groceries and other such needs, **Supermercado Playero** (Carretera Sosúa-Cabarete Km 1, tel. 809/571-1821) has a larger branch on the main highway; the smaller one is closer to the hotels and the main drag.

Health and Emergencies

For emergencies in the DR, you can dial 911, just as in the United States. You'll find the 24-hour **Centro Médico Bella Vista** (Carretera Sosúa-Cabarete, tel. 809/571-3429, 8am-9pm Mon.-Sat., 8am-8:30pm Sun.) on the road between Sosúa and Cabarete; pharmacies are on Calle Pedro Clisante—try **Farmacia Sosúa** (tel. 809/571-2350, 8am-7pm Mon.-Sat.).

Money

There's a **Banco Popular** (Dr. Alejo Martinez 1, tel. 809/571-2555, 9am-4pm Mon.-Fri., 9am-1pm Sat.) as well as **Banco Progreso** (Calle Pedro Clisante) with ATMs.

GETTING THERE

Most fly into Puerto Plata's **Aeropuerto Internacional Gregorio Luperón**, then catch a *guagua, carro público,* hotel shuttle, or taxi for the 20-minute ride to Sosúa. Cab fare is around US$35. Check the boards as you exit customs at the airport for the latest official fare.

Caribe Tours (Autopista Puerto Plata-Sosúa, tel. 809/571-3808) has a station in the nontouristy area of Sosúa, known as Los Charamicos. Buses head out to Santo Domingo daily, leaving every hour starting at 5:20am and running until 6:20am, or try **Metro Tours** (Calle Dr. Rosen, tel. 809/571-1324).

GETTING AROUND

It's easy to walk around Sosúa and get to the beaches on foot. That's the good news. If you need to go farther, all of the public transportation options abound from motorbikes—there are many in these parts—to private taxis, which often park on Calle Pedro Clisante.

You can flag down a *carro público* heading to either Cabarete or Puerto Plata (RD$50 or US$1.10); they pass up and down along the highway. To head to Puerto Plata (RD$50 or US$1.10), stand in front of the big Playero Supermarket on main road or go to the main departure hub one block or two up, which is a gas station across from the Texaco. The *carritos* to Cabarete are immediately adjacent to the ones heading to Puerto Plata. Ask anyone for help, and they'll point you in the right direction. If you'd rather take an expensive taxi, call **Taxi Sosúa** (tel. 809/571-2797). To rent a car for road trips to neighboring towns like Cabarete or Río San Juan, try contact **Pionia Rent Car** (Av. Malecón, Puerto Plata, a block from La Sirena, tel. 809/586-3809, pioniarentcar@gmail.com, 8am-6pm Mon.-Sat., US$35).

Cabarete

Cabarete is referred to as the water sports capital of the Dominican Republic, and sometimes even of the Caribbean. It is indeed one of the world's top windsurfing and kitesurfing hubs. Thousands descend on this beachfront town throughout the year from around the world to spend their days splashing in the sun along the glorious white sand and skimming over incessant waves and constant trade winds. Yearly competitions like the Windsurf Classic and Master of the Ocean keep Cabarete at the top of the world's water sports scene. By night, the adrenaline rush is tempered with plenty of libations and dancing in outdoor bars lining the beach. It's the perfect vacation for the young and restless—or the young-at-heart and restless. Yes, it is touristy, but you'll also find a solid expat community of all ages, many of whom made their home here in search of the perfect beach life.

ORIENTATION

The Cabarete area is essentially split into three main parts: Cabarete proper, Kite Beach, and Encuentro Beach. If you want to stay close to the action—the heart of town with bars, restaurants, clubs, and El Choco National Park—stay in **Cabarete.** In Cabarete, you'll find all your needs from windsurfing schools to swimmable beaches and fine dining along the main drag, both roadside and beachfront. As you continue west, it gets less and less crowded. **Encuentro** is by far more isolated, where you'll find boutique resorts. **Kite Beach** has more hotels and kitesurfing schools, as well as boutique resorts. The waves are rough here, so it's really not a leisurely swimming type of spot. Going east in Cabarete, you'll find an area known as **La Punta,** where the sunsets are lovely and there are romantic hotels and restaurants that are an ideal escape from the noise, but still walking distance from the heart of Cabarete.

SIGHTS
El Choco National Park

It's pretty amazing that just a 10-minute drive from the main strip of Cabarete and its water sports-jammed beaches will bring you to a 77-square-kilometer (30-square-mile) national park and protected area where you can hike, ride horses, mountain bike, or bathe in jade-colored waters. Set in the local neighborhood Callejón de la Loma, **El Choco National Park** (Callejón de La Loma, tel. 809/454-3072, 9am-5pm daily, US$1.10) greets visitors with a beautiful freshwater lagoon by the entrance, which is a popular swimming spot for locals on the weekends.

Over 100 families once inhabited El Choco, until the government decided to turn it into a national park and relocated many. Today there are only a handful of inhabited homes that remain within the park, closer to the entrance, and they offer insight into traditional Dominican living. Hiking through El Choco takes you past various fruit trees, including cacao and coffee, medicinal plants, birds, and tropical jungle foliage. Along the way are two water caves—known as **Las Cuevas de Cabarete**—entered by means of ladders and wooden steps with incredible stalactite formations. These are said to be the deepest water caves on the entire island of Hispaniola, and certified cave divers can explore them. The entire park feels like one big jungle, virtually untouched and waiting to be discovered.

The easier, main entrance to the park is close to town. Get there by taking the Callejón de la Loma down from La Roma Restaurant and continuing all the way to the end, or about a 20- to 25-minute walk from the center of Cabarete. I recommend you visit the park with **Iguana Mama** (www.iguanamama.com) for a more informative 2.5-hour hike (US$35 pp, US$25 children) or a **"Choco Loco" mountain bike ride** of 44 kilometers (27 miles) (US$55 pp). If you head there solo, ask for one of the bilingual local guides at the entrance of the park when you pay your entrance fee—**Levi Martinez** (tel. 809/972-1162) is a good one.

Zipline and animal lovers will appreciate **Monkey Jungle and Zip Line Adventures** (Carretera El Choco, tel. 809/649-4555, www.monkeyjungledr.com, 9am-4pm daily, US$50 zipline only or US$70 combo, cash only, with own transport, or Runners Adventures excursion US$90). This nature sanctuary is tucked 9 kilometers (6 miles) into the lush forest of El Choco. The 1.1-square-kilometer (280-acre) farm is also home to a 1,372-meter (4,500-foot) certified zipline with seven stations, a five-acre botanical garden, and 45 squirrel monkeys you'll get to feed and watch crawl over you.

El Choco National Park

Cabarete

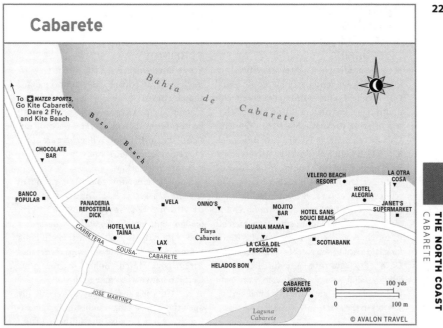

To WATER SPORTS,
Go Kite Cabarete,
Dare 2 Fly,
and Kite Beach

Bahía de Cabarete

Bozo Beach

CHOCOLATE BAR

BANCO POPULAR

PANADERIA REPOSTERÍA DICK

HOTEL VILLA TAÍNA

VELA

ONNO'S

Playa Cabarete

LAX

HELADOS BON

JOSE MARTINEZ

CARRETERA SOUSA-CABARETE

VELERO BEACH RESORT

HOTEL ALEGRÍA

MOJITO BAR

HOTEL SANS SOUCI BEACH

IGUANA MAMA

LA CASA DEL PESCADOR

SCOTIABANK

LA OTRA COSA

JANET'S SUPERMARKET

CABARETE SURFCAMP

Laguna Cabarete

0   100 yds
0   100 m

© AVALON TRAVEL

All profits from visits go directly to an onsite medical and dental clinic for locals, where health care teams have volunteered since 2009 and treated over 21,000 patients.

BEACHES

There are three main beaches in the Cabarete area, each with its own atmosphere. **Playa Cabarete,** on the eastern end and facing the Cabarete bay, is the social beach, with a fun row of bars, restaurants, and water sports shacks. It's popular for windsurfing, but there's plenty of space to swim and relax as well. It's wide, allowing for plenty of lounge-type setups. You won't see any kiting on this main portion of Cabarete Beach, for the safety of all swimmers, particularly kids. At night, it's even prettier with colorful lights and island ambience as folks come out to eat and dance in flip-flops.

On the eastern edge of the beach, about 15 steps from the heart of the stretch, you'll begin to spot kitesurfing school after kitesurfing school, and plenty of kites resting on the beach or up in the air—this is where beginners take their lessons. This beginners' area is known as **Bozo Beach.** It can get supercrowded so watch your feet (and sometimes your head) as you walk along the stretch.

Continue walking west and you'll hit **Kite Beach**—with more kitesurfers, although fewer beginners. The waves are stronger and this isn't really a swimming beach like Cabarete. The shoreline has also eroded quite a bit, so you may end up wading through water in some parts when walking from the Cabarete end. There are a couple of nice bars out the way, but more small hotels and resorts.

Playa Encuentro is the farthest from Cabarete town on the western end. It's the surfer's beach—one of the best in the country for its water and wind conditions. It's rocky—you can't enter the water without water shoes—and not for relaxed swims. But it's still a fun beach to visit and beautiful at that. Take a surfing lesson or watch the pros catch a wave or two.

SPORTS AND RECREATION
★ Water Sports

KITESURFING

If you're heading to Cabarete specifically to kitesurf by day (and party by night), you'll find excellent schools lining the shore with multilingual instructors and often onsite hotels offering packages. Start with **Go Kite Cabarete** (Extreme Hotels, Kite Beach, tel. 829/644-8354, www.gokitecabarete.com, 9am-6pm, US$550/7 hours), locally owned and operated by native Richard Diaz. The school gets rave reviews for its ideal location on the premises of an adventure hotel and with plenty of space for beginners to learn off its beach. Another solid pick on Kite Beach for a laid-back lesson away from the crowds is **Dare 2 Fly Cabarete** (Agualina Resort, tel. 809/571-0805, www.daretofly.com, 9am-6pm, US$520/9 hours), one of the first kiteboarding schools in the area.

WINDSURFING

Vela Windsurf Resorts (beachfront, tel. 809/571-0805, www.velacabarete.com, 9am-6pm daily, US$45/hour private or US$140/6-hour group lesson) is the popular choice for windsurfing classes, right on Cabarete Beach, tucked amid all the lounges and restaurants where you can come and go as you please.

SURFING

Playa Encuentro is the place to be for surfing. This beach is lined with vibrantly painted thatch-roofed shacks, which are surfing schools. These shacks are set in the shade with benches facing the most glorious waves on this side of the North Coast. While there are a host of options for surfing lessons, two of the best picks are listed below.

Your best bet for your first round of surfing classes is **321 TakeOff School of Riding Waves** (tel. 809/963-7873, 6:30am-6pm daily, US$50/day program or US$190/7-day). If you're smart, you'll book a one-on-one private lesson with owner and surf master Marcus Bohm—a gregarious German native who came to the DR in 1990 at age 20 to windsurf and stayed to eventually open the first surfing schools on Encuentro Beach. Marcus is also the founder of the now world-renowned Master of the Ocean world competition taking place every year in Cabarete, and filmed last year by ESPN, and of the nonprofit Happy Dolphins program, funding local kids' swimming and lifeguard training classes. Note that surfing classes

Playa Cabarete is the windsurfing hub of the Caribbean.

Kitesurfing Schools

The hottest and fastest-growing water sport in the Caribbean is kitesurfing. The sport first made its appearance in Cabarete in the 1990s, introduced by a couple of adventurous Frenchmen, and it soon captured attention as the popularity of windsurfing slowly declined. Less wind is needed to kitesurf than to windsurf, which provided more days of the year to practice. With perfect wave conditions, and a growing number of IKO-certified schools, this northern piece of the DR has established its dominant position in the kiting world.

Cabarete's sought after kitesurfing schools are lined along the beachfront, stretching from Cabarete town to neighboring Kite Beach. What school you choose to kitesurf with, as a beginner in particular, will depend on your language ability—there are schools catering to the French-, or German-, or English-speaking. It isn't so much a question of expertise, since all schools are IKO certified, as it is a matter of comfort and fit for the student. Here are recommended schools that will offer you a great jumpstart into this adrenaline sport, with a focus on both safety and fun.

Kitesurfing schools abound on the western end of Playa Cabarete.

Dominican owned and operated **Go Kite Cabarete** (Extreme Hotels, Kite Beach, tel. 829/644-8354, www.gokitecabarete.com, 9am-6pm daily, US$550/7 hours) is one of the best on the stretch. It specializes in beginners and has experienced, Dominican instructors, including the popular Richard Diaz. The school has a laid-back atmosphere and is ideally located on an all-adventure hotel's premises—with on=site gym facilities, a yoga studio, and even a circus school. There's plenty of space for everyone's equipment on the beachfront, where training begins. Advanced kiteboarding lessons are also offered.

A hip and lively female pro kiteboarder-owned school, **Laura Eastman Kiteboarding** (tel. 809/571-0564, www.laureleastman.com, 9am-6pm daily, US$71/hour or US$630/10 hours) is where the cool kids hang out—including from the neighboring Millenium Resort. The atmosphere is fun throughout the day, with music and kitesurfers going to and from the beach. Beginners are welcome, and you're only charged for the minutes actually spent learning from your coach. Kiteboarding for kids is offered (over 8) as well as advanced lessons.

From beginners to pros, **KiteClub Cabarete** (tel. 809/571-9748, www.kiteclubcabarete, 11am-6pm daily, US$240/3 hours) has a solid, long-running reputation with owner Jon Dodds, who is an IKO examiner. Aside from the usual beginner lessons, the school offers two-way radio helmets, whereby students stay in contact with their instructor while kitesurfing. The vibe is social and there's an excellent onsite cafeteria.

The multilingual, friendly instructors and staff at **Dare 2 Fly Cabarete** (Agualina Resort, tel. 809/571-0805, www.dare2fly.com, 9am-6pm daily, US$190/3 hours) teach on a beautiful stretch of Kite Beach, beside the popular VacaBar.

begin at dawn, so if you want to pop in unannounced, which is welcomed, the morning is your best bet. Water shoes are provided for the rocky shores, and you'll have a great time whether you're learning the basics of surfing in his "Feel It" program—which begins on shore and continues in hip-deep water—or taking off with the pros.

Next door, **LG Surf Camp** (tel. 809/986-6454 or U.S. tel. 321/392-2273, www.lgsurf-camp.com, 6am-6pm daily, US$1,200 for week-long all inclusive package with lodging, meals, and lessons) also provides lessons and surfing vacation packages with owner Luciano Gonzalez, a Red Bull-sponsored Dominican pro surfer who is a four-time winner of the Master of the Ocean competition and has traveled worldwide to compete from Hawaii—where he was crowned Red Bull King of the Air in 2003 an 2009—to Europe. His story is one of humble beginnings to soaring success. This is a unique opportunity to learn from a local whose life was transformed thanks to sports.

Fishing

Captain Freddy (tel. 809/613-4177, www. dominicanfisherman.com, US$25-125) offers reef trolling along the reefs of Sosúa, Cabarete, and Sabaneta, as well as deep-sea fishing—think mahimahi and marlin—shore fishing, and family trips for freshwater fishing in remoter villages.

Diving and Snorkeling

Dive Cabarete (Calle Principal, tel. 809/915-9135, www.divecabarete.com, 10am-6pm Mon.-Sat., US$100/2-tank dive) offers PADI scuba lessons (US$456 Open Water) as well as dive excursions, the majority of which are off the coast of Sosúa. There's also cave

diving possibilities at the Dudú Blue Lagoon in Río San Juan for the experienced. Two-hour snorkeling trips (US$35 pp) take you to Sosúa Bay, where you can see a variety of Caribbean critters.

Stand-Up Paddleboarding

Kayak River Adventures (Calle Principal, Cabarete, tel. 829/305-6883, www.kayakriveradventures.com, US$59-89) takes you on guided SUP tours down Cabarete's Jamao and Yásica Rivers, for a half or full day. Beginners are welcome, as are children eight years old and up.

With **321 TakeOff Surf School** (Encuentro Beach, tel. 809/963-7873, US$60) you can try a **Sosúa SUP Adventure,** gliding from Cabarete to Sosúa's gorgeous bay for an excursion of three hours.

A handful of kitesurfing and windsurfing schools on Cabarete Beach also rent out SUP boards—right in town, try **Vela** (Calle Principal, tel. 809/571-0805, www.velacabarete.com, 9am-6pm daily, US$20/hour or US45/half day).

Yoga

Yoga classes abound in Cabarete. Find weekly 90-minute sessions on Encuentro Beach

surf shacks at Playa Encuentro

at **Natura Cabana** (Paseo del Sol 5, Perla Marina, tel. 809/571-1507, info@naturacabana.com, US$10, no reservations required); contact them for the latest schedule. Closer to town, at Kite Beach, **Rogue Fitness' Yoga Loft** (Extreme Hotel, tel. 809/571-0330, http://yogacabarete.com/schedule, US$15) offers beachfront sessions.

Canyoning, Waterfall Rappelling, and Caving

Iguana Mama (Calle Principal, tel. 809/654-2325, www.iguanamama.com, 7:45am-3:30pm Mon. and Fri., US$80-159) is the DR's top adventure company and the longest-running one on the North Coast. You can't go wrong with one of their adrenaline-inducing activities and friendly guides. Try the full-day **Big Bastard** adventure, where you'll test your endurance canyoneering in a stunning river valley, with rappels of up to 160 feet and jumps of up to 60 feet. You'll likely be the only ones onsite. Other waterfall trips head to 27 Charcos de Damajagua, the Magic Mushroom, and Ciguapa Falls. Iguana Mama also offers hiking trips to El Choco National Park in Cabarete, where you can spelunk in two water caves.

The smaller eco-adventure company **Kayak River Adventures** (Calle Principal, tel. 829/305-6883, www.kayakriveradventures.com, US$89-129) also takes you hiking and canyoning to the Magic Mushroom or Ciguapa Falls. Also on tap is caving at one of their "off-the-beaten-track" caves called La Cueva, which requires four rappels before you even start spelunking in chambers ranging from 10 to 50 meters (32 to 165 feet) in height. Once you reach the cave floor, the caving continues as you will make your way through for two hours give or take, guided only by your headlamp and your experienced guides. The cave is huge! The ceiling of the cave is between 10-50 meters high (33-164 feet).

Kayaking

You'll experience the real DR by kayaking or SUPing downstream 10 kilometers (6 miles) along jungle and farmland with **Kayak River Adventures** (tel. 829/305-6883, www.kayakriveradventures.com, US$59-89). It's a half-day excursion on the Jamao and Yassica Rivers, at the foothill of the Cordillera Septentrional. A great trip for families—you'll learn about a variety of Dominican flora and fauna, including birding, on this ecotour. Impromptu stops allow for dipping into fresh river water, of course. There's also a full-day version.

You can also rent single or double kayaks from **Vela Windsurf Resorts** (beachfront, tel. 809/571-0805, www.velacabarete.com, 9am-6pm daily, US$10-15/hour) and go exploring on your own; just beware of the busier kitesurfing end.

Ziplining

The closest zipline is within El Choco at the 1.1-square-kilometers (280-acre) **Monkey Jungle and Zip Line Adventures** (9 km up Carretera El Choco, tel. 829/649-4555, ww.monkeyungledr.com, 9am-4pm daily, US$50 zipline, cash only). There are seven stations and a certified 1,372-meter-high (4,500-foot) zipline. If you choose to continue the adventure, onsite are a botanical garden where squirrel monkeys reside and a cave. All profits go to charity. You can venture here in your own car, or you can sign up with **Runners Adventures** (tel. 809/320-1061, www.runnersadventures.com) for US$35 more, which usually includes all these attractions.

Horseback Riding

Go horseback riding in the Dominican countryside with **Bávaro Runners** (tel. 809/320-1061, www.bavarorunners.com, US$120), out of nearby Puerto Plata—they offer a triple adventure day with waterfalls, horses, and ziplining.

Cultural Tours

Cabarete Coffee Company (Bahia de Arena, between Kite Beach and town, tel. 809/571-0919, www.cabaretecoffee.com, 8:30am-2pm every Tues. and Thurs., US$75) offers tours of an organic cacao farm, as well as a coffee plantation—two of the DR's major exports.

Spa

N Day Spa (Plaza El Patio, Calle Principal, across from Panadería Reposteria Dick and across from Friends, tel. 809/905-6510, www.cabaretespa.com, 9am-6pm Mon.-Sat., US$45-95), short for Naomie Day Spa, is in the center of town, but its facility is tucked away from the traffic noise on the main street. This full-service spa is small but cozy, offering two treatment rooms, with options for a couples massage. The staff here is friendly and bilingual.

Attabeyra Spa (Natura Cabana, Paseo del Sol 5, Perla Marina, tel. 809/571-1507, info@ naturacabana.com, 10am-6pm daily, US$30-80) is set amid the quiet oasis of a boutique resort on Encuentro Beach. Treatments range from after-sun wraps and Turkish baths to chocolate exfoliations and various kinds of massage, including hot stone and reflexology. Mani-pedis and waxing services are also offered.

ENTERTAINMENT AND EVENTS
Nightlife

Cabarete is the place to be for all-night partying and boozing like you're forever young, if that's your fancy. Cover-free lounges, bars, and discos line the stretch, which becomes one big outdoor *va-et-vient* of partygoers from tourists to local out-of-towners, shuffling in the sand as they hop around their favorite venues. Others lounge by the water with treats bought at the liquor store. Whether you prefer a game of pool or an all-out rave, you'll find your fun in Cabarete. Prostitution isn't as prevalent or in your face as it is in Sosúa, and the scene is international. Here are a few spots to check out.

Mojito Bar (Cabarete beachfront, tel. 809/571-9327, www.mojitobar-cabarete. com, 11am-11pm Wed.-Mon.) is a great pick to start the night off with some freshly made mojitos on the beach. It's hard to beat this affordable, lively spot. There are daily happy hours from 4pm-8pm with two for one mojitos, Cuba libres, margaritas, piña coladas, and more, as well as a drink special every day of the week. Green Friday is popular, with local bands performing on a small stage inside the open-air restaurant. Nearby, **voyvoy!** (Cabarete beachfront, tel. 809/571-0805, www.voyvoycabarete, 9am-2am daily) has friendly bartenders and a cozy space serving excellent happy hour specials, starting at US$2.25 a cocktail.

Havana Club (Cabarete beachfront, tel. 809/882-3144, 9pm-2am daily) is a bit of a dive, with no air-conditioning or fans, but the DJ spins excellent Latin sounds and drinks are cheap. If you're willing to sweat it out, it's not a bad spot. Just don't expect a stellar crowd.

The open-air **Lax Ojo** (beachfront Cabarete, tel. 829/745-8811, www.laxojo. com, 10pm-2am Sun.-Wed., later close Thurs.-Sat.) is the largest and most packed nightclub on the strip, featuring two large floors where DJs spin a variety of music. Thursdays are Latin night and attract locals from neighboring Puerto Plata. It can get unbearably packed on the weekends, especially on the ground floor. **Onno's** (beachfront, tel. 809/571-0461, www.onnosbar. com, 9am-3am daily) is another favored dance spot, especially among the locals—the smaller space gives it more of a lounge feel. Music ranges from R&B to *dembow* and merengue. Thursday is ladies' night, with half-price drinks. You can also hop over to **Bambú Bar** (beachfront, tel. 809/982-4549, 10pm-2am daily) for more dancing.

Arriba Bar (Av. Principal, tel. 809/571-9592, 12pm-2am daily) is a great chill-out spot where you can play pool with locals and expats, throw back some drinks, and listen to a DJ spinning music, at times with videos on screen. When it isn't busy you can find enough space to dance on the floor beside the bar. It's a wind down after the madness of Cabarete Beach across the street.

Voodoo Lounge (entrance of Callejón

de La Loma, tel. 809/874-0615, 5pm-midnight Wed.-Sun.) is a casual, unpretentious local spot to mingle with Dominicans and expats away from the tourist club strip on the beach. Wednesdays are popular for open mic, and there are occasional live music nights on Saturday—keep an eye out on social media pages.

Festivals and Cultural Events

Every January around the middle of the month, over 30 master sailors from both the DR and abroad gather to compete at the **Caribbean Laser Midwinter Regatta,** an ISAF grade 3 event consisting of nine races and organized by The Laser Training Center in Cabarete. Entering its 14th edition as of 2016, the race takes place a week prior to the Miami Olympic Regatta, in which many also participate. Cabarete has also hosted the **World Cup of the Windsurfing Association** for several years.

One of the most popular annual events in all the Dominican Republic is the **Dominican Republic Jazz Festival** (www.drjazzfestival.com) held the first week of November, with performances from both Dominican and international jazz artists taking place in Puerto Plata, Sosúa, and Cabarete. It's a great time to be on the North Coast and enjoy the mix of both Dominican and international vibes that this area represents so well.

The annual **Master of the Ocean** competition (321 TakeOff, Playa Encuentro, tel. 809/963-7873 or 809/856-4798, www.masteroftheocean.com) launched in 2003 and brought even more international attention to the North Coast of the Dominican Republic. The brainchild of Marcus Bohm, owner of 321 TakeOff surfing school, it now takes place every February featuring 12 teams of four athletes per team, who come from around the world as well as across the DR to compete for the title by mastering four water sports: windsurfing, surfing, stand-up paddleboarding, and kiteboarding. It's a fun time to be in Cabarete—last year ESPN was there filming the event.

SHOPPING

Kana Rapai Art Studio (Calle Principal, across from Onno's, tel. 809/852-0757, www.kanarapai.com) is very Cabarete in its original, handmade gifts made out of recycled material. You'll find casual jewelry, purses, and magnets, among other handmade gifts. A few steps away, across the street, is the more traditional **Taina Joyería Shop** (Calle Principal, tel. 829/678-3595, 10am-7pm daily), a small boutique with locally made wood carvings, larimar and other handmade jewelry, Taíno and Haitian art—including statues of Taíno gods—and run-of-the-mill souvenirs like mugs. Get your cigars at **D'Angel Cigar Lounge** (Calle Principal, facing Scotiabank, tel. 809/571-9761, angelcigarlounge@hotmail.com, 9am-5pm Mon.-Sat.), where you'll find a humidor and a couple of chairs where you can cool off while enjoying your purchase.

For groceries, you'll find all your need to stock your fridge at **Janet's Supermarket** (Calle Principal, tel. 809/571-9774, www.janetssupermarket.com, 8am-8pm Mon.-Sat., 8:30am-1pm Sun.) in Cabarete town, or closer to Kite Beach there's the smaller, local **Supermercado La Rosa** (tel. 809/571-0361, 8am-10pm Mon.-Sun.).

FOOD
Cafés

Breakfast on the beach never looked so good as the open-air, casual beachfront **voyvoy!** (next to Vela Windsurfing School, tel. 809/571-0805, www.voyvoycabarete, 9am-2am daily, US$1.50-4), facing Cabarete's beautiful stretch with crowds walking past and windsurfers dotting the sea. The menu ranges from omelettes to coconut pancakes and fresh smoothies. Of course there's coffee as well. Bury your toes in the sand and enjoy the moment.

On the main drag, an all-around traditional breakfast can be had at **Panadería Repostería Dick** (Calle Principal 31, tel. 809/571-0612, panarolfdick@yahoo.com, 6:30am-5pm daily, US$2-10), be it—English, French, or Dominican. This popular casual café has a sidewalk terrace on the main drag. The service and atmosphere are authentically Cabarete.

The Belgium Bakery (Plaza Popular, next to Banco Popular, tel. 829/571-8198, www.belgiumbakery.com, US$3-10), boasts a shaded outdoor terrace blessed with the delicious aroma of freshly baked pastries, quiches, cakes, and other artisan desserts, to be washed down with coffee or a Belgian beer. The glass display alone is enough to make you grab a seat. Aside from breakfasts, there's a daily coffee and dessert special for under US$4 (RD$150) and two for one happy hour hamburgers noon-2pm.

Cabarete Coffee Company (Bahia de Arena, between Kite Beach and town, tel. 809/571-0919, www.cabaretecoffee.com, 7am-3pm daily, US$3-10) organic coffee is grown in the mountainous Madre de las Aguas region, considered to be the most important watershed on all of Hispaniola. Try the dark roast "Surfer's Blend" to take home, or stay in and enjoy a healthy breakfast or lunch with your java or smoothie. Choices range from sandwiches to bagels and salads.

Chocolate Bar (across from Banco Popular, Calle Principal, tel. 809/603-8354, chocolatebardr@gmail.com, 8am-6pm Mon.-Sat., 8am-2pm Sun., US$2-10) is good whether you need a cacao fix or healthy fruit juices and smoothies.

Dominican

Located at Xtreme Hotel, **Casa Mami's** (Carretera Sosúa-Cabarete Km 10.5, next to Police Station, Kite Beach, tel. 809/618-6987, 9am-10pm daily, US$3) serves daily Dominican dishes at local prices, including fish fillets, barbecue chicken, salad, and rice and beans.

La Parilla Luis (across from Ocean Dream, Callejón de La Loma entrance, tel. 809/857-5527, 5pm-10pm Fri.-Wed., closed Thurs., US$4-8), affectionately known as the Chicken Shack, doesn't disappoint either. It serves up one the cheapest meals and tastiest grilled barbecue chicken in town, with

yucca, rice, plantains, or sautéed veggies for just over US$2.

Arriba Bar (Av. Principal, Cabarete, tel. 809/571-9592, US$2.50, 12pm-2am daily) is a casual, second-floor bar and restaurant where you can grab a cheap lunch of the day to go—rice and beans with a meat stew. Take it over to the beach and enjoy.

La Casita de Papi (Cabarete beachfront, tel. 809/986-3750, noon-10pm Tues.-Sun, US$7-20) is one of the busiest dining spots on the beach, and for good reason. Their signature seafood dishes, Shrimp a la Papi and Langostino a la Papi are finger-licking good, as are the desserts—try the banana flambé, lit up at your table. There's a cozy interior with a couple of white linen-covered wooden tables, facing an open kitchen, but the best setting is under the blue sky or stars along the white sand beach. You can now also find a branch of this restaurant in Santo Domingo's Colonial City.

Reached by boat, ★ **Wilson's La Boca Restaurant** (Camino del Sol, tel. 809/571-9594 or 809/667-1960, noon-3pm daily, US$7, boat ride provided) offers fresh fish Dominican-style with an ambience to match. Hop in a taxi from Cabarete town (US$10 one-way) and head to the south side of the beach, about 2.5 miles away, at the mouth of the Yásica de Sabaneta River. There, you will hop in a small motorboat to cross over the water and reach the rustic, open-air shack of a restaurant. In a town that sometimes feels like it has more tourists than locals, it's a nice escape and reminder of the real DR. Options for lunch are the catch of the day—lobster when in season, mahimahi, or crab—with typical sides of rice and beans, salad and plantain.

International

On the road between Cabarete and Sosúa, stop by **Parada Típico El Choco** (across from Ocean Village, Carretera Sosúa-Cabarete, tel. 809/854-5562 or 809/571-3534, paradaelchoco@diconti.com, 8am-11:30pm daily, US$5-10) is a solid pick for meals any time of day and a popular expat haunt. Try the omelettes for breakfast, or the steaks, barbecue, or burgers. Portions are huge, and the atmosphere is convivial under a cozy thatched roof.

You could quickly become a regular at the lagoon-facing, casual restaurant inside ★ **Ali's Surf Camp** (Calle Bahia 11, ProCab, tel. 829/548-6655, www.cabaretesurfcamp.com, 7:30am-9:30pm daily, US$4-10). Tucked to the back of the ProCab expat neighborhood an easy walk from town, the romantic candlelit tables on the thatch-roofed wooden deck are matched with a flavorful menu. You'll find it written in chalk on small boards pinned around the dining area. Juicy grilled steaks or *parillada,* seafood and finger-licking side dishes (the spiced, sautéed potatoes and rice are some of the best I've had in Puerto Plata) will keep you returning, as will the cocktails. Bring mosquito repellent.

★ **Mojito Bar** (Cabarete beachfront, tel. 809/571-9327, www.mojitobar-cabarete.com, 11am-11pm Wed.-Mon., US$3-10) has the best drink specials (two for one at happy hour) and most affordable sandwich deals in town with daily "combo" specials: grab a mojito and a sandwich for under US$5. There's interior seating but the beachfront is delightful, with a perfect view of windsurfers up ahead.

With a cozy beachfront setup made up of sofas and chairs, **Onno's** (beachfront, tel. 809/571-0461, www.onnosbar.com, 9am-3am daily, US$5-7) is a classic, with its burgers, sandwiches, pizza, and seafood entrées. The food is decent but the local atmosphere is great. Happy hours last 5pm-9pm, with mojitos for US$2.

For a taste of Mexico on the go, the local favorite ★ **Gordito's Fresh Mex** (Plaza Ocean Dream, tel. 809/571-0128, www.gorditosfreshmex.com, 11:30am-8:30pm Mon.-Sat., US$3-10) doesn't disappoint, serving up delicious tacos—the fish ones are delicious— burritos with veggie options, rice bowls, and even margaritas.

For tasty Italian-style pizza or pasta, **Pomodoro** (Cabarete Beach, tel. 809/571-0085, pomodoropizzacabarete@gmail.com, 4pm-11pm Wed.-Mon., 11:30am-11:30pm Sat.-Sun., US$10-15) is the long-standing, consistent pick. Add on some wine and gelato to your order. They also deliver.

On the less-crowded Kite Beach end, expat fave **VacaBar** (next to Hotel Agualina, tel. 809/889-1198, vacabarcabarete@gmail.com, 8:30am-5pm Mon., 8:30am-9pm Tues.-Sat., 8:30am-2pm Sun., US$4-15) is a small spot serving breakfasts and burgers—look for the chalkboard menu—on a wooden platform with a deck extending steps from the sea. If you're staying in the area, it's an ideal spot to start the day watching kitesurfers roam the sea and catching the breeze.

Want an unforgettable dinner? You'll get just that when you head to ★ **La Otra Cosa** (La Punta de Cabarete, tel. 809/571-0607, www.otracosarestaurant.com, dinner only 6:30pm-10pm daily, US$10-35), especially at sunset. Located on a scenic edge in La Punta just past Velero Beach Resort, you'll walk past the main entrance and suddenly come upon a stunning open-air, multilevel thatched-roof dining room with panoramic views of the Atlantic below. As if the scenery isn't romantic enough, the menu is a delight. Try the tuna tartare tempered by mango chutney, or the seared tuna in a ginger and flambé rum sauce. It's a real treat to dine here to the sound of world music beats.

Miro's (Cabarete beachfront, tel. 809/571-9345, mirobeach@hotmail.com, 11am-11:30pm Tues.-Sun., US$10-30), though slightly pricey, is a standout amid restaurants serving similar fare for its sophisticated ambience on the beach and its Mediterranean and seafood menu including paella, tuna tartare, and sushi.

On the streetside, the small but übermodern **Yalla** (next to Panadería Dick, Calle Principal, tel. 809/571-9357, noon-11pm Thurs.-Tues., US$7.65-12) impresses with its creative tapas and sandwiches. Try the pineapple pork, diced chorizos, manchego cheese croquettes, or chicken skewers, among other tapas options. The chocolate churros are a must for dessert.

Go for steaks and seafood at the beachfront **Chez Arsenio** (Hideaway Beach Resort, tel. 809/571-9948, lagan.anne@gmail.com, 11am-10pm Mon.-Fri., 9am-10pm Sat.-Sun., US$5-20), even if the slow service might taint your experience on a busy night. Options also include curries and pastas. Set under a thatched palapa flanked by the beautiful and breezy Encuentro Beach and the resort swimming pool, it's a good choice for a romantic meal al fresco, away from Cabarete's busy beachfront.

Vegan and Vegetarian

★ **Clorofila** (Callejón de La Loma, on left side next to Voodoo Lounge, first tel. 829/993-5607, 9am-4pm Mon.-Sat. closed Sun., US$5.50-6) is earning its raves as the latest and welcome addition to the eclectic Cabarete food scene in the more locally frequented (and affordable) part of town, a stone's throw off the main tourist strip. The small, green-colored restaurant owned by a local community power couple specializes in Dominican-inspired vegan and vegetarian dishes that will suit anyone who loves food—with all ingredients sourced locally. The menu—displayed on a chalkboard outdoors—changes daily and includes tasty, creative picks like the eggplant ceviche, papaya and cilantro salad, spicy Thai soup with tofu and vegetable rolls. The presentation is equally pleasing and worthy of a fine dining establishment. —You'll also enjoy the reggae beats while you sip on a *morir soñando*—the Dominican smoothie made here with coconut milk (in lieu of cow's milk), orange juice, brown sugar, and honey.

Vegans and even non-vegans will also enjoy **Fresh Fresh Café** (Calle Principal, tel. 809/571-0283, freshfreshcabarete@gmail.com, 8am-9pm daily, US$3-10). The most popular items, enjoyed on covered terrace or indoors with air-conditioning, are their breakfast bagels and their healthy detox smoothies and salads. You'll also find veggie burgers and wraps. The meat eaters can enjoy the fish bowls or chicken sandwiches, or veggie curries and grilled fish for dinner. Don't miss sampling the coconut brownies. There's also a Sosúa location.

ACCOMMODATIONS
Under US$50

Casa Blanca Hotel (Calle Principal, tel. 809/571-0934, www.casablancacabarete.com, US$25-55) offers a range of rooms, albeit dated, ranging from single-bed hostel types to larger, self-catering apartments. There's a small pool on the grounds and restaurant for guests.

The budget **Hotel Alegría** (tel. 809/571-0455, www.hotel-alegria.com, US$40, air-conditioning additional) has an ideal location, on the eastern edge of Cabarete beach, steps from Janet's Supermarket, and a stone's throw from the sand and its activities, yet away from the mayhem. Standard rooms are basic, with wireless Internet, fan, and small TVs, but if you're just looking for a safe and relatively clean roof over your head, they'll suffice. Those who wish can upgrade to oceanview rooms, with optional air-conditioning for an extra fee. There's a restaurant onsite, good for breakfasts, although you're so close to the beach you might as well venture out.

Get a feel for a local neighborhood and stay at **Casa Carmen** (Callejón de La Loma, tel. 809/879-2415, h.perez@hotmail.com, US$25). This hostel type of accommodation is ideal for the non-fussy, light traveler who wants to immerse. Rooms are basic, with fans and a communal kitchen. You'll be around plenty of local shops, fruit markets, and a mixed Dominican and expat population. The main Cabarete Beach is a 10-minute walk away.

Kite Beach Hotel (Carretera Sosúa-Cabarete, tel. 809/571-0878, www.kitebeach-hotel.com, $50-160, includes breakfast) offers a range of rooms to fit every budget, from basic pads with no air-conditioning to superior rooms and deluxe apartments. A beach-facing pool and restaurant complete the setting. You'll be a bit isolated from the town's social corner, but it's an easy shared taxi hop away.

US$50-100

Cabarete Palm Beach Condos (beachfront Cabarete, tel. 809/571-0758, www.cabaretecondos.com, US$85-198) offer a range of beachfront apartments, studios, and penthouses with delightful summer furniture, oceanfront patios, full kitchen facilities, and an onsite swimming pool. To top it off, you're a stone's throw from all of Cabarete's amenities from restaurants to kitesurfing schools, yet set back enough from the beach to get some tranquility. It's a great spot for families and groups.

★ **Hotel Villa Taina** (Playa Cabarete, tel. 809/571-0722, www.villataina.com, US$97-163, includes breakfast) is a solid pick for families, with 57 rooms set facing Cabarete Beach conveniently close to restaurants and activities. Options range from standard to partial oceanfront suites, all of which are tastefully decorated in tropical colors. Expect in-room fridges, TV, air-conditioning, and free wireless Internet. Other amenities onsite are a restaurant, swimming pool, windsports school, and the full-service Tranquila Spa. Yoga, a gym, and volleyball are offered as activities.

Extreme Hotel (Kite Beach, tel. 809/571-0330, www.extremehotels.com, US$59) is everything its name suggests: a nontraditional ecofriendly (solar-powered) escape where you'll find an active vacationer's playground, including kitesurfing lessons, an onsite gym with regular Zumba and yoga classes, and the Kaiceitos Circus—where you can learn how to swing from a trapeze like a pro. Rooms are clean and basic, yet just right for a fun, active beachside vacation. With a solid restaurant onsite serving Dominican and Spanish specialties, Extreme Hotel is its very own getaway.

On the beginning edge of Playa Encuentro is **Natura Cabana Boutique Hotel & Spa** (Paseo del Sol 5, tel. 809/571-1507, www.naturacabana.com, US$90, breakfast included), popular for its palapa bungalows—doubles and triples available—with kitchenettes and beachfront setting, as well as its onsite yoga classes. The rooms are fan only (an ecofriendly measure, although there is 24-hour generator power), with full baths, a couple of water bottles a day, and wireless Internet. There is a breakfast palapa, as well as a separate, pricey gourmet restaurant—unless you're cooking in your apartment or take a taxi to town, you will have to dine here, as the resort is remote. Note that the ocean is rough and rocky so you can't swim, but you can still relax beachside and read a good book in the breeze or take a dip in the small swimming pool. Don't walk the deserted beachfront trail to the surf school area by yourself or even as a pair—opt for a quick taxi or bike ride on the roadside instead.

Over US$100

★ **Velero Beach Resort** (Calle La Punta, tel. 501/571-9727, www.velerobeach.com, US$135) is my favorite in Cabarete—a gorgeous, immaculately clean boutique-size resort close enough to the action but set apart from the madding crowd. The infinity swimming pool is the main draw, with all the rooms' balconies facing it and the Atlantic. The view from the onsite restaurant is equally stunning. Rooms are cozy and include all the comforts from air-conditioning to flat-screen TV, without being over the top.

Ultra Violeta Boutique Residences (next to Cabarete Coffee Company, tel. 829/931-5555, http://ultravioletacabarete.com, from US$165) takes the boutique resort scale up a notch. Tucked on a quiet corner of Kite Beach, the all-white and purple escape has 21 one- to three-bedroom seafront apartments facing an infinity pool and looking out over the beach. No amenities are spared, from the gourmet kitchens to music equipment, outdoor showers, and Jacuzzi tubs.

An oasis on Encuentro Beach is **Hideaway Beach** (Playa Encuentro, U.S. tel. 212/627-2878, www.hideawaydr.com, US$175), a gated resort a short walk away from the surf schools (within view from the hotel's stretch). The property is small and has 15 one- and two-bedroom self-catering suites and a sprawling lawn with peacocks and towering coconut trees before you reach the beach. If you're seeking a quiet, secluded escape this could be a good pick. There is swimming pool, and tasty meals are provided at Chez Arsenio.

INFORMATION AND SERVICES

Health and Emergencies

The tourist police, POLITUR (Gaspar Hernandez, tel. 809/571-0713) has a presence in town, but the office itself is actually outside of town. To reach the police, you can contact 809/571-0810 or simply dial 911.

In town Servi Med Cabarete (tel. 809/571-0964, 24-hour) has various multilingual staff doctors. You can also contact Centro Médico (tel. 809/571-4696).

Money

There's a branch of Scotiabank right in Cabarete town (Calle Principal, tel. 809/571-0292, 8:30am-4pm Mon.-Fri., 9am-1pm Sat.), with 24-hour ATMs. You'll also find a Banco Popular (Calle Principal, 809/571-0903, 9am-5pm Mon.-Fri., 9am-1pm Sat.).

Laundry

If you've been on the road for a while and need clean clothes, head to Family Laundry (across from Janet's Supermarket, 8am-6pm Mon.-Sat., US$5.50/load).

GETTING THERE AND AROUND

To get to Cabarete from Puerto Plata, you can take an airport taxi for US$35 (for 1-4 people, one-way) or you can hop in a *carrito* or shared cab for less than a dollar, and get an interesting cultural experience while you're at it.

Once there, getting around Cabarete and its various beaches is easy on foot, but there may be times when you'd rather take a break from long walks in the hot sun. When that happens, you have a few choices. The shared taxis go up and down the main drag and are easy to flag down anywhere. You can go up and down from Cabarete to Kite Beach for 30 pesos (US$0.65), for instance. The cars usually have a "Sosúa Río San Juan" top, but it's not always visible from a distance, so just keep a close eye on the road as they approach.

If you need to get from Cabarete to Sosúa or Puerto Plata, it's equally simple to catch a *carrito*—you'll have to switch in Sosúa to continue on to Cabarete, but the switch takes place immediately adjacent to the last stop in Sosúa, at a gas station across from the Texaco. Fares range between 45-50 pesos (US$0.98-1.09) for each leg, before dark.

If you'd rather pay a lot more to go by taxi to nearby towns or farther, contact Taxis Cabarete (tel. 809/571-0767 or 809/571-0824), or the reliable Gabriel Polanco (tel. 809/602-6568), who might be willing to negotiate with you if you're a solo traveler. Rates range from 300 pesos (US$6.55) from Cabarete up the drag to Encuentro Beach to US$100 to Río San Juan.

East of Cabarete

RÍO SAN JUAN

About 100 kilometers (62 miles) east of Puerto Plata, or just an hour's drive east from Cabarete, Río San Juan is a stunning, refreshing little corner on the North Coast. A fishing town where nature is still splendid, Río San Juan has a Mediterranean-like rocky coastline, diamond white sand beaches, and mangrove lagoons home to herons and vultures. Aside from having the most breathtaking daily sunsets, it's a place that has retained its Dominican authenticity with fishing as its main industry. You'll see more Dominicans out and about enjoying their beach, while others drive here on weekends for a peaceful family getaway. The electricity shortage is an issue here—power cuts take place almost daily from 11am to about 4pm—and there isn't a whole lot to do. But who needs indoor activities or organized tours when you're surrounded with natural sights to enjoy? Río San Juan's slow pace and natural beauty are likely to change soon. Several resorts are being furiously built along the coast. A seven-star Aman Resort opened at Playa Grande in December 2015. My advice? Visit now and enjoy this gift of nature before the secret's out.

Getting around Río San Juan and finding your way around the small town is super easy, as most of the town, including its three beaches, is centered on a couple of main streets. The highway links Río San Juan to Playa Grande, Cabrera, and Laguna Dudú to the east. Calle Duarte is the main road in town, where restaurants, shops, and the Gri Gri Lagoon can be found.

Sights

LAGUNA GRI GRI

A peaceful, small lagoon sitting between the heart of Río San Juan and the Atlantic Ocean, the **Laguna Gri Gri** flows through dense, mazelike rows of red mangrove trees. Above black turkey vultures hang high and fly above gri gri trees during the day. The lagoon is brackish: made up of part salty and part freshwater.

Steps going down from the main street of Calle Duarte in town take you to the

Laguna Gri Gri

entrance of the lagoon. This is where locals hang out on the benches and plenty of wooden motorboats park on the western side. Kids like splashing about in the water on the eastern corner where the freshwater is. The onsite office **Sindicato de Boteros de la Laguna Gri Gri** (tel. 809/589-2277, 8:30am-5pm daily, US$18 for 1-3 persons or RD$800, US$26.60 for two or RD$1,200) is where you pay for the boat ride down the lagoon—a handful of captains are always on standby. The excursion will take you past the mangroves and along various scenic stops like the **Cueva de las Golondrinas,** a natural turquoise sandbank or *piscina natural,* and **Playa Caletón** where you're free to stay until sunset if you choose. Snorkeling (US$40) and fishing (US$75) can be added on. Enjoying the view of the lagoon or bathing in it is free—just do as the local kids do and engage in backflip contests.

Although cruising down the river is a short 10-minute ride, the sight of the dense trees and vultures coupled with the hissing sound of white herons passing above calm waters is a mesmerizing experience. Soon enough, the river opens up onto the Atlantic Ocean, and the stunning cliff coastline and turquoise sea of Río San Juan. Don't miss spotting the white rock sculptures set on the cliffs, created by artist Persio Checo in honor of the DR's first Taíno inhabitants. There's also a natural *cara del indio*-shaped rock that resembles the face of a native.

Take the boat tour around 4pm if you want to see as much bird activity as possible. They come out to play on the open lagoon when the sun begins to fade.

If you're lucky, your captain might show you **El Pontón.** This dead-end cliff-side channel just around the bend from the lagoon has water that is cold and fresh, making it a great spot to swim. It's not normally part of the tour. You can also hike to El Pontón. Ask a local to show you. You'll even be able to continue on foot to Playa Caletón, right around the corner, if you like.

Beaches
PLAYA GRANDE

Just eight kilometers (five miles) east and a 25 pesos (US$0.55) *guagua* ride from Río San Juan is one of the Dominican Republic's top 10 most beautiful beaches: **Playa Grande.** It's also one of the most frequented on this coast and well guarded. If you want fewer crowds, as always, head here on a weekday.

If you come here by bus, you'll get off at the main entrance sign, then hike just five more minutes downhill to the parking lot and main entrance to Playa Grande and the adjacent Playa Preciosa. Walking down Playa Grande, you'll pass a food vendor area serving excellent fresh catch, a bar, a surf shack where you can rent boards, and a rocky part of the beach before you see its full grandeur: the mile-long and wide golden sand expanse stretching into the distance. The tides have created a thick and tall slope of sand before you step down and get into the water. Entry is smoother on the eastern end of the beach. Chairs are about 100 pesos (US$2.18) each. The waves at Playa Grande are real—this beach is known for its swells and undertows—so be sure you're a good swimmer and don't venture too far from shore.

OTHER BEACHES

Playa Los Minos is one of three beaches in town, and right beside Hotel Bahia Blanca. It's a shallow one, and therefore a favorite of families with small kids, as well as adults who come here at 6am to begin their morning workouts. The sun sets directly in front of this beach—red ball sinking into the horizon—and the atmosphere is lively on the weekends, with a small onsite bar and merengue and bachata echoing along the shoreline.

Continue walking on the road past Hotel Bahia Blanca, and you'll end up on a small but idyllic stretch known as **Playa de los Guardias.** There's virtually no shade here, save for one tree where you can set up a couple of beach chairs and a barbecue pit, but you can park the car, Dominican-style, and play your stereo as you please. The water is lovely, and

Río San Juan

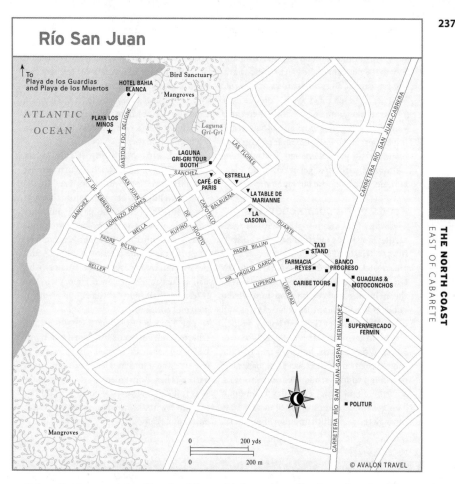

it doesn't get as crowded as Playa Los Mino on this side. The lagoon's bird sanctuary sits at the very back and makes for an interesting side visit. Just watch your feet for red crabs.

It has a morbid name due to the couple of graves still remaining at the back of the beach, but **Playa de los Muertos** is a gorgeous, curvy white sand stretch reached by walking well behind Hotel Bahia Blanca and Playa de los Guardias. You'll see a footpath past the bird and mangrove swamps. The water is a glorious turquoise, in part rocky but with easy entry openings. Trees for shade run all along its edges and make it popular with families who bring their food and

drinks on the weekends or after a long day. Kids like to leap off the small rocks on the edges of the beach.

Reached by road via public bus or by boat—you can ask to include this stop on your tour of the Laguna Gri Gri—**Playa Caletón** is within Río San Juan. This lovely small crescent is flanked by cliffs, covered in sponge-like sands—rocky in part—and idyllic during the week. At the back of beach you'll find a series of *casitas* all selling fresh fish and drinks, including your regular beachside piña colada in a pineapple. It is not surprisingly supercrowded on Sundays when Dominicans descend with their coolers and hot lunches dished out of big pots, while a DJ with mega speakers blasts the area.

A two-minute walk down a narrow pathway to the far right of the Playa Grande parking lot leads to **Playa Preciosa,** a deserted white sand beach that's a sight for sore eyes. There are no guards nor facilities here, so if you're solo, don't stay too long by yourself and leave your valuables at home. It's a gorgeous blond and turquoise scene and good for strong swimmers with stronger waves than Playa Grande. Don't venture out far alone.

Food and Accommodations

You won't find another place with as spectacular a view or location as **Hotel Bahia Blanca** (Gaston Fernando Deligne, off Calle Duarte, tel. 809/589-2563, US$31) flanked by two stunning bays, a five-minute walk from the main drag, and equally close to and from either of Río San Juan's three beaches, as well as the Laguna Gri Gri. A friendly French Canadian owner, resident of the DR for over 30 years, manages the hotel. It's true that the rooms are dated; don't expect great mattresses or locking windows, and there are only fans. And there's no power every day 11am-5pm. The generator comes on at 5pm and lasts through the night until mid-morning. But it's decent for a night or two, and frankly, you'll forget about any minor inconveniences when you're out and about enjoying all the beaches or sitting on one of several wide terraces facing the glorious panoramic view of the ocean and the sunset every single day. There's a small restaurant here that serves breakfast and dinner with a view and cold beers or soda when you need them.

La Table de Marianne (Calle Duarte 15, tel. 829/494-4445, latabledemarianne@ hotmail.com, 8am-5pm Mon.-Fri., US$2-10) is a friendly, surprisingly affordable spot for a morning coffee and pastry outdoors or inside, as well as crepes, baguette sandwiches, and other breakfast and lunch treats. The pink and white interior is inviting, and the Belgian owner is a wonderful host who will make you feel welcome. There's wireless Internet, albeit spotty at times, and plenty of gourmet coffee.

The French restaurant **Estrella** (Calle Duarte 7, tel. 809/589-2303, 8am-11pm daily, US$4-20) has a casual bakery and pizzeria on one side and a formal open-air dining room on the other. Conveniently set on the main street, it's one of the few consistent dining spots in town. Choices range from burgers to pastas and seafood.

Playa Grande

La Casona (Calle Duarte 6, tel. 809/589-2597, lacasonarsj@gmail.com, 9am-10pm daily, US$3.30-5) cafeteria-style restaurant is the best in town for affordable and tasty Dominican food, served from a buffet. Portions are generous for rice n' beans, your chosen stew of the day, and yucca chips. They also have cheap and finger-licking good empanadas stuffed with chicken or fish. There's inside seating or you can pop up on the counter and watch the news from a distance.

Café de Paris (Calle Duarte, tel. 809/778-0687, 9am-11pm daily, US$4-6) serves a full menu ranging from seafood to steaks, and hosts a street "sidewalk" party every Sunday facing its terrace and the lagoon.

Getting There and Around

Shared taxis run the highway east from Puerto Plata to Río San Juan. You'll have to make a couple of switches, but it's easy. Getting around the main sights in town only requires walking or taking the public bus off the main highway to head to Playa Grande or in the direction of Cabrera and Laguna Dudú.

Caribe Tours (tel. 809/589-2644, www.caribetours.com.do, US$7) has a terminal on the main highway close to the entrance to town and offers daily departures from Río San Juan

to Santo Domingo. Check the online interactive map for the latest schedule.

CABRERA
Laguna Dudú

The attraction of **Laguna Dudú or El Dudú** (8am-6pm daily, US$3.32 or RD$150) is one of the most beautiful natural sights on this North Coast. Three stunning freshwater blue lagoons of varying depth and surrounded with caves and a verdant tropical forest have been turned into a park. As you pass the front gate, you'll be amazed at the well-manicured gardens dotted with hammocks, benches, and thatch-roofed seating areas. There are signs directing you to the various lagoons. Two require taking a staircase down to the lower level, but the screams you hear will likely be coming from **El Dudú Blue Lagoon,** the biggest pool of all with 90 percent freshwater and 10 percent salt on the eastern end. There's a zipline directly above the gorgeous emerald and turquoise expanse 8 meters (25 feet) deep and 1,900 square meters (0.5 acres) wide, and you can hang on to a tiny bar, with no other supportive gear, and zip your body down the line until you reach a point of no return and have to let go, jumping approximately 10 meters (33 feet) down into the water. It's a real

Enjoy the view at the Hotel Bahia Blanca.

adrenaline rush. Not to worry: you can bypass the madness and go down the stone staircase to bathe in the lagoon below instead.

On the other side of the park, you'll find two more lagoons. One is a shallow sinkhole with fish swimming beneath a near crystal surface reflecting stalactites and bats scurrying at the back of the cave. There are more rocks and the water is shallow, but it's a gorgeous sight and the water is cold. A few steps over is my favorite of the pools, a gem of an emerald lagoon sitting at the foot of a towering limestone cliff, surrounded by wild trees and with a rocky entrance. The view is breathtaking, as is taking a swim in this cold, freshwater body. There are kayaks for rent (US$2.21 or RD$100) if you want to circle the lagoon. (There's no exit, but it can be fun for two to four people per kayak.) There's also a wooden platform with seating overlooking the lagoon, usually busy on the weekends when the onsite outdoor bar is open.

Besides all the refreshing water, you'll find a dry cave that you can explore solo. Cueva Taína isn't much to see except it has an interesting arched entrance and some giant stalactite formations, an enclosure with ostriches and turkeys, and an onsite restaurant with restroom and very basic shower facilities serving lunch during park hours.

The park, east of Cabarete and Rio San Juan in the town of Cabrera, can be reached easily by hailing the *guaguas* (US$70 pesos from Río San Juan) running up and down the highway between Río San Juan and Cabrera. The trip is about 45 minutes from Río San Juan and 10 minutes from Cabrera.

Zipline into one of Laguna Dudú's freshwater lagoons.

Playa Diamante

Playa Diamante is of the most unusual beaches in the country because a river flows almost into the sand as you approach the beach. Walk from east to west on this small stretch, and you'll go from warm to cold water. The sand is sticky and wet, the water supershallow out for miles. It makes for a favorite Dominican spot to talk, swing back some drinks, and bathe with the kids. There's a sign for the turnoff right off the main highway in Cabrera, and it's a short drive from there.

West of Puerto Plata

PARQUE NACIONAL LA ISABELA

Located in Luperón and hugging the Atlantic shoreline, **Parque Nacional La Isabela** (9am-5pm daily, US$2.21 or RD$100)—not to be confused with the Villa Isabella municipality farther south—comprises of a museum and archaeological site preserving the ruins of the first European settlement in the "New World." It's where Christopher Columbus' second voyage landed him in 1493, and he named it after the Spanish queen Isabel La Católica, who funded his voyages. The small museum displays the history of Columbus' times, the Taíno people, and details on the ruins left behind by Columbus that are on display in the park. The hike begins just past the museum, and takes you to a beautiful oceanfront display of both replicas of Spanish homes and original stones from what was once the first church where the first mass was held in 1494, and, perched on a bluff, Columbus' first home here.

Farther up from the park, you'll find the rebuilt Templo de las Américas, a replica of the original church. Walk up the winding interior staircase and admire a view of the deserted, white sand Castillo Beach in the distance. If you're already in the area, it's worth a quick stop here; if not, you can skip it.

★ ESTERO HONDO MARINE MAMMAL SANCTUARY

If you only make it to one natural sight on the North Coast, I highly recommend the natural wonder and protected area at the **Estero Hondo Marine Mammal Sanctuary** (tel. 829/492-3362, 9am-5pm daily, US$5.54 or RD$250, includes guided tour) consisting of a lagoon and park covering nearly 49 square kilometers (19 square miles) and located approximately 69 kilometers (43 miles) west of Puerto Plata. This is six miles west of where Christopher Columbus first landed in the DR. The drive to this northwestern edge of the Puerto Plata province is one of the loveliest, passing through fishing villages and farming communities where local scenes abound from small *colmados* to passing cows, men on

the lookout tower at Estero Hondo Marine Mammal Sanctuary

Kitesurfing in Buenhombre

An isolated beach community under a two-hour drive west from Punta Rucia, Buenhombre boasts a kitesurfing school, kite camp, and a handful of fish shacks. It's worth coming here to get a slice of the old DR in a true fishing village. If you have a day to spare, kick back and spend it around local fishers and the occasional kitesurfers who come here to try new waters with Kite Buenhombre (tel. 829/325-5250, www.kitebuenhombre.net, US$65/class or US$500 for full course/12 hours, day trips from Cabarete also offered). Beware of the beach—there's coral, including deep sinkholes with occasional currents, especially closer to the eastern side where the fishing boats are moored. It isn't always as shallow as it seems close to shore. There have been accidents in the recent past with weak swimmers.

The quickest way to get to Buenhombre is along a very poorly indicated route that begins past Punta Rucia along a gravel road. You'll have to ask directions at every point because there are literally no signs for this shortcut to Buenhombre, but it's the most interesting and picturesque, taking you past villages and countryside scenes. Locals are used to it so don't fret. Go a couple of kilometers on the gravel road until you hit what seems like the top of a hill where you'll see a paved road; turn right. Keep going until you spot a gas station—la bomba—but ask locals because it will otherwise be harder to find. On spotting the gas station, make a left toward it but at its corner, turn clockwise (like a u) to continue on the road. It will wind into one of the next highway coastal roads in the country with stunning panoramic views as you descend to Buenhombre's coastline and bay.

---

donkeys or horses, and pastel-colored homes surrounded by hills and subtropical landscape. Arriving to the park, your first sight will be a stunning and often-deserted wide turtle-nesting beach—Playa Marisa—to the left, stretching all the way to the entrance and hugging the lagoon.

Your tour will begin at the main sanctuary park ranger office where you pay your entrance fee and explore a small indoor and outdoor display about the sanctuary, from its four mangrove species to the birdlife. Read about manatees and look at a glass-enclosed skeleton of a 1,300-kilogram (2,866-pound) male manatee found dead of old age (approximately 70) in 2011. There are over 50 manatees that are a constant presence within this protected lagoon. Knowledgeable head guide Freddy Garcia will lead you through the first trail known as El Sendero del Cangrejo because of all the crab holes in the ground. There are hermit crabs, and blue crabs only come out at night or when it rains. This is a 20-minute hike through an incredibly rich landscape including all three types of mangroves found in the Dominican Republic from red mangroves

to white buttonwood and white, one of only two places in the country to have them in one place. The hike will also take you past medicinal and native Taíno trees and plants like the saladillo, which the Taíno used to spice their food. The second hike known as the Sendero del Manatí requires a one-minute ride to the other side of the park just 1 kilometer (0.62 miles) away, where an observation deck awaits and you are guaranteed to spot manatees rising to the surface every few minutes. Bring your camera.

While you can visit the park solo and hike with a guide, the best way to appreciate the splendor of Estero Hondo is to explore the lagoon on a 1.5 hour kayak or paddleboard jaunt as part of a full-day Paddle Manatee Adventure tour with Bávaro Runners (Puerto Plata, tel. 809/320-1061, www.runnersadventures.com, US$95). You'll get to paddle off the beach and cruise along the waters, appreciating its grandeur and breathtaking surrounding landscape while heading toward the "palo de la garza" or a dense maze of mangroves home to cattle egrets. Beside it is a natural pool where you can park your kayak

Cayos Siete Hermanos (Seven Brothers Cays)

Starting one kilometer (0.6 mile) off the shores of Monte Cristi is a set of islets that few get to experience. The Seven Brothers Cays or Cayo Siete Hermanos, are seven tiny cays where deserted, idyllic beaches are home to various migratory birds and sea turtles: Tororu, Muertos, Ratas, Terrero, Monte Grande, Monte Chico and Arenas. Surrounding the islands are some historic shipwrecks ideal for diving excursions. Trips to the cays are costly, but that's the price of seeing one of the most unique spots in the DR. Particularly if you have a large group, it's money well spent. Contact the locally owned, ecotour-focused **Soraya y Santos Tours** (Bugalu 3, tel. 809/961-6343 or 829/221-0453, www.ssmontecristitours.com, 7am-7pm, US$266 for 1-8 persons) to arrange for a day out to the cays with the only main tour operator in Monte Cristi. Divers will want to contact **Galleon Divers** (across from Cocomar Restaurant, Calle Juan de Bolaños 8, tel. 809/579-2623, galleondivers@galleondivers.com, US$75 2-tank dive).

and hop into the delightful water. There's a small beach and hut beside the natural pool, where you can also take a rest if you wish, and if you're lucky, a manatee might come close to shore. In the mangroves, you'll see birds soaring and spider crabs crawling with beautiful seashells covering the bottom.

You'll then head to the mouth of the lagoon where it meets the sea, closer to where the majority of manatees reside, and glide around from a safe distance (absolutely no motorized boats are allowed on the protected lagoon). You might also spot barracuda leaping out of the water as they consume the small fish inhabiting the lagoon.

LA ENSENADA

A 15-minute drive farther west past Estero Hondo will bring you to the beautiful beach of La Ensenada. The stunning **Playa Ensenada** has soft, white sand and supershallow, calm waters—you can literally walk out several miles—making it a favorite of families coming from Santiago, Puerto Plata, and other northern towns. The beach is lined with the usual plastic chairs and tables, as well as dozens of local *frituras*, all offering the traditional fried or steamed fish meals. The atmosphere is busy and lively, in true Dominican fashion. The beach has shower and bathroom facilities. As always, come on a weekday if you're not into crowds and rowdiness.

It's also one of the jumping-off points for speedboat excursions to Cayo Paraíso or Cayo Arena. For snorkel trips to Cayo Arena, contact **Capitán Josy** (tel. 829/712-2835, US$75 for two, but less with up to 13 people, three-hour tour). There are facilities here, including showers for 25 pesos or US$0.55.

PUNTA RUCIA

Just past the beach at La Ensenada, barely a five-minute drive west and up a long and dusty dirt road, begins the beachfront community of **Punta Rucia.** This village is an ideal spot to get away from it all, especially during the week before locals descend on the area from Santiago, Puerto Plata, or even as far as Santo Domingo. The first sign you'll see is for the upscale Punta Rucia Lodge on the right hand side. Again, the highlight here is a beautiful, uninterrupted white sand beach—prettier than La Ensenada and with fewer, if any, crowds—with gloriously flat turquoise waters and floating fishing boats. There's seaweed and corals in some parts on the eastern end of the beach, but entry is easy. Dotting this coastline are quite a number of B&Bs and guesthouses, fish shacks, and a couple of Italian and French restaurants. Some of the guesthouses are no-frills cabins and rooms tucked higher up in the hills but offering a splendid panoramic view of Punta Rucia's bay.

Another option to overnight cheaply

is the solar powered and colorful **Casa Libre** (shortly after entering Punta Rucia, on the right side, look for a small sign, tel. 809/693-5010, casitamariposa@hotmail.com, US$26.75, includes full breakfast), also known as Casita Mariposa. This German and French-owned bed-and-breakfast lodge perched above the bay has three no-frills rooms in brightly painted wooden cabins, separate outdoor shower facilities (with views to make up for it), waterfront porches, and a short, stony path to the Punta Rucia beach below offering absolute privacy. It's rustic and not for everyone: you'll sleep with a single oscillating fan in your cabin and on thin foam mattresses (with mosquito nets), but you're surrounded with nature and sea views. Shutters open if you choose. It's a good option in the winter months if you can't stand the heat of summer. For food, two decent choices are **Restaurant Damaris** (tel. 849/251-2709, US$6.55 for buffet) for local fare and **Lino's** (tel. 809/704-3045, US$7.80-12.30) for delicious Italian homemade pizza and freshly baked bread on the beach. Lino's delivers for an extra US$1.20.

★ Cayo Arena

Punta Rucia is also a primary jumping-off point to **Cayo Arena** (also called Cayo Paraiso), and there are various hotels and outfitters offering the excursions from Punta Rucia or Puerto Plata. Cayo Arena is essentially a sandbank sitting out at sea about 7 kilometers (4.35 miles) off the coast where you'll experience some of the best snorkeling in the DR. The corals, critters, and waters glow in true Caribbean fashion right offshore. Cayo Arena is part of the National Park of Monte Cristi, and thus a protected area. A series of thatch huts line the small island, where outfitters lay out their gear and entertain their respective day-trippers. It's a fun day out surrounded by a gorgeous island landscape, but don't expect to have a solo Robinson Crusoe experience unless you head out here very early in the morning to avoid all the tour groups and various boats that end up docking here by 11am. Still, it's an excursion that is absolutely worthwhile. Contact the local fishermen's association for reasonable prices at **Cooperativa de Pescadores Punta Rucia** (Cesar, president, tel. 809/866-4079 or Captain Francisco, tel. 829/943-7457, US$78 1-4 persons). The tour includes all of the regular offerings of snorkeling stops, park entry fees, a ride along the mangroves of the Monte Cristi National Park and a full day out on Cayo Arena or as long as you'd like to stay. The association also offers fishing trips from spearfishing to deep-sea fishing (half day 6am-1pm, US$112 for two).

At the far western end of Punta Rucia beach, **Paradise Island** (tel. 809/320-7606 or in Punta Rucia tel. 809/841-7606, www.paradiseisland.do, US$50 pp for 1-5 persons, US$40 pp for more) also offers an all-day excursion to Cayo Arena with lunch, snacks, drinks, and the usual mangrove and snorkeling tour stops. They also have seven rooms if you decide to overnight, slightly tucked at the back of the beach but just a few steps away, with air-conditioning, breakfast, hot and cold water, balconies if you choose, but no TV. From Puerto Plata, you can also hop on a catamaran cruise to the cay with **Bávaro Runners** (tel. 809/320-1061, www.bavarorunners.com, Tues., Thurs., and Sat., US$95 pp).

PARQUE NACIONAL MONTE CRISTI

Most visitors don't go farther than Punta Rucia on their adventures west of the North Coast. In doing so, they miss one of the most unique landscapes and authentic parts of the Dominican Republic just an additional hour's drive west. It's a ride that will have you driving past mountainous and wild rocky scenery. This cactus-filled landscape dotted with banana plantations, rice fields, and salt mines is an ecotraveler's dream tucked on the western edge of the North Coast and within view of Haiti. It's an entirely different DR: one where rural life dominates and massive resorts with vendor-filled beaches are far away.

As you enter town, you'll spot piles of salt on either end of the main road, before you arrive at the small but picturesque Malecón with a long dock where locals like to take in the breeze in this hot town. In the near distance is a view of El Morro—Monte Cristi's iconic landmark.

El Morro is a majestic 242-meter (793-foot) mesa—the tallest in the DR. Some might say it resembles Table Mountain in Cape Town. It features prominently from almost anywhere in town and the surrounding area. As you enter the **Parque Nacional Monte Cristi** boundary, a stone's throw from the Malecón, the rather deserted landscape will make it seem as if it's just you, the sea, and the mountains. You can either continue down the road—you'll eventually come to a parking lot—and hang out at the gorgeous **Playa El Morro,** or you can tour the park.

Touring the park's waters and mangrove swamps can only be done by boat. An overall tour of the Monte Cristi National Park known as the **Ruta El Morro y Los Caños** is offered by the Dominican family-owned **Soraya y Santos Tours** (Bugalu 3, tel. 809/961-6343 or 829/221-0453, www.ssmontecristitours.com, 7am-7pm, US$156 for 1-8 persons), specializing in ecofriendly excursions around the parks natural gems. The trip begins with cruising along the mangroves for a good 15 minutes or so, followed by swimming stops at two natural pools where the waters turn into a clear turquoise and you'll find it hard to leave. One is known as **the platform** (*la plataforma*)—just a half-mile boat ride into the park, and there is literally a wooden platform set up beside the swimming area and mangroves where you can dock and jump in to enjoy fresh water. There's a picnic table and a grill that locals use on the weekends. The second natural pool stop is known as **La Avena,** translated as oats, because its floor is covered with an oatmeal-textured sand. Locals bottle up this sand to use it as a body scrub—or you can scrub away right there. It's the only place in the Dominican Republic where you'll find this.

The tour continues onto the open water of the Atlantic Ocean, and you'll cruise across

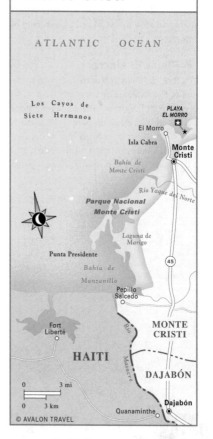

a spectacular Mediterranean-like landscape past Playa del Morro and its towering rocks. You'll stop next at an offshore island across from Playa El Morro known as **Isla Cabra.** There's an old lighthouse here and a small shaded stretch of white sand where you can picnic, swim, and pretend you're on your own deserted island. The water is a gorgeous clear turquoise, and you'll even see the fish scurrying past your feet.

Make the effort: a day trip from Puerto Plata or Punta Rucia to Monte Cristi is just about a 2.5-hour drive and easy to do round-trip. However, staying overnight is the best way to fully take in the unique preserved landscape of this authentic part of the North Coast. This is also one of the best spots to indulge in the freshest seafood or traditional spicy goat stew (*chivo picante*), a specialty of this region.

★ Playa El Morro

You'll reach **Playa El Morro** by driving to the end of the road, where there will be a parking lot. You'll have to hike a few easy steps down the rocks below the parking lot to reach the beach. With its reddish brown sand on one end, blondish stretch on the other, and a dramatic spray of waves crashing against towering rocks, Playa El Morro is a sight for sore eyes. The cliffs of El Morro hug the shore on the northwest—be sure to prepare your camera for this stunning landscape.

Before you descend, take in the spectacular view of the sea, sand, and El Morro's imposing presence—there are no vendors here, no man-made structures of any kind. Get here during the day before the shadows set and the sun begins to lower. On one end of the beach, you'll see piles of soft stones covering the sand—sometimes they move to the left, sometimes to the right, according to how the tide shifts them.

Playa El Morro

Santiago and the Cibao Valley

Look for ★ to find recommended
sights, activities, dining, and lodging.

Highlights

★ **Monumento a los Héroes de la Restauración:** Climb to the top of Santiago's most famous landmark to learn more about the heroes in the War of Restoration and take in 360-degree views of the city on the wraparound terrace (page 253).

★ **Carnival in La Vega:** Buy a devil's mask and join in the frenzy at the country's largest and most colorful carnival, which takes place every weekend in February (page 266).

★ **Saltos de Jimenoa:** Used as the filming locations for the opening scene in *Jurassic Park,* these two stunning waterfalls are not to be missed (page 268).

★ **La Confluencia:** Bring your picnic fare and take a dip in swirling freshwater pools at this park, where three of Jarabacoa's rivers meet (page 270).

★ **River Rafting on the Río Yaque del Norte:** Get soaked rowing and tumbling down the DR's longest river (page 272).

★ **Manabao and La Ciénaga:** Experience the beauty of the real Dominican countryside in the villages of Manabao and La Ciénaga, where you can visit agricultural farms and swim in the Río Yaque del Norte (page 279).

★ **Hiking Pico Duarte:** Visit the Parque Armando Bermúdez for a two-day hike to the highest point in the Caribbean. At the top you can proudly take a selfie with a statue of Juan Pablo Duarte, father of Dominican independence (page 280).

★ **Parque Nacional Valle Nuevo:** Escape civilization at one of the most impressive and biodiverse parks in the DR. Spend a night at Villa Pajón Eco-Lodge to truly appreciate the park's landscape (page 288).

This region is often called "the Dominican Alps" because it's hugged by the Cordillera Septentrional and central mountain ranges. It's a delightful and surprising departure from the stereotypical image of the DR as a sun, sea, and rum destination. Affluent locals escape from the heat and buzz of Santiago to the peaks and valleys of El Cibao, as Dominicans refer to it. El Cibao, which means "mountain rock" in Taíno, is blessed with the highest mountain in the Caribbean: Pico Duarte, at 10,128 feet above sea level. Pico Duarte is the crown jewel of the region, and the most intrepid explorers will opt to spend a night on the peak.

The country's most important national parks, such as Valle Nuevo, are also found in the highlands where the most valuable rivers supply the country with water. A handful of them are even classified as scientific for their biodiversity. These parks are home to mountainside villages that offer prime material for outdoor and photography enthusiasts. The Cibao's land makes it the breadbasket of the Dominican Republic; over 90 percent of the country's vegetables are cultivated and produced in the stunning, green, cool hills of Constanza, dubbed "the Switzerland of the Caribbean" for its stunning views of rolling farmlands and cabins. This area is surrounded by imposing, mist-covered mountains up to 2,134 meters (7,000 feet) above sea level—easily the highest inhabited elevation across the Antilles. The Cibao Valley is also made up of rolling tobacco hills, where the world's best cigar leaves are grown and hand rolled to perfection.

As if its natural gifts weren't enough, culture is plentiful in these parts, too. The largest and most vibrant carnival in the country takes place in La Vega. Roadside *lechoneras*, or roast pork eateries, are here in abundance. And the DR's second largest city, Santiago—possibly the least touristy part of the country—is a sweet spot for night owls, cigar aficionados, and baseball enthusiasts.

As it's the birthplace and home to the Mirabal sisters, from Salcedo, it's no wonder Cibaeños are so proud; there's a bold claim that the most beautiful Dominican women come from this

---

Previous: Constanza; view from the Monumento a Los Héroes de la Restauración. **Above:** Salto Baiguate in Jarabacoa.

Santiago and the Cibao Valley

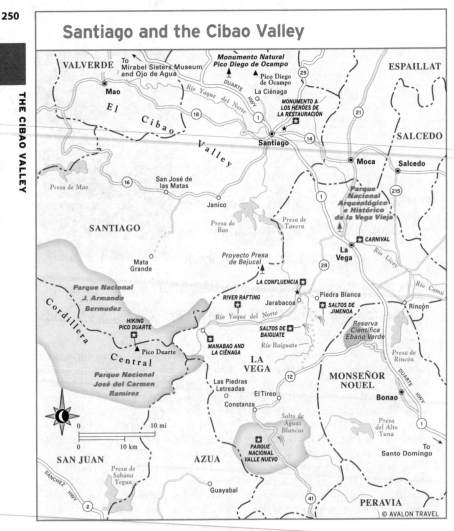

region. If you haven't been to the Cibao, the cultural heartland of this country, you haven't been to the Dominican Republic. Squeezing in this side of the country, if only for a day or two, will give you a better view and understanding of this stunning island's incredible topography and friendly inhabitants.

PLANNING YOUR TIME

If you're coming to the heartland of the Dominican Republic, it's to experience outdoor adventure, scenic rides, and the country's most spectacular landscape. You can easily skip Santiago—unless you're a cigar and nightlife lover, in which case one night is the minimum. Otherwise, make Jarabacoa your base, where there's enough to do that you could be busy for well over a week. From Jarabacoa, explore the mountains—hike El Mogote, if you dare—waterfalls, rivers, and *campo* villages. Save at least three full days for this place. From your Jarabacoa base, you could go to nearby Manabao and La Ciénaga, which easily have the most showstopping scenery. These two villages are also departure points for the hike to Pico Duarte. If you are braving the tallest peak in the Caribbean, you'll need to put aside at least three full days—two for the hike and one to rest. Plan it ahead of time by contacting one of the major organizers; it will save you a lot of effort and precious vacation time.

Put aside at least a day and a night for Constanza, an hour and 20 minutes south of Jarabacoa, where you'll find little tourism but more stunning landscapes across flower plantations and vegetable and strawberry fields. Hike the pine forest-filled Valle Nuevo National Park, which has the coolest temperatures in the Caribbean, and spend the night by a chimney fire for a unique Caribbean experience.

The Cibao Valley, as you'll soon realize, is its own getaway. If you're combining it with a beach stay, split your days and spend three on this side, at a minimum.

Santiago de los Caballeros

The Dominican Republic's second largest city after Santo Domingo, Santiago de los Caballeros—which citizens call *la Ciudad Corazón* or "heartland city"—is a massive, sprawling, scorching hot, traffic-filled maze. It isn't much of a destination for tourists, except that it's a primary gateway to the mountainous, adventure-filled towns of Jarabacoa and Constanza. It's an industrial city for the most part. Because of its location in the fertile Cibao region, it's a leading exporter of major Dominican products such as rum, cigars, and textiles. Tobacco aficionados will find their pleasure here at premium cigar outlets like La Aurora.

With attractive mountain towns like Jarabacoa and Constanza just over an hour away, Santiago's primary use for the visitor is as a public transit stop en route to those regions. It's just good enough for a day's visit, perhaps to see the Monumento a los Héroes, tour a couple of museums, and buy what you need at the mall. It doesn't have much more to offer unless you're a major cigar lover, a baseball fan (this is home to the Cibao Eagles), or a night owl.

The city's main shopping drag, Calle del Sol, is easily explored on foot. Lined with Chinese fashion apparel, American fast-food chains, as well as the all-around pedestrian shuffle of hawkers and shoppers, when you're here you'd almost think you're on one of New York City's streets, except for the security guards with shotguns standing outside of jewelry stores. There's a local sidewalk market tucked at the back of this area with much more local color. Here Dominican and Haitian vendors hawk fruits and vegetables. The Monumento a los Héroes is the main landmark, and surrounding it are numerous restaurants, bars, and lounges. Along with Calle del Sol, it's the only pedestrian-friendly area. The rest of the city is spread out, with large avenues and plenty of traffic, so you'll need a car or a taxi to get around, especially in the scorching Santiago heat.

Established in 1495 and named by Columbus in honor of 30 Spanish aristocrats who helped found the city, Santiago's history bears mentioning because of its important role in the country's independence. It was once the capital of the Dominican Republic during the War of Restoration between 1863 and 1865, and it was also the site of the Battle of March 30, 1844, when the Dominican Republic fought and won independence from Haiti.

SIGHTS
Parque Duarte
Parque Duarte, the city's most popular park, is a wide, shady expanse, noisy during the day

Santiago de los Caballeros

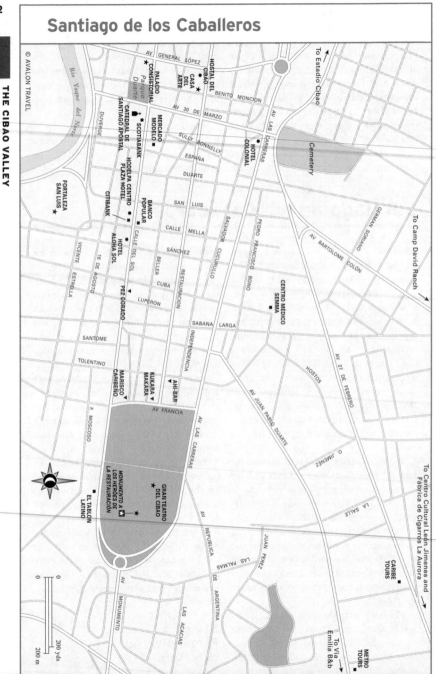

© AVALON TRAVEL

Río Yaque del Norte

To Estadio Cibao

AV GENERAL LÓPEZ

PALACIO CONSISTORIAL

Parque Duarte

HOSTAL DEL CIBAO

CASA DEL ARTE

BENITO MONCION

AV 30 DE MARZO

DUVERGE

CATEDRAL DE SANTIAGO APOSTAL

SCOTIABANK

MERCADO MODELO

SULLY BONNELLY

AV LAS CARRERAS

HOTEL COLONIAL

Cemetery

ESPAÑA

HODELPA CENTRO PLAZA HOTEL

CITIBANK

BANCO POPULAR

DUARTE

SAN LUIS

SALVADOR CUCURULLO

PEDRO FRANCISCO BONO

GERMAN SORIANO

To Camp David Ranch

FORTALEZA SAN LUIS

HOTEL ALOHA SOL

CALLE DEL SOL

CALLE MELLA

AV BARTOLOME COLÓN

VICENTE ESTRELLA

16 DE AGOSTO

PEZ DORADO

BELLER

SÁNCHEZ

CUBA

RESTAURACIÓN

CENTRO MÉDICO SEMMA

LUPERON

SANTOME

SABANA LARGA

TOLENTINO

INDEPENDENCIA

AV 27 DE FEBRERO

HOSTOS

F. MOSCOSO

MARISCO CARIBEÑO

KUKARA MAKARA

AHI-BAR

AV FRANCIA

AV LAS CARRERAS

AV JUAN PABLO DUARTE

O. JIMENEZ

To Centro Cultural León Jimenes and
Fábrica de Cigarros La Aurora

LA SALLE

MONUMENTO A LOS HÉROES DE LA RESTAURACIÓN

GRAN TEATRO DEL CIBAO

EL TABLON LATINO

AV

REPUBLICA

JUAN PEREZ

CARIBE TOURS

0   200 yds
0   200 m

AV MONUMENTO

DE

ARGENTINA

LAS ACACIAS

LAS PALMAS

To Vía
Emilia B&b

METRO TOURS

but a favorite respite from the hot sun. It's surrounded by gorgeous architecture from the Palacio Consistorial to the cathedral, but it's also on the end of busy Calle del Sol. Expect plenty of foot traffic and keep an eye out while walking in these parts, day or night.

Catedral de Santiago Apóstol

Adjacent to the central park is the **Catedral de Santiago Apóstol** (Calle 30 de Marzo) an all-white gothic and neoclassical building from the late 19th century. Its most impressive feature is its stained-glass windows. Also onsite are the marble tombs of former Dominican dictator Ulises Heureaux and General Jose Maria Imbert. Opening hours vary as there are often special masses held here.

Palacio Consistorial

Across from Parque Duarte is the two-story **Palacio Consistorial** (Calle Benito Monción, corner of Calle del Sol, free). Built between 1895 and 1996, this renovated 19th-century neoclassical building was once the city' town hall. The most interesting room here is the Salon del Carnaval de Santiago on the ground floor, with displays of life-size mannequins decked out in carnival costumes and masks explaining the importance of carnival culture in this part of the Dominican Republic. Unfortunately for the monolinguals, all labeling is in Spanish and there aren't any audio translations. The second floor hosts rotating photography and art exhibits. Head up here if only to enjoy the outdoor balcony views onto the Parque Duarte and the cathedral.

★ Monumento a los Héroes de la Restauración

Atop a hill on the eastern side of the city, the 67-meter-tall (220-foot) white marble **Monumento a los Héroes de la Restauración** (Av. Coronel Juan Maria Lora, tel. 809/241-1391, http://monumento-mhr.com, 9am-6pm Tues.-Sun., RD$60 or US$1.30) is the most impressive and

recognizable building in Santiago. Locals simply call it El Monumento de Santiago. It's worth a stop if you have a couple of hours in the city. This structure was completed in Trujillo's time, and the dictator himself named it the Monumento a la Paz de Trujillo. When his regime fell, it was rededicated to the Heroes of the War of Restoration (or Guerra de España, 1863-1865). The statue at the very top of the monument represents the Angel de la Paz, the peace angel, facing what is considered to be the center of Santiago.

Designed by architect Henry Gazón Bona, the Monument's construction began in 1944 on the centennial of the DR's independence, and was completed in 1952. There are five floors in the monument, and each floor recounts the history of the Dominican Republic and its major battles, depicted in various glass displays, as well as the most significant players in the War of Restoration. You'll also see large paintings by Spanish artist Vela Zanetti created while he was in exile during the Spanish Civil War.

If you manage to traverse the 347 steps to reach the fifth floor (bring water), you'll enjoy the **Mirador Santiaguero**—a wraparound terrace with glorious views of the city below. There are telescopes you can use for 10 pesos (US$0.22). The outdoor area at the base of the monument is perhaps even more impressive, with life-size statues of Dominican heroes hugging the building. It is also of more use to residents, with sprawling lawns and benches that have a 360-degree view over the city and the distant Cordillera Central. Lovers and families take a moment out of their busy day to relax here or enjoy a Sunday afternoon.

There are unfortunately no English audio devices available, and the elevator is often out of service.

Fortaleza San Luis

Originally built in 1804, Santiago's **Fortaleza San Luis** (Calle Duverge, 9am-5pm daily, free) is close to the center of town and has a gorgeous, imposing, yellow-walled entrance with two canons facing the city. This fortress

Cigar Country

It's no exaggeration to say that the DR is the number one exporter of premium cigars in the world. In fact, Dominican cigars account for over half of the cigars sold in the United States alone. These fine, hand rolled products have been judged over the past years to be well superior in quality and flavor to those made in Cuba.

The history of tobacco cultivation and cigar making in the country goes back centuries. The indigenous inhabitants used tobacco in religious ceremonies, before the arrival of the Spaniards. During the 20th century, when Cuban tobacco growers were threatened by the Castro regime, which was seeking to seize their operations and eventually would result in their being boycotted by the United States, they moved over to the Dominican Republic. Thanks to the DR's fertile soils and ideal temperatures, the seeds were here to stay and thrive.

Some of the best tobacco is grown outside of Santiago in the Cibao Valley, particularly, in the Yaque Valley and Villa Gonzalez, home to tobacco fields from which sought-after, award-winning cigars are made: Davidoff Nicaragua Toro, Arturo Fuente Don Carlos, and Fernando Leon Family Reserve Belicoso, among others. The ideal breezy and sunny climate, along with good drainage and fertile lands, have helped production. Today, cigar brands of various strengths come out of such respected factories as Tabacalera de García, Tabacalera La Aurora, and La Flor Dominicana, where they are hand rolled and assembled by artisans who are passionate about and meticulous in their application of traditional craftsmanship.

In 1992, the country's top cigar manufacturers created the Asociación de Fabricantes de Cigarros de la República Dominicana—currently at 11 members, each of whom produce at least six or more cigar brands—to establish and help maintain high-quality production standards. Every year, they put on a prestigious **ProCigar Festival**, a weeklong cigar retreat celebrating the product and taking visitors across some of the most visited regions from Punta Cana to La Romana.

To sample or experience a Santiago cigar factory—a must while in the DR if you partake—be sure to visit one of the top outlets in the country and purchase directly from them, as counterfeit cigars are all too frequent in tourist areas. It is an easy ride from downtown Santiago to the renowned **La Aurora** (Av. Tamboril-Santiago, Parque Industrial Tamboril, tel. 809/575-1903, www.laaurora.com.do, free, reservations required), offering one-hour tours of the oldest cigar factory in the country established in 1903. You'll learn how to smoke a cigar, observe the rolling process, and perhaps even try your hand at making your own starting in late 2016. For a smaller boutique factory, visit **PDR Cigars** (Pinar del Río Cigars, no phone, www.pdcigars.com, 8am-noon and 2pm-4pm Mon.-Fri., free tour) in the town of Villa Gonzales about nine miles northwest of Santiago producing four Dominican *puro* (made with DR tobacco) cigars, as well as blends with Brazilian tobacco. Across the street is another common visitor stop to watch the process at **Tubano's** (Villa Gonzales, no phone, 8am-noon and 2pm-4pm Mon.-Fri., free tour). Besides simply having access to quality products, prepare to be impressed with how quickly and yet precisely cigar rollers make and finish each piece. The sampling that ensues isn't too bad, either.

is one of the city's most historical sights since it is where numerous battles took place during the War of Restoration. It's also where over 1,000 U.S. Marines took over the city during the United States occupation of the DR in 1916, which lasted until 1924.

The entrance is always open, if guarded, and leads into a spacious parking lot after you pass the three busts of independence heroes Sanchez, Melia, Duarte, and, behind them, a whole row of statues of important historical figures. It makes for an interesting walk, but don't do it in the hot Santiago sun.

On the other side of the parking lot, away from the impressive display of army tanks, the Museo de la Fortaleza (donation suggested RD$150 or US$3.27, with guide) might surprise you when you see just how spacious and well stocked it is. Opened in 2005, its displays show off Taíno items dating back 500 years including items used in everyday life, rituals, containers, and carvings of witch doctors'

Monumento a los Héroes de la Restauración

faces. At the back are items dating from World War II. Between you'll see shotguns and swords used by conquistadores like Drake and Columbus and pirates. The first U.S. Marine occupation of the DR in 1916 is documented with black and white photographs taken at the fortress. There are gorgeous paintings, as well as displays of various carnival and folklore figures. The museum's well-informed guide, **Etnaras Sarante** (tel. 829/871-6478, etnaras39@hotmail.com), speaks enough English to explain various items in the museum and their historical context.

Casa del Arte

You'll find Dominican artists' works displayed at the **Casa del Arte** (across from Parque Duarte, Calle Benito Monción, 3pm-8pm daily, free), a renovated Victorian building in this historic part of downtown Santiago. You'll recognize it by the colorful mural that covers its front walls and entrance. The opening hours can be random and the curator isn't the friendliest chap you'll meet, so prepare to just wander around alone and take in the drawings. There are paintings by Luis Jimenez and Ofemil Abreu, among others.

Directly across from it is **La 37 por Las Tablas** (Benito Monción 37, tel. 809/587-3033, www.la37porlastablas.blogspot.com, from US$1), a renovated cultural space dedicated to Dominican performing arts. It's ideal for those who speak Spanish and want to catch some theater. Even if you don't, you can call ahead for some historical background on Dominican arts and drama before grabbing drinks on the patio at adjacent sidewalk bars. Check before you go for hours as they vary.

Centro Cultural León Jimenes

The **Centro Cultural León Jimenes** (Av. 27 de Febrero 146, tel. 809/582-2315, www. centroleon.org.do, 10am-7pm Tues.-Sun., RD$150 or US$3.27) was built by the tobacco empire that is the León Jimenes family. There are three permanent exhibit rooms on the ground floor. The Sala de Antropología displays Taíno artifacts, ceramics, and deities, as well as background on the sugarcane industry and its African origins. An adjacent exhibit room displays Dominican cultural items and lifestyle photos. The Sala de Artes Visuales showcases creations of Dominican artists who participated in the León Jimenes art contest, which goes back to 1964 when Eduardo León Jimenes created the event in the hopes of promoting art and creativity in new generations of artists in the DR.

Walk through the cafeteria and cross over the patio to the second building to find out more information on the León family on the second floor. On display are old machines and tools used for cigar making.

Unfortunately, the center isn't as informative if you're not a Spanish speaker: there are no bilingual guides on permanent staff (you'd have to call ahead to book one) and there were no English audio devices available as of the time of writing. The souvenir shop, however, has a few worthwhile items authentic to the area and the DR, including *merenguero* hats, cigars, coffee, and history books.

A taxi to Centro León or other major sights within the city shouldn't cost more than RD$150 (US$3.27). There are also shared taxis—catch the one labeled Route A and be sure to confirm your drop-off location.

Fábrica de Cigarros La Aurora

A free one-hour factory tour at the oldest cigar factory in the country is a must for cigar smokers or anyone curious about one of the country's main exports and the number one producer and exporter of premium cigars in the world. Founded in 1903, **La Aurora** (Av. Tamboril-Santiago, Parque Industrial Tamboril, tel. 809/575-1903, www.laaurora. com.do, free, reservations required) exports to at least 64 countries, and imports about 20% of the tobacco used. On the tour you'll get a history of the founding León family and see the various factory floor rooms where cigar rollers turn around about 200 cigars by hand every day (for RD$5,000 or US$100 a week salary), including the humidor and the vintage cigar gallery, among other sections. While you tour, you'll get a complimentary cigar, and learn how to light, hold, and smoke in true cigar smoker swag (the guide Eugenio Hernandez is quite amusing in his demonstrations). Starting in November 2015, classes will be offered on how to roll your own cigar—so be sure to inquire if that's of interest. Pick up a box of Aurora Preferidos or León Jimenes Prestige from the shop for the tobacco lovers in your life. Tours are complimentary, as are pickups, but you must call ahead and make a reservation.

Estadio Cibao

Home to the Cibao Eagles (Águilas Cibaeñas), one of the most successful of the six baseball teams in the country, the **Estadio Cibao** (Av. Imbert, tel. 809/575-1810, http://aguilas. lidom.com/main/estadio-cibao, from RD$150 or US$3.27) is the largest baseball facility in the DR with at least 18,000 seats. It hosts pro baseball games two to three times a week in the Dominican from mid-October to late January. Dubbed "el valle de la muerte" or the valley of death, it was built in 1958 and expanded in 1974. In 2014, the stadium suffered a major fire; luckily it was closed at the time.

Gran Teatro del Cibao

Across from the Monumento a los Héroes, the two marble and mahogany halls of the **Gran Teatro del Cibao** (Calle Daniel Espinal, esq. Av. Las Carreras, tel. 809/583-1150, 9am-4pm Mon.-Fri.) play host to national and

rolling cigars at La Aurora

Santiago's Cabaña Culture

one of Santiago's infamous *cabañas*

You can't miss the big, bold, and flashy signs for *cabañas turísticas* (some call themselves *aparta-hotel* officially, but if you're paying by the hour, there's no confusion as to what the place is and the highway signs are clear). By-the-hour hotel rooms for trysts and other illicit encounters are common throughout the DR, but Santiago takes them to a whole new level. Some of these *cabañas* are so fancy and fabulous—complete with themed executive spa suites—they make Punta Cana's most luxurious suites seem standard. You will want to move in immediately.

Just for kicks—or heck, for real—visit a couple of them and stay for a few hours to get a sense of just how big this market is and how huge of a cultural trend it reflects. The way they operate is all part of the fun: there is no reception check-in, just drive straight into the private garage, which shuts down after you enter (so no one sees you arriving or exiting). Enter your suite, lock the door behind you, and escape for four hours at a time or up to a week! Everything is provided: food, condoms (from a secret swinging box in your suite, accessible immediately after you turn over the cash), spa tubs, full kitchens, disco lights, and outdoor patios with cascading swimming pools. You name it, it's all here.

One of Santiago's most luxurious and popular *cabaña* complexes is **Bora Bora** (Autopista Duarte Km. 5 1/2, tel. 809/570-7000, www.borabora.com.do, US$40/4 hours). Like its name, the interior of each presidential suite is exotic and themed (I loved the Samurai Suite) with varying features, including bedroom balconies looking down into hot spa tub on the ground floor. **Horus** (Carretera Las Palomas, off Autopista Duarte, tel. 809/241-0606, www.horusapartahotel.com, US$50/4 hours) is another to offer fancy digs. The latest is **Fenix Aparta-Hotel** (Carretera Canabacoa, US$77/4 hours) with its ridiculously lavish driveway featuring giant, cast-iron animal figures. Its stunning, new executive suites feel like a penthouse, with a disco-lit floor and pole in the living room and a swimming pool outdoors.

Illicit love is not mandatory: you can share the suite with friends, stock up on food and drinks, and have one heck of a private party.

international artists. Check the theater's social media pages for the latest events. Dominican architect Teofilo Carbonell designed the building in 1995 and is said to have modeled it after Santo Domingo's national theater. It has a capacity of 1,600 seats.

Monumento Natural Pico Diego de Ocampo

Not one for museums and prefer the great outdoors? Get to the **Monumento Natural Pico Diego de Ocampo** (tel. 829-799-7839, lisandromichael1998@hotmail.com, US$10), declared a biological reserve in 1996—to make the 2-hour hike up the 1,249-meter-tall (4,097-foot) peak. Named after a maroon who fought against Spanish colonialists from these mountains back in the 16th century, it's the highest point on the Cordillera Septentrional and a perfect way to get your body ready for the peaks of Jarabacoa, especially if you're going to climb Pico Duarte later in your journey. The 45-minute ride 15 kilometers (9.3 miles) north of Santiago to the entrance of the monument is quite a challenge—you'll need an all-terrain vehicle—but the vistas are gorgeous and the countryside life you see, as you get deeper in, is worthwhile.

Get on Highway 1 from the city, and continue onto the Carretera al Pico Diego. After about 40 minutes when you reach yellow Colmado Checo (good place for a water stop), you'll know you're just a minute away from the start of the hike. The trick: guides are only around on the weekends, Friday through Sunday. There's signage to the entrance of the hike; the guides sit and wait at the top of the hill during that time. The view from the top of Pico Diego over the Cibao Valley is spectacular taking in the Septentrional range, part of the Cordillera Central, and Santiago in the distance. To arrange for a car and a ride to take you up to the peak, contact taxi driver Hancis Beato (tel. 829/902-3244), who knows these parts well.

Mirabal Sisters Museum

The heroines of Dominican history, the Mirabal sisters—Patria, Minerva, Maria Teresa, and Bélgica also known as the Butterflies—were from Salcedo and fought to overthrow former dictator Rafael Leonidas Trujillo before three were eventually murdered by his men on their way back home from visiting their husbands in prison. Their killing triggered a revolt that ultimately led to the assassination of Trujillo in 1961.

The surviving sister, Bélgica Adela Mirabal, affectionately known as Doña Dede, founded a **Mirabal Sisters Museum** (tel. 809/587-8530, 9:30am-4:30pm Tues.-Fri., call ahead) in 1994 in her native city of Ojo de Agua, to commemorate her family. She passed away in 2014 at the age of 88. The museum is in the sisters' former second home. Sitting amid immaculate gardens, the home houses displays of the family's personal effects from handkerchiefs to dresses and teacups. The kitchen and other rooms are kept in their original condition. The most moving showcase is of the items recovered from the murdered sisters' bodies—including a bloodstained handkerchief, shoes, and a braid from Maria Teresa's head that her sister cut and kept. There's a gift shop onsite, as well as a bookstore.

SPORTS AND RECREATION
Hiking

If you're not headed to Jarabacoa, then your best bet for some outdoor activity is to hike the **Pico Diego de Ocampo**. It's a tricky spot to find; contact local taxi driver **Hancis Beato** (tel. 829/902-3244) to drive you up the hills from the city, on a 45-minute, part-paved and part-bumpy ride to the trail entrance at **Monumento Natural Pico Diego de Ocampo** (tel. 829-799-7839, lisandromichael1998@hotmail.com, US$10). At least that is clearly marked with a giant sign. Follow the trail on foot to meet up with the guides that wait here on weekends, before starting your two-hour journey that will give you a feel for the glorious mountainous landscape of this Cibao region and the city of Santiago's backdrop. There isn't much else

a costumed devil at Carnaval de Santiago

to do here, so begin the hike in the morning, and return by early afternoon in time for lunch.

Horse-drawn Carriage Tour

Tour the city while shielding yourself from the harsh sun for a couple of hours in a traditional **horse-drawn carriage tour.** You'll find them outside or around the Monumento a los Héroes, as well as around Parque Duarte, waiting to whisk visitors away. Don't pay more than RD$400 (US$8.72).

ENTERTAINMENT AND EVENTS

Santiago is known to have one of the most active nightlife scenes in the country. There are certainly more clubs, bars, and corners to hang out in than are listed below, but these are the safest for first-time visitors, especially those who aren't bilingual. Even by this fearless traveler recommends that you don't venture into local neighborhoods and clubs unaccompanied.

You'll find the majority of popular, trendy bars surrounding the Monumento a los Héroes, an area that comes alive at night. The largest outdoor lounge is **Puerta del Sol** (but note they don't serve Presidente beer), which fills up from late afternoon on. Under a flamboyant tree, the best ambience is at the outdoors **Ahí Bar** (Calle Tolentino corner of Calle Restauración, tel. 809/581-6779, www.ahi-bar.com, 4pm-2am Mon.-Fri., noon-4am Sat.-Sun.). It is a popular stop for a cold drink any day of the week with music, video screens, and smaller space that's tucked away from the main streets. An indoor Ahí nightclub opens across the street from the bar on the weekends.

Colinas Mall is home to **22 VIP Club** (Av. 27 de Febrero, tel. 809/576-0170, http://twentytwovipclub.com, 10pm-2am Thurs.-Sun.) overlooking the city on its top fourth floor, while a few blocks north, **Rancho Típico Las Colinas** (no sign, look for merengue concert posters on its outside walls) hosts live merengue on the weekends and the occasional Dominican recording artist. **Pasión** (Autopista Duarte Km 7 1/2, 809/612-6411, 10pm-3am daily) is the fancier club option.

Tabú Room Club (tel. 809/724-4671, 8pm-8am daily) and **Trio** are both located within the longtimer **Matum Hotel & Casino** (Av. Las Carreras) grounds. Tabu is the more popular and packed one, despite its smaller size. If you're up for a casino night, head to the onsite casino.

Festivals and Events

The grandest outdoor show in the city is **Carnaval de Santiago.** And it gets more elaborate and popular every year, despite nearby competition in La Vega as the biggest carnival destination in the country. Santiago's Carnival is one of the most colorful and culturally authentic you can attend. If you're here in February, every weekend of the month you can enjoy watching Dominicans from all walks of life celebrating in the streets of the city and revelers in colorful folkloric costumes and handcrafted masks with spiky horns representing Santiago's *lechones* or devils, as well as other popular Dominican carnival personalities.

The celebrations take place around the city's most popular sight, the Monumento a los Héroes de la Restauración (Monumento de Santiago), giving the already-colorful event a gorgeous, green backdrop. Everything kicks off on Sundays between 3pm and 4pm and lasts until 8pm. Crowds spread out either along the barricades of the parade or up on the lawns of the monument to watch from above. You can show up as early as 2pm if you like and enjoy the sponsoring rum company's bar shelling out mixed drinks for 50 pesos (barely over a dollar) while a DJ spins the latest Dominican and Carnival tunes. Once the parade begins, look out for those *lechones* and the long sisal rope whips they swing at high velocity. As long as you're standing behind the barricaded sidewalks you will be safe. Security is plentiful all along the parade route and around the monument, and food vendors are numerous. It's a fun time to visit this otherwise hectic city.

ProCigar Festival (third week of February, tel. 809/580-4754, www.procigar. org, US$895 for full program) is celebrated during one week across several locations across the DR, includes a stop in Santiago as the birthplace and capital of the world's best cigars. Over 400 participants come from around the world to indulge in a fun time that includes cigar factory excursions, local cuisine and nightlife, and plenty of entertainment. Check the website for each year's schedule of activities, full program, and cost.

SHOPPING

Calle del Sol is the main shopping street in Santiago, where you'll find fast food, electronic junk, Chinese fashion stores, and plenty of vendors on the street trying to sell you something, anything. Don't be surprised to see security guards with shotguns in front of jewelry stores. In the heart of Calle del Sol, the **Mercado Modelo** is a bit less hectic than the rest of the street and offers locally made souvenirs. Inaugurated in 1942 by Trujillo, the covered yet bright market complete with a fountain and rest area hosts over 400 vendor shops, ranging from jewelry and Dominican larimar and amber stones to merengue instruments you can take home.

For a colorful food market experience, and a look into why this area is known as the breadbasket of the DR, head to the largest outdoor **Mercado Hospedaje Yaque** (Calle Capotillo, off Calle del Sol), where you'll find all the local vegetables and fruits you can think of and might not know, herbal shops with over a dozen *botánicas* where locals buy healing potions (believer beware), cafeteria shacks for cheap lunches, and men playing dominoes in corners while waiting to make a sale. It's a noisy, busy, crazy corner of the city, but a wonderful peek into daily Dominican life.

You'll find your fair share of shopping malls in Santiago with the requisite shoe stores, movie theaters, and food courts, but they're not terribly impressive compared to Santo Domingo's. Try the popular **Plaza Internacional** (Av. Juan Pablo Duarte), home to Caribbean Cinemas and decent fashions, **Bella Terra Mall** (Av. Juan Pablo Duarte, near corner of Estrella Sadhala, tel. 809/336-2903, www.bellaterra.com.do), or **Las Colinas Mall** (Av. 27 de Febrero, corner of Av. Imbert, tel. 809/576-6555, www.colinas-mall.com.do).

The gift shop inside **Centro León** (Av. 27 de Febrero 146, tel. 809/582-2315, www.centroleon.org.do, 10am-7pm Tues.-Sun.) carries typical Santiaguero and Dominican items worth checking out, including La Aurora cigars and *merengue típico* hats.

Just 15 minutes outside of Santiago, in the village of **Higüerito** (off Carretera 1/ Autopista Duarte towards Ortega, after Rancho Chito Restaurant), you'll find some delightful pottery, hand made by Dominican artisans who use a potter's wheel. You can sit and watch them if you like, and it's an easy stop on way from or to the airport. These

The Faceless Dolls of Higüerito

You've probably spotted them in souvenir shops, intrigued at these ceramic dolls with hats and zero facial features. The concept was born right here, in the village of El Higüerito, just 15 minutes outside of Santiago south of the airport. The Jose Marte Polonia family, who still run their own workshops, have manufactured the *muñecas sin rostro* since 1983, after a woman from their neighborhood came up with the idea of producing a doll representing the average Dominican woman. That is to say, one who could be of many diverse roots—Dominicans have African, Spanish, Taíno blood in their veins—so that it would be impossible for her to have any distinct facial features. The dolls act as a reminder that this is an all-inclusive culture, a melting pot that is embraced. For the past 35 years, the Marte family are just one of a handful who make these dolls right out of their homes turned ateliers, and you can walk right in and watch **"Jose muñequito"** (Calle Camboya, tel. 809/216-5955, 8am-5pm)—as the workshop is also known in the vil-

one of Higüerito's faceless dolls

lage—spinning the wheel as he begins to shape each one, later turned over to their painter for the colorful shades. The earth used to make the dolls comes from Bonao, mixed with Higüerito's own.

There used to be up to 100 doll makers in this village, but competition and recessions proved tough and now only five remain. The Marte family's dolls sell in major tourist zones, including Punta Cana. A small doll of varying skin color as you prefer costs about RD$100 (US$2.18), and a larger one is RD$600 (US$13.08).

pottery makers and artisans are unique to this area. The vases and other house items are painted in vibrant colors and make a beautiful addition to any home. Visit the small, Dominican-owned ceramic workshop **Arte en Barro Jimenes** (Calle Bonagua Abajo 145, tel. 809/409-1006 or 829/655-9982, 7:30am-12:30pm, 1:30pm-5:30pm daily). The main potter, Guancho, has worked here for 22 years and uses earth brought in from nearby Bonao to make the pots—about 150 pots are made by hand daily. You can walk to the back and watch the oven they use to solidify the pots. Across the street, the painter decorates and covers them in various colors and patterns. This is also where you can purchase the finished items.

FOOD

If you're in the city center, grab coffee and dessert at **Pan y Galletas Piki** (across from

Parque Duarte, Calle del Sol, tel. 809/582-2334, 6:30am-7:30pm daily, US$2-4), set on the corner of a pedestrian-only alley lined with historic buildings. You can enjoy your treats in the Parque Duarte.

An even better option, away from the madness of Calle del Sol, is **La Campagna** (Av. Duarte 21, tel. 809/581-5056, www.lacampagna.com.do/panaderia, 7am-10pm daily, US$3-10), a nicely shaded open terrace coffee shop with gourmet java as well as sandwiches, burgers, and small bites. The quiet atmosphere is perfect for those who want to bring their laptops and surf the net. There's an adjacent restaurant if you need more options.

Set on a row of trendy bars and restaurants across from the Monumento de Santiago, **El Tablón Latino** (Calle del Sol 12, tel. 809/581-3813, 11am-11pm daily, US$5-12) serves up a wide range of Latin dishes—think Peruvian ceviche, Dominican pork *chicharrón*, or

Spanish risotto—in a casual chic atmosphere. Eat on the outdoor terrace or indoors with tightly spaced seating and freezing air-conditioning. They also offer a solid range of salads, flatbread sandwiches, and desserts. Portions are large, and you can't go wrong with much of their menu. Wash it all down with a fresh juice. Service can be slow when busy.

Max's Delicias (pronounced "Mas," Calle del Sol 28, tel. 809/971-5574, 9am-10pm daily, US$3-10) is a casual, Dominican cafeteria where you can eat well and cheaply. It's a one block walk up from the monument, yet hidden because a giant tree hangs over the restaurant's sign. Keep your eyes peeled when walking or driving there.

On par with Dominicans' love for hanging out by a gas station, Square One (Av. Estrella Sahlada, by Shell Gas, tel. 809/241-5384, www.square1rd.com, US$5-15) is the most popular diner in the city, open 24 hours with a decent, affordable menu of breakfast treats, sandwiches, burgers, and more. The 20- to 40-something crowd is as hip and urban, you might think you're back in the United States.

In the city center, Pizzeria Monti (corner of Duarte and Beller) you can get a decent, large slice of pizza for just RD$60 (US$1.09). The small, cozy restaurant also has a second floor for additional space.

Kukara Makara (Av. Francia 7, tel. 809/241-3143, www.kukaramacara.net, 10am-1am daily, later on weekends, US$10-15) looks like a tourist trap with its cowboy saloon-themed exterior and interior. The food is average at best—the eclectic menu ranges from seafood to salads, mofongo, steaks, and pastas, and yet crowds constantly stream in and out, perhaps due to its convenient location facing the Monumento de Santiago. There are honestly better options around this area.

A longtime favorite in Santiago and popular spot for business folks and groups, Pez Dorado (Calle del Sol 43, tel. 809/582-2518, noon-11pm daily, US$5-12) specializes in Chinese cuisine, as well as Dominican seafood dishes and steaks. And it has a more formal atmosphere than most restaurants.

An excellent alternative for seafood is ★ Marisco Caribeño Restaurant (Calle del Sol 1, corner of Av. Francia, tel. 809/971-9710, www.mariscocentro.com, 10am-midnight daily, US$6-15), close to the Santiago Monument. There's an excellent seafood buffet on Sundays (RD$600), as well as an à la carte menu. You can listen to live music while you dine on Saturdays.

★ Camp David Ranch (Carretera Gregorio Luperón Km 7.5, tel. 809/275-6400, 7am-midnight daily, US$5-15) has the nicest restaurant setting, within a 10- to 15-minute drive out of town and up into the hills. The panoramic mountain view from the outdoor dining terrace is just one of the reasons to come and dine here. (There's also cozy indoor seating.) The menu delights with appetizers like pork belly taquitos or shrimp soaked in a passion fruit sauce and served with spicy guacamole. Entrées could be yucca gnocchi stuffed with beef or paella. It's popular among Santiagueros on Sundays, so come early if you want to find space, or reserve ahead.

ACCOMMODATIONS

Hotel accommodations are surprisingly pricey in Santiago—perhaps because it's primarily a business traveler's destination.

The two-person operation at ★ Via Emilia B&B (Calle Estado de Israel 16, tel. 809/806-6609, www.viaemiliasantiago.com, US$35-39) is a find in a city filled with big hotels. A stone's throw from the main bus stations and Calle Duarte yet out of plain sight, this small guesthouse provides all you need for a safe, comfy place to stay. Small, immaculately clean rooms include private bath, flatscreen TV, fan and air-conditioning (though not strong), and wireless Internet. There's an onsite dining room offering meals at an extra charge if you choose. Staff are friendly and accommodating. Look for the Italian flag on the front door when you're first trying to locate the place. You'll need a car or taxi to get here.

Hodelpa Centro Plaza Hotel & Casino (Calle Mella and Sol, tel. 809/583-6666, www.hodelpa.com, US$90-130, includes breakfast)

Santiago's *Lechoneras*

Lechoneras specialize in pork.

Meat lovers alert: Santiagueros love their pit-roasted pork. There are three renowned *lechoneras*, as they're called, in the city. All are casual, open-air restaurants right off a main road or highway and serve foods other than pork (in case you're only interested in seeing the setup). Note that this isn't food for the poor: roasted pork is a Dominican delicacy. A plate goes for about RD$200-300 (US$4.36-6.54) for a quarter, or RD$600 (US$13.08) for a pound. Go early if you want to see how the meat is made (as early as 6am); after lunchtime it's all gone.

Lechonera Milito (Av. Hispanoamericana, tel. 809/626-0140, 7am-6pm daily) is perhaps the farthest out from downtown and used to be a much bigger restaurant before the owner passed and they move to their current location. Still, it's a popular pit stop—with casual restaurant seating or counter service. A second option is **El Embrujo** (Av. Rafael Vidal, across Century Plaza Hotel, tel. 809/581-4099, 7am-midnight). Santiagueros agree that **Rancho Chito** (Autopista Duarte Km 12 1/2, tel. 809/276-0000, www.ranchochito.com, US$3.65-20) is the best option of the three, and the more modern, fancy setting certainly proves it. The spacious thatched-roof restaurant—with two rooms—offers cafeteria-style dishes, where you can pick your pork cuts among numerous other local options, or from an extensive à la carte menu. It's a family favorite and fills up on Sundays for its buffet option (RD$230 or US$5).

is right at the heart of the city's main commercial shopping street Calle del Sol. It's good for those who want to be in the middle of the action, as well as close to the city's few sights. You'll find all the classic hotel room furnishings and comfort here—though rooms are small—including minibars and coffeemakers. Perks include a free airport shuttle and an onsite casino and restaurant.

Hotel Platino (Av. Estrella Sadhala, tel. 809/724-7576, www.hotelplatinord.com, US$53-130) gets rave reviews for its staff and provides good value for those passing through the city but not looking to stay in the center. The slightly dated rooms are clean and provide mini fridges, TV, and wireless Internet. If you want to take it up a notch, go for the suites.

Those who want to escape or bypass Santiago for the day while transiting, can head to **Camp David Ranch Hotel** (Carretera Gregorio Luperón Km 7.5, tel. 809/276-6400, www.campdavidranch.com, US$90-115, includes breakfast), sitting 457 meters (1,500 feet) above sea level overlooking the bustling city. The hotel's 17 modern rooms are well appointed with king beds, neutral wall colors, wood furniture, flat-screen TV, air-conditioning, iron, wireless Internet, safe boxes, and outdoor verandas with views onto the valley. The bathrooms, while small, have marble sinks and glass showers. On display in the lobby—attached to the onsite restaurant's glorious outdoor terrace—are original vintage cars belonging to former dictator Rafael Leonidas Trujillo, including his black 1956 Cadillac Fleetwood.

INFORMATION AND SERVICES

You'll find plenty of shopping on Calle del Sol, the main commercial street in the city. Avenida Duarte is home to shopping malls and restaurants, cafés and various stores, including **La Sirena** (Calle España, 8am-10pm). Parallel Avenida 27 de Febrero houses numerous services from banks to bus stations.

For 24-hour medical care, in town your options are **Centro Medico Semma** (Padre Francisco Bono, tel. 809/688-6646 or 809/226-1053) or **Hospital Jose Maria Cabral y Baez** (Av. 27 de Febrero, tel. 809/724-7555) close to the center. If you have the time to spare, a better bet is on Autopista Duarte, at **Hospital Metropolitano de Santiago** (Autopista Duarte Km 2.8, tel. 829/947-2222, www.homshospital.com).

GETTING THERE AND AROUND

Air

Aeropuerto Internacional del Cibao (www.aeropuertocibao.com.do) is just a 20-minute drive out of the city, and services airlines such as American, Delta, JetBlue, United, Copa, and Spirit. Airport taxis to the city cost around US$25.

Bus

Getting to Santiago is quite easy from Santo Domingo or Puerto Plata. **Caribe Tours** (Av. 27 de Febrero, tel. 809/576-0790, www.

caribetours.com.do, US$2.39-5.88) sends a bus nearly every hour from Santiago to Santo Domingo—check the website for departure times. Get off at the second and final stop in Santiago in the city center, as there are two. **Metro Tours** (Av. Duarte, tel. 809/587-3837, http://metroserviciosturisticos.com, US$2.39-5.88), just a block away, also has departures throughout the day, even if not every hour like Caribe. Whichever bus you opt for, bring a scarf or jacket of some kind since the air-conditioning can be stupidly high. Other possible destinations from Santiago by bus include Puerto Plata, Sosúa, and Monte Cristi. Arrive at least 45 minutes prior to your bus departure.

A third way of reaching Santiago from Puerto Plata, particularly if you plan on connecting to other small towns such as La Vega or San Francisco de Macorís, is to hop on a **Javila Tours** minibus. It's popular with the locals and comfortable, with air-conditioning and wireless Internet on board. The vans depart every 15 minutes from 6am through 5pm. The fare is just RD$120 or US$2.60, and you can hop off at Parque Los Chachases in Santiago for the next round of connections.

Taxi

Santiago's taxis charge a set fare of about US$3.27 (RD$150) for one-way rides within city limits. You'll usually see them parked outside major supermarkets, sights, and bus stations. You can also call **Santiago Taxi** (tel. 809/581-8888) or Santiago native taxi driver **Hancis Beato** (tel. 809/902-3244), with whom you can negotiate for out-of-town rides or all-day fares.

Car

Getting around Santiago isn't hard if you remember the key drags: Calle del Sol, the main shopping street, runs east into the Monumento a los Héroes. The main avenues are 27 de Febrero and Duarte, where you'll find all the malls, movie theaters, and supermarkets. You can rent a car from the airport (booked online to ensure better rates) through **Avis** (tel. 809/233-8154, www.avis.com), **Alamo** (tel. 809/233-8163, www.alamo.com), **Europcar** (tel. 809/233-8150, www.europcar. com), or **Honda Rent-a-car** (tel. 809/233-8179, www.nationalcar.com).

La Vega

A hot, dusty city, and the third largest in the DR, La Vega is essentially a transportation and commercial center. There's no reason to visit—*unless* it's February, and then you can witness one of the most vibrant and traditional carnivals in the country. Despite the fact that it doesn't have much going on, La Vega is home to two historically significant sights: the Holy Hill of Santo Cerro and the archaeological ruins of La Vega Vieja, the original city founded by Columbus himself in 1494 as a gold mining base. An earthquake leveled it in 1562, and the population relocated to its current spot along the Río Camú.

SIGHTS

In this city itself, **Casa de la Cultura** (across from Parque Duarte, tel. 809/573-1021, casadelaculturadelavega@gmail.com, 8am-5pm Mon.-Fri.) displays local art every month; there was no schedule when I visited, so don't expect too much if you happen to stop in here. Within the Parque Duarte compound a few steps north is the city's well known and imposing **Catedral Inmaculada Concepción**. This towering, odd, faded old gray stone building is a serious eyesore on the outside. It's much more attractive on the inside, with an impressive 15-foot-tall statue of Jesus. The ceiling lit up to look like a starry sky took 15 years to complete from 1977 to 1992. The cathedral has a 1,000-person capacity.

The Holy Hill of Santo Cerro

Whether you're into history or religion or neither, if you're lucky enough to pass through Santo Cerro northeast of La Vega and Highway Duarte and indulge in the views over the Valle de La Vega, you will not be sorry. It's absolutely breathtaking. But Santo Cerro

is also one of the holiest sites in the country and one of the most significant historically. This was one of the first three dioceses in the "New World." A major pilgrimage takes place every year on September 24 to the **Nuestra Señora de Las Mercedes Church** (mass 6:30am and 5pm Mon.-Fri., 7am and 4pm Sat., 6:30am, 9am or 11am, 4pm Sun.) following nine days of *fiestas patronales* or patron saint celebrations that begin around September 16. Thousands of Dominicans come from all corners of the country and from abroad.

Legend has it that Santo Cerro was the site of a miracle in the Spanish colonial days. Columbus had received a cross from Queen Isabela of Spain when he set sail, and he planted it on this hill overlooking the Cibao upon arriving. When the Taíno fought the Spaniards in 1495, they attempted to burn the cross, but it wouldn't take fire and the Virgin de las Mercedes appeared before them on this very cross. The Taíno are said to have fled in fear, and it brought an end to the war with the indigenous population (you can tell whose version of the story this was). The original cross, made of níspero wood, is no longer here. It is thought to have ended up in private hands in Rome, among various stories which can't be verified, but you can still see the Holy Hole or *Santo Hoyo* where it was originally planted inside the church. Before reaching the church, look out for a fenced off *árbol de níspero*—a tree originally planted by Columbus in 1495.

Be sure to walk behind the church to the lookout terrace for unbelievable views over the valley. Take the staircase down to admire the 14-meter-high (46-foot) cross from up close. Built just a couple of years ago, its base hugged by a giant rosary, its mosaic tiles are covered in depictions of the passion of Christ.

Look down at the steps and observe the intricate verses sculpted into each one. On your way out, buy some local *croquetas de maís* snacks—sweet corn crackers—from vendors.

Parque Nacional Arqueológico e Histórico de la Vega Vieja

At the **Parque Nacional Arqueológico e Histórico de la Vega Vieja** (Carretera Juan Bosch, 8am-5pm, US$2.18 pp), you can walk amid the 500-year-old ruins of the old city, named Concepción de La Vega, that Christopher Columbus founded as a gold mining base and turned into one of the most prosperous cities in the Americas. Declared a national park in 1976, it's tucked off the highway before La Vega's center (there's a hard-to-spot sign for the turnoff to the park along the highway). A young, Spanish-speaking guide will show up as you arrive at the parking lot to collect your entrance fee and take you through the ruins. He will tell you the story of Columbus' old fort where he kept his precious gold, now in ruins, and old sentinel towers. It's pretty incredible to think that you're standing on some of the oldest colonial settlements in the Americas. If you position yourself in front of the fort facing west, you can spot the new Santo Cerro cross in the distance.

The first archaeological studies of this site began in 1994, with the help of researchers from the Florida Museum of Natural History. These determined the size and location of the original city, along with cataloging over 200,000 items recovered from excavations. It was later found that it was the largest settlement in the "New World" until at least 1520. At the back of the park is a museum—more of a room, really—filled with ancient Taíno artifacts and tools, Franciscan stones and early Spanish tools, telescopes, and random items from various periods.

ENTERTAINMENT AND EVENTS
★ Carnival in La Vega

Dating back to the 1500s, **El Carnaval de La Vega or Carnaval Vegano** (www.carnavalvegano.do) is the biggest, oldest, most vibrant and culturally authentic Carnival celebration in the Dominican Republic. Every Sunday in February, no detail is spared in this festival in the third city of the DR. Any other time of year it is a noisy, dusty place with not much happening other than day-to-day commerce. But for those six weekends of the year, culminating with independence weekend at the end of February, the heart of the city along

the view from the Holy Hill of Santo Cerro

Parque Duarte and the main avenues surrounding it transforms into the most exuberant scene you've ever witnessed in the Caribbean. La Vega's celebrations reflect the DR's mixed African, Taíno, and European heritage. Expect music and drumming, parades of colorful costumes with signature devilish masks with horns—the making of which is true art and begins months prior—pageant contests to crown a king and queen of Carnival, and large concerts. This is also one of the most commercially sponsored Carnivals in the country.

Arrive by noon in front of Parque Duarte along a block of Calle Juan Bosch to catch La Vega's smaller, lesser-known **Carnaval de La Boa**—a traditional version celebrating how Carnival used to be feted 50 years ago—with plenty of families and kids and costumed devils. This smaller carnival lasts until about 2pm. The bigger La Vega carnival celebrations with tents stretching down Calle General Juan Rodriguez and parallel streets kick off around 3pm, but the crowds are already streaming through from 1pm. You'll see the various *cuevas* or headquarters of each devil group, as well as bars where you can purchase drinks and dance. If you mingle on the sidewalks with the crowd, look out for those devil whips or *vejigazos*! Carnaval de La Vega is one massive street party worth seeing at least once.

FOOD AND ACCOMMODATIONS

El Zaguán (Av. Pedro Rivera, tel. 809/573-5508, 9am-10pm daily, US$2-3) is a favorite for its *mofongo*, and generous portions of Dominican and Creole dishes. On **El Naranjo's** (Calle Padre Adolfo, tel. 809/573-7751, elnaranjocafe@hotmail.com, 8am-11:30pm daily, US$3-10) outdoor patio, you can enjoy a small menu of tacos, burritos, and sandwiches, ideal if you're in a rush and on the go. Directly across the street is a **Pollo Licey** (tel. 809/242-3090, 11am-10pm daily, US$1.50-3) for a cheap box of rice and beans.

Hotels are scarce in La Vega. If you must stay here, which would be for Carnival, **Hotel El Rey** (Calle Don Antonio Guzman 3, tel. 809/573-9797, US$50) is the best option, a straight 10-minute walk to the city's parks and area restaurants. There is also one onsite (closed Sunday). Rooms include double beds or a queen-size, with flat-screen TV, fridge, decent working air-conditioning, and private baths with shower. The surrounding area is a bit run-down but go out walking in daylight hours and you'll be fine. A block south is the budget **Hotel Zitro** (Av. Antonio Guzman Fernandez, tel. 809/573-7731, US$15), offering spacious rooms but no air-conditioning or restaurant.

GETTING THERE AND AROUND

There are various transport options to La Vega. **Caribe Tours** (Av. Pedro Rivera 37, tel. 809/573-6806, www.caribetours.com.do) provides transport to or from Santo Domingo, as well as the northern cities of Puerto Plata and Santiago. There's also service—at 8:30am, 11:30am, 3:30pm, and 6pm—from La Vega to the more tourist-ready Jarabacoa (RD$70 or US$1.53). Check the website for current times and prices. From Santiago, **Expreso Quito Patio** minibus line departs throughout the day (5am-5pm) for La Vega across from Parque Los Chachases and offers service regularly between the two cities. The ride is just 20 minutes with light traffic. Purchase your RD$75 or US$1.65 ticket at the window before boarding.

The north-south running **Autopista Duarte** linking to Santo Domingo is always a good bet for catching a *guagua* off the main road, going in either direction. Stay in the center of the city and you'll be able to get around on foot; alternatively, you can hire a taxi to get you around La Vega and Jarabacoa. Call driver **Hancis Beato** (tel. 829/902-3244), or ask your hotel for referrals.

Jarabacoa

Easily one of my favorite parts of the DR, Jarabacoa (pronounced HA-ra-bah-ko-ah) takes your breath away with its mountainous landscape, rolling hills, fresh air, and friendly people who live in colorful villages along three rivers—the Río Yaque, the Baiguate, and the Jimenoa. After all, the city name is Taíno for "place of waters." You won't tire of the sweeping *campo* fields where goats, turkeys, and birds roam and chew, and where wooden shacks dangle on mountain edges, attached to the earth with wooden footbridges. Roads are lined with flowers and fields of fragrant cilantro, *tayota* (chayote), and other natural delights. Fresh water, fresh food, fresh and cool mountain air: it's hard to beat the center of the Cibao Valley, and Jarabacoa is a wonderful introduction to it.

There's no shortage of social activity either. *Parilladas* or steak houses are packed with folks enjoying the grilled meats the area is known for. Kids are always jumping off the handful of cascades that bless Jarabacoa. Weekends mean tubing down rivers in old tires while families barbecue riverside. When the sun goes down, bars blast merengue and bachata out under the starry, chilly skies.

On the flip side, Jarabacoa is also where you'll spot some of the most extravagant mountain vacation homes, perched so high you'll wonder how amazing the view is from the inside. This town is indeed the rich Santiaguero and Santo Domingo *capitaleño's* weekend escape. There are numerous privately owned cabins and villas, some with pools and infinite mountain vistas.

Downtown Jarabacoa is an intimate pedestrian-friendly town easy to explore in a day. Whatever you do, don't leave without getting a motorbike ride through some of the most scenic areas outside the center of town, including Pinar Quemado, Manabao-La Ciénaga, and the neighborhoods lining the Río Yaque del Norte. This City of Eternal Springs was made not just for freshwater bathing, but also exploring on motorbike or mountain bike, the wind blowing through your hair.

SIGHTS

One of the landmarks here, as in most Dominican towns, is the **Parque Central** or **Parque Duarte,** a small but clean space with a bust of the independence hero, plenty of benches, and lovely mountain views in the distance. Locals hang out here in the day as much as the nighttime. Traffic, especially motorbikes, is always whizzes around.

★ Saltos de Jimenoa

It is said that if you haven't been to the Jimenoa waterfalls, you haven't been to Jarabacoa. There are two **Saltos de Jimenoa:** Jimenoa Uno and Jimenoa Dos. Jimenoa Dos is easy to reach from town and doesn't require much of a hike thanks to a series of bridges. The entrance to the **Salto de Jimenoa Dos** (8am-5pm, RD$50 or US$1.09) is reached after a gorgeous ride through the Pinar Dorado community, past chayote fields, grazing cows, gorgeous green dotted with distant mountain cabins, just outside Jarabacoa. You'll need a car, taxi or bike ride.

Once at the entrance after paying the park fee, you'll proceed behind the booth and begin your hike along the river on footbridges and steps until the last portion where the waterfall is located. Along the way, you'll spot riverbanks where you can descend and sit if you choose (no benches) before you continue your hike. The views of the suspension and wooden footbridges against towering rocks make for great photo ops here. You can't swim in this 40-meter (131-foot) waterfall's pool, unfortunately. The currents below the falls are strong, and there have been incidents in the past that resulted in drowning. The lookout point is fenced off with wood and quite high, but allows admiring

Jarabacoa

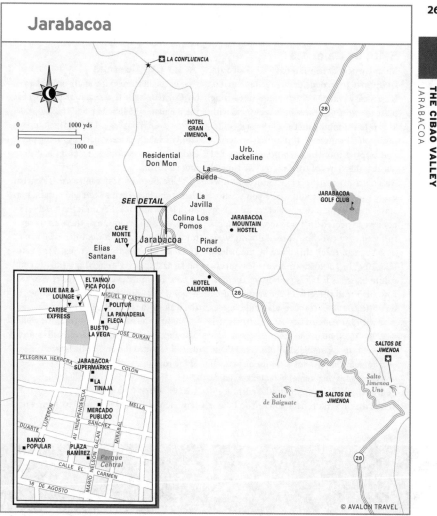

© AVALON TRAVEL

the waterfall from a close enough distance. Locals have been known to hop the fence for photo ops. The water levels are lower than in previous years, due to the general lack of rain that the country and island have suffered in the past two years. It used to be that you'd be sprayed all over if you stood by the railing area.

Salto de Jimenoa Uno is a lot steeper, tucked inside a ravine with water cascading down 75 meters (246 feet) on the way to

Constanza. You can't see the waterfall from the road, only the sign indicating where to begin your hike down. It reads *"El gran salto proyecto comunitario,"* on the left-hand side after about 4.5 miles along the Constanza Road. You'll hike a steep hill down to the bottom. Wear good shoes, and keep in mind that you'll have to come back up.

Which of the two is better? It's really hard to say—if you're intent on swimming, head to Jimenoa Uno. Jimenoa Dos is more of a scenic ride and hike, and you'll get to see one of the most beautiful neighborhoods of Jarabacoa.

Salto de Baiguate

My favorite place in Jarabacoa is **Salto de Baiguate,** tucked inside a gorgeous canyon. It's an easy place to reach and a refreshing place to swim, and the vibe is very local with kids often climbing up the dark rocky cliffs under the 25-meter-tall (82-foot) waterfall and leaping into the deep pool below. But it's also the views of this impressive flow of water against a lush, rocky landscape towering over you that will make you want to stay longer. The water is clean and crispy cool as expected in Jarabacoa, and it's a fun and easy two-hour break during your day. You can reach this place by motorbike (US$10). The 15- to 20-minute ride is an absolute blast, as it takes you down the narrow, lush trail directly to the steps leading down to the fall. You can also ride horses here with **Jarabacoa Eco Adventures** (tel. 849/917-7638, http://jarabacoamotoadventures.blogspot.com, US$15 pp). There's no entrance fee, as it's not a national park. If you drive your own rental here, take Avenida Pedregal, which leads you to the entrance if you're driving south from town. You'll have

to leave the car by the big Salto de Baiguate sign, then hike the trail for about 10-15 minutes to the steps.

★ La Confluencia

One of the most relaxing spots in Jarabacoa, **La Confluencia** is a spacious park where the Baiguate, the Jimenoa, and the Yaque del Norte rivers converge. Locals flock to this family-friendly place, especially on the weekends. On the weekdays it's quiet and even more blissful.

There are picnic tables and a small local bar shack, and locals bring their coolers and pots and plates, just like they do at the beach. It's a great place for swimming—there are various mini pools amid the rocks where you can sit and relax in refreshing water, just like a natural Jacuzzi spa, while enjoying a *trago* (drink) or two. There are even horses for rent (US$7/ hour) if you want to go on a ride along the river, along the back of La Confluencia.

Finding the park is easy—from the center of town, Avenida La Confluencia will lead you directly toward the park, which is at the end of the road.

Café Monte Alto

Jarabacoa's **Café Monte Alto** (Carretera

Salto de Jimenoa Dos

Belarminio Ramirez, Altos del Yaque, tel. 809/574-2618, www.ramirezcoffee.com, 8am-6pm Mon.-Fri., 8am-4pm Sat., US$3.31 or RD$150) is a hit in the Cibao region. And their coffee only sells in this particular part of the country. Founded in 1943 by the Ramirez Coffee Company, the factory oversees 350 hectares (865 acres) of coffee in the Cordillera Central. They produce two types of Arabica ground coffee: Monte Alto, a regular coffee brand, and Café Monte Alto Orgánico, which is harvested at the highest altitude on their farm (793-1,494 meters [2,600-4,900 feet]) and guaranteed to be chemical-free.

If you're a coffee lover, take a short ride from Jarabacoa to this family-owned coffee factory for a one-hour tour of the facility, where you'll see their cleaning, roasting, and grinding machinery. You'll learn about the coffee making process from bean to cup and even get to taste the final product at their onsite café. You can purchase the various coffee brands (including certified organic) there as well. The guided tour is in Spanish only, unfortunately, so you'll have to bring along a bilingual guide or friend if you're not fluent.

SPORTS AND RECREATION
Tours

Rancho Baiguate (tel. 809/574-4940, www.ranchobaiguate.com) and **Rancho Jarabacoa** (tel. 809/222-3202, www.ranchojarabacoa.com) are the most complete adventure tour operators in town. Both offer similar excursions such as river rafting, canyoning, and horseback riding to waterfalls. Rancho Baiguate has plenty of English-speaking guides. Other independent tour guides offer similar services and usually attract smaller crowds, or will customize trips for you. I highly recommend David Durán of **Jarabacoa Eco Adventures** (tel. 849/917-7638, http://jarabacoamotoadventures.blogspot.com), a young Dominican guide who knows the area well and offers reasonable prices. He can take you to all of the well-known places but also to off-the-beaten-track ones—including secret waterfalls (I've sworn not to tell about the one I experienced). Some activities only require that you have transportation, which could be a cheap motorbike taxi, a regular taxi, or your rental car.

La Confluencia

★ River Rafting on the Río Yaque del Norte

Besides being Jarabacoa's signature activity, river rafting is a fun way to enjoy the beautiful scenery along the DR's longest river, the Río Yaque del Norte. **Rancho Baiguate** (tel. 809/574-6890 or U.S. tel. 646/727-7783, www.ranchobaiguate.com, US$50) offers river rafting trips that will take you to the river entry point, about a 30-minute drive, and then give you basic rafting training and tips (you will also watch a safety video at the ranch before departure). From there, it's directly in the raft and onto the river. Toss and tumble and paddle your way down while your guide shouts out instructions as you go over rapids and small falls. The ride isn't too crazy, but it will get your adrenaline pumping.

The river is flanked by cliffs and lush vegetation. *Garzas* soar overhead, cows graze along the banks, and ramshackle huts sit dangerously perched high above the river. There are a couple of stops along the riverbank: one for snacks, and another for picking mangoes. Rancho Baiguate's tireless guides make it a lively trip. Bring a change of clothes and shoes and leave your things at the office, unless you're staying at the ranch itself. Wear what you wouldn't mind getting wet. Long pants are recommended in case you fall into the river (take it from me).

The gift shop at Rancho Baiguate sells water shoes, but you can wear your sneakers if you don't mind getting them wet. Just be sure to wear closed-toe shoes.

Hiking

The hiking opportunities are numerous in Jarabacoa. Getting close to nature comes as easily as walking along the roads or veering off into local villages. The only question is, how much vacation time do you have to spare? You can climb the mighty **El Mogote,** with the second highest peak in the DR after Pico Duarte. It is an extremely steep hike to the 1,163-meter (3,815-foot) peak and not for the faint of heart. The summit can be reached in about 2.5 hours; if you're not an experienced hiker, double that estimate. En route you will have breathtaking views of the mountain range covered in pine trees and Jarabacoa below. You'll pass lots of vegetation as you get higher, such as coffee trees and blackberry bushes (you can snack on the blackberries). The last 30 minutes are the toughest, but once at the top by the caretaker's cabin, you can climb yet another 9 meters (30 feet) up a steel lookout tower to take in 360-degree views of

local kids tubing down the Rio Yaque del Norte

the surrounding valleys and mountains, all the way to Constanza. Every ache or pain will disappear. An even better experience, if you have the time, is to camp there overnight so you can witness the most glorious sunrise before making your way back to town.

Contact David Durán of **Jarabacoa Eco Adventures** (tel. 849/917-7638, http://jarabacoamotoadventures.blogspot.com) to take you on this hike. Your guide will bring plenty of water, but make sure you have snacks as well, especially as you'll need more strength when you prepare to hike back down. Remember it's as tricky going down as it is going up. Wear long hiking pants, solid sneakers that fit well around the toes (or you'll end up bruising them), a hat, and sunscreen.

Mountain Biking

Ride a mountain bike to the area's falls with **Rancho Baiguate** (tel. 809/574-4940, www.ranchobaiguate.com, US$25-40 pp). You can bike to either Salto Baiguate or Salto Jimenoa, or a combination of both, depending on your fitness level.

Horseback Riding

You can ride to many of the town's main sights, including to Salto Baiguate or Salto Jimenoa with **Rancho Baiguate** (tel. 809/574-4940, www.ranchobaiguate.com, US$10-15 pp). There are also horses for rent at **La Confluencia** (about US$8/hour or RD$350), so you can ride around the park.

Paragliding

There are two paragliding operations in town. **Flying Tony** (tel. 809/848-3479, www.flyindr.com, US$60 pp, US$800/course) is the longest running, and takes you on a 25-minute drive up to the Paso Alto area on the scenic highway between Jarabacoa and Constanza to the take-off point, where you're outfitted with equipment and prepped to fly in tandem with your paragliding guide (ask ahead for guidelines on body positioning and overall paragliding, as I received little instruction beforehand). The feeling of floating and flying above Jarabacoa's

breathtaking scenery is unlike any other you'll have during your time here. If you've never done it, I highly recommend it. Liftoff is easy and returning to ground is gradual, requiring you to land on your butt, legs straight out, but there's nothing to worry about—the guides have over 30 years of experience all together.

The other recommended operation in town is **Hawk Paragliding** (tel. 849/867-3212, www.hawkparagliding.com, US$60).

Motorbike Tours

Negotiate with a motorbike taxi and go on a ride along some of the most gorgeous scenery in Jarabacoa. One of them is off the Carretera Jarabacoa-Manabao. From here, turn right onto the backcountry road, running along the back of the Río Yaque in Vera del Yaque. The wide pasturelands, the views of cows, sheep, piglets, and donkeys against a perfectly-green background and the Mogote Mountain in the distance: you won't want to leave. You'll get to pose next to footbridges leading to wooden shacks, contrasting against the green river beneath. Make sure you look for the mango trees. There are usually dozens of mangoes on the ground, waiting to be enjoyed. You might even spot kids floating down the river in their own homemade tubes. Other scenic motorbike rides are through El Pinar Dorado and along the road leading to Salto Jimenoa Dos.

MotoCaribe (Calle Las Palmas 3, Pinar Dorado, tel. 809/574-6507, US$1,795) organizes a six-day motorbike excursion around the North Coast and the Cibao, starting with exploring the central mountains in Jarabacoa for one day before continuing on to Samaná. Dates are set well in advance.

Golfing

If you're intent on golfing, head to **Jarabacoa Golf Club** (Piedra Blanca, tel. 809/782-9883, www.jarabacoagolf.com, 8am-7pm daily)—the only mountain golf club in the Caribbean! Surrounded with a pine tree landscape and boasting cool temperatures year-round, there are two par 3, five par 4, and two par 5 holes on 43 acres. It's a membership course but visitors

Extreme Adventures in Jarabacoa

If you're an adrenaline junkie, you've come to the right place. No other corner of the DR compares to what's offered in this natural landscape of rugged terrain, high peaks, and dense forests covered in pine hiding waterfalls and gushing rivers.

- **River raft** down the Yaque Norte with **Rancho Baiguate** (tel. 809/574-4940, www.ranchobaiguate.com). Prepare to get tossed around frequently as you maneuver the raft with your partners. You might even end up falling into the cold river when you tumble over gushing falls!

- **Go canyoning** down to the Baiguate Falls with **Rancho Baiguate** (tel. 809/574-4940, www.ranchobaiguate.com, US$50pp) on a four-hour thrilling adventure.

- **Hop on a mountain bike** with **Rancho Baiguate** (tel. 809/574-4940, www.ranchobaiguate.com, US$25-40pp) and head out to Baiguate or Jimenoa Falls. If you dare, combine both falls for up to 30 kilometers (18.3 miles) and 3.5 hours of riding.

- **Paraglide** (in tandem) over the incredible mountain vistas of Jarabacoa and peek at the Jimenoa Falls from above. Contact **Flying Tony** (tel. 809/848-3479, www.flyindr.com, US$60 pp) or **Hawk Paragliding** (tel. 849/867-3212, www.hawkparagliding.com, US$60).

- **Hike to the summit of Pico Duarte**, the highest peak in the Caribbean and the mother of all challenges. You can sign up for a group hike through **Rancho Baiguate** (more frequent hikes if you visit in the winter time), or with **independent tour guides** (tel. 849/917-7638, http://jarabacoamotoadventures.blogspot.com), with whom you'll save more if you're on a budget.

are able to sign up at special rates. After you play take a ride down to Salto Jimenoa Dos nearby, or just enjoy a drive around this gorgeous neighborhood.

ENTERTAINMENT AND EVENTS

Jarabacoa isn't exactly known as a party town. It does have its corners, of course, where locals hang out and booze, especially as Thursday rolls around and announces the weekend. But in comparison to Constanza, it's surprisingly quieter during the week. There are few spots where you can get your drinks and mingle with the mountain crowd.

Bars and Clubs

Parque Central is the liveliest part of town, and as in most Dominican towns, it's surrounded with casual sidewalk bars and *colmados*. **D'Chano,** across from the park, seems to attract beer lovers throughout the day.

Downtown Jarabacoa Lounge & Grill (Norberto Tiburcio or Av. La Confluencia,

tel. 809/365-8746) has a sidewalk terrace and quite possibly the iciest cold beers in town, including imported options. The vibe is trendy but laid-back. Latin hits play loudly all day and evening, with occasional DJs on the weekends. You can dance the night away on the weekends only at **Venue Bar & Lounge** (Av. La Confluencia, Fri.-Sun. 10pm-1am).

Festivals and Events

The annual **Rancho Baiguate Horse Rally** or **Rally a Caballo** takes place on Saturday during Easter weekend. It's a fun day of food, music, and watching hundreds of participants compete in horse races.

Every year in the last week of June, Jarabacoa hosts a **Festival de las Flores** (the Jarabacoa Flower Festival). Expect horseback parades, folkloric dances, food, art, merengue and bachata concerts, and of course a flamboyant flower-decorated truck parade! There are fun contests for best flower decorated hat, umbrella, and horse. The event lasts four days and is in its seventh year.

Bonao Carnival

East of Jarabacoa and Constanza in the Cibao Valley, the scenic city of **Bonao** (www.carnavalbonao.net) is known for hosting one of the most original, lively, and well-organized Carnivals in the Dominican Republic since the 1930s. The main character is the Macarao—the *diablo cojuelo* or limping devil—with a face resembling a monstrous animal. Its unique costume is made of satin, shining with lamé and sequins, and ringing with miniature bells and whistles.

You'll see various groups of Maracaos during the Carnival parades, which take place every Sunday starting the last weekend of January through the second weekend of March. Head to Parque Duarte and anywhere along the main drag of Calle Duarte. Although Bonao Carnival had humble beginnings, it's been the fastest growing of all Carnival celebrations in the country, bringing together individuals from all walks of society. It's a fun, intimate Carnival experience, much more so than the bigger, commercialized ones in La Vega or Santo Domingo.

SHOPPING

Plaza Ramirez (across from Parque Duarte) has several shops, including a coffee counter where locals quickly sip and go, an Internet center, a hair salon, and fashion clothing stores within the plaza.

Calle Duarte, the main drag in town, is lined with a variety of stores, from fashionable Chinese apparel to pharmacies and *colmados*. You'll also find Jarabacoa's **Mercado Público** is a small and friendly local market filled with all the vegetables and fruits, chicken and pork counters found in most Dominican outdoor markets. A block past the market, on the main drag, is **Jarabacoa Supermarket** (Av. Independencia or Duarte, tel. 809/574-2780, 8am-10pm Mon.-Sat., 9am-1pm Sun.).

FOOD

La Panadería Fleca (next to the police station and Esso gas, Calle Independencia, 7am-10pm daily, US$3-5), smack in the middle town, offers a nice range of pastries, cakes, croissants, and chocolates to nibble on. Wash it all down with a cup of gourmet coffee. It can get hot inside, with just two ceiling fans, but there's limited shaded outdoor seating if you don't mind traffic noise and bustle.

El Taíno (Av. la Confluencia, tel. 809/574-6620, noon-5pm, US$3-5) is an excellent and cheap Dominican cafeteria in town, serving homemade dishes for a mere 100 pesos a plate of rice and chosen meat for lunch or dinner. The later in the day you stop by, the fewer the options.

The longtimer **Super Cafeteria La Tinaja** (Av. Independencia, tel. 809/574-2311, 8am-11pm daily, US$4-10) is a popular option for a range of Dominican dishes, as well as over 20 flavorful sandwiches (including choice of pita or whole wheat bread) and burgers when you tire of rice and beans. They also offer Dominican breakfast of *mangú*, and local desserts, *batidas* or milky fruit shakes, and cold local or imported beers and wine.

El Burrito Mexicano (off Av. La Confluencia, turn right after Vivero Jarabacoa, tel. 809/307-8026, 5pm-11pm Sat., 1pm-11pm Sun., US$5-7) is set out in the owner's dining and living rooms (literally), with panoramic window views of the hills below. The food is phenomenal if you're lucky enough to find this hidden restaurant. The trick is to come here early, and certainly avoid the weekends unless you want to wait for an hour even without drinks. Service is slow and basic, but the delicious, flavorful food in generous portions makes it worth it. Order the steaming fajitas "Pancho Villa" or the enchiladas—the most popular dish here. There's also a vegetarian menu and a kids menu. The margaritas come in various fruit flavors.

Do *not* miss treating yourselves to a sunset dinner at ★ **Aroma de la Montaña** (Jamaca de Dios, between Palo Blanco and Pinar Quemado, tel. 829/452-6879, www.aromadelamontana, 11am-10pm

Sun.-Thurs., 11am-11pm Fri.-Sat., US$9-35). Whether you come here for a cocktail or stay on for a fantastic meal, this mountaintop restaurant is a gem in Jarabacoa and even the whole of the DR. You'll understand as you wind up the mountain roads and enter the property to get to view from the terrace after passing the gorgeous fountain-lobby. All of Jarabacoa sits below as you sip on and enjoy one of the most romantic dining spots and table views in the entire DR. The food is no less impressive, nor the service. Try the eggplant parmesan or goat or steak dishes, all of which are excellent. I can tell you, it's hard to come by a place such as this one. Only one warning: their credit card machine is known to be faulty due to the altitude and Internet connections, so bring sufficient cash to avoid any inconvenience. A taxi ride to the restaurant averages one-way US$7 for up to four persons.

On the main road to Jarabacoa just outside of town are a string of *paradas* or restaurant stops specializing in grilled meats. You can even smell the delicious aroma as you drive past. Stop at **Parada Corazon D'Jesus** (Carretera Jarabacoa-La Vega Km. 9, tel. 809/757-4811, US$5-10) for a T-bone steak or other grilled flesh of your choice.

ACCOMMODATIONS
Under US$50

If you have time to spare, spend a night or two at ★ **Sonido del Yaque** (Carretera Manabao Km. 10.5, tel. 829/727-7413, sonidodelyaque@gmail.com, US$22pp, includes 3 meals a day), run by a local women's cooperative and offering six charming wooden cabins tucked into lush gardens and the gorgeous hilly backdrop. The property is an inspiring green initiative–it runs off the grid, using renewable energy and water sources. They have a riverfront restaurant that provides organic, locally sourced meals and they also provide local excursions.

Hotel California (Carretera Jarabacoa-Constanza 99, tel. 809/574-6255, www.hotelcaliforniajarabacoa.com, US$26.50/fan only) will do just fine if you're on a budget and passing through town. Rooms include fan, cable TV, and dated bathrooms, but linens are clean. There's a swimming pool and a nice outdoor relaxation area. Service is friendly, and there's a convenient *colmado* down the road.

Don't be duped by the name or the incredible rates at Molly and Rudolfo's ★ **Jarabacoa Mountain Hostel** (Calle de los Pintores 2, close to Rancho Ruiseñor, tel. 809/574-6117, www.jarabacoahostel.com, US$32-36). Molly and Rudolfo's guesthouse is

Try the delicious food at Aroma de la Montaña.

a plush, gorgeous place to stay. Off the beaten track, yet a stone's throw from Jarabacoa's bustling center in a neighborhood known as La Joya, two olive-colored villas set in a gated compound offer self-catering units that share a living room, dining room, and fully equipped kitchen. It's by far the best value in Jarabacoa, with an interior of wood and leather furnishings, and perks so great you might not want to leave: Tempur-Pedic mattresses, flat-screen TVs with Netflix in each room, free local calls and wireless Internet, laundry facilities, and hot water. Because the kitchen and living areas are shared, you'll feel as if you are staying with friends, always meeting fellow travelers when not mingling with the owners and sharing in their longtime knowledge of the area. If you're able, ask for the room with the en suite bathroom, complete with a soaking spa tub as well as a large rain shower.

It's a five-minute motorbike taxi ride from the hostel to town, unless you're up for walking 20-30 minutes. It's well worth the comfort of returning here after a long day out exploring Jarabacoa's great outdoors. Molly also provides an extensive list of activities with plenty of details, including driver and guide info that allow you to plan your stay easily. Their onsite guide, **David Durán** of **Jarabacoa Eco Adventures,** knows the area inside out and is able to take you anywhere on his motorbike or in your car.

US$50-100

Rancho Baiguate (off Avenida Pedregal, tel. 809/574-4940, www.ranchobaiguate.com, US$80, includes all meals) is one of the most well-known resorts in town, particularly with foreign tourists, and offers a large number of trained guides and outdoor adventures. The most popular are the river rafting down the Río Yaque del Norte and the expedition to Pico Duarte. It's a well-run operation, and 27 rooms range from standard to bigger, newer suites at the back, with essential amenities, including glass showers, fans, screened windows, and either double or king-size beds. There are cheaper dormitory rooms; if you're a backpacker, inquire about those. The property's nicely landscaped acres allow for hiking or relaxing by a large pool area to the back (though unshaded). There's a macadamia farm, kids' playground, horses, pisciculture ponds, and shaded trails. The restaurant serves up meals buffet-style with open-air shared picnic tables.

★ **Jarabacoa River Club & Resort**

Jarabacoa River Club & Resort

(Carretera Jarabacoa-Manabao Km. 4, tel. 809/574-2456, www.riverclubjarabacoa.com, US$44-65, breakfast included) looks like big, bright amusement park as you approach and first see the children's park on the left, followed by the lodge's mini soaking pools and larger swimming pools, all perched over the river. The views are gorgeous! The restaurant also faces the river, and there's a bridge you can cross to find more relaxation areas. It's popular with locals, and the merengue blasts as couples randomly dance along the river or soak in one of the several bathing spots. You might even see the river rafting tour groups descend as they pass under the river club's bridge on the tail end of their adventure.

The brown-brick one-level **Hotel Brisas del Yaque** (Calle Independencia, corner of Calle del Carmen, US$45-53, includes breakfast), not to be confused with Brisas del Yaque II which shut down, has 19 guest rooms all on the ground floor with double beds and white and green bedding, air-conditioning, TV, mini fridges, and a small bathroom. There's not much to see or do here, so the price isn't justified; it's essentially a place to rest your head. The parking lot is disproportionately huge compared to the small hotel. There's a restaurant onsite serving meals throughout the day.

Hotel Gran Jimenoa (off Av. La Confluencia, tel. 809/574-6304, www.granjimenoahotel.com, US$62-100) is the fanciest of the lot, although it's also one of the older properties. Its setting impresses with the gushing streams of the Río Yaque del Norte crossing the heart of the hotel. Its dining room gets particularly exciting river views. Rooms range from deluxe to suites. The atmosphere is family-friendly, with breakfast buffets offered with the rate. There's a small swimming pool, open wireless Internet, and plenty of seating areas around the river.

INFORMATION AND SERVICES

In the center of town, **Ecofarma** (Av. Independencia, tel. 809/365-9595 or 809/365-9500) is available 24 hours for any medication needs you might have. Remember that you can call the pharmacy and order for delivery if you prefer (delivery hours are 6am-11pm).

Nynet Cafe (Plaza Ramírez, across from Parque Duarte, tel. 809/574-7972, www.nynetcafe.com, 8am-11pm daily, US$0.81 per hour) provides Internet on tightly spaced desktops in a nicely air-conditioned room.

The **Jarabacoa Tourist Information Center** (tel. 809/574-6810, 8am-noon, 2pm-6pm Mon.-Fri., 8am-1pm Sat.) has information on the town as well as hotels and excursions, but no handouts and maps of Jarabacoa cost 150 pesos or US$3.30. They sell a few random artisan gifts, including ceramics and fruit wines.

An office of the tourist police **CESTUR** is near Clínica Los Rios, and can be reached at tel. 809/574-2412. The **police station** (tel. 809/574-2540) is across from the Esso gas station smack in the center of town.

Plaza La Confluencia (Av. Norberto Tiburcio, tel. 809/365-9391) is a bit of an oddity with its modern concrete buildings dating from 2012. It is not much to write home about, but here you'll find a **Banco Popular,** as well as a couple of pizza and Italian eateries.

GETTING THERE AND AROUND

Across from Punto del Arte Bar and the Panadería, you'll spot numerous **motorbike taxis** waiting to whisk you away. As is the custom, they will call out to you as you walk to see if you want a ride. In that same area, a few steps from the bakery, is the **Expreso Jarabacoa** (tel. 809/574-6464) bus terminal for heading to nearby La Vega, as well as the **Jaraba Taxi** stand (tel. 809/574-6464).

Sindi-Taxi (Calle Jose Duran 2, tel. 809/574-4242 or cell tel. 829/285-4243) can get you from point A to B in town, with 24/7 service. Ask for the price before they pick you up; rates are set.

The **public guaguas** or **minibuses** for

Constanza leave across from the Shell station. If you want to head there for a day trip, be sure not to miss the last *guagua* back from Constanza at 3pm. Still, there are worse things than to get stuck in that gorgeous mountain town.

Caribe Tours (Calle Jose Duran, tel. 809/574-4796, www.caribetours.com.do, RD$270 or US$5.88) offers daily trips to and from Santo Domingo, leaving Jarabacoa at 7am, 10am, 1:30pm and 4:30pm. Check their website or call for the latest schedules.

Around Jarabacoa

★ MANABAO AND LA CIÉNAGA

Take a dreamy trip to the gateway villages to Pico Duarte, **Manabao and La Ciénaga.** Manabao—meaning "water springs" in Taíno—is approximately 17 miles south of Jarabacoa, or about an hour away, and La Ciénaga is another 4.3 miles or 15 minutes southwest from Manabao. Pack your lunch before you leave Jarabacoa, as there isn't much in the way of restaurants in these parts. If you've rented a car, head out of Jarabacoa via the Manabao Road as it crosses through town (Highway 28 going south) and take it all the way until you reach Manabao. Continue on that same winding road to La Ciénaga. Otherwise, contact local guide David Durán of **Jarabacoa Eco Adventures** (tel. 849/917-7638, http://jarabacoamotoadventures.blogspot.com, US$25 pp), who will take you on a splendid, slow motorbike ride along the Carretera Jarabacoa-Manabao. The ride will take you higher and higher up on the winding roads bordering the rolling hills and peaks of the Cordillera Central. Expect to stop multiple times.

Along the way you'll pass **Balneario La Cortina,** a vertical freshwater pool and cascade right off the road. A dip in the water is very refreshing. You will then pass a coffee farm—stop at Finca Altagracia if you'd like a closer look—and the landscape will turn to pine and majestic *grayumbo* trees. Soon you'll be riding alongside the Río Yaque del Norte next to cows and horses relaxing on riverbanks, by shacks lining colorful bridges,

The views from Manabao make it worth a day trip.

and through fields of trees growing guava, banana, avocado, and green *tayota*, or chayote—the main vegetable crop here. This is the real Dominican *campo*.

The ride alone could take up to two hours, stops included. Once you reach Manabao, feel free to pull over and hike your way down the side of the road (it isn't steep) for a swim in the river sourced from Pico Duarte. After you're done in Manabao, continue on to La Ciénaga, where you'll see a big entrance sign for the Parque Nacional Armando Bermúdez. Veer left, rather than enter the park, and spot at a bridge leading to another public river bathing spot known as **Balneario Boca de los Ríos**. There are benches where you can leave your belongings before walking a couple of steps below to the river. It's an ideal place to cool off one more time before heading back to Jarabacoa or on to Pico Duarte. All in all, this trip makes for a blissful day in the countryside.

PARQUES NACIONALES BERMÚDEZ Y RAMÍREZ

Established in the 1950s as the country's first national parks, Parque Nacional Armando Bermúdez and Parque Nacional José del Carmen Ramírez encompass 1,500 square kilometers (579 square miles) of the central, mountainous heart of the Dominican Republic. This area is often described as "the Dominican Alps" for being home to the tallest peaks in the country and the entire Antilles. More importantly, you'll find the highest point in all of the Caribbean here: the infamous **Pico Duarte**, which has outdoor adventure travelers flocking to the region in order to reach the summit of its 10,128-foot peak.

At 767 square kilometers (296 square miles), **Parque Nacional Armando Bermúdez** (tel. 809/974-6195, www.ambiente.gob.do/ambienterd/eco-parque/parque-nacional-armando-bermudez, 8am-5pm Mon.-Sat., US$2.18) is the larger of the two, extending from La Ciénaga de Manabao province to the bottom of Maco National Park and to the Artibonite River Basin in the north.

This protected park has several rivers and streams sourcing within its limits, including the Yaque del Norte and the Mao Bao and its tributaries. Aside from Pico Duarte, it's home to three more of the Caribbean's highest peaks: La Pelona (3,085 meters [10,120 feet]), La Rucilla (3,038 meters [9,967 feet]), and Pico Yaque (2,760 meters [9,055 feet]). Here you'll find a humid subtropical forest filled with endemic *criollo* pine trees. Spring-like temperatures range from 12°C (53°F) in the early morning to -8°C (17°F) at night with the occasional frost. Fauna include numerous species of birds, such as the Hispaniolan parrot, the palmchat or *cigua palmera* (the DR's national bird), and the Hispaniolan woodpecker.

Parque Nacional José del Carmen Ramírez (8am-5pm Mon.-Sat., US$2.18) is south of Parque Bermúdez and covers 764 square kilometers (295 square miles). It also harbors rivers such as the Yaque del Sur, Mijo, and San Juan in a similar humid subtropical forest. Most enter north from Jarabacoa into Parque Nacional Armando Bermúdez.

Spending time in these parks with a guide (guides are mandatory) will show you the Dominican Republic's mountainous side, lush flora and fauna, and mountain *campo* lifestyle, which not many visitors get to see. Hiking here requires that you save up at least 2-3 of your vacation days, but the adventure is well worth it.

★ Pico Duarte

The tallest peak in the Caribbean—once renamed Pico Trujillo by the eponymous dictator—is one for the bucket list traveler. Even if you don't keep tabs, accomplishing the hike to the highest summit of the Antilles earns you lifetime bragging rights. Should you do it? That will depend on your level of fitness, as well as how many days you have to spare on your trip. You'll need at the very least two full days for Pico Duarte (and possibly a full third to rest your bones from the hike). While there are several hiking routes to the peak, it's easier to take the one that departs from La Ciénaga or Mata Grande, through the entrance of Parque Bermúdez, simply because the climate is cooler on this side, with more rain and breezes likely, and there are several river sources that run through it. Day one of the hike usually goes from La Ciénaga to Compartición (18 kilometers [11 miles], up to 2,438 meters [8,000 feet] elevation), and day two, from Compartición to Pico Duarte and back.

The latest official rates for guides and mules per day are listed outside the **Bermudez park office in La Ciénaga.** The national park entrance fee is RD$100 (US$2.18), a guide costs RD$800 (US$17.44) per day, and mules RD$400 (US$8.82) per person and RD$450 (US$9.81) per carrier mule. Two mules per person are mandatory, as you might tire or need help, and provisions need to be carried separately. It's much simpler and safer to hop on an arranged expedition with one of the tour companies and individual guides listed below.

Last but not least: if you've never attempted such a hike, be prepared in terms of knowing what to pack. It's not a super-technical hike, but it does require endurance and good fitness. Do your research and ask your hotel or guide for advice. The two most important elements are proper hiking boots and proper clothing to accommodate for the cold nights, which sometimes reach below freezing. You should also remember to bring a waterproof bag and gear, swimwear, sunscreen, toilet paper, and bug repellent. Stay hydrated and keep your own pace—don't kill yourself trying to achieve the hike in a shorter time than allotted.

TOURS

If you're independent travelers looking to save a buck and not leave your vacation fortune on a single hike (it's incredibly pricey to hike Pico Duarte), contact the young **David Durán of Jarabacoa Eco Adventures** (tel. 849/917-7638, http://jarabacoamotoadventures.blogspot.com). He's one of the most reasonably priced tour guides. David grew up in Jarabacoa and knows the mountains and their hiking conditions like the back of his hand. Through his company, and working along with guests of Jarabacoa Mountain Hostel, he has guided numerous visitors to Pico Duarte and back, as well as to other peaks in the area. David takes care of all your arrangements, including transportation to the park entrance, mules, meals and water, and tents for the two-day expedition. The journey up to Pico Duarte takes two days and one night at a minimum. If you choose to space out the hike, it will cost more—just discuss your needs with the guide beforehand. It goes without saying that you should be in good health before embarking on this journey. It's no easy hike, and you'll be on your feet for at least eight hours in one stretch on the first day. But the evening spent next to the bonfire and under the stars is as unforgettable as reaching the summit itself.

Rancho Baiguate (tel. 809/574-6890 or U.S. tel. 646/727-7783, www.ranchobaiguate.com, US$255/3-day, 2 night pp) is the other major organizer of hikes to Pico Duarte, for hotel guests as well as anyone wishing to join their groups. They have a minimum of 2 nights, and an expedition stretching up to five days and four nights if you'd rather space it out that long.

From Cabarete, **Iguana Mama** (tel. 809/654-2325, www.iguanamama.com, 9am-5pm Mon.-Sun.) offers a three-day, two-night excursion to Pico Duarte (US$425, all-inclusive). Note you are on your own getting to Jarabacoa. You can easily reach town via public transport or a rental car.

GETTING THERE AND AROUND

Most who visit Pico Duarte come through or choose Jarabacoa as their base. The latter is probably the easiest due to the number of organized tour operators; you'll have more luck finding groups to join in high season. The drive to the visitor center at **La Ciénaga de Manabao** to reach Parque Bermúdez and the hiking entrance to Pico Duarte on this side is one of the most spectacular rides surrounding Jarabacoa. It's even more enjoyable by motorbike, if you've got time to spare and can spend a half day here—bathing in the Río Yaque del Norte along the way—before beginning your hike the next morning. There are overnight bunk beds at the park office, or you can inquire there for cabanas to rent (call park ranger Herman, tel. 809/271-8929, US$10 for four).

Constanza

If you thought Jarabacoa's hills were stunning, brace yourself for mountainous, lush Constanza, just 38 kilometers (23.5 miles) south of Jarabacoa and 90 kilometers (56 miles) from Santiago. Named after a 16th-century Taíno chief's daughter, Constanza is where you'll revel in the most breathtaking countryside views in the DR—blessed with mountain range-hugging farmlands everywhere your eyes look, made even prettier with fields of flowers.

A relatively young municipality founded in the 19th century, it saw its first inhabitants arrive in the 1750s. In the 1950s, former dictator Rafael Trujillo brought Japanese immigrants to the country to help build and design the farming community in Constanza, and the rest, as they say, is history. Agriculture is the primary industry here. In addition to Japanese immigrants, Spaniards and Hungarians also came here, and each culture brought international flair to the small town. You can see this reflected today in the fun bistros and restaurants. Aside from its farming, Constanza is the country's most vital nature conservation zone in the DR—the rivers Nizao, Constanza, Las Cuevas, Tireo, and Yuna have their sources here and provide more than 70 percent of the water needed for farmland irrigation in the country.

Cabins sit atop verdant hills and laborers work in fields of cabbage, strawberries, corn, carrots, and potatoes. It's an image you won't see anywhere else in the country, let alone the Caribbean. The same goes for the cool average temperature of 18°C (64°F) year-round and falls down to -5°C (23°F) in the mountains from December to April. Constanza, which locals call Valle Encantado, or the "enchanted valley," is also a nature lover's and adventurer's paradise, being home to four national parks, including two scientific reserves, which protect the untouched, biodiverse environment of this area. Parque Nacional Valle Nuevo alone boasts over 400 river sources, as well as cloud forests and pine trees where the hiking is unparalleled. Birders in particular can spot at least 80 bird species out here. Trujillo himself owned a cabin in Valle Nuevo and a hotel in Constanza (the old Hotel Suiza).

Navigating the interior roads of Constanza is no small undertaking: you'll need an all-terrain truck to explore these mountainous hills, particularly the parks. You will also require clothing suited for the cooler temperatures, as nights in the valley require chimney fires. The effort is worth it for Constanza's incredible charm. Its downtown is filled with buzzing bars, which get packed on the weekends with city dwellers. Its *colmados* offer fresh strawberry shakes. Its mist-filled skies arc above fragrant fields of cilantro and garlic, and the song of the *cigüita de Constanza* or rufous collared sparrow accompanies exploration of its pine forests. An effort is being made to expose more visitors to agro- and ecotourism activities around Constanza's gorgeous natural sights, so get here while it's still unknown to outsiders.

A trip to Constanza, also known as the ecological sanctuary of the Antilles, shows you a community that embraces visitors, even though little English is spoken here. This is a place where you'll be granted access to someone's home, despite being a stranger (a good thing to know if you're on the road and dying to find a bathroom—take it from me).

If you're planning on spending time in

Constanza

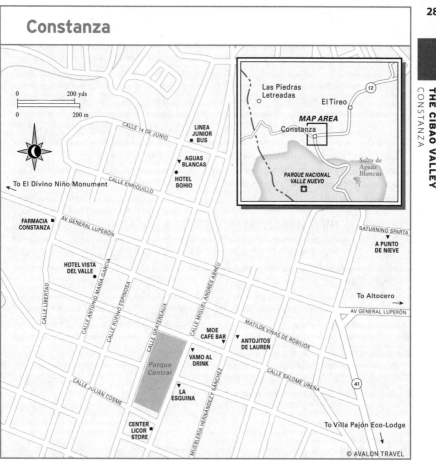

Jarabacoa, don't leave without at least spending a day in Constanza.

SIGHTS

Constanza's downtown sights are easily accessed and explored on foot. If you're heading out of the town for sightseeing or other adventures, however, you'll either need your own vehicle or to plan your trip with one of three extreme adventure companies. Sights are plentiful, but when it comes to tour activities, note that this area isn't as commercialized as the more popular tourist zones in the DR, so a little dose of patience goes a long way. Renting your own vehicle is by far the

best option at this time. Still, for those who'd rather not drive, try one of these two outfitters based in Santo Domingo during the week: **Constanza Extreme Adventures** (tel. 809/480-4837 or 809/480-4836, constanzaextremeadventure@gmail.com) specializes in four-wheel ATV rides through Valle Nuevo to Aguas Blancas and El Divino Niño Monument, and **Ecoturismo Constanza** (tel. 809/786-3681 or cell tel. 829/801-7199, www.ecoturismoconstanza.net) takes you to thermal pools, canyoning, paragliding, and horseback riding through parks and to other off-the-beaten-track locations. Be sure to contact the tour company in advance.

Parque Central

For a small town, Constanza's **Parque Central** is quite a sizable and lively square-shaped landscaped expanse. People and pigeons gather here daily, and young shoeshine boys roam looking for their next customer. As in most Dominican towns, the nights are more alive, when locals bring their own beverages and music and socialized on corners with their friends. Across from the town's most popular bar—La Esquina—as well as the church, this area is your best bet to hang out with the locals. Annual events are often staged here as well.

El Divino Niño Monument

El Divino Niño Monument (El Gajo de Maiz, tel. 809/585-3080 or cell tel. 809/910-0101, mdivinonino.blogspot.com, amcamilo-camilo@hotmail.com, 10am-5pm Sat.-Sun. and holidays, no fee) is worth the stop, not least for its spectacular view over the entire Constanza valley. The backstory of this monument which pays tribute to Jesus and the power of faith is as moving as it gets. Facing death from two bouts of advanced cancerous tumors, Antonio Manuel Camilo, a former vice minister of agriculture and longtime civil servant who traveled often to Constanza for work, had a dream that his deceased mother advised him of the following: "Son! Hold on to El Divino Niño, and he will cure you." He was an atheist, but after failed surgery attempts to remove the tumors and a determination to live, he decided to have faith and listen to his mother. He was miraculously healed, and lives today without a trace of cancer. In gratitude, he decided to build a monument paying tribute to Christ in a town he loves deeply, despite being originally from Salcedo.

The construction of the 15-meter-high (48-foot) and 12-ton El Divino Niño at the hands of Dominican sculptor Ramon Osorio began in January 2011 and ended in October 2011. At the foot of the monument is an offering chamber, where candles burn and photos of loved ones are left with a prayer or two. There are bathroom facilities, and a spacious gift shop where you can purchase souvenirs with El Divino printed on them, as well as books authored by Camilo himself on how the monument was built and how cancer brought him peace. Along the side wall of the gift shop is a pharmacy, La Botica Divina, where free medicine is handed out to those who need it in the community, courtesy of his cardiologist brother.

There's a mass at El Divino Niño the last

El Divino Niño Monument

Aguas Blancas Waterfall

along these bumpy dirt roads. You'll see the laborers at work, many of whom are Haitian immigrants, harvesting or cleaning weeds.

Aguas Blancas Waterfall

About 10 kilometers (6 miles) from Constanza, **Salto de Aguas Blancas** (or Agua Blancas Waterfall) is one of the town's principal sights and pride. You'll see various artistic renderings in restaurants and hotels around town of the 83-meter-tall (272-foot) waterfall. At 1,676 meters (5,500 feet) it's the highest-altitude waterfall in the Caribbean. The drive to the falls is one of the most picturesque, soaring above sweet corn and carrot fields and hills blanketed in pine, hugging local villages and farmers' shacks. Some of the pine appears to be dark maroon; that indicates a recent fire that devastated a portion of the plains. Once at the top, it's an easy walk over from the parking lot to a couple of foot bridges that will take you to a main platform where you can observe the gushing falls in all their glory. It is not advisable to swim here, due to the cold temperature of the water and the risk for hypothermia. It's enough to pose for photos and admire the scenery. There's no fee to enter, and there are a couple of bathroom facilities we hope will be improved soon.

The bad news is that the road leading to the falls, particularly the last 30 minutes, is incredibly rough and steep, a winding edge-of-the-cliff-type of ride with gaping holes and rocks that require a very sturdy, all-terrain truck (not even a 4x4 will do) and a good driver to get to the top. The better news is that there are imminent plans to begin improving this path, and you can get here by *motoconcho* (US$20 for two, round-trip).

If you're taking your own truck, you'll drive the main road going south from Constanza (Route 41) through Colonia Japonesa village. The road will split after about a half mile past the village, and you will take the left road towards Salto Aguas Blancas. Keep driving for about 30 minutes and you will see a big sign for the waterfall road on the left. This is a really tough road that will put your tires to the

Sunday of every month at 11am, and it often fills up fast. Soon there will be lodging offered below the monument, at a hotel called La Posada Divina. You can imagine what waking up to those views will be like!

Getting to the monument is quite simple but will require, again, a solid truck until the planned road paving takes place. Drive along Avenida Gregorio Luperón, the main road as you enter town, and continue straight up until you come across an open residential gate that says "Hacienda Ecológica." Pass through and head to the top of the hill, where you'll end up at El Divino Niño.

El Tireo

Constanza is a dream for scenic drives around the villages, agricultural and flower fields. Take a turn through **El Tireo,** one of the most breathtaking *pueblos,* and nicknamed the Switzerland of the Caribbean, to cruise by cabins and homes lining vast vegetable fields of potatoes to garlic and cabbage. Prepare to take plenty of photos of the spectacular views test. Go slow. And if you get lost along the way, don't hesitate to stop and ask locals.

Reserva Científica Ébano Verde

The **Reserva Científica Ébano Verde** (tel. 809/350-5372 or 809/567-4300, areas.protegidas@ambiente.gob.do, no fee, permission required) is about an hour's drive from Jarabacoa on the way to Constanza, sandwiched between two towns and tucked in the heart of the Cordillera Central. There are virtually no signs to this protected reserve established in 1989 and for good reason: it's not generally accessible to the public. You'll need to obtain a permit or announce your visit, at the very least, ahead of time from Santo Domingo. The majority of those who come here are scientists from around the country and the world, as the reserve is used for active study of the country's over 600 species of flora and fauna. If you do venture here, you'll be one of the lucky few to enjoy one of the greenest and most protected areas of the DR, even if all you get to do is drive to the entrance and its surrounding river. At an altitude of approximately 914 to 1,524 meters (3,000 to 5,000 feet) and covering 29 square kilometers (7,100 acres) in one of the most humid areas of the country, its habitat includes broadleaf cloud and riparian forests, home to the sources of the Camu, Jimenoa, and Jatubey Rivers.

The reserve is named after an endemic tree growing only in this northwestern central area of the Dominican Republic and subsequently endangered due to felling: the Ébano Verde or *Magnolia pallenscens* species found only in broadleaf cloud forest and producing valuable wood. There's a small but interesting museum onsite (all in Spanish, I'm afraid), displaying the reserve's rich life, including various plants and over 100 bird species, some endangered species. Other endangered species that have a home here are frogs such as the giant tree frog and lizards like the *Anolis insolitus*. Among the flora are 81 species of orchids.

Adjacent to the park office, within the gated grounds, is a well-kept garden where

The Ébano Verde tree species is endemic to the Cordillera Central.

various Ebano Verde species are on display and labeled. Ask the caretaker to show you the tree he planted 18 years ago when he started working here. After you've explored the museum and the garden, head out the gate and hike left toward the end of the path, where you'll find an entrance to the emerald green **El Arroyazo**, a gorgeous bathing spot where streams cascade down from the Río Camú (it's crispy cold!). The pool attracts locals who come swim here on weekends.

When you make your way to the reserve from Jarabacoa, you'll head down the Constanza Road, and about an hour later, turn left at a small sign that says El Arroyazo, just past a green building that says Panadería La Palma. Continue uphill through the Las Palmas community of fields of tomatoes and flower outlets followed by lush forests lining the dirt road. Continue all the way down until you end up on the entrance to the reserve's national park office. Note that hiking within the reserve requires permission from the main office in Santo Domingo, but if you ask nicely

Saving the Golden Swallow

These nesting boxes were created to help save the endangered *golondrina verde*.

Established in 2010, The **José Delio Guzmán Foundation** (tel. 809/334-6935, www.fundacionjdg.org) was launched by the owners of Villa Pajón Eco-Lodge, longtime landowners in part of what is now Valle Nuevo National Park, in 2010. The organization aims at raising conservation awareness in local communities. This includes preservation of forests, rivers, mountains, as well as contributing to the scientific research and education of rural zones when it comes to Dominican flora, fauna, and endangered species.

Enter the **Golden Swallow Project** (www.thegoldenswallow.org) to save the *golondrina verde* or green swallow (*Tachycineta euchrysea*), an endangered, endemic species. This bird has an iridescent crown and a metallic blue green back, its long wings allowing it to stay in the skies for extended periods of time, where it also feeds. But it is at risk from rats and limited nesting locations—this bird doesn't have the ability to build its own nest cavities. The foundation collaborated with Cornell University to build and place approximately 172 wooden nesting boxes at various locations along 31 kilometers (19 miles) of Valle Nuevo. You can spot these boxes as you explore the park. They are fixed to metal posts and stand at head level above the ground. Thanks to this project, each year the golden swallows have not only nested but also returned in greater numbers. Surrounding communities are now more educated on the importance of bird conservation, and interest in birding has increased as a tourism activity.

A female can lay from one to four eggs, and incubate them with her body heat within 18 days. If you do spot a nesting box that's occupied, remember to not try and disturb it under any circumstances. Do not touch, get too close, or tamper with the box or its contents.

The José Delio Guzmán Foundation has offices both in Santo Domingo and in Constanza. Contact them directly if you are interested in volunteering or bringing volunteer groups to Valle Nuevo.

enough, you can at least see the museum and the grounds by the park office, before proceeding to the river.

Las Piedras Letreadas

Northwest of Constanza, after the village of La Culata and a steep hike through forests, you'll find the largest Taíno carvings in the Caribbean—essentially gargantuan rocks with petroglyphs of Taíno faces (presumably gods) all over them. It's an impressive sight, if you have the time to spare. Contact

Constanza Extreme Adventures (tel. 809/480-4837 or 809/480-4836, constanzaextremeadventure@gmail.com), to arrange for an excursion; call them at least a week ahead as this tour doesn't take place as frequently as most tours.

★ Parque Nacional Valle Nuevo

If you only make it to one spot in Constanza, it should be the **Parque Nacional Valle Nuevo** (or Parque Juan B Perez Rancier, areas.protegidas@ambiente.gob.do, 100 pesos or US$2.18 pp), one of the most impressive national parks in the DR. Stretching across four provinces—La Vega primarily, Monseñor Nouel, Azua, and San José de Ocoa—the park is southwest of the Cordillera Central, and at 1,981 to 2,134 meters (6,500 to 7,000 feet), the highest plateau in the region. The park is known as Madre de las Aguas, "mother of the waters," for being home to over 500 sources of freshwater. Major rivers like Río Nizao and Río Constanza supplying the country with vital water have their sources here. Average temperatures during the year hover between 14°C (57°F) and 22°C (71°F) in the park, but in December you can expect temperatures below zero, as well as ice.

Outside of its importance as a watershed, the biodiversity of Valle Nuevo cannot be overstated. The park's 902 square kilometers (348 square miles) are in majority covered in *criollo pine*, king of this landscape but also include savannas, river forests, cloud forests and highland plains. Over 531 species of plants have been identified, of which 138 are endemic to Valle Nuevo. Of fauna, there are 17 amphibian species, 27 species of reptiles, over 70 species of butterfly, and between 66 and 72 species of birds. You'll hear the sharp alarm sounding whistle of the *jilguero* bird and possibly spot many colorful species like the Antillean siskin.

Hop on the **Sendero de los elechos** for a short but eye-opening walk through *criollo* pines and a humid cloud forest. Seeing the trees from the car and walking among them are two entirely different experiences. A second hike, **Sendero de la cañada,** continues on to the right as you exit the first trail, taking you deeper into the park.

Going farther you'll find a small tribute bust of Colonel Francisco Alberto Caamaño Deño, who hid in the mountains to fight President Joaquín Balaguer's regime. The statue marks the very spot he was shot dead. Camaaño was actually also buried there for

The Villa Pajón Eco-Lodge is tucked inside the Parque Nacional Valle Nuevo.

many years before anyone knew, and his body was only later moved to the National Pantheon in Santo Domingo. Just beyond this, you'll find the DR's very own pyramids. Well, sort of—local communities built the two stone, cone-shaped structures known as **Las Pirámides** in gratitude to Trujillo in 1957 when he built the Constanza-Ocoa Highway linking the two areas. Some say it's the geographical center of the country, and I'm not sure they are wrong—particularly if you look on the map of the Dominican Republic. The office behind the monument provides a small museum-style display with information on Valle Nuevo. Better yet, take a seat and watch an informative 10-minute video describing the park and its environment, in English or Spanish. A few more miles south of the pyramids, the scenery changes to fern trees—some call this area Jurassic Park—dotted with stunning, vibrant bromeliads.

There have been various devastating forest fires in Valle Nuevo recently: in 2014 and in April and May 2015. Fortunately, surrounding villages had received training on how to fight a major fire, but tens of thousands of acres of pine were burned—hence their current maroon hue.

The beautiful **Villa Pajón Eco-Lodge** is tucked inside the park—hikers, wildlife and nature enthusiasts, and anyone interested in ecotourism should consider spending a night here.

SPORTS AND RECREATION
Mountain Biking

Hop on a bike loaned or rented from your hotel and ride the **Ruta Bicicleta** along the El Valle community. It starts behind the airstrip and passes along all of the vegetable fields, from carrots, to potatoes, cabbage and onions, that wind along the road. The route will lead you to the entrance of La Sabina community, for more scenic views. The ride is fairly flat and of moderate difficulty. You'll end up taking a left at the Polytechnic School Deligne and ending up past Las Auyamas, all

the way to the Colonia Japonesa. Feel free to stop along the way to snap photos.

Paragliding

Ecoturismo Constanza (www.ecoturismo-constanza.net, US$55 pp) can take you flying over the Constanza Valley for more spectacular views of the villages and fields.

ENTERTAINMENT AND EVENTS
Nightlife

Constanza comes alive at night from Thursday straight through to Sunday. From the corner bars with karaoke and liquor stores with a sidewalk audience to disco lights, it's all here.

The **Parque Central** is a favorite meetup spot at night, and locals gather here with their speakers, rum bottles, and mixers. Some are happy just hanging out outdoors and enjoying the cool air with their friends. Across the park, **La Esquina** (Calle Miguel Abreu, corner of 27 de Febrero, tel. 809/539-1711, laesquinard@gmail.com, 4pm-12am Mon.-Thurs., 4pm-2am Fri., 11am-2am Sat., 11am-12am Sun.) is the busiest and funkiest bar. There's no dancing here, but plenty of eclectic Euro-Latin music. It's more of a mingling and people-watching spot—a great place to start the evening off. Over at the indoor **Moe Cafe Bar** (Mueblería Hernández y Sánchez, corner of Salomé Ureña, 8pm-2am Thurs.-Sun, no cover), you can twirl the night away, but some locals don't like its smoky atmosphere. Those who want to club the night away instead head to **Alcoholegio** (tel. 809/991-8036, 10pm-2am Thurs.-Sat., no cover) after midnight, for a mix from merengue to house, including hookahs for the trendy. Feel like laughing hard? Head to karaoke at the ultra-local **Mi Drink** (7pm-midnight Sun.-Thurs., 7pm-2am Fri.-Sat.). You can hear the off-tune singing a block away.

Festivals and Events

The annual town fair or *fiestas patronales* are held the third weekend of September, usually in the Parque Central facing the church. Events range from sports activities for kids as well as live merengue concerts and local food vendors. It's a lively time to be in Constanza.

SHOPPING

The good news about most of the purchases you'll make here is they will be mostly edible and sweet, since it's an agricultural town. Also what you invest directly supports the local communities who produce the goods.

If you're into coconut sweets, pass by **Dulces de Doña Benza** (Av. Jimenez Moya 13, tel. 809/924-8902, 10am-5pm daily) on the way out of town. Locals often stop here on their way back to their respective cities. She's been making *dulce con coco* for the past 75 years out of her small kitchen.

Pick up some strawberry or guava liqueur at **La Montaña de Chenco** (Av. Antonio Duverge, corner of Salomé Ureña, tel. 809/539-3538, 8am-noon and 2pm-6pm Mon.-Fri., 8am-5pm Sat., 9:30am-2pm Sun., from US$5) along with numerous other locally made products at this lovely all made-in-Constanza store, including strawberry vinegar, coffee, guava or pear puree, and macadamias. Contact **Villa Pajón** (Valle Nuevo,

tel. 809/334-6935, www.villapajon.do) to pick up some jars of locally made strawberry marmalade (US$5.50).

FOOD

Grab a cup of coffee or hot chocolate and dessert at **A Punto de Nieve** (on side street after Dilenia's, tel. 829/936-4763, 10am-5pm daily)—a darling, vintage-feel café tucked away from the town's noise yet a stone's throw from its center. It's inside a garden casita with a pink interior set in the owner's outdoor garden with distant mountain views—you can see her house set in the back. The shop serves up sweet Latin treats, from churros or *tres leches* among several desserts, fresh fruit juices and smoothies. Salsa music plays lightly in the background as you sip from porcelain cups and step back to the 1950s.

You will find flavorful home-cooked food at a super-affordable price at the immaculately clean **Pura Leña Comedor** (Calle Antonio Garcia, across from D'Ruth salon, 12pm-4pm, US$3.31). Try the meatballs with a choice of various rice options or grilled chicken among other daily specials displayed on a chalkboard. Dishes can be ordered to go or enjoyed at one of just five tables. It's a small joint but the best in town.

The food at Pura Leña Comedor is cheap and delicious.

★ **Aguas Blancas Restaurant** (Calle Rufino Espinosa 54, 809/539-1561, aguasblancasrestaurante@gmail.com, 9am-10pm daily, US$3.30-11) is easily the best pick in town or a nice fine dining experience. Set in a cozy all-wood interior with a mountain tavern feel right in the middle of town, the menu serves up various options from seafood to steaks (oh so tender) and pasta, including a tasty "criollo corner" with Dominican dishes like *sancocho* and *chivo picante*. The service is top-notch. You must not leave here without trying waiter Manuel's homemade hot sauce (a rare find in the DR and the best I've tasted here). Last but not least, the strawberry flan is a must for dessert, made fresh from Constanza's strawberries, including the coulée.

★ **Antojitos de Lauren** (Calle Duarte 15, tel. 809/539-2129, 11am-10pm daily, US$4-13) is virtually synonymous with Constanza. This locally owned restaurant is run by a well-known family whose parents emigrated from Lebanon to the mountain town many moons ago. Their specialty is pizza. You can watch it being made through the glass counter. Order the Pizza Constanza, the only all-vegetarian pizza in town, topped with all things green grown right here.

Owned by the Ferrer family, who are Spanish and Dominican, ★ **La Esquina** (Calle Miguel Abreu, corner of 27 de Febrero, tel. 809/539-1711, laesquinard@gmail.com, 4pm-12am Mon.-Thurs., 4pm-2am Fri., 11am-2am Sat., 11am-12am Sun., US$5-10) reflects a surprisingly Euro-cool vibe yet with Dominican spirit. This cozy, small "gastro bar" is the most popular hangout in town and attracts a laid-back, trendy crowd from Santo Domingo on the weekends as well as the area's locals who stop here after a long day of work for a cold beer or a burger. There are sidewalk benches for those who want to watch the buzz around the central park or interior seating hugged by walls with sketches of popular Dominican and Spanish singers. The music is diverse and not so loud you can't hear each other. Last but not least, they brew their own Constanza-made beer, *Ferringer*—ask for *una negra* like a local and indulge in the dark ale. On Sundays, everyone flocks here for the Spanish Dominican buffet, with paellas being the primary attraction.

The colorful **Miguelito Grill and Tapas** (tel. 809/539-2442, 8am-11pm Tues.-Sun., US$3.25-10) might be harder to find because there's no outdoor sign and it sits below a *ferreteria* or hardware store run by the same place. But this diner-style restaurant decorated in New York-Paris prints earns its popularity with a wide range of menu options, including excellent steaks and one of the best burgers in town. It's quite modern for a small town like Constanza—but again, this place is full of surprises.

ACCOMMODATIONS

Perhaps thanks to being a popular city dweller's getaway, Constanza offers some of the best accommodation value in the country. Options range from staying right in town with more noise but basic rooms all providing amenities such as TV, hot water guaranteed (rare in other parts of the DR outside of resorts), and wireless Internet to staying up in a mountain lodge and enjoying the remoteness, cool weather, and stunning landscape that the area offers. Rates listed are for double occupancy.

Under US$50

The pink-and-white ★ **Hotel Vista del Valle** (Calle Antonio Garcia 41, in front of Comedor Luisa, tel. 809/365-7273, hotelvistadelvalle@hotmail.com, US$19.90) is a budget hotel that offers the beast deal and value in town for its cleanliness, inviting narrow, leafy lobby entrance, and tastefully decorated rooms. There are 12 that are split across three floors, offering all the amenities you'd need from hot water to closets, TV, and cheerful linens. Rates go up to US$33 on the weekend (Fri.-Sun.), as with most hotels here.

Hotel Bohio (Calle Rufino Espinosa, tel. 809/539-2696, US$25-30) is another budget option if the Vista del Valle is booked. Its location across from the excellent Aguas Blancas Restaurant and around the corner from a bus line to Santiago is probably the only advantage here. Rooms are dated (you might even find the seat missing from your toilet), and service is average at best. If you're just looking for a place to crash for a night, this could work.

US$50-100

★ **Altocerro** (Colonia Kennedy, tel. 809/539-1553 or 809/530-6192, www.altocerro.com, US$54-120, breakfast included) offers self-catering villas sitting atop the hills of Constanza with gorgeous balcony views over the town. The buildings—including bathroom facilities—are a bit dated but under renovation. The service is warm, and the restaurant offers equally delightful views. You'll need a car or a bike to get into town, unless you're up for a long hike. Wireless Internet, hot water, and cable TV are offered, of course. Just pick a villa closer to the ground if you must use the Internet or if you'd rather not walk too far to and from the restaurant. Altocerro is a favorite of city dwellers, so be sure to book in advance if you're visiting on the weekend.

Hotel Constanza Villas & Club (Carretera Constanza-Valle Nuevo Km. 1, Las Auyamas, tel. 809/563-5048, http://hotelconstanza.net, US$90, breakfast included) is smaller than its name sounds, with 10 self-catering villas, which can be split as needed, and a total of 25 rooms. It's a cozy alternative close to town at a five-minute drive out. The rooms are comfortable and spacious with raised ceilings, wireless Internet, cable TV though spotty due to the mountains, mini fridges, and a separate sunroom with views onto the Constanza vegetable fields and mountain range in the distance. It can get a bit rowdy on the weekends when the locals fill the place up or when a wedding takes place, but noise usually dies down after midnight. It's pricey for what it is. Decide whether you'd rather be right in town or outside of it.

★ **Villa Pajón Eco-Lodge** (Valle Nuevo, tel. 809/334-6935, www.villapajon.do, US$66-77 for two; higher on weekends) has been recognized as a "Dominican Treasure." You'll understand why if you stay here. 20 kilometers (12.4 miles) from Constanza and 2,286 meters (7,500 feet) above sea level, this lodge feels like the remotest, lushest, and most untouched corner of the country. Tucked inside the lush and biodiverse Parque Nacional Valle Nuevo, amid its mix of cloud forest, pine forest, and vast savannas of alpine grass hugged by rocky mountains, this longtime family-owned land—the Guzmans have owned 40,000 acres of it since the 1955 era of Trujillo—used to be

the villas at Altocerro

Villa Pajón Eco-Lodge

the site of a sawmill and then a flower plantation before the area was deemed protected in 1994. The business eventually turned into ecotourism and cabin lodging on 28 hectares (70 acres).

The lodge is named after a type of spiky bush you'll spot all over the ground at the foot of pine trees. The fragrant grounds are perfectly landscaped with vibrant hortensias, agapanthus, and daisies, surrounding seven self-catering cabins named after the area's birds. The lodge is named after a type of spiky bush you'll spot all over the ground at the foot of pine trees. These range from one bedroom to three; all are equally enchanting. It's all brick and stone design, with chimneys and wood fires that are started for you in the evening. There are front porches with rocking chairs and outdoor grills. Warm home-cooked meals—often Dominican specials—can be served in your cabin if you order in advance, but you are also free to bring your own groceries and utilize your fully equipped kitchen. The lodge switched to solar power in March 2015—electricity is available from 7pm until about 10am.

Onsite, you'll find a central dining room with a porch for relaxation, an organic garden, with lettuce, cooking herbs, and tea. You'll also spot various farm animals roaming the grounds—usually a favorite for kids—and more than 70 bird species, including the year-round *ciguera de Constanza,* fluttering about in the flower and fruit bushes.

Two trails are currently offered which take you directly from outside the lodge into the park. You can also choose a horseback ride or a trip to local farms.

To get to the lodge, you'll have to first pass through the entry gate for the national park, where they will collect 100 pesos (US$2.18) per passenger in park fees (bring small change) before you proceed straight up the long, winding road to the lodge. The trip itself from Constanza town up to Valle Nuevo is one of the most scenic drives in the DR and one you won't forget.

INFORMATION AND SERVICES

Rent wheels right in Constanza from **Hidalgo Rent A Car** (Av. Antonio Abud Isaac 3, tel. 829/204-5290).

Within the local airport compound, the Tourist Information Center run by the **Cluster Ecoturístico Constanza** (Av. Comandante Jímenez Moya, Aerodromo Expedición 14 de Junio, tel. 809/539-1022 or 829/741-2535, clusterecoturisticoconstanza@gmail.com) has useful maps, flyers, and information, and the pulse of the latest and greatest things to do.

For a pharmacy, contact **Farmacia Constanza** (tel. 809/539-2880) or **Farmacia San Jose** (tel. 809/539-2516).

You'll find a **Banco Popular** (tel. 809/544-5000) right at the entrance of town. For emergencies, the **Politur** has presence here (tel. 809/539-2485), and the local **police** can be reached at tel. 809/539-1000.

GETTING THERE AND AROUND

From Jarabacoa, take the scenic mountain highway known as the Carretera Jarabacoa-Constanza, which will carry you along glorious vistas of the Cordillera Central and through the various villages. When you reach a fork in the road after a 1.25-hour drive, you can go left to head to Las Palmas village and eventually reach the Ébano Verde Scientific Reserve, or take a right and continue to the scenic El Tireo village, Constanza, and Valle Nuevo. If you're looking for a driver from Jarabacoa to Constanza, negotiate a rate with **César of Sindi-Taxi** (cell tel. 829/285-4243 or tel. 809/574-4242).

Public bus services abound to connect to various big cities. If you're coming from Santiago or La Vega, contact **Línea Junior** (Calle 14 de Junio, tel. 809/582-2134 in Santiago, tel. 809/539-2177 or 809/539-2777 in Constanza, 400 pesos or US$8.72), a private bus service that departs daily at 5am and 2pm from Santiago. They'll pick you up right from your front door. Just arrange the day prior by leaving your name, phone number, and location in person at the office or by phone in case you miraculously get an answer. For Constanza to Santiago, the bus also departs daily at 5am and 2pm. The journey each way is around 3.5 hours long, including all the individual pickups.

If you're heading to or from Santo Domingo, contact **Expreso Constanza** (tel. 809/539-2134) or **Caribe Tours** (Calle Duarte, next to Antojitos D'Lauren, tel. 809/539-2554 or 809/539-3180, www.caribetours.com.do) which has daily departures to the capital at 7am and 5:30pm, as of publication time, and the same departure times from Santo Domingo to Constanza.

Getting around downtown Constanza is easy on foot, but if you're heading out of the center of town and on excursions, you will definitely need your own all-terrain vehicle. There are no taxis here. Negotiate with a motorbike taxi (ask your hotel or locals), which you'll have to call because they don't generally congregate on corners as in other parts of the DR. Constanza is still developing tourism-wise so take a strong dose of patience with you; the experience will be worth it.

Barahona and the Southwest

Look for ★ to find recommended
sights, activities, dining, and lodging.

Highlights

© AVALON TRAVEL

★ **Las Calderas Sand Dunes:** Climb a series of tall sand dunes and take in views of the Caribbean Sea on one end and the Bay of Las Calderas on the other (page 300).

★ **Barahona-Enriquillo Coastal Highway:** Drive down Barahona's stunning shoreline and marvel at mountains, sea, and forests while passing through Dominican *pueblos* and fishing towns (page 305).

★ **Minas de Larimar:** Visit a mining area where over 200 men work daily to extract Larimar, a unique blue stone found only in this region of the country (page 307).

★ **Cueva de la Virgen:** Hike to a huge cave at the foot of the Bahoruco mountain range, swim in the cavernous chambers, and learn about the mysterious legends surrounding this mystical place (page 308).

★ **Social Impact Tourism in La Ciénaga:** A local cooperative arranges homestays in the beautiful coastal town of La Ciénaga, as well as unique excursions in South Barahona (page 311).

★ **Balneario de San Rafael:** Bathe in this river's multilevel emerald pools and cascades or grab a table for a cold beer and a plate of seafood and admire the scenery (page 312).

★ **Parque Nacional Sierra de Bahoruco:** Hike amid cloud forests and experience the best birding in the country at this untouched national park (page 317).

★ **Bahía de las Águilas:** This beach, frequently referred to as the best in the DR, lives up to all the superlatives with five miles of brilliant white sand and clear turquoise waters (page 321).

★ **Laguna Oviedo:** Get up close and personal with flamingos on a boat ride along the largest salt water body in the country (page 326).

Journeying to this isolated region just to visit Bahia de las Águilas is worth it—it's the number one rated beach in the Dominican Republic—but there's much more to explore in the southern pearl of the DR.

Rarely a first or even second timer's choice, this region actually offers the remotest, least developed, and most breathtaking landscape in the country. Over 70 percent of its land is protected by national parks: the *sur profundo,* or deep south as it's known, is the greenest, most biodiverse area of the country. It's home to the DR's first UNESCO Biosphere Reserve, stretching 5,770 square kilometers (2,228 square miles) across the Barahona and Pedernales provinces. A surprising panoply of ecosystems coexist within this one region, where temperatures can reach below zero in the Sierra de Bahoruco and rise to sweltering heat in the dunes of Baní or Jaragua Park. It's a world of abundant rivers, interior lagoons teeming with crocodiles, coral reefs, mangrove-lined shores, coastal lagoons, pebble beaches, pine trees in cool cloud forests, and dry, desertlike landscapes.

It's the wild, wild west: this peninsula is very far from the stereotypical image of the DR. One scenic fishing and agricultural municipality leads to the next on the Barahona highway, winding along the coastline dotted with cactus and views of the *balnearios,* or natural swimming holes, where rivers run to meet the sea. Barahona's pebblestone beaches are no less magnificent, and towering bluffs hug this spectacularly natural landscape so close they seem to almost collapse into the sea. Deeper in the countryside and up into the mountains, nature lovers are enthralled with the birds of the Bahoruco Sierra, the flamingos gliding on Laguna Oviedo, and the Lago Enriquillo, a giant saltwater lake where rhinoceros iguanas and alligators roam. Banana fields add to the verdant scenery—the *plátano barahonero* is known to be the best in the country. In Polo, coffee thrives at the cool temperatures over 610 meters (2,000 feet). Take a tour and hike through coffee trees into the cloud forests of Cachote.

Previous: the coastal town of La Ciénaga; Playa San Rafael. **Above:** rhinoceros iguanas at Parque Nacional Lago Enriquillo.

Barahona and the Southwest

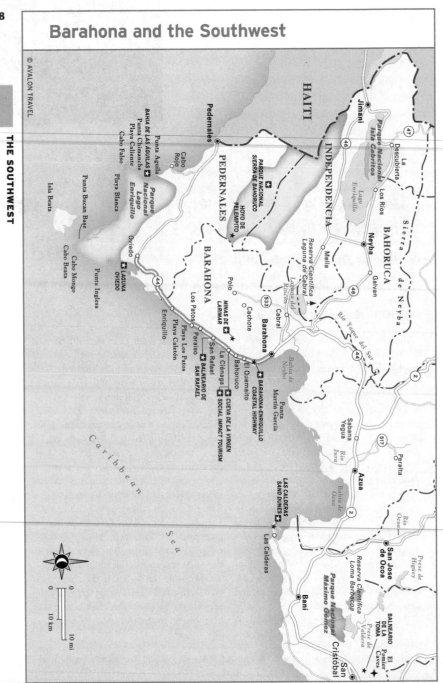

HAITI

Jimaní

La Descubierta

47

46

Parque Nacional Isla Cabritos

Los Ríos

Lago Enriquillo

Neyba

BAHORUCA

Galván

48

Sierra de Neyba

Río Yaque del Sur

INDEPENDENCIA

Pedernales

Cabo Rojo

PEDERNALES

PARQUE NACIONAL SIERRA DE BAHORUCO

HOYO DE PELEMPITO

Mella

Reserva Científica Laguna de Cabral

Laguna del Rincón

Cabral

44

2

BAHIA DE LAS ÁGUILAS
Punta Águila
Punta Chimanché
Playa Caliente
Cabo Falso

Playa Blanca

Parque Nacional Lago Enriquillo

Oviedo

LAGUNA OVIEDO

BARAHONA

Polo

533

Cachote

MINAS DE LARIMAR

Barahona

Punta Bucan Base

Punta Inglesa

Cabo Mongo
Cabo Beata

44

Los Patos
Paraíso
San Rafael
La Ciénaga
Bahoruco
El Quemaíto

Playa Los Patos
Playa Caletón
Enriquillo

BALNEARIO DE SAN RAFAEL

CUEVA DE LA VIRGEN

SOCIAL IMPACT TOURISM

BARAHONA-ENRIQUILLO COASTAL HIGHWAY

Bahía de Neyba

Punta Martín García

Sabana Yegua

Río Jura

Azua

517

2

Peralta

Isla Beata

Caribbean Sea

Bahía de Ocoa

LAS CALDERAS SAND DUNES

Las Calderas

Baní

Río Ocoa

San José de Ocoa

Presa de Higüey

Reserva Científica Loma Barbacoa

Parque Nacional Máximo Gómez

Presa de Valdesia

BALNEARIO DE LA TOMA

El Pomier Caves

San Cristóbal

N

0   10 mi
0   10 km

History isn't thin in these parts, either. It starts with the mystery of thousands of petroglyphs inside El Pomier's caves. This is also where Taíno cacique Enriquillo (Guarocuya) fought the Spanish for decades. It encompasses the Afro-Dominican heritage of music and dance through Casandra Damirón and, in San Cristóbal, the dismal memory of once dictator Rafael Leonidas Trujillo.

The pace is at its absolute slowest in arid Pedernales—you'll feel a million miles away from the rest of the country.

PLANNING YOUR TIME

Get a car (you'll need it) and begin your travels from Santo Domingo. If you're strapped for time, head straight to your guesthouse or hotel in Barahona—it's a three-hour drive to Barahona province. The highways are good on this side of the country. Travel should be relatively smooth, as long as you watch for cows and motorbikes. Aside from a couple of difficult to reach areas like the larimar mines, you'll be set with a solid truck.

Your drive down the Barahona province is along a scenic highway the passes various municipalities that hug the sea. You can see the southwest's main sights in a couple of days. Spend a few homestay nights with the local cooperative COOPDECI as a base. Visit the Larimar mines with the cooperative's guides. Quemaito and San Rafael are must-stops to enjoy the river and sea. You could spend all day surfing Playa San Rafael or hiking in the Sierra de Bahoruco. Cruise the bay of La Ciénaga and take a boat ride across the Lago Enriquillo.

Aside from Barahona's seaside municipalities, save at least half of a day for a trip up to Polo—not just to visit the coffee plantations, but also to see this scenic mountain town and enjoy its cool air and friendly people. Organize a hike with local tour guides and explore Polo's hills on foot. Plan an entire day for Bahía de las Águilas—it's a long trip that takes you all the way to edge of the southwest, past Cabo Rojo and onto La Cueva, where boats depart.

West of Santo Domingo

A few towns that you'll pass as you drive from Santo Domingo to Barahona are worth a pit stop.

SAN CRISTÓBAL

Approximately 17.3 miles west of Santo Domingo, San Cristóbal is the town whose primary claim to fame (or shame) is being the birthplace of Dominican dictator Rafael Leonidas Trujillo Molina, who terrorized the country for 31 years from 1930 to 1961. On a more positive historical note, the first Constitution of the DR was drafted here in 1844. Today, you can actually visit Trujillo's decaying old homes if you want: the three-story, seafront La Casa Caoba, which he used to meet his lovers and has since been vandalized, and the extravagant Castillo del Cerro, which he built but never moved into. San Cristóbal also offers beaches, Taíno caves, and swimming holes.

El Pomier Caves

A 1.5-hour drive from Santo Domingo, the anthropological reserve of **El Pomier** (9:30am-5pm daily, RD$100 or US$2.18 for entrance, additional RD$300 or US$6.54 for a guide) is said to contain the highest number of petroglyphs in the Dominican Republic—across 55 caves, though only a handful are accessible—and indeed the Caribbean region. Don't expect it to be overrun by tourists, however, because few venture to the southwest of the DR. A welcome center and a landscaped park are on the hike to the cave entrance. Petroglyphs of birds, animals, and other mysterious geological formations are what you'll observe in

Castillo del Cerro: Trujillo's Home

In the city of San Cristóbal, the Castillo del Cerro looks like a dull government building from the outside. But it is actually a five-story home built in 1949 for Rafael Leonidas Trujillo. The dictator didn't fall in love with it or use it, and today it serves as a training center for penitentiary guards. The rooms are a display of opulence in the Baroque style, including imported green and rose marble from Italy, granite staircases, and marble floors. There are also "salons" similar to those of the Palacio Nacional in Santo Domingo. On the last floor is a museum with displays on Dominican history, including replicas of some chilling items like the electric chair the dictator used to torture his opponents. Take Avenida Luperón going west from the central park, and turn south at Isla Gasolina.

the three linked caves, including lots of bats. The first cave has railings and is easier to explore. It is estimated there are more than 600 animals represented in this one. To get here solo, you could catch a motorbike taxi from the central park up to the cave entrance. If you're driving from Santo Domingo, take Autopista 6 to the *cruce de La Toma*, turn right at the crossroads, and continue until you reach a bridge, where you'll then turn left and continue straight until you hit the entrance. You can also sign up for an organized tour to the caves through **Viator Travel** (www.viator.com, US$159).

South of San Cristóbal are beaches, black or grayish in color—Palenque, Najayo, and farther south, Playa Cocolandia, which is safer and better for swimming. These beaches are popular with locals who day trip from the capital.

Balneario de la Toma

A favorite spot to cool off in the area is La Toma of San Cristóbal, a jade-colored, river-fed pool about 6 kilometers (4 miles) north of the city, sitting at the foot of a rocky hill. There are ladders, as well as toboggan slides for the kids that drop directly into the swimming hole. You'll find food and drinks for sale as well, and multilevel terraces with plenty of seating overlooking the pool. The entire scene looks like a giant water park on the weekends. It's a good spot to visit after your trek at the Pomier caves.

AZUA

The town of Azua is hot and dusty, and not much happens here to make you stay long—unless you head east of town to the gorgeous **Bahia de Ocoa** in **Palmar de Ocoa,** a bay area that is set to develop in the future with more hotels and real estate developments as folks start paying attention to the stunning landscape in these parts. Wine is being harvested here, for the first time in the DR (www.ocoabay.com.do), as part of an agritourism project. Stroll by the scenic docks for a quick photo op. And perhaps swim in Playa Chiquita before you hit the road again.

BANÍ

Birthplace of 19th-century Dominican hero Generalissimo Máximo Gomez, revered for his role in Cuban independence, the town of Baní—meaning "abundance of water"—is mostly known for its to salt mines, an important naval base in Las Calderas facing a gorgeous bay with adjacent sand dunes (generally known as Dunas de Baní), and the country's sweetest tasting mangoes (known as the *mango banilejo*), of which it produces hundreds of species, enjoyed during an annual mango festival in the summertime.

★ Las Calderas Sand Dunes

Have you ever seen a desert in the Caribbean, or a landscape of sand dunes overlooking the sea, towering over you while the intense heat wave envelops your body? You'll find just such a surprising landscape in Las Salinas, a half-hour outside of Baní. Head out of Baní going west to the naval base of Las Calderas. You'll actually go through the gates of the base—it's just fine, but no pictures—to get to the small village of Las Calderas with splendid views of the bay to your right. Keep an eye out for the main entrance to the sand dunes. You'll pay a small entrance fee (RD$100 or US$2.18) before proceeding to explore the dunes. Make sure you first head to the lookout point behind the main office to get a gorgeous porch view of Las Calderas Bay.

Once you're ready to brave the heat, head down and begin your hike to the sand dunes—walk to the left, past goats in the bush, and climb up the sandy hill. Just when you're almost out of breath, the sea reveals itself before you on the other side. It's a gorgeous scene, even if you can't swim in the strong currents at Las Salinas beach.

Getting there by public transportation is quite easy. Take the Expreso Baní minibus or *guagua* from Parque Enriquillo in Santo Domingo (US$2.86 or RD$130); it leaves pretty much every 15 minutes on the hour starting at 7am (ask the cab driver to drop you at the Baní stop). Note that you can also catch this same express bus right off Santo Domingo's Malecón as it runs down the boulevard—technically, you could flag it down from outside one of your hotels. Once you approach Baní, 1.5 hours away, ask the driver to drop you at the *guagua* stop for Las Salinas, which is on the way. This second bus ride to Las Salinas (US$1.21 or RD$55) is just about 20-25 minutes; be sure to remind the driver to drop you at the national park/the sand dunes so he doesn't forget. The minibuses are air-conditioned and comfortable. Bring plenty of small change for the buses and park entrance fee.

Las Calderas Sand Dunes

Barahona City

There's Barahona *province,* made up of various municipalities, and then there's Barahona city—a dusty, polluted, and chaotic urban hub. The municipalities, or small towns, on the other hand, are the chief attractions in this area:

SIGHTS

There are no major sights in the city of Barahona. For visitors, this is mostly an area to pass through on the way to the region's more blissful coastal and beach scenery, fishing villages, and national parks.

El Malecón

The city's waterfront is in a sad state—partially abandoned in the daytime, part polluted on the beach side. Still, locals hang out along its bars and on the small stretch of sand under the shade. If you happen to be stuck in town go to a cleaner and prettier beachfront at Hotel Costa Larimar to grab a cocktail or meal and enjoy the shore.

ENTERTAINMENT AND EVENTS
Nightlife

Most of the nightlife around Barahona and especially in its various towns and fishing villages consists of roadside bars and the typical thatch-covered *terrazzas* blasting merengue and bachata so loud you won't need directions to find them. In Barahona city, the bars and dance spots line the Malecón and filter back on its side streets. Popular picks are the **Big Tree Sports Bar** (Malecón, tel. 809/707-7228, 7pm-2am Thurs.-Sun.), which occasionally hosts live concerts, and a block up from its corner, **La Fábrica Liquor Store** (Av. Bahia, off Malecón, no phone, 9am-midnight daily, later close on weekends), which fills up with its outdoor veranda and flat-screens showing sports and other entertainment. Enjoy your drinks onsite or take them to go. Also on the waterfront, you'll find pool tables at **Club de Billar La Casita.**

Festivals and Cultural Events

Barahona's Carnaval (February) takes place every Sunday afternoon along the seafront boulevard. This is probably the liveliest you'll ever see this city. Expect plenty of colorful devil costumes, as well as the award-winning Pintaos de Barahona—a group easily recognized for their painted bodies, representing the maroons who fought against slavery and persecution. The parades begin around 4pm and last into the early evening.

The oldest carnival in the southwest is the **Cabral Carnival** (March), one of the most African-inspired in the DR and also known as Carnaval Cimarrón, spanning three days at the end of Holy Week. It's the last of all the carnivals to be celebrated in the country, as it's held during Easter. Expect to see the Cachuas of Cabral, the main characters wearing a mask made out of vibrant crepe paper and flapping bat-shaped wings, as they roam all weekend starting at midnight on Holy Saturday. They crack their whips—look out—and it all ends with a big, loud folkloric ceremony on Monday after Holy Week, when they burn Judas in effigy in the village cemetery.

The **Feria Nacional de la Uva** or **Neyba Grape Fair** (end August) takes place over a weekend in the town of Neyba, known for its delicious grapes. You can find them on sale in the town's central park, along with the wines and marmalades and juices made out of the fruit. Aside from all things grapes, the festival includes music, local food, and grape grower exhibits. If you're not in town in August, you can always buy some grapes from the central park on your way to or from an excursion to Lago Enriquillo.

Barahona City

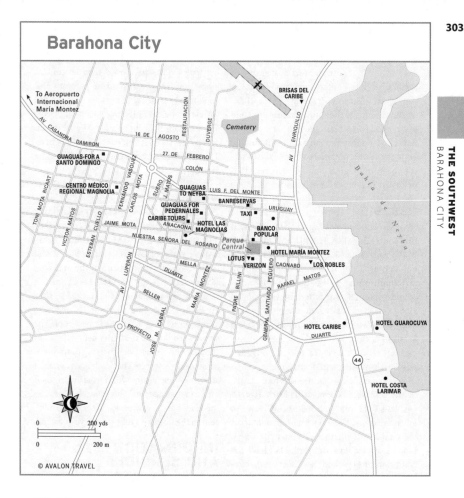

To Aeropuerto
Internacional
María Montez

AV. CASANDRA DAMIRON

16 DE AGOSTO

RESTAURACIÓN

DUVERGE

Cemetery

ENRIQUILLO

AV.

BRISAS DEL
CARIBE

Bahia de Neyba

27 DE FEBRERO

COLÓN

GUAGUAS-FOR A
SANTO DOMINGO

FERNANDO VASQUEZ

SUERO

J. MATOS

CARLOS MOTA

CENTRO MÉDICO
REGIONAL MAGNOLIA

GUAGUAS
TO NEYBA

LUIS F. DEL MONTE

BANRESERVAS

URUGUAY

TONI MOTA RICART

VICTOR MATOS

ESTEBAN CUELLO

JAIME MOTA

GUAGUAS FOR
PEDERNALES

CARIBE TOURS

ANACAONA

HOTEL LAS
MAGNOLIAS

TAXI

BANCO
POPULAR

NUESTRA SEÑORA DEL ROSARIO

Parque
Central

HOTEL MARÍA MONTEZ

AV. LUPERON

MELLA

DUARTE

LOTUS

VERIZON

CAONABO

LOS ROBLES

MARÍA MONTEZ

PADRE BILLINI

RAFAEL MATOS

BELLER

PROYECTO

JOSE M. CABRAL

DUARTE

GENERAL SANTIAGO PEGUERO

HOTEL CARIBE

HOTEL GUAROCUYA

44

HOTEL COSTA
LARIMAR

0   200 yds
0   200 m

© AVALON TRAVEL

FOOD

Unless you're eating at your hotel or resort where there might be restaurant, don't set your expectations high when it comes to dining out. Remember that tourism in the southwest is still very much a work in progress. Aside from the few decent selections in the city, you'll mostly find far and few in-between local restaurants along the highway after leaving town and plenty of fresh seafood shacks by the beaches and rivers outside the city.

For cheap eats, a block behind the central park find the diner-style **Cafetería La Esquina de Fidel** (US$1.74-5.45), which claims to be the best sandwich spot in the city. It dishes out various types of meat fillings in toasted baguettes. Come early if you don't want a long wait, as it's popular with locals. Also available are fresh juices and fruit milk shakes or *batidas*.

Melos Café (across from Hotel Las Magnolias, Calle Anacaona, 8am-2pm and 6pm-9pm Mon.-Wed., lunch only Thurs.-Sat., US$5) is the closest you'll find to a Dominican-style local *comedor* or small restaurant, serving a rice n' beans plate of the day. You'll have to buzz the front door to be allowed in; there's seating and it's a clean, friendly spot.

ACCOMMODATIONS

You have two general options when considering an overnight in the Barahona region: spend the night in Barahona city at one of the budget hotels and drive to and from the sights you want to visit along the coastline, or stay in one of the municipalities outside of Barahona—such as Quemaito, Paraíso, or Bahoruco. I'd recommend avoiding Barahona city—it's a noisy, polluted gateway to an otherwise beautiful region. But if you do, note that prices are higher on the weekends.

US$25-50

If you're bent on staying in the city, you'll find solid value at ★ **Hotel Las Magnolias** (Calle Anacaona 13, tel. 809/524-2244, magnolia.cdm@hotmail.com, US$26), offering air-conditioning, full bath with hot water, wireless Internet, free coffee and water in the lobby areas, and daily housekeeping service. The owner is a friendly Dominican lady. The location is close to a local cafeteria and supermarkets and the central park. If you're just passing through, it will do just fine.

A popular pick for location despite the unjustified price, is the no frills **Loro Tuerto** (Av. Luis Del Monte, tel. 809/524-6600, www.lorotuerto.com, US$42) with nine rooms that are set back off an otherwise busy city street, motel-style, facing a backyard. They have air-conditioning (a perk in these hot parts), wireless Internet, an old TV, and a bath. There's a bar and plenty of tables in a former restaurant space where guests can relax.

Across from Barahona city's Malecón, the four-story **Hotel Caribe** (Av. Enriquillo, tel. 809/524-4111, www.hotelcaribe.do, US$40) and its blue and white exterior covered in bougainvillea offers simple and clean rooms that come at a price that includes both breakfast and dinner from the adjacent, average restaurant. Wicker furniture, blue walls, and dated bathrooms are what you'll get for the rather expensive price—but you'll also get a view of the boulevard.

Directly across the street is the larger, recently renovated **Hotel Guarocuya** (Av.

Enriquillo, tel. 809/524-4121, guarocuyahotel@gmail.com, US$29-44), set in from the road. It still keeps its feel of old days gone by, but with a new, spacious, and pastel-colored lobby that leads to ground-floor rooms and an outdoor terrace with sea views. Rooms are simple and clean, offering queen-size beds, TV, air-conditioning, and shower. Pick an oceanview room if you're going to stay here. The onsite restaurant was not up and running at print time.

US$50-100

The blue and white **Hotel Costa Larimar** (Av. Enriquillo, tel. 809/524-1111, www.hotelcostalarimar.com, US$90, includes breakfast) resembles a condo tower in Miami and is tucked at the farthest end of the Malecón. Rooms here are not necessarily any fancier than the rest of the hotels in the zone—they are slightly dated—but the resort is directly on a clean beach and offers the largest pool. The sea view rooms are the better bet, with newer showers and connections to living room suites if you need the space. The beach is a nice, small stretch a stone's throw from fishering canoes, but don't wander off the grounds alone, as there are bushes at the back of the beach adjacent to the hotel and robberies have occurred.

INFORMATION AND SERVICES

Stock up at the **Jacobo Supermarket** (Calle Padre Billini, corner of Calle Anacaona, tel. 809/524-2645, supermercadojacobo@hotmail.com) in Barahona city before you head out of town, especially if you're a picky eater. It can be a big noisy outside the supermarket with rows of motorbike taxis hollering at passersby, but just ignore it all and shop away. There's an ATM inside the supermarket, though it's been known to be out of service.

Across the city's central park, you'll find a 24-hour ATM at **Banco Popular** (tel. 809/544-5555, www.popularenlinea.com). There are two machines and on Friday it can be supercrowded; try to go at off hours or during the weekdays.

For medical care, head to **Clínica Magnolia**, also known as **Centro Médico Regional** (Calle José Francisco Peña Gómez, tel. 809/524-2470). You'll find medicine at **Farmacía Méndez** (Calle Jaime Mota, tel. 809/524-2318). The tourist police branch **CESTUR** can be reached at tel. 809/754-3003.

GETTING THERE AND AROUND

Caribe Tours (tel. 809/524-4952, www.caribetours.com.do, US$6.85 one-way) offers daily departures from Santo Domingo to Barahona and back, at 6:15am, 9:45am, 1:45pm and 5:15pm. It's a three-hour trip, with enough time for a coffee stop when the bus unloads at Azua. Bring a cardigan or scarf as the air-conditioning can get super-cold on the bus. You'll get dropped off at the Caribe Tours office in the heart of Barahona city, close to many of the smaller guesthouses. Check the website for the latest schedule in case of changes.

You'll need to rent a car to get around at your leisure in the southwest, especially as the chief activity in these parts is exploring up and down the coast and taxis are stupidly expensive as in the rest of the country. There are local buses or *guaguas* running up and down the highway, but they don't always run frequently and you'd be losing a lot of travel time waiting around. It all depends on your schedule and patience level. Getting around Barahona city itself, if you must stay there, is easily done on foot.

Barahona Province

The beauty of Barahona province is in the various scenic fishing towns dotting the highway you'll get to drive through. Stop along the way, as these spots are sights in and of themselves, in addition to natural attractions you'll find across the area. Your ride will take you to the following in this order: Quemaito, Bahoruco, La Ciénaga, Paraíso, San Rafael, Los Patos. How often you pause and take in the views is entirely up to your schedule, but you won't want to miss the sights that make the southwest stand out from the rest of the country.

There are only two main bodies offering organized excursions in this region. One is **Guanaventuras** (La Ciénaga, tel. 829/560-3560, www.guanaventuras.com), part of a local cooperative in La Ciénaga and made up of two Dominican tourism-licensed guides. They offer an exciting and affordably priced catalog of their own off-the-beaten-track tours, as well as jaunts to the more well-known sights. The second is **Ecotour Barahona** (tel. 809/243-1190, www.ecotourbarahona.com), a private French-owned tour operator with slightly higher prices and the advantage of having one fluent English-speaking guide. You will have just as great a time with either, but the cooperative's guide can take you to some lesser-known sites and your dollars would go directly to supporting the local community of La Ciénaga.

★ BARAHONA-ENRIQUILLO COASTAL HIGHWAY

If ever there was ever a highway that constituted as a sight in and of itself, it would be the Barahona-Paraíso, or **Barahona-Enriquillo Coastal Highway 44,** which offers breathtaking views of mountains, sea, and green forests while passing through Dominican *pueblos* and fishing towns. As soon as you depart from the chaos that is Barahona city, you'll find yourself immersed in a landscape unlike any other in the DR. The sea and dramatic cliffs fill your eyes all the way down the coastline. It gives a whole new meaning to a scenic drive, and it's best enjoyed if you rent a car and drive at your own pace. Just watch out for motorbikes, which are easy to miss, and cows; they occasionally like to sit in the road as if they are themselves admiring the scenery.

EL QUEMAITO
Playa El Quemaito

About six miles from Barahona, Playa El Quemaito, stretching 1.2 miles, is the safest beach for swimming and not just wading. It has lovely Caribbean Sea views as you descend into the parking lot from the main highway—you'll see a big turquoise sign for Playa El Quemaito—and immediately spot the great expanse of white rocks against turquoise seas. A walking wooden walkway leads to the beach and various thatch-covered seating areas.

For food, the kiosks at Playa El Quemaito dish out fresh catch, rice and beans, and other Dominican options, including alcoholic beverages. Grab a shaded palapa on the beach after ordering and enjoy—without even swimming.

Accommodations

Six miles outside of the city, Hotel Casablanca (El Quemaito, tel. 829/740-1230, www.hotelcasablanca.com.do, US$70, includes breakfast) is a funky, cozy hotel run by a Swiss lady, tucked at the end of a stony path off the main highway and perched over the Atlantic with stunning views of the cliffs and crashing waves below. Rooms offer queen beds, white linens, and tasteful pastel furniture. There's a lounge to relax in and wireless Internet. It's a half mile to the nearest swimmable (pebble stone) beach, Playa El Quemaito. Note that there are no stores around, so be sure to shop in town before heading here. If you're looking for a simple oasis in the southwest, this is fine, but rent your own car to get around easily. Dinners are an addition US$30, but most rave about them.

Unpretentious Hotel Panorámica Barahona (Carretera Barahona Paraíso, US$70-210, includes breakfast) has a lovely cliff-top setting, with a large swimming pool facing the sea and immaculate, spacious grounds. It's adjacent to Playa La Meseta tucked away from the highway for the ultimate vacation respite. Rooms range from deluxe to presidential suites and include all the amenities from wireless Internet to air-conditioning and mountain or sea views. The suites have balconies.

BAHORUCO

Aside from being known for its pro surfer waves, Bahoruco is the site of the only larimar mines in the world, a precious stone found

the Barahona-Enriquillo Coastal Highway

only in the DR. It's also home to Casa Bonita Tropical Lodge, the only luxury resort in these parts. Along with neighboring La Ciénaga, it's a good base for excursions around the region.

Sights

PLAYA DE BAHORUCO

Bahoruco's main beach is a surfer's haven and has hosted surf championships in the past. It's not a place for swimming and there aren't any facilities, but the views of palm trees and distant hills are gorgeous—great for a photo op. And it's a pretty stretch to come down and enjoy watching fishers at work or chill with locals hanging out along the pebblestone beach. Look out for an eastbound exit sign from the main highway leading you to the beach.

★ MINAS DE LARIMAR

The semiprecious blue stone known as *larimar* is unique to the Dominican Republic. It can *only* be found here, in the hills of Bahoruco—part of La Ciénaga municipality of Barahona, about 13 miles south of Barahona city. Larimar is believed to be a type of pectolite, a rock made up of acid calcium silicate hydrate and sodium. Its uniqueness comes from the fact that it's a blue not found in other pectolites around the world. Its benefits? Dominicans believe it's a feminine stone that brings healing, calmness, and equilibrium to one's environment, as well as love, serenity, and creativity.

Although larimar stones were spotted by locals as early as 1916, legend has it that around the mid-1970s a man known as El Ciego—some say his name was Miguel Mendez—from Bahoruco, alongside a Peace Corps volunteer, picked up blue stones along the beach and later in the river. It led him to follow the stream to the mountains, where he found the source. His daughter's name was Larissa, and he decided to call the stone *larimar,* with *mar* referencing its sea blue color.

Larimar remains Bahoruco's primary economic activity, alongside fishing. You'll spot various larimar workshops as you drive around Bahoruco—including a recently opened official **Escuela Taller Museo Larimar** on the main highway in Bahoruco. It is a President Danilo Medina initiative in sustainable income-producing activities where locals or students work the stone to your liking.

But the more interesting visit is to the actual larimar mines, where the stone is extracted from the Bahoruco hills. You'll need a guide as well as their excellent truck for the off-roading required to get there. **Guanaventuras** (La Ciénaga, tel. 829/560-3560, www.guanaventuras.com, US$110/1-5 persons) are the only ones with a truck sturdy enough for the adventure; it's even rented out to the other tour company, **Ecotour Barahona** (tel. 809/243-1190, www.ecotourbarahona.com, US$119, includes stop at Villa Miriam and larimar workshop). If you can understand Spanish and want to support the local cooperative, sign up with Guanaventuras.

A visit to the mines is fascinating. There are up to 200 miners working here daily, both Haitians and Dominicans (no minors allowed), starting around 8am until usually the end of the day, sometimes late into the night if the production is spectacular. There are up to 80 holes of to 46 meters (150 feet) deep, a portion is government-owned—you'll see the tunnel entrance as you reach the area—and the rest are privately owned holes. You can walk into some of the horizontal openings, and go deeper if you choose, to watch the men.

Beyond being able to hike alongside hard-working miners into this gritty, unpolished scene, you can also see how they live in their makeshift mining community. Many overnight onsite in shacks rather than commuting back to the village every day. You'll find everything here—*colmados,* hardware stores, *comedores,* men cooking outdoors and, out of plain sight, prostitutes.

You can buy the rock straight from the source (US$11/just under one pound)—but stick to the miner recommended by your tour company to ensure you get a high-quality piece. Word is that the amount of larimar available is getting lower and more expensive in the stores, and no one knows what will happen if it were to run out. You might as well get your stone while you can.

★ CUEVA DE LA VIRGEN

Immersed in the subtropical forests of Bahoruco, the hike to **Cueva de la Virgen** (Guanaventuras, local guide Aurelino, tel. 829/560-3560, info@guanaventuras.com, US$88 pp for 1-5 persons, including transport; or US$44 pp with own car)—or the Virgin's Cave—begins just beside the entrance to Casa Bonita Tropical Lodge. The lodge also offers this tour, but be sure to contact the Guanaventuras cooperative instead to book—they are the first ones who knew of and opened up this trail for visitors and deserve the support. This stunning cave, originally called Hell's Gorge or Garganta del Diablo (they changed the name to make it more attractive), is blessed with small cascades and rivers from the Bahoruco range. It is a sight that was known to the members of the cooperative of La Ciénaga and local residents, and with much effort and collaboration with the local tourism body, they transformed into a tourist attraction and official trail in early 2015.

The adventure begins with a 30- to 35-minute ride down a woodsy, bumpy shaded path to the beginning of the hike, and this pre-hike journey is certainly part of the attraction. You'll enter a humid forest and pass milk farms, colorful foliage, and flowers with butterflies flutter about against the backdrop of the Bahoruco mountain range. The terrain is part flat, part rocky and a fun, bumpy course (especially on a motorbike). Guide Aurelino Feliz of Guanaventuras grew up visiting this area and will explain all of the flora (over seven species of ferns, avocado trees, yaorumbo tree, passion fruit, mango, and fig trees once considered a witch refuge) and fauna (grass snakes, centipedes, 49 species of birds such as the *cigua palmera*—the national bird of the DR—white crowned pigeons, white-winged ciguita, and hummingbirds) along the hike. It takes about

Cueva de la Virgen

four hours total or a half-day—and the hiking trail is well indicated in both English and Spanish.

The area surrounding the Cueva de la Virgen consists of a series of 33 falls as yet unexplored due to dangerous heights, but you can see the last three with make up the cave via two chambers connected by a ladder. The flow will also depend on the time of year and rainfall. The legends behind the Cueva de la Virgen are haunting, told to you while you stand at the mouth of the cave staring at its dark chambers and listening to the rush of the water.

There are two legends—though one is perhaps more real than the other. The cave was discovered years ago and according to the elders, it was during the time that dictator Rafael Trujillo ordered the mass murder of Haitians in 1937 to remove them from the country. Many Haitians refused to leave, having families and homes in the DR, and were afraid for their lives so they hid in this cave. They were the first to discover it.

Unfortunately, they were eventually found by Trujillo's guards who showed up with machetes—women were raped, men killed, and their bodies left in the open. Many locals believe their souls continue to roam in the cave. The more fictional legend tells of the appearance of a woman with long hair around the largest rock in the first chamber. She was feared because she could seduce you into approaching her, and if you fell into her spell and touched her, you'd turn to stone. When locals came to collect water, along a slippery and rough terrain, they were afraid of ending up stuck here.

The size of the cave is impressive. Sit in a corner and take it all in before or after you take a swim, and imagine what must have happened years ago.

Sports and Recreation
MOUNTAIN BIKING
You can hop on a bike and explore the southwest's great outdoors when staying at **Casa Bonita Tropical Lodge** (Km. 17 Carretera de la Costa, Bahoruco, U.S. tel. 800/961-5133 or tel. 809/540-5809, www.casabonitadr.com).

Food and Accommodations
★ **Casita Bonita Tropical Lodge** (Km. 17 Carretera de la Costa, before La Ciénaga U.S. tel. 800/961-5133 or tel. 809/540-5809, www.casabonitadr.com, US$176-280) is the only luxury resort in these parts and attracts a crowd who wants plush accommodations and facilities, like the infinity pool and lounge-like restaurant overlooking Bahoruco's Caribbean waterfront in the distance, when they're not venturing out during the day. Twenty-three years ago, the resort was the dream of a former Dominican government official from Santo Domingo who was in love with the southwest. There are 12 deluxe double or king rooms with private balconies and oceanview suites with kitchenettes and open-air showers. Sixteen new suites have been added, and there are currently plans to expand into luxury villas adjacent to the hotel. If you can afford it, it's worth splurging for a stay here.

There's an onsite, outdoor spa, **Tanama Eco Spa,** set in the woodsy grounds below the hotel under a thatch palapa, accessed by golf cart. Two steps away from the massage bed is a post-massage Jacuzzi filled with bubbles.

The **onsite restaurant** (US$9-18) is available to guests and the public. They use farm to table ingredients from their organic garden and offer a range of excellent dishes for all meals, from pastas to seafood and steaks and sandwiches. The open-air, all-white trendy setting with a wooden dining platform adds to the romance of the place.

LA CIÉNAGA
Not to be confused with La Ciénaga in Jarabacoa, this La Ciénaga is a small coastal and fishing town, which neighbors Bahoruco to the south and is tucked at the foot of the eastern slope of the Sierra de Bahoruco. It has splendid views and a tight-knit community known for its local cooperative COOPDECI (Cooperativa para el Desarrollo de La Ciénaga) with the tour operating arm Guanaventuras.

Sights
PLAYA LA CIÉNAGA
Fishering canoes, kids splashing along the shoreline while adults idle away in the shade, La Ciénaga's beach is a sight for sore eyes when you approach the hill and take in its view from the Malecón above. Walk down the steps and you'll notice litter on the beach, but the water is a clean, beautiful turquoise, especially nice for a morning swim. Grab a snorkel mask and explore the white sea urchins underwater.

EL MALECÓN
As small as La Ciénaga is, there's still a Malecón or waterfront boulevard, and the views going down the highway approaching this town are breathtaking. At sundown, locals descend on this area to take in the breeze, have drinks, or play games (including teens taking part in local boxing matches). It's a great place to get a feel of La Ciénaga's community.

Sports and Recreation

With **Guanaventuras** (tel. 829/560-3560 or 809/461-3424, www.guanaventuras.com, US$88/1-5 persons), you'll hop into a fishering canoe for a boat ride along La Ciénaga's gorgeous bay, and jump into the waters off the beach to explore corals as well as white sea urchins. Those who want to can fish the traditional Barahona way, with a string (yarn and hook). The views of the shore and village behind are as memorable as the feel of the Caribbean Sea.

Nightlife

La Ciénaga nights get lively starting on Thursdays along its small waterfront—as well as surrounding bars with many folks hanging out in the street. Head to **La Bodeguita de la Esquina,** a local bar and *colmado* right off the Malecón. Classic merengue and bachata blast through its open wooden doorways, attracting a hilarious cast of neighborhood characters. Locals tend to sit across from the bar on the street corner with their drinks. It's a fun atmosphere that feels like a street party on weekend nights.

Food and Accommodations

★ **Delicias De Mi Siembra** (tel. 829/560-3560, www.demisiembra.com, noon-3pm daily, US$3), run by the friendly ladies of La Ciénaga's local cooperative COOPDECI, serves daily Dominican breakfast and lunch for a great price. Anyone is welcome to come and dine at their open-air, casual eatery right off the highway. The location used to be ideally seafront on the town Malecón, but the building was eventually sold by the owner and they relocated to their current spot. They also have a fresh juice of the day, and while you're there, pick up a couple of bottles of the artisan marmalade—with flavors like soursop, passion fruit, and guava, among others.

A fantastic opportunity to not only save bucks but get a cultural experience is to sign up for a homestay or *hospedaje en casa de familia* in the fishing town of La Ciénaga with ★ **COOPDECI** (tel. 829/560-3560 or guide Aurelino Feliz at 809/461-3424, www.guanaventuras.com, US$14.30 pp, includes breakfast). You get a cozy, clean room to yourself, with full bath, at one of the cooperative member's homes, located ideally within a short walk to La Ciénaga beach and off the main highway in a wonderful and typical Dominican neighborhood. Breakfasts are served daily and you're welcome to mingle with your hosts or just relax on the porch

Delicias De Mi Siembra

★ Social Impact Tourism in La Ciénaga

Visiting the beautiful balnearios, beaches, cliff-front hotels, and national parks is awe-inspiring, but staying with a Dominican family and spending time with the women of La Ciénaga's local cooperative will be the most memorable part of your trip to the southwest.

The **COOPDECI** or **Cooperativa Para el Desarrollo de La Ciénaga** began as a mothers' club with 35 members from La Ciénaga. They had the idea of developing their club into a micro enterprise and community tourism initiative in order to help contribute to the development of their community and empower themselves economically. They decided to focus on sustainable agriculture, capacity building, and environmental protection. This grand idea turned into reality in 2008, with funding help, in part, from the Taigüey Foundation and the French Embassy.

Today, La Ciénaga's cooperative runs a local restaurant, where they also produce and sell artisan marmalade, arrange homestays, and offer unique tours through their excursion arm. This collection of offerings reflects the cooperative's idea of a better "all-inclusive"—and is a one-stop shop ideal for the visitor seeking immersion.

- **Eat at a local restaurant** that serves Dominican specialties. **Delicias De Mi Siembra** (www.demisiembra.com), adjacent to the cooperative's office, serves a daily lunch for just US$2.25 and attracts plenty of locals in an area otherwise lacking in *comedores* along the highway.

- **Buy artisan marmalade,** produced and sold at De Mi Siembra. The marmalades are made from fruits collected in the nearby Sierra de Bahoruco, and the members rotate days when they make mango, soursop, guava, or orange. The marmalades are their primary income producer; the cooperative signed a two-year contract to produce for a national supermarket chain in Santo Domingo, which was a huge success for them.

- **Arrange a homestay,** or *hospedaje en casa de familia.* You'll get your own room and bathroom at the house of a cooperative member, usually less than a 10-minute walk from the beach. A full breakfast is included in the modest fee (US$14.31 or RD$650 per night). To arrange a homestay, call the cooperative at tel. 829/560-3560 or 809/461-3424. They speak a little English—enough to get by and for you to arrange and enjoy your stay.

- **Take a tour** through their excursion arm, **Guanaventuras,** which offers unique and popular tours. You can go snorkeling at La Ciénaga's gorgeous bay, hike to the Cueva de la Virgen on a trail created by the cooperative, or visit the larimar mines. To contact Guanaventuras, the coop's tour excursion arm, call head guide Aurelino Feliz at tel. 809/461-3424 or visit www.guanaventuras.com.

Every dollar you spend goes directly into the cooperative and toward sustaining and empowering its members financially, and helping an entire community continue to thrive. It doesn't get any better than that. To reach La Ciénaga from Barahona on public transportation, hop on a *guagua* from Calle Colon and ask to get dropped off at *"donde la cooperativa de la Ciénaga,"* which is on the left-hand side along the highway. The cooperative's headquarters is right on the highway in La Ciénaga, a short drive south of Bahoruco (and south of Casa Bonita Lodge).

THE SOUTHWEST
BARAHONA PROVINCE

when you're not off on sightseeing tours with the coop.

SAN RAFAEL
Sights
PLAYA SAN RAFAEL

Make a leisurely stop at **Playa San Rafael,** just five minutes south from Paraíso. You'll hit its spectacular views as you take the curve on the Barahona-Paraíso highway and see its towering green bluffs contrasting against a stunning turquoise sea. There are various entry points for enjoying the San Rafael River. The most popular is the first where the river cascades down into the sea through a series of multileveled freshwater pools. You can choose to bathe in cold water or head over to the seaside where you'll find folks dipping in along the edges of the pebblestone Playa San Rafael.

Don't swim on the beach side if you're not a strong swimmer—it's deep and there are strong waves. The entire scene is one of the prettiest in this southwest region with natural infinity views. You'll find a convivial ambience with plenty of food vendors (US$7 a plate of fish and sides) and seating areas around the river and beach. Expect lots of crowds and music on the weekends when locals and out-of-town travelers head here to relax. To have it nearly to yourself, come early in the week. Expect to pay a small fee to the parking attendant if you're driving; otherwise there's no fee to enjoy this sight—but note that there are no changing facilities.

★ BALNEARIO DE SAN RAFAEL

One of the most popular sights in this region is the stunning emerald cascades and pools of the San Rafael River tumbling down to meet the Caribbean Sea. The **Balneario de San Rafael** is located in the eponymous town is set up like a giant outdoor natural spa escape, and you'll want to stay all day. Dip in one of the freshwater tiered pools, stand against

one of the mini falls for a back massage or cool off along the edges of the river where it meets with the pebblestone San Rafael Beach. There are numerous fish vendor shacks and bars dotting the river attraction and plenty of plastic chair and table seating spaced out enough that you don't feel crowded (but avoid Sundays).

There's a second smaller spot to enjoy San Rafael's river pools less than a half mile up from the first on the right-hand side of the road. Here you can bathe and relax with seating and a couple of food shacks. A third location is the private, gated **Villa Miriam** (tel. 809/524-4141 or 829/868-8828, US$2.20), another block up on the right, where the small entrance fee assures you more privacy and access to bathroom and changing facilities.

Sports and Recreation
SURFING

Hook up with **San Rafael Surf School y Eco Tours** (tel. 829/729-8239, raylinsurf@gmail.com. US$17.50/hour) run by an inspiring young Dominican, Raylin Romero, for a fun time in the waves whether you're a novice or experienced surfer. His modest but professional school operating out of a colorful

Balneario de San Rafael

Afro-Dominican Roots in the Southwest

The country's African heritage remains strong in Barahona, once home to brave maroons who successfully rebelled against slavery and neighbor to Afrocentric Haiti. At the various carnivals in the region, including during Holy Week, Afro-influenced dances and rituals prevail. In Cabral, the Cachúas appearing during **Semana Santa** are characters wearing colorful masks, armed with whips, and performing rituals and dances from midnight on Holy Friday all the way to Monday, when they reenact the burning of Judas in the cemetery.

Another significant event is the **Gagá**—both a ritual and a dance influenced by neighboring Haiti—celebrated in Polo, the western border province of Elias Piña, but mostly in the *bateyes* of the southwest because they were often linked to sugarcane production. It's a celebration of productivity and harvest coinciding with the start of spring. The celebrations begin at midnight on Holy Thursday and last through Resurrection Sunday. The dances are circular, and the chants are in Creole and Spanish to the beat of the *tambu* and *catalie*—different types of traditional Dominican drums—accompanied by a special-made four-foot-long (1.2 meter) bamboo trumpet for bass. The women wear white, and the elders don colorful garb. The Gagá represents sacrifice, protection, baptism, and blessing. The Máscaras del Diablo from Matayaya, in the province of San Juan, and in Elias Piña province perform a land fertility ritual by burning their masks and scattering the ashes on fields.

beach shack is open on the weekends or by reservation. You can rent a board and/or get some lessons with him. Ask Raylin about combining your surfing experience with one of his hiking tours in the mountains of San Rafael (US$17 pp). Bahoruco's beach has some of the best surf in the area. The village is just 10 miles south from Barahona, off the highway.

Accommodations

Feel like camping and taking in all of Barahona's natural splendor? Contact Raylin Romero of **San Rafael Surf School y Eco Tours** (tel. 829/729-8239, raylinsurf@gmail. com, US$8.75 pp). He can arrange for tents on the beach, along with fresh local meals, and you might just end up dancing merengue under the stars. It's a true local experience. Backpackers who insist on staying in the city can look up **Hotel Cacique** (Calle Jose Francisco Peña Gomez, Barahona city, tel. 809/524-4620, US$18), close to the city Malecón. It has worn rooms and bathrooms, air-conditioning, and is just a basic roof over your head. With the homestay in nearby La Ciénaga, it doesn't make much sense to stay in the gritty city.

PARAÍSO

Of all the stops along the southwest, Paraíso is among the most pedestrian-friendly areas and provides opportunity to meander down its seafront as well as through its neighborhood streets. There are fast-food vendors and *colmados* all around (which blast music on the weekend nights). Paraíso's **Fiestas Patronales** (mid-January) held for a week are for the hard-core partiers, with plenty of music, dancing, and boozing, of course.

Sights
PLAYA PARAÍSO

Like most beaches in this coastal area, this is where fishers take off at sunrise to hunt for their catch. It's a striking turquoise against white scene, good for a breezy stroll in the morning or at sunset.

EL MALECÓN

The waterfront is just a block facing a small central park and adjacent to Hotel Piratas del Caribe. Nonetheless it's the gathering spot for locals, particularly fishers who relax here between their runs and kids who dare to play close to shore (the currents are dangerous to swim in).

Food and Accommodations

★ **Hotel Piratas del Caribe** (Calle Arzobispo Nouel 1, tel. 809/243-1140, www. hotelpiratasdelcaribe.com, US$99-179) is a darling, five-room villa turned boutique guesthouse tucked beside the town's small Malecón and park facing the Atlantic and Paraíso's pebblestone beach (even if you can't swim there due to the currents). The intimate, luxurious waterfront suites behind a tall gate feature four-poster beds with mosquito nets, flat-screen cable TV, air-conditioning, spacious bathrooms with shower, and private balconies. Meals can be ordered ahead, and breakfasts are served on your terrace. Throw in a swimming pool in the verdant courtyard and it's hard to find a better pick in this area with few accommodation options. If you're a light sleeper, keep in mind that there's a local bar across the park that blasts music on the weekends.

In the mountains northwest of Paraíso ★ **Rancho Platón** (Paseo de los Locutores, www.ranchoplaton.com, US$120-140, all-inclusive meals) is a hydro-powered eco-lodge and a good pick for families. Surrounded by rivers, falls, and various mountain-fed pools, tastefully decorated cabanas—including treehouses—offer cozy accommodations with air-conditioning and hot water, but no TV. Food is decent and all meals are included at an additional cost. The highlight is the onsite activities, including a waterslide ideal for kids, hiking, tubing on the Nizao River, and horseback riding, when you're not dipping in fresh river water. (The road getting there is only for sturdy pickup trucks so you're better off getting a ride.)

LOS PATOS
Sights
PLAYA LOS PATOS

Much like Playa San Rafael, **Playa Los Patos** offers a river and sea combo. The river is probably more popular than the beach due to the same issues of safety and temperature. The view is beautiful from the highway, even if the river isn't as deep or fun as San Rafael's. Expect a small parking fee (US$1.10) and options for seafood and drinks. You'll spot ducks—*patos* in Spanish—and egrets around the river. At time of my visit, the village of Los Patos was experiencing water shortages in homes, and as a result some were actually soaping up and bathing in the river.

LOS PATOS RIVER

Another popular balneario (swimming hole) along the coast, also a place where the river

Los Patos

meets the Caribbean Sea, is Los Patos located in the village of the same name about 21 miles south of Barahona city. The one large freshwater pool that stretches all the way to the sea is also the world's shortest river, at just 500 meters or 0.11 miles long. The river is fed by Paraíso's mountains making it cold and clear. You'll find various species of fish swimming alongside you as well as ducks (*patos*). Ask about the nearby Taíno cave, home to bats and petroglyphs. A handful of newly built shacks here serve typical Dominican fish plates and drinks. There are public bathroom facilities. Expect to pay a couple of bucks for parking. At the time of my visit, residents of Los Patos were in dire need of water in their homes due to unrepaired aqueduct and were bathing in the river.

Food

There are multiple vendor shacks surrounding the Patos River attraction, offering fresh fish, chicken, rice and beans, and plenty of rum or beers.

West of Barahona City

The options are endless with the numerous national parks that cover more than half of the southwest region. Many are home to endemic flora and fauna. Hike at Parque Jaragua, home to Taíno caves. Look for birds at Laguna Oviedo and numerous other dry flora. Explore the cloud forests of Cachote. If you're up for more challenge, walk from Polo to Paraíso with local guides and test your mountain endurance. Another gorgeous site to hike is the Parque Sierra de Bahoruco, offering a blend of ecosystems and overnight camping options.

To weigh all of these hiking options, contact **Guanaventuras** (tel. 829/560-3560 or head guide Aurelino Feliz at tel. 809/461-3424, www.guanaventuras.com) run by the local cooperative of La Ciénaga, and with two licensed guides who know these woods like the back of their hands. Their latest tour offerings catalog is available in the office; the one online is accurate in descriptions but the prices are out of date. Other hiking opportunities are offered with **Ecotour Barahona** (tel. 809/243-1190, www.ecotourbarahona.com) or **Tody Tours** (tel. 809/686-0882, www.todytours.com, US$200/hour), which specializes in birding in the region and takes you on hikes through the Sierra de Bahoruco.

POLO
Polo Magnético

Turn the engine off and the car rolls all by itself—that's what draws visitors to the **Polo Magnético** or Magnetic Hill, barely a couple of feet long where the phenomenon occurs. Some say it's an optical illusion, while others swear by the magnetic fields in this particular part of the DR. You'll see a sign for it as you head toward the mountains of Polo. To be honest, it's only worth coming here to experience it if you're also headed to Polo for the coffee experience.

LAGUNA DEL RINCÓN

Although it has suffered through droughts in the last couple of years, **Laguna Cabral** or **Laguna del Rincón**—tucked behind the community of Cabral or about 20 kilometers (12 miles) from Barahona—is a scientific reserve and the DR's largest freshwater lagoon at 65 square kilometers (25 square miles). It's home to a variety of marine and wildlife surrounded as it is by dry subtropical forest. As a source of water, its importance cannot be overstated; it feeds from the Yaque del Sur and spills into the Enriquillo Lake. Among flora spotted at Laguna Rincón are red mangroves, rhinoceros iguanas, frogs, ducks and white herons. Communities used to survive from the fishing the lake provides, but it has

Polo's Coffee Trail

The best coffee of the Dominican Republic is produced in the magnificently verdant mountains and birding haven of Polo, a town over 762 meters (2,500 feet) above sea level and approximately 35 kilometers (21.7 miles) from Barahona. Polo's economy once relied on sugarcane, thanks to its fertile and cool lands, but eventually those same conditions allowed for coffee to thrive. Today, aside from agricultural produce including beans, citrus, and pumpkin, Polo's dark and fragrant organic coffee is the number one product to come out of these hills. Polo is responsible for at least a third of all the coffee to exported from the Dominican Republic.

To fully appreciate the community of Polo, you'll want to drive up slowly, taking in the winding, scenic views of one the most beautiful areas of the southwest, riding past yellow flowers or *flor de campo* spilling slightly over the road, not to mention orchids, colorful wooden shacks, and tranquil, cool air year-round.

Once in Polo, you have various alternatives for exploring the coffee trail. One is to head to **Cafe Toral** (tel. 849-858-1231, cafetoral.com, calidad@cafetoral.com, call ahead to arrange a free tour), located at 702 meters (2,303 feet) above sea level, where you can experience **La Ruta del Café**—a comprehensive one-hour tour of the Spanish family-owned coffee plantation, taking you through its various coffee plants outdoors, teaching you about the origins of coffee, the production process, the seven types of coffee they produce, all the way to the final product. The trail is in both English and Spanish, and Jose Miguel Medina, manager of product quality control, will accompany you. Your second option is to head into the village to visit the Dominican-run cooperative **Cooperativa Simona Esmeralda Feliz** (Calle Duarte, tel. 809/993-2811, sucreperez@gmail.com) who produce their own coffee and own their own machinery. Their headquarters are at the *"colmado de la cooperativa"*—they run a convenience store as well—and at the back of it is their coffee machinery. The cooperative counts 286 members, and is a mix of women, men, and adolescents. The pleasant Señor Sucre Perez, manager of the cooperative, is usually at the store; you can watch their process during the months of November through January

If you'd like to experience another, local coffee trail—like Cafeto Madre in La Lanza farm, contact the **Asociación de Guías La Plataforma Juvenil de Polo** (head guide Brulee, tel. 829/719-3603, US$20 with transport). They can also take you on hikes down various coffee trails, including the Ruta del Café at Cafe Toral (US$13.25/up to 6 people or RD$600). The guides can also conduct outdoor hikes through nearby Cachote.

proven to be a double-edged sword with overfishing resulting.

CACHOTE

In the mountains 25 kilometers (16 miles) above Paraíso and La Ciénaga is one of the southwest's ecotourism and biodiversity jewels, an spot few tourists or even Dominicans get to see: the protected area and community of Cachote up in a cloud forest of up to 1,097 meters (3,600 feet) above sea level where approximately 30 families live on the outer limits of Padre Miguel Fuertes Natural Monument. It is here that most of the region's rivers begin, including the Cortico and Nazito.

A welcoming center called **Canto del Jilguero** (Ecoturismo Comunitario Cachote, tel. 829/721-9409 or 809/524-6609, ecoturismocomunitariocachote@yahoo.com, US$55/1-3 persons for two nights, includes three meals per day, and hiking; no hot water) and run by the Cachote local cooperative provides a visitor's info area as well as two basic overnight wood cabins. This is also the departure point for up to five hiking trails and excursions. Many will delight birders with opportunities to spot at least 31 birds endemic to the island. The five trails (US$33 pp/1-3 persons, includes lunch) range from 30 minutes to an entire day—from the coffee trail to birdwatching and nature hikes.

The reserve is also an important home to species of the precious *ébano verde* wood. It can get chilly, so bring warm clothing, as well

Polo's coffee is said to be the best in the DR.

If you're lucky enough to be in the Barahona area in late September, look out for Polo's annual **Festicafe** (www.festicafe.org). This coffee festival celebrates the end of the harvesting season and brings together more than 200 coffee producers to celebrate the region's blends. Hundreds of Dominicans from around the country head this way for this colorful festival, hosted in Polo's baseball field (*el play municipal*) during the last weekend of September. The festival is in its 11th season, with its second year held in September (the festival used to take place in June, but the rains were a nuisance). You'll want to come here to get your share of Polo's organic coffee as they sell out soon after the festival. Polo's coffee is also exported to the United States and Europe.

If you're tempted to stay overnight to enjoy the temperatures and views of Polo, the cooperative has one private room with bath, and shared rooms with bunk beds and shared bathrooms for up to 40 people (US$7.75 pp)

as extra blankets, and a rain jacket. To get to Cachote, look out for the sign on the right-hand side of the main Barahona-Paraíso highway. The drive is about 1.5 hours, and you'll need a four-wheel-drive truck. Don't attempt it on your own if you're not an experienced driver.

★ PARQUE NACIONAL SIERRA DE BAHORUCO

Parque Nacional Sierra de Bahoruco together with the Parque Nacional Jaragua and Parque Nacional Lago Enriquillo constitutes the Jaragua-Bahoruca-Enriquillo Biosphere Reserve, the first UNESCO Biosphere Reserve in the Dominican Republic.

This park west of Barahona in Duvergé has a total surface area of 1,225 square kilometers (473 square miles) an encompasses a variety of ecosystems from pine forests to broadleaf, thorn, and cloud forests rising to 2,286 meters (7,500 feet) above sea level. The Sierra de Bahoruco actually stretches enough that it carries over into Haiti, where it's known as the Massif de la Selle. The average temperature in these hills is 19°C (67°F).

Birding is the primary activity here, thanks to the presence of 112 species. You can spot 32 of the DR's 34 endemic birds. Among them are about 14 endangered species such as the Hispaniolan parrot, the Hispaniolan parakeet, the western chat-tanager, Bicknell's thrush, the white-fronted quail-dove, the golden swallow, the Hispaniolan trogan, the white-winged warbler, the palm crow, and the Hispaniolan crossbill.

There are over 10 species of endemic, endangered amphibians, not to mention more than 1,100 plant species, among which are at least 180 of orchids, at least 10 percent of which are endemic to the park. The rhinoceros iguana is represented here as well as a few snakes. **Tody Tours** (Calle José Gabriel Garcia 105, Colonial Zone, tel. 809/686-0882, www.todytours.com, US$200/hour) offers birding trips to the reserve at Puerto Escondido and runs a bird-watching base camp within the reserve at **Villa Barrancoli** (US$25/pp, includes dinner). Six screened cabins sit at 400 meters (1,312 feet), offering single beds and a bath house with hot water, as well as a shared living, dining, and kitchen facilities. Independent travelers are welcome to book the cabins when there are no scheduled tours. Inquire ahead, and know that you'll have to supply your own breakfast and lunch. To get there on your own, from Barahona you'll head toward Duvergé, south of Lago Enriquillo. In Duvergé, look for a left turn, where there is a colorful mural of birds. The road will take you to Puerto Escondido in 20 minutes, where you'll find the park office (RD$50/pp), before continuing on to a T-intersection indicating a left toward Rabo de Gato. Continue right at the following intersections until you reach the campsite.

HOYO DE PELEMPITO

The main reason you should come all the way out to **Hoyo de Pelempito** or the Pit of Pelempito, if you have the time to spare, is for the spectacular views over the Sierra de Bahoruco. This pit is a geological depression at 700 meters (2,296 feet) below sea level and now a flora and fauna sanctuary.

The hole formed from the collapse of a cave millions of years ago due to the energy released along the fault lines in this region. At night temperatures drop and it gets quite chilly. There's an observation deck from which to take in the vistas. The road to get here is poorly indicated and requires a solid truck; you're better off taking a local guide with you, unless you're traveling in a group. Contact guide Aurelino Feliz with Guanaventuras (La Ciénaga, tel. 829/560-3560, info@guanaventuras.com).

PARQUE NACIONAL LAGO ENRIQUILLO

Parque Nacional Lago Enriquillo (tel. 809/815-8162, 8am-5pm, RD$100 or US$2.21)

The Parque Nacional Sierra de Bahoruco is a top birding area.

is home to the largest lake in the Caribbean region. The lake is approximately 260 square kilometers or 100 square miles To give you an idea, that's a little over the size of Manhattan! The park is part of the trio that constitutes the country's first UNESCO Biosphere Reserve (along with Parque Nacional Jaragua and Parque Nacional Sierra de Bahoruco). You'll quickly notice the park's most famous resident: the rhinoceros iguana. You'll find them roaming around as soon as you enter the park limits, and even on the stretch of road before the park. If you can, get a snapshot of the iguana crossing road sign.

Tucked between the Sierra de Neiba to the north and the Sierra de Bahoruco at nearly 700 feet (213 meters) above sea level to the south, **Lago Enriquillo** is 40 meters (130 feet) below sea level. The lake is named after the valiant Taíno chieftain whose rebel forces fought the Spanish. It's the primary and only remaining home for the American crocodile in the DR (they used to be found in the northwest as well, but no longer), due to the water's hyper salinity. You'll spot numerous crocs of various sizes as you cruise across the part of the lake known as "*los borbollones*," to the left of the main dock. They tend to get out on the banks during the winter mating season;

hiking in this area is now avoided during this time, after an incident in which a croc chased a guide.

The lake's water levels have risen dramatically over the years, nearly doubling in an eight-year span to reduce its salinity, which is normally over two times higher than that of the sea. Some say the shift due to climate change and increased humidity in the region, though deforestation is said to be the likely culprit by other scientists. So serious is this expansion that you'll immediately notice the hundreds of palms now partly submerged, their tips sticking out of the water and giving the entire lake an eerie, prehistoric feel, as living creatures crawl beneath and above the shimmering surface in the hot sun. These rising levels have also taken over hundreds of acres of land once used for crops—sugarcane, potatoes and plantain—thus taking away from the livelihood of surrounding villages.

Flora around the lake include various cactus species and mangrove shrubs. At least 62 bird species soar above, including sandpipers, roseate spoonbills, white-cheeked pintail duck, and glossy ibis. There used to be flamingos, but they left when the water level began to rise, and can now be found over on

Lago Enriquillo

Laguna Oviedo at Parque Nacional Jaragua. In addition to the rhinoceros iguana, Ricord's iguana lives here, as well as other wildlife such as the Hispaniolan slider turtle, Hispaniolan brown racer, and Hispaniolan yellow-mottled frog. Beneath the surface, the primary fish to be found is tilapia and other smaller tropical species. When cruising the lake, you'll spot a few fishers hanging on barely-there wooden planks, hunting away.

At the heart of this lake **Isla Cabritos** (Goat Island) is home to more iguanas and cactus. Visitors were allowed to visit this plot up until two years ago, when the island officially closed. Some say it's for scientific research; others say it's the dangerously rising water levels of Enriquillo. There also used to be a popular high sulfur pool at the entrance of Parque Enriquillo, **La Azufrada,** where visitors could swim and feel the therapeutic waters, but it has also since closed. These two closures have caused a decline in visits to the park, which is a shame because there's still plenty of top birding, crocodile sighting, and all-around adventure to be had.

The drive from Barahona or Paraíso to Parque Enriquillo itself is a beautiful and culturally interesting experience, beginning with the statue of valiant chieftain Enriquillo himself. You'll pass through various villages including Villa Jaragua and Los Rios, where Dominican scenes unfold, including vendors selling grapes in Neyba, ladies sitting in the shade while getting their hair done, and reforested road tunnels like the Tunel Ecológico and in Río Postrer village. Just before getting to the park panoramic views of the lake unfold before you as you drive.

To arrange for a boat ride, head into the park, and after paying your entrance fee, go with local guide and passionate conservationist **Manuel Medina** (tel. 809/815-8162, US$77.40/1-10 persons with Cabritos Island when open, but negotiable for one). Make sure you wear plenty of sunscreen and a hat, closed-toe shoes, long pants, long cotton sleeves, and sunglasses. This is the most intense heat you'll ever feel in the DR, even by Caribbean standards.

On the way back from Enriquillo, a popular stop is **Las Caritas de los Indios**—right off the main highway. A series of wooden stairs allow you to climb to the cliff-top platform, where you can observe impressive petroglyphs carved centuries ago. The view of the lagoon and scenery from up there is also spectacular.

Pedernales Province

PEDERNALES

Pedernales town is at the border, the last frontier of the southwest before you reach neighboring Haiti, with a crossing at Anse-a-Pitres about 1.5 kilometers (0.9 miles) from the town center. The eponymous province is where one of the major natural parks—Parque Nacional Jaragua, which includes Laguna Oviedo—is located, though it is most often visited from Barahona because it's a better pick as a base and can be done as a day trip.

The road journey from Barahona to Pedernales town can only be described as excruciatingly long. This is where the coastal highway ends; it's at least a 2.5-hour trek all the way down to these parts on a straight road. Of course, if you're heading to Bahia de las Águilas or one of the natural sights most visited from Barahona, you'll have something to look forward to and it won't matter that the drive is uneventful, dry, and only lined with cactus. But that's also what's unique about Pedernales, its unusual desert landscape, allowing you to see a completely different side to the DR. Expect to stop at a handful of military posts along the way; this is mostly because you're so close to the Haitian border and surveillance is tight.

If you're taking a *guagua*, which don't run up and down that often due to the distance, you're in for an even longer ride. Aside from the glorious beaches, there's really not much reason to overnight in Pedernales town—unless you're in need of a place to crash as you come in from Haiti, want to peak at the Monday and Friday Haitian market (not as popular as it used to be), or want to linger for much longer at the national parks without setting up a base in Barahona.

Beaches

If there's one thing Pedernales has, it's gorgeous, pristine beaches where you're not likely to see another soul—even aside from Bahia de las Águilas. One of the prettiest is on the way to the Bahia: **Playa Cabo Rojo.** The long stretch of fine white sand is a great place to stop and swim before you take that left turn to head to La Cueva (de Los Pescadores) and Bahia de las Águilas. The partly dismal view of the bauxite plant ahead will evaporate from your mind once your eyes fixate on the phosphorescent turquoise water. The beach departure point for all boats to Bahia de las Águilas at **Playa La Cueva** is also gorgeous with its powdery stretch. You can enjoy it while munching at Rancho La Cueva facing the beach or at the new and trendy Ecomar Restaurant which recently received a controversial permit to build a 228-villa resort on La Cueva Beach within the park. Closer to the city is the eponymous **Playa Pedernales.**

★ BAHIA DE LAS ÁGUILAS

Touted to be the most beautiful beach in the entire Dominican Republic, this beach has nearly eight meters (five miles) of ultra-fine, powder-soft white sand and heavenly Caribbean turquoise waters so clear you can see your toes. Sitting inside the protected Jaragua National Park, you can't imagine anyone else has been here, where a magnificent rocky karst landscape hugs the beach and sea.

The road to get to the jumping-off point of La Cueva, where the boats depart, is long—at least two hours from Barahona province—and reveals a surprising landscape of cactus against bright skies with the sea in the

distance. The road veers to Cabo Rojo, down a path that's a dark rust color due to the controversial bauxite mine in the area. After the port of Cabo Rojo and the small airstrip for private planes, another left turn takes you to La Cueva, where the departure beach—another pristine stunner—and a couple of restaurants await. The boat ride across the Bay of Eagles is one of the most beautiful you'll experience in the DR. The towering cliffs, dozens of birds, and the sheer magnitude of this body of water lined with white sands are dreamy.

You can also reach Bahia de las Águilas beach by car. There's a road that lets you drive up to La Cueva and continue down to the beach past Rancho La Cueva Restaurant. You'll just have to pay the park entrance fees, and drive about 40 minutes down a dirt path. The only downside to this alternative is that you'll only get as far as the main beach strip, which is where most people hang out (you'll notice a sort of lookout tower by it). By boat, leaving from either of the two restaurants on the beach, you can go farther into the bay and take in its real splendor, not to mention find more private swimming spots away from the crowd. Note that there is no shade here, but there are often constant breezes. Still, bring an umbrella and plenty of sunscreen.

Sports and Recreation

Because most of the excursions to the national park are out of Barahona town or province, there aren't many organized tours in these parts and no public transportation to the sights. If you're carless, you can contact **Jopaka Tours** (Hostal Doña Chava, Calle Segunda 5, tel. 809/524-0332, www.donachava.com) to arrange for outings to Hoyo Pelempito and Bahia de las Águilas or fishing trips. If you're into cave diving, contact **Golden Arrow Technical Dive Center** (Calle Victor Garrido Puello 12, Santo Domingo, tel. 809/566-7780, denis@cavediving.com.do, from U$50/nontechnical dive), in operation since 1999 and offering dives off Pedernales at Cabo Rojo, Bahia de las Águilas, and Cabo Falso.

Shopping
HAITIAN MARKET

Haitians are authorized sell goods at the border of Pedernales, on the Dominican side, every Monday and Friday under a covered space. It really isn't anything so unusual you'd need to make your way here. If anything, it's as chaotic as any other vegetable or thrift market you might encounter in a bustling Dominican town. Given the recent immigration conflict between the two countries, check ahead on the latest situation to make sure it's a good idea to even stop here.

Food

When you're heading this way, you might as well veer off to Cabo Rojo and continue on to eat some fresh seafood at one of two restaurants facing Playa La Cueva. **Rancho Típico La Cueva de las Águilas** (tel. 809/753-8058, 11am-10pm daily, US$10-20) is the longest-running restaurant and jumping-off point to Bahia de las Águilas where you can enjoy the best of Pedernales' seafood, including a delicious *paella de mariscos* or a plate of fish with *tostones*.

Before you reach Rancho La Cueva is the adjacent newcomer, trendy Italian-owned and beachfront **Eco del Mar** (tel. 809/576-7740, www.ecodelmar.com.do, 11am-10pm daily, US$10-15), sitting on a breathtaking stretch of the beach, also offering a delicious menu of fresh-made pizza, risotto, and numerous other options if you're looking for something other than the usual Dominican fare. The owners are superfriendly and will even let you get behind the bar to mix your own drink if it's the kind not found here; the bar carries premium liquor of all sorts. If you have time, hop on a boat from either of these restaurants and enjoy the renowned Bahia de las Águilas.

Another excellent spot for seafood that's actually in Pedernales town and close to the main beach is the contemporary **King Crab Café** (Calle Fernando Dominguez, formerly Duarte, tel. 809/256-9607, kingcrabcafe@restaurante.com.do, US$10-15). Try the seafood soup or grilled lobster. It's a nice spot (probably the best in town) for a romantic dinner. A more casual but solid option in town is **Comedor Perla Negra** (Calle Central, off Av. Duarte, tel. 809/750-0241), also serving the area's renowned seafood dishes, including chicken and goat options.

Accommodations

Your best bet in Pedernales town is **Hostal Doña Chava** (Calle Segunda 5, tel.

Bahia de las Águilas

809/524-0332, www.donachava.com, US$22), an immaculate, colorful guesthouse with a charming setup that makes you feel like you're a world away from the concrete jungle. Think thatch-roof corridors, wooden railings, leafy courtyard, simple and colorful rooms with single beds, cable TV, air-conditioning from 8pm-8am, wireless Internet, bath, and lounge areas. There's a generator for the frequent power cuts. It's centrally located, while also just 15 minutes from Bahia de las Águilas, and great value for independent travelers.

Up for a little more adventurous and memorable stay? Camp out on gorgeous Playa La Cueva at the new **Eco Del Mar** (tel. 809/576-7740, www.ecodelmar.com.do, US$10/night), a restaurant and bar offering good value camping for those who want to enjoy the great beaches of the Pedernales for a little longer. The tents are set on the beach, with a reasonable distance to the back of the public restaurant, and have single beds. The bathroom facilities are separate and outdoors, clean, and provide hot water. The food is delicious, and the service impeccable. The advantage is getting to stay overnight after your boat trip to Bahia de las Águilas (also offered through Eco Del Mar) and taking in the sunset and the stars rather than hitting the long road back to Barahona.

Getting There and Around

After reaching Barahona from Santo Domingo via the local bus leaving from Parque Enriquillo throughout the day, **Caribe Tours** (tel. 809/524-4952, www.caribetours.com.do, US$6.85 one-way, 6:15am, 9:45am, 1:45pm and 5:15pm), or with your own car, expect an additional 2.5 hours south to reach Pedernales. Again, there's really no reason to overnight in Pedernales town proper. Many of the excursions to this province depart from the neighboring Barahona province.

Getting around is difficult without your own car, unless all you want to do is hop on a few organized excursions. These will be expensive and leave you to see a lot less than you might on your own. There are local *guaguas* that run up and down the coast, but they might not always show up when you need and you might be waiting a while on the roadside (not to mention they don't run after sundown). To rent a car, do it from the Las Américas airport in Santo Domingo.

OVIEDO
Parque Nacional Jaragua

Undoubtedly among the country's most significant and largest natural reserves **Parque Nacional Jaragua** (Juancho, tel.

Eco Del Mar offers overnight "glamping" on Playa La Cueva.

Wind Energy in the DR

Parque Eólico Los Cocos is the first wind farm in the country.

It's an unmistakable sight as you venture deeper down the highway into Pedernales province. Gargantuan white wings, turning slowly in the distance, towering over green farmland and adding to the already-mesmerizing coastal views. What you're looking at is one of the most groundbreaking, privately funded renewable energy projects in the country, if not the Caribbean. Sited on an elevated ridge between 10-100 meters (33-328 feet) above sea level, the **Parque Eólico Los Cocos** is the country's first wind energy producer connected to the national grid. Located in the community of Juancho up to 40 wind turbines provide electricity to the region and the country, displacing approximately 160,000 tons of carbon dioxide emissions per year and generating and annual 220,000 mwh of clean energy.

The Dominican Republic has suffered through frequent power outages due to a rise in electricity demands over the past 20 years, coupled with high generation costs, poor management, and rising fuel costs. In 2007, the government approved a renewable energy law giving tax exemptions to renewable energy projects in an attempt to encourage infrastructure that would lessen dependency on fossil fuels. A study by the National Energy Renewable Lab of the U.S. Department of Energy revealed that the Dominican Republic's wind capacity could produce up to 30,500 megawatts, mostly in the southwest region and in the northwest. But the strongest source is in the region of Pedernales. EGE Haina, behind the Parque Eólico Los Cocos, began operating in the DR in 2009 in various parts of the country, acquiring four power plants and investing over US$83 million in maintenance and upgrades. Construction of the wind farm in Los Cocos began in March 2010. Transporting all of the wind turbines and substations to such a remote area as Juancho proved to be a challenge, and thus began the million-dollar renovation of the nearby port of Cabo Rojo.

The first installation of 14 wind turbines at Los Cocos, injecting 25 megawatts into the national power network at an investment of US$100 million, took place in February 2011, with official inauguration in October 2011. The project was expanded in 2012, tripling generation capacity to 77 megawatts. To say the park and its turbines are an impressive sight as you drive through one of the poorest areas in the country is an understatement. The website for Los Cocos (www.egehaina.com/plantas/loscocos) has a fun interactive screen explaining how the wind transforms into energy.

809/601-7979, www.ambiente.gob.do/ambienterd/eco-parque/parque-nacional-jaragua, 8am-5pm daily, US$2.20 or RD$100), at over 1,295 square kilometers (500 square miles), became part of the first UNESCO Biosphere Reserve in the Dominican Republic alongside two other parks, named the Jaragua-Bahoruco-Enriquillo Biosphere Reserve. Named after a Taíno chief, Parque Jaragua has been co-managed by the Dominican nonprofit **Grupo Jaragua** (www.grupojaragua.org.do) since 1987, encompasses a handful of Barahona's and Pedernales' most breathtaking features. Driving through the park on the highway linking to Pedernales reveals just how much of an ecotourism hot spot this area is.

The landscape ranges from towering limestone seafront cliffs to desertlike surroundings to cays—including the isles of Beata and Alto Velo. Bahia de las Águilas runs 5 kilometers (3 miles) northwest of the Jaragua and harbors manatees, turtles, conch, lobster, and colorful Caribbean critters. Pristine white sands and lagoons such as Oviedo surround the bay. Other beaches include Playa Mongo (a surfer haven), San Luis, Beata and Lanza So isles, and Mosquea. The park's total sea surface is 905 square kilometers (349 square miles).

The varied ecosystems found inside the park include subtropical dry forest, with plenty of cactus, thorn forest, wetlands, white and black mangroves, cays, beaches, sea grass, and coral reefs. The flora numbers over 400 species, many of which thrive in dry, desert environment. Bird lovers will find over 130 species, of which 10 are endemic and 47 migratory. They are primarily large populations of American flamingos at Laguna Oviedo, little blue herons, sooty terns, white ibis, belted kingfishers, osprey, black-crowned night herons, and the showy roseate spoonbill. The park is also known to have the biggest Caribbean population of the white-crowned pigeon. Endangered reptiles such as the rhinoceros and Ricord's iguana call this haven their home. You may also spot the shrew-like insect-eating Hispaniolan solenodon or the Hispaniolan hutia, a large rodent.

Last but not least, four species of sea turtles make their presence known here the hawksbill, the loggerhead, the leatherback, and the green sea turtle.

Parque Jaragua is home to several caves— La Cueva, El Guanal, La Poza, and Cueva

flamingos on Laguna Oviedo

Mongó—with petroglyphs that reveal the presence of Taíno as far back as 2590 BC.

★ LAGUNA OVIEDO

The largest saltwater body in the Dominican Republic at 27 square kilometers (10.4 square miles) and 1.5 meters (4.9 feet) deep, **Laguna Oviedo** marks the beginning Parque Nacional Jaragua and is the main reason visitors come to the park. This hypersaline lagoon has a salt level three times higher than the sea; it even crystallizes during the dry season from January through March. It is a major nesting site and refuge for endemic and migratory birds, including American flamingos, West Indian whistling ducks, and the roseate spoonbill.

While the lagoon is protected, there's a co-management plan to allow the families who live around the lagoon to sustain themselves; as such the lagoon is divided into various zones, each with its own stipulated use or nonuse. Pupfish, snook, and tilapia are taken by local fishers.

If you sign up through the main tour operators in town, you'll likely just do the boat ride down the lagoon with a swim. But if you get here with your own car, the possibilities widen. The entrance to Laguna Oviedo is well marked; there's a giant sign along the highway on the left. There's also an informative makeshift museum-type display at the park entrance, all in Spanish I'm afraid. This is also the main Parque Jaragua office and the base for local community guides who are well versed in the area's flora and fauna and can take you out on excursions from the nearby pier or on foot. Note that many speak only Spanish. Ask for the park's licensed tour guide **Juan Carlos Santana** (tel. 809/601-7979); he is often at the main office if he's not out giving a tour. A visit to the lagoon is often included in other organized tours on the way to Bahia de las Águilas.

Bird-watching is a great here, but there is much more to be enjoyed. Three main hiking trails traverse the area and lead to sulfur water pools. There are several excursion options. Boat rides go out to smaller isles and caves. You'll have to decide among them based on how much time you have. A complete tour of the lagoon by boat can take up to 2.5 hours (US$78 for 1-5 people, plus park entrance fee). A one-hour option is available for less (US$55). Solo travelers should not be afraid to bargain with the guides. A complete list of prices is posted at the park office. The sunrise at the park is spectacular, so ask about camping here.

You can also hike along the shores to view the flamingos on a **Paseo Flamencos** walk (US$20/pp). It takes about an hour. The turtle-nesting season within the park is from March through September, with egg observation possible from April 1 through July, usually at 8pm and 6am.

Background

The Landscape

GEOGRAPHY

The Dominican Republic is blessed with the most diverse topography of the Caribbean region. Consider it one mini-region from place to place, from warm sun and beaches to cool mountain climates that drop below zero at night, desertlike sand dunes and regions with cactus sprouting out of the roadside, and both the highest and lowest point in the Caribbean with Pico Duarte and Lago Enriquillo, respectively. Throw in subtropical and cloud forests, hypersaline lakes, rivers and waterfalls, and you could experience an entire Caribbean region's landscape in a single weeklong visit.

Occupying the eastern two-thirds of Hispaniola Island at 48,442 square kilometers or 18,704 square miles (about half the size of Portugal), the DR is the second largest country in the Caribbean after Cuba and sits in the middle of the Caribbean region. To the north are the Bahamas, while Jamaica and Cuba lie to the west, a 388 kilometer (241 mile) border with neighboring Haiti and then Puerto Rico to the east, and South America is well south. The northern coast faces the Atlantic, while the south basks beside the Caribbean Sea.

There are 31 provinces, plus a National District (Santo Domingo). The country is essentially demarcated by its five major mountain ranges—part of what makes the Dominican landscape so stunning and helps bear the brunt of major storms—extending through the country from north to central and south.

On the North Coast is the **Cordillera Septentrional** rising above the coastal plains to stretch along the northern region from Monte Cristi to Nagua. It slopes south to give way to the Cibao Valley, which runs from Manzanillo Bay in the northwest to the northeastern Samaná Peninsula. Swampy lowlands separate the Samaná Peninsula from the Septentrional, but the peninsula is made up of mountains as well, with elevations of up to 579 meters (1,900 feet).

Below the Septentrional, deep in the heart of the Dominican Republic like its solid spine, the **Cordillera Central** dominates as the biggest and most rugged mountain range. It's home to the tallest peak in the region, Pico Duarte, and has elevations ranging from 1,829 meters to 3,170 meters (6,000 to 10,400 feet), starting at the Haitian border and running south to Constanza Valley, and down to the southern Sierra de Ocoa. Home to additional prominent peaks, such as La Rucilla, it's the source of major rivers such as the Yaque del Norte, Yaque del Sur, and Nizao. Its reach extends further through the **Cordillera Oriental** and the Sierra de Yamasa.

Bordering the Cibao Valley to the south, separated by the San Juan Valley is the **Sierra de Neiba** mountain range, rising to about 2,200 meters (7,218 feet), its waters draining in part into Lago Enriquillo, while the southernmost **Sierra de Bahoruco**, the second largest range rising to 1,600 meters (1 mile), stretches east from the Haitian border and runs parallel to the Cordillera Central.

Aside from forests and mountains, limestone cliffs, lakes, and rivers, the DR has approximately 789 kilometers (490 miles) of beaches out of its 1,865 kilometers (1,159 miles) of coastline, the primary reason visitors descend on the country, and offshore islands that are straight out of a postcard. Off the coast of Bayahibe, in the southeast, sit Saona and Catalina Islands. Beata is south of Pedernales, while up north are Cayo Arena

---

Previous: Many Haitians survive in the DR by selling fruit, sweets, and other goods; a riverfront home in Manabao.

The Caribbean

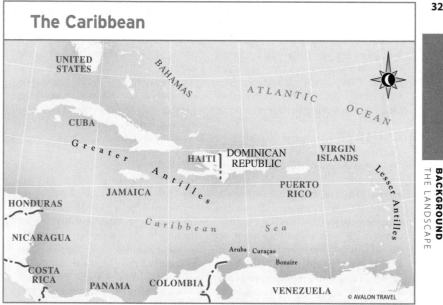

(or Paradise Island) and the Cayos Siete Hermanos, off the Monte Cristi shoreline.

Rivers and Lakes

The Dominican Republic has *ríos* running in the mountains and over the plains, with seven major drainage basins—six of which are out of the Cordillera Central. Wherever you go, there always seems to be a river and its tributaries nearby for one's swimming enjoyment. The longest of them all is the **Yaque del Norte,** at 298 kilometers (185 miles) with a basin area of 7,044 square kilometers (2,720 square miles), in the central Cibao Highlands. It rises out of the tallest peak of the Caribbean—Pico Duarte—and runs north through Santiago, then winds its way west into the mountain retreat town of Jarabacoa river rafting is one of the attractions. The relatively shallow Yaque empties into the Bahia de Monte Cristi of the Atlantic Ocean at the northwestern edge of the country. It's an important source of irrigation for rice farming and agriculture in the central region. The **Yuna River** is the second largest and most important, at 210 kilometers (131

miles), forming within the Cibao Valley and emptying into the Bay of Samaná.

In the east and southeast of the country are the Ozama, Chavón, Soco, and Magua. You can see the **Río Ozama** when visiting Santo Domingo—Columbus himself explored it—driving or taking in the views from the Colonial Zone. At 15 kilometers (9 miles) long, boats can navigate it before it empties into the Caribbean through the capital city, home to the largest port of the country. The **Chavón,** running through La Romana and hugging Altos de Chavón, appeared in *Apocalypse Now* and is one of the most beautiful bodies of water in the country.

The southwest region has its own share of rivers running from the Neiba Valley. Perhaps the most intriguing body of water is the **Lago Enriquillo,** the lowest point below sea level and the largest lake in the Caribbean region with over three times the salt level in ocean water and home to hundreds of bird species. Its drainage basin includes 10 river systems, covering an area of over 3,000 square kilometers (1,158 square miles). Up north, you'll find gems such as the **Laguna Gri Gri,** in Río San

Juan, teeming with birds and mangroves that are delightful to explore at sunset.

Rivers are a popular gathering spot for families on the weekend as beaches for the cooler water temperatures they offer in hot weather. Groups come out with large pots and cook riverside while the children splash around and couples hug or dance in the shade.

CLIMATE

The Dominican Republic's motto should be "365 days of sunshine." For the most part, the country's tropical climate is as ideal as it gets for a vacationer: the average annual temperature is 25°C (77°F), with warm and sunny days for most of the year. The only slight variation comes in the "winter" months—November through April—when temperatures cool off slightly in the evenings (20°C [68°F]) and early mornings, and rainfall is more frequent. In the interior, up in the mountains of the Cordillera Central and the hills of the southwest, it gets a lot chillier—dipping below freezing at night, with frost-covered mountain peaks. If you're heading this way in the summer months, brace yourself: it is uncomfortably hot and humid, but sunny nonetheless, with average daily temperature of 31°C (88°F). Rain has been scarce during the summer and even year-round the last two years, and this unprecedented drought is worrisome, affecting rivers, waterfalls, and pastures.

Up in the Cibao Valley, folks enjoy an eternal spring, which makes it an attractive place to live. The area is blessed with constant breezes such that it never feels unbearably humid. If you're staying in the twin towns of Jarabacoa and Constanza, you'll need a jacket and pants for nights—especially in the winter months.

Over in the northwest around Monte Cristi or southwest in Barahona and Pedernales, burning hot weather awaits and desertlike temperatures can rise up to 28°C (100°F) or more. Rain is frequent from November through April on the North Coast, while other areas are supposed to get precipitation from May to November. Most rainfall comes in unexpected bursts and doesn't last all day or night. The southwest is the driest, hottest part of the country, as evidenced by the cacti shooting up from roadsides in Barahona and Pedernales.

Of course, no place has perfect weather and you could stumble on a couple of days with gray skies, but even that is rare! Blue skies, sun, and glorious days abound in the Dominican Republic.

Hurricanes

The hurricane season generally runs from June 1 through November 30, although there's a small chance one could form outside of those dates. The Dominican Republic has been hit with approximately 11 hurricanes over the span of the last century—in other words, not that many—and most have had an impact on the southwestern or eastern coast. Hurricane Georges struck in September 1998 as a Category 3 and was one of the most devastating. It hit the capital of Santo Domingo and the Punta Cana coast, causing over 300 deaths and billions of dollars in damage, particularly to agricultural lands. It was the worst storm since Hurricane David, a Category 5 storm that made landfall in 1979 and killed at least 2,000 people.

Hurricanes that hit the DR usually begin in the Atlantic off the western coast of Africa as tropical depressions or tropical storms, with the possibility of progressing into hurricanes and making their way slowly to the Caribbean. It can take up to two or three weeks to form into a serious hurricane, so there's plenty of time for evacuation if needed. While the possibility exists in the summer months and the Dominican Republic is located in the storm belt—September tends to be the peak period—the chances of a hurricane hitting are minimal and certainly shouldn't affect your trip planning. Hotels and airlines are well prepared by now with contingency plans, so they will be informed before you are. Summer is also a great time for hotel specials and flight discounts.

You can keep up with weather conditions at

all times by following the National Hurricane Center (www.nhc.noaa.gov) on social media, and sign up for the State Department's SMART Traveler Enrollment Program to receive notifications in case of extreme emergency situations.

NATIONAL PARKS

Revealing a growing consciousness of the country's rich biodiversity and the need to preserve it for future generations, the Dominican Republic now oversees 18 national parks, nine natural monuments, and six scientific reserves. The first UNESCO Biosphere Reserve was established in 2009, combining three of the country's most biodiverse national parks—Jaragua, Bahoruco, and Enriquillo—in the southwest region. The protection of all this land was in part the result of the government stepping up to the plate after environmentalists' warned in the 1970s that much of the DR's forests would vanish by the 1990s if no changes were made due to illegal forestation, fires, and pollution, among other causes. Challenges and abuses have not gone away in certain national parks in the southwest, but for the most part, the country is a staunch protector of its natural resources, recognizing their vital role in ecotourism.

You will be able to explore a handful of the most diverse and unique national parks of the Dominican Republic during your visit, whether you're headed north, south, east, or into the heart of the country. The government manages the parks and entry at each location costs a usual RD$100 (100 Dominican pesos) per person or about US$2.21.

Two of the most important parks protect the mountains and pine forests of the Cordillera Central and the most rugged landmass: **Parque Nacional Armando Bermudez,** founded in 1956 and home to the 3,088-meter-tall (10,128-foot) Pico Duarte, and the adjacent **Parque Nacional Jose del Carmen Ramirez,** founded in 1958. Many come here to hike the tallest peak of the Caribbean and check that item off a bucket list, but the parks offer plenty for birders and those who want to take in some of the most spectacular views of the DR.

The southwest region is where you'll find the crown jewel of the DR's parks, where the greatest numbers of endemic flora and fauna are found, including over 50 species of birds and up to 166 species of the country's orchids, at **Parque Nacional Sierra de Bahoruco.** The park is a variation of dry forest becoming cloud forest and Hispaniolan pine forests at high elevations. It is one of the most fascinating parks for scientists because of its limestone subterrain. While it is currently under threat due to illegal farming and felling in the southern portion, there's hope that the damage done is being identified and stopped before it's too late.

On the southern tip of Pedernales, **Parque Nacional Jaragua** provides a habitat for the cute pink flamingo, among other species. It also encompasses mangroves, beaches, Taíno caves, and the Oviedo Lagoon.

Parque Nacional Isla Cabritos, also in the southwest and a popular excursion from Barahona province, is a tiny island within Lago Enriquillo, the largest lake in the Caribbean in which roams the largest population of American crocodiles, endemic iguanas, and over 60 bird species. While the island itself is currently closed to visitors as of publication time, Lago Enriquillo remains open and is a great choice for birders and crocodile lovers.

The east coast of the DR, off the Samaná Peninsula, is home to the mystical **Parque Nacional Los Haitises** with its rich variety of mangroves but also its giant rock formations jutting out of the water, best explored by boat. It is home to populations of frigates and brown boobies. Along its shores, some tucked away and others seafront, are Taíno caves with cavernous chambers filled with petroglyphs and bats.

Equally impressive on the southeastern tip of the DR below the Punta Cana region is the **Parque Nacional del Este,** starting in Boca de Yuma and stretching out to Bayahibe. It consists of dry, flat terrain with tropical forests and limestone bedrock. There are Taíno caves to explore on foot or underwater. The park also comprises the stunning offshore islands of Saona and Catalina and their coral reefs, supporting frigate populations, the endangered *paloma coronita* (white crowned pigeon), and the most important turtle-nesting site of the country at Isla Saona.

Along the northwestern coast of the country is the **Parque Nacional Monte Cristi,** a range of subtropical dry forest with towering cliffs rising dramatically over the Atlantic. The most impressive is El Morro, a limestone mesa towering 213 meters (700 feet) above sea level and facing a gorgeous stretch of beach. The park also counts offshore islands, including Cayos Siete Hermanos, which protect colonies of brown pelicans, great egrets, and frigate birds, coastal lagoons with mangroves, and freshwater pools. Coral reefs stretch from El Morro to Punta Rucia. It's one of the least visited parks despite its uniqueness. Northeast of Monte Cristi is another of my favorite protected areas, the **Estero Hondo Marine Mammal Sanctuary** with the largest population of manatees. You can observe them from a lookout tower or go paddleboarding on the lagoon. For even more off-the-beaten-track national parks, look into **Parque Nacional Saltos de La Jalda** in Miches, protecting stunning waterfalls, and **Parque Aniana Vargas** in Cotuí.

Just 12 miles east of Santo Domingo, adjacent to the international airport, is one of the first and smallest national parks. **Parque Nacional Submarino La Caleta** is a popular dive excursion from Boca Chica for its marinelife and shipwreck—though not better than the diving you'll find off the coast of Bayahibe within the Parque Nacional del Este.

ENVIRONMENTAL ISSUES

Today, the Dominican Republic faces a handful of environmental issues ranging from deforestation due to illegal felling and soil erosion to a lack of water and serious droughts.

Approximately 25 percent of Dominican Republic land has been designated as protected area, and since 1967, the law prohibits commercial tree cutting. However, some national parks have proven to be preserved on paper only and are under serious threat from illegal actions—some say from the government itself—including illegal farming and sale of protected lands, with issuance of permits to private individuals. These abuses have been brought to light in the last couple of years in the Parque Nacional Sierra de Bahoruco. They have led to the destruction of southern portions of the most biodiverse park in the country, affecting endemic fauna and birds.

Thankfully, in the summer of 2015, the government decided to begin looking into these violations by creating a technical committee to draw up a plan to address the park's issues. A group was sent to tour the park and its surrounding communities for fact finding, along with the help of the U.S. Fish and Wildlife Service as observers and Dominican conservation body Grupo Jaragua (www.grupojaragua.org.do). Overpopulation and the need have drawn mostly Haitian sharecroppers working for Dominicans who claim to have title to lands within the park. They have been planting avocado while simultaneously destroying the soil when they burn the land to clear it.

Forest fires are another unfortunate issue for the DR's forests, particularly in the pine forests of the Cordillera Central, where arson has taken place in the recent past. Farmers and communities have now been trained to fight fires to minimize destruction when disaster strikes.

Another major source of concern is the increasingly dry weather and lack of water—as in much of the Caribbean region. The nation has faced shortfalls in the last three years, with the most serious droughts occurring in 2015. Some river basins and streambeds have gone dry, Certain waterfalls that once gushed away are smaller or thinned out (even at El Limón and Damajagua Falls). Homes and farms are facing water shortages. The change in weather is blamed on El Niño, while others point to environmental abuse of riverbeds, by removing sediments and other important natural resources from them.

A growing tourism industry also means a need for additional monitoring to prevent pollution and damage, and thankfully governmental efforts have increased to raise awareness among visitors about their own environmental impacts. There are also more ecoconscious travelers and Dominican resorts than in past years, and while there is a passion for showing the rich "nature" of the country away from resorts, care needs to be taken to prevent overvisiting of natural sites and destructive impact on these fragile ecosystems.

Plants and Animals

Travel outside of any major city and venture inland to take in the country's impressive richness in flora, The Dominican Republic is home to 5,600 plant species, of which 1,800 are endemic. The country's fauna counts 166 species of reptiles (144 endemic), 74 species of amphibians (71 endemic), and over 300 bird species of which 10 percent are only found right here in the DR. And that is not even counting mammals and land and marine invertebrates. This makes the country an important site for scientific studies and for great potential in ecotourism.

PLANTS
Trees
The most common type of vegetation in the country is the subtropical forest. It is what you will find in the Cibao Valley, the Bahoruco range, and on the Samaná Peninsula, for instance.

Subtropical forests are home to the national West Indian mahogany (*Swietenia mahagoni*) or *caoba* as they call it here. It is native to the island of Hispaniola but not endemic to the DR. These can grow up to 11 meters (36 feet) tall. Mahogany was used to build the first cathedral in Santo Domingo. Other common trees are the West Indian cedar, the wild olive, the ceiba (silk cotton tree), the bija, and the mammon tree. The Taíno cultivated the higuero or calabash tree, which they used to make their utensils and ceremonial masks.

Palm trees of various species are impossible to miss. A signature of the DR, tall coconut palms originally from Africa tower above its diamond white sand stretches or filling entire forests. The royal palm (*Roystonea borinquena*) is found in deeper soil, but also seen planted along boulevards in big cities. Other types of palm include the sabala, the cana, the guano, and the yarey, all native to the island and often used for making furniture. The Spanish introduced several trees such as the African tulip and the *poinciana*, also called the flamboyant tree, which blooms in the summer and looks spectacular along countryside roads.

In the highlands, pine trees dominate the mountainous landscape. The Creole pine is the most common species. Many trees are festooned with bromeliads and orchids.

Mangroves proliferate in coastal and estuary areas in all varieties and constitute an important barrier against hurricanes and erosion, as well as their supporting a marinelife and bird populations. You'll find these in Parque Los Haitises, Parque Monte Cristi, and Parque Jaragua. However, because the DR coastline also includes cliffs and rocks, there aren't as many mangrove spots as in the other Caribbean countries.

Flowers and Fruits
The array of flowers and fruits encountered is mind-boggling, thanks to the diversity in environments and altitudes across the country, from the highest in the Cibao Valley to the lowest on Isla Cabritos in the southwest. You're never far from fresh fruit in the DR,

and passion fruit in particular is as common and affordable as an orange. Dominicans love to drink fruit smoothies blended with sugar and condensed milk into *batidas*. In Santo Domingo, fruit carts are a dime a dozen, and they'll even cut and slice your chosen produce on the spot for a to-go snack or breakfast. The country is blessed with pineapples, passion fruit, oranges, melons, guavas, papayas, mangoes, bananas (called *guineo*), and grapefruit, among others.

Vegetables are equally ubiquitous, grown mostly in the Cibao region. Avocados are a common find, as well as cabbage, onions, eggplant, plantains, and sugarcane. The indigenous Taíno were the first to cultivate and use *yuca* (cassava), an important ingredient for many Dominican dishes, including the traditional *sancocho* soup.

Flower lovers will be thrilled to see all the blooms that surround them. Over 300 species of orchids grow in the DR. You can view them at Santo Domingo's Botanical Gardens, the largest in the Caribbean, or at Punta Cana's Scape Park. Even more gorgeous blooms are grown in Constanza, where entire fields are as vibrant as a kaleidoscope. Japanese immigrants helped grow these flowers back in the late 1950s during the Trujillo regime. Over 50 percent of endemic orchids are found in the Sierra de Bahoruco in the deep southwest, or go see the bromeliads in Valle Nuevo. With the rise in cultivation of cacao, coffee, and other products and the accompanying illegal felling of trees, several floral species are now critically endangered, including the *Pereskia quisqueyana*—the country's national flower—which you can only spot in Bayahibe.

ANIMALS
Land Mammals

Almost all of the mammals you'll see in the Dominican Republic are nonnative, initially brought in by the Spaniards centuries ago. The two that are the exception are in danger of extinction: the **solenodon** and the **hutia.** The solenodon is a weird-looking, shrewlike small furry creature with an elongated snout and a long, scaly naked tail. It can grow up to 30 centimeters (one foot) in length, not including that tail, which can add 25 centimeters (10 inches). It feeds on insects and worms, as well as roots and vegetables. This is actually one of the rarest and oldest mammals of North America. There are only two living species of the solenodon; the other is the Cuban solenodon (*Solenodon cubansus*). Because it is mostly nocturnal, it's hard to

There are at least 300 species of orchids in the DR, of which half are endemic.

La Rosa de Bayahibe

la rosa de Bayahibe

The country's national flower is the *Pereskia quisqueyana* or the rose of Bayahibe, as of 2011. This gorgeous, delicate pink bloom is actually a species of cactus that grows only in the Dominican Republic, in the Altagracia province and mostly in Bayahibe on the southeastern coast of the country. It's one of the few cacti to carry leaves—the flower's petals can reach up to 2.2 centimeters (0.87 inches) in length. Sadly, it's also in danger of extinction. As a result, the Bayahibe community, as well as several regional hotels, has made efforts to replant and grow this flower. You can find plenty of it planted by the church on the edge of Bayahibe town, known as La Punta de Bayahibe.

spot this creature, and when it's on the go, it runs in zigzags. Last but not least, the males do have spurs on their ankles that release venom, which they use against prey. The hutia is a small rodent, also nocturnal, and roams around tree trunks and in caves. Aside from these, you'll spot an abundance of pigs, cows, goats, horses, chickens, and way too many cats and dogs.

Marine Mammals

Of the 1,668 kilometers (346 miles) of coastline in the Dominican Republic, including offshore islands, 1,264 kilometers (785 miles) are protected. And the stars of the Dominican Republic's coastal waters are the **humpback whales,** drawing thousands of visitors every year during their mating season, mid-January through mid-March, when about 3,000 of them faithfully return to the Bay of Samaná.

The humpback whales can weigh up to 60 tons and measure up to 15 meters (49 feet). They bask in the Caribbean waters simply to mate; they do all there feeding the rest of the year while in the Arctic Circle, building up to 20 centimeters (8 inches) of fat to sustain them.

The **West Indian manatee** is another precious marine mammal, spotted along estuaries and coastal areas. In the DR, the largest population of manatees can be seen at Estero Hondo Reserve on the northwest coast. These endangered herbivores, also known as "sea cows," are as gentle as you can imagine, despite their gargantuan size. Outside of the reserve areas, they remain at risk from hunting and interference from tour boat excursions.

Last but not least, **four species of turtles** roam around the reefs of the Dominican Republic: the green sea turtle, the leatherback turtle, the loggerhead, and the hawksbill turtle. Major turtle nesting sites are Isla Saona—where you'll find an active turtle conservation center on Mano Juan—and Parque Nacional Jaragua, where they come ashore at night to lay eggs from May through October. The hawksbill is the most endangered because of demand for its shells, which are illegally sold in jewelry and other accessories. Please always be aware of what you are purchasing.

Coral Reefs

The growing threats to the country's reef systems from overfishing, agriculture, tourism, and coastal development have caused the government to create marine protected areas, including at Parque Monte Cristi, Los Haitises, Parque Nacional del Este and Parque Jaragua. Despite over 60 percent of the reefs being protected, the problems continue, and some areas, particularly Punta Cana where tourism is thriving, have begun to implement coral reef gardening systems to help regrow healthy coral.

The largest reef formation in the country is in the northwestern Monte Cristi region, with a length of 64 kilometers (40 miles) stretching from El Morro to Punta Rucia. Along this coastline are extensive sea grass beds and red mangroves. Off Punta Rucia are coral keys, teeming with marinelife. Additional reefs are found in Sosúa, off the north shore of the Samaná Peninsula, off Las Galeras at Cabo Cabrón, off the Bávaro-Punta Cana-Macao region, in Parque Nacional del Este with its islands, at Boca Chica, and in Parque Nacional Jaragua.

Diving and snorkeling are popular activities—cave diving in particular—but in the most touristed regions, overdiving of sites and lack of monitoring has led to serious reef damage from visitors being careless. This is particularly evident in Sosúa and the surrounding areas. Make sure you heed all instructions on how to position your body properly and not touch anything with your fins or hands, potentially hurting yourself in the process. Look, appreciate, and keep it moving.

Birds

Birding enthusiasts are increasingly drawn to the DR, and rightly so—it is a home to a whopping 300 plus species, of which 27 are endemic. Frequently spotted endemic birds you should look out for include the national bird *cigua palmera (Dulus dominicus)* or palmchat, the black-crowned tanager *(Phaenicophilus palmarum),* the

Birding is becoming increasingly popular in the DR.

Hispaniolan amazon *(Amazona ventralis)*, the vervain hummingbird *(Mellisuga minima)*, the Hispaniolan lizard-cuckoo or *pájaro bobo (Saurothera longirostris)*, and the Hispaniolan parakeet *(Aratinga chloroptera)*. Top birding and conservation sites include the Parque Nacional Los Haitises, the Sierra de Bahoruco where 26 of the 27 endemics are present, Parque Jaragua, Lago Enriquillo, and Parque Nacional Valle Nuevo.

Reptiles and Amphibians

Among the DR's well-known reptiles—there are 1,411 species—are the **American crocodile,** the **rhinoceros iguana,** and the **Ricord's iguana.** The rhinoceros iguana, so named because of the horns on the male snouts, can reach lengths between 61 and 127 centimeters (24 and 50 inches). You can spot all three creatures in abundance in the southwest region of the country at Lago Enriquillo. There are no poisonous snakes in the country (good news), and frogs are plentiful—coming out at night in the bushy areas, including the hills of Puerto Plata and around coastal areas like Las Galeras where they seem particularly huge and are horrendously loud. **Lizards** are a common sight, of which up to 21 species exist in a variety of bright and dim colors. It's actually fun discovering a new kind every time you're out hiking or sitting on the porch of your mountain lodge. They're very territorial and inflate their throats when they feel threatened.

History

To know the history of a country is to understand a place and its people—and nowhere is this truer than in the Dominican Republic. It took many years for the country to reach the democratic system in now enjoys—despite continued corruption woes—and its steady development. Independence only came in 1844, after 22 years of occupation from neighboring Haiti and decades of a mix of foreign intervention, despotism, and terror lasted until 1961. Eventually, the democratic process improved along with the country's economic boom. But understanding why the DR now stands where it is today in relation to its neighbors as well as in the world, you'll need to understand its tumultuous history.

PRE-COLUMBIAN PERIOD

As we all know, Christopher Columbus wasn't the first visitor to the island of Hispaniola or present-day Dominican Republic. Thousands of years before he arrived, various groups of Amerindian origin moved to and occupied the Antilles. They are believed to have traveled from the Caribbean coasts of Central and South America. Various groups lived here over thousands of years, one replacing or mixing with the other.

The first believed to have settled in the current DR are the Ciboney *(ciboneyes or barreroides)*. Their utensils and remains have been discovered in the southwest in Azua. Originally from Central America, they settled in Pedernales, Barahona, and Azua. They didn't practice agriculture or know much about it, but rather survived from fishing and hunting small animals. They lived near coastlines in transient settlements, particularly near river mouths and mangroves. Other Amerindian groups who arrived here known as the Banwaroides originated in Trinidad and headed to San Pedro de Macorís and on to the north and east of the DR.

Centuries later, two new tribes immigrated to the island. One is believed to be from the Yucatán (the Caribs), and the other, the Arawak from the Amazon in South America, essentially became the ancestors to the Taíno people.

The Taíno

The Taíno were the most advanced of all the groups to settle on the Dominican portion of the island. They practiced complex agriculture, built ceremonial plazas, and practiced sophisticated rituals, art, politics, and entertainment. They planted yucca (cassava), of which they made bread, as well as corn, sweet potatoes, and garlic primarily. They also harvested fruits—papaya, guava, soursop—and lived by hunting and fishing. They didn't write but spoke a common language. In the caverns they used, they drew symbolic images as rock art or petroglyphs, which remain around the country, inside the Parque Nacional del Este and at El Pomier, for instance.

Their homes, known as *bohíos*, were nearly circular with a cone-shaped, thatched roof with palm leaves. The rectangular *caney*, however, was where the cacique lived and would receive his guests. Hammocks can be attributed to the Taíno, too, who called them *hamaca*; other words they used were *barbacoa, tobacco,* and *canoe,* which were later incorporated into Spanish and English. Chances are, you've used and said them all without knowing their origin.

The Taíno had their own hierarchical structure and maintained a peaceful relationship among the various tribes. The cacique was at the top, and servants at the bottom, but none of this caused conflict. Instead, everyone had their assigned roles: women made pottery vases, cups, and spoons, while men built canoes and utensils for fishing, hunting or fighting. As seen in various caves and archaeological sites in the DR, the Taíno were talented artists and craftspeople. They also made amulets made out of stone, conch, or wood. In ceremonies, they wore gold crowns, and dressed up with fine cotton belts and collars.

They believed in a variety of gods, and the cacique communicated with them through the Rito de la Cohoba, a ritual whereby the chieftain would first induce vomit with a wooden or manatee-rib spatula to purge impurities, then inhale a hallucinogenic substance—made out of the ground seeds of the *Anadenanthera peregrina* tree—while participants adorned and painted his body. They believed this state of semi-unconsciousness gave them visions and insights into matters of political importance, disputes, or predictions of agricultural yield. The Museo del Hombre Dominicano, in Santo Domingo, has a nice visual display on this ritual. Other respected figures were the

a Taíno cave

behiques, who organized religious rites and cured the ill.

Caves were sacred to the Taíno; they had numerous beliefs related to them, including making offerings to the spirits before entering one. Perhaps the most notorious Taíno contribution is tobacco—which they rolled and smoked like the cigars that are a prime Dominican product today.

It's unclear how many lived on the island. Estimates range from 200,000 to the millions by the end of the 15th century, and there were five Taíno kingdoms when Columbus arrived. Their peaceful life took a sad turn with the arrival of the Europeans. Between diseases such as smallpox, genocide, and suicide to avoid slavery, it's believed that the Taíno of the Dominican Republic were completely extinguished. But their culture and heritage isn't forgotten and remains preserved in the museums, caverns, forests, agricultural fields, musical or home instruments, and festivals of the DR.

COLONIALISM: COLUMBUS' ARRIVAL

Christopher Columbus set sail for the "New World" from Spain on August 3, 1492, on behalf of the Spanish crown, in the hopes of discovering new riches in Asia. Instead, with his men and three ships—*Santa Maria,* captained by the admiral himself, *La Niña,* and *La Pinta*—he stumbled on the Bahamas first, followed by Cuba, before eventually arriving and settling on the north coast of the Dominican Republic on December 5, 1492. He named it "Española," and thus the Dominican Republic became the first Spanish settlement in the Americas and the launchpad for more conquests in the Caribbean region. The term "colonialism" was even coined after Columbus (Colon in Spanish).

Enamored with the beautiful land of mountains, sea, rivers, and valleys before him, Columbus also took note of the warm welcome of the Taíno, the gold they were wearing, and their lack of weapons, and decided to stay on to exploit the land for more gold. By December 1492, Columbus and his men were preparing to return to Spain to report their findings and good news. Their relationship with the Taíno was still peaceful at this point. The eve of their return to Spain, however, the *Santa Maria* hit a reef and sank (other accounts say it was stuck and they dismantled the ship). The Taíno helped, and Columbus decided to build a fort right along that north coast, leaving his 39 sailors there to hold it down. The settlement was called La Navidad, to mark the Christmas day they ran aground. La Navidad is believed to have been on the north coast of present-day Haiti, though the original fort site has yet to be uncovered.

During the admiral's absence, tensions arose between the Taíno and the Spanish sailors who began to abuse the natives, forcing them into service or killing them and raping their wives. Cacique Caonabo led an attack against the Spanish, and by the time Columbus returned in 1493 with over a dozen ships and 1,200 men to further expand the settlement, La Navidad had been abandoned and burned to the ground. Determined to keep chasing after gold deposits of the Cibao Valley, Columbus and his men settled 115 kilometers (71 miles) east of their previous location on the north coast in a new enclave which Columbus named La Isabela, after the queen of Spain. But again, there were numerous challenges there—including droughts and disease, which affected both Spaniards and Taíno—and Columbus decided to abandon the area. By this time, in the mid-1490s, the Taíno were already enduring hard labor, having been forced to work in mines. You can visit the ruins of La Isabela and what remains of Columbus' home, now a protected site and with a comprehensive museum, while in Puerto Plata.

The Spaniards headed south where it was reported that gold was found, eventually settling along the west bank of the Río Ozama or what is now the Colonial Zone of Santo Domingo.

MASSACRE OF THE TAÍNO

Nicolas de Ovando, governor of Santo Domingo, was considered the chief mastermind behind the extermination of the Taíno (ironically, there's a luxury hotel named after him in the Colonial Zone). Ovando instituted the *encomienda* system in 1503, per the Spanish crown, whereby all land was considered Spain's property and the Taíno were its tenants. The land would be granted to Spanish settlers or *encomenderos*, along with some Taíno for labor. Their owners were entrusted with educating the natives about Catholicism and paying them wages. But that didn't happen; instead, the Taíno were abused for work, unpaid, and stripped of their possessions.

As if this weren't enough, Ovando was determined to get rid of the Taíno and orchestrated a mass murder by tricking Anacaona, cacique and wife of the former Caonabo, into gathering all Taíno chiefs, at least 80 of them, and meeting with him for a feast. The house was set on fire and those who escaped, including Anacaona, were hung. With no leaders left, the Taíno became weak from hard labor, the inability to feed themselves from their own agriculture, and disease. Some also committed suicide. It's believed that the smallpox epidemic in 1518 finally wiped them out.

THE SLAVE TRADE

The extermination of the Taíno resulted in profound consequences. This period also coincided with the decline in Santo Domingo's prestige—more exciting was the conquest of Mexico by Hernán Cortés in 1521 and the discovery of more gold and silver in Latin America. Many Spanish colonialists left for these destinations, and the population of Santo Domingo dwindled.

The shortage of Taíno needed for labor, particularly in the development of the sugar industry, meant that the Spanish turned their eyes toward Africa. In a continuous quest to regain riches, they began the importation of African slaves in 1503. The colonialists set out from European ports to West Africa's coast with the goods they used to trade for people. They captured a half million slaves who were brought to the island and sold. African labor was used exclusively between 1520 and 1801. All the horrors of the transatlantic slave trade are part of the history of the Dominican Republic. African men and women chained in the galleons of ships in horrifying conditions made a three-month voyage to the Caribbean. Many died on the way from disease and despair, and those who survived were no better off at the hands of the Spanish once on Hispaniola. They suffered and were denied the practice of their culture and language, while the riches were transported back to Spain in ships filled with coffee, tobacco, rum, rice, and sugar.

Thus the mixing of populations began in the 16th century, leading to the majority *criollo* population in the DR's today.

But it wasn't long before the enslaved began to revolt. The first rebellion took place in December 1521 under Diego Colón, and was squashed. But much defiance continued to occur, along with attempted escapes, which were cruelly punished. The movie *Roots* sums up the experience of enslaved Africans on the island. Groups began to form, known as maroons, fighting the Spanish from the mountains—the most famous of these was led by Enriquillo in the Bahoruco range of the southwest.

Aside from slave rebellions, the late 16th century saw French and English pirates attacking ports in the Spanish side of the island, which led Spain to fortify Santo Domingo. But in 1586, the buccaneer Sir Francis Drake captured the city which he occupied and pillaged for a month while demanding a ransom for its return to Spanish control. He took refuge in the cathedral, and once he was paid, he burned it, Colon's home, and a third of the city to the ground before leaving.

TUGS OF WAR AND INDEPENDENCE

Over on the western end of the island, neighboring Saint-Domingue—under the Treaty of Ryswick, Spain had ceded the western third of the island to France—was actually the most productive agricultural colony for France and thus brought in the most riches, also through use of enslaved Africans. It had a huge impact on the economy of France, and for this reason, there were at least three times as many slaves in Haiti than there were in Santo Domingo, a smaller colony with little influence on Spain. French landowners had enriched themselves by the end of the 18th century, unlike their counterparts in Santo Domingo, who exported less and had less demand from the market and thus fewer slaves. Spanish law also allowed the enslaved to purchase their freedom for a small fee. This resulted in many obtaining their freedom by the turn of the century, and freed Africans made up a good portion of the population, unlike in the neighboring French colony.

Inspired by the French revolution of 1789, Saint-Domingue (present-day Haiti) saw the biggest African slave rebellion in the Western Hemisphere in 1791, whereby the enslaved formed their own armies and slaughtered the French slave masters. This rebellion shook the institution of slavery throughout the Americas. Over in Santo Domingo, news of this rebellion led many Spaniards to flee the island. The Spanish crown saw it as an opportunity to invade the western end of the island, only to be met by the forces of Toussaint L'Ouverture and General Dessalines, who quashed them. Napoleon Bonaparte dispatched forces in 1802 in an attempt to end Toussaint's rule as general of Haiti and reinstate slavery, and the French were again met by Toussaint's forces.

The Haitian Revolution continued under Dessalines and Boyer. France had lost two-thirds of its men fighting, not to mention to disease. In January 1804, Haiti became the first independent black nation. Dessalines ordered the death of all the surviving French in Haiti. To distinguish them from the Creoles, they were subjected to a test requiring them to say *Nanett alé nan fontain, cheche dlo, crich-a li cassé* (Nanette went to the fountain, looking for water, but her jug broke). Ironically, a century later, Haitians would be subjected to a similar language test before meeting their death under Trujillo.

Many Spaniards returned to Santo Domingo and sought to regain control of eastern end of the island and reestablish Spanish sovereignty. With the help of the British, Spanish rule was restored in 1809. Meanwhile, Spain's economy was on the decline under

The Puerta del Conde in Santo Domingo is a symbol of DR's independence.

Ferdinand VII. With weakened Spanish rule and interest, in 1821 Spain announced the colony to be independent. But within just a few weeks, Haitian troops under President Jean-Pierre Boyer invaded Santo Domingo and declared the entire island to be Haiti.

The 22 years of Haitian occupation of the DR began to shape the complex relations between Haitians and Dominicans that run so deep today. One of Boyer's first actions was to abolish slavery on this side of Hispaniola, leading to freedom for many enslaved Dominicans—a fact that is often lost today in the immigration feud between the countries. These people were the first to receive redistributed plots of land to farm and feed and sustain their families. But the Haitian president grew unpopular among the elite because he seized land belonging to exiles and the Catholic church and redistributed it for farming purposes, forced the official language to be French, and invited freed blacks from the United States to settle in Santo Domingo (most of them moved to present-day Samaná). Land was also given to members of the military and government officials. Churches were closed and priest salaries suspended.

Another aspect of Boyer's legacy was the agreement he signed with France in 1825, under military duress and desperate to regain access to European markets, stating that France would recognize Haiti as an independent country if it paid a fee of 150 million francs within five years, a sum ultimately reduced to 90 million francs. This was the beginning of the end for Haiti's economy, despite the fact that it had defeated French forces. Boyer borrowed the first amount from France itself and during his rule of the island attempted to force Dominicans to help in paying the debt. Boyer's economic vision focused on increasing agricultural production and replacing the Dominican focus on livestock, while shutting down the cockfights which took the men away from laboring. This was seen as an attempt to change Dominican culture and caused additional friction.

In 1838, an organized movement began against Haitian rule of the DR—at the center of which was a young man from a prominent Santo Domingo family who had returned home after studying abroad: Juan Pablo Duarte. After capturing Santo Domingo and claiming independence from Haiti in 1844, Duarte was forced into exile by General Pedro Santana. Yet another period of turbulence began, with various factions fighting to obtain control of the government under Santana and General Buenaventura Baez. The era of *caudillos* began simultaneously—strongmen on a horse" who ruled their own areas internally with armies made up of peasants. The Dominican economy was in shambles as Baez left the country and General Santana declared himself president and sought annexation from Spain.

Spanish rule was reinstated in 1861. However, a Guerra de la Restauración (War of Restoration) led by Dominican rebels with the help of Haitians pushed Spain out again in 1865. The border town of Restauración, in the province of Dajabón, was named to recognize Haitian's help in the War of Restoration.

But this wasn't the end of Dominican troubles. In 1882, a dictator by the name of General Ulises Heureux came along, brutalizing his people before he was assassinated in 1889. He had also borrowed money from the United States and Europe to finance the army and build up the sugar industry. The United States entered into a debt repayment treaty with the DR, and political instability continued to rock the country, until 1916 when U.S. president Woodrow Wilson sent troops to Santo Domingo to take control and occupy the country until 1924. The occupation was resented on all sides, both Dominican and American, and turned out to be a double-edged sword: it brought stability to the country, but also played a part in bringing to power Rafael Trujillo, dictator from 1930 to 1961. He got his start in the U.S.-trained Dominican National Guard in 1918 and rose to become head of the armed forces after the United States pulled out.

THE TRUJILLO ERA

The Trujillo Era is one that remains firmly planted in Dominican's minds. There isn't one tour you can take without hearing a reference to the former dictator. Rafael Leonidas Trujillo Molina terrorized the country and ruled with an iron fist during his 31-year oppressive regime. Some say he also developed and built up the country unlike any other leader; and that crimes were low in this day, despite the fact that he also expropriated property and the country's riches for himself and his family. In fact, many of the architectural structures still standing today, and that you'll likely visit, were his doing.

The Trujillo Era was a period of persecution and suppression of civil rights, when anyone who dared oppose "El Jefe"—one of his numerous nicknames—would disappear, along with their families, never to be found again. The dictator renamed buildings and cities after himself—including Santo Domingo, which became "Ciudad Trujillo," and Pico Duarte, as "Pico Trujillo." Worse, households had to carry his portrait, stating their allegiance to El Jefe (the chief), children had to greet him with "Papa," as if he were their father, and his secret police and spies were everywhere. Speaking ill of him was a very dangerous, and deadly, proposition.

Besides being a giant womanizer—he could choose and demand any girl he wanted, and those who resisted suffered retaliation—Trujillo was also known for being a racist. He hated that Haitians were growing in number in the DR, and thus "diluting" the Spanish race. He wanted to "whiten" the Dominican race, and many of his actions were driven by this, including the most atrocious of them all and part of his *blanquismo* or "whiteness" policy when he orchestrated the massacre of an estimated 20,000 Haitian sugarcane workers in 1937, coinciding with a slump in the sugar economy during the Great Depression. In distinguishing them from dark-skinned Dominicans, Trujillo's soldiers would ask the victims to pronounce the word *perejil* or parsley in Spanish—difficult for those who are French Creole speaking. Their bodies were then dumped in the Massacre River.

Trujillo's reputation was tarnished by these shameless murders, and he attempted to make up for it in 1940 when he offered asylum and land in Sosúa to 100,000 Jews during World War II. But few were fooled by his actions, once again suspected as an attempt to whiten the Dominican race. Trujillo's true demise and the ultimate beginning to the end of his era occurred when he had the three popular, revolutionary Mirabal sisters murdered in 1960 as they returned from visiting their husbands in prison. It was made to look like a car crash, but their bodies had been beaten. On May 30, 1961, he was assassinated by members of his own regime who had grown resentful. Some say the CIA had a hand in it as well, with the United States in fear of the dictator turning into another Castro situation in the Caribbean region.

POST-TRUJILLO AND THE U.S. INTERVENTION

After Trujillo, Joaquín Balaguer came to power, but was a puppet and not an elected president. General unrest and strikes led Balaguer to share power with a seven-member council in 1962. The council led the country into the first free general elections of the DR in a long time. Juan Bosch Gaviño became president, a liberal scholar and poet who supported workers and students. He made numerous changes that conservatives disliked, including crafting a constitution that separated church and state and legalized divorce, enforcement of civil and individual rights, and distribution of Trujillo's estates to peasants. After just seven months in office, Bosch was toppled from office. But he didn't give up, and with the help of Constitutionalists and Colonel Francisco Caamaño Deño, attempted to take back the National Palace and radio stations and reinstate his presidency. Complete mayhem and a civil war ensued. U.S. president Lyndon Johnson intervened by sending in 23,000

U.S. Marines on April 24, 1965, to restore peace and hold elections. The occupation lasted until September 3, 1965. The April War—la Guerra de Abril—is celebrated in the DR on April 24; you can head to the Colonial Zone to see official parades, and there is usually an official mass held at the cathedral which the president attends but isn't open to the public.

Balaguer was put back in power and won successive elections (some say through intimidation) such that he was president for 22 years over six presidential terms. A protégé of Trujillo, he was known as a strongman and also ruled with an iron fist, though not quite as brutal, and repressed opposition, particularly in the first decade of his rule. He continued to work until he was well in his 80s and turning blind. It was Balaguer who saw fit to develop the tourism industry in the DR, set up the industrial zones, and also squandered a lot of the country's money—he was the one who built the widely criticized (to this day) million-dollar lighthouse shaped like a cross in Santo Domingo, at a time when the country was suffering from electricity shortages and high unemployment. After Balaguer, the Constitution was amended to bar the successive reelection of presidents.

In 1996, Leonel Fernandez, born and raised in the United States, won the election. He focused on squashing corruption, but he wasn't hugely popular. In 2000, businessman and agronomist Hipólito Mejía Dominguez became president. The economy worsened—a massive bank fraud undermined confidence in the government and the country took a turn for the worst financially, with the peso falling to RD$52 to the dollar. Fernandez returned to the presidency in 2004, and later in 2008—ironically thanks to a constitutional amendment made during the Mejía administration, once more allowing the successive reelection of presidents. The country also entered into the free trade agreement with the United States and Central American nations, and economic conditions improved.

THE DOMINICAN REPUBLIC TODAY

In 2012 a new era was ushered in for the Dominican Republic, with a new president from the same party as outgoing Fernandez (the DLP): Danilo Medina Sánchez, former secretary of state for two terms under Fernandez. He was also the party's presidential candidate in 2000 but had lost to Hipólito Mejía. This time around, he promised opportunities for all Dominicans, with more trickling down of wealth, and on the campaign trail vowed to spend 4 percent of the country's GDP on education as the key to lifting people out of poverty.

For the past four years, President Medina has come through with his 4 percent investment promise. Schools have been sprouting up like mushrooms, but the quality and availability of teachers remain a problem. Initially, his popularity soared for being the first Dominican president to have ever spent so much on the country's educational system. He also was known for paying surprise visits around the countryside—well documented on social media and online—interacting with all levels of Dominican society, to support and fund local cooperatives in communities and assist with job creation programs. The country's fiscal deficit was reduced, with a steady GDP growth of 5 percent. These achievements made Median popular among Dominicans. After he first took office, he was named the most popular Latin American leader in 2014 in various media outlets.

But Medina's popularity has suffered since in the eyes of his people, even though he is likely to get reelected in 2016. In 2015, accusations of corruption and inefficiency against high levels in his government, including the courts and judges as well as in the police force, along with the country's increased crime levels and frequent power outages have tarnished his image. And this is despite his being the first president to tackle and face the growing Haitian immigration crisis—particularly, the status of Haitians born in the DR—and propose a solution. After a controversial

2013 court ruling stripped citizenship from Dominican-born Haitian children of illegal migrants, he attempted to remedy the issue by allowing illegal residents to apply for residency permits, including those who had been in the country since before 2011. Whether he will have made a significant change on these controversial Haitian matters is yet to be seen.

Presidential elections are scheduled for May 2016, and some predict Medina will once again win. In the meantime, the DR continues to grow financially and is more politically stable than it has ever been.

THE DR AND HAITI: AN INTERTWINED FATE

Ask about the Haiti-DR immigration situation while you're visiting the Dominican Republic and the response usually begins with: it's *complicated*. Indeed, to understand the evolution of the Haitian illegal migrant worker crisis and get a good feel for present-day relations between Dominicans and Haitians, you'll need to know about the history of and between the two countries, as well as the politics and economics of the DR and its neighbor. Two nations sharing an island, yet separated by a once easily crossed border as well as major cultural differences, becomes grounds for a precarious relationship. Both have bloody trails in their past, thanks to politics and power-drunk leaders—from Haiti's 22-year occupation of the DR that sought to suppress the Dominican way of life to the tragic massacre of over 20,000 Haitians under the Trujillo regime. And then there's the fact that the DR obtained its independence in 1844 not after fighting Spain, but rather its neighbor Haiti (making it the only Caribbean nation to have obtained independence from another Caribbean nation). Last but certainly not least, the United States played its part in the mess that exists today—it occupied both countries twice, and Haitian cane workers began arriving in the Dominican Republic en masse in the early 20th century to work in the U.S.-created sugar industry. The United States also meddled in political affairs and supported

the selection of presidents according to what served U.S. economic interests best.

It's a difficult situation for both populations, one that the DR and Haiti will be grappling with for years to come. To go so far as saying that Dominicans are racist or believe the U.S. media propaganda that spread in 2015 is erroneous—the majority of Dominicans are rational and hospitable people, and certainly not xenophobes. When you visit the country, you'll realize this for yourself. At the population level both groups have been known to help each other in times of dire need. The Dominicans were the first to rush to help Haiti during the devastating earthquake of 2010. Many also risked their lives hiding their Haitian friends during Trujillo's massacre hunt. The Haitians were the ones who abolished slavery in the DR, a fact often lost on the masses.

An easy read and excellent resource to begin to understand the historical background and events that shaped the relations between Haiti and the DR is *Why The Cocks Fight: Dominicans, Haitians, and the Struggle for Hispaniola*, by Michele Wucker. She explains that "Even now, it is nearly impossible for Dominicans and Haitians to think of each other without some trace of the tragedy of their mutual history. . . ."

There's no clear number on how many undocumented workers live in the DR, but it was estimated at about 500,000 in 2013, and they are the majority of the DR's total immigrant population. They worked in sugarcane fields as the U.S.-created sugar industry boomed, in what is known as *bateyes*, and others later followed to work in construction—all hard, poor-paying jobs that Dominicans avoid. Still others, particularly after the 2010 earthquake, hopped over in desperate search of food and survival—selling fruit and other small items on the streets, hustling to survive day by day.

The Haitian illegal immigration crisis in the DR isn't new. Nor are politicians' tactics of using fearmongering among Dominicans—that Haitians are always plotting to invade the DR again and unite the island—as well as addressing the Haitian immigrant issue to distract from domestic issues. After Trujillo, President Balaguer—clearly anti-Haitian but diplomatic—eventually also took to Haitian workers in 1991. As retaliation against Haitian president Aristide for denouncing the slave-like conditions of Haitian migrant sugarcane workers in the DR and painting the country in an ugly light with international bodies abroad including the UN, Balaguer issued a decree that Haitians over the age of 60 and those under 16 had to be deported. His soldiers went through cane fields and villages to find them. It's estimated that over 50,000 fled or were expelled, and some months after, Aristide was overthrown by military coup.

President Danilo Medina's attempt to tackle the immigration crisis is also, some say, politically motivated with Dominican presidential elections ahead of him in 2016. The main argument thrown to the masses is that one poor country (DR) can no longer bear the needs of a poorer country (Haiti) nor support illegal immigrants who are essentially availing themselves of resources (including better health care) without paying taxes.

The issue came to light again and landed in international media in 2013, when the Dominican Republic's highest court ruled to retroactively revoke the citizenship of children of illegal Haitian migrants born after 1929, whose births were never registered in the DR. It relied on a constitutional clause stating that citizenship is determined on the mother's nationality. This decision, on its face, essentially rendered over 200,000 people stateless—many of whom had lived in the Dominican Republic their whole life and had never since returned to Haiti. After an international outcry, a new law was introduced to soften the blow: the National Plan for the Regularization of Foreigners (or PNRE in Spanish). This plan allowed those Haitians who are undocumented but born in the DR to apply for the *cédula* or the Dominican residency card/national ID so they can legally remain in the country. They were given until July 6, 2015, to file for regularization. Those who did not have a *cédula* by that date would be deported back to Haiti, but the date was thankfully extended.

As of fall 2014, it is estimated that around 290,000 Haitians applied for legal residency. In the spring and summer of 2015, lines were long outside governmental offices. Hundreds of Haitians waited to discover their fate. It's hard to say what really happened or how, but over 25,000 packed up and "voluntarily" returned to Haiti on their own, in fear of being thrown out into the streets by the police when the deadline expired. Many have simply set up camp close to the border, having nowhere else to go, as refugees in their own country. Haiti's government can also be blamed for its failure in providing its citizens with documentation and lacking a way of providing for them.

By mid-September, an estimated 289,000 applications had been received, about 27 percent of which were denied. What the future holds is anyone's guess, but at the end of the day, it's a sad situation with two poor nations struggling to find a solution for a decent life, and yet at the mercy of political maneuvering.

Government and Economy

GOVERNMENT

The DR has a democratic government, with three branches: executive, legislative and judiciary. The president is the head of the executive branch, appoints a cabinet, and also serves as the country's commander in chief. Both the president and vice president hold four-year terms, with possibility to run again for a nonconsecutive term. In 2015, an amendment to the Constitution was made specifically to allow President Danilo Medina to run for a second consecutive term in light of the upcoming 2016 presidential elections. Many already predict it will be Medina. Some support him for the biggest economic and educational strides the country has made in many years during this tenure, while others denounce corruption at all levels of his government.

The National Congress consists of the Senate, with 32 members, and a Chamber of Deputies, with 150 members. The country's Supreme Court has nine judges who are elected by the Senate.

The country's three political parties are the Partido Revolucionario Dominicano (PRD), the Partido de la Liberacion Dominicana (PLD), and the Partido Reformista Social Cristiano (PRSC). As of publication time, the current president is Danilo Medina, a member of the PLD.

Governors are presidential appointees and run the 31 provinces and the National District. The provinces consist of municipalities, with each municipality electing its own council and holding a little autonomy.

ECONOMY

The Dominican Republic has long depended on agriculture—mainly sugarcane to start. But in the 1970s, it began diversifying its economy by increasing mining (gold, silver, ferronickel, and bauxite), manufacturing, and tourism. The cigar production industry, along with coffee and cacao, has grown significantly in the last few years with nearly 60 percent of all exports going to the United States.

In 2003, the country faced a major banking fraud scandal that led to the collapse of the Banco Intercontinental (BANINTER), the country's second largest commercial bank, and a complete loss of confidence in the government and the country's economy. Losses amounted to over US$2 billion. The Dominican peso tumbled, the country's credit rating downgraded, and poverty levels worsened.

It's extraordinary then, that over the past years, the Dominican Republic has made a comeback from ruin to become one of the fastest-growing economies in the Latin America and Caribbean regions, with GDP growth averaging around 5.4 percent annually between 1992 and 2014. Tourism has played a large role in this rise—revenues from tourism surpassed sugar earnings for the first time in 1984. A major boom that has continued in the last three years under President Danilo Medina has placed the country as the undisputed king of Caribbean travel. Tourism revenues in 2014 were US$5.6 billion, and are predicted to continue going up.

The country has diversified its exports as well, and "industrial free zones" or manufacturing plants have been set up to make goods solely for the U.S. market, primarily textiles, tobacco and medical products. In 2005, the DR ratified the CAFTA agreement with the United States and Central American neighbors. The free zones now bring in billions in annual revenue. On the other hand, they've been criticized for using cheap labor and for the benefits of trade with the neighbors not reaching the workers.

Public services have improved—in particular, education and health. A budget consisting of 4 percent of the GDP was committed to the educational system under President Medina, a

The Dominican Flag

The Bible sits in the heart of the Dominican Flag.

The flag of the Dominican Republic was adopted in 1844. A thick white cross, representing salvation and the struggle for a free Dominican people, divides the flag in four rectangles. The ultramarine quarters stand for progress and liberty, the vermillion for the blood shed by the country's heroes. At the center of the flag is the Dominican coat of arms, and therein lies a unique element: this is the only flag in the world featuring the Bible. The Bible is flanked by six spears with a golden cross above it. If you're at the restaurant and see "Dominican flag" or *bandera dominicana* on the menu, don't be alarmed! It's also the name of the national dish, consisting of a plate of rice, beans, and chicken stew.

first in Dominican history, which has allowed for the construction of schools and classrooms, and children now attending school full days. With near 30 percent of the population under the age of 15, this is good news indeed. Last but not least, banking practices have improved—along with growth driven by the country's largest private and capital bank Banco Popular Dominicano. Dominicans living abroad support the economy by sending in over US$3 billion a year to their relatives.

Despite this all-around improved performance, poverty remains higher today than ever—according to the World Bank, soaring from 32 percent in 2000 to 41 percent in 2013. Basic services remain out of reach from the poorest, and the gap between rich and poor continues to widen, in part due to stagnant low wages.

Tourism

It might be difficult to believe, but the Dominican Republic is relatively new in the tourism game, even if it is now the undisputed top destination of the Caribbean. It wasn't until 1971 that the government began promoting tourism, and only in 1984 that tourism replaced sugar as the country's leading foreign-exchange earner. During this time, the country reaped the benefits of being close the United States and the general boom in Caribbean tourism tied to a strong U.S. economy.

The DR became and continues to be seen as the king of the budget all-inclusive vacation, in large part thanks to Punta Cana's fame around the world. This has attracted the type of traveler who would remain confined behind resort walls, with access to everything from food to drinks and an exhaustive number of pools and beaches. But in the late 2000s, the tourism game started shifting, with more visitors interested in an upscale experience—from destination weddings to honeymoons. Luxury travel has also risen in the DR, from Punta Cana to the revived North Coast, where swank hotels continue to sprout. The first Aman Resort in the DR opened in November 2015.

The potential for DR tourism continues to grow. There's increasing interest in ecotourism—lesser-known corners of the islands such as Samaná and Jarabacoa are coming to light—educational and volunteer travel, adventure and sports travel, and immersive experiences. Sustainable community tourism groups have started to develop in various parts of the country, in an effort to empower communities while also providing the authentic experiences that visitors now crave.

Agriculture

Agriculture and *campo* life were the backbone of the Dominican Republic for centuries, until its slight decline in the 1980s when tourism, mining, and manufacturing took on important roles. But while you might have images of resorts and beaches swirling in your head, the truth is that a significant number of Dominicans are still farmers. The country is blessed with rich soil and high elevations, and grows its own rice, vegetables, tropical fruits, and flowers—unlike many countries in the Caribbean. Up to a third of the land is used for cultivation. It also supplies its needs for chickens, eggs, dairy products, and beef. Agriculture was always the main driver of the economy for centuries, particularly through sugarcane. But when sugar prices fell in the 20th century, coffee, cacao, and tobacco took a more prominent place in the industry. Making a living is tough for farmers, who may be forced to supplement their income with other trades such as making crafts.

Agriculture is a major part of Dominican life.

People and Culture

THE PEOPLE

The Dominican Republic population is a diverse mix of various ethnicities: Taíno, African, and European. This melting pot of cultures and backgrounds makes for a fascinating destination with various influences showing up in cuisine to music, dance, and religious ceremonies. The majority of the population is considered *criollo* or a mix of African and Spanish, but there are also many Dominican Haitians, as well as those of a more Spanish descent (usually in the upper echelons economically). Perhaps it's this multi-continental blend that makes Dominicans such a warm, hospitable people with a zest for life I haven't seen anywhere else.

Dominicans believe in courtesy, hospitality, and kindness to strangers. The more you travel into the countryside, the more evidence of this you'll see. Folks will welcome you into their homes. I was once desperate for a bathroom while driving in the hills of Constanza and stopped at a Dominican home to ask if I could use their toilet and their answer was, of course! Life for Dominicans is about making the most of every day, no matter how little you have and giving thanks to God. It's about smiling, enjoying, dancing the days and nights away, and loving with all they have—they are die-hard romantics. You'll always hear music playing and people laughing or joking around. And if you think Parisians have perfected the art of sidewalk people watching, then you need to come to the Dominican Republic. Sitting on the corner and watching the world go by with a cup of rum or a Presidente is the number one activity (which many criticize as laziness, but you have to appreciate their ability to be "in the now"), perhaps followed closely by playing dominoes.

Family is the core of Dominican life. At any chance they get, Dominicans will tell you it's all about *la familia* (and they show grave concern if you say you don't have children or a spouse). On the weekends, especially Sunday, it's on full display with everyone flocking to the beach or the river, cooking together, playing, and enjoying their time off. Nothing is ever done "solo"—that's just a foreign concept. Sticking together, through thick or thin, is

Dominicans spend a lot of time with their families.

Things You Might Not Know About Dominicans

Dominicans have their own way of interacting and doing things, some of which might surprise you and others that will make you chuckle.

- They often calls others *"mi amor"* (my love) or *"cariño"* (darling).

- Dominican time is real—*ahorita* might translate into "right now" but it could mean tomorrow or some point in the future.

- Whenever entering a public space, Dominicans greet everyone with *"saludos"* or *"buen día,"* whether it's a bus, a taxi, a restaurant, or a clinic. Not to do so would be considered rude.

- Sunday is the noisiest day of the week and the biggest for partying and drinking. It's also family day.

- Dominicans often use facial expressions in lieu of words—they will move their lips forward to point to a place, or wag their index finger to say no.

- Whatsapp is king—phone credits cost money, so most Dominicans use their smartphones with Wi-Fi.

- It's never loud enough—big speakers are popular, in the shops, at home, or even placed in the back of the car.

- Dominicans love their beaches as much as you do. And they have legal access to all of them because all beaches are public.

- Superstition runs deep—certain things you do or don't do can cause bad luck, including opening the fridge while ironing, putting your purse on the floor, or not saying "God bless you" to a newborn.

second nature for Dominicans. The mother is the central glue that keeps the unit together. Her children worship her, and she would do anything for them.

While Dominicans are all about sharing their plate of food or drinks, watching their neighbors' kids, or running to the aid of a friend who calls in need, it's not all roses all the time—there are issues of race and class, and many upper-class folks don't mix with anyone who isn't in their circle, as judged according to their family's history and wealth. That's true of most of the once-colonized Caribbean.

Dominicans are often criticized for being too focused on race and color. They call people by their skin color, for instance, and it is considered completely normal here. While it isn't usually intended in a discriminatory manner, it can be surprising and even offensive to foreigners, especially from the United States. If you're darker skinned, you'll hear folks calling out to you with "negro" or "morena," and if you're lighter skinned, "rubio." And there are a dozen other words for all the shades in between. Many Dominicans, however, recognize the beauty in their mixed heritage and will invite you to do the same.

THE CULTURE
Language

The official language of the Dominican Republic is Spanish. If you're traveling to tourist areas such as Punta Cana, La Romana, and Puerto Plata, you'll find plenty of other languages are understood or spoken a little by hotel employees and tour guides. But for the majority of the country, Spanish is it—more precisely, Dominican Spanish, which can be difficult to understand. That's because Dominicans have their own colloquialisms. They're also known for speaking fast—really fast—swallowing syllables and not pronouncing the "s" at the end of a word. For instance, you'll hear *Como tu ta?* instead of *Como tu estás?* The more pronunciation, the more foreign you'll sound. If you don't understand, just ask them to speak slowly—*más despacio por favor*—or flat out tell them you don't speak Spanish. They'll gladly try to help how they can (even pulling out a piece of paper when necessary). Dominican phrases can be filled with innuendos and double meaning, and the more you learn about the culture, the more you'll understand how to speak or what is being said to you. Review the phrase book in the Essentials chapter and you'll be set for your first trip.

Religion

Dominicans are a people of faith—all you have to do to pick this up is listen to them speak. Their sentences are always accompanied with a *Si Dios quiere* (If it is God's will) or *gracias a Dios* (thanks to God). The majority of Dominicans are Roman Catholic, as a result of the past Spanish colonial days. But that's been changing, with other denominations growing in popularity, including Evangelicals and Jehovah's Witnesses.

On the other hand, most Dominicans from the countryside—but even those from the city—practice a form of syncretic religion, blending African traditions with Christianity. They consult *curanderos* or folk healers, who "open the way" to any life difficulties faced, and they wear charms. You'll notice the numerous *botánicas* or herb shops inside markets, carrying tons of obscure-looking potions and bottled concoctions, candles, and herbs for sale. Ceremonies involve African-inspired spiritual dances and drums.

Merengue and Bachata

Music and dance—more precisely, merengue and bachata—are at the core of Dominican life every day, in every neighborhood, in every corner. They top all the other DR cultural elements including cockfighting and baseball. It's no exaggeration to say that there is no life without twirling your body to music coming from either deafeningly loud speakers or from a live band. Sometimes it seems as if every day is a party in the DR. You'll be hard pressed to find a Dominican, male or female, who doesn't know how to dance merengue or bachata—it's simply not possible. They have their favorite artists and songs, and the older the generation, the longer that list seems.

Beyond the party aspect, merengue and bachata have a deeper significance culturally. Lyrics reflect social aspects of life and can talk about love, sex, politics, humor, and everyday struggles. Romance tops it all, though, as Dominicans are as poetic as it gets.

Merengue is the national music and dance of the Dominican Republic and has become a word and worldwide genre that is synonymous with the country itself. Merengue is the essence of being Dominican: its instruments reflect the mixed heritage of the country: an accordion (European), a two-sided drum (African) placed on one's lap, and a *güira* (Taíno), a sort of metal cylinder with holes, with a brush that is run up and down across its surface. The accordion was brought over by the Spanish, but it was later retuned to play merengue notes.

Some say the word originated during the colonial period, from African dances. Merengue's 2/4 beat is danced as a couple and has an intoxicating rhythm that can range from moderately fast to really fast. That's because there are various types of this genre. The folkloric, traditional kind is known as *Perico ripiao* or *merengue típico*. It is believed to have originated in the Cibao region (while others say it might have come from Cuban influences) at the end of the 19th century, and can be considered the "country music" of the DR. One well-known, award-winning *perico ripao* performer is Facundo Peña, from the village of Guananico in the Puerto Plata province, birthplace of generations of *merengue típico* performers and instrument makers, still going today. If you're lucky to be in this area in late November, contact the **UMPC** (tel. 809/696-6932, local tourism network for

Puerto Plata)—for information on the annual *merengue típico* festival.

Ironically, merengue was rejected by the upper classes at first, considered as music of the masses with vulgar movements (the same was later considered of bachata). But Trujillo arrived and changed all of that, putting merengue on center stage any many of his events and parties.

How do you dance the merengue? The man leads—holding the woman's waist with the right hand—and the couple dances by swaying their hips sensually left and right, but without swinging the torso. They turn, step side to side occasionally, but never release hold of both hands—only one at times. If you're a woman, your job is simply to follow the cues and keep swaying your hips while maintaining the steps and your posture. If anything, it's a great workout. It's relatively easy as well. You can take lessons in various parts of the country if you'd like to practice before you brave the dance floor.

Juan Luis Guerra, today one of the greatest Grammy-winning and world-renowned Latin artists, is perhaps the biggest merengue figure of the 1980s and 1990s. He took the genre and mixed it with the modern sounds of pop and jazz. One of his classic songs is *Ojalá que llueva cafe* (I wish it would rain coffee). Other typical merengue songs include *La dueña del swing* by Los Hermanos Rosario, *Dominicano Soy* by Fernando Villalona, and *Vamo' hablar inglés* by Fefita La Grande.

While the younger generation is leaning toward a more modern merengue with guitars and saxophones or toward the "dancehall" version of Dominican music—known as *dembow*—*merengue típico* continues to be appreciated and to vibrate in the Cibao region's cities and villages along the *rancho típicos*, as well as in the capital of Santo Domingo.

Bachata grows more popular every year and was recently declared the national patrimony of the DR. Bachata is a more sensual, slow genre that was made popular among the working class for the longest time before it received fuller recognition. Bachata was influenced by the Cuban bolero, but originated in the DR and is unique to this country. It was looked down on by the upper class for a long time, considered the music of bars and brothels, with lyrics about romance, sex, and poverty. Plenty of double entendre *(doble sentido)* and sexual connotations are hallmarks of bachata, which took shape in the 1980s, and for this reason is culturally entrenched. It's the music of love and heartbreak.

Instruments used in bachata, a three-step dance with a fourth tap step, are numerous: guitars (lead, electric bass, rhythm), bongos or drums, and the *güira*. The dance takes two partners, with the man leading as always. They stay close together when they move their hips, as if forming a square or box with their feet, then engage in a push and pull with the hands, depending on one's style. Artists credited for taking bachata to the international stage are Juan Luis Guerra, with his album *Bachata Rosa*, and more recently, Romeo is blazing his way through the charts. Among other famous bachata artists are Aventura, Raulín Rodríguez, Frank Reyes, Anthony Santos, and Luis Vargas.

Other genres you'll hear in the DR include salsa, son (especially in Santo Domingo), *dembow*, the popular reggaeton, and even Dominican jazz—often at the Dominican Republic Jazz Festival on the North Coast. A great way to experience all the various folkloric dances of the DR, in a historical timeline and one sitting, is to watch the two-hour performance by the Ballet Folklórico del Ministerio de Turismo. The group performs a free dance show, complete with live instruments, twice a week in the Colonial Zone (Fri. and Sat. starting at 7pm), by Plaza de España, and it goes over all of the dances and music of the DR—including African—in colorful costumes. You'll even get to dance with the group members at the end.

For an album with a mix of merengue, bachata, and other Dominican genres, a good pick is Latin Hits 2015 Club Edition. For *merengue típico*, look up *El Mero Merengue—Lo mejor del perico ripao* (1995).

Ritmo Dominicano: Carnivals and Festivals

JANUARY

In San Pedro de Macorís, the first day of the year kicks off with the Guloya Festival when Afro-Dominican revelers–descendants of late 19th-century migrants from British-speaking Caribbean islands–dressed in vibrant Junkanoo-like costumes dance their way through the streets, to various drums and flutes. The Guloyas' dance is classified by UNESCO as a Masterpiece of the Oral and Intangible Patrimony of Humanity.

FEBRUARY

An absolute cultural treat is a visit to the DR during this most festive month of the year: Carnaval celebrations take place in major towns and cities across the island every Sunday afternoon of the month, including Santo Domingo (east and west), Santiago, La Vega, Bonao, Río San Juan, La Romana, Punta Cana, and Puerto Plata. Each of these regions has their local carnival personality and traditional devil costumes–such as the Lechones in Santiago or the Taimáscaros of Puerto Plata–as well as comparsas and Dominican folklore characters. You could literally hop around the country all month and experience the carnival revelry every Sunday. The season culminates at the end of the month, sometimes the first Sunday of March, with a big national parade on Santo Domingo's Malecón featuring the winning carnival groups from each region competing for the grand prize while entertaining spectators.

MARCH

Santo Domingo's Ciudad Colonial is where Easter Semana Santa parades take place–often on Good Friday–including a national evening mass at the Cathedral on Easter Saturday. Semana Santa is a celebrated time for Christians around the country, although these days it's also a reason for Dominicans to skip the cities, head to the beach, and party. It's a good time to be in Santo Domingo if you want to see the religious processions and a special Easter Saturday evening mass at the cathedral.

Easter Week in Cabral displays the DR's surviving syncretic religion and African traditions with the Cimarrón Festival, when the cachuas come out with whips and devilish multicolor masks with horns, impersonating the colonial master as well as the abused slave.

JUNE

Glimpse the Dominican Republic's Afro-Caribbean pulse at various festivals and ceremonies around the country. Samaná's annual, outdoor summer harvest festivals, hosted by the local church, is where African American descendants continue their ancestors' 19th-century celebrations of thanks for crops, rain, and earth with the beat of drums, chanting, and traditional foods like johnnycakes, ginger beer, and coconut rice.

Puerto Plata's annual cultural festival is a great time offering folk music, traditional African tribal dances, salsa, and merengue. There are also many crafts exhibits by local artists.

AUGUST

The Merengue Festival or Festival del Merengue y Ritmos Caribeños takes over

Literature and Film

Perhaps as a result of all the strife in their history, coupled with their eternal romantic spirit, Dominicans have great skill with the written word. The earliest writers came from within the church, understandably because they were in charge of leading colonies and the Taíno during difficult colonial times. Friar Bartolomé de las Casas was among the first, with his accounts in *Historia de Las Indias* of the Spanish atrocities committed against the Taíno, pleading to the crown to intervene. Early poets include Leonor de Ovando—recognized as the first poet in the

Santo Domingo's Malecón at Plaza Juan Barón park, with over 30 or artists performing all night over a weekend-long fest of all things Dominican.

SEPTEMBER

Puerto Plata hosts the annual **Festival del Merengue**–usually at the end of the month–with a range of the best of Dominican artists.

Cattle festivals are a more authentic expression of the DR's still dominating agricultural and countryside spirit, when cowboys and their families descend on the town and festivities include horseback riding for all ages and games with plenty of music. Puerto Plata's **Feria Ganadera El Cupey** is a great example.

OCTOBER

The biggest concert in the country, **Festival Presidente,** is an all-out party till the wee hours of the morning at the Olympic Stadium, where the beer flows and Dominican fans dance in the aisles, screaming out lyrics under the stars and occasional fireworks. The event takes place every two years over three nights, from around 6pm to 3am.

NOVEMBER

The annual **Dominican Republic Jazz Festival** (www.drjazzfestival.com) attracts local Dominican as well as international artists with incredible jazz performances across various cities over the course of five days. From Santiago to Sosúa, Puerto Plata city and Cabarete–on the beach–it's a nice time out. Book you rooms in advance as hotels sell out quickly.

Colonial Fest (www.colonialfest.org) is a celebration of arts, crafts, cuisine, and all things Dominican, and takes place in Santo Domingo's Colonial Zone. Nights are filled with outdoor concerts on Plaza de España or at Parque Colón. They can be late in posting schedules, so don't miss out on rooms while waiting on that.

In November, an annual **Merengue Típico Festival** takes place in the heart of Guananico. It's an authentic insight into Dominican culture.

DECEMBER

New Year's Eve (December 31) is just as big in the DR as other countries: Dominicans take to the streets and celebrate on the Malecón and in local bars with all-night music and dancing.

YEAR-ROUND

The **fiestas patronales** or patron saint festivals are held at various times of the year in the various towns, and are a great expression of the modern side of the DR's Latino culture–from foods to live music, drumming, and all-night partying. These parties last a little over a week (known as the *novena* or nine days prior to the actual patron saint day). Barahona's are held in January, for instance, while Constanza's take place in September.

"New World"—and Salomé Ureña, who was revered for championing women's education in the late 19th century by opening the first women's higher education center in the country.

Félix María del Monte is considered the father of Dominican literature in the Independence era. Close to the Trinity, with whom he worked—the three Fathers of Independence—he was also a journalist, poet, and playwright. Some of his famous works include "El banilejo y la jibarita" and "Las Vírgenes de Galindo." The harsh Trujillo days gave birth to a new wave of creatives and poets, including Juan Bosch Gaviño, who eventually became president of the DR in 1963.

On the contemporary side are award-winning artists like Junot Díaz and Julia Alvarez, who emigrated to the United States and became world renowned. Alvarez's *In the Time of Butterflies* tells the tale of the Mirabal sisters, and Diaz won the 2008 Pulitzer Prize for *The Brief Wondrous Life of Oscar Wao.*

While the DR doesn't itself have a strong film industry—only a couple of Dominican-made movies come to mind, like *Sanky Panky* in 2007—Pinewood Studios built one of the largest filming studios in Juan Dolio in 2011, valued at $70 million, and as of 2013 it is home to the world's second largest water tank for underwater filming.

The country has also been a favorite backdrop of Hollywood movies and reality series, particularly of the *Survivor* kind. Movies that were filmed in the DR include *Apocalypse Now* (1979), *Jurassic Park* (1993), *The Good Shepherd* (2006), and *Miami Vice* (2006).

Essentials

Transportation

GETTING THERE
Air

The Dominican Republic is blessed with 10 international and domestic airports (www.aerodom.com) in key areas of the country. You're never too far from a flight. When planning your trip, be sure to consider the most convenient arrival and departure point according to your itinerary and budget. Sometimes people forget how big the island really is.

The most affordable airport to fly into is usually Santo Domingo's **Aeropuerto Internacional de Las Américas** (SDQ, tel. 809/947-2225). It's the largest of the lot, and because it is just outside the capital city, it is well connected in terms of public transportation to various parts of the country, including Samaná and Punta Cana by bus.

Aeropuerto Internacional Punta Cana (PUJ, tel. 809/959-2376) receives an astounding near two million passengers a year and serves Punta Cana and Bávaro, where the bulk of visitors to the DR end up.

If you are headed to the Puerto Plata, opt for **Aeropuerto Internacional Gregorio Luperón** (POP, tel. 809/291-0000), just a 15-minute ride from downtown Puerto Plata town and the best pick for Playa Dorada, Cabarete, Sosúa, and visits to the North Coast. Some also opt to fly into the Santiago area, at **Aeropuerto Internacional del Cibao** (STI, tel. 809/233-8000)—just remember that the airport is at least a 30-minute ride to downtown Santiago, and from there it is another hour ride to Puerto Plata. That would mean an expensive cab ride to Puerto Plata, depending on your arrangements and itinerary.

For the southeastern DR, those heading to La Romana, including Casa de Campo, or Bayahibe and Dominicus beach areas can fly into **Aeropuerto Internacional La Romana** (LRM, tel. 809/813-9000). Over on the Samaná Peninsula is the relatively new **Aeropuerto Internacional El Catey,** also known as **Aeropuerto Internacional Presidente Juan Bosch** (AZS, tel. 809/338-5888), outside Samaná town and ideal for stays around the peninsula. **Aeropuerto Arroyo Barril** (ABA, tel. 809/669-6100) and **Aeropuerto Constanza** (COZ, tel. 809/539-1022) are for domestic charters.

A host of airlines fly to the DR, including **American Airlines** (tel. 809/542-5151, www.aa.com), **Delta Airlines** (tel. 809/200-9191, www.delta.com), **Air Canada** (tel. 809/959-0200, www.aircanada.com), **British Airways** (tel. 809/959-0254), **Spirit Airlines** (tel. 809/549-0200), and **JetBlue** (tel. 809/200-9898, www.jetblue.com). Flights out of the DR (especially from Santo Domingo) head not just the United States but also directly to other Caribbean islands and Latin America. Find affordable tickets online, and stay tuned to airline websites and social media for any special deals.

Ferry

An overnight ferry service between Santo Domingo and Puerto Rico (San Juan or Mayaguez) is offered by **America Cruise Ferries** (Puerto Don Diego, tel. 809/688-4400, www.acferries.com, US$190 adults, US$174 children). The 12-hour journey begins at the port in Santo Domingo, across the Fortaleza Ozama.

GETTING AROUND
Air

If you want to save time or are traveling in a group, it might be a good bet to charter a

---

flight. There are domestic airports and air-strips around the country that can get you from, say, Punta Cana to Puerto Plata. Contact **Air Century** (tel. 809/826-4333, www.aircentury.com) or **Dominican Quest** (tel. 809/523-9630), offering charters as well as shuttle services.

Bus and *Guagua*

The bus service in the DR is impressive; there's always a bus or *guagua* that will take you to your destination, even if you have to connect. There are three general types of bus service in the Dominican Republic: 1) the large and comfy coach buses that travel long distance between key cities; 2) privately owned and run minivan services that offer express runs to and from destinations; and 3) the in-city or in-town, usually beat-up white minivans that cram in as many people as possible. The last two are usually known as *guaguas*.

The two major coach bus companies are **Caribe Tours** (tel. 809/221-4422, www.caribetours.com.do), **Metro Tours** (tel. 809/227-0101, http://metroserviciosturisticos.com), and **Bávaro Express** (tel. 809/682-9670, www.expresobavaro.com). Caribe Tours offers more destinations and departures. You can expect comfortable seats, air-conditioning (often uncomfortably cold), wireless Internet, and bathrooms on board. Tickets can be reserved in advance and purchased at the counter at least an hour before departure.

The more local private bus services are decent with comfortable minivans holding about 25 (no being squashed here) offering the same perks and with some colorful curtains and Dominican music playing. All you have to do is ask the locals, and they will tell you which service is best from your destination if you are in a small town.

The local buses—the real definition of a *guagua*—are probably the least comfortable and offer the most chaotic yet interesting social scene, which makes it fun even if you only do it a couple of times. The merengue beats on, above the interior chatter, while the driver stops anytime someone hollers or stands on the side of the road, while the conductor leans halfway out the door calling out for customers and collecting fares. Unless it's an express, they'll stop anywhere along the road to pick up or drop off passengers, so you're often in for a longer ride than in a taxi. More than likely, you'll be squeezed like sardines (if you're claustrophobic, this could be a problem!). The only local *guaguas* I don't recommend are the ones in Santo Domingo—unless you are accompanied by a local.

When riding on public transportation, always have small change ready for your rides. Drivers might not have change for large bills. Also ask about fares ahead of time from anyone, including other passengers, so you don't get ripped off.

Rental Car

Be warned: driving in the Dominican Republic is doable if you have experience driving in the Caribbean, but even then it's tricky. The roads and highways are some of the best in the Caribbean, but you will need to drive defensively and constantly be on the lookout for obstacles—motorbikes, cattle, dogs, pedestrians, or anything that could leap from the side, back, or front! And many times, road rules don't apply. Defensive driving and speeding lead to a high number of road accidents, one of the highest in the world.

If you are unsure, this option isn't for you. But if you do decide to rent a car and explore the island—and it is the best way to enjoy its great outdoors and the countryside at your own pace—you will find that all the international rental companies such as Hertz, Alamo, and Dollar have outlets here. They have offices at the international airports, as well as in the tourist areas. Your best bet is to rent a sturdy four-wheel drive. A good map and knowing Spanish go a long way when you are lost (likely to happen the more you go off the beaten track).

TAXI

Taxis abound all over the Dominican Republic, and you will soon realize that not all taxis are created equal. Some are shiny vans, and others are beat-up Toyota Corollas. To be safe, hop into one that is tourism certified, particularly for airport rides. Locally that won't always be possible. The most important thing when it comes to taxis is to know the rate to your destination and agree on a fare before you board, because there are no meters.

In-city taxis are generally affordable at under US$5 a trip—with rates slightly higher after 5pm—and there are general taxi central numbers you can call in each area. In Santo Domingo, they run 24-hour dispatches (Apolo Taxi, Santo Domingo, tel. 809/537-0000, www.apolotaxi.com). Many times, local rates within cities are set by the taxi association. But when it comes to longer distances, you can openly barter and negotiate. Drivers are usually decent folks, but there are plenty trying to abuse the system and overcharge. Knowing some Spanish and the fare will save you some bucks.

Carritos (Shared Taxis)

Shared taxis, which are four-door cans usually of the Toyota type, operate like *guaguas*. They stop anywhere along their routes to pick up or drop off. Fares are only slightly higher than the bus, and they cram a maximum of 4-5 people in the back and two in the front, not including the driver. Carry small change and announce your destination as you hand the money over to the driver (while he is at the wheel) shortly after you enter the car.

Motoconchos (Motorbike Taxis)

They are all over the Dominican Republic, parked on street corners, by bus stations, along *guagua* stops and near major intersections: *motoconchos,* or bike taxis. They'll take you the same destinations as taxis for chump change. Of course, it's a lot more dangerous. They don't carry helmets for their passengers (and don't wear any themselves—despite it being a law). Don't hesitate to tell the *motoconcho* to slow down if he's going too fast for your liking. You can have two passengers on the back of the bike, and it's common to see Dominicans squeezing in their entire family. It's simply one of the most affordable ways for them to get around. The countryside roads are safer to explore on motorbike taxis, because of lighter traffic. It is nice enjoying the landscape this way, but you will be riding at your own risk.

Visas and Immigration

All arriving tourists will need a passport, valid for at least six months and with sufficient pages for entry and exit stamps. More importantly—and sometimes missed by travelers in a rush to exit the airport—you will need to purchase a US$10 tourist card as soon as you enter the immigration area and *before* getting in line for immigration. If you want to cut your wait, have the exact bill ready and purchase the card from one of the automated machines, rather than standing in line at the ticket counter. Tourist cards are valid for 30 days. Should you overstay that limit by a few weeks or months, you will simply face a scaled exit charge at the airport when you leave.

The customs line can be a pain or easy, depending on the airport. Santo Domingo usually has the longest lines, but they usually don't go through your things if you are traveling light and a short-term tourist. Those who arrive on a visa and overstay will have to pay a fee—check with your embassy if this is a concern.

Travel Tips

CONDUCT AND CUSTOMS

Dominicans love to laugh, joke around, and spend time with their families and friends on the water. They celebrate life through music, dancing, and plenty of drinks (but they can handle their liquor). Sharing is an important aspect of Dominican culture. Always begin a conversation, even if just a question, by greeting the person and asking how they are. Greeting people by saying *Buen día* or *Buenas noches* when entering a public space, even buses, is considered polite and a must. Learn all the courtesy words. Decline an offer you do not want by saying *No, gracias.*

If you'd like to take photographs of people, always ask first. Dominicans are generally fine with this and will indulge you, but you must request politely first. Do not photograph military or police officers for fun; it's prohibited unless you ask nicely and they agree (the Pantheon guards in the Colonial Zone seem to be an exception to this). When tipping, be generous. Wages are incredibly low for Dominicans, and the 10 percent service fee added to restaurant bills, for instance, might not reach their pockets at all. If you receive excellent service or even if it is basic, feel free to tip. At the market, haggling for clothing and other items (besides produce) can be fun, but keep it reasonable.

VOLUNTEERING ON VACATION

You may want to travel, but feel a nudge to give back to the communities you're visiting, or to immerse yourself and learn more about the culture. One of the best ways to do this is to share what is most valuable: your talent and time. There are plenty of organizations offering voluntourism opportunities. Just be careful in selecting the ones that are a good fit for your skills as well as reliable. Wherever you end up volunteering, your expenses should be affordable. The key is to obtain as much detail as you can.

One that I highly recommend is the local tourism cooperative **Red de Turismo Comunitario de Puerto Plata** (tel. 809/261-2993) with various communities and opportunities to choose from. You can contact the network and custom design your volunteer time and interests. At the same time, you'll get to enjoy the great outdoors of the North Coast. For more information on the UMCP, see the Puerto Plata chapter. Another great option, out of Cabarete, is the **Mariposa DR Foundation** (tel. 809/571-0610, www.mariposadrfoundation.org) working with local adolescent girls to educate and empower them economically. They welcome volunteer help in various aspects of their operations ranging from teaching to gardening. Submit their online form for more details.

The DR is challenged in its educational system, above all else, and there's always a dire need for English teachers. One organization that would be interested is **COOPDECI— Cooperativa para el Desarrollo de La Ciénaga,** the local cooperative of La Ciénaga, in the Barahona province. Those heading to the Punta Cana region can volunteer in environmental and sustainable programs with the **Puntacana Ecological Foundation** (tel. 809/959-9221, fepc@puntacana.com). Contact them in advance for a current list of opportunities and matching.

TRAVELING WITH CHILDREN

Children will need a valid passport. As a general precaution, if a minor is traveling to the DR without one parent, carry a notarized document from the absent parent. It is generally fine traveling with nonparents as long as the children return with the same adults, but it is better to be safe and carry an authorizing document from the parents there as well.

Responsible Travel

To travel responsibly is to travel not just to enjoy a place but to realize that your presence has an impact on every person, thing, and place you encounter or visit and to want to make as positive an impact as possible. This is particularly key when traveling in developing countries with heavy tourism, such as the Dominican Republic, where the majority of the population lives in poverty and tourism wealth doesn't trickle down far enough.

So how can you travel responsibly while in the DR? Here are a few suggestions:

- **Pick Dominican-owned businesses**—from local restaurants to guesthouses—as much as you can.

- **Shop at the neighborhood *colmados*.** These Dominican-owned corner stores/bars/slash snack shops are the crux of Dominican culture and help sustain entire neighborhoods. They are also fun to hang out in with a cold beer and merengue or bachata blasting. Look for what you need here, whether snacks, rum, or a phone card, before heading to the supermarket.

- **Learn a few phrases of Spanish** and interact with Dominicans. They are hospitable people and will gladly interact with you.

- **Tour with local community tourism organizations** (such as UMCP in Puerto Plata, www.popreport.com/turisopp) or licensed Dominican tour operators. The various chapters mention options. Not only will you get a more authentic look at life in the Dominican country-side, but your tourism dollars will go directly to the communities you're visiting.

- **Shop from local artisans and artists** and purchase handmade products. Be careful not to buy any prohibited products such as turtle shells or red coral.

- **Use public transportation** where feasible, or hire a local driver. I've recommended names in each chapter of this book.

- **Attend local festivals,** where you'll get insight into the culture as well as find shopping options for local food and arts.

- **Make your stay as green as possible.** Recycling has a long way to go in this country, but you can try not to contribute to the issue by reducing the amount of plastics and other such containers you use. Eat inside the restaurant rather than taking food out, and try to use one refillable water bottle.

- **Be conscious of your electricity and water usage** in your hotel room or otherwise. Be reasonable, even if it is available to you without limit. Turn off the lights and air-conditioning while you are out exploring. Stay in hotels that are ecofriendly and environmentally conscious.

- Last but not least, **appreciate the people** who are receiving you and **respect their culture.**

With a myriad of all-inclusive resorts at all budget levels, the DR can be an easy family vacation. When selecting a resort, make sure you look into the activities offered and whether there's a special Kids Club or a Preferred Family Club for additional fee. The perks are usually worth it. But don't stay cooped up in resorts either—Dominicans love and understand the family concept, and getting out and about to see how they enjoy themselves is a great way to share time with your kids. In Samaná, Puerto Plata, or Jarabacoa, families like swimming together at the beach, at the river, and by waterfalls, while cooking out and listening to music. There are plenty of water sports for teenagers, especially on the North Coast. If you're visiting in winter, you can take the kids to a baseball game at a number of professional stadiums in Santiago, La Romana, or Santo Domingo. Cultural experiences also

Getting Married In the DR

It's difficult to top the DR's gorgeous scenery, not to mention the array of all-inclusive or boutique hotels offering bridal and honeymoon packages, often with an onsite coordinator. Packages usually include all you need, including judge, license, flowers, cake, champagne, and music, in addition to accommodations. Popular destinations are La Romana and Punta Cana, but you'll find plenty of more secluded options in Puerto Plata and Samaná. Before the fun begins, you'll need to comply with the formalities. To marry in the DR, the bride and groom need to bring a notarized statement of their marital status certified by the Dominican consulate in their respective countries. Valid passports and birth certificates for the couple, of course, and copies of any divorce decrees will be needed where applicable. You'll need two witnesses, and all of the relevant documents will need to be translated into Spanish once in the DR. Church weddings are a possibility—imagine the riverfront backdrop of the gorgeous St. Stanislaus Church at Altos de Chavón, or the colonial buildings in Santo Domingo. A handy list of the complete requirements can be found online. For an up-to-date list of the complete requirements, inquire with the resort that interests you, as hotels keep up with these.

abound when you visit the countryside, usually a favorite for kids, where there are plenty of fresh fruits and hiking trails. If you are relying on taxis, use one of the referrals in this book (according to where you are staying) and ask ahead whether the vans have working seat belts.

TRAVELING WITH PETS

To travel with your dog or cat, you'll need to bring a recent health certificate from your veterinarian, certified by the Agriculture Department of your state and apostilled by the state government. You must also show a rabies certificate. For up-to-date information and more details, contact the Embassy of the Dominican Republic in the United States (www.domrep.org) or in your country of residence. The website hispaniola.com can also provide more details.

WOMEN TRAVELERS

Ladies, the good news is that it is safe to travel the Dominican Republic solo or in groups. I did it myself multiple times countrywide and have not encountered any issues. Of course, I stay as vigilant as I am at home and don't take unnecessary risks (such as walking alone at night). Travel during the day, whether on public transport or on excursions, so you're not isolated. Staying at independently run hotels and guesthouses is also an excellent way to meet fellow travelers and get local tips from owners who will have more time for their solo guests than a massive all-inclusive. That said, all-inclusive resorts also often have an entertainment crew who are more than willing to accompany the solo female.

Look out for the *sanky panky*—a term used for local men who go after foreign women of any adult age and romance them (through selfless acts of generosity and love) for the sole purpose of getting money or, better yet, a visa and a way out of the country. They are often good-looking, well groomed, and display plenty of muscles. They roam the beach or work at hotels on the entertainment crew. This phenomenon is common in many tourism-driven destinations. Just be smart and realistic about whom you are befriending. The only major nuisance for female travelers in the DR is the machismo displayed by Dominican men in the streets. Hollering, ogling, and whistling are common practice. But don't worry, it is just talk and considered normal to admire and gawk at women, particularly foreign ones. Ignore it and keep moving.

SENIOR TRAVELERS

Senior travelers love the DR for the well-rounded variety of activities it offers—particularly in terms of sports. The North

Coast, for instance, is a dream for its hiking, kayaking, and sailing opportunities, as well as plenty of golfing. Continuously ranked as the Golf Destination of the Year by the International Association of Golf Tour Operators, as recently as 2015, golfers will find plenty of options on top-rated courses around the country, including world-renowned Teeth of the Dog at Casa de Campo. Seniors are also welcome to rest up at all-inclusive resorts, some of which offer preferred club options for more privacy and luxury. Samaná is ideal for senior travelers as well, for its less crowded, powdery beaches and affordable fine dining options.

GAY AND LESBIAN TRAVELERS

The Dominican Republic is surprisingly more tolerant than most other Caribbean countries when it comes to gay and lesbian travelers—a world apart from Jamaica or Grenada. Hotels all welcome gay couples. Gay bashing or violence is rare, and you will find many openly gay Dominicans, both male and female. The current U.S. ambassador to the DR, James Brewster, is gay and lives here with his partner. Still, public displays of affection are not acceptable, and you should be conservative while out and about as a couple. Do not hold hands or kiss outside in order to avoid unwanted attention.

Santo Domingo has the most gay-friendly options, especially in the Colonial Zone—check out www.monaga.net and www.gaytravel.com.

TRAVELERS WITH DISABILITIES

As in most of the region, independent travel (getting around on public transport for instance) for those who are disabled is extremely limited. If the goal is to relax at an all-inclusive resort, these are well equipped with elevators and usually have special rooms for travelers with disabilities. The DR is a welcoming destination, so don't be afraid to ask for what you need. If going on tour excursions, check that they offer appropriate vehicles and can meet your requirements ahead of time.

Food and Accommodations

FOOD

The Dominican national meal is called the Dominican flag or *bandera dominicana*: a plate of rice and beans, with a stewed meat sauce and a side salad. Also called the *plato del día* at the local restaurants (special of the day), it is the most affordable meal aside from fried chicken and, well, anything fried roadside. Cafeterias or *comedor* abound in towns and cities, and offer delicious buffets of Dominican and international foods (ordering alone is a cultural experience) for an incredibly low price (usually under US$5). On the weekends, you will notice more street foods—including chicken and pork being grilled roadside. One advantage of many European expats living in the DR is a greater variety of cuisines than on other Caribbean islands, though not all are created equal. Wherever you end up, you're never too far off from an Italian or French restaurant. Cafés and pastry shops are popular too, given that Dominicans have a super sweet tooth.

If you are staying at an all-inclusive resort, the food will be predominantly non-Dominican, but some have Dominican restaurants à la carte on the list. When that happens, you should make a reservation for it. Be sure to step out and try the local food in town as well.

ACCOMMODATIONS

The hotel choices in the Dominican Republic are as varied as it gets, from luxurious all-inclusive resorts with preferred club perks to nature lodges, guesthouses, and local by the hour "cabanas."

Dominican Drinks: Beers, Rum, and Mamajuana

Dominicans love their **Presidente** beer, made by the national brewery Cervecería Nacional Dominicana around since 1935. It is the iconic brand of the island, pretty much synonymous with being Dominican. The name and the green bottles pop up pretty much everywhere at concerts, the local *colmados*, restaurants, and even on plastic chairs on the beach. The custom is to purchase a "grande" or big bottle and share it with friends—more importantly it must be served and consumed really cold to the point that the bottle has a light white frosting. The lightweights can opt for a Presidente Light. The latest brand in the Presidente family is the Presidente Black, a thicker-bodied beer with 6 percent alcohol. Aside from Presidente, other brands are popular, such as **Bohemia,** a pilsner-based beer with 5 percent alcohol but made in Mexico, and **Quisqueya,** made by the Cervecería Vegana in the DR, a pilsner-type beer at 6 percent alcohol. If you find yourself in Constanza, you'll also find a popular thick, dark craft beer made and sold at La Esquina bar called **Ferringer,** a play on the owners' family name.

Equally as popular, and as expected in the Caribbean, is **rum**—or *romo* as they like to say here. And the DR produces several popular brands: **Brugal, Barceló,** and **Macorix.** Brugal 1888 has ranked on many a list of top Caribbean rums. When you head to a local bar, it's customary to buy a bottle (of any size you choose), your mixer, and enjoy with your group. Cuba libres, Santo libres, Brugal Añejo (a popular pick) or Extra Viejo, or on the rocks—everyone has their preference.

Perhaps the most Dominican of all drinks is **mamajuana**—and almost every souvenir store will pounce on you to sample and buy a bottle. Sample away but beware: this concoction is a potent, fermented mix of cured tree barks and herbs soaked in red wine and rum. The herbs and barks could include canelilla (*Cinnamodendron ekmanii*), marabeli (*Securidaca virgata*), bojuco caro (*princess vine*), and *clavo dulce* (whole clove), among other ingredients. There are as many varieties of mamajuana as there are makers of this local drink. Dominicans like to say it's an aphrodisiac or a liquid Viagra. Whatever it is, the right mamajuana is tasty, strong, and makes for an excellent aperitif (some restaurants offer it free post meal), if you can handle it. If you plan on taking a bottle home, make sure you are purchasing from a reputable store, keep the receipt, and only bring back liquid mamajuana because the tree or bark-only packages are considered plants and not allowed into the United States. Last but not least: don't consume more than a couple of shots at a time—it's superpowerful and there's a danger of alcohol poisoning if you overindulge.

ESSENTIALS
FOOD AND ACCOMMODATIONS

High-season rates are higher (prices listed in this edition are for double occupancy in high season, unless otherwise noted), and you will need to plan ahead of time for the busiest times of the year, namely Christmastime and Easter. Keep your eye on websites and hotel social media channels for deals.

Although the DR is best known for its wide choice of all-inclusive resorts facing powdery beaches, there are lots more options all over the island to fit every budget. You should give these a try whenever possible. It's the best way to get a feel for the country and its incredible people, rather than staying trapped in an all-inclusive. There's a rise in luxurious accommodations, particularly boutique hotels and luxury, condo-style resorts. The first Aman resort opened in Río San Juan in November 2015, and fancy digs continue to sprout like mushrooms. But there are also charming, affordable lodges offering the best of the DR's great outdoors. Look into Puerto Plata or Jarabacoa, for instance. My recommended best picks are indicated in each chapter. Camping is not common or recommended in the DR, except when clearly organized for overnight hikes or on the beach through kite-surfing schools or as part of a trip to Bahia de las Águilas, for example. Take your time in researching your chosen accommodations so you get not only a great deal but also good food, service, and location for your buck.

Traveling on a Budget

Budget travelers will love the DR: it can be incredibly cheap to explore if you know how.

- **Planning your vacation:** Schedule your vacation in the off-season from mid-April through October. You'll find hotel rates discounted, even at all-inclusive resorts. For local guesthouses and hotels, just showing up often gets you an even lower rate, and unless it's a public holiday, you won't have trouble finding rooms.

- **Getting around:** Take public transportation. Taxis are prohibitively expensive and tend to overcharge tourists. Catch the local shared taxis (*carrito*) or buses (*guagua*) in small cities and towns to get around like Dominicans do. There's always one going to popular sights, beaches, or shops. Long-distance bus companies **Caribe Tours** (tel. 809/221-4422, www.caribetours.com.do) and **Metro Tours** (tel. 809/227-0101, http://metroserviciosturisticos.com), as well as smaller private bus lines (depending on your destination) charge under US$5 per person for comfortable, air-conditioned vans, often with wireless Internet.

- **Eating:** Eat at the local *comedor* or cafeteria, where the dish of the day is under US$4 with sides. If you're vegetarian, you can stick to the avocado salads or the rice and beans. Fruits sold streetside on carts or at the market–RD$10 (US$0.21) for five bananas, depending on the area–and fresh squeezed juices are equally cheap. Another solid spot for a quick fill is the *pica pollo* or fried chicken joint; there's always one on the main drag in your town, just like the local cafeterias. *Colmados*–the corner stores–also offer a daily dish; you'll need to speak a little Spanish to ask.

- **Sleeping:** Stay in locally owned guesthouses or hostels. Backpackers will find hostels in various areas such as Samaná, Santo Domingo, and even Bávaro. Superaffordable local hotels that are the equivalent of hostels sometimes even provide an amazing bang for your buck (with wireless Internet and hot water). Camping is not a big (or safe) thing here in the DR compared to other Caribbean and Central American destinations like say, Belize. But there are the occasional locations, in the southwest, for instance, offering beachfront camping. Sleeping al fresco is also popular in the mountains of Jarabacoa on hikes of Pico Duarte or El Mogote.

- **Getting the lowest price:** Bargaining is an art form in the DR. Learn a little Spanish and haggle away—whether when hiring local taxis for a private ride or shopping at the markets.

Health and Safety

SAFETY
Emergencies

Use 911 in an emergency. Dispatchers can connect to ambulances, firefighters, and the police. Depending on how remote you are, it may be better not to wait for assistance. Head to the nearest emergency room when possible. Clinics with 24-hour ER rooms include **Centro Médico Bournigal** (Calle Antera Mota, Puerto Plata, www.bournigal-hospital.com, tel. 809/586-2342), **Clínica Corazones Unidos** (Calle Fantino Falco 21, Ensanche Naco, Santo Domingo, tel. 809/567-4421, www.corazonesunidos.com.do), **Hospiten Bávaro** (Carretera Veron-Punta Cana, tel. 809/686-1414, www.hospiten.com.do), **Centro Médico La Romana** (tel. 809/523-3333, www.centralromana.com.do), and **Centro Médico Regional Barahona** (Jose Francisco Pena Gomez 71, tel. 809/524-2470). Note that in the Dominican Republic, you have to pay before receiving clinical care.

Crime

Leave valuables at home and remember that commonsense rules: don't walk around flashing expensive clothes, jewelry, or accessories, and keep your wits about you. Petty theft and robberies by passing motorcycle or scooter do happen. Staying aware and low key will help prevent that.

For crime emergencies, contact the nearest CESTUR (Cuerpo Especializado de Seguridad Turistica) office—the specialized tourist police corps assigned to each major area. They are trained in handling visitors and often speak or understand more than just Spanish. You can also grab a glossy copy of *La Cotica* handbook from airports, hotels, or tourism offices for all the latest emergency numbers and tourist information countrywide. The emergency number is 911, just as in the United States. Numbers for regional CESTUR offices are:

- Santo Domingo: 809/685-0508 or 809/689-6464
- Bávaro: 809/754-3082
- Bayahibe: 809/754-3012
- La Romana: 809/754-3033
- Puerto Plata: 809/754-3101
- Cabarete: 809/754-2992
- Sosúa: 809/754-3274
- Las Terrenas: 809/754-3042

HEALTH

Carry a small medical first aid kit with you; it could come in handy for minor injuries. Good-quality sunscreen and mosquito spray are a must, along with your preferred painkillers. Other personal necessities you are used to could be hard to find, including birth control. Bringing a pack of wipes wouldn't hurt, particularly since public bathrooms don't always carry toilet paper.

Water

You cannot drink the tap water in the DR. Always go for filtered, bottled water, even to brush your teeth—better to take these precautions than invite illnesses. Whether on or off the resort, limit the amount of ice cubes in your drinks or salad consumption if you feel unsure that the hotel or restaurant is using tap water for these and depending on your stomach sensibilities. Bottled water is cheap and available at local stores and supermarkets, in the rare case that your hotel doesn't provide it or you need more. Stay hydrated throughout the day—the intense sun and high humidity, particularly in the summer, can cause serious dehydration.

Diarrhea

Avoid traveler's diarrhea by avoiding tap water, and being aware of the raw fruits and vegetables you are consuming. Stay hydrated with lots of water for flushing out the toxins form your body. If it persists beyond a day, go to the nearest clinic and see a doctor.

Dengue

A rise in dengue cases has caused concern for several Caribbean countries in the second half of 2015, and the DR is no exception with 57 dengue-related deaths so far in 2015. This mosquito-borne virus causes fever, severe headaches, and serious joint and muscle pain.

Malaria

There's little risk of malaria in the DR, especially if you are heading to tourist areas. You only need to be concerned and prepared if you are headed to the border areas of Dajabón or San Juan and are staying there. In the latter case, get prescription malaria pills from your doctor. Treatment often begins before departure and continues for up to a month after your return.

Women's Health

The local pharmacies and supermarkets carry most women's products in major brands you recognize from plastic tampons to panty liners. For other medical needs, such as creams or remedies for yeast infections, you'll have to go to the pharmacy and request them (no prescription needed) as these are not sold over the counter. Your best bet is to see an ob-gyn at the nearest clinic.

Pharmacies

The DR has a host of **pharmacies** across the country, and you're never too far from medication when you need it. Most big resorts have their own first aid kids and pain relievers for basic aches and pains, but you can look to the nearest city for more options. The added bonus is that most pharmacies in the DR also offer a delivery service. 24-hour pharmacies include **Farmacia Trizza** (Higüey, tel. 809/554-4242), **Farmacia Los Hidalgos** (Santo Domingo, tel. 809/338-0700), or **Farmacia Carol** (Las Terrenas), among many others in various major towns and cities, such as Jarabacoa, Santiago, and Puerto Plata.

Information and Services

MONEY

The currency of the Dominican Republic is the Dominican peso (RD$). It fluctuates, so you'll have to check it before your trip, but it is generally RD$45 to US$1 dollar. The peso is divided into 100 cents; coins run into 1, 5, 10, and 25 pesos. Bills come in 20, 50, 100, 200, 500, 1,000, and 2,000 pesos. You'll find major banks and 24-hour ATMs in most areas—including Scotiabank branches and Banco Popular. These last two tend to work best with American cards. When using ATMs, do it in busier areas and during daylight; avoid the weekends when lines tend to be longer. The maximum you can withdraw with each transaction is RD$10,000 or about US$220.

While the American dollar is accepted in major tourist areas, shops and supermarkets in smaller towns and cities might not so ask ahead. If they do, you will need to know the currency exchange to check on what you're getting back and paying. Major department stores and restaurants generally accept debit or credit cards, but try to limit your usage of plastic and stick to cash where possible unless at a major resort, shopping mall, or fine dining spot.

TIPPING AND TAXES

A 16 percent sales tax is tacked on to food and drinks in restaurants, plus a 10 percent service charge by law. The latter is supposedly the waitstaff tip, but it is unclear whether they always receive it. So when you're eating out, look for that extra added to your check (sometimes on rare occasions, it is already included). Avoid using your credit or debit cards wherever possible and use cash, especially in smaller cities or towns. Expect sales taxes of 28 percent on hotel bills and 16 percent in shops. You should add at least 5-10 percent for waitstaff tip, and don't forget the hotel maid (at least US$1-2 a day).

COMMUNICATIONS

Wireless Internet and computers are ubiquitous in the DR and easily used for Skype or Facetime calls. But if you are in an all-inclusive, you might find that they charge exorbitant prices for usage per hour—avoid this ridiculous fee by researching where you stay ahead of time and ensuring that wireless Internet is included or at least free in common areas. Cybercafés and restaurants or coffee shops with wireless Internet are everywhere in the big cities and tourist areas. The only places that are a bit challenged with connections are the mountains of Constanza. Mac users might find it handy to know that there is an Apple authorized retailer in the DR, I-Zone (tel. 809/955-3237, www.izone.com.do), with various locations islandwide and carrying various Apple accessories as well as electronics.

For news on the DR, you will find daily articles and travel information in English on **Dominican Today** (www.dominicantoday.com). **Newspapers** include *Listin Diario* (www.listindiario.com), *Diario Libre* (www.diariolibre.com), and *El Nacional* (www.el-nacional.com.do).

Forget about the **post office**—it just doesn't function well at all for important packages or documents. Your best bet is to pay for DHL or FedEx if you really need it. You can also receive packages from North America through private shipping services like Caripack, depending on your location.

MAPS AND TOURIST INFORMATION

The Ministry of Tourism has various offices in the main tourist destinations around the island. It also has a useful website (www.godominicanrepublic.com), in various languages, with background and activity information on each region that you can download and save. All relevant local tourism office locations are indicated in the respective chapters of this book. If you can, however, I recommend you grab free tourism publications and maps when you spot them in hotels, tour operator offices, and at the airports when you arrive. You will find additional useful websites and sources in the Resources chapter.

Resources

Glossary

Avenida: Avenue.
Ballenas: Humpback whales.
Buen provecho: Enjoy your meal/drink.
Calle: Street.
Carnaval: Carnival.
Cerveza: Beer.
Chicharrón: Deep-fried pork.
Chivo: Goat.
Colmado: Corner store/neighborhood grocery store.
Conuco: Plot of farming land.
Fiestas patronales: Patron saint festivals.
Freiduras/frituras: Fried food shacks/vendors.
Guagua: Bus.
Hostal: Guesthouse.
Cuba libre: Rum and coke.
La capital: The capital/Santo Domingo.
Limpiabotas: Shoe shine boy.
Malecón: Seafront boulevard.

Mamajuana: A traditional, potent herbal drink.
Merengue: The DR's national music and dance, along with bachata.
Merengue típico: The original (folkloric) merengue genre.
Mofongo: A mashed plantain dish.
Motoconcho/concho: Motorbike taxi.
Museo: Museum.
Parada: Stop (bus/taxi).
Parque central: Central park.
Peso: DR currency.
Plato del día: Dish of the day/special of the day.
Playa: Beach.
Presidente: The most popular Dominican beer.
Santo libre: Rum and sprite.
Sendero: Hiking trail.
Una fría: A cold one (beer).

Spanish Phrasebook

Learning a few words of Spanish will make your stay a much more enjoyable one and less frustrating. If you're planning on traveling independently around the island, then it's a must to know a few words. Few Dominicans understand English outside of the cities and tourist zones, especially when it comes to public transportation and basic needs.

BASIC EXPRESSIONS AND GREETINGS

Greetings are important in the DR! Walking into a public space without saying *Buen día* or approaching someone without saying hello first can be considered rude. Keep in mind also that Dominicans tend to chop words and leave out the "s." So it wouldn't be strange to hear *Pa'tra* for *para atras* or for the use of expressions in unexpected ways (*te llamo pa'tra* for I'll call you back.) When in doubt, ask them to speak slowly: *más despacio, por favor!*

For pronunciation, plenty of free online resources allow you to listen to and get a sense of basic Spanish grammar and vocabulary. A solid one is www.studyspanish.com.

Hola Hello.
Buenos días / Buen día Good morning.
Buenas tardes Good afternoon.
Buenas noches or "Noches" Goodnight.
Como esta usted? How are you?
Muy bien, gracias Very well, thank you.
Bien Good.
Todo bien? Everything good/cool?
Todo bien, gracias Everything is good, thanks.
Mal Not good, bad.
Y usted? And you?
Gracias Thank you.
Muchas gracias Thank you very much.
De nada You're welcome.
A la orden You're welcome (a Dominican way of saying it)
Adios Goodbye.
Hasta luego See you later.
Por favor Please.
Si Yes.
No No.
No sé I don't know.
Momentito por favor One moment, please.
Disculpe/Con permiso Excuse me please (when trying to get attention or trying to pass someone).
Perdon/Lo siento I'm sorry/Excuse me (when you've made a mistake or bumped into someone).
Mucho gusto/Un placer Pleased to meet you/It's a pleasure.
Encantado/a Charmed/Thrilled to meet you.
Como se dice...? How do you say ...?
Como se llama usted? What is your name?
Me llamo... My name is...
Usted habla inglés? Do you speak English?

Hablo poco espanol I speak little Spanish.
Quisiera usted...? Would you like... ?
Quieres? Do you want... ? (informal)
Ven conmigo/Vamos Come with me/ let's go.

PEOPLE
Yo I.
Tu You (informal).
Usted You (formal).
El He/Him.
Ella She/her.
Nosotros We/us.
Ustedes You (plural).
Ellos They/them (males).
Ellas They/them (females).
Señor Mr.
Señora Mrs./Madam.
Señorita Miss.
Esposo/esposa Wife.
Amigo/Amiga Friend (male/female).
Novio/novia Boyfriend/Girlfriend.
Hijo/Hija Son/Daughter.
Hermano/hermana Brother/Sister.
Padre/Madre Father/Mother.
Abuelo/Abuela Grandfather/ Grandmother.
Sobrino Nephew.
Primo/Prima Cousin.
Nieto Grandchild.
Chica Girl.
Chico Boy.
Mujer Woman.
Hombre Man.

TIME
What time is it? Que hora es?
It's five o'clock in the afternoon Son las cinco de la tarde.
It's four in the morning Son las cuatro de la manana.
For one hour Por una hora.
Seven thirty Siete y media.
At what time...? A que hora...?
How many hours? Cuantas horas?

DAYS AND MONTHS

Lunes Monday.
Martes Tuesday.
Miércoles Wednesday.
Jueves Thursday.
Viernes Friday.
Sábado Saturday.
Domingo Sunday.
Hoy Today.
Mañana Tomorrow.
Ayer Yesterday.
La próxima semana Next week.
El próximo mes Next month.
Enero January.
Febrero February.
Marzo March.
Abril April.
Mayo May.
Junio June.
Julio July.
Agosto August.
Setiembre September.
Octubre October.
Noviembre November.
Diciembre December.
Una semana A week.
Un mes A month.
Después After.
Antes Before.

TRANSPORTATION

Guagua Public bus in the DR (white minivans).
Carro-concho/Carrito Shared taxi.
Motoconcho Motorbike taxi.
Vehículo/Carro A car.
Jeepeta An SUV.
Donde está... ? Where is... ?
A que hora sale... ? What times does the (bus/taxi/etc.) leave?
A cuanta distancia está.... ? How far to... ?
Cuantas cuadras más? How many more blocks?
El camino para... The road/way to...
La parada de... The stop for...
El barco The boat.
El muelle The dock.

La lancha Speedboat.
El aeropuerto The airport.
La boletería The ticket office.
La entrada The entrance.
La salida The exit.
Está lejos? Is it far?
Está cerca? Is it near?
A la derecha To the right.
A la izquierda To the left.
Derecho/todo derecho Straight ahead.
Al lado de Next to.
Al frente de In front of.
Atrás/Pa' tra Behind/At the back.
En la esquina In the corner.
En el semáforo At the traffic light.
Una vuelta A turn.
Dale Give it some gas! Speed up.
Aqui Here.
Donde pueda, chofer Pull over where you're able, driver (especially in a local bus/taxi).
Por allá Over there.
Calle Street.
Punte/Cuota Bridge/toll.
La carretera The highway.
Kilómetro Kilometer.
Cual es la dirección? What's the address?
Norte/Sur North/South.
Este/Oeste East/West.

ACCOMMODATIONS

Hotel Hotel.
Cabana A motel, can be luxury or basic (rooms by the hour, if you know what I mean).
Hay cuarto? Do you have room? Is there an available room?
Necesito un cuarto por ___ noches I need a room for __ nights.
Habitación sencilla/doble Single room/Double room.
Puedo verlo? Can I see it?
Cual es el precio? What's the price?
Hay más económico? Is there anything cheaper/more affordable?
Con baño With bath.
Ducha Shower.
Hay agua caliente? Is there hot water?

Televisión TV.
Con aire With A/C.
Con abanico solamente With fan only.
El desayuno incluido Breakfast included.
Toallas Towels.
Jabón Soap.
Papel higiénico Toilet paper.
Mantas Blankets.
Sábanas Sheets.
La llave The key.
El gerente The manager.

HEALTH

Estoy enfermo/enferma I'm sick (male/
  female).
Como se siente? How do you feel?
En que le puedo ayudar? How can I help
  you?
No me siento bien I don't feel well.
Ayúdame, por favor Help me, please.
Llame un doctor Call a doctor.
Emergencia Emergency.
Sientese y espere Take a seat and wait.
*Donde está el hopital/centro
  medico?* Where is the hospital/clinic?
La farmacia Pharmacy/drugstore.
Fiebre Fever.
Me duele... My___ hurts.
Dolor de cabeza Headache.
Dolor de estómago Stomachache.
Quemadura Burn.
Medicina Medicine.
Antibiótico Antibiotics.
Pastilla Pill.
Algodón Cotton.
Pastillas anticonceptivas Contraceptive
  pills.
Condones Condoms.
Crema dental Toothpaste.
Dientes Teeth.
Dentista Dentist.
Dolor de muelas Toothache.

COMMUNICATIONS

Tarjeta de crédito Credit card.
Efectivo Cash.
Teléfono Telephone.
Quisiera llamar a... I'd like to call... .

Una carta A letter.
Correo aereo Airmail.
Registrado Registered.
Paquete/caja Box/package.
Un giro A money transfer.
Paquete internet An Internet package.

AT THE BORDER

Frontera Border.
Aduana Customs.
Migración Immigration.
Tarjeta de turista Tourist card.
Inspección Inspection.
Pasaporte Passport.
Cédula Dominican ID card or used to
  mean ID card (can be your driver's
  license for non-Dominicans) .
Licensia de manejar Driver's license.
Título Title.
Profesión Profession.
Estado civil Marital status.
Casado/a Married.
Soltero/a Single.
Divorciado/a Divorced.
Viudado/a Widowed.

AT THE GAS STATION

La bomba The gas station.
Gasolina Gas.
Lleno, por favor Full, please.
Goma Tire.
Gomeria Tire repair shop.
Aire Air.
Agua Water.
Aceite (cambio) Oil change.
Batería Battery.
Radiador Radiator.
Alternator Alternator.
Generator Generator.
How much do you charge? Cuánto
  cobran?

DOMINICAN EXPRESSIONS

Que lo que? What's up/What's going on?
  (Also abbreviated as "klk" or KLK.)
Pana! Hey buddy/bro.
Tiguere A slick man/Hustler (in other

words, look out for anyone described this way). Can also be used among friends when teasing each other. Can be used in feminine *tiguera*.

Loco Crazy (also used affectionately among friends).

Como tu'ta? How are you? (The Dominican way of chopping words).

Tranquilo Everything cool (I'm fine).

Que chevere/Que chulo! How cool/wonderful/great.

Ya tu sabe You know it/That's right.

Dímelo Tell me/Talk to me.

Está bien That's fine/OK.

Entonces? So?

Que fue? What happened? What's wrong?

Mi amor My love (used for anyone and everyone)

Cariño Darling.

Que vaina! What a thing! (In surprise or disgust; vary your tone accordingly).

Coño! An exclamation expressing surprise or disgust similar to "Damn!"

Maleducado, déjame tranquila! Rude man, leave me alone!

Carajo! Hell or damn! Can add emphasis by saying, "Coño, carajo."

Sanky panky Term used to describe men who go after tourists (usually white women) for money/green cards, etc. They often work at hotels and hang in the tourist beach areas.

Suggested Reading

HISTORY

Roorda, Eric Paul, and Lauren Derby. *The Dominican Republic Reader: History, Culture, Politics.* Durham and London: Duke University Press, 2014. A unique compilation of the most important aspects of Dominican history and culture, this book examines various themes through excerpts from reliable sources. It also provides interesting background and history on some of the country's cultural symbols from baseball to bachata.

Wucker, Michele. *Why the Cocks Fight: Dominicans, Haitians, and the Struggle for Hispaniola.* New York: Hill and Wang, 2000. An excellent, easy read that examines the history of both Haiti and the DR, the evolution of their relationship, and the cause of friction between the two nations. It also gives an excellent historical recap in an engaging manner even for those who are not history buffs. If you pick just one history book for background, make it this one.

CULTURE

De Feliz, Lindsay. *What about Your Saucepans?* Great Britain: Summertime, 2013. A British expat tells the tale moving to the DR to make a change from her life in the UK, taking on a dive master position, and meeting then marrying a younger Dominican man who eventually goes into local politics. The book is a page-turner for sure, an easy read with plenty of humor and excellent depictions of Dominicans, their culture, relationships, and way of life.

ECOLOGY

Latta, Steven, Christopher Rimmer, et al. *Birds of the Dominican Republic and Haiti.* Princeton Field Guides: 2006. This is the go-to guide for all the bird species on Hispaniola island.

FICTION

Alvarez, Julia. *In the Time of the Butterflies.* Chapel Hill, NC: Algonquin Books, 1994. Alvarez recounts the life story of the famous three Mariposas or the Mirabal sisters, who rebelled against Trujillo and were eventually murdered on the dictator's orders. The movie based on this novel is also excellent.

Alvarez, Julia. *How the Garcia Girls Lost Their Accents*. Chapel Hill, NC: Algonquin Books, 1994. This truly enjoyable, award-winning read tells the tale of four Garcia daughters from a wealthy family who fled their native DR under the Trujillo regime to take refuge in the United States. The stories weave the past with the present and cultural identity issues with immersion in a new culture.

Díaz, Junot. *The Brief Wondrous Life of Oscar Wao*. New York: Riverhead Books, 2007. The Pulitzer Prize-winning novel tells the tale of a Dominican family in the United States through the eyes of an overweight teenager/nerd growing up in New Jersey. The novel offers interesting DR historical context through the lives of the various generations within Oscar's family.

Vargas Llosa, Mario. *The Feast of the Goat*. New York, NY: Farrar, Straus and Giroux, 2001. Weaving various story lines from both past and present, this novel tackles the tumultuous days of General Rafael Leonidas Trujillo and his brutal rule over the Dominican Republic for three decades.

Internet Resources

Access DR
www.accessdr.com
An excellent online English-language resource and travel blog with visitor tips and articles on sights, hotels, and things to do around the country. It's also a solid source for tourism-related news. They produce a print version guide you can pick up in many tourist locations from airports to hotels.

Active Cabarete
www.activecabarete.com
A website for all water sports enthusiasts heading to Cabarete, with information on lodging, weather, events, and more.

Caribe Tours
www.caribetours.com.do
Though in Spanish, this website for one of the main long-distance bus companies in the DR has an interactive map that's easy to use and understand to quickly view routes with departure point, schedules, and ticket prices. You can also email them via the website to reserve a spot.

Colonial Zone DR News Blog
www.colonialzone-dr.com
A handy website on all things Colonial Zone in Santo Domingo. It also has a super news blog frequently updated with details on monthly events taking place in the Colonial Zone and other relevant news.

Discover Puerto Plata
www.discoverpuertoplata.com
The Puerto Plata private tourist cluster's website on the best of the North Coast, including hotel, food, and nightlife information.

Dominican Today
www.dominicantoday.com
An English-language news resource on Dominican current events and the latest happenings around the country.

DR Ministry of Tourism: Go Dominican Republic
www.godominicanrepublic.com

DR1 Dominican Republic Travel Information
www.dr1.com

An old go-to resource for all English-speaking expats for everything from news to travel information. Its most useful feature is the forums organized by region where you can ask for travel advice as well as find a gazillion useful tips. The travel section has useful general information on the DR.

Embassy of the Dominican Republic in the United States
www.domrep.org

Go Samana
www.gosamana-dominicanrepublic.com

The private tourist cluster's website providing information on member hotels, restaurants, tour guides, and general history and activities on the Samaná Peninsula.

Guia Constanza
www.guiaconstanza.com

The private tourism cluster for Constanza offers a colorful website filled with information on sights, restaurants, and member hotels for those exploring this lovely mountain town in the central DR.

Hispaniola.com

A website on all things tourism and travel around the DR, including general information on flora, fauna, and history.

Que Hacer Hoy
www.quehacerhoy.com.do

If you're looking for the latest and greatest of every single day in Santo Domingo categorized by art, bars, concerts, and other events, this is your website. It also lists all the best daily happy hour locations . . . pretty nifty.

Index

List of Maps

Acknowledgments

I want to express my sincere gratitude to the wonderful friends and contacts in the DR who offered their support and assistance with my work on this book. Your willingness to assist during my year of research and living in the DR and to share your expert insights—on tourism, the environment, politics, wildlife, cultural anecdotes, and more—on your respective regions and pueblos and on your country is deeply appreciated.

A handful of these wonderful folks have become friends and are also some of the most model Dominicans I know, whether native or longtime residents: Tim Hall, Ambra Abbott, Alejandro Guzmán, Mara Sandri, Shirley Padilla, Francisco Duluc, Molly and Rodolfo Cruz, David Durán, and Yonathan Reyes, who sadly passed tragically in January 2016 before this book came to life. May he rest in peace.

A big thanks to Cathy Resek, an exemplary tourism public relations professional, for inviting me to the annual DATE travel trade show at the start of my yearlong project, and for becoming a lifelong Dominican ally and believer in my work in the process.

I want to thank all the folks I will never forget—the taxi drivers who looked out for me on the road, the tour guides who helped carry my gear and went out of their way to make sure I had the information I needed, the locals who showed me their favorite spots in each part of the country, and the small business owners and women's cooperatives who showed me their community initiatives and are making a difference in the DR.

I also want to thank the Dominican Republic Ministry of Tourism for their assistance in Punta Cana and La Romana, and for sharing my photography, video, and DR work on social media. Thanks to Milka Hernández, for always being available to help and offering assistance with such spirit. Thanks to the Constanza Tourist Cluster and Señor José Delio Guzmán, for their dedication in showing me their beautiful, up and coming region. And thanks to host Juan Musa from Puerto Plata's Channel 10, for inviting me on his popular cable television show to talk about the book and my travels in the country.

Last but not least, a big thanks to my two families: my parents, for their constant support in my journey as a travel and guidebook author, and my publishing family at Avalon Travel, for their constant encouragement and hard work—Grace Fujimoto, Elizabeth Hansen, Rachel Feldman, Darren Alessi, Kat Bennett, Molly Conway, and the rest of the team.

Also Available

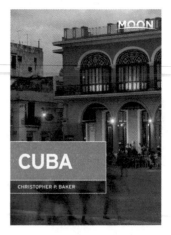

MAP SYMBOLS

≡≡≡	Expressway	○	City/Town	✈	Airport	⚓	Golf Course
—	Primary Road	◉	State Capital	✗	Airfield	℗	Parking Area
—	Secondary Road	⊛	National Capital	▲	Mountain	≜	Archaeological Site
- - - -	Unpaved Road	★	Point of Interest	✦	Unique Natural Feature	♟	Church
—	Feature Trail	•	Accommodation				Gas Station
- - - -	Other Trail	▼	Restaurant/Bar	🕱	Waterfall		Glacier
··········	Ferry	■	Other Location	♠	Park		Mangrove
≡≡≡	Pedestrian Walkway			▣	Trailhead		Reef
▥▥▥	Stairs	Λ	Campground	⛷	Skiing Area		Swamp

CONVERSION TABLES

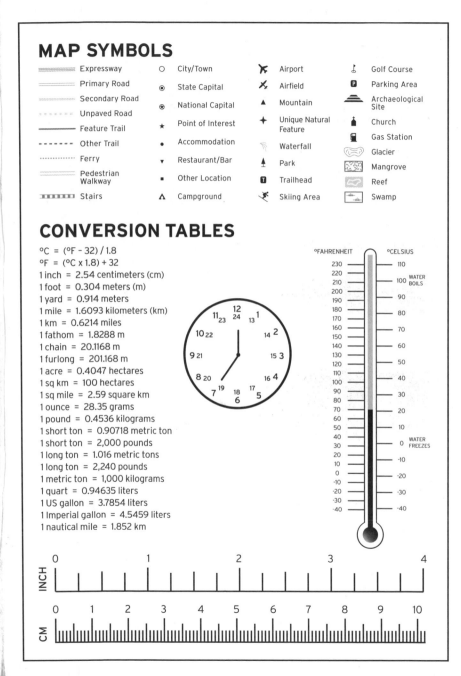

°C = (°F – 32) / 1.8
°F = (°C x 1.8) + 32
1 inch = 2.54 centimeters (cm)
1 foot = 0.304 meters (m)
1 yard = 0.914 meters
1 mile = 1.6093 kilometers (km)
1 km = 0.6214 miles
1 fathom = 1.8288 m
1 chain = 20.1168 m
1 furlong = 201.168 m
1 acre = 0.4047 hectares
1 sq km = 100 hectares
1 sq mile = 2.59 square km
1 ounce = 28.35 grams
1 pound = 0.4536 kilograms
1 short ton = 0.90718 metric ton
1 short ton = 2,000 pounds
1 long ton = 1.016 metric tons
1 long ton = 2,240 pounds
1 metric ton = 1,000 kilograms
1 quart = 0.94635 liters
1 US gallon = 3.7854 liters
1 Imperial gallon = 4.5459 liters
1 nautical mile = 1.852 km

MOON DOMINICAN REPUBLIC

Avalon Travel
An imprint of Perseus Books
A Hachette Book Group company
1700 Fourth Street
Berkeley, CA 94710, USA
www.moon.com

Editor: Rachel Feldman
Series Manager: Kathryn Ettinger
Copy Editor: Ashley Benning
Graphics Coordinator: Darren Alessi
Production Coordinator: Darren Alessi
Cover Design: Faceout Studios, Charles Brock
Interior Design: Domini Dragoone
Moon Logo: Tim McGrath
Map Editor: Kat Bennett
Cartographers: Austin Ehrhardt and Brian Shotwell
Indexer: Deana Shields

ISBN-13: 978-1-63121-287-1
ISSN: 1092-3349

Printing History
1st Edition — 1997
5th Edition — November 2016
5 4 3 2 1

Some photos and illustrations are used by permission and are the property of the original copyright owners.
Front cover photo: Puerto Plata © Lebawit Lily Girma
Back cover photo: © Donyanedomam | Dreamstime .com
Interior photos: © Lebawit Lily Girma except page 21 © Cfarmer | Dreamstime.com

Printed in Canada by Friesens